HUMAN RIGHTS IN THE
WORLD COMMUNITY

HUMAN RIGHTS

in the

WORLD COMMUNITY

Issues and Action

edited by

Richard Pierre Claude and
Burns H. Weston

UNIVERSITY OF PENNSYLVANIA PRESS
Philadelphia

Published with the assistance of the Jacob Blaustein Institute for the Advancement of Human Rights

Library of Congress Cataloging-in-Publication Data

Human rights in the world community.

   Includes bibliographies and index.
   1. Human rights.   I. Claude, Richard Pierre,
1934–   .   II. Weston, Burns H., 1933–   .
K3240.4.H838   1989   342'.085   88-37844
ISBN 0-8122-8163-2   342.285
ISBN 0-8122-1283-5 (pbk.)

3rd paperback printing, 1991

To Monique Weston Clague
& Gregor Pierre Claude

Contents

I S S U E S

CHAPTER 3   **BASIC HUMAN NEEDS, SECURITY RIGHTS, AND HUMANE GOVERNANCE   115**

A C T I O N

CHAPTER 6   **NONGOVERNMENTAL ORGANIZATION, CORPORATE AND INDIVIDUAL APPROACHES TO IMPLEMENTATION 287**

APPENDIX: SELECTED DOCUMENTS 333

Preface

The United Nations Educational, Scientific and Cultural Organization (UNESCO) sponsored an international congress on "Teaching Human Rights" in 1978. Persons attending the Vienna Congress from all over the world adopted the view that the United Nations' objective of promoting human rights internationally could be achieved, in significant part, through education and the development of appropriate texts and teaching materials.[1] This book seeks to bring such materials together in one place for use in political science, international relations, and international law classes. We hope it will be of interest to the general reader as well.

The volume aims to facilitate effective human rights education in several ways. It relies on a broad distinction between *issues* associated with international human rights problems and *action* that seeks to implement human rights standards at the international, national, and individual levels. Each of six chapters containing essays by leading scholars is preceded by an editors' introduction designed to orient the reader and to survey the field within which the excerpted readings fit. Each reading is followed by "Questions for Reflection and Discussion," which we hope will be helpful in critically analyzing the readings, in prodding new thinking, and in stimulating fresh research beyond the scope of the existing literature.

At the end of each of the chapters is an annotated bibliography, emphasizing more recent publications as well as selected "classics."[2] On the theory that human rights is made tangible by eyewitness experience, an appropriate annotated filmography also is set out after each of the chapters.[3] Films are an important teaching device in our television age when, by way of international satellite hook-ups, TV brings into our homes, broadcasts of "Live Aid" in response to hunger in Africa, superpower officials talking to one another over ideological dividing lines, and top performers (for instance, "U2" from Great Britain and the "Jazz Group" from Czechoslovakia) rallying support for international human rights. One way or another, we all have become eyewitnesses to human rights problems. Because the promotion of human rights depends on everyone, the reader should familiarize herself or himself with

1. UNESCO, *The Teaching of Human Rights* (Paris, 1980).

2. For additional bibliography, see UNESCO, *Human Rights Documentation, Data Bases and Bibliographies,* (Paris, 1987); and Julian R. Friedman and Marc I. Sherman, eds., *Human Rights: An International and Comparative Law Bibliography* (Westport, Conn.: Greenwood Press, 1985); and Center for the Study of Human Rights of Columbia University, *Human Rights: A Topical Bibliography* (Boulder, Colo.: Westview Press, 1983).

3. Persons interested in using such films should consult college or local libraries or video film outlets to secure the mailing addresses of nonprint media distributors. This information is also available in Anne Gelman and Milos Stehlik, *The Human Rights Film Guide,* from Facets Multimedia, Inc., 1517 West Fullerton, Chicago, Ill. 60614.

the many groups that serve human rights causes.[4] They are easy to join and need new members' help.

Human rights is not an abstract field of study. It is a field of work. It requires everyone's work, support, and commitment. Thankfully, as individuals, we do not have to begin from scratch. The United Nations took the first step in 1948 toward committing all governments to human rights by formulating internationally defined norms. These standards form the grounding in which the study of human rights should be rooted. Hence, this volume concludes with an appendix of the leading documents that specify the rules upon which the world seeks to build a community respectful of human dignity.

Whether the world is up to the task of building a global community respectful of human dignity remains to be seen. That it should try to do so is imperative. A credible case for this view can be made by those who have seen its opposite. An Argentine judge who served on the court that convicted the military rulers in his country for human rights violations between 1976 and 1983 argues that it is time to view human rights from a global perspective. According to Justice Jorge Antonio Bacqué:

> It has become obvious that technological idiocy, unbridled fanaticism and Realpolitik have pushed humanity, for the first time in its history, to the brink of a precipice where the mode and conditions of life are at risk. This danger may be averted only by paying unconditional respect to human dignity.[5]

4. The *Human Rights Internet Reporter*, published four times a year, details the work of thousands of nongovernmental organizations and supplies mailing addresses as well. Such groups are profiled in the regional directories published by the Human Rights Internet, Harvard Law School, 401 Pound Hall, Cambridge, Mass. 02138.

5. Supreme Court of Argentina, Buenos Aires, Judgment of 22 June 1987. (*Causa No. 547 incoada en virtud del Decreto No. 280/84 del Poder Ejecutivo National.*) Constitutionality of the Law of "Due Obedience," Justice Jorge Antonio Bacqué, dissenting. The full opinion is published in English in "Supreme Court of Argentina, Buenos Aires," *Human Rights Law Journal* 8 (1987): 430–71.

Acknowledgments

This book started life as a glimmer in Sidney Liskofsky's eye and was initially nurtured with support from the Jacob Blaustein Institute for the Advancement of Human Rights. The project has also benefited from support by the General Research Board of the University of Maryland at College Park and a grant from W. H. and Carol Bernstein Ferry. In its formative stages, the enterprise was evaluated by several anonymous survey respondents—teachers of human rights—whose comments substantially influenced the design of the volume. Among those to whose names we can attach valuable comments or other forms of scholarly first aid are Christian Bay, Lawrence Ward Beer, Thomas Buergenthal, Christina Cerna, Roger Clark, Karen Dawisha, Jack Donnelly, Tom Farer, David Forsythe, the late Julian Friedman, William Goodfellow, Jo Marie Griesgraber, Louis Henkin, Michael Klein, Bert Lockwood, Jr., Mary Malzkuhn, Raul Manglapus, Steven Marks, J. Paul Martin, Ji Won Park, Mary Rayner, George Rogers, the late Harry Scoble, Eric Stover, Ronald Terchek, Richard Alan White, and Laurie Wiseberg. Alexander von Cube's devotion to human rights deserves four star recognition.

Graduate students in the Government and Politics Department at the University of Maryland who were helpful were Tasneem Bakhshi, Tom Bode, Michael Cain, John Crotty, David R. Davis, Patricia Davis-Giehrl, Franke Hess, Garry Jennings, Paul Koloc, David E. Morrison, Paul Parker, the late Michael Reilly, Marcheta Wright, and Elaine Yanotti. The following students at the University of Iowa College of Law have earned our thanks as well: Martin Christopher Dolan, Kelly M. Hnatt, Andrew Mark Johnson, and Robin Ann Lukes. The energy and enthusiasm of these students supplied the editors with a satisfying endorsement of the project.

For expert typing, manuscript preparation, and great tolerance for professorial eccentricities, we are indebted to several secretaries, including Mary Q. Lewis and Mary E. Sleichter in Iowa City, and Kay Klein, Denise D. DiLima, and Rebecca Mattis in College Park, Maryland. Any eccentricities of errors in this volume are the copyright of the editors; grateful acknowledgment to those on whom we leaned and from whom we gleaned writings and comments, we happily place in the public domain.

Chapter One

International Human Rights: Overviews

THE full realization of human rights worldwide is a distant dream. A truly just world order is not easily or quickly achieved. But the drive for social justice on a global scale, spurred by the experience of Nazi atrocity and ever more revealed in internationally defined human rights norms and procedures, persists nonetheless. As Adolfo Perez Esquivel put it on the occasion of receiving the Nobel Peace Prize in 1980, "[T]he last few decades have seen a more extended and internationalized conscience in respect of human rights, such that we are confronted with and increasingly forced toward a deeper understanding of what the struggle for human rights means.[1]

In this introductory chapter, we seek to provide a "deeper understanding of what the struggle for human rights means" by looking at the topic from two broad vantage points. First, we look at human rights in the context of changing historical concepts and international law. In his essay, Burns H. Weston shows that internationally defined human rights, and the systems established for their implementation, have come to occupy a central position in contemporary world affairs in general, and in the field of international law in particular. Here we are concerned mainly with the promise of human rights. Second, turning from law to politics, we focus on performance. Richard A. Falk assesses the prospects for achieving human rights, both domestically and internationally, in the context of diverse "normative logics" or controlling perspectives that are simultaneously arenas of struggle and foundations of authority for the realization of human rights in the contemporary world. "In essence," he contends, "the protection of human rights is an outcome of struggle between opposed social forces and cannot be understood primarily as an exercise in law-creation or rational persuasion." Both readings are intended to provoke rather than soothe. The reader is urged to reflect, discuss, and debate after studying these essays critically and carefully, taking into account the questions posed at the end of each reading.

To deepen our understanding of the struggle for global justice, it is important to appreciate at the outset that international human rights bespeak, at bottom, a multidimensional program of legal and political struggle that takes human suffering seriously. Far from defining a static or monolithic state of affairs, the term "international human rights" is code language for a number of different—ever expanding, ever accelerating—initiatives: (a) an attack upon the concept of state sovereignty as traditionally conceived; (b) a goal-setting agenda for global policy; (c) a standard for assessing national behavior and therefore for judging political legitimacy; and (d) a spirited movement of concerned private individuals and groups that transcends political boundaries (an increasingly significant factor in international relations). Let us take an exploratory look at some aspects of these four meanings of international human rights.

---

1. Adolfo Perez Esquivel, "Afterword," in *The International Bill of Rights*, ed. Paul Williams (Glen Ellen, Calif.: Entwhistle Books, 1981), 105.

HUMAN RIGHTS AS A CHALLENGE TO STATE SOVEREIGNTY

International law, a complex process of authoritative and controlling decision operating across national and equivalent frontiers, exists, at a minimum, to maintain world order. To this end, by way of an interpenetrating medley of command and enforcement structures both internal and external to nation-states, classical international law has come to rely upon a variety of doctrines, principles, and rules to minimize interstate conflict and otherwise guarantee a world order system of separate territorial states.

Many, if not most, of these doctrines, principles, and rules—and the institutions and procedures that apply them—have been altered in meaning, challenged in usage, and otherwise thrown into question by the field of international human rights. Consider, for example, the classical international law doctrine of state sovereignty and its corollary of nonintervention, the central props of our inherited state-centric system of world order. The values associated with this doctrine (a legal license to "do your own thing") and its corollary (an injunction to "mind your own business") rest in uneasy balance with human rights concerns (which seem to tell us that "you are your brothers' and sisters' keeper"). The problem typically arises in the context of the question: Is it inappropriate interference for one state to criticize the human rights performance of another?

South African diplomats from Pretoria protest when the case of Nelson Mandela (a black political leader long imprisoned because of his opposition to that country's practice of racial apartheid and discrimination) is publicized at the United Nations. They point to Article 2(7) of the UN Charter, which says that the United Nations may not intervene "in matters which are essentially within the domestic jurisdiction of any state."[2] Many countries use this ploy. The governments of Iran, Paraguay, Romania, Uganda, and others ritually call upon the doctrine of state sovereignty and the principle of nonintervention, particularly when they are on the defensive in respect of their international human rights obligations. Those governments that abuse human rights typically plead for restraints, asking outsiders to refrain from interfering, directly or indirectly, individually or collectively, with their internal or external affairs.

The tension between the claims of those who criticize human rights violations and those who protest such interference was the topic of extended analysis by the late Sir Hersch Lauterpacht of the United Kingdom. A dominant trend of the last half of the twentieth century, he observed, is one that involves the sovereign state yielding to the "sovereignty of humankind." In Lauterpacht's words:

> In so far as the denial of fundamental human rights has been associated with the nation-state asserting the claim to ultimate reality and utterly subordinating the individual to a mystic and absolute personality of its own, the recognition of these rights is a brake upon exclusive and aggressive nationalism, which is the obstacle, both conscious and involuntary, to the idea of a world community under the rule of law.[3]

The claim made by Lauterpacht is readily understood when we note some of the major historical trends upon which Lauterpacht relied.

With the inception of the modern state system in the mid-seventeenth century, the relation of citizen ("subject") to government was seen to fall within the exclusive jurisdiction

2. See the Appendix.
3. Hersch Lauterpacht, *International Law and Human Rights* (New York: Garland Publishing, 1973), 47.

of the territorial state, although absolute sovereignty was by no means an historical accident. Religious jealousies and rivalry between kingdoms made the 1600s a century fraught with war, including one of the most destructive civil and international wars in the annals of human history, the Thirty Years War (1618–48). This calamity led princes and potentates to decide that the cycle of violence had to be broken; the territorial integrity of kingdoms had to be insulated from interference from without.

The sixteenth-century French social and political philosopher Jean Bodin (1530?–1596) is best remembered for giving the notion of state sovereignty its classic formulation: The sovereign prince exercises power simply and absolutely and cannot be subject to the commands of another, for it is the sovereign prince who makes the law for the subject. It is only by voluntary agreement that the sovereign can incur an obligation from abroad.

So conceived, the late-seventeenth-century world of nation-states would provide each kingdom with a defense of absolute power to overcome the centrifugal forces of jealousy and threat from without. Of course, though this new safety barrier between nations was motivated in part by humanitarian concerns and though it served the cause of human rights by reducing arbitrary killings based on religious and political rivalries, it also was an arrangement that suited well the interests of royal absolutism of European monarchs who sought to expand their power often at the expense—indeed the abuse—of their subjects.

Yet, just as the pre-seventeenth-century forces of political centrifugalism provoked the counterpoint of sovereign absolutism, so also did the unchecked and commonly abusive displays of sovereign absolutism provoke their own counterpoint. As Weston points out in his essay, the philosophy of natural rights associated with John Locke and others began to take hold in much of Enlightenment Europe and America even before the eighteenth century. Against unlimited claims of power in the guise of "the divine right of kings," philosophers began to speak of natural rights. In this spirit, Thomas Jefferson wrote from Paris to James Madison: "[A] bill of rights is what the people are entitled to against every government on earth."[4] Jefferson's Lockean turn of mind made him realize that natural rights were of limited value if they were not reflected in the fundamental structure of a nation's laws.

It was not, however, until after World War II—after the rise and fall of Nazi Germany—that the doctrine of state sovereignty changed dramatically, taking its most radical turn since the Peace of Westphalia (1648) when the state system first emerged. In *Beyond Sovereignty*, Marvin Soroos notes that, in stark contrast to an earlier reverence for the state sovereignty doctrine that "discouraged outside efforts to intervene on behalf of populations victimized by even the most cruel and tyrannical of rulers,"[5] the defense of unrestricted sovereignty was increasingly challenged during the twentieth century, "especially in the aftermath of revelations of the horrors of the atrocities committed by the Nazis against the Jews during World War II, which led many commentators to conclude that state sovereignty is not an absolute principle, but rather was subject to certain limitations in regard to human rights."[6]

In short, as Weston makes clear, human rights came of age as a legitimate international concern with the close of World War II, the founding of the United Nations, and the adoption of the Universal Declaration of Human Rights by the UN General Assembly in 1948 [7] and

---

4. In P. L. Ford, ed., *Writings of Thomas Jefferson,* 10 vols. (New York: G. P. Putnam, 1892–99), 4: 477. See generally Richard P. Claude, "The Classical Model of Human Rights Development," in *Comparative Human Rights,* ed. Richard P. Claude (Baltimore: Johns Hopkins University Press, 1976), chap. 1.
5. Marvin S. Soroos, *Beyond Sovereignty* (Columbia, S.C.: University of South Carolina Press, 1987), 230.
6. Ibid. See generally Richard L. Rubenstein, *The Age of Triage: Fear and Hope in an Overcrowded World* (Boston: Beacon Press, 1983).
7. See the Appendix.

as a consequence such weighty issues as the proper limits of state sovereignty came to occupy a central place on the agendas of most international institutions. In the postwar period, individuals have become a focus of international concern, not only as the charges of a sovereign state, but directly and in their own right; and on this radical foundation, the scaffolding of contemporary international human rights law and policy has been erected. It is a modern structure, cantilevered and often fundamentally at odds with the classical international law doctrine of state sovereignty. No longer can it be said, in the late twentieth century, that the state may treat its own citizens however it may wish, unaccountable to the international community beyond. No longer can it be said internationally that "the king can do no wrong."

AN AGENDA FOR PREFERRED WORLD POLICY

The field of international human rights has achieved a comprehensive and elevated global quality of preferred world public policy. It supplies a framework for a world order of human dignity.

Such is the thesis, at any rate, of international human rights scholars Myres S. McDougal, Harold Lasswell, and Lung-chu Chen who have led the way in urging others to facilitate the development of global policy by exploring the values that "are being ever more insistently expressed in the rising common demands . . . of people everywhere"[8] and that consequently supply the menu for global human rights study and action. Demands for *respect* (insisting, for example, on nondiscrimination), for *power* (reflected in appeals for wider political participation), and for *wealth* (including calls to accumulate and employ wealth for productive purposes) are among the more obviously important value demands recognized. But also important and sometimes primary are those relating to *enlightenment* (involving the enjoyment of knowledge and information), *well-being* (embracing assurances of individual and group survival), *skills* (for example, seeking to optimize talents and to overcome handicaps), *affection* (including the freedom to give and receive loyalty to groups of one's choice), and *rectitude* (requiring, optimally, a public order in which one can act responsibly for the common interest). Human rights, conceived in terms of these eight values, involve the underlying concerns of a world public order of human dignity, and they delineate the focus for intellectual inquiry and appraisal in the field we have come to call human rights. According to McDougal and his colleagues, we live in an era characterized by "an overriding insistence, transcending all cultures and climes, upon the greater production and wider distribution of all basic values, accompanied by increasing recognition that a world public order of human dignity can tolerate wide differences in the specific practices by which values are shaped and shared, so long as all demands are effectively appraised and accommodated in terms of common interest.[9]

Complementing the eight values underlying the human rights world of McDougal, Lasswell, and Chen is a more reductive model that concentrates on three values. Described by Weston in his essay in this chapter and referred to throughout this book, the model relates to the notion of "three [accumulating] generations" of human rights elaborated by French

8. Myres S. McDougal, Harold Lasswell, and Lung-chu Chen, *Human Rights and World Public Order: The Basic Policies of an International Law of Human Dignity* (New Haven, Conn.: Yale University Press, 1980), p. 90.
9. Ibid., 6.

human rights specialist Karel Vasak,[10] and tracking the French revolutionary slogan *liberté, égalité, et fraternité*. The civil and political rights of pre-nineteenth-century origin belong to the first (*liberté*) generation. The economic, social, and cultural rights largely surfacing in the last one hundred years comprise the second (*égalité*) generation. The third generation of rights, which is currently emerging from both the rise and decline of the nation-state in these twilight years of the twentieth century, parallels the notion of *fraternité*. The notion is born of the kinship and indispensible solidarity of men and women everywhere—for example, claims of right to political and economic self-determination; claims of right to the "common heritage of mankind"; claims of right to a clean and healthy global environment; and claims of right to national and international peace.

The values implied by the global human rights agenda relative to human needs have stimulated considerable scholarly analysis among such philosophers as Henry Shue and Amartya Sen, and such social scientists as Peter L. Berger, Adamantia Pollis, and Peter Schwab.[11] Johan Galtung and Anders Helge Wirak also have elaborated a model of human values linked to human needs and concepts of rights that is particularly useful in the analysis of economic and political development.[12] Their model is set out in the introduction to Chapter 3 of this text, where it helps guide our thoughts about basic human needs relative to second- and third-generation human rights, with particular attention to issues vital to developing countries.

The second essay in this chapter, by Richard Falk, is designed to sharpen our focus on the politics of human rights. From a political science perspective, Falk argues that legal and related cultural variables are not the most important factors to clarify in raising questions about the scope and universality of human rights. More important, he contends, are political factors that explain the differences in goals from one extrenched elite leadership group to another. Thus, in an ambitious exploratory effort, he seeks to link human rights performance with diverse social and political systems.

Falk's essay is grist for the political science mills, setting out six different regime scenarios, which he calls "normative logics"—statist, imperialist, nationalist, globalist, transnationalist, and populist. In characterizing the "statist logic," for example, he makes explicit the normative underpinnings of a regime type. His analysis suggests that, from the regime (or logic) premises specified, various human rights prospects logically flow. Thus the statist regime is likely to be jealous of sovereign prerogatives and quick to reject external human rights concerns as interventionist. Claim and response patterns are discussed, with telling contrasts emerging where human rights are involved. A reader interested in systematically applying Falk's framework to current world affairs could do so profitably by utilizing it with reference to any one or more of the nineteen countries profiled in-depth in the *International Handbook of Human Rights*.[13] Of course, Falk accepts the view that States are not the only significant

10. Karel Vasak, "A 30-Year Struggle: The Sustained Efforts to Give Force of Law to the Universal Declaration of Human Rights," *UNESCO Courier* (Nov. 1977): 29–32. See the related analysis by Stephen P. Marks, "The Peace-Human Rights-Development Dialectic," *Bulletin of Peace Proposals* 4 (1980): 339–47.

11. Henry Shue, *Basic Rights, Subsistence, Affluence, and U.S. Foreign Policy* (Princeton, N.J.: Princeton University Press, 1980); Amartya Sen, *Poverty and Famines: An Essay on Entitlement and Deprivation* (Oxford: Oxford University Press, 1981), and "The Right Not to Be Hungry," in *The Right to Food*, ed. Philip Alston and Katarina Tomasevski, (The Hague: Martinus Nijhoff Publishers, 1984), 69–77; Peter L. Berger, "Are Human Rights Universal?" in *Human Rights and U.S. Foreign Policy*, ed. Barry M. Rubin and Elizabeth P. Spiro (Boulder, Colo.: Westview Press, 1979); Adamantia Pollis and Peter Schwab, eds., *Human Rights: Cultural and Ideological Perspectives* (New York: Praeger Publishers, 1979).

12. Johan Galtung and Anders Helge Wirak, "Human Needs and Human Rights—A Theoretical Approach," *Bulletin of Peace Proposals* 1 (1977): 251–58.

13. Jack Donnelly and Rhoda E. Howard, eds., *International Handbook of Human Rights* (Westport, Conn.: Greenwood Press, 1987).

actors in international relations and accordingly reserves one of his analytical categories for international organizations and another for nongovernmental organizations.

Efforts by scholars to analyze human rights in terms of regimes, values, and political systems are not ivory-tower exercises. Scholarly analysis is needed because those active in international human rights have passed beyond the stage of mere wishful thinking; they have embarked on a global effort to construct a workable program of action.

HUMAN RIGHTS AS A STANDARD FOR ASSESSING NATIONAL BEHAVIOR

In an essay surveying positive international human rights law, Theodoor C. van Boven, former Director of the UN Division of Human Rights, correctly notes that the mandate extended to the UN Commission on Human Rights in 1946 to prepare an "international bill of rights" was inspired by, among other things, "the desire to establish a comprehensive system for the promotion and protection of human rights."[14] The resulting 1948 Universal Declaration of Human Rights, 1966 International Covenant on Economic, Social and Cultural Rights, and 1966 International Covenant on Civil and Political Rights,[15] which together have come to be called the "international bill of rights," went a long way toward this end.

But these trailblazing instruments were clearly only the beginning, not the end, of international human rights law-making in the United Nations and elsewhere. Supplementing the Universal Declaration and the two covenants, in the years preceding and since, have been literally scores of other human rights conventions less well known to the general public but nonetheless representative, in their totality, of what is considered the international "*corpus juris* of social justice."[16] These include, but are not limited to, treaties that fall into the following four categories of human rights instruments:[17]

14. Theo C. van Boven, "Survey of the Positive Law of Human Rights," in *The International Dimensions of Human Rights,* 2 vols., ed. Karel Vasak, revised and edited for the English edition by Philip Alston (Westport, Conn.: Greenwood Press for UNESCO, 1982), 1:87.
15. See the Appendix.
16. van Boven, "Survey of the Positive Law of Human Rights," 88.
17. Starting with the American Declaration on the Rights and Duties of Man [Mar. 30–May 2, 1948, O.A.S. Off. Rec. OEA/Ser.L/V/I.4 Rev. (1965)] and shortly thereafter the Universal Declaration of Human Rights (see the Appendix), a lengthy list of declarations and resolutions has shaped and defined the content of fundamental rights. While declarations and resolutions, adopted by such international organizations as the United Nations and the Organization of American States, do not always give rise to "rights" in the positive law sense that treaties are said to do, they invariably contain "rights" in the aspirational sense that are expected to be respected globally and consequently afford a basis for evolving standards of *customary* international human rights law. In contrast to the obligations implied by declarations and resolutions, conventions are theoretically legally binding treaties carrying the full weight of international law for signatory State parties. The process and politics of formulating a human rights declaration or resolution (sometimes setting a foundation upon which a later human rights convention may develop) are ably described by Sidney Liskofsky in "The U.N. Declaration on the Elimination of Religious Intolerance and Discrimination: Historical and Legal Perspectives," in *Religion and the State: Essays in Honor of Leo Pfeffer,* ed. James E. Wood, Jr. (Waco, Tex.: Baylor University Press, 1985), 441–83.

For a convenient source of international human rights instruments, including declarations and resolutions as well as treaties, see United Nations, *Human Rights: A Compilation of International Instruments* (New York: United Nations Publications, 1983) (hereafter *UN Compilation*). See also Richard B. Lillich, ed., *International Human Rights Instruments: A Compilation of Treaties, Agreements, and Declarations of Especial Interest to the United States* (Buffalo, N.Y.: W. S. Hein, 1983).

1. *General conventions* which concern all or a large portion of human rights and have been adopted at both the universal and regional levels.[18]
2. *Topically specific conventions* which are intended to guard against particular human rights abuses, e.g., genocide, war crimes, and crimes against humanity, slavery, traffic in persons, forced labor, and torture.[19]
3. *Conventions on group protection* which correspond to the special needs of distinct groups, such as refugees, stateless persons, migrants, workers, women, children, and combatants, prisoners, and civilians in time of armed conflict.[20]

18. At the universal level: International Covenant on Economic, Social and Cultural Rights, International Covenant on Civil and Political Rights, Optional Protocol to the International Covenant on Civil and Political Rights (see the Appendix). At the regional level: European Convention for the Protection of Human Rights and Fundamental Freedoms, Nov. 4, 1950, E.T.S. No. 5; European Social Charter, Oct. 18, 1961, E.T.S. No. 35; American Convention on Human Rights, Nov. 22, 1969, O.A.S.T.S. No. 36, at 1, O.A.S. Off. Rec. OEA/Ser.L/V/II.23 doc. 21 rev. 6 (1979); African Charter on Human and People's Rights, June 28, 1981, OAU Doc.CAB/LEG/67/3/Rev. 5 (1981).
19. See, e.g., Convention on the Prevention and Punishment of the Crime of Genocide, Dec. 9, 1948, 78 U.N.T.S. 277; Convention on the Non-Applicability of Statutory Limitations to War Crimes and Crimes Against Humanity, Nov. 26, 1968, 754 U.N.T.S. 73; Slavery Convention, Sept. 25, 1926, 60 L.N.T.S. 253; Protocol of Amendment to the Slavery Convention, Dec. 7, 1953, 212 U.N.T.S. 17; Supplementary Convention on the Abolition of Slavery, the Slave Trade and Institutions and Practices Similar to Slavery, Sept. 7, 1956, 266 U.N.T.S. 3; Convention for the Suppression of the Traffic in Persons and of the Exploitation of the Prostitution of Others, March 21, 1950, 96 U.N.T.S. 271; ILO Convention (No. 29) Concerning Forced or Compulsory Labor, June 10, 1930, 39 U.N.T.S. 55; ILO Convention (No. 105) Concerning the Abolition of Forced Labor, June 25, 1957, 320 U.N.T.S. 291; Convention Against Torture and Other Cruel, Inhumane or Degrading Treatment or Punishment, Dec. 10, 1984, U.N.G.A. Res. 39/46, 39 U.N. GAOR, Supp. (No. 51) 197, U.N. Doc. A/39/51 (1984).
20. See, e.g., Convention Relating to the Status of Refugees, July 28, 1951, 189 U.N.T.S. 137; Protocol Relating to the Status of Refugees, Dec. 16, 1966, 606 U.N.T.S. 267; European Agreement on the Abolition of Visas for Refugees, Apr. 20, 1959, Europ. T.S. No. 31; European Agreement on Transfer of Responsibility for Refugees, Oct. 16, 1980, Europ. T.S. No. 107; Convention Relating to the Status of Stateless Persons, Sept. 13–23, 1954, 360 U.N.T.S. 117; Convention on the Reduction of Statelessness, March 24–Apr. 18, 1959 and Aug. 15–28, 1961, U.N. Doc. A/CONF. 9/15 (1961); ILO Convention (No. 97) Concerning Migration for Employment, Revised, June 8, 1949, 120 U.N.T.S. 71; ILO Convention (No. 143) Concerning Migrations in Abusive Conditions and the Promotion of Equality of Opportunity and Treatment of Migrant Workers, June 4, 1975, reproduced in ILO, *International Labour Conventions and Recommendations* 1919–1981 (Geneva: International Labour Organization, 1982), 11; European Convention on the Legal Status of Migrant Workers, 1977, Europ. T.S. No. 93; ILO Convention (No. 87) Concerning Freedom of Association and Protection of the Right to Organize, July 9, 1948, 68 U.N.T.S. 17; ILO Convention (No. 98) Concerning the Application of the Principles of the Right to Organize and Bargain Collectively, July 1, 1949, 96 U.N.T.S. 257; ILO Convention (No. 100) Concerning Equal Remuneration for Men and Women Workers for Work of Equal Value, June 29, 1951, 165 U.N.T.S. 304; ILO Convention (No. 122) Concerning Employment Policy, July 9, 1964, 569 U.N.T.S. 65; Convention on the Political Rights of Women, Mar. 31, 1953, 193 U.N.T.S. 135; Inter-American Convention on the Granting of Political Rights to Women, May 2, 1948, O.A.S. Treaty Series No. 38, at 8, Ser. X/8 (1948); O.A.S. Convention on the Nationality of Women, Dec. 26, 1933, O.A.S. Treaty Series No. 38, at 1, Ser. X/8 (1933); Convention on Consent to Marriage, Minimum Age for Marriage and Registration of Marriages, Dec. 10, 1962, 521 U.N.T.S. 231; European Convention on the Legal Status of Children Born Out of Wedlock, Oct. 15, 1975, Europ. T.S. No. 85; Geneva Convention for the Amelioration of the Condition of the Wounded, and Sick in Armed Forces in the Field, Aug. 12, 1949, 75 U.N.T.S. 31; Geneva Convention for the Amelioration of the Condition of the Wounded, Sick and Shipwrecked Members of the Armed Forces at Sea, Aug. 12, 1949, 75 U.N.T.S. 85; Geneva Convention Relative to the Treatment of Prisoners of War, Aug. 12, 1949, 75 U.N.T.S. 135; Geneva Convention Relative to the Protection of Civilian Persons in Time of War, Aug. 12, 1949, 75 U.N.T.S. 287. See also Protocol Additional to the Geneva Conventions of 12 August 1949, and Relating to the Protection of Victims of International Armed Conflicts (Protocol I); and Protocol Additional to the Geneva Conventions of 12 August 1949, and Relating to the Protection of Victims of Non-International Armed Conflicts (Protocol II). For the texts of Protocols I and II, see Diplomatic Conference on the Reaffirmation and Development of International Humanitarian Law Applicable in Armed Conflicts, Final Act (1977), reprinted in *International Legal Materials* 16 (1977): 1391, 1442.

4. *Conventions prohibiting discrimination* based on race or sex, and in education, employment, and occupation.[21]

In van Boven's words, "international human rights law," since War II especially, "has been developing in an unprecedented way and has become a very substantive part of international law as a whole."[22]

Proof that international human rights law "has become a very substantive part of international law as a whole," serving as a standard against which to measure national behavior, is found, of course, in the human rights protestations of states, international governmental institutions, transnational professional associations, corporations, trade unions, churches, nongovernmental organizations, and others who variously respond to distress signals from abroad on the basis of these instruments. Mindful that human rights assessments can be politically as well as juridically significant because they can appreciably enhance or detract from the legitimacy upon which governments depend to retain and exercise power, all of these actors believe themselves to be, particularly in this age of relatively easy access to sophisticated international communications technology, more or less free to criticize governments for their human rights failings and to use state assent to treaties and other sources of international human rights law as the warrant of their disapproval.

Fault-finding, however, can be a dangerous enterprise, marred by dogmatism and self-righteousness and consequently capable of exacerbating international tensions in the most severe way. International human rights law, therefore, ought not to be invoked for the imposition of one set of values to the detriment of others. With the accessibility of improved international communications, global politics is taking on the aspects of a highly pluralized debate, and that debate includes the issue of how, in a world of diverse cultures, the basic demands for human dignity can be satisfied while simultaneously accommodating widely differing views of what human dignity means. As Rhoda Howard and Jack Donnelly emphasize, it is well to be skeptical of the popular wisdom that internationally prescribed human rights are common to all cultural traditions and adaptable to a great variety of social systems and structures.[23] The essay by Richard Falk in this chapter touches upon this theme.

Still, while no political regime is without its shortcomings where human rights performance is concerned, neither is any political regime today inclined to disavow internationally prescribed human rights standards, or at least not publicly, as if to confirm La Rochefoucauld's wise observation that "hypocrisy is the homage which vice pays to virtue." Even

---

21. See International Convention on the Elimination of All Forms of Racial Discrimination, Mar. 7, 1966, 660 U.N.T.S. 195; International Convention on the Suppression and Punishment of the Crime of "Apartheid," Nov. 30, 1973, U.N.G.A. Res. 3068 (XXVIII), 28 U.N. GAOR, Supp. (No. 30) 75, U.N. Doc. A/9030 (1974); International Convention Against Apartheid in Sports, Dec. 10, 1985, U.N.G.A. Res. 4064 (XXXIV), 40 U.N. GAOR, Supp. (No. 53) 37, U.N. Doc. A/40/53 (1985); Convention on the Elimination of All Forms of Discrimination Against Women, Dec. 18, 1979, U.N.G.A. Res. 34/180 (XXXIV), 34 U.N. GAOR, Supp. (No. 46) 193, U.N. Doc. A/34/46 (1980); UNESCO Convention Against Discrimination in Education, Dec. 14, 1960, 429 U.N.T.S. 93; Protocol Instituting a Conciliation and Good Offices Commission to be Responsible for Seeking a Settlement of Any Disputes Which May Arise between States Parties to the Convention against Discrimination in Education (1968), reprinted in *UN Compilation*, 36; ILO Convention (No. 111) Concerning Discrimination in Respect of Employment and Occupation, June 4, 1958, reprinted in *UN Compilation*.
22. van Boven, "Survey of the Positive Law of Human Rights," 87.
23. Rhoda E. Howard and Jack Donnelly, "Human Dignity, Human Rights, and Political Regimes," *American Political Science Review* 80 (Sept. 1986): 801–18. For a vigorous reply to the authors' thesis that internationally defined human rights require the existence of a liberal regime, followed by a spirited rejoinder by the authors, see Neil Mitchell, "Liberalism, Human Rights and Human Dignity," *American Political Science Review* 81 (Sept. 1987): 921–27.

though the human rights achievements of different political regimes vary and even though they do not yet represent the realization of a comprehensive conception of human dignity, the human rights standards that have been adopted internationally have become a major feature of the world's political landscape. As Weston points out in his essay, these standards, representing the most inclusive recognition of rights possible within the political, ideological, and cultural constraints of our late-twentieth-century state system, reflect a consensus among states as to the existence of certain minimal rights of individuals and groups within their respective jurisdictions, rights that member states of the UN have agreed to recognize, promote, and protect, and for which, therefore, states are properly held accountable. Today, the legitimacy of political regimes—hence their capacity to rule non-coercively—is judged less by the old standards of divine right, revolutionary heritage, national destiny, or charismatic authority, and more by new standards informed and refined by the language of international human rights.

HUMAN RIGHTS AS A POPULIST WORLDWIDE MOVEMENT INFLUENCING INTERNATIONAL RELATIONS

In concluding that international human rights law has been generated largely in response to "political or social concerns of a widely-felt character," Theodoor van Boven cites the work of many nongovernmental organizations.[24] The persistent pressure of Amnesty International on the UN General Assembly to adopt a Convention Against Torture and Other Cruel, Inhumane, or Degrading Treatment or Punishment, for example, or of the American Jewish Committee to win the General Assembly's acceptance of a Declaration on the Elimination of All Forms of Intolerance and of Discrimination Based on Religion or Belief, for another, lends credence to the conclusion that international human rights law has been greatly advanced by global popular support. In van Boven's words, "one of the specific traits of international human rights law is that this branch of international law extends well beyond the domain of international judicial decisions and intergovernmental practice.[25] It is directly influenced and advanced by an international movement. And as James Avery Joyce has written, as states and the United Nations fall short in the defense of human rights, "it is the *non*-governmental groups who are steadily forming a global if not yet systematized movement of investigation, protest and reform."[26] Such groups, in no way bound by the norms of nonintervention applicable to states, maximize the free flow of information across borders, spreading the word on human rights violators. While governments dally with "quiet diplomacy," nongovernmental human rights groups turn up the volume on complaints to mobilize neighborly shame and to enlist world public opinion against egregious rights violations.[27]

Such human rights interest groups are proliferating. In the 1980s, the Human Rights Internet, now a project of the Harvard Law School, has published directories enumerating and profiling nongovernmental organizations active in international human rights through-

24. van Boven, "Survey of the Positive Law of Human Rights," 88.
25. Ibid., 110.
26. James Avery Joyce, "Mobilization of Shame," in *The New Politics of Human Rights* (New York: St. Martin's Press, 1978), 79.
27. For pertinent discussion, see Reading 22 in Chapter 6 in this volume.

out the world. Internet lists about eight hundred such groups in Western Europe; more than five hundred in the United States and Canada; nearly four hundred in Latin America, Africa, and Asia; and in excess of two hundred unofficial as well as "approved" groups in Eastern Europe and the Soviet Union,[28] with many others remaining unlisted for fear of political reprisals. All of these organizations greatly increase the numbers of people worldwide who are engaged in human rights activities that have global impact. The international law of human rights, has in other words, an attentive global constituency.

These human rights interest groups are also diverse. They include trade unions and business organizations, professional societies, single-issue and policy reform groups, political organizations, and ethnic, ideological, and religious entities. A minority deal exclusively in the human rights field. Most are human rights "part-timers," special purpose groups that make human rights activities a significant but not exclusive part of their concerns—religious organizations as well as trade unions and political parties, for example (such as the Union of Councils for Soviet Jews, the Human Rights Office of the National Council of Churches in Korea, Pax Romana—the International Movement of Catholic Lawyers, the International Human Rights Program of the Disciples of Christ, and so forth). Indeed, the humanitarian concerns of various churches, including Buddhist, Islamic, Hindu, and Bahai groups, have drawn their faithful into promoting human rights through action as well as through education. As one observer of the international human rights movement, José Zalaquett, has remarked, "a union, by virtue of its own nature, will have the central objective to advance the interest and labor rights of its members; a political party will aspire, by definition, to political power; a given church will not regard the task of defending and promoting human rights as necessarily its exclusive or central programme."[29]

In fact, however, numerous trade unions and political parties do have goals and programs that touch significantly upon human rights concerns as a matter of routine. As Zalaquett himself observes, many such organizations, with memberships and affiliations crossing national frontiers, have in recent years reformulated existing projects or started new ones using the language of human rights or invoking international standards.[30] Many of these and equivalent transnational groups, such as the American Association for the Advancement of Science, have incorporated human rights objectives into their scheme of goals, and many have institutionalized these interests by setting up human rights offices to monitor the problems of their counterparts, confreres, or co-religionists in distant lands.[31]

This proliferation and diversification of human rights groups lends support, logically, to a new perspective on international relations. It emphasizes the significance of non-state actors and rejects the conventional wisdom of international relations defined exclusively or near-exclusively by the behavior of states and of international organizations composed of states. Modern communication and transportation technologies have made the classical notion of world politics obsolete. Territorial boundaries, however much bolstered by doctrines of sovereignty, are no longer impregnable—being, indeed, downright porous. Drugs,

---

28. See *Human Rights Directory: Western Europe* (1972), *North American Directory* (3d ed., 1984), *Latin America, Africa, Asia* (1981), and *Eastern Europe and the USSR* (1987)—all available from Human Rights Internet, Harvard Law School, Cambridge, Mass. 02138.
29. José Zalaquett, *The Human Rights Issue and the Human Rights Movement* (Geneva: Commission of the Churches on International Affairs, World Council of Churches, 1981), 30–31. See also Pontifical Commission, "Justicia et Pax," *The Church and Human Rights,* Working Paper No. 1 (Vatican City, 1975); *Theological Perspectives on Human Rights* (Geneva: Lutheran World Federation, 1977).
30. See, e.g., Jean Mayer, "The Concept of the Right to Work in International Standards and the Legislation of International Labour Organization Member States," *International Labour Review* 124 (Mar.–Apr. 1985): 225–42.
31. See, e.g., Mark R. Rosenzweig, "Psychology and United Nations Human Rights Efforts," *American Psychologist* 43, no. 2 (Feb. 1988): 79–86.

pollutants, illegal aliens, and terrorists manage to get through these boundaries, to be sure; but so too, and more importantly in the long run, does information. No longer does the world consist of independent sovereign states, impenetrable to anything but the influence of other states in direct proportion to the size and resources of such other states (what British international relations theorist John W. Burton calls "billiard-ball-like states"[32]).

In 1987, for example, the Paris-based League for Human Rights set up a twenty-four-hour international hot line for information on major human rights issues. In another recent development, an international computerized information-sharing network, called the Human Rights Information and Documentation System (HURIDOCS), has become operational.[33] Electronically stored and transmitted information is used by a network of institutions that participate in gathering and disseminating the data. The system has been made widely accessible through the creation of coordinating structures in Western Europe, Latin America, and elsewhere. In short, human rights groups everywhere are developing improved capabilities in rapid international communication such that private individuals and groups from throughout the world can and do participate in international relations directly. Indeed, insofar as human rights issues are at stake, governments are often the last to get into the act.

In sum, the contemporary international human rights law and policy process reflects a globe webbed by networks of interconnected and interconnecting state and non-state actors who, in the words of one of Burton's colleagues, "see politics on the surface of the earth as an integrated process operating in a single community."[34] In this process, states constitute an important subsystem in the global social community, but they are by no means the only, or even the principal, actors. Non-state actors, such as human rights nongovernmental organizations, have become significant influences on the international scene. If gross violations of human rights in one part of the globe drive refugees in unmanageable numbers elsewhere in search of asylum, human rights groups, sometimes more reliably than governments, may send the early warning signals. Church groups may supply essential sanctuary despite government apathy or hostility. Private organizations, such as the Refugee Policy Group, may supply the most reliable accounts of the social costs at both the sending and receiving ends. And all those involved will, as suggested above, likely allocate blame and urge responsibility for the displaced.

1. BURNS H. WESTON *Human Rights*

It is a common observation that human beings everywhere demand the realization of diverse values to ensure their individual and collective well-being. It also is a common observation that these demands are often painfully frustrated by social as well as natural forces, resulting in exploitation, oppression, persecution, and other forms of deprivation. Deeply rooted in these twin

32. In Michael Banks, "The International Relations Discipline: Asset or Liability for Conflict Resolution?" in *International Conflict Resolution, Theory and Practice*, ed. Edward A. Azar and John W. Burton (Boulder, Colo.: Lynne Rienner Publishers, 1986), 18–19. See also R. J. Vincent, *Human Rights and International Relations* (Cambridge: Cambridge University Press, 1986).
33. See "French League Establishes Human Rights Hotline," *Human Rights Internet Report* 11, no. 5/6 (Winter–Spring 1987): 38; Bjorn Stromarker, *HURIDOCS: Standard Formats for the Recording and Exchange of Information on Human Rights* (Dordrecht: Martinus Nijhoff Publishers, 1985).
34. Christopher Hill, "Implications of the World Society Perspectives for National Foreign Policies," in *Conflict in World Society: A New Perspective on International Relations*, ed. Michael Banks (New York: St. Martin's Press, 1984), 174–91.

observations are the beginnings of what today are called "human rights" and the legal processes, national and international, associated with them.

HISTORICAL DEVELOPMENT

The expression "human rights" is relatively new, having come into everyday parlance only since World War II and the founding of the United Nations in 1945. It replaces the phrase "natural rights," which fell into disfavor in part because the concept of natural law (to which it was intimately linked) had become a matter of great controversy, and the later phrase "the rights of Man," which was not universally understood to include the rights of women.

Most students of human rights trace the historical origins of the concept back to ancient Greece and Rome, where it was closely tied to the premodern natural law doctrines of Greek Stoicism (the school of philosophy founded by Zeno of Citium, which held that a universal working force pervades all creation and that human conduct therefore should be judged according to, and brought into harmony with, the law of nature). The classic example, drawn from the Greek literature, is that of Antigone, who, upon being reproached by Creon for defying his command not to bury her slain brother, asserted that she acted in accordance with the immutable laws of the gods.

In part because Hellenistic Stoicism played a key role in its formation and spread, Roman law may similarly be seen to have allowed for the existence of a natural law and, with it, pursuant to the *jus gentium* ("law of nations"), certain universal rights that extended beyond the rights of citizenship. According to the Roman jurist Ulpian, for example, natural law was that which nature—not the state—assures to all human beings, Roman citizen or not.

It was not until after the Middle Ages, however, that natural law doctrines became closely associated with liberal political theories about natural rights. In Greco-Roman and medieval times, natural law doctrines taught mainly the duties, as distinguished from the rights, of "Man." Moreover, as evident in the writings of Aristotle and St. Thomas Aquinas, these doctrines recognized the legitimacy of slavery and serfdom and, in so doing, excluded perhaps the most central ideas of human rights as they are understood

today—the ideas of freedom (or liberty) and equality.

For the idea of human (i.e., natural) rights to take hold as a general social need and reality, it was necessary that basic changes in the beliefs and practices of society take place, changes of the sort that evolved from about the thirteenth century to the Peace of Westphalia (1648), during the Renaissance and the decline of feudalism. When resistance to religious intolerance and political-economic bondage began the long transition to liberal notions of freedom and equality, particularly in relation to the use and ownership of property, then were the foundations of what today are called human rights truly laid. During this period, reflecting the failure of rulers to meet their natural law obligations as well as the unprecedented commitment to individual expression and worldly experience that was characteristic of the Renaissance, the shift from natural law as duties to natural law as rights was made. The teachings of Aquinas (1224/25–1274) and Hugo Grotius (1583–1645) on the European continent, and the Magna Carta (1215), the Petition of Right of 1628, and the English Bill of Rights (1689) in England, were proof of this change. All testified to the increasingly popular view that human beings are endowed with eternal and inalienable rights, never renounced when humankind "contracted" to enter the social from the primitive state and never diminished by the claim of "the divine right of kings."

It was primarily for the seventeenth and eighteenth centuries, however, to elaborate upon this modernist conception of natural law as meaning or implying natural rights. The scientific and intellectual achievements of the seventeenth century—the discoveries of Galileo and Sir Isaac Newton, the materialism of Thomas Hobbes, the rationalism of René Descartes and Gottfried Wilhelm Leibniz, the pantheism of Benedict de Spinoza, the empiricism of Francis Bacon and John Locke—encouraged a belief in natural law and universal order; and during the eighteenth century, the so-called Age of Enlightenment, a growing confidence in human reason and in the perfectability of human affairs led to its more comprehensive expression. Particularly to be noted are the writings of the seventeenth-century English philosopher John Locke—arguably the most important natural law theorist of modern times—and the works of the eighteenth-century Philosophes centered mainly in Paris, including

Montesquieu, Voltaire, and Jean-Jacques Rousseau. Locke argued in detail, mainly in writings associated with the Revolution of 1688 (the Glorious Revolution), that certain rights self-evidently pertain to individuals as human beings (because they existed in "the state of nature" before humankind entered civil society); that chief among them are rights to life, liberty (freedom from arbitrary rule), and property; that, upon entering civil society (pursuant to a "social contract"), humankind surrendered to the state only the right to enforce these natural rights, not the rights themselves; and that the state's failure to secure these reserved natural rights (the state itself being under contract to safeguard the interests of its members) gives rise to a right to responsible, popular revolution. The Philosophes, building on Locke and others and embracing many and varied currents of thought with a common supreme faith in reason, vigorously attacked religious and scientific dogmatism, intolerance, censorship, and social-economic restraints. They sought to discover and act upon universally valid principles harmoniously governing nature, humanity, and society, including the theory of the inalienable "rights of Man" that became their fundamental ethical and social gospel.

All this liberal intellectual ferment had, not surprisingly, great influence on the Western world of the late eighteenth and early nineteenth centuries. Together with the practical example of England's Revolution of 1688 and the resulting Bill of Rights, it provided the rationale for the wave of revolutionary agitation that then swept the West, most notably in North America and France. Thomas Jefferson, who had studied Locke and Montesquieu and who asserted that his countrymen were a "free people claiming their rights as derived from the laws of nature and not as the gift of their Chief Magistrate," gave poetic eloquence to the plain prose of the seventeenth century in the Declaration of Independence proclaimed by the thirteen American Colonies on July 4, 1776: "We hold these truths to be self-evident, that all men are created equal, that they are endowed by their Creator with certain unalienable Rights, that among these are Life, Liberty and the Pursuit of Happiness." Similarly, the Marquis de Lafayette, who won the close friendship of George Washington and who shared the hardships of the American War of Independence, imitated the pronouncements of the English and American revolutions in the Declaration of the Rights of Man and of the Citizen of

August 26, 1789. Insisting that "men are born and remain free and equal in rights," the declaration proclaims that "the aim of every political association is the preservation of the natural and imprescriptible rights of man," identifies these rights as "Liberty, Property, Safety and Resistance to Oppression," and defines "liberty" so as to include the right to free speech, freedom of association, religious freedom, and freedom from arbitrary arrest and confinement (as if anticipating the Bill of Rights added in 1791 to the Constitution of the United States of 1787).

In sum, the idea of human rights, called by another name, played a key role in the late eighteenth- and early nineteenth-century struggles against political absolutism. It was, indeed, the failure of rulers to respect the principles of freedom and equality, which had been central to natural law philosophy almost from the beginning, that was responsible for this development. In the words of Maurice Cranston, a leading student of human rights, "absolutism prompted man to claim [human, or natural] rights precisely because it denied them."

The idea of human rights as natural rights was not without its detractors, however, even at this otherwise receptive time. In the first place, being frequently associated with religious orthodoxy, the doctrine of natural rights became less and less acceptable to philosophical and political liberals. Additionally, because they were conceived in essentially absolutist—"inalienable," "unalterable," "eternal"—terms, natural rights were found increasingly to come into conflict with one another. Most importantly, the doctrine of natural rights came under powerful philosophical and political attack from both the right and the left.

In England, for example, conservatives Edmund Burke and David Hume united with liberal Jeremy Bentham in condemning the doctrine, the former out of fear that public affirmation of natural rights would lead to social upheaval, the latter out of concern lest declarations and proclamations of natural rights substitute for effective legislation. In his *Reflections on the Revolution in France* (1790), Burke, a believer in natural law who nonetheless denied that the "rights of Man" could be derived from it, criticized the drafters of the Declaration of the Rights of Man and of the Citizen for proclaiming the "monstrous fiction" of human equality, which, he argued, serves but to inspire "false ideas and vain expectations in men destined to travel in the obscure walk of laborious life." Bentham, one of the founders of Utilitarianism and a nonbeliever, was no less scornful. "Rights," he wrote, "is the child of law; from real law come real rights; but from imaginary laws, from 'law of nature,' come imaginary rights. . . . Natural rights is simple nonsense; natural and imprescriptible rights (an American phrase), rhetorical nonsense, nonsense upon stilts." Hume agreed with Bentham; natural law and natural rights, he insisted, are unreal metaphysical phenomena.

This assault upon natural law and natural rights, thus begun during the late eighteenth century, both intensified and broadened during the nineteenth and early twentieth centuries. John Stuart Mill, despite his vigorous defense of liberty, proclaimed that rights ultimately are founded on utility. The German jurist Friedrich Karl von Savigny, England's Sir Henry Maine, and other historicalists emphasized that rights are a function of cultural and environmental variables unique to particular communities. And the jurist John Austin and the philosopher Ludwig Wittgenstein insisted, respectively, that the only law is "the command of the sovereign" (a phrase of Thomas Hobbes) and that the only truth is that which can be established by verifiable experience. By World War I, there were scarcely any theorists who would or could defend the "rights of Man" along the lines of natural law. Indeed, under the influence of nineteenth-century German Idealism and parallel expressions of rising European nationalism, there were some—the Marxists, for example—who, although not rejecting individual rights altogether, maintained that rights, from whatever source derived, belong to communities or whole societies and nations preeminently. Thus did F. H. Bradley, the British Idealist, write in 1894: "The rights of the individual are today not worth serious consideration. . . . The welfare of the community is the end and is the ultimate standard."

Yet, though the heyday of natural rights proved short, the idea of human rights nonetheless endured in one form or another. The abolition of slavery, factory legislation, popular education, trade unionism, the universal suffrage movement—these and other examples of nineteenth-century reformist impulses afford ample evidence that the idea was not to be extinguished even if its transempirical derivation had become a matter of general skepticism. But it was not until the rise and fall of Nazi Germany that the idea of rights—human rights—came truly into its

own. The laws authorizing the dispossession and extermination of Jews and other minorities, the laws permitting arbitrary police search and seizure, the laws condoning imprisonment, torture, and execution without public trial—these and similar obscenities brought home the realization that law and morality, if they are to be deserving of the name, cannot be grounded in any purely Utilitarian, Idealist, or other consequentialist doctrine. Certain actions are wrong, no matter what; human beings are entitled to simple respect at least.

Today, the vast majority of legal scholars, philosophers, and moralists agree, irrespective of culture or civilization, that every human being is entitled, at least in theory, to some basic rights. Heir to the Protestant Reformation and to the English, American, French, Mexican, Russian, and Chinese revolutions, the last half of the twentieth century has seen, in the words of human rights scholar Louis Henkin, "essentially universal acceptance of human rights in principle" such that "no government dares to dissent from the ideology of human rights today." Indeed, except for some essentially isolated nineteenth-century demonstrations of international humanitarian concern to be noted below, the last half of the twentieth century may fairly be said to mark the birth of the international as well as the universal recognition of human rights. In the treaty establishing the United Nations (UN), all members pledged themselves to take joint and separate action for the achievement of "universal respect for, and observance of, human rights and fundamental freedoms for all without distinction as to race, sex, language, or religion." In the Universal Declaration of Human Rights (1948), representatives from many diverse cultures endorsed the rights therein set forth "as a common standard of achievement for all peoples and all nations." And in 1976, the International Covenant on Economic, Social and Cultural Rights and the International Covenant on Civil and Political Rights, each approved by the UN General Assembly in 1966, entered into force and effect.

DEFINITION OF HUMAN RIGHTS

To say that there is widespread acceptance of the principle of human rights on the domestic and international planes is not to say that there is complete agreement about the nature of such rights or their substantive scope—which is to say, their definition. Some of the most basic questions have yet to receive conclusive answers. Whether human rights are to be viewed as divine, moral, or legal entitlements; whether they are to be validated by intuition, custom, social contract theory, principles of distributive justice, or as prerequisites for happiness; whether they are to be understood as irrevocable or partially revocable; whether they are to be broad or limited in number and content—these and kindred issues are matters of ongoing debate and likely will remain so as long as there exist contending approaches to public order and scarcities among resources.

Nature

Despite this lack of consensus, however, a number of widely accepted—and interrelated—postulates may be seen to assist, if not to complete, the task of defining human rights. Five in particular stand out, although it is to be noted that not even these are without controversy.

First, regardless of their ultimate origin or justification, human rights are understood to represent individual and group demands for the shaping and sharing of power, wealth, enlightenment, and other cherished values in community process, most fundamentally the value of respect and its constituent elements of reciprocal tolerance and mutual forbearance in the pursuit of all other values. Consequently, they imply claims against persons and institutions who impede realization and standards for judging the legitimacy of laws and traditions. At bottom, human rights limit state power.

Second, reflecting varying environmental circumstances, differing worldviews, and inescapable interdependencies within and between value processes, human rights refer to a wide continuum of value claims ranging from the most justiciable to the most aspirational. Human rights partake of both the legal and the moral orders, sometimes indistinguishably. They are expressive of both the "is" and the "ought" in human affairs.

Third, if a right is determined to be a human right it is quintessentially general or universal in character, in some sense equally possessed by all human beings everywhere, including in certain instances even the unborn. In stark contrast to "the divine right of kings" and other such conceptions of privilege, human rights extend, in

theory, to every person on Earth without discriminations irrelevant to merit.

Fourth, most assertions of human rights—arguably not all—are qualified by the limitation that the rights of any particular individual or group in any particular instance are restricted as much as is necessary to secure the comparable rights of others and the aggregate common interest. Given this interdependency, human rights are sometimes designated prima facie rights, and it makes little or no sense to think or talk of them in absolutist terms.

Fifth and finally, human rights are commonly assumed to refer, in some vague sense, to "fundamental" as distinct from "nonessential" claims or "goods." In fact, some theorists go so far as to limit human rights to a single core right or two—for example, the right to life or the right to equal freedom of opportunity. The tendency, in short, is to de-emphasize or rule out "mere wants."

In several critical respects, however, this last postulate raises more questions than it answers. What does it mean to say that a right is fundamental? Does it entail some bare minimum only, or, more plausibly, does it admit to something greater? If the latter, how much greater and subject to what conditions, if any? In other words, however accurate, this last postulate is fraught with ambiguity about the content and legitimate scope of human rights and about the priorities, if any, that obtain among them. Except for the issue of the origin and justification of human rights, no cluster of preliminary human rights considerations is more controversial.

Content

It cannot be disputed that, like all normative traditions, the human rights tradition is a product of its time. It necessarily reflects the processes of historical continuity and change that, at once and as a matter of cumulative experience, help to give it substance and form. Therefore, to understand better the debate over the content and legitimate scope of human rights and the priorities claimed among them, it is useful to note the dominant schools of thought and action that have informed the human rights tradition since the beginning of modern times.

Particularly helpful in this regard is the notion of "three generations of human rights" advanced by the French jurist Karel Vasak. Inspired by the three normative themes of the French Revolution, they are: the first generation of civil and political rights (*liberté*); the second generation of economic, social, and cultural rights (*égalité*); and the third generation of newly called solidarity rights (*fraternité*). Vasak's model is of course a simplified expression of an extremely complex historical record; it is not intended as a literal representation of life in which one generation gives birth to the next and then dies away.

The First Generation

The first generation of civil and political rights derives primarily from the seventeenth- and eighteenth-century reformist theories noted above, which are associated with the English, American, and French revolutions. Infused with the political philosophy of liberal individualism and the economic and social doctrine of laissez-faire, it conceives of human rights more in negative ("freedoms from") than positive ("rights to") terms; it favors the abstention rather than the intervention of government in the quest for human dignity, as epitomized by the statement attributed to H. L. Mencken that "all government is, of course, against liberty." Belonging to this first generation, thus, are such claimed rights as are set forth in Articles 2–21 of the Universal Declaration of Human Rights, including freedom from racial and equivalent forms of discrimination; the right to life, liberty, and the security of the person; freedom from slavery or involuntary servitude; freedom from torture and from cruel, inhuman, or degrading treatment or punishment; freedom from arbitrary arrest, detention, or exile; the right to a fair and public trial; freedom from interference in privacy and correspondence; freedom of movement and residence; the right to asylum from persecution; freedom of thought, conscience, and religion; freedom of opinion and expression; freedom of peaceful assembly and association; and the right to participate in government, directly or through free elections. Also included is the right to own property and the right not to be deprived of one's property arbitrarily, each fundamental to the interests fought for in the American and French revolutions and to the rise of capitalism.

Of course, it would be error to assert that these and other first-generation rights correspond completely to the idea of "negative" as opposed to "positive" rights. The right to security of the person, to a fair and public trial, to asylum from persecution, and to free elections, for example, manifestly cannot be assured without some affirmative government action. What is constant in this first-generation conception, however, is the notion of liberty, a shield that safeguards the individual, alone and in association with others, against the abuse and misuse of political authority. This is the core value. Featured in almost every constitution of today's approximately 160 states, and dominating the majority of the international declarations and covenants adopted since World War II, this essentially Western liberal conception of human rights is sometimes romanticized as a triumph of Hobbesian-Lockean individualism over Hegelian statism.

The Second Generation

The second generation of economic, social, and cultural rights finds its origins primarily in the socialist tradition that was foreshadowed among the Saint-Simonians of early nineteenth-century France and variously promoted by revolutionary struggles and welfare movements ever since. In large part, it is a response to the abuses and misuses of capitalist development and its underlying, essentially uncritical, conception of individual liberty that tolerated, even legitimated, the exploitation of working classes and colonial peoples. Historically, it is counterpoint to the first generation of civil and political rights, with human rights conceived more in positive ("rights to") than negative ("freedoms from") terms, requiring the intervention, not the abstention, of the state for the purpose of assuring equitable participation in the production and distribution of the values involved. Illustrative are the claimed rights set forth in Articles 22–27 of the Universal Declaration of Human Rights, such as the right to social security; the right to work and to protection against unemployment; the right to rest and leisure, including periodic holidays with pay; the right to a standard of living adequate for the health and well-being of self and family; the right to education; and the right to the protection of one's scientific, literary, and artistic production.

Yet, in the same way that all the rights embraced by the first generation of civil and political rights cannot properly be designated "negative rights," so all the rights embraced by the second generation of economic, social, and cultural rights cannot properly be labeled "positive rights." The right to free choice of employment, the right to form and to join trade unions, and the right freely to participate in the cultural life of the community, for example, do not inherently require affirmative state action to ensure their enjoyment. Nevertheless, most of the second-generation rights do necessitate state intervention in the allocation of resources because they subsume demands more for material than for intangible values according to some criterion of distributive justice. Second-generation rights are, fundamentally, claims to social equality. Partly because of the comparatively late arrival of socialist-communist influence in the normative domain of international affairs, however, the internationalization of these rights has been somewhat slow in coming; but with the ascendancy of the Third World on the global stage, intent upon a "revolution of rising expectations," they have begun to come of age.

The Third Generation

Finally, the third generation of solidarity rights, while drawing upon, interlinking, and re-conceptualizing value demands associated with the two earlier generations of rights, are best understood as a product, albeit one still in formation, of both the rise and the decline of the nation-state in the last half of the twentieth century. Foreshadowed in Article 28 of the Universal Declaration of Human Rights, which proclaims that "everyone is entitled to a social and international order in which the rights set forth in this Declaration can be fully realized," it appears so far to embrace six claimed rights. Three of these reflect the emergence of Third World nationalism and its demand for a global redistribution of power, wealth, and other important values: the right to political, economic, social, and cultural self-determination; the right to economic and social development; and the right to participate in and benefit from "the common heritage of mankind" (shared Earth-space resources; scientific, technical, and other information and progress; and cultural traditions, sites, and monuments). The other three third-generation rights—the right to peace, the right to a healthy and balanced environment, and the right to humanitarian disaster relief—suggest the impotence or inefficiency of the nation-state in certain critical respects.

All six of these claimed rights tend to be posed as collective rights, requiring the concerted efforts of all social forces, to substantial degree on a planetary scale, and implying a quest for a possible utopia that projects the notion of holistic community interests. Each, however, manifests an individual as well as collective dimension. For example, while it may be said to be the collective right of all countries and peoples (especially developing countries and non-self-governing peoples) to secure a new international economic order that would eliminate obstacles to their economic and social development, so also may it be said to be the individual right of all persons to benefit from a developmental policy that is based on the satisfaction of material and nonmaterial human needs. Also, while the right to self-determination and the right to humanitarian assistance, for example, find expression on the legal as well as the moral plane, the majority of these solidarity rights tend to be more aspirational than justiciable in character, enjoying as yet an ambiguous jural status as international human rights norms.

Thus, at various stages of modern history—following the "bourgeois" revolutions of the seventeenth and eighteenth centuries, the socialist and Marxist revolutions of the early twentieth century, and the anticolonialist revolutions that began immediately following World War II—the content of human rights has been broadly defined, not with any expectation that the rights associated with one generation would or should become outdated upon the ascendancy of another, but expansively or supplementally. Reflecting evolving perceptions of which values, at different times, stand most in need of encouragement and protection, the history of the content of human rights also reflects humankind's recurring demands for continuity and stability.

LEGITIMACY AND PRIORITY

This is not to imply that each of these three generations of rights is equally acceptable to all or that they or their separate elements are greeted with equal urgency. First-generation proponents, for example, are inclined to exclude second- and third-generation rights from their definition of human rights altogether (or, at best, to label them as "derivative"). In part this is due to the complexities that inform the process of putting these rights into action. The suggestion of greater feasibility that attends first-generation rights because they stress the absence rather than the presence of government is somehow transformed into a prerequisite of a comprehensive definition of human rights, such that aspirational and vaguely asserted claims to entitlement are deemed not to be rights at all. The most forceful explanation, however, is more ideologically or politically motivated. Persuaded that egalitarian claims against the rich, particularly where collectively espoused, are unworkable without a severe decline in liberty and quality (in part because they involve state intervention for the redistribution of privately held resources), first-generation proponents, inspired by the natural law and laissez-faire traditions, are partial to the view that human rights are inherently independent of civil society and are individualistic.

Conversely, second- and third-generation defenders often look upon first-generation rights, at least as commonly practiced, as insufficiently attentive to material human needs and, indeed, as legitimating instruments in service to unjust domestic, transnational, and international social orders—hence constituting a "bourgeois illusion." Accordingly, while not placing first-generation rights outside their definition of human rights, they tend to assign such rights a low status and therefore to treat them as long-term goals that will come to pass only with fundamental economic and social transformations to be realized progressively and fully consummated only sometime in the future.

In sum, different conceptions of rights, particularly emerging conceptions, contain the potential for challenging the legitimacy and supremacy not only of one another but, more importantly, of the political-social systems with which they are most intimately associated. As a consequence, there is sharp disagreement about the legitimate scope of human rights and about the priorities that are claimed among them.

On final analysis, however, this liberty-equality and individualist-collectivist debate over the legitimacy and priorities of claimed human rights can be dangerously misleading. It is useful, certainly, insofar as it calls attention to the way in which notions of liberty and individualism can be, and have been, used to rationalize the abuses of capitalism; and it is useful, too, insofar as it

highlights how notions of equality and collectivism can be, and have been, alibis for authoritarian governance. But in the end it risks obscuring at least three essential truths that must be taken into account if the contemporary worldwide human rights movement is to be objectively understood.

First, one-sided characterizations of legitimacy and priority are likely, over the long term, to undermine the political credibility of their proponents and the defensibility of their particularistic values. In an increasingly interdependent and interpenetrating global community, any human rights orientation that does not genuinely support the widest possible shaping and sharing of all values among all human beings is likely to provoke widespread skepticism. The last half of the twentieth century is replete with examples.

Second, such characterizations do not accurately mirror behavioral reality. In the real world, despite differences in cultural tradition and ideological style, there exists a rising and overriding insistence upon the equitable production and distribution of all basic values. U.S. President Franklin D. Roosevelt's Four Freedoms (freedom of speech and expression, freedom of worship, freedom from want, and freedom from fear) is an early case in point. A more recent demonstration was the 1977 Law Day speech by then U.S. Secretary of State Cyrus R. Vance, in which he announced the U.S. government's resolve "to make the advancement of human rights a central part of our foreign policy" and defined human rights to include "the right to be free from governmental violation of the integrity of the person, . . . the right to the fulfillment of such vital needs as food, shelter, health care, and education, . . . [and] the right to enjoy civil and political liberties." Essentially individualistic societies tolerate, even promote, certain collectivist values; likewise, essentially communal societies tolerate, even promote, certain individualistic values. Ours is a more-or-less, not an either-or, world.

Finally, none of the international human rights instruments currently in force or proposed say anything whatsoever about the legitimacy or rank-ordering of the rights they address, save possibly in the case of rights that by international covenant are stipulated to be nonderogable and therefore, arguably, more fundamental than others (for example, freedom from arbitrary or unlawful deprivation of life, freedom from torture and from inhuman or degrading treatment and punishment, freedom from slavery, freedom from imprisonment for debt). There is disagreement, to be sure, among lawyers, moralists, and political scientists about the legitimacy and hierarchy of claimed rights when they treat the problem of implementation. For example, some insist on certain civil and political guarantees, whereas others defer initially to conditions of material and corporeal well-being. Such disagreements, however, partake of political agendas and have little if any conceptual utility. As the UN General Assembly has repeatedly confirmed, all human rights form an indivisible whole.

In short, the legitimacy of different human rights and the priorities claimed among them are a function of context. Because people in different parts of the world both assert and honor different human rights demands according to many different procedures and practices, these issues ultimately depend on time, place, setting, level of crisis, and other circumstance.

INTERNATIONAL HUMAN RIGHTS: PRESCRIPTION AND ENFORCEMENT

BEFORE WORLD WAR II

Ever since ancient times, but especially since the emergence of the modern state system, the Age of Discovery, and the accompanying spread of industrialization and European culture throughout the world, there has developed, for economic and other reasons, a unique set of customs and conventions relative to the humane treatment of foreigners. This evolving International Law of State Responsibility for Injuries to Aliens, as these customs and conventions came to be called, may be understood to represent the beginning of active concern for human rights on the international plane. The founding fathers of international law—particularly Francisco de Vitoria (1486?–1546), Hugo Grotius (1583–1465), and Emmerich de Vattel (1714–1767)—were quick to observe that all persons, outlander as well as other, were entitled to certain natural rights; and they emphasized, consequently, the importance of according aliens fair treatment.

Except, however, for the occasional use of treaties to secure the protection of Christian minorities, as early illustrated by the Peace of Westphalia (1648), which concluded the Thirty Years War and established the principle of equal rights for the Roman Catholic and Protestant religions in Germany, it was not until the start of the nine-

teenth century that active international concern for the rights of nationals began to make itself felt. Then, in the century and a half before World War II, several noteworthy, if essentially unconnected, efforts to encourage respect for nationals by international means began to shape what today is called the International Law of Human Rights (which for historical but no theoretically convincing reasons has tended to be treated separately from the International Law of State Responsibility for Injuries to Aliens).

Throughout the nineteenth and early twentieth centuries, numerous military operations and diplomatic representations, not all of them with the purest of motives but done nonetheless in the name of "humanitarian intervention" (a customary international law doctrine), undertook to protect oppressed and persecuted minorities in the Ottoman Empire and in Syria, Crete, various Balkan countries, Romania, and Russia. Paralleling these actions, first at the Congress of Vienna (1814–15) and later between the two world wars, a series of treaties and international declarations sought the protection of certain racial, religious, and linguistic minorities in central and eastern Europe and in the Middle East. During the same period the movement to combat and suppress slavery and the slave trade found expression in treaties sooner or later involving the major commercial powers, beginning with the Treaty of Paris (1814) and culminating in the International Slavery Convention (1926).

In addition, toward the end of the nineteenth century and continuing well beyond World War II, the community of nations, inspired largely by persons associated with what is now the International Committee of the Red Cross, concluded a series of multilateral declarations and agreements designed to temper the conduct of hostilities, protect the victims of war, and otherwise elaborate the humanitarian law of war. At about the same time, first with two multilateral labor conventions concluded in 1906 and subsequently at the initiative of the International Labor Organization (ILO, established in 1919), a reformist-minded international community embarked upon a variety of collaborative measures directed at the promotion of human rights. These included not only fields traditionally associated with labor law and relations (for example, industrial health, safety, and welfare; hours of work; annual paid holidays) but also—mainly after World War II—in respect of such core human rights concerns as forced labor, discrimination in employment and occupation, freedom of association for collective bargaining, and equal pay for equal work.

Finally, during the interwar period, the Covenant establishing the League of Nations (1919), while not formally recognizing "the rights of Man" and while failing to lay down a principle of racial nondiscrimination as requested by Japan (owing mainly to the resistance of Great Britain and the United States), nevertheless committed the League's members to several human rights goals; fair and humane working conditions for men, women, and children; the execution of agreements regarding traffic in women and children; the prevention and control of disease in matters of international concern; and the just treatment of native colonial peoples. Also, victorious powers who as "mandatories" were entrusted by the League with the tutelage of colonies formerly governed by Germany and Turkey accepted as "a sacred trust of civilization" responsibilities for the well-being and development of the inhabitants of those territories. (The arrangement was carried over into the UN trusteeship system and had serious repercussions more than a half century later in relation to the mandate entrusted to South Africa over the territory of South West Africa [now Namibia].)

As important as these pre–World War II human rights efforts were, however, it was not until after the War—and the Nazi atrocities accompanying it—that active concern for human rights on the international plane truly came of age. In the proceedings of the International Military Tribunal at Nuremberg in 1945–46, German high officials were tried not only for "crimes against peace" and "war crimes" but also for "crimes against humanity" committed against any civilian population even if in accordance with the laws of the country where perpetrated. While the tribunal, whose establishment and rulings subsequently were endorsed by the UN General Assembly, applied a cautious approach to allegations of "crimes against humanity," it nonetheless made the treatment by a state of its own citizens the subject of international criminal process.

HUMAN RIGHTS IN THE UNITED NATIONS

The Charter of the United Nations (1945) begins by reaffirming a "faith in fundamental human rights, in the dignity and worth of the human person, in the equal rights of men and women and of nations large and small." It states that the purposes of the United Nations are, among other things, "to develop friendly relations among nations based on respect for the principle of equal rights and self-determination of peoples . . . [and] to achieve international cooperation . . . in promoting and encouraging respect for human rights and for fundamental freedoms for all without distinction as to race, sex, language, or religion. . . ." And, in two key articles, all members "pledge themselves to take joint and separate action in cooperation with the Organization" for the achievement of these and related purposes. It is to be noted, however, that a proposal to ensure the protection as well as the promotion of human rights was explicitly rejected at the San Francisco Conference establishing the United Nations. Additionally, the Charter expressly provides that nothing in it "shall authorize the United Nations to intervene in matters which are essentially within the domestic jurisdiction of any state. . . ," except upon a Security Council finding of a "threat to the peace, breach of the peace, or act of aggression." Moreover, although typical of major constitutive instruments, the Charter is conspicuously general and vague in its human rights clauses, among others.

Thus, not surprisingly, the reconciliation of the Charter's human rights provisions with the Charter's drafting history and its "domestic jurisdiction" clause has given rise to not a little legal and political controversy. Some authorities have argued that, in becoming parties to the Charter, states accept no more than a nebulous promotional obligation toward human rights and that, in any event, the United Nations has no standing to insist on human rights safeguards in member states. Others insist that the Charter's human rights provisions, being part of a legally binding treaty, clearly involve some element of legal obligation; that the "pledge" made by states upon becoming party to the Charter consequently represents more than a moral statement; and that the "domestic jurisdiction" clause does not apply because human rights, whatever isolation they may have "enjoyed" in the past, no longer can be considered matters "essentially within the domestic jurisdiction" of states.

When all is said and done, however, it is clear from the actual practice of the United Nations that the problem of resolving these opposing contentions has proved somewhat less formidable than the statements of governments and the opinions of scholars might lead one to assume. Neither the Charter's drafting history nor its "domestic jurisdiction" clause nor, indeed, its generality and vagueness in respect of human rights has prevented the United Nations—on the basis of individual petitions, statements from witnesses, state complaints, and reports from interested nongovernmental organizations—from investigating, discussing, and evaluating specific human rights situations. Nor have they prevented it from recommending or prescribing concrete action in relation to them, at least not in the case of "a consistent pattern of gross violations" of human rights, provided there has been a majority persuasive enough to force the action desired (as in the imposition by the Security Council in 1977 of a mandatory arms embargo against South Africa). Of course, governments usually are protective of their sovereignty (or domestic jurisdiction). Also, the UN organs responsible for the promotion of human rights suffer from most of the same disabilities that afflict the United Nations as a whole, in particular the absence of supranational authority and the presence of divisive power politics. Hence, it cannot be expected that UN actions in defense of human rights will be, normally, either swift or categorically effective. Nevertheless, assuming some political will, the legal obstacles to UN enforcement of human rights are not insurmountable.

Primary responsibility for the promotion of human rights under the UN Charter rests in the General Assembly and, under its authority, in the Economic and Social Council and its subsidiary body, the Commission on Human Rights, an intergovernmental body that serves as the UN's central policy organ in the human rights field. Much of the commission's activity, initiated by subsidiary working groups, is investigatory, evaluative, and advisory in character, and the commission annually establishes a working group to consider and make recommendations concerning alleged "gross violations" of human rights referred to it by its Sub-Commission on Prevention of Discrimination and Protection of Minorities (on the basis of communications from individuals and groups, pursuant to Resolution 1503 [1970] of the UN Economic and Social Council, and sometimes on the basis of investigations by the subcommission or one of its working groups).

Also, the commission has appointed special representatives and envoys to examine human rights situations on an ad hoc basis, who, in the course of preparing their reports, examine reliable information submitted in good faith, interview interested persons, or make on-site inspections with the cooperation of the government concerned.

In addition, the commission, together with other UN organs such as the International Labor Organization (ILO), the UN Educational, Scientific and Cultural Organization (UNESCO), and the UN Commission on the Status of Women, drafts human rights standards and has prepared a number of international human rights instruments. Among the most important are the Universal Declaration of Human Rights (1948), the International Covenant on Civil and Political Rights (together with its Optional Protocol, 1976), and the International Covenant on Economic, Social and Cultural Rights (1976). Collectively known as the International Bill of Rights, these three instruments serve as touchstones for interpreting the human rights provisions of the UN Charter.

The Universal Declaration of Human Rights

The catalog of rights set out in the Universal Declaration of Human Rights, which was adopted without dissent by the General Assembly on December 10, 1948, is scarcely less than the sum of all the important traditional political and civil rights of national constitutions and legal systems, including equality before the law; protection against arbitrary arrest; the right to a fair trial; freedom from ex post facto criminal laws; the right to own property; freedom of thought, conscience, and religion; freedom of opinion and expression; and freedom of peaceful assembly and association. Also enumerated are such economic, social, and cultural rights as the right to work and to choose one's work freely, the right to equal pay for equal work, the right to form and join trade unions, the right to rest and leisure, the right to an adequate standard of living, and the right to education.

The Universal Declaration, it must be noted, is not a treaty. It was meant to proclaim "a common standard of achievement for all peoples and all nations" rather than enforceable legal obligations. Nevertheless, partly because of an eighteen-year delay between its adoption and the completion for signature and ratification of the two covenants, the Universal Declaration has acquired a status juridically more important than originally intended. It has been widely used, even by national courts, as a means of judging compliance with human rights obligations under the UN Charter.

The International Covenant on Civil and Political Rights and the Optional Protocol

The civil and political rights guaranteed by this covenant, which was opened for signature on December 19, 1966, and entered into force on March 23, 1976, incorporate almost all of those proclaimed in the Universal Declaration, including the right to nondiscrimination. Pursuant to the covenant, each state party undertakes to respect and to ensure to all individuals within its territory and subject to its jurisdiction the rights recognized in the covenant "without distinction of any kind, such as race, colour, sex, language, religion, political or other opinion, national or social origin, property, birth or other status." Some rights listed in the Universal Declaration, however, such as the right to own property and the right to asylum, are not included among the rights recognized in the covenant. Similarly, the covenant designates a number of rights that are not listed in the Universal Declaration, among them the right of all peoples to self-determination and the right of ethnic, religious, or linguistic minorities to enjoy their own culture, to profess and practice their own religion, and to use their own language. To the extent that the Universal Declaration and the covenant overlap, however, the latter is understood to explicate and help interpret the former.

In addition, the covenant calls for the establishment of a Human Rights Committee, an international organ of eighteen persons elected by the parties to the covenant, serving in their individual expert capacity and charged to study reports submitted by the state parties on the measures they have adopted that give effect to the rights recognized in the covenant. As between the state parties that have expressly recognized the competence of the committee in this regard, the committee also may respond to allegations by one

state party that another state party is not fulfilling its obligations under the covenant. If the committee is unable to resolve the problem, the matter is referred to an ad hoc conciliation commission, which eventually reports its findings on all questions of fact, plus its views on the possibilities of an amicable solution. State parties that become party to the Optional Protocol further recognize the competence of the Human Rights Committee similarly to consider and act upon communications from individuals claiming to be victims of covenant violations.

The International Covenant on Economic, Social and Cultural Rights

Just as the International Covenant on Civil and Political Rights elaborates upon most of the civil and political rights enumerated in the Universal Declaration of Human Rights, so the International Covenant on Economic, Social and Cultural Rights elaborates upon most of the economic, social, and cultural rights set forth in the Universal Declaration: the right to work; the right to just and favorable conditions of work; trade union rights; the right to social security; rights relating to the protection of the family; the right to an adequate standard of living; the right to health; the right to education; and rights relating to culture and science. Unlike its companion International Covenant on Civil and Political Rights, however, this covenant is not geared, with modest exception, to immediate implementation, the state parties having agreed only "to take steps" toward "achieving progressively the full realization of the rights recognized in the . . . Covenant," and then subject to "the maximum of [their] available resources." The covenant is essentially a "promotional convention," stipulating objectives more than standards and requiring implementation over time rather than all at once. One obligation is, however, subject to immediate application: the prohibition of discrimination in the enjoyment of the rights enumerated on grounds of race, color, sex, language, religion, or political or other opinion; national or social origin; property; and birth or other status. Also, the international supervisory measures that apply to the covenant oblige the state parties to report to the UN Economic and Social Council on the steps they have adopted and the progress they have made in achieving the realization of the enumerated rights.

Other UN Human Rights Conventions

The two above-mentioned covenants are by no means the only human rights treaties drafted and adopted under the auspices of the United Nations. Indeed, because there are far too many to detail even in abbreviated fashion, it must suffice simply to note that they address a broad range of concerns, including the prevention and punishment of the crime of genocide; the humane treatment of military and civilian personnel in time of war; the status of refugees; the protection and reduction of stateless persons; the abolition of slavery, forced labor, and discrimination in employment and occupation; the elimination of all forms of racial discrimination and the suppression and punishment of the crime of apartheid; the elimination of discrimination in education; the promotion of the political rights of women and the elimination of all forms of discrimination against women; and the promotion of equality of opportunity and treatment of migrant workers. (For particular agreements, see *Human Rights: A Compilation of International Instruments*, 3rd ed. [1978], published by the United Nations.)[1] Many of these treaties are the work of the UN specialized agencies, particularly the International Labor Organization (ILO), and many also provide for supervisory and enforcement mechanisms—for example, the Committee on the Elimination of Racial Discrimination established under the International Convention on the Elimination of All Forms of Racial Discrimination of December 21, 1965.

UN Human Rights Declarations

In addition to developing human rights standards and procedures through treaties, the UN General Assembly, impressed by the impact of the Universal Declaration of Human Rights, also has resorted to the proclamation of declarations as a means of promoting human rights. Adopted in the form of a resolution of the General Assembly, which technically is not binding on the member states in the sense of a treaty, a declaration, particularly when it enuciates principles of great and solemn importance, may nevertheless create within the international community strong expectations about authority and control. Perhaps the best known examples subsequent to the Universal Declaration, while not devoted exclusively to human rights considerations, are the Declaration on the Granting of Independence to Colonial Countries and Peoples (1960) and the Declaration on Principles of International Law Concerning Friendly Relations and Co-Operation Among States in Accordance with the Charter of the United Nations (1970).

HUMAN RIGHTS AND THE HELSINKI PROCESS

Post–World War II concern for human rights also has been evident at the global level outside the United Nations, most notably in the proceedings and aftermath of the Conference on Security and Cooperation in Europe, convened in Helsinki on July 3, 1973, and concluded there (after continuing deliberations in Geneva) on August 1, 1975. Attended by representatives of thirty-five governments that included the NATO countries, the Warsaw Pact nations, and thirteen neutral and nonaligned European states, the conference had as its principal purpose a mutually satisfactory definition of peace and stability between East and West, previously made impossible by the period of the Cold War. In particular, the Soviet Union was concerned with achieving recognition of its western frontiers as established at the end of World War II.

There was little tangible, however, that the Western powers, with no realistic territorial claims of their own, could demand in return, and accordingly they pressed for certain concessions in respect of human rights and freedom of movement and information between East and West. Thus, at the outset of the Final Act adopted by the conference, in a Declaration of Principles Guiding Relations Between States, the participating governments solemnly declared "their determination to respect and put into practice," alongside other "guiding" principles, "respect [for] human rights and fundamental freedoms, including the freedom of thought, conscience, religion or belief" and "respect [for] the equal rights of peoples and their right to self-determi-

---

1. [The current edition of the *Compilation* is the 4th ed. (1983).]

nation." It was hoped that this would mark the beginning of a liberalization of authoritarian regimes.

From the earliest discussions, however, it was clear that the Helsinki Final Act was not intended as a legally binding instrument. "Determination to respect" and "put into practice" were deemed to express moral commitments only, the Declaration of Principles was said not to prescribe international law, and nowhere did the participants provide for enforcement machinery. On the other hand, the Declaration of Principles, including its human rights principles, always has been viewed as at least consistent with international law. Additionally, the fourth of four sections (commonly known as "baskets") of the Final Act provides for the holding of periodic review conferences in which the participating states are called upon "to continue the multilateral process initiated by the Conference," But most importantly, ever since their adoption, the Final Act's human rights provisions have served as important and widely accepted yardsticks for external scrutiny and appropriate recourse to perceived violations.

In sum, like the Universal Declaration of Human Rights and other such declarations of the UN General Assembly, the Helsinki Final Act, though not a treaty, has created widespread expectations about proper human rights behavior, and consequently it has inspired and facilitated the monitoring of human rights policy. Assuming some cordiality between East and West, the Helsinki Process may be said at least to hold out the potential for modestly beneficial results in the human rights arena.

REGIONAL DEVELOPMENTS

Action for the international promotion and protection of human rights has proceeded at the regional level in Europe, the Americas, Africa, and the Middle East.[2] Only the first three of these regions, however, have gone so far as to create enforcement mechanisms within the framework of a human rights charter. The Permanent Arab Commission on Human Rights, founded by the Council of the League of Arab States in September 1968 but since then preoccupied by the rights of Arabs living in Israeli-occupied territories, has not brought a proposed Arab Convention on

Human Rights to a successful conclusion and so far has tended to function more in terms of the promotion than the protection of human rights.

European Human Rights System

On November 4, 1950, the Council of Europe agreed to the European Convention for the Protection of Human Rights and Fundamental Freedoms, the substantive provisions of which are based on a draft of what is now the International Covenant on Civil and Political Rights. Together with its five additional protocols, this convention, which entered into force on September 3, 1953, represents the most advanced and successful international experiment in the field. A companion instrument, similar to the later International Covenant on Economic, Social and Cultural Rights, is the European Social Charter (1961), whose provisions are implemented through an elaborate system of control based on the sending of progress reports to, and the appraisal of these reports by, the various committees and organs of the Council of Europe. The instrumentalities created under the European convention are the European Commission of Human Rights and the European Court of Human Rights. The convention also makes use of the governmental organ of the Council of Europe, the Committee of Ministers.

The commission may receive from any state party to the convention any allegation of a breach of the convention by another state party. Also, provided its legal competence to do so has been formally recognized, the commission may receive petitions from any person, group of individuals, or nongovernmental organization claiming to be the victim of a violation of the convention. In such cases, the commission is charged to ascertain the facts and to place itself at the disposal of the parties to secure "a friendly settlement . . . on the basis of respect for Human Rights." If no such solution is reached, the commission is called upon to draw up a report, stating its opinion as to whether the facts disclose a breach, and to recommend action to the Committee of Ministers, including referral of the case to the European Court of Human Rights.

The jurisdiction of the court extends to cases referred to it by a state party whose national is

---

2. [For greater detail, see Reading 16 in Chapter 4 in this volume.]

alleged to be a victim of a violation, by a state party against whom a complaint has been lodged, and by any state party that may have referred the case to the commission. The court may not, however, receive a complaint by an individual applicant. Moreover, it may receive state complaints only if the defendant state has accepted its jurisdiction. This may be done ad hoc for a particular case or by a general declaration accepting the compulsory jurisdiction of the court. In either event, and in cases referred by the European commission as well, the judgment of the court is final. If a question is not or cannot be referred to the court, then the Committee of Ministers of the Council of Europe makes a final decision on human rights complaints.

The instrumentalities of the European convention have, over the years, developed a considerable body of case law on questions regulated by the convention, and the provisions of the convention are deemed, in some European states, part of domestic constitutional or statutory law. Where this is not the case, the state parties to the convention have taken other measures to make their domestic laws conform with their obligations under the convention.

Inter-American Human Rights System

In 1948, concurrent with its establishment of the Organization of American States (OAS), the Ninth Pan-American Conference adopted the American Declaration on the Rights and Duties of Man, an instrument similar to, but coming a full seven months before, the Universal Declaration of the United Nations and setting out the duties as well as the rights of the individual citizen (a throwback, perhaps, to Greco-Roman and medieval natural law theories). Subsequently, in 1959, a meeting of consultation of the American Ministers for Foreign Affairs created, within the framework of the OAS, the Inter-American Commission on Human Rights, which has since undertaken important investigative activities concerning human rights in the Americas. Finally, in 1969, the Inter-American Specialized Conference on Human Rights, meeting in San José, Costa Rica, adopted the American Convention on Human Rights, which made the existing Inter-American Commission on Human Rights an organ for the convention's implementation and

established the Inter-American Court of Human Rights, which sits in San José.

Both the substantive law and the procedural arrangements of the American convention, which entered into force in 1978, are strongly influenced by the UN covenants and the European convention, and they were drafted also with the European Social Charter in mind. Under the American convention, however, unlike its UN and European predecessors, the right of petition by individuals, groups of individuals, and nongovernmental organizations operates automatically. Under the UN system, the right of petition applies only when the state concerned has become a party to the Optional Protocol to the International Covenant on Civil and Political Rights, and under the European system a special declaration by the states concerned is required. On the other hand, again in contrast to the European system (but not the UN system), interstate complaints under the American convention operate only among states that have expressly agreed to such procedure.

African Human Rights System

In 1981, following numerous pleas by the UN Commission on Human Rights, interested states, nongovernmental organizations, and others dating as far back as 1961, the Eighteenth Assembly of Heads of State and Government of the Organization of African Unity (OAU), convening in Nairobi, Kenya, adopted the African Charter on Human and Peoples' Rights. The Charter entered into force on October 21, 1986, and, as of this writing, has been ratified by thirty-one of the fifty OAU member states.

Like its European and American counterparts, the African charter provides for the establishment of an African Commission on Human and Peoples' Rights, with both promotional and protective functions and with no restriction on who may file a complaint with the commission (signatory states, individuals, groups of individuals, and nongovernmental organizations, whether or not they are victims of the alleged violation). In contrast to the European and American procedures, however, concerned states are encouraged to reach a friendly settlement without formally involving the investigative or conciliatory mechanisms of the commission. Also, the African charter does not call for a human rights court. African customs and traditions, it is said, emphasize mediation, conciliation, and consensus rather than the adversarial and adjudicative procedures common to Western legal systems.

Four other distinctive features of the African charter are especially noteworthy. First, it provides for economic, social, and cultural rights as well as civil and political rights. In this respect it bears resemblance to the American convention, but is distinctive from the European convention. Next, in contrast to both the European and American conventions, it recognizes the rights of groups in addition to the family, women, and children. The aged and the infirm are accorded special protection also, and the right of peoples to self-determination is elaborated in the right to existence, equality, and nondomination. Third, it uniquely embraces two third-generation, or "solidarity," rights "as belonging to all peoples": the right to economic, social, and cultural development and the right to national and international peace and security. Finally, it is so far the only treaty instrument to detail individual duties as well as individual rights—to the family, society, the state, and the international African community.

INTERNATIONAL HUMAN RIGHTS IN DOMESTIC COURTS

Using domestic courts to clarify and safeguard international human rights is a new and still evolving approach to human rights advocacy. In addition to the inevitable interpretative problems of applying conventional and customary norms that are fashioned in multicultural settings, controversial theories about the interrelation of national and international law plus many procedural difficulties—carrying such labels as "standing," "act of State," and the "political questions doctrine"—burden the party anxious to invoke international human rights norms in the domestic context. To be sure, considerable progress has been made, as perhaps best evidenced in the far-reaching decision handed down by the U.S. Court of Appeals for the Second Circuit in 1980 in *Filártiga v. Peña-Irala*, in which the court held that the international prohibition of torture is unequivocally established in the law of nations and therefore to be honored in U.S.

courts. But as human rights scholar Richard Lillich has cautioned, "in all likelihood the [national] judiciary will have to experience much more international human rights law consciousness-raising before [wholesale resistance to its domestic application] is rejected."

CONCLUSION

Whatever the current attitudes and policies of governments, the reality of popular demands for human rights, including both greater economic justice and greater political freedom, is beyond debate. A deepening and widening concern for the promotion and protection of human rights, hastened by the self-determinist impulse of a postcolonial era, is now unmistakably woven into the fabric of contemporary world affairs.

Substantially responsible for this progressive development has been, of course, the work of the United Nations, its allied agencies, and such regional organizations as the Council of Europe, the Organization of American States, and the Organization of African Unity. Also visibly helpful, however, particularly since the early 1970s, have been three other factors: the public advocacy of human rights as a key aspect of national foreign policies, made initially legitimate by the example of U.S. President Jimmy Carter; the emergence and proliferation of activist nongovernmental human rights organizations such as Amnesty International (winner of the Nobel Prize for Peace for 1977), the International Commission of Jurists, and diverse church-affiliated groups; and a worldwide profusion of courses and materials devoted to the study of human rights both in formal and informal educational settings. Indeed, in light of the weaknesses that presently inhere at the intergovernmental level of global and regional organization, it is likely that each of these factors will play an increasingly important role in the future.

To be sure, formidable obstacles attend the endeavors of human rights policymakers, activists, and scholars. The implementation of international human rights law depends for the most part on the voluntary consent of nations; the mechanisms for the observance or enforcement of human rights are yet in their infancy. Still, it is certain that a palpable concern for the advancement of human rights is here to stay, out of necessity no less than out of idealism. As Nobel laureate and political dissident Andrey Sakharov once wrote from his internal exile in the Soviet Union:

The ideology of human rights is probably the only one which can be combined with such diverse ideologies as communism, social democracy, religion, technocracy and those ideologies which may be described as national and indigenous. It can also serve as a foothold for those . . . who have tired of the abundance of ideologies, none of which have brought . . . simple human happiness. The defense of human rights is a clear path toward the unification of people in our turbulent world, and a path toward the relief of suffering.

QUESTIONS FOR REFLECTION AND DISCUSSION

1. Among indigenous cultures in Africa and elsewhere, it is believed that individual rights do not exist outside the group structure, hence the Xhosa saying: "Umntu ngumntu ngabantu" (a person is a person only through other people). Other, including Marxist, societies agree. Judeo-Christian and Islamic societies contend, on the other hand, that individual rights and duties are derived from divine sanction or nature. Given such radically different assumptions about the origins of rights, is it possible for the world's cultures to understand one another, let alone come up with long-term human rights accords?

2. Why is the determination of the nature and scope of human rights an important inquiry? Is the answer to the question in any way suggested by the following two statements by Burns Weston?

[I]f a right is determined to be a human right it is quintessentially general or universal in character, in some sense equally possessed by all human beings everywhere, including in certain instances even the unborn.

[T]he legitimacy of different human rights and the priorities claimed among them are necessarily a function of context. Because different people located in different parts of the world both assert and honor different human rights demands according to many different procedures and practices, these issues ultimately depend on time, place, institutional setting, level of crisis, and other circumstance.

Whatever your answer to the foregoing question, can the two statements be reconciled?

3. If, "[a]t bottom, human rights limit State power," as Weston contends, or if human rights are "fundamental" in character, addressing needs rather than "mere wants," why is it considered permissible to place limitations on them? See, for example, Article 29 of the 1948 Universal Declaration of Human Rights and Article 4 of the 1976 International Covenant on Civil and Political Rights (in the Appendix).

4. Catholic philosopher Jacques Maritain subdivides human rights into the rights of the human person as such (e.g., to existence, to personal liberty); the rights of the civic person (e.g., to self-determination, to free association); and the rights of the social person (e.g., to free choice of work, to just wages). How does this typology differ from the "generational" breakdown set forth in Weston's essay? What purpose does it serve?

5. Are economic, social, and cultural rights really "rights"? Are so-called solidarity (third-generation) rights? Is it better to think about such rights as "social goals" rather than "rights"? Why? Why not?

6. Weston refers to the recent emergence of "third-generation" or "solidarity" rights, as "[f]oreshadowed in Article 28 of the Universal Declaration of Human Rights, which proclaims that 'everyone is entitled to a social and international order in which the rights set forth in this Declaration can be fully realized.' . . ." Philip Alston ("A Third Generation of Solidarity Rights: Progressive Development or Obfuscation of International Human Rights Law?," *Netherlands International Law Review* 29 [1982]: 322) is skeptical:

In many respects the concept of third generation rights smacks rather too strongly of a tactical endeavor to bring together, under the rubric of human rights, many of the most pressing concerns on the international agenda and to construct an artificial international consensus in favour of human rights by appealing to the "favorite" concerns of each of the main geopolitical blocs. . . . In sum, the concept of third generation solidarity rights would seem to contribute more obfuscation than clarification in an area which can ill afford to be made less accessible to the masses than it already is.

What is your view?

7. Is it possible and/or desirable to set a hierarchy of rights or categories of rights? Why does "property" occupy such an important place among Western rights theorists? Should "property" be treated the same as "life" and "liberty"? Should economic, social, and cultural rights be secured before civil and political rights? Before solidarity rights? The other way around? Why? Why not?

8. To what might the "right to property" refer if not simply to land and personal possessions? John Locke suggested that every man is a "[p]roperty in his own Person" that "nobody has a right to but himself." Does it make sense to expand the notion of property rights to rights in one's person? What might be the implications of doing so?

2. RICHARD A. FALK *Theoretical Foundations of Human Rights*

In most respects national sovereignty at the state level is stronger than ever. Such a political reality restricts the potential scope for applying rules of international law to those subject matters where governments give their consent to be bound and are prepared to implement their consent with a high degree of compliance. The protection of human rights is in a very special category. For various reasons associated with public opinion and pride, governments are quite ready to endorse (even formally) standards of human rights despite their unwillingness to uphold these standards in practice. Occasionally, for internal political reasons, the reverse situation pertains, such that a government is unwilling to endorse in a formal manner standards of human rights that are characteristically upheld: the United States, of course, is the prime instance of this latter observation, beset by social forces with political leverage that are reluctant to validate any external claims on the shape and substance of the internal governing process.

At the heart of the matter is the peculiar status of enforcement in international society. Given the absence of community enforcement capabilities, the system depends on voluntary patterns of compliance, the effectiveness of which depends, in turn, on perceived self-interest. Normally, governments don't agree to norms unless, at least at the moment of their creation, compliance seems consistent with the national interest. But human rights are different, at least for many governments. In this instance, some governments have an interest in subscribing to the norms even when there is absent any serious intention to comply, and vice versa: some have an interest in avoiding subscribing even when their intention to comply is evident. In the former case, the absence of any *real* enforcement prospect makes it feasible to give lip service to human rights, while in the latter case the *theoretical* possibility of enforcement inhibits certain governments from regarding human rights as binding rules of international law.

Such a situation creates the temptation to adopt a cynical view of efforts to protect human rights, a view to some qualified extent justified by patterns of state practice. However, a more subtle appreciation of the relationship between norms of law and the behavior of states in international society suggests that the protection of human rights through their formulation as norms may achieve certain limited results. The tension between normative aspiration and political constraint in relation to the protection of human rights needs to be better understood.

To depict this tension requires an image of the overall system of world order, defined here as the main patterns and principles by which sovereign states and other actors interact with one another.

One dimension of world order consists of a series of competing normative logics, each of which purports to provide an independent basis for structuring behavior in prescribed directions. A normative logic refers to a set of propositions about what ought to happen with respect to the exercise of authority in the world political system.[1] In a sense, each normative logic can be thought of as an independent line of ethical or legal argument about how to relate values or societal goals to behavior, given the reality of sovereign states.

These several complementary ordering logics are of greatly unequal political weight. Each logic generates a distinctive normative approach. The assessment of these distinct logics determines the relationship of human rights to the world legal order at a given period in international history. . . . It should be emphasized that the protection of human rights . . . is an outcome of struggle between opposed social forces and cannot be understood primarily as an exercise in law-creation or rational persuasion. Similarly, the ordering logics specified below are arenas of struggle, as well as foundations of authority.

STATIST LOGIC

The predominant ordering logic since the Peace of Westphalia has been associated with the "will" of the territorial sovereign state. The government of a state has been its exclusive agent with respect to formulating its will in external relations. The juridical framework of relations worked out in the West has been gradually generalized to apply throughout the globe. The mainstream of international law has evolved out of the predominance of the state and of the states system. Notions of rights evolved within the context of domestic political struggles. However, from Greek, Stoic, and Christian roots came ideas of humane governance associated with relations between rulers and ruled anywhere. While medieval ideas of Christian unity and natural law were influential, theorists of the emergent states system were ambivalent about such critical issues as rights of resistance, tyrannicide, and humanitar-

ian intervention. That is, the prerogatives of the state were balanced against notions of "higher law."

Jean Bodin, writing in the sixteenth century, set forth the decisive argument in favor of centralized secular authority, prefiguring the actual emergence of strong governments enjoying the realities of sovereign control over domestic society. The Swiss eighteenth-century jurist Vattel extended Bodin's views of sovereignty to the external relations of states, providing an application of statist logic to the conduct of interstate or international relations accepted as authoritative virtually until the present time. He separated natural law from positive law, placing emphasis on the requirement of governmental consent as critical to the formulation of international law obligations. Also, Vattel underscored the importance of accepting a government's own interpretation of its obligations, especially in relation to its own citizenry, or those present within its territory. External actors had no standing to complain in the absence of very specific agreements affording protection to aliens.

That is, human rights were not a fit subject for global concern unless a particular government so agreed. The positivist idea of sovereignty shielded abuses of rights committed within state territory. Some tension arose from the status of aliens abused by the territorial government, especially when the abuse was committed outside the European center of the world political system. Thus, "capitulary regimes" and doctrines on "the diplomatic protection of aliens abroad" complemented notions of nonintervention in the colonial period. With the collapse of colonial legitimacy, ideas of granting special status to privileged aliens and the more general approach of diplomatic protection lost their influence. Powerful governments continue to maintain a residual claim to intervene to protect their nation[als] in a situation of jeopardy, but the claim is controversial and regarded by the Third World as colonialist behavior. . . .

The pure morality of the states system is, in its essence, both antiinterventionary and antiimperial. The main contention, which continues to attract modern champions, is that only imperial

1. Perhaps the word *logic* conveys an overly rigorous image of the relationships between premises and application. It seems preferable, however, to *approach* or *perspective*, since the main intention is to suggest that a line of analysis *follows from* (in a logical sense) the adoption of an initial premise about the foundation of political authority in the world system.

actors have, in general, the will and capabilities to do anything significant about abuses of human rights, and yet it is precisely these actors that are least trustworthy because of their own wider, selfish interests. R. J. Vincent upholds the morality of nonintervention even "in the face of outrageous conduct within the state" (as in relation to Nazi persecution of Jews or mistreatment of blacks as a result of apartheid). Vincent argues that there are, on balance, insufficient grounds for trust in the impartiality of the intervenor and that there are reasons to suppose that the consequences of intervention will extend beyond the correction of the perceived evil.[2] In effect, an absolute doctrine of nonintervention (at least by forcible means) is an ordering choice that acknowledges that some particular instances might justify intervention, but not sufficiently to create a precedent that other potential intervenors could invoke.

This view of world legal order rests heavily on the juridical ideas of equality of states and sanctity of treaties and on the geopolitical ideology of a pure states system. It presupposes the absence of imperial actors serving as global enforcers, or, put differently, of strong states assuming the role of assuring compliance by weak states. This model of juridical and political equality, of a world of states mutually respectful of each other's sovereign prerogatives, necessarily precludes any missionary claim to intervene for humanitarian purposes. The highest goal in such a system is the autonomy of state actors protected through maximum adherence to the norm of nonintervention.

The statist matrix of political life also means that the most substantial contributions to the realization of human rights arise from the internal dynamics of domestic politics. Far more significant than imposing human rights policies from outside is an effective commitment to their protection arising from within the body politic. Political theorists as different as Kant and Lenin have argued that the realization of human rights is an automatic consequence of adopting the proper form of domestic government: in Kant's case, a liberal republic, and in Lenin's a radical socialist state established after an armed struggle that overcame the old order. That is, the achievement of human rights is a matter primarily for domestic reform; global concern is neither necessary nor effective.

Of course, there are connections between domestic political changes and external stimuli. The point, however, is that a repressive structure of governance cannot be transformed by marginal, voluntary remedial steps taken under pressure from without of the sort associated with human rights initiatives. The maximum impact of human rights pressures, absent enforcement mechanisms, is to isolate a target government, perhaps denying it some of the benefits of trade and aid. There are no positive examples where such pressure has led to abandonment of the pattern of violation or to a collapse of the governing process responsible for such abuses of human rights. . . . However, a domestic challenge, if it succeeds, may indeed lead to a new political arrangement untainted by human rights abridgments. . . .

The critical political arena for human rights, then, is most often internal to sovereign states. To the extent that repressive regimes are sustained by outside support via arms and capital, however, policies of governments and international financial institutions have some relationship to ongoing struggles between those who seek to promote human rights and those opposing them. An important implication of this way of thinking is that noninterference with the dynamics of self-determination is the most solid external contribution foreign governments can make to the promotion of human rights. Noninterference includes, of course, refraining from covert operations intended to alter the domestic play of forces.

But what of antirepressive interference? Here, I think, the reality of hegemonial and transnational patterns of self-interest are such that likely intervenors are predisposed in favor of the status quo or of some new configuration of control manipulated from outside. States are by and large oriented around selfish ends of power, wealth, and prestige; they are not reliably enough committed to human rights to be endowed with interventionary discretion, at least in the absence of a global community mandate that would shift the ordering logic to that of supranationalist logic (see below).

And what of counterinterventionary moves designed to neutralize the intervention of others? The interdependence of international political life means that to stay out while others go in can amount to a form of intervention. The dictates of

2. R. J. Vincent, "Western Conceptions of a Universal Moral Order," in *Moral Claims in World Affairs*, ed. Ralph Pettmann (New York: St. Martin's Press, 1979), 52–78, esp. 68–72.

statist logic suggest that if one state intervenes in a given country, counterintervention of a proportional character may be appropriate. Of course, such relations are imprecise, and each side is interested in prevailing over rather than neutralizing its adversary. Nevertheless, these considerations inevitably enter into an assessment of what must be done to allow the domestic arena to operate as effectively as possible to uphold human rights in light of statist logic.

HEGEMONIAL LOGIC

Juridical equality has been up against the geopolitical reality of gross inequality since the inception of the states system. As a consequence, some polities have been much more penetrated than others. The colonial system, assimilated into world legal order with different degrees of formality in the nineteenth century, upheld imperial patterns of control. These patterns were justified by the colonizers, as had been the conquest of the New World some centuries earlier, by humanitarian, civilizing claims, and were formalized in such legal doctrines as state responsibility, diplomatic protection, and extraterritoriality. These humanitarian rationalizations and their doctrinal embodiment have been totally discredited during the decolonizing period, losing by now their earlier status of legal and moral right. Both international law and morality rest to some extent on a consensus among actors; if that consensus is eroded or shattered, the norms it had earlier supported are weakened or destroyed. The hegemonial relationship persists in informal and covert patterns, although it is everywhere renounced as a valid ordering logic, except possibly in the form of support for humanitarian intervention undertaken by states. Nevertheless, the United States proclamation of a human rights diplomacy to be implemented as an element of its foreign policy entails a hegemonial attitude toward the internal affairs of some other foreign countries to the extent that the attitude has consequences, as through diplomatic pressure, withholding aid or credits, and giving aid and comfort to dissident elements. Of course, unintended consequences occur. The promotion of human rights by the Carter Administration was never intended to overlook strategic considerations by undermining or alienating governments friendly to the United States; in fact, however, the evidence suggests that opposition groups in such countries as Iran, South Korea, and Tunisia were emboldened by Carter's encouragement of human rights in foreign societies. . . . Nevertheless, such interactions with internal struggles do not contradict earlier assertions that the destiny of human rights is overwhelmingly shaped by domestic factors.

The hegemonial outlook is not a reciprocal tolerance of the sort appropriate to contractual relations among equals in the statist framework. On occasion, it may involve some efforts to bargain concessions in human rights for economic assets with foreign states (such as the Soviet Union) of equivalent power; the effectiveness and side-benefits (and costs) of "linkage" geopolitics are controversial and should be considered a special instance of statist behavior rather than an exercise in hegemony. Hegemonial logic is an acknowledgment of the structuring role of power in a political system lacking an established governing process. In this regard, it is international relations as explained by Thomas Hobbes. In essence, there is no such thing as equality in international life on the level of states, no matter how much equality is achieved on the level of persons.

Hegemonial claims may be promoted by regional or even subregional actors, possessing relatively greater power within their relative domain and possibly motivated, in part at least, by human rights concerns. . . . The principal locus of this hegemonial capacity and disposition is in the leading global states, which take a definite interest in events in all regions of the world, but exceptional circumstances of abuse and relative capability to act . . . may create a much more geographically limited conception of hegemonial role in certain settings, as between neighboring small countries.

The normative underpinning for the hegemonial logic is connected with "leadership": the supposition that there is some implicit correlation between power and virtue giving powerful states a mandate to impose their will on weaker states and that, on balance, this works out positively. Such a hegemonial process may obtain the acquiescence, tacit approval, and/or cooperation of other like-minded states. This kind of support, even if limited to the absence of censure for violating nonintervention norms, operates to confer a weak form of legitimation on *certain* hegemonial claims based on human rights abuses. Usually the hegemonial features are omitted from any argument in justification. The claim is projected as a matter of acting to overcome societal evil elsewhere, as the adoption of a policy by a given government to promote the well-being of others. . . . The United States, given its political traditions, is peculiarly prone to suppose that its exertions of influence on other societies are selfless undertakings for the benefit of foreign peoples. . . . On the other side of the struggle, the Soviet pattern of response amounted to an ideological mirror image of the Western crusade. The Soviet conception of freedom has been associated with nothing more substantive than the pro-Soviet orientation of a foreign government. . . .

The more elusive case for hegemonial claims arises in relation to building up a defense against international aggression. Here the argument is that the overriding normative issue is maintaining a context for national self-determination in the face of a serious threat posed by an expanding imperial actor. As such, weaker countries are faced with an either/or prospect and would serve the cause of domestic political virtue by accepting a subordinate relationship to the more benign of the rival imperial actors. Such was the diplomatic posture of the United States in the first phases of the Cold War, dramatized by John Foster Dulles's contentions that nonalignment by Third World governments was "immoral." Such a hegemonial logic vindicates for *its* constituency the overthrow of Dubček in Czechoslovakia, Allende in Chile, or Mossedegh in Iran, as well as support for their far more repressive successor regimes. Of course, the more severe repression that arises after the hegemonial intervention is never acknowledged by the intervening government(s). Hence the contradiction between the liberating claim and the oppressive reality is never confronted. It is inevitable that the intertwining of hegemonial logic and statist behavior would produce these patterns of behavior. In one central respect, "hegemonial logic" is nothing more than an exemption for the strong from the constraints of "statist logic." Its "justifications," based on benevolent motivation, have not been validated by patterns of great power practice through history and seem flawed by the difficulty of separating the pursuit of interests at the expense of a weaker foreign society from the promotion of its well-being. In this regard, a case could be made for stripping away the normative pretensions that cover the exercise of power in international re-

lations with fig-leaf claims of moral and legal purpose. . . .

NATURALIST LOGIC

Far less consequential in its behavioral impact than either statist or hegemonial logic is the naturalist notion that certain rights inhere in human nature and should be respected by all organized societies. Here, the basis of human rights is prior to politics; the absence of consent by a sovereign authority is not necessarily an excuse for nonobservance. To the extent that human rights rest on a moral imperative, their status is both prior to and independent of their formal acceptance by a government. If a legal imperative is asserted, most jurists require some form of acceptance of norms to occur, although the process can be an implied one, as through the formation of customary international law. In part, the naturalist case is an appeal to the conscience of the rulers, or, more broadly, to the conscience of every political actor in the world, including private citizens, and even more, a plea to all to become "political" in their actions as they regard rights. It is the essential ground for claiming that human rights are universally valid.

Whereas statist logic accords primacy to jurisdictional principles, naturalist logic accords primacy to normative standards. Ideally, the state machinery would use its power to act within the guidelines of natural rights. The main difficulty with naturalist logic relates to the vagueness of the norms and ambiguity of the mandate. Those with power lay down what often appear as self-serving interpretations of what natural law requires, usually on the basis of nonnaturalist goals that rest on statist or hegemonial analysis. In this regard, disembodied naturalism (that which is right) is disregarded by policymakers and leaders as sentimental and moralistic. At the other extreme, a naturalist justification for controversial behavior may provide a government with a normative rationalization for what appears from an impartial perspective to be an imperial adventure.

In recent years, claims to topple regimes in Uganda and Cambodia raised an extreme naturalist case for outsider intervention. In effect, the naturalist contention was that the regimes in place were so shockingly bad by objective moral standards that the only appropriate question for outsiders was whether in the specific circumstances it was possible to intervene effectively. Vietnam's role in "liberating" Cambodia was not phrased by its leaders in Hanoi in naturalist/humanitarian terms, but rather as a matter of statist prerogatives to uphold its own sovereign status. Tanzania's role in toppling Amin's regime was more directly justified along naturalist lines. It was only because Amin's barbaric practices caused such widespread outrage that Tanzania's violation of Uganda's sovereign rights was overlooked. In Third World settings, especially Africa, the noninterventionist features of statist logic are generally given precedence over naturalist claims because of the fear that such claims could generate warfare and new patterns of imperial abuse disguised by a regional variant of hegemonial logic.

Given this sensitivity about hegemonial behavior in the Third World, it is necessary to organize interventionary missions of this sort with wide community support if possible. The difficulty of doing this effectively even in extreme cases suggests the vitality of statist logic, or put differently, the political weakness of naturalist logic standing on its own. If a course of action dictated by naturalist logic also coincides with the perceived implications of other logics (especially, statist and hegemonial), an improved prospect for effective action exists. In such an instance, however, motives are clouded, and cynical observers (often accurately) attribute the real motive to the practical influences and dismiss the naturalist argument as window-dressing. This either/or style of analysis misses the instances where naturalist considerations exert some influence, but not necessarily *sufficient* or *decisive* influence that might have been sufficient on its own to explain an interventionary act.

Naturalist logic does have a bearing on public opinion, and may inhibit some repressive policies. It may provide the most effective case to build popular support for taking human rights seriously. In addition, the influence of naturalist logic may express itself in relation to the normal desire that most rulers and ruling groups have to be regarded with respect, if not esteem. With transnational groups active in publicizing gross violations of human rights, there seems to be some incentive to avoid censure even when no government or international institution is prepared to object strenuously to a pattern of violation in a particular foreign society.

A final aspect of naturalist logic is its attractive doctrine that all persons, not just citizens, should be protected against state abuse. As such, the particular politics associated with the serious promotion of human rights contributes to the formulation of a movement for global reform in which the central objective is the well-being of people rather than the sanctity of juristic persons called states.

Governing by naturalist logic is up against a variety of constraints, especially to the extent that the existing national systems of political order lose legitimacy in the eyes of the masses. Given the dynamics of power and economic scarcity, there is a persistent need to coerce and mystify to protect the rich and deter the poor. The bureaucratic character of the modern state also renders naturalist logic less relevant to the decisional process. Political leadership in large organizational settings tends to be dominated by a variety of competing pressure groups representing differing parts of the government. Under these conditions a government will more readily use the rhetoric of high ideals while ignoring them in practice. Public policy is set by reference to a pragmatic calculus, partly shaped by pressure, partly by perceptions of interest. The spirit of doing right by doing good cannot prevail in such an atmosphere. Yet there is a subsidiary trend, exemplified by the notion of war crimes as prosecuted at Nuremberg in 1945, that violations of minimum rights are criminal acts even if committed by the highest public officials acting in the course of their bureaucratic duty. Although the Nuremberg Judgment was set in a framework of positive law, its validity rested more on the public consensus that Nazi leaders had acted in defiance of naturalist logic.

Naturalist logic remains, however, the underpinning of human rights, validating in the most fundamental way certain minimum standards of behavior. Such validation is prior to and takes precedence over any agreement to uphold certain rights that may exist, even if it is binding by way of treaty commitment. There is in all societal spheres an active moral force that is sensitive to patterns of abuse deemed contrary to nature; such patterns are perceived as wrong, as justifying resistance, opposition, and even outside financial and military assistance. The various forms of support given by outsiders to those engaged in the struggle against apartheid in South Africa draws on this naturalist logic. There is a core sense of decency and fairness that gives human rights their motive power in the popular imagination despite an understanding that the influence of these norms on governmental policy often tends to be at most honorific, minimal. It is this potency attached to moral claims that produces various forms and enthusiasms for populism, including shouts of "power to the people," "take it to the people," and so forth.

SUPRANATIONALIST LOGIC

Here, we move to a different kind of logic, based on the inability to deal with the questions of human rights by reference to the relations among and within sovereign states. The creation of a supranational logic as an act of will by national governments complements the traditional language of diplomacy by a metalanguage of supranationalism. Whereas the lines of argument arising from statist, hegemonial, and naturalist logic are based on the *horizontal* ordering of separate states, supranational logic aspires to vertical ordering from above.

A weak sense of supranational community is operative at both the regional and global level and has been given increasing institutional expression in recent decades. This sense is conventionally associated with expressions of collective action by governments representing states in permanent international organizations. The League of Nations and the United Nations are the most prominent examples of such organizations; their shortcomings rarely lead even their critics to propose a world without such a central global actor. Globalist logic also characterizes various groupings of governments sharing a common position (Third World, OECD [Organization for Economic Cooperation and Development]) or goal (nuclear suppliers, OPEC [Organization of Petroleum Exporting Countries]). Also, regional logic is operative to a limited and uneven extent in different parts of the world, with an impressive record of achievement and growth in Western Europe.[3] . . .

With respect to human rights, the main global arena of supranationalist logic is the General Assembly of the United Nations.[4] In its initial decade, dominated by the United States, the General Assembly was principally a bearer of Western hegemonial logic. Since then, it has become increasingly a bearer of both statist and naturalist logic, being an arena dominated by governments concerned with the protection of state sovereignty and at the same time being a forum in which the principal normative concerns of world public opinion were given expression. As such, it transmits contradictory signals, exhibiting strong rhetoric, selective moral perception, and, finally, expressing a political will that is constrained by the overall calculus of statist and hegemonial interests. . . .

An aspect of this limitation on supranationalist logic arises from the inability of the United Nations to escape from its womb of hegemonial and statist logic. The activities of the United Nations are deeply constrained by the *will* of hegemonial actors, especially the two superpowers, and by deference to a statist conception of the *structure* of world order. . . . Some activity by the General Assembly suggests the opposite potentiality, namely, the inability of formal constraints alone to prevent the United Nations from playing an active norm-related role where a consensus of governments exists (as was the case with respect to demands for a new international economic order). Whether perceived as the conscience of the world or as an unconstitutional encroachment on statist prerogatives, the reality of the General Assembly's role in certain human rights contexts is undeniable, principally because it establishes a climate of concern about particular patterns of abuse that encourages sanctions or even intervention.

In addition, the rhetoric of the secretariat of the United Nations creates a weak independent sense of global identity that arises from some identification with longer range planetary concerns. The secretary general . . . speaks as a voice of conscience oriented toward the morality of the whole human species, rather than on behalf of a particular segment. Although constrained by practical inhibitions, the secretary general is expected to be a voice of globalist logic, reinforced by the content of a naturalist logic. . . . The secretary general does not now possess an important voice. It is not expected to challenge successfully the main policies of the superpowers, except in

---

3. [For details about regional logic, see Reading 16 in Chapter 4 in this volume.]
4. [For details concerning supranationalist logic and the United Nations, see Reading 15 in Chapter 4 in this volume.]

very marginal ways, and the effort to mount such challenges is more likely to weaken the United Nations than inhibit a hegemonial actor like the Soviet Union or the United States. . . .

What the United Nations does in the human rights area is to set standards and generate norms, as well as put pressure on a few politically isolated states whose abuses are serious (e.g., Chile, Israel) although by no means the worst, if severity of abuse were the principal criterion for agenda attention. In this regard, the United Nations' role is restricted and arbitrary, and its impact quite limited even where its concern is great (e.g., southern Africa). . . .

TRANSNATIONAL LOGIC

A variety of ordering activities in world society occur across national boundaries, reflecting neither statist territoriality nor the universalist sweep of globalist logic. In essence, the distinctive transnational aspect is the initiation of a stimulus in one state so as to have an impact elsewhere. The growing significance of a transnational perspective reflects the increasing interdependence of international life combined with the persisting weakness of global institutions. The transnational focus is an ordering halfway house responding to global needs, yet accepting the territoriality of power and authority. Transnational order as a logic is intermediate between the horizontal language of statism and hegemony, and the vertical language of supranationalism. Although they often base their claims on an alleged universality of outlook detached from other ordering logics, transnational actors are situated within sovereign states and subject to their control, except to the extent that some transnational economic actors can overwhelm the statist capabilities of weak states either on their own or through the support of hegemonial actors. . . .

The transnational context of human rights is obvious. Interventionary obstacles restrict what governments or intergovernmental institutions will do, while geopolitical considerations may insulate some polities from human rights criticism or make their leaders reject such criticism as politically motivated. Therefore, it is not surprising that nongovernmental organizations devoted to the promotion of human rights have emerged in recent years. Amnesty International, International League for Human Rights, and the Inter-

national Commission of Jurists are among the most significant transnational actors whose special concern is the human rights field. By issuing reports, applying informal pressure on foreign officials, and keeping in touch with victims of human rights abuse, these organizations exert an important, if selective, influence. Of course, statism intrudes as a constraint. Access to facts can be seriously curtailed by governments eager to avoid adverse publicity. No enforcement or sanctioning processes are directly available, although the impartial disclosures by these transnational actors may create a climate in some countries that builds pressure for more coercive stands on human rights in official arenas. The various moves against racism in southern Africa reflect this interactive process.

Transnational actors in the human rights area are private associations that depend for their existence on voluntary contributions of money. Their stature is partly a reflection of the quality of their work, their freedom from partisan causes, and their commitment to widely shared values. Hence, their influence results from having an impact on public opinion in all relevant arenas.

These initiatives focus on civil and political rights that have been globally and nationally endorsed through their embodiment in the Universal Declaration, the main global and regional human rights covenants, as well as in national constitutions and statutes. As a consequence, even many repressive governments are technically committed to these norms, and may be marginally vulnerable to arguments from within or without that the call for human rights is nothing more than the call for domestic law enforcement.

Within the wider conception of human rights as extending to the right of every person to the basic necessities of life, especially those transnational groups associated with religious and educational organizations have been important. The World Council of Churches, the National Council of Churches, the Third World Forum, and the World Order Models Project are examples of transnational actors seeking to generate support for humane patterns of governance that center on the full realization of human rights. Some of these groups take an active stand that is political in character: for instance, church organizations that give funds to liberation groups engaged in armed struggle, especially those in southern Africa.

In terms of ordering logics, normative transnationality is fragile and vulnerable, depending for its very formal existence on statist indulgence and voluntary private financing. And yet, given the "space" available in democratic polities, these transnational initiatives are relatively well established, enjoying a large measure of autonomy, and able to maintain contact with oppositional groups in many repressive societies. Awarding Amnesty International the Nobel Peace Prize in 1977 confirmed, in one sense, the contribution and prominence of the transnational approach to the promotion of human rights.

POPULIST LOGIC

The weakest, potentially most subversive, of ordering logics is that of "the people," taken in Rousseau's sense of being the ultimate repository of sovereign rights. Governments, institutions of any character, are derivative, and corrupting to the extent that they substitute various particular interests for the promotion of general interests. All political institutions are imperfectly representative, whatever their claim. And yet governments, especially, have at their disposal overwhelming capabilities to resist all challenges except occasionally those that arise from revolutionary groups seeking themselves to take over control of state power.

At the margins of power are a growing number of individuals and loosely organized groups that distrust the capacity, *in general*, of any government to uphold basic human well-being, including individual and group rights. These individuals and groups deny governmental and intergovernmental claims to possess a monopoly of legitimated authority. Often in the context of human rights these groups react to the failure of governments to follow through on their own promises, such as those contained in the Nuremberg Principles or the Helsinki Accords. Positive populist initiatives include the Bertrand Russell War Crimes Tribunal (originally organized in response to the Vietnam War, more recently perpetuated as a commission of inquiry into the denial of human rights in Latin America and West Germany, and now carried forward in a proposed permanent form by the Lelio Basso Foundation), the proclamation at Algiers on July 4, 1976, of the Universal Declaration of the Rights of Peoples (which supplements conventional international law with a series of claims based on the inalien-

able rights of peoples), and aspects of the counterconferences at major United Nations conclaves on global policy issues. Various individuals and groups adopt a perspective of planetary citizens, especially in imperial actors who tolerate oppositional activity, to emphasize the degree to which supranationalist logic needs to be strengthened by agitational activity.

At this stage, populist initiatives are significant mainly as thorns in the side of certain state and imperial actors. In human rights contexts, this means mobilizing public awareness about certain categories of abuse. It is a moral logic based on declaring what is right, as such, drawing its inspiration from naturalist logic.

The populist approach is distinguished from the transnationalist approach by its rejection of statist legitimacy. Transnational actors tend to accept the legitimacy of the overall world order system, seeking to induce governments to do what they are obliged to do with respect to specific claims of right. Populist actors insist that statist prerogatives are derivative from popular sovereignty and fully accountable to it; their thrust is more radical, and often their attacks on abuses of human rights rest upon more fundamental indictments of repressive structures of governance (e.g., imperialism, fascism). Of course, the interaction of logics is evident here. Some transnational actors have arisen as a consequence of populist pressure and have adopted as their goal a populist program of action. Environment groups, especially those with an antinuclear focus, such as Friends of the Earth, are illustrative of this admixture of populism and transnationalism. Other forms of populism become co-opted by statist logic, operating virtually as an adjunct to governmental authority and accepting as a constraint the consent of the territorial sovereign; the International Red Cross, for instance, has assumed this basic character. Still other types of populism act essentially as pressure groups on behalf of supranationalist logic, as is the case with the United World Federalists, or, perhaps, the United Nations Association.

In effect, populism is a protean logic that can act either independently or to reinforce the thrust of any of the other logics in a wide variety of respects. It can also act to oppose other logics, as is the case of the interaction between revolutionary populism, with its antecedents in movements associated with philosophical anarchism, and statism.

Conceived of as a logic, then, populism, like supranationalism, is operative at a different level of social organization. If supranationalism provides a metalanguage or logic in relation to logics associated with statism, then populism provides a sublanguage, taking a stance that is "below" the state. . . .

The main conclusion, at once obvious and fundamental, is that the cause of human rights in the present world system is overwhelmingly dependent on the normative orientation of the governing process at the state level. Some pressures can be brought on this process from outside, as by impartial transnational organizations whose motives are harder to discredit in certain situations, especially where the leadership in the target polity seeks to avoid having an international reputation as repressive and the abuse can be corrected without seeming to erode the quality of governmental control. Yet this pressure can only be marginal, perhaps leading to some cosmetic changes in judicial procedures, in improved conditions of confinement, or possibly even release for prominent prisoners of conscience. Nevertheless, the governing orientation of states is primarily shaped by internal factors, especially by attitudes of domestic leaders relating to the retention of power and maintenance of domestic order, what has been called "the rulers' imperative."

The world order limits on the promotion of human rights seem firm, at least in the short run of say five to ten years. A different perspective arises if one considers the present historical period to be one of transition to a new political frame of reference that involves some drastic changes in the state, regional, and supranational levels of organization. There is disagreement about the extent, pace, and even reality of transition. Some consider the "crisis of world order" to be one of simply adjusting to the passing of American primacy that helped organize international relations after World War II. Such adjustments, involving a more pluralistic, complex variant of world order, require neither structural change nor normative shifts in emphasis.

A second more fundamental view of transition suggests that the interdependent character of security, and of economic and ecological life requires greater capabilities for "management," perhaps even central guidance. Here, too, the functional shift toward central guidance does not imply any reduction in the internal political autonomy of state actors. Perhaps, over time, a more integrated world system would begin to translate awareness about abuses of human rights into a more formidable role for the supranational ordering logic at the expense of both statist and hegemonial logic. This move toward the "management of interdependence" is sometimes described as a "moderate" (as compared to the present and past) world order system in which cooperative aspects of relations between state actors are augmented while competitive aspects are diminished. It may be that the attainment of moderation would encourage gentler modes of governance, resting on more consent and less coercion. Such a development is feasible if the relationship between economic and demographic growth can be reconciled with improved life circumstances for most inhabitants of most polities in the world.

A third, even deeper, view of transition exists. Its time horizon is a matter of decades. It views the crisis of world order as involving the disintegration of the state system as it emerged from European regional politics in the middle of the seventeenth century, a development often conveniently associated with the Peace of Westphalia, concluded in 1648 at the end of the Thirty Years War. From this perspective a new world order system is emergent that will combine an organizational framework suitable for a planetary polity with appropriate new beliefs, values, and myths. The essence of such a system, if it is to achieve transition, is the attainment of stability on a planetary scale. This could take either of two principal forms. It could be a centralized tyranny that imposes its will on the various peoples of the world. It could also be a relatively decentralized form of central guidance (combining functional specialization with the deconcentration of power at the state level) premised on a symbiotic link between leadership and consent, which manages to combine stability with equity as the essence of the new world order system. The idea of "equity" covers a range of substantive arrangements proceeding from a minimalist commitment to assure satisfaction of basic material needs as a matter of right for everyone to a maximalist commitment to a just polity that achieves substantial equality among its inhabitants, as well as equality among such collectivities as sovereign states. Nonutopian conceptions of equity could not do more than reach a compromise between a basic needs approach and the achievement of genuine equality.

In the negative variant of the poststatal system, human rights will be denied in more systematic and flagrant ways than is currently the case. In terms of ordering logics, the supranational logic (or conceivably the hegemonial logic via world conquest, condominium, or oligopoly) would be greatly expanded at the expense of both statist and populist logic, the latter being already trivial. Supranational logic would assume a hierarchical relationship of repressive superiority that would extend to the strict control of even regional and subregional expressions of supranational logic. In the positive variant, the essence of world order will be the progressive realization of human rights by means of a combined strengthening of populist and global logic, mainly at the expense of statist logic.

In this conjectural spirit it is worth noticing the following aspect. The protection of human rights in a given world order system is not rigidly the exclusive preserve of any one of the ordering logics. It all depends on the value base that animates a given political actor at any level of social organization. As racist and religious militants' movements have demonstrated, repressive intolerance can rise from below (via populist logic) as well as be imposed from above (via statist logic). Similarly, holders of effective power may, under certain circumstances, act to remove human rights abuses within their own policy (e.g., civil rights in the United States).

From a formal point of view, a balance among ordering logics is important as a check against tendencies to abuse authority. The present world order system, confronted by an insidious mixture of inequality, misery, and scarcity, is most profoundly obstructed by the imbalanced domination of ordering logic by the sovereign state. Yet supplanting the state by a centralizing mutation is unlikely to diminish its repressive features for very long. Besides, the state helps to neutralize certain adverse features of the hegemonial logic. Strengthening weak states and weakening strong states seem like reasonable short-term approaches to the role of the state in the world system. It is for this reason that the positive direction of global reform at this historical stage seems to require a simultaneous strengthening of supranational (global and regional), naturalist, transnational, and populist logics at the expense of the statist and hegemonial logics.

In one respect, strengthening the naturalist logic may be the most important emphasis at this point in the transition process. It helps to orient other ordering logics around emergent values, building a normative foundation and social consensus that will help create the sort of community sentiments needed if a beneficial form of world order is to be brought into being some time early in the twenty-first century.

QUESTIONS FOR REFLECTION AND DISCUSSION

1. Why does Richard Falk describe the theoretical foundations of human rights in terms of "ordering logics"? What are the identifying characteristics of each logic? To what extent do the logics overlap?

2. In an omitted paragraph, Falk remarks that "[t]o think of human rights in the world as a whole, as distinct from some particular transgression (treatment of Indians, slavery, genocide), is a recent phenomenon and, to date, partly an American preoccupation. . . ." Why is this so? Indeed, if, as Falk suggests elsewhere, it is essentially internal forces that bring about regimes committed to redressing human rights violations, how and why has a world view of human rights even come about?

3. To what extent might hegemonial claims be used to achieve goals quite unrelated to human rights? Consider, for example, Falk's observation that

> [t]hroughout the Cold War, interventionary diplomacy in all forms was justified in large part by United States policymakers as a commitment to "freedom" (by which was meant, as it became increasingly clear in the Vietnam era, merely that the regime was non-communist or non-Marxist, no matter how repressive of elemental human rights it might be otherwise).

Can you think of other situations in which a human rights rationale has been used to rally support for a particular geopolitical struggle? If so, is hegemonial human rights logic subject to criticism? Why? Why not?

4. What role do normative standards play in naturalist logic? Might such standards be used, similar to hegemonial claims, for purposes unrelated to human rights? How might naturalist logic be used as a more positive force?

5. What difficulties inhere in supranationalist logic? Why is the United Nations the most dominant force in supranationalist logic? How does the United Nations pose limits on supranationalist logic?

6. What human rights role is played by transnational actors? Is it a strong role? Why? Why not? Can it be made stronger? How is transnationalist logic to be distinguished from populist logic? Why is the populist force so weak?

7. What does Falk say about the future of human rights from a world order point of view? Do you agree with his assessment? Which of his "ordering logics" holds out the greatest promise for human rights? Why? Which offers the least? Why?

SELECT BIBLIOGRAPHY

Bilder, Richard. "Rethinking International Human Rights: Some Basic Questions." *Wisconsin Law Review* 1 (1969): 171–217. Professor Bilder makes explicit several assumptions underlying human rights that deal with the instrumental connections between peace and human rights.

Blaustein, Albert P., Roger S. Clark, and Jay A. Sigler, eds. *Human Rights Sourcebook*. New York: Paragon House Publishers, 1987. A comprehensive collection of human rights documents.

Brownlie, Ian. *Basic Documents on Human Rights*. 2d ed. New York: Oxford University Press, 1981. A large but accessible handbook of human rights documents containing most of the relevant international instruments on human rights.

D'Amato, Anthony. "The Concept of Human Rights in International Law." *Columbia Law Review* 82 (1982): 1110–59. A critical analysis of the sources of international human rights law with particular attention to custom.

Falk, Richard A. *Human Rights and State Sovereignty*. New York: Holmes and Meier Publishers, 1981. Integrates human rights into a political perspective to generate a theoretical framework for analysis and practical recommendations.

Forsythe, David P. *Human Rights and World Politics*. 2d ed. Lincoln, Neb.: University of Nebraska Press, 1988. A wide-ranging and highly readable introduction to the law and politics of international human rights.

Frost, Mervyn. *Towards a Normative Theory of International Relations*. New York: Cambridge University Press, 1986. Frost argues that settled norms serve as "background theory" from which one may derive solutions to "hard cases" in international relations. His argument relies on the theory of rights advanced by Ronald Dworkin in *Taking Rights Seriously*.

Hennelly, Alfred, and John Langan. *Human Rights in the Americas: The Struggle for Consensus*. Washington, D.C.: Georgetown University Press, 1982. Essays on the philosophical and theological roots and origins of human rights in the context of political conflict in the Western Hemisphere.

McDougal, Myres S., Harold D. Lasswell, and Lung-chu Chen. *Human Rights and World Public Order— The Basic Policies of an International Law of Human Dignity*. New Haven, Conn.: Yale University Press, 1980. Places human rights in a highly sophisticated jurisprudential perspective to generate a theoretical framework for scholarly analysis and policy recommendation.

Macfarlane, L. T. *The Theory and Practice of Human Rights*. London: Temple Smith, 1985. Macfarlane argues that human rights differ from other moral claims by virtue of their universality, individuality, paramountcy, practicality, and enforceability; however, he concludes that most such claims are thwarted by the existing framework of sovereign nation-states.

Meron, Theodor, ed., *Human Rights in International Law: Legal and Policy Issues*. 2 vols. New York: Oxford University Press, 1984. A teacher's guide to international human rights, including analytical essays by experts with their pedagogical suggestions and syllabi.

Pollis, Adamantia, and Peter Schwab, eds. *Human Rights: Cultural and Ideological Perspectives*. New York: Praeger Publishers, 1979. Asks whether human rights are universal, and to what extent their implementation is contingent on socioeconomic factors; also shows how different historical experiences and varied cultural patterns lead to diverse notions of human rights.

Rosenbaum, Alan S., ed. *The Philosophy of Human Rights: International Perspectives.* London: Aldwych Press, 1980. Explores the foundations of contemporary human rights in Jewish, Catholic, Islamic, and other ethical and cultural sources.

Ruggie, John G. "Human Rights and the Future International Community." *Daedalus* 112, 4 (1983): 93–110. A political science analysis of the "new international normative status of human rights," which remain closely dependent upon "the nature of the international community."

Schwab, Peter, and Adamantia Pollis. *Toward a Human Rights Framework.* New York: Praeger Publishers, 1982. Looks at human rights in three different state contexts: liberal, socialist, and Third World. Identifies patterns of human rights norms as well as abuses in each of the three contexts.

Sieghart, Paul. *The International Law of Human Rights.* Oxford: Clarendon Press, 1983. Comprehensively reviews more than forty internationally defined rights, with interpretation and explanation relying on international institutions and the superior courts of thirty countries.

———. *The Lawful Rights of Mankind: An Introduction to the International Legal Code of Human Rights.* New York: Oxford University Press, 1985. The international law on human rights—what it says, how it was made, and how it works; a guidebook for the nonspecialist reader.

UNESCO. *Human Rights, Comments and Interpretations.* New York: Columbia University Press, 1949; reprint, Westport, Conn.: Greenwood Press, 1973. Post–World War II comments on the importance of human rights for world peace by Jacques Maritain, Harold J. Laski, Quincy Wright, F. S. C. Northrop, Aldous Huxley, Mahatma Gandhi, and others.

Vasak, Karel, ed. (revised and edited for the English edition by Philip Alston) *The International Dimensions of Human Rights.* 2 vols. Westport, Conn.: Greenwood Press for UNESCO, 1982. Essays on international human rights and the institutions that implement them by academics and specialists from all parts of the world.

SELECT FILMOGRAPHY

Human Rights. Thames Television, producer. U.K.: Media Guild, 1984. 120 min., color; videotape. British television documentary traces the development of human rights since the 1948 adoption of the UN Universal Declaration of Human Rights. Interviews with diplomats, human rights advocates, and victims of violations around the world who discuss the concept of universal and inalienable human rights.

Judgment at Nuremburg. Stanley Kramer, producer. U.S.A.: CBS/Fox, 1961. 178 min., color; Beta, VHS videotape. A powerful dramatization of the trials of Nazi war criminals at Nuremburg following World War II. Reveals the extent of the atrocities committed, which, in turn, set in motion the movement to draft the "International Bill of Rights." Stars Marlene Dietrich, Burt Lancaster, Maximillian Schell, and Spencer Tracy.

Memory of Justice. Marcel Ophuls, producer. France: Films Inc, 1976. 278 min., color, French (English subtitles); 16 mm. Landmark documentary of the Nazi war crimes trials at Nuremburg. Filmmaker Ophuls traveled throughout Germany searching for peoples' attitudes about the past, and about other atrocities of war, probing the questions of guilt and responsibility.

Sophie's Choice. Alan J. Pakula, producer. U.S.A.: CBS/Fox, 1982. 150 min., color; Beta, VHS videotape. Meryl Streep won an Academy Award for "best actress" for her extraordinary portrayal of a survivor of a Nazi concentration camp.

ISSUES

Chapter Two

Basic Decencies and Participatory Rights

IN this chapter we consider the grave problems raised by twentieth-century genocide, torture, and discrimination based on race, sex, and religion, as well as that directed against refugees and indigenous or "aboriginal" peoples. Our concern is with the root value of simple human respect or, more precisely, with those modern-day deprivations of human respect that show contempt for the basic decencies of life—personal security and survival—and for claims to equality in the pursuit of life.

Suffering characterizes much of human history, but during the twentieth century we have managed to propagate misery on a global scale. Two world wars, complete with fire bombings and atomic blasts, claimed sixty million lives. Through genocide, mass purges, arbitrary killings, and barbarous torture under the regimes of Adolph Hitler, Josef Stalin, Idi Amin, and, most recently, Pol Pot, and through race, sex, and other forms of arbitrary discrimination, as well as through the abuse of powerless minorities of all descriptions, the processes of dehumanization have further revealed themselves in all their stark invidiousness. The patterns of indecency and marginalization continue today.

Against this appalling background, however, there is some good news. For, though unparalleled in its treachery, our era is also the first in which people are trying to do something about it on a global scale. In the name of human rights, insistence upon basic decency and equality has established a minimum global standard that is now an integral part of contemporary international law. Thus does the Preamble to the UN Charter, responding to death camps, torture chambers, abused minorities, and helpless peoples fleeing misery and oppression, "reaffirm faith in fundamental human rights, in the dignity and worth of the human person, in the equal rights of men and women and of nations large and small."

The first step from preambulatory rhetoric to legal action was taken at Nuremberg in 1945, when Nazi leaders captured as criminals of war were convicted not only for violations of the laws and customs of war, a time-honored standard imposed by military victors, but also for "crimes against humanity." They were convicted for political, racial, and religious persecutions committed against *any* civilian population (i.e., against German citizens as well as other nationals) and their convictions were justified "whether or not in violation of the domestic law of the country where perpetrated."[1] In other words, in contrast to pre–World War II times when "international law allowed each equal sovereign an equal right to be monstrous to his [sic] subjects,"[2] the law of Germany, however authoritative, constituted no defense. As Leo Gross has put it, "[t]hese [Nuremberg] trials were in a profound sense a demonstration against the totalitarian subjection of the individual to 'nationalized' truth; they were a protest against the erasure of the individual as a subject, mediate or immediate, of international law, and as a responsible member of the international community."[3]

Drawing upon the principles of Nuremberg, the United Nations developed the Convention

1. Article 6(c) of the Agreement for the Prosecution and Punishment of the Major War Criminals of the European Axis, Aug. 8, 1945, 59 Stat. 1544, 1547–48, E.A.S. No. 472. *The Nuremberg Trial,* 6 F.R.D. 69, 110 (International Military Tribunal, 1946).
2. Tom J. Farer, "Introduction," in *The International Bill of Human Rights,* ed. Paul Williams (Glen Ellen, Calif.: Entwhistle Books, 1981), xiii.
3. Leo Gross, "The Punishment of War Criminals: The Nuremberg Trial," *Netherlands International Law Review* (1954): 34.

on the Prevention and Punishment of the Crime of Genocide.[4] Genocide is defined as "acts committed with intent to destroy in whole or in part, a national, ethnical, racial, or religious group as such,[5] and the Contracting Parties to the Convention "confirm" that, even if perpetrated by a government against its own inhabitants, it "is a crime under international law which they undertake to prevent and punish."[6] Genocide is a violation of human rights on the most hideous scale.

In the first reading in this chapter, provocatively entitled, "The Sovereign Territorial State: The Right to Genocide," Leo Kuper indicts the continuing passivity of the international community in the face of large-scale genocides in the post–World War II era. Citing the mass killings attributable to Idi Amin in Uganda, Pol Pot in Cambodia, and to the government of Alfredo Stroessner in its callous mistreatment of the Ache Indians in Paraguay, he observes that none have provoked effective international action or even formal condemnation. His documented and melancholy conclusion is that the United Nations' response to genocidal crimes is "deeply disillusioning," but understandable in view of political and ideological divisions within the organization. The United Nations, Kuper observes, has made too few advances from its staid protection of state sovereignty and its "corollary [requirement] of non-intervention in . . . domestic affairs." He therefore invests his hopes for dealing with genocide in "regional intergovernmental associations, and the international non-governmental agencies, the first and perhaps main line of defense against genocide. . . ."

The historical record on genocide is explained, at least in part, by what sociologist Helen Fein describes as the tendency of people to act within a restricted "universe of obligation" (i.e., that circle of people with reciprocal obligations to protect one another) set by friendship, family, tribe, nation, culture, religion, or other bonds of fraternity and to dehumanize "outside others."[7] Also, because it is so atrocious, genocide raises fundamental questions about whether other acts contemptous of human life are properly within the scope of survival rights. What other life-threatening acts, it may be asked, are today sought to be prevented and punished, if any? Does the desideratum of basic decency include survival rights beyond the right to be free from genocide?

Both the Universal Declaration of Human Rights and the International Covenant on Civil and Political Rights[8] specify that "no one shall be arbitrarily deprived of his [sic] life," and, in *The Right to Life in International Law*, B. G. Ramcharan shows that the word "arbitrarily" was carefully chosen "with the intention of providing the highest possible level of protection to the right to life and to confine permissible deprivations therefrom to the narrowest of limits.[9] He asserts that, today, there is an international consensus as to deprivations of life that are manifestly arbitrary[10] that they include (in addition to genocide, crimes against

4. Dec. 9, 1948, 78 U.N.T.S. 277.
5. Ibid., art 2.
6. Ibid., art 1.
7. Helen Fein, *Accounting for Genocide* (New York: The Free Press, 1979), 7–9.
8. See the Appendix.
9. B. G. Ramcharan, *The Right to Life in International Law* (The Hague: Martinus Nijhoff Publishers, 1985), 20.
10. Consensus is lacking, however, on problems arising from developments of medical technology that touch on the very nature of human life: the experimental use of fetal tissue, test tube fertilization and embryo transfer, surrogate motherhood, and so on. A troublesome issue of medical ethics is whether heroic medical efforts (routinely used for a normal child) should be denied to severely deformed and grossly retarded neonates and newborns. In "Biotechnology and The Law," Justice M. D. Kirby (Australia) writes: "Before the courts intervened . . . , 'compassionate infanticide' was a common practice in many hospitals." The author cites and critically discusses cases in Australia, England, Canada, and the United States in which "orders have been made requiring operations to be performed on neonates or young children, despite the disinclination of medical staff and parents." *The Review* (International Commission of Jurists) 39 (Dec. 1987): 46–50. See also Elsie L. Bandman and Bertram Bandman, *Bioethics and Human Rights: A Reader for Health Professionals* (Boston: Little, Brown, 1978).

humanity, war crimes, deaths resulting from acts of aggression, executions carried out in the absence of due process, and enforced or involuntary "disappearances") torture-related deaths and those resulting from degrading treatment or punishment in prison or other detention. Torture, it may be assumed, is within the scope of survival rights under contemporary international law, both customary and conventional.

Matthew Lippman's essay on the problem of torture traces the history of torture and describes the "new torture." Whereas the practice of torture was once a *public* function of crude moral instruction, a matter of public display supervised and done for more or less specific reasons (e.g., the winning over of heretics and the verification of "unreliable witnesses"), the "new torture," shrouded in secrecy and often unsupervised, serves the *private* function of crude moral instruction, generally to intimidate political opponents. This change in role suggests changed public attitudes. Once torture was a legitimate governmental act. Now, by virtually any standard of human decency, it is considered illegal as well as immoral—a proposition that even governments have come to accept. All of which stands, of course, in sharp contrast to contemporary realities. Modern torture employs sophisticated techniques used by governments to abuse and intimidate political opponents. What is more, modern professional codes of ethics notwithstanding, psychological and medical knowledge is sometimes employed in political efforts to "break" prisoners.[11]

Expressing reservations about the United Nations' efforts to curb the practice of torture, Lippman confirms these contemporary realities. However, three promising UN efforts, essentially postdating the Lippman essay, merit notice.

First, after an intensive campaign by nongovernmental organizations, especially Amnesty International, the UN General Assembly adopted, in 1975, the Declaration on the Protection of All Persons from Being Subjected to Torture and Other Cruel, Inhuman or Degrading Treatment or Punishment, and, thereafter, in 1984, building upon the declaration, it adopted the Convention Against Torture and Other Cruel, Inhuman or Degrading Treatment or Punishment.[12] When the convention enters into force, upon the ratification of twenty countries, it will move state-sponsored torture into the poisoned circle of "crimes against humanity," and it will do so with a tough provision recognizing "universal criminal jurisdiction" (which is to say that any signatory country apprehending a torturer may bring him or her to justice). Specifically, per Draft Convention Articles 6 and 7, the state parties will be required to take alleged offenders into custody, make preliminary inquiries, notify the state from which the accused comes, and, unless the accused is to be extradited by the arresting state, submit the accused to her or his own state authorities for prosecution.

Second, the UN Commission on Human Rights has established the office of Special Rapporteur on Torture. An independent investigator (since 1985, Professor P. H. Kooijmans of the Free University of Amsterdam) is authorized to respond to complaints of torture on an "urgent action" basis by questioning governments about reliance on cruelty. The Rapporteur's confidential challenges on specific allegations have made a difference. As Rapporteur Kooijmans himself has noted, after reporting to the United Nations about "people who have been released and have not been tortured":

11. Four relevant reports were published in 1987 by the American Association for the Advancement of Science (Human Rights Program): Richard P. Claude, Eric Stover, and June P. Lopez, *Health Professionals and Human Rights in the Philippines*; Gregg Maxwell Bloche, *Uruguay's Military Physicians: Cogs in a System of State Terror*; Eric Stover, *The Open Secret: Torture and the Medical Profession in Chile*; and Mary Rayner, *Turning a Blind Eye? Medical Accountability and the Prevention of Torture in South Africa*.
12. Dec. 9, 1975, U.N.G.A. Res. 3452 (XXX), 34 U.N. GAOR, Supp. (No. 34) 209, U.N. Doc. A/10034 (1975); Dec. 10, 1984, U.N.G.A. Res. 39/46, 39 U.N. GAOR, Supp. (No. 51) 197, U.N. Doc. A/39/51 (1984). See Ahcene Boulesbaa, "An Analysis of the 1984 Draft Convention," *Dickinson Journal of International Law* 4, no. 2 (Spring 1986): 185–211.

Whenever one approaches a government with a concrete case, that action by the U.N. Rapporteur is considered, at least by the government involved, as an activist attitude. . . . Yet, I never received a reply that it was none of my business, and [that] I was interfering with the internal situation. The general shame felt for the practice of torture obviously is so great that no government at this time feels that the most appropriate reply is to make a reproach of interference. . . . Even when governments flatly deny that torture has taken place, it means that they feel they are subject to the rule that torture is prohibited. If you compare that response with the situation of a few years ago, when governments would protest interference in internal affairs, it is real progress.[13]

Third, in recent years, the United Nations has sought also to help the victims of torture. In 1981, the General Assembly set up a Voluntary Fund for Victims of Torture, relying upon voluntary contributions of governments, private groups, and individuals. Among the projects of the fund are grants to psychiatric and medical centers for the treatment and rehabilitation of victims of torture.[14] For example, the International Rehabilitation Centre for Torture Victims, established in Denmark in 1982, maintains facilities at the University Hospital of Copenhagen, treats both victims and their families, and trains health professionals from other countries in the latest methods of therapy.

A problem related to torture is the phenomenon of "disappearances," whereby a government assumes the power to end life, criminally, without cause or responsibility. The problem was most common in the 1970s, but it has persisted, tragically, into the 1980s in Argentina, Brazil, Chile, Guatemala, and the Philippines, as well as in Afghanistan, Cambodia, and Ethiopia. The "desparecido" or "disappeared" (a term first used by the Guatemalan press and intended to refer to the presumed victims of political violence) in reality have not disappeared. Even though their fate is, typically, violent (often illegal) arrest, torture, secret detention, and death,[15] their whereabouts are ordinarily well known to the governments responsible for their "disappearance." Evidence collected by Amnesty International, the International League for Human Rights, and the United Nations Working Group on Involuntary Disappearances, among others, documents the point ad nauseam. The uncovering of mass graves of people previously believed to have "disappeared" and the testimony of survivors of secret detention camps have helped not only to fill in the factual vacuum left by each individual "disappearance" but also to refute denials of accountability on the part of governmental authorities in countries, such as Argentina, where the practice once was widespread.[16]

The two essays in this chapter by Richard B. Lillich and Jack Greenberg track the range of those governmental acts, other than and in addition to torture and "disappearances,"

13. "Interview with Professor Kooijmans, Special Rapporteur on Torture for the U.N. Commission on Human Rights," *SIM Newsletter* (Netherlands Institute of Human Rights) 16 (Nov. 1986): 6–7.
14. See Elena O. Nightingale and Eric Stover, "Toward the Prevention of Torture and Psychiatric Abuse," in *The Breaking of Bodies and Minds: Torture, Psychiatric Abuse and the Health Professions* ed. Eric Stover and Elena O. Nightingale (New York: W. H. Freeman, 1985), 229–52. See also Hans Danelius, "The U.N. Fund for Torture Victims," *The Review* (International Commission of Jurists) 37 (Dec. 1986): 35–42.
15. See, e.g., Amnesty International, *Disappearances: A Workbook* (New York, 1981).
16. The fate of the "disappeared" and the more than sixteen thousand human rights victims of the Argentine military regimes (1976–83) is poignantly detailed in the report of the Argentine National Commission on Disappeared People, written under the supervision of the well-known Argentine writer, Ernesto Sabato, and sponsored by the democratically elected government that displaced the military in 1983. *Nunca Mas!* is the most detailed report that any government ever has published on the human rights transgressions of a prior regime. It portrays in sad detail the slippery slope from the violations of individual freedoms toward more and more grotesque violations of all civil rights. See *Nunca Mas! (Never Again): A Report by Argentina's National Commission on Disappeared People* (London: Faber and Faber, in association with the Index on Censorship, 1986).

that show contempt for the basic decencies of life and for claims to equality in the pursuit of life.

Lillich sets out the international standards designed to safeguard the rights to life, liberty, and security of the person as well as the civil rights to equality implicit in the rule of law. He explains how these and other rights—the right to a remedy, the right to a fair trial, the presumption of innocence, the right to freedom of movement, the right to nationality, the right to marry and found a family—are protected under international law so as to ensure everyone's claims for respect and equal participation in the fundamental freedoms set forth in the Universal Declaration of Human Rights.

Greenberg clarifies the international norms applicable to the broad topic of race, sex, and religious discrimination. According to Article 2 of the Universal Declaration of Human Rights, "[e]veryone is entitled to all the rights and freedoms set forth in this Declaration, without distinction of any kind, such as race, color, sex, language, religion, political or other opinion, national or social origin, property, birth or other status."

The focus on racism is essential. In 1967, the United Nations Education, Scientific and Cultural Organization (UNESCO) convened a committee of distinguished experts to assess issues of racial discrimination worldwide, to disseminate scientific facts about race, and to combat racial discrimination. The committee agreed that racist doctrines lack any scientific foundation whatsoever and adopted the position that racism stultifies the development of those who suffer it, perverts those who apply it, divides nations within themselves, aggravates international conflict, and threatens world peace.[17] The UNESCO experts confirmed the obvious, of course: Racial discrimination, however widespread and wherever found, degrades and fetters all humans.

Accordingly, having defined "racial discrimination" as "any distinction, exclusion, restriction or preference based on race, color, descent, or national or ethnic origin which has the purpose or effect of nullifying or impairing the recognition, enjoyment or exercise, on an equal footing, of human rights and fundamental freedoms in the political, economic, social, cultural or any other field of public life," the 1966 International Convention on the Elimination of All Forms of Racial Discrimination,[18] which entered into force in 1969, set forth appropriate remedies, in some cases penal sanctions and in others education and community action, to combat this social abomination. Also, pursuant to the convention, a Committee on the Elimination of Racial Discrimination was established to (a) review and analyze state reports, (b) examine state complaints relative to the performance of other states parties, and, subject to appropriate recognition of the competence of the committee, (c) consider complaints and communications from individuals or groups claiming to be victims of racial discrimination.

Extreme forms of racism have cast a pall upon modern history, having been used to justify colonial exploitation, scapegoat Jews in Nazi Germany, exile Asians from Uganda,

---

17. UNESCO, *Statement on Race and Racial Prejudice* (Paris, 1967). The UNESCO experts also reached a consensus on the following propositions:
   · All people living today belong to the same species and descend from the same stock.
   · The division of the human species into "races" is partly conventional and partly arbitrary and does not imply any hierarchy whatsoever.
   · Current biological knowledge does not permit us to impute cultural achievements to differences in genetic potential. The peoples of the world today appear to possess equal biological potentialities for attaining any level of civilization.
   · The human problems arising from so-called "race relations" are social in origin rather than biological. Racism involves antisocial acts and beliefs that are based on the fallacy that discriminatory intergroup relations are justifiable on biological grounds.
18. Mar. 7, 1966, 660 U.N.T.S. 195.

and repress blacks in South Africa. Today, South Africa, both internally and in Namibia, rejects outright the notion that it should seek justice, equality, and other protection of human rights for all of its citizens. The doctrine of apartheid systematizes racial segregation and, through elaborate arrangements, restricts all aspects of the domestic, social, political, and economic life of nonwhites who, in South Africa proper, constitute four-fifths of the population.[19]

Carried out with harsh rigor and determination, apartheid has been condemned by the United Nations as a policy that amounts to "the organization of society on the principles of slavery." In South Africa and Namibia, blacks are denied political rights, freedom of movement and residence (and forced to live in conditions of humiliating indignity and squalor), freedom to work, and freedom to marry. In addition, every African over the age of sixteen is compelled to carry a "pass book" so the Government can maintain tight control. Strikes in the gold, diamond, platinum, and uranium mines have been brutally crushed. Ninety percent of workers in the mines are black; they earn below-subsistence wages and work under subhuman health and safety conditions.

Since 1962, there has been a growing demand for the adoption of antiapartheid enforcement measures by the United Nations. On several occasions, the General Assembly has recommended, by more than a two-thirds majority, the imposition of economic and diplomatic sanctions against South Africa, and the Security Council has called upon all member states not to supply arms to South Africa.[20] None of these measures has produced any dramatic turnaround, to be sure, but every day South Africa is feeling itself more and more isolated. Whether it can be persuaded to reverse its perilous course in time to avoid a bloodbath still is not known.[21]

Less dramatic, perhaps, but no less important, is the issue of sex discrimination, particularly of women. In the introduction to her *Sisterhood Is Global* anthology, Robin Morgan powerfully delineates women's issues worldwide.[22] The facts being insufficiently well known, her commentary merits extended quotation:

> "While women represent half the global population and one-third of the labor force, they receive only one-tenth of the world income and own less than one percent of world property. They also are responsible for two-thirds of all working hours," said former UN Secretary General Kurt Waldheim in his "Report to the UN Commission on the Status of Women." This was a diplomatic understatement of the situation.
>
> Two out of three of the world's illiterates are now women, and while the general illiteracy rate is falling, the female illiteracy rate is rising. One third of all families in the world are headed by women. In the developing countries, almost half of all single women over age fifteen are mothers. Only one third of the world's women have any access to contraceptive information or devices, and more than one half have no access to trained help during pregnancy and childbirth. Women in the developing world are responsible for more than 50 percent of all food production (on the African continent women do 60 to 80 percent of all agricultural work, 50 percent of all animal husbandry, and 100 percent of all food processing). In industrialized countries, women still are paid only

19. See *Apartheid: The Facts* (London: International Defense and Aid Fund for Southern Africa, in cooperation with the United Nations Center Against Apartheid, 1983). See also *South Africa in the 1980's: State of Emergency* (London: Catholic Institute for International Relations, 1987).
20. See Ozdemir A. Ozgur, *Apartheid, the United Nations and Peaceful Change* (Dobbs Ferry, N.Y.: Transnational Publishers, 1982).
21. For pertinent discussion, see Reading 23 in Chapter 6 in this volume.
22. Robin Morgan, "Planetary Feminism: The Politics of the 21st Century," in *Sisterhood Is Global: The International Woman's Movement Anthology* (Garden City, N.Y.: Anchor Press/Doubleday, 1984), 1–37.

one half to three quarters of what men earn at the same jobs, still are ghettoized into lower-paying "female-intensive" job categories, and still are the last hired and the first fired; in Europe and North America, women constitute over 40 percent of the paid labor force, *in addition* to contributing more than 40 percent of the Gross Domestic Produce in *un*paid labor in the home. As of 1982, 30 million people were unemployed in the industrialized countires and 800 million people in the Third World were living in absolute poverty; most of those affected are migrant workers and their families, youth, the disabled, and the aged—and the majority of all those categories are women. Approximately 500 million people suffer from hunger and malnutrition; the most seriously affected are children under age five and women. Twenty million persons die annually of hunger-related causes and one billion endure chronic undernourishment and other poverty deprivation; the majority are women and children. And this is only part of the picture.

Not only are females most of the poor, the starving, and the illiterate, but women and children constitute more than 90 percent of all refugee populations. Women outlive men in most cultures and therefore *are* the elderly of the world, as well as being the primary caretakers of the elderly. The abuse of children in virtually all cultures, and also because women bear responsibility for children, is a women's problem because it is mostly female children who are abused—nutritionally, educationally, sexually, psychologically, etc. Since women face such physical changes as menarche, menstruation, pregnancy, childbearing, lactation, and menopause—in addition to the general health problems we share with men—the crisis in world health is a crisis of women. Toxic pesticides and herbicides, chemical warfare, leakage from nuclear wastes, acid rain, and other such deadly pollutants usually take their first toll as a rise in cancers of the female reproductive system, and in miscarriages, stillbirths, and congenital deformities. Furthermore, it is women's work which must compensate for the destruction of ecological balance, the cash benefits of which accrue to various Big Brothers: deforestation (for lumber sales as export or for construction materials) results in a lowering of the water table, which in turn causes parched grasslands and erosion of topsoil; women, as the world's principal water haulers and fuel gatherers, must walk farther to find water, to find fodder for animals, to find cooking-fire fuel. This land loss, combined with the careless application of advanced technology (whether appropriate to a region or not), has created a major worldwide trend: rural migration to the cities. That, in turn, has a doubly devastating effect on women. Either they remain behind trying to support their children on unworkable land while men go to urban centers in search of jobs, or they also migrate—only to find that they are considered less educable and less employable than men, their survival options being mainly domestic servitude (the job category of two out of five women in Latin America), factory work (mostly for multinational corporations at less than $2 U.S. per day), or prostitution (which is growing rapidly in the urban centers of developing countries). Since women everywhere bear the "double job" burden of housework in addition to outside work, we are most gravely affected by the acknowledged world crisis in housing—and not only in less developed countries. In Britain, the Netherlands, and the United States, women were the founders of spontaneous squatters' movements; in Hungary the problem is so severe that women have been pressuring to have lack of housing declared as a ground for abortion; in Portugal, Mexico, and the USSR, women have been articulating the connections between the housing crisis, overcrowding, and a rise in the incidence of wife battery and child sexual abuse.

But the overlooked—and most important—factor in the power of women as a world political force is the magnitude of suffering combined with the magnitude of women: *women constitute not an oppressed minority, but a majority—of almost all national populations, and of the entire human species.* As that species approaches critical mass and the capacity to eradicate all life on the planet, more than ever before in recorded history, that majority of humanity now is mobilizing. The goal not only is to change drastically our own powerless status worldwide, but to redefine all existing societal structures and modes of existence.[23]

An important step toward the attainment of the goal of equal rights for women was taken on December 18, 1979, when the UN General Assembly adopted the Convention on the Elimination of All Forms of Discrimination Against Women.[24] The thirty-article convention, reflecting the extent of the exclusions and restrictions inflicted on women solely because of their sex, calls for equal rights for women, regardless of their marital status, in all fields—political, economic, social, cultural, civil, and health. In addition, for the international supervision of the obligations accepted by the states parties, the convention sets up machinery comparable to that of the International Convention on the Elimination of All Forms of Racial Discrimination.[25] A committee of experts, elected by the states parties and serving in their personal capacity (i.e., not under instructions from their respective governments), monitors progress made toward the objectives of equal rights. In Fran Hosken's opinion, "[t]here is no doubt that in the international context, this convention is the single most important document speaking for the human rights of women that has ever been devised."[26]

Like race and sex discrimination, religious bigotry is an affront to human dignity and a disavowal of the principles of the UN Charter. This was the view adopted by the UN General Assembly on November 25, 1981, in the Declaration on the Elimination of All Forms of Intolerance and Discrimination Based on Religion or Belief.[27] In propounding a right to "freedom of thought, conscience and religion," the declaration, in Article 1, states:

> This right shall include freedom to have a religion or whatever belief of [one's] . . . choice, and freedom, either individual or in community with others and in public or in private, to manifest [one's] religion or belief in worship, observance, practice and teaching.

Moreover, for purposes of the declaration, "intolerance and discrimination based on religion or belief" is explained in Article 2 to include "any distinction, exclusion, restriction or preference" based on religion and *intended or having as its effect* the "nullification or impairment of the recognition, enjoyment or exercise of human rights and fundamental freedoms on an equal basis." In placing religious liberty squarely in the context of human rights, the declaration affirms the seamless fabric of all human rights. The underlying presumption is that one need not be a "believer" to acknowledge religious freedom as a basic human right; one has only to take the notion of human rights seriously.

Invidious discrimination of all kinds has directly or indirectly caused wars and great suffering. Racism, sexism, and religious bigotry also have contributed to the flood of refugees that currently besets the international community. Since most of the world's refugees are women and their children, it is ironic that a woman is the symbol of freedom and refuge in the United States: the Statue of Liberty, "Mother of Exiles." The human rights issue of

---

23. Ibid., 1–3.
24. U.N.G.A. Res, 34/180 (XXXIV), 34 U.N. GAOR, Supp. (No. 46) 193, U.N. Doc. A/34/46 (1979).
25. See n. 18, above.
26. Fran P. Hosken, "Toward a Definition of Women's Human Rights," *Human Rights Quarterly* 3, no. 2 (Spring 1981): 1–10, at 6.
27. Nov. 25, 1981, U.N.G.A. Res. 36/55 (XXXVI), 36 U.N. GAOR, Supp. (No. 51) 171, U.N. Doc. A/36/55 (1981). For background on the declaration and exploration of the topic, see Leonard Swidler, ed., *Religious Liberty and Human Rights in Nations and in Religions* (Philadelphia: Temple University, Ecumenical Press, 1986).

these refugees is the focus of the essay in this chapter by Animesh Ghosal and Thomas M. Crowley.

For the last decade or so, the sheer numbers of refugees and displaced persons, whose primary goal is to be able to participate equally in the contemporary global system, have been such as to cause increasing concern in such receiving nations as the United States, Canada, Honduras, Somalia, Pakistan, and Thailand. According to a UN study, "by the beginning of the 1980's, numbers of refugees exceeded ten million, with the exodus from certain countries reaching hemorrhage proportions, and "[i]ncreasingly large migratory movements within countries and regions have begun to pose economic and social problems not hitherto experienced on quite the same scale."[28] The impact of these ballooning exoduses has been substantial on the work of the United Nations High Commission for Refugees (UNHCR). Initially set up during World War II to assist persons fleeing from the Soviet Union and Nazi Germany, the early work of the High Commission was primarily legal and technical, involving the determination of who was a "bona fide refugee" and advocating national resettlement based on the individual case work of "protection officers." Today, as pointed out by David Kennedy,

> [t]he westward flow of Eastern Europeans has been eclipsed by sudden, large scale trans-boundary migrations in the Third World—the so-called south-south refugee flows. This shift has drawn into question almost every assumption about international refugee work. Refugees today are less often middle-class people who need legal assimilation in a second European culture than destitute people with a wide variety of special needs. Assistance, rather than protection, has come to comprise by far the greatest portion of the UNHCR's work. The Office must devise solutions for groups of people rather than for individual refugees. In fact, individual determination of refugee status has become increasingly impractical and beside the point.[29]

Ghoshal and Crowley present a critical assessment of U.S. policies regarding refugees and immigrants and show how thousands of refugees who have fled to American shores in recent years—among them Afghans, Cubans, Ethiopians, Haitians, Iranians, Salvadorans, and South Africans—have been entitled to secure refuge in the United States under American and international law. The authors note, however, that the pressures of public opinion and social service systems overwhelmed by the influx of refugees place restrictions on migration. Such pressures, the authors observe, test the limits of internationally defined concepts of the "right to sanctuary" based on "a well-founded fear of being persecuted for reasons of race, religion, nationality, membership of a particular social group or political opinion. . . ." The authors examine the supposed distinction in U.S. policy between "political refugees" and "economic migrants" and analyze the advantages of the former and the problems of the latter; they conclude by comparing U.S. policies with those of other governments.

The last issue addressed in this chapter on basic decencies and participatory rights is the survival and protection of aboriginals, Native Americans, and other tribal peoples referred to by the Minority Rights Group (London) as the "Fourth World."[30] These are the marginalized peoples outside the periphery of modern civilization who are generally recognized to be the largest (300 to 500 million) and most disadvantaged group whose status has not

---

28. Sadruddin Aga Khan, UN Special Rapporteur, *Study on Human Rights and Massive Exoduses* (UN Commission on Human Rights, 38th sess., 1981), 1. See also Frances D'Souza and Jeff Crisp, *The Refugee Dilemma*, Report No. 43 (London: The Minority Rights Group, 1985).
29. David Kennedy, "International Refugee Protection," *Human Rights Quarterly* 8, no. 1 (Feb. 1986): 1–69, at 5–6.
30. See Ben Whitaker, ed., *The Fourth World: Victims of Group Oppression* (New York: Schocken, 1972).

yet been fully addressed by international legal standards and mechanisms pertinent to the values of basic decency and equality. Because of this failure, the United Nations, in 1971, appointed a Special Rapporteur to study the policies pursued in various countries toward their indigenous populations. Additionally, in 1982, the Human Rights Commission authorized the establishment of a Working Group on Indigenous Populations to review developments pertaining to the promotion and protection of indigenous rights and to submit its conclusions to the UN Sub-Commission on Minorities.[31]

In his wide-ranging essay in this chapter, Christian Bay argues that the survival of indigenous peoples represents the most urgent category of human rights issues today. Professor Bay examines the plight of indigenous peoples through the case of the Yanomami, the largest group of forest-dwelling native people in South America who still preserve their original way of life. The Yanomami are distributed throughout the outlying areas of Brazil and Venezuela. Victims of colonial aggression and the blight of unfamiliar European diseases, they have been forced to relocate without benefit of a territory they can call their own. Of course, these disabilities take their toll not just on individuals; they disrupt, even extinguish, the culture that provides the Yanomami with identity and community. Bay argues, first, for the natural priority of survival rights. He then urges that these rights require that high priority be given to the protection of vulnerable peoples such as the Yanomami. He argues, too, that a state committed to the advancement of human rights must de facto be on a collision course with the large commercial enterprises that actively try to influence governments to sacrifice human rights to corporate legal claims and interests by, for example, displacing customary tribal lands for agribusiness. Bay also draws attention to the fact that ecologically minded scientists have made a strong case for using indigenous rather than imported models for the development of the Amazon. Are the Yanomami, who have learned to balance population and resources and who have lived for centuries in the Amazon without poisoning its waters and lands, to be denied a future because of modern civilization's heedless "conquest of nature"?

The readings in this chapter explore a broad array of issues affecting people everywhere: civil liberties, equality rights, and standards of decency that reject genocide, torture, "disappearances," and multiple affronts to human dignity. All these issues, in the present generation as in earlier generations, are dealt with by cultural prohibitions, religious norms, and elite standards of noblesse oblige. But as our world has become more unitary, the emerging international law of human rights has sought to rise above parochialism by fixing a minimum normative foundation of basic decency and to establish a range of claims defining everyone's participation in basic human rights. Fewer and fewer of humankind's compelling problems have solutions that are viable in national isolation. Increasingly, they call for cooperative global solutions, solutions that recognize that we are a single species and that each of us has a stake in the human interests emerging globally alongside national and regional interests. The discovery that human interests can best be fostered by united action is beginning to have a major impact on political thinking. Minimal norms of basic decency and equal participation by all in the enjoyment of human rights has moved to the center

---

31. See José R. Martinez-Coba, UN Special Rapporteur, *Study on Indigenous and Tribal Populations*, U.N. Doc. E/CN.4/sub. 2/1986/7; Asbjorn Eide, "Indigenous Populations and Human Rights: The United Nations Efforts at Mid-Way," in *Native Powers, The Quest for Autonomy and Nationhood of Indigenous Peoples*, ed. Jens Brosted (Bergen: Universitetsforlegt, 1985), 196–212. See also Menno Boldt and J. Anthony Long, eds., *The Quest for Justice: Aboriginal Peoples and Aboriginal Rights* (Toronto: University of Toronto Press, 1985). On problems and perspectives in the United States, see the thoughtful essay by Felix S. Cohen, "Americanizing the White Man," in *The Legal Conscience: Selected Papers of Felix S. Cohen*, ed. Lucy Kramer Cohen (New York: Archon Books, 1970), 315–27.

of the international agenda. No ideology has refuted nor has any national action effectively taken exception to the proclamation in the 1948 Universal Declaration of Human Rights that basic freedoms and human rights represent "the highest aspiration of the common people."

3. LEO KUPER *The Sovereign Territorial State: The Right to Genocide*

The main thesis of this [essay] is that the sovereign territorial state claims, as an integral part of its sovereignty, the right to commit genocide, or engage in genocidal massacres, against peoples under its rule, and that the United Nations, for all practical purposes, defends this right. To be sure, no state *explicitly* claims the right to commit genocide—this would not be morally acceptable even in international circles—but the right is exercised under other more acceptable rubrics, notably the duty to maintain law and order, or the seemingly sacred mission to preserve the territorial integrity of the state. And though the norm for the United Nations is to sit by and watch, like a grandstand spectator, the unfolding of the genocidal conflict in the domestic arena right through to the final massacres, there would generally be concern, and action, to provide humanitarian relief for the refugees, and direct intercession by the Secretary-General. Moreover, some of the steps presently taken by the United Nations in the field of human rights may have the effect of inhibiting the resort to massacre; and there are indications of changing attitudes in the United Nations, though this may be too optimistic an assessment. In the past, however, there was small comfort to be derived from the Genocide Convention,[1] or from the commitments of the United Nations, by peoples whose own rulers threatened them with extermination or massacre.

The almost perennial complaint is that the world remains indifferent to the genocide or the genocidal massacres, and that the United Nations turns a deaf ear. I suppose it may be unrealistic to expect the representatives of the nations, great and small, gathered in imposing session on world affairs, to be unduly concerned over charges of the imminent extermination of a small Indian people in Paraguay. . . . [T]he complaint filed for the Aché Indians by the International League for the Rights of Man resulted in a light flurry of verbal interest among some human rights–oriented "experts" and delegates in United Nations corridors, but . . . no formal action was taken; and . . . the plea by the Anti-Slavery Society of Great Britain in August 1974 did not succeed in securing a recommendation for even an investigation of conditions in Paraguay. But reactions were by no means totally negative. Some years later, in closed meeting during its thirty-fourth session (February/March 1978), the United Nations Commission on Human Rights did decide on action in respect of a number of countries, including Paraguay. While the nature of the action was not disclosed, it appears from a report of the United States government to have been a recommendation for intercession with the government of Paraguay by the Secretary-General. Moreover, the Inter-American Human Rights Commission of the Organization of American States had adopted a resolution in May 1977 calling attention to reports of serious abuses and requesting the government of Paraguay to take measures to protect the rights of the Aché Indians. There has been some response by the government to these expressions of international concern.

In the Burundi genocide, the situation was very different from the extermination of small bands of hunters and gatherers, deemed expendable in the march of "progress." The Hutu were a large settled population of peasants, the massacres took place on a vast scale, and they were immediately known to the outside world, given the presence of diplomatic representatives, missionaries and expatriates. Again, there were

---

1. Convention on the Prevention and Punishment of the Crime of Genocide. Adopted by the U N General Assembly on Dec. 9, 1948, and entered into force on Jan. 12, 1961. 78 U.N.T.S. 277.

many charges of indifference by the outside world. But I would rather describe it, not as indifference, but as a curious mixture of condemnation, of support and of inaction, which permitted the massacres to take their seemingly uninhibited course over the years.

The attempted coup and the massacres by Hutu were on 29 April 1972. Tutsi counteraction was immediate, the suppression of the revolt being followed by the systematic slaughter of selected Hutu strata, with of course much general slaughter. The Belgian government, as the former mandatory power, was most directly concerned. As early as 19 May 1972, the Belgian Prime Minister had informed his cabinet that according to the information at his disposal Burundi was confronted with a veritable genocide; and the Foreign Minister had declared before the Senate Foreign Relations Committee on 24 May that the Belgian Ambassador in Burundi was instructed to express Belgian concern and hope for the restoration of order and peace: accounts in the French press found their echo in the French National Assembly on 2 June, when deputies urged the government to take energetic action to bring an end to the massacre in Burundi. But in fact, France lent support to the Burundi government, as did China and North Korea. The U.S.A., on 1 May, declared Burundi to be a disaster area, and engaged in humanitarian relief and diplomatic approaches. Members of the diplomatic corps in Burundi, with notable exceptions, made representations. In his Sunday address on 28 May, Pope Paul referred to the bloody battle of brothers against brothers of the same nation, and on 29 May the Papal Nuncio in Burundi presented the government with a remarkably diplomatic (and insipid) letter of protest on his own behalf and that of other diplomats.

There was also activity in the United Nations. The Secretary-General expressed the United Nations' concern to the representative of Burundi at the United Nations. In the last week of May, he offered assistance for the launching of a United Nations aid program. On 22 June the first of two small UN missions arrived in Burundi, and on 4 July, the Secretary-General reported to a press conference in Geneva that the humanitarian mission had confirmed the enormous suffering; though precise figures could not be obtained, different sources estimated the number of the dead as between 80,000 and 200,000.

Apart from the active concern of the Secretary-General of the United Nations, the various diplomatic approaches, and the provision of humanitarian relief, no serious steps were taken to halt the massacres in either 1972 or 1973. At its meetings in 1973, the Sub-Commission on Prevention of Discrimination and Protection of Minorities forwarded to the Commission on Human Rights a complaint against Burundi of consistent patterns of gross violations of human rights. But when the Commission met in 1974, it effectively shelved the matter by appointing a new working party to communicate with the government of Burundi, and to report back to the next annual meeting of the Commission. The structure and ideology of the United Nations, particularly its protective stance in relation to the sovereign rights of the territorial state, stood in the way of effective action. Moreover, there had been the catastrophic experience of earlier intervention in the Congo. But a major preliminary obstacle was presented by the Organization of African Unity, given the policy of the United Nations and of western diplomats that this body should be primarily responsible for mediating in the conflict, and for initiating appropriate policy.

Whatever representations may have been made privately by members of the Organization of African Unity, its official releases were supportive of the Burundi regime. The Secretary-General of the O.A.U., on a brief visit to Burundi on 22 May 1972, accompanied by the Tanzanian Prime Minister and the President of Somalia, announced that his presence signified the total solidarity of the O.A.U. with President Micombero of Burundi. The O.A.U. summit meeting in Rabat the following month adopted a resolution to the effect that the Council of Ministers was convinced that, thanks to Micombero's saving action, peace would be rapidly re-established, national unity consolidated and territorial integrity preserved. Lemarchand suggests that since most African states are, to a greater or lesser extent, potential Burundis, none would wish to establish a precedent that might prevent it dealing with similar crises by means of its own choosing. There would also have been the overriding preoccupation with action against the racist regimes of Southern Africa, and resentment against any involvement which might deflect from that purpose, or reflect on the domestic policies of African states. Whatever the explanation for the attitude of the O.A.U. towards the Burundi massacres, one can well understand the anguish of the victims, confronted with the seeming indifference of African rulers. It is conveyed in the following letter written on 8 September 1972 by the *Mouvement des Etudiants Progressistes Barundi* in Belgium, to heads of African states meeting in Tanzania:

Tutsi apartheid is established more ferociously than the apartheid of Vorster, more inhumanly than Portuguese colonialism. Outside of Hitler's Nazi movement, there is nothing to compete with it in world history. And the peoples of Africa say nothing. African heads of state receive the executioner Micombero and clasp his hand in fraternal greeting. Sirs, heads of state, if you wish to help the African peoples of Namibia, Azania, Zimbabwe, Angola, Mozambique and Guinea-Bissau to liberate themselves from their white oppressors, you have no right to let Africans murder other Africans. . . . Are you waiting until the entire Hutu ethnic group of Burundi is exterminated before raising your voices?

According to a U.S. report, there was more active concern by a few African heads of state following the ethnic violence in April–May 1973. Perhaps this may have restrained, in some small measure, the fury of genocidal massacre. But one cannot help wondering whether more lives might have been saved if there had been no Organization of African Unity, and whether there might have been more effective humanitarian intervention in the absence of both a United Nations Organization and a Genocide Convention.

[Editors' note: Kuper next describes the "reticence" of the international community in the face of the "mass slaughter" of Ugandans under the military rule of General Idi Amin beginning immediately after Amin's successful coup in January 1971. He suggests that it is no exaggeration "to describe the actions of the UN Commission on Human Rights and the Organization of African Unity as having the effect of condoning the mass slaughter." He then turns his attention to the case of Kampuchea (Cambodia).]

In the case of Cambodia (Democratic Kampuchea), there would appear to have been an expeditious response by the Commission on Human Rights. . . . [I[n 1979, the Commission had before it a careful analysis prepared by the Chairman of the Sub-Commission on Discrimination. The institution of any action at all, and as speedily as within a period of three years, was quite remarkable. But in terms of the needs of the people of Cambodia, it constituted interminable delay and inhuman indifference. After all, the forced

evacuation of Phnom Penh in April 1975 was immediately known to the outside world, and refugees' accounts soon gave abundant testimony to the harshness of the regime and its brutal destruction of human life. Yet the procedures followed were of such a leisurely and administratively protracted nature that Cambodia had been invaded and conquered by the time the Commission could initiate further action. Moreover, the resolution of March 1978 seems virtually to have been forced on the Commission by extreme pressure. There were the submissions by the governments of Canada, Norway, the United Kingdom, the United States of America and Australia, and by two major non-governmental organizations, with supporting documentation, which I assume could not easily be dismissed by the majority of the members. And the debate itself supports this interpretation.

The original resolution proposed by the United Kingdom delegation asked simply that a study of the human rights situation in Democratic Kampuchea should be made with the cooperation of the government of that country and of any other government, non-governmental organization or individual who might be able to provide objective and reliable information on the situation. In support of the resolution, the representative of the United Kingdom argued that the Commission "had not hesitated to examine the situation in certain countries, such as Chile and South Africa, under other procedures. There were, however, other gross violations of human rights which were as bad as, if not worse than, the cases just mentioned, and which the Commission never considered. . . . If the Commission continued to turn a blind eye to those situations, it was in danger of discrediting itself, and the United Nations generally, in the eyes of world public opinion." He then commented on the reports of systematic and arbitrary executions and other flagrant violations of human rights involving thousands of deaths, and systematic brutality at the whim of the authorities, with the slaughter in many cases of entire families. "All those atrocities had aroused the conscience of the world, but the Commission had disregarded them for political reasons." If the Commission was to fulfill its functions, it would have to bring the allegations into the open by instituting a full and impartial investigation.

The proposed resolution was innocuous enough, but it aroused opposition of a most disquieting nature. A compromise was arrived at (seemingly in the corridors with much diplomatic frou-frouing) which resulted in the revised resolution to which I have already referred, an almost totally debilitated resolution. The adoption of this resolution may have represented progress and created an important precedent for the Commission, as the United States representative commented; but to the outside observer it appears simply as a stalling operation, with a polite face-saving bow in the direction of the supporters of the original proposal.

In March 1979, during the annual meetings of the Commission . . . representatives of Australia, Canada, Sweden and the United Kingdom tabled a motion, which, in its revised form, would record the Commission's view that, on the basis of the evidence available, gross and flagrant violations of human rights had occurred in Democratic Kampuchea, and which would note the Commission's decision to keep the situation under review at its next meeting (in 1980) as a matter of priority.

Neither the original nor the revised resolution, though deliberately moderate in tone, were debated. Yugoslavia, acting on behalf of the sponsors (Benin, Egypt, Pakistan, Senegal, Syria and Yugoslavia) tabled a draft decision to postpone consideration of the report on Kampuchea to the next session in 1980. This was carried by a large majority. As for the revised resolution, which carefully refrained from reference to the Sub-Commission's report, it was guillotined on a motion by the Chairman of the Commission, carried by an overwhelming majority, that the Commission should decide not to vote on the resolution. Only Australia, Austria, Canada, France, West Germany, Sweden and the U.S.A. opposed this motion.

The issue was not controversy over the facts. There seemed to be fairly general agreement that the government of Democratic Kampuchea had committed gross violations of human rights. The Soviet representative, using the occasion to attack both the U.S.A. and China, described the Kampuchean government as a "cut-throat regime" which had established a system of slavery of a new type, and had subjected the people of Kampuchea to "generalized genocide" (presumably in the sense of genocide against *all* strata, the distinction between political and ethnic slaughter seemingly abandoned in this, as in much other contemporary, discussion). The issue was rather

one of *realpolitik* connected with the invasion of Cambodia by Vietnam. In any event, whatever the motivations of the members, the Commission had succeeded in evading even a mildly phrased condemnation of the Cambodian regime. Once again, the Commission had "risen above principle."

It was left to the successor Cambodian regime, installed by the Vietnamese, to initiate action, and in August 1979 the new government instituted criminal proceedings against the former Prime Minister and Deputy Prime Minister—in absentia—on charges of genocide. The indictment cited massacres by the accused and their associates of nearly all the officers, soldiers and officials of the previous administration, along with their families, and a systematic plan to eliminate ethnic minorities, including a large number of Thai and Cham, and also all those who opposed the regime. It detailed the forced evacuation of the towns; the unprecedented apparatus of repression, reducing the population to a state of slavery; the abolition of all social relations, forcing the population to focus on only one central point of authority; the elimination of Buddhism and Islam, the abolition of culture and education, the systematic killing of religious converts and intellectuals; "corrupting adolescents in order to make them torturers"; and the destruction of the economy. There was evidence of massacres, executions, torture, mass graves, and survivors' accounts to support the indictment, and the accused were found guilty of genocide by the People's Revolutionary Tribunal.

But the crimes of the regime proved no barrier to continued participation in the General Assembly of the United Nations. In September 1979, a majority of 71 (against 35, with 34 abstentions) voted to continue the assignment of the Cambodian seat to the ousted government. Among nations supporting the resolution were governments that had previously denounced the regime before the Commission on Human Rights—Australia, Canada, the United Kingdom and the U.S.A.. One can only ask—is genocide a credential for membership in the General Assembly of the United Nations? Meanwhile, the Cambodian people were threatened with near extinction by famine and disease, in another chapter in the politics of starvation, reminiscent of the Biafran tragedy in the last stages of the Nigerian civil war.

In Bangladesh, as in Uganda and Cambodia, slaughter pursued its relatively uninhibited course, until invasion by a foreign power, with supporting local forces. The massacres, starting in March 1971, took place under the full gaze of the outside world, with observer reports, and charges of genocide, filtering through to the world press. Yet the United Nations General Assembly and Security Council were only "seized" of the matter, and then from a quite different aspect, in December 1971 following the escalating of the conflict between India and Pakistan into open warfare, and the invasion of Bangladesh by India. As for the Sub-Commission on Prevention of Discrimination and Protection of Minorities, meeting in August 1971, it speedily disposed of a written request by twenty-two international non-governmental organizations that the Sub-Commission examine the available information and recommend measures for the protection of human rights in East Pakistan. A plea presented in person by the representative of the International Commission of Jurists similarly fell on deaf ears. Only one member is reported as having argued that the Sub-Commission should not remain silent. I found it almost unbearable to read this discussion by a United Nations body of one of the major genocides of the twentieth century; it was so procedural and so devoid of human compassion.

The Secretary-General of the United Nations had been deeply concerned. In July 1971, in a memorandum to the President of the Security Council, he drew attention to the tragic situation in the India-Pakistan sub-continent, and its possible consequences as a potential threat to peace; but no Security Council action resulted from this approach. Indeed, the only effective action taken by the United Nations in relation to the massacres was the mounting of a massive program of humanitarian relief which continued after the cessation of hostilities. Some perspectives on the failure to take action, arising out of the alignment of the great powers—with the U.S.A. and China supporting Pakistan and Soviet Russia supporting India—and the considerations shaping the United States policy of delicate diplomacy behind the scenes, are given in the United States Congress Hearings before the Subcommittee on International Organizations and Movements.

I have not dealt with all the cases of genocide or genocidal massacres since the Second World War. . . . Sometimes the massacres were so precipitate, as in the massacres of Ibo in Northern Nigeria or of Arabs in Zanzibar, that there was no possibility of preventive action by the United Nations. In Rwanda, United Nations missions had the unfortunate effect of further polarizing relations between Tutsi and Hutu. In Vietnam, there were obstacles to the involvement of the United Nations, and its role was both marginal and intermittent. The Secretary-General had good cause to record, in his introduction to the Annual Report for 1971–72, his deep concern that the United Nations, created in the aftermath of a world war to safeguard international peace and security, should appear to have no relevance to what was happening in Vietnam. And we recall that charges of genocide against the United States were heard by a privately instituted tribunal. In the Sudan, there was seeming indifference to the struggle of the Southern Sudanese, in contrast to the Algerian revolutionary forces, who succeeded in internationalizing their war of liberation. The Turkish genocide against the Armenians preceded the United Nations by many years, and here the contribution of the U N was to give the genocide a gentle push down the memory hole.

I have also not mentioned the recent cases of Equatorial Guinea and East Timor. In March 1978, the Commission on Human Rights decided, under its confidential procedures, on some unspecified form of action relating to Equatorial Guinea. Here a dictator of about ten years' standing had been engaged in slaughtering, torturing, repressing and pillaging his people. In August 1979, he was overthrown in a coup, then tried before a military tribunal, found guilty (of genocide, multiple murders, treason, the violation of human rights, and the misuse of public funds) and executed. In East Timor, there had been an invasion of the country by Indonesia in December 1975, and massive slaughter of its inhabitants. The government of Indonesia failed to comply with repeated calls by the United Nations to withdraw its armed forces from East Timor, so as to enable the people of the territory freely to exercise their right to self-determination. In a statement presented to the Fourth Committee of the U N General Assembly, Noam Chomsky contrasts the protective stance of the U.S.A. and the West towards the atrocities of the Indonesian occupation with their denunciation of the Khmer Rouge regime in Cambodia.

I have also not mentioned the . . . expulsion of Chinese by the Vietnamese government, with great loss of life through the denial of refuge in adjoining countries, and by drowning, starvation and disease. This recalls the many other expulsions of minority groups in recent years, and the danger that, with increasing pressure of population on resources, mass expulsion may become a regular feature of the international scene.

The major and important contribution of the United Nations has been in the provision of humanitarian relief for the survivors of the genocidal conflicts. And I should add also the contribution of its peace-keeping forces, which have no doubt averted many massacres. But taken as a whole, the United Nations performs a quite negligible role in the direct prevention or punishment of the crime of genocide, and the Genocide Convention is virtually a dead letter. In the comments which follow, I seek to explore some of the reasons for this failure.

The performance of the United Nations Organization in the suppression of the crime of genocide is deeply disillusioning, particularly against the background of the humanitarian ideals which inspired its founding, and which the organization continues to proclaim—ideals in which the suppression of war, of crimes against humanity and of genocide were quite central. But of course the United Nations is not a humanitarian, but a political, organization, and its humanitarian goals are at the play of political forces, pressure groups and blocks, in an arena where delegates pursue the divisive interests of the states they represent. Added to this, its ideological commitment to the protection of the sovereignty of the state, with the corollary of non-intervention in its domestic affairs, stands in the way of effective action against "domestic" (internal) genocide. And above all, it is the rulers of the states of the world who gather together at the United Nations, and it is mainly, though not exclusively, the rulers who engage in genocide.

. . . [T]he political conflict in the debate on the Genocide Convention . . . resulted in the emasculation of its provisions in two important respects—the exclusion of political groups as potential victims of genocide, and the elimination of effective enforcement procedures. I have stressed [elsewhere] the rather obvious argument that political division within a society has been, and continues to be, a significant source of systematic massacre, and that there is no valid theoretical reason for denying political groups the protection of the Genocide Convention. Political groups are as vulnerable and identifiable as ethnic groups; moreover, what seems to be a purely eth-

nic conflict usually has a political dimension, as, for example, in Burundi, and the seemingly purely political may be interwoven with ethnic antagonisms, as to some extent in both Indonesia and Cambodia. One can only suppose that many of the governments represented in the debates on the Convention did not wish to be denied the right to dispose of their political opponents, by radical means if necessary, and with the minimum of outside interference.

But the issue of the exclusion of political groups from the protection of the Genocide Convention is somewhat academic, since the protection, as matters stand at the present time, is quite spurious. The initial draft of the Convention incorporated the principle of universal enforcement, and made provision for both national and international jurisdiction. It was watered down by the exclusion of the principle of universal enforcement and by other modifications, and now provides for trial by a competent tribunal of the state in the territory of which the act was committed, "or by such international penal tribunal as may have jurisdiction with respect to those Contracting Parties which shall have accepted its jurisdiction." Where there has been a change of government, action within the state against the former rulers becomes feasible, and I have referred to two such cases, Cambodia and Equatorial Guinea. In the ordinary course, however, the effect of the present provisions is that the rulers, the main universe for genocidal murderers, would be expected to prosecute themselves or to submit to the jurisdiction of an international penal court, which does not exist, though more than thirty years have passed since the framing of the Genocide Convention. . . .

The barrier to the effective implementation of the Genocide Convention lies not only in the emasculation of the enforcement procedures. It is deeply embedded in the structure and performance of the United Nations as a whole, and of the bodies primarily "seized" with complaints of human rights violations. These bodies are the Commission on Human Rights, and the Sub-Commission on Prevention of Discrimination and Protection of Minorities. The Deputy Director of the Human Rights Division explained to me that the complaints might be classified in three categories—those handled within confidential procedures, those sent for processing, also within the confidential procedures, but published by the authors, and complaints made directly to the Commission by governmental representatives or by observers. As regards the third category of open complaint, he recalled only one recent case, where a charge of genocide had been made against Democratic Kampuchea. Because of the confidentiality of closed meetings and the diplomatic style of reporting in the open meetings, it is not easy to unravel the proceedings of the Commission, or to know how much of the discussion has surfaced. . . . The Commission on Human Rights consists of members who represent their governments and are accountable to them. Members of the Sub-Commission on Discrimination and Protection of Minorities, on the other hand, serve as experts in their individual capacities and not as representatives of their governments. But this is only in theory; they too are nominated by their governments and, no doubt, many respond to the interests of these governments. In practice, both the Commission and Sub-Commission are heavily politicized. By this, I do not mean to imply that these bodies do not include highly principled members, deeply dedicated to the promotion of human rights. But there is a sharp tension between a universal ethic and the power interests of sovereign states. And there are many divisions within the United Nations—between capitalist and socialist countries, between the wealthy industrialized nations and the struggling Third World, and between regional alliances—which serve as the basis for voting blocks, exposing the most tragic issues to "regional and ideological protection rackets" and to the "disguised barter of one atrocity for another."

The subordination of human rights issues to quite naked political interests . . . has provoked repeated comment in the Commission and Sub-Commission. An important speech along these lines was that made at the opening of the thirty-fifth session of the Commission, on 12 February 1979, by the Acting Chairman, Mr. Keba M'Baye, President of the Supreme Court of Senegal, and a long-standing member of the ad hoc working group of experts on Southern Africa. The meeting was held shortly after the celebration of the thirtieth anniversary of the Declaration of Human Rights, and Mr. M'Baye reviewed the world situation—the continued atrocities of war; the Third World, as exploited victims of the egoism of the rich countries, stagnating in underdevelopment and given over to despair and rancor; fear, poverty, torture; violations of the right of peoples to self-determination; massacres, punitive expeditions, the malpractices of apartheid; thousands of African and Asian children killed every day by malnutrition and disease; the continued persecution of national or foreign minorities in a world which claimed to aspire to the civilization of the universal; and mass deportation of foreign minorities serving as scapegoats for despotic and unpopular regimes. It was a sad commentary on the current state of human rights. . . .

The speech makes reference to a central ideological commitment of the United Nations, respect for the sovereignty of the state. It is enshrined in Article 2(7) of the United Nations Charter, which provides that "nothing contained in the present Charter shall authorize the United Nations to intervene in matters which are essentially within the domestic jurisdiction of any state or shall require the Members to submit such matters to settlement under the present Charter; but this principle shall not prejudice the application of enforcement measures under Chapter VII." The former colonial territories have good reason to fear intervention, and the injunction against such intervention is elaborated in the General Assembly's Declaration on the Inadmissibility of Intervention in Domestic Affairs of States and Protection of their Independence and Sovereignty.[2] The protection of domestic jurisdiction is almost inevitably invoked by any state charged with violating the human rights of its subjects. But Chapter VII of the Charter, vesting the Security Council with the right to impose sanctions against any threat to the peace, already constitutes a substantial modification of the principle of non-interference in the internal affairs of a state. And the recognition of such international crimes as genocide or crimes against humanity similarly implies limitations on the powers of the sovereign state. Human rights are a matter of legitimate international concern. Yet the United Nations remains highly protective of state sovereignty, even where there is overwhelming evidence, not simply of minor violations, but of widespread murder and genocidal massacre. It is

---

2. [Resolution 2131 (X), Dec. 21, 1965.]

no wonder that it may seem to be part of a conspiracy of governments to deprive the people of their rights.

A second central ideological commitment is to the right of peoples to self-determination. It appears in the first article of the Charter, and in many resolutions of the General Assembly, notably in 1952, in a resolution entitled The Right of Peoples and Nations to Self-determination, and again in 1960, in the Declaration on the Granting of Independence to Colonial Countries and Peoples.[3] The right to self-determination, to freedom from alien subjugation and exploitation, was an inspiring, crusading call in the world movement for decolonization. But the situation is quite changed in the successor states to the former colonial societies, most of which are multiethnic. Now a political movement by an ethnic group to realize the "inalienable" right to self-determination is seen as a reprehensible attack on the sovereignty and territorial integrity of the state—secession, not liberation. . . . I can well appreciate that there could be anarchy if every group, however small, sought to exercise the right of self-determination. There is certainly a need to define the self which would be entitled to claim the right to self-determination, the conditions for the exercise of that right, and the forms such exercise might take. But as it is, some of the most destructive and genocidal conflicts have been waged precisely in the repression of claims for greater autonomy or for independence by large, distinctive, regionally separate peoples. And one has to ask whether the slaughter of millions in Bangladesh, Biafra, the Sudan and now in Eritrea can possibly be justified by the interests of the Territorial State in the relatively unrestrained exercise of its internal sovereignty and in the preservation of the domains it has conquered or inherited? Or is there a need for the United Nations to abandon a dehumanized scale of values which effectively condones the sacrifice of human victims to the Territorial State?

The general argument in this [essay] is that the United Nations provides no protection against genocide, and that the Commission on Human Rights, though vested with a primary responsibility, actually condones the crime by delay, evasion and subterfuge. A weapon available to the Commission is the urgent condemnation of gross violations of human rights, and the exposure of those responsible to the opprobrium of international public opinion. But it is precisely this step that the Commission is reluctant to take. It uses the confidential procedures to hide, in the maximum secrecy it can attain, its own, often disreputable, deliberations; and through the same procedures, it protects its fellow rulers, as a club or a clique might protect its delinquent members. Yet the United Nations is the most appropriate body for protection against, and punishment of, genocide, and the problem is what developments and pressures might render it somewhat effective, and how to bridge the immense distance which presently separates proclaimed ideal from actual practice.

Given the structure and performance of the United Nations, it is perhaps naive to anticipate significant change. Yet there are indications of imminent change. Two new U.N. covenants have now come into force, the International Covenant on Economic, Social and Cultural Rights and the International Covenant on Civil and Political Rights. An optional protocol, attached to the second covenant, enables individuals in a state which ratifies the protocol to have recourse to a Human Rights Committee. As for the Commission on Human Rights, it has somewhat improved its procedures, and it has finally begun to initiate action beyond the boundaries of its three scapegoat nations. There could be appreciable further progress if some of the suggestions were taken up for a more efficient division of functions, and for the appointment of a High Commissioner for Human Rights, or a High Commissioner for the Prevention of Genocide and Torture.

Some significance is also to be attached to the fact that in two countries, Cambodia and Equatorial Guinea, the successor regimes actually instituted proceedings against the former rulers on charges of genocide. As countries overthrow tyrannical and murderous rulers, who seem to be more abundant than ever, we may anticipate that the representatives of the new regimes are likely to show greater moral and militant concern for protection against massacre and genocide. Thus it would seem that the intervention of the new President of Uganda, at the summit meeting of

3. [See Louis B. Sohn and Thomas Buergenthal, eds., *International Protection of Human Rights* (Indianapolis, Ind.: Bobbs-Merrill, 1973), 535–39.]

the Organization of African Unity in July 1979, must have contributed to the belated decision to write an African Charter of Human Rights, and to establish an African Commission on Human Rights. . . .

Regardless of the actual and potential contri-

bution of the United Nations, the regional intergovernmental associations, and the international non-governmental agencies, the first, and perhaps main, line of defense against domestic genocide lies within the countries themselves. . . .

QUESTIONS FOR REFLECTION AND DISCUSSION

1. In an omitted portion of his essay, Leo Kuper quotes a Ugandan official as asking: "Is systematic genocide an internal matter or a matter for all mankind?" How would you answer this question? If you think it is a matter for all "mankind" (let us say, "humankind"), what would be appropriate for the international community to do to stop genocidal activity within the boundaries of a sovereign state? Or do you think that the absolute sovereignty of the state should be maintained? Why? Why not?

2. Kuper maintains that the failure of the UN complaint machinery, in particular the UN Commission on Human Rights, to condemn openly and vigorously all acts of genocide has the effect of condoning genocidal activity. What factors might prevent the United Nations from acting efficiently in this regard? If concerted international action is not forthcoming, do you agree that an individual country, acting on its own, should have the right to intervene in another country to stop what it perceives as genocidal activity? Why? Why not?

3. The 1948 Convention on the Prevention and Punishment of the Crime of Genocide (78 U.N.T.S. 277) defines "genocide" in Article 2 as follows:

> In the present Convention, genocide means any of the following acts committed with intent to destroy, in whole or in part, a national, ethnical, racial or religious group, as such:
>
> (a) Killing members of the group;
> (b) Causing serious bodily or mental harm to members of the group;
> (c) Deliberately inflicting on the group conditions of life calculated to bring about its physical destruction in whole or in part;
> (d) Imposing measures intended to prevent birth within the group;
> (e) Forcibly transferring children of the group to another group.

Kuper observes that, though as vulnerable and identifiable as ethnic groups, political groups are not protected by the convention. Why might this be so?

4. What motivates political elites to engage in genocide? What rationales do they use to excuse their acts? Are any of these rationales convincing? During the Inquisition of the twelfth and thirteenth centuries, largely because the Inquisitors sincerely believed that God was directing them to murder the Infidels, whole populations were slaughtered for departing from orthodoxy. Is it reasonable to expect any of the contending factions in the Middle East to act any differently toward their adversaries, given that they, too, believe their ultimate political legitimacy to be derived from a divine authority?

5. The Soviet Union is a party to the Genocide Convention, as is the United States. Yet each day, in keeping with the strategy of nuclear deterrence, each threatens, because of perceived political differences, to annihilate the other with nuclear weapons. Does this amount to a genocidal intent toward one another? Toward the rest of the world? Does the capacity for "overkill" afford proof of this intent?

6. Are saturation bombings, widespread defoliation, and rural pacification programs, as used by the United States in Vietnam and the Soviet Union in Afghanistan, evidence of genocidal activity?

7. Wars and massacres are not the only way people are wiped out. Systematic and purposeful ecological change, such as the disruption of a rain forest that eliminates or radically reduces the economic and cultural life of an indigenous population, can do the same thing. Would this constitute genocide? What about a systematic and purposeful absorption of one culture by another, resulting in the total loss of the unique and distinctive characteristics of the people of the culture so absorbed?

4. MATTHEW LIPPMAN *The Protection of Universal Human Rights: The Problem of Torture*

The practice of torture is prohibited in virtually all comprehensive international human rights instruments. The Universal Declaration of Human Rights (1948) provides that "[n]o one shall be subjected to torture or to cruel, inhuman or degrading treatment or punishment." The fundamental nature of the human right of freedom from torture is emphasized by the fact that under the major international human rights instruments no derogation is permitted from this right either in times of "public emergency which threatens the life of the nation";[1] or "in time of war, or other public emergency threatening the life of the nation";[2] or "in time of war, public danger, or other emergency that threatens the independence or security of a State Party."[3]

In addition, the Geneva Conventions of 1949 contain a common Article 3 which prohibits torture and other humiliating and degrading treat-ment during an armed conflict "not of an international character."[4]

In the light of the prohibition against torture contained in virtually every comprehensive human rights instrument and the fact that the use of torture has been condemned by numerous influential nongovernmental organizations, the prohibition against torture has correctly been referred to by Michael O'Boyle as "a specific example of *ius cogens* or a peremptory norm of general international law from which there can be no treaty derogation."[5]

THE INCIDENCE OF TORTURE IN THE WORLD

Despite the fact that the practice of torture arguably is prohibited under international law, the

1. International Covenant on Civil and Political Rights, Article 4 [in the Appendix].
2. European Convention for the Protection of Human Rights and Fundamental Freedoms, Nov. 4, 1950, E.T.S. No. 5, Art. 15.
3. American Convention on Human Rights, Nov. 12, 1969, O.A.S.T.S. No. 36, at 1, O.A.S. Off. Rec. OEA/Ser.L/V/II. 23 doc. 21 rev. 6 (1979), Art. 27.
4. Art. 3 reads in part:

> In the case of armed conflict not of an international character occurring in the territory of one of the high contracting parties, each party to the conflict shall be bound to apply, as a minimum, the following provisions: (1) Persons taking no active part in the hostilities, including members of armed forces who have laid down their arms and those placed *hors de combat* by sickness, wounds, detention, or any other cause, shall in all circumstances be treated humanely, without any adverse distinction founded on race, colour, religion, or faith, sex, birth or wealth, or any other similar criteria. To this end the following acts are and shall remain prohibited at any time and in any place whatsoever with respect to the above-mentioned persons: (a) *violence to life and person, in particular, murder of all kinds, mutilation, cruel treatment and torture,* . . . (b) *outrages upon personal dignity, in particular, humiliating and degrading treatment of any kind.* . . .

See Convention for the Amelioration of the Condition of the Wounded and Sick in Armed Forces in the Field (12 Aug. 1949), 6 U.S.T. 3217, T.I.A.A no. 3363, 75 U.N.T.S. 85; Convention Relative to the Treatment of Prisoners of War (12 Aug. 1949), 6 U.S.T. 3316, T.I.A.A no. 3364, 75 U.N.T.S. 135; Convention Relative to the Protection of Civilian Persons in Time of War (12 Aug. 1949), 6 U.S.T. 3516, T.I.A.A no. 3365, 75 U.N.T.S. 287.

It should also be noted that Art. 31 of the Convention on the Protection of Civilian Persons in Time of War provides that "[n]o physical or moral coercion shall be exercised against protected persons, in particular to obtain information from them or from third parties." Art. 32 of the same convention provides that each high contracting party is "prohibited from taking any measure of such a character as to cause the physical suffering or extermination of protected persons. This prohibition applies not only to murder, torture, corporal punishment, mutilation and medical or scientific experimentation not necessitated by the medical treatment of protected persons, but also to any other measures of brutality whether applied by civilian or military agents."

5. Michael O'Boyle, "Torture and Emergency Powers Under the European Convention on Human Rights: *Ireland v. United Kingdom,*" *American Journal of International Law* 71 (1971): pp. 674–706 at 687. O'Boyle cites the Vienna convention on the Law of Treaties to support this proposition: "A treaty

Reprinted, with changes, from Matthew Lippman, "The Protection of Universal Human Rights: The Problem of Torture," *Universal Human Rights* 1 (Oct.–Dec. 1979): 22–55. Copyright © 1979 by Johns Hopkins University Press. Reprinted by permission.

General Assembly has noted the plethora of United Nations reports of torture, and Amnesty International has documented the widespread use of torture by states. An analysis of Amnesty International's data indicates that torture is used against detainees by over fourteen African nations, eleven Asian nations, and four countries in Western Europe, as well as over twenty countries in the Americas, eight countries in the Middle East, and three countries in Eastern Europe and the Sovet Union.[6]

Despite the widespread use of torture in the world, it must be remembered that the use of torture is not a historically unique phenomenon. In past eras, torture has been used to "test" the veracity of "unreliable witnesses," such as slaves, or to extract confessions of guilt from suspected criminal offenders, or to force heretics to admit to or recant their religious beliefs. In all such cases the use of torture was relatively strictly supervised and regulated. In contrast, the "new torture," which originated in the Third Reich, is characterized by the systematic and widespread use of sophisticated scientific techniques against a regime's political opponents. Torture thus has become a tool of regimes seeking to govern by the "reign of terror." At the same time, no regime will admit to using torture and the practice of torture generally remains covert and unregulated.

WHY TORTURE IS USED

According to a recently published study, *The Technology of Political Control,* the "new torture" is used by contemporary regimes for one or more of four purposes: namely,

. . . extraction of information from a determined person, preparation of the prisoner for a "show trial," ending (or even reversing) the political effectiveness of the prisoner, and the inculcation of a climate of generalized fear among certain sections of the population. The standard method of achieving any of these goals has been, and generally still remains, the "breaking of the prisoner" through a process of mounting stress, imposed classically by physical means, but more recently by psychological ones.[7]

The rationale for the use of torture to "extract information" is typified by the statement of English Labour Minister Roy Hattersely: "Let's imagine 250 people in an aeroplane, let's say we know some terrorists mean business because one bomb has gone off already, let's assume we've got a man and could save twenty-two odd lives by finding out where the second bomb is. If he wouldn't tell me I'd have to think very hard before I said don't bring any pressure to bear on that man that might cause him pain."[8] The thrust of this argument is that "if one places a value on human life, indeed the highest value, one is really

is void if, at the time of its conclusion it conflicts with a peremptory norm of general international law. For the purposes of the present convention, a peremptory norm of general international law is a norm accepted and recognized by the international community of states as a whole as a norm from which no derogation is permitted and which can be modified only by a subsequent norm of general international law having the same character."

6. My data indicate that in 1979 torture was utilized in sixty-one countries . . . :

> *Africa:* Burundi, Cameroun, Ethiopia, Ghana, Malawi, Morocco, Rhodesia, South Africa, Namibia, Tanzania, Togo, Tunisia, Uganda, Zambia.
> *Asia:* Cambodia, India, Indonesia, North Korea, South Korea, Laos, Pakistan, Philippines, Singapore, Sri Lanka, North Vietnam, South Vietnam.
> *Western Europe:* Cyprus, Portugal, Spain, Turkey. (Note: Belgian soldiers involved in NATO operations in November 1971 allegedly "tortured" twelve [Belgian] "enemy soldiers" for twenty-four hours and were later found guilty of assault by a military tribunal.)
> *Eastern Europe and the Soviet Union:* Albania, German Democratic Republic, Romania, USSR.
> *Middle East:* Bahrain, Egypt, Iran, Israel, Oman, Syria, Yemen.
> *Americas:* Argentina, Bolivia, Brazil, Colombia, Chile, Costa Rica, Cuba, Dominican Republic, Ecuador, El Salvador, Guatemala, Honduras, Mexico, Nicaragua, Panama, Paraguay, Peru, Uruguay, Venezuela.

7. Carol Ackroyd, Karen Margolis, Jonathan Rosenhead, and Tim Shallice, *The Technology of Political Control* (Middlesex, U.K.: Penguin, 1977), 230.

8. Ibid, 231. A similar hypothetical was suggested by Jeremy Bentham to justify the "practice of torture," in M. Ruthven, *Torture: The Grand Conspiracy* (London: Wiedenfeld and Nicolson, 1976) 19:

> Two men are caught setting fire to a house, one of them escapes. His re-arrest becomes a matter of urgency for there are grounds for suspecting that he may set fire to another house. The captured arsonist refuses to name his accomplice, what is to be done? The prisoner cannot be threatened with

obliged to hurt one person to save many lives." Whatever the merits of the application of torture in such a clear-cut situation, the "balancing-test" approach can be carried very far. It can be used to rationalize the application of torture to prevent future harm and can lead to the torture of suspected "potential bombers," to the torture of persons suspected of being friends with or sympathetic to "potential bombers," and to the torture of friends of persons suspected of being sympathetic to "potential bombers." Such abuse of torture is most likely to occur in situations involving internal guerilla warfare where there is an urgent need for information concerning the guerillas' plans, tactics, and organizational structure.

Torture is also often used to prepare defendants for "show trials." The classic example is the 1936–38 Stalinist "show trials" in which former Bolshevik Party leaders were coerced into publicly confessing their guilt to charges of which, it appears, they were innocent.[9] Kircheimer argues that such trials are used to legitimize regimes' repression of dissident elements and to generate popular support for the regime.[10]

Torture may also be used to incapacitate an individual psychologically or physically and thereby render the individual politically ineffective. Ackroyd et al. present a detailed description of this process:

Breaking a prisoner by a combination of increasing physical pain and/or anxiety neutralizes the victim even long after release. It produces a psychiatric condition similar to that occurring after excessive combat in wartime, technically known as "anxiety neurosis" . . . including "spells of uncontrollable emotions," especially of anxiety and frequently of rage, occasionally even convulsive attacks. . . . Anxiety can produce gastrointestinal, cardiovascular and genito-urinary symptoms and muscular disorders such as tremors. . . . [S]uch symptoms may be very long-lasting, if not permanent.[11]

On the other hand, "mind control" techniques may be used to "rehabilitate" and "brainwash" a prisoner. The prisoner's confidence in his or her existing "belief system" is broken down and the individual is supplied with a "new ideological perspective." Upon release, such "rehabilitated" dissidents may become spokespersons for the regime and attempt to discredit their former fellow dissidents and political viewpoint. In addition, the very act of subjecting an individual to interrogation and torture may politically neutralize the individual, since other "dissidents" may suspect that the individual cooperated with the authorities or is a "double agent" and can no longer be trusted. Others also may avoid fraternizing with individuals who have been subjected to interrogation since they may fear that any such relationship may render them "politically suspect."

The major function of torture today is its use by many regimes lacking popular support who desire to inculcate a climate of fear and political apathy in the general population. In the analysis of Amnesty International, "[t]o set torture as the price of dissent is to be assured that only a small minority will act. With the majority neutralized by fear, the well-equipped forces of repression can concentrate on an isolated minority."[12]

Regimes' justification for the use of abusive techniques against individuals perceived as "posing a threat" to them often is presented on the basis of self-defense and on the basis of maintaining police morale. The Wuillaume Report on methods of French interrogation at the Lambèse, Bathana, Guelma, and Constantine prisons in Algeria concluded that "to cast aspersions upon a body of public servants who have so much devotion and indeed so much heroism to their credit, would be unwise and might lead to serious consequences,"[13] and to "forbid any methods of interrogation other than those which are strictly legal . . . [would be to] plunge the police into a

---

punishment, for (as this is the eighteenth century) he is already liable to the utmost penalty of the law. There are only two options: either he must be bribed to reveal his accomplice in return for commuting the death sentence (which, from a sense of honour, he still might not accept) or, says Bentham, he must be subjected to instant pain. Even if he were to accept the bribe, the public interest would scarcely benefit—for in order that the second arsonist be apprehended, the eventual release of the first must be conceded; torture is therefore the preferable alternative on utilitarian grounds.

9. See Roy Medvedev, *Let History Judge* (New York: Knopf, 1971).
10. Otto Kircheimer, *Political Justice* (Princeton, N.J.: Princeton University Press, 1961), 6.
11. Ackroyd et al., *The Technology of Political Control*, 232–33.
12. Amnesty International, *Report on Torture* (New York: Farrar, Straus and Giroux, 1975), 21–2.
13. Office of the Governor General, Civil Inspectorate-General in Algeria, "The Wuillaume Report," (Algiers, March 2, 1955), reported in Pierre Vidal Naguet, *Torture: Cancer of Democracy*, trans. Barry Richards (Middlesex: Penguin, 1963), 117.

state of disorder and paralysis.''[14] In viewing the behavior of the police, the Wuillaume Report alluded to the threat posed by Algerian terrorists and cautioned that the benefits of police effectiveness were sufficient justification for the human costs exacted.

The Compton Committee in England prefaces its report on the alleged use of "physical brutality" against interned Northern Ireland "terrorists" by pointing out the threat such terrorists pose to "the preservation of the peace or the maintenance of order.''[15] In contrast, Herman argues that governments use such "atrocity management" as a device to generate increased animosity towards the "enemy," to rationalize governmental failures to defeat the dissident forces, and to justify the harsh treatment of detainees.[16]

Regimes' practice of torture generally is covert and is denied by government officials. However, when faced with documented allegations of the torture and harsh treatment of detainees that cannot easily be denied, regimes have argued not only that such harsh treatment is required for reasons of self-defense and police morale, but also that legal regulation and institutionalization of such techniques is required so as to ensure that the techniques are not abused. The Parker Committee in Great Britain recommended that ''(1)

the techniques should only be applied in conformity with the Directive [on Military Interrogation] and guidelines should be drawn up to assist personnel; (2) the techniques should only be applied under express authority of a U.K. Minister; (3) a Senior Officer should be in control at the interrogation centre and would carry personal responsibility; (4) a panel of highly skilled interrogators should be available to reduce the need to use the techniques; and (5) a doctor with psychiatric training should be present.''[17]

SOME ADDITIONAL ASPECTS OF THE "NEW TORTURE"

In addition to the use of torture as a device of "government by terror," the "new torture" is characterized by a number of additional attributes which in combination appear to distinguish it from the torture used in previous eras.

1. Torture often involves the application of sophisticated psychological and pharmacological techniques which result in intense pain but at the same time leave few overt signs of physical abuse.

2. In many countries, individuals engaged in the practice of torture have developed a "slang" of torture and have "ritualized" the use of torture. This appears to be a psychological attempt

---

14. Ibid., 117.

15.

At the beginning of February this year the I.R.A. began to increase the ferocity of their well-established campaign of violence. . . . This campaign of murder and intimidation has included gun attacks on military and police patrols, explosive attacks on offices and buildings, together with indiscriminate bombing of occupied buildings in the cities, killing and injuring members of the general public. More recently there has been a concerted attack on individual police officers, police premises and the homes of police officers. Since August 1969, 104 civilians, 12 members of the R.U.C. and 38 members of the Armed Forces are known to have been killed; and many civilians and members of Armed Forces have been injured, some seriously. There have been over 1,000 incidents involving explosives; and the weight of explosives used by the terrorists so far has been calculated at about 11,000 lbs. Up to the morning of 10th November 1971, the security forces had uncovered 293 pistols and revolvers, 234 rifles, 24 machine guns, 116 shotguns, 123,614 rounds of ammunition, . . . 1,607 pipe, petrol and nail bombs, 154 grenades, 26 gallons acid, and large quantities of fuses, detonators and electric cable.

The aims of the I.R.A. are to intimidate the population by brutal terrorism and so to prevent any co-operation with the Government, the police and the courts of law; to inhibit normal political activity and constitutional progress; and to cause the public in Great Britain to become so sickened by the ceaseless bloodshed and destruction that the Army's withdrawal will come to be seen as the lesser of two evils. No responsible Government can afford to yield to pressures of this kind.

Report of the enquiry into allegations against the security forces of physical brutality in Northern Ireland arising out of events on the 9th August 1971 (London: H.M. Stationery Office, Cmnd 4823 of 1971), "The Compton Report," iii–iv.

16. Edward S. Herman, *Atrocities in Vietnam* (Philadelphia: Pilgrim Press, 1970), 17–18.

17. *Report of the Committee of Privy Councillors appointed to consider authorized procedures for the interrogation of persons suspected of terrorism* (London: H.M. Stationery Office, Cmnd 4901 of 1972), "The Parker Report," 7–9.

by torturers to deny that torture is being used and to distance themselves from their "victims."

3. The practice of torture has become internationalized and standardized. Experts, training, and equipment often are provided by one government to another. For instance, United States advisors have been involved in training security forces in various countries in techniques of torture.

4. In some countries, the intervention of the military into the area of domestic security has resulted in application of counter-insurgency techniques against political dissidents. Special military interrogation units have been organized in countries such as Uruguay, Brazil, Indonesia, Greece, and Turkey. As a result, techniques previously applied in warfare or against colonial populations now are being used against domestic populations.

5. The application of torture and military techniques to domestic populations has been accompanied in many countries by the abrogation of due process and "natural justice" principles. This has been accomplished through "Special Powers Acts" and application of constitutional provisions providing for martial law and for state of siege in times of "internal rebellion."

6. In some countries, widespread torture is carried out by quasigovernmental, vigilante-type groups. This permits the governments involved to deny any responsibility for the practice of torture.

7. The practice of torture often is accompanied by inflammatory political, racial, and ethnic attacks on particular groups. These attacks place such groups "outside the pale of humanity" and help rationalize the use of torture against them.

TECHNIQUES OF TORTURE

Some of the most frequently used techniques of the "new torture" include:[18]

PHYSICAL ABUSE

Submarine: The prisoner's head is immersed continuously in a tub of filthy water, urine, excrement, and petroleum while the victim's sexual organs are squeezed.

Electric shock: Electric shocks are delivered to the sensitive portions of the victim's body.

Body extension: The victim is fastened by the knees or ankles to a bar suspended from the ceiling and beaten or subjected to shock treatment or sexually abused. Often another prisoner or the victim's spouse is forced to witness the torture. Eventually, the victim is "cut down" and experiences severe pain on impact with the floor resulting from the fact that all the blood has drained into the victim's arms.

Water pipe: The victim is bound and secured. Then the eyes are bandaged, the nose is plugged up, a tube is thrust into the mouth, and a strong stream of water is injected into the mouth until the victim is "inflated" and loses consciousness. The victim is then "pumped out" and the process is again initiated.

Falange: The prisoner is secured to a bench and the soles of the prisoner's feet are beaten with sticks or pipes by five or six men. Such prolonged beating leads to a painful swelling of the feet, but, other than broken and fractured bones, no lasting overt physical impairment is likely to result. During the torture process the victim is forced to run around the bench periodically and is continuously beaten. These beatings are accompanied by pouring water down the victim's mouth and nose, rubbing detergent, soap, or pepper in the victim's eyes, banging the victim's head on the bench or floor, and beating other portions of the victim's body.

Extraction: Teeth, nails, and pubic hair are torn out.

Sexual abuse: Women are raped and objects such as bottles are jammed into females' vaginas.

18. The application of various torture techniques is described and documented in Amnesty International, *Report on Torture,* and in the following specific country reports published by Amnesty International: *Report of an Amnesty International Mission to Argentina, 6–15 November 1976; Report on Allegations of Torture in Brazil,* 3d ed. (1976); *Chile* (1974); *Human Rights Violations in Ethiopia* (1978); *Torture in Greece: The First Torturers' Trial, 1975* (1977); *Indonesia* (1977); *Report of an Amnesty International Mission to the Republic of Korea, 27 March–9 April 1975,* 2d ed. (1977); *The Republic of Nicaragua: An Amnesty International Report, Including the Findings of a Mission to Nicaragua, 10–15 May 1976* (1977); *Report of an Amnesty International Mission to Northern Ireland, 28 November–6 December 1977* (1977); *Political Imprisonment in the People's Republic of China* (1978); *Amnesty International Mission to the Republic of the Philippines, 22 November–5 December 1975* (1976); *Political Imprisonment in South Africa* (1978); *Human Rights in Uganda* (1978); *Prisoners of Conscience in the USSR: Their Treatment and Conditions* (1975). See also Amnesty International briefings on *Iran* (1976), *Paraguay* (1976), *Uruguay: Deaths Under Torture, 1975–1977* (1978), *Singapore,* 2d ed. (1978).

Males' genitals are subjected to beatings and electric shock treatment. In one torture a string is tied to the prisoner's testicles and the other end of the string is tied to a jack which is "dropped."

Roll-up: The prisoner is tightly strapped into a bed with damp sheets; the sheets dry out and squeeze and suffocate the individual. This process is repeated over a period of days.

PSYCHOLOGICAL TECHNIQUES

Sensory deprivation: A hood is placed over the prisoner's head or the prisoner is incarcerated in a drab, monochromatic environment with no sensory stimulation. These sensory deprivation techniques are occasionally accompanied by a bread and water diet, sleep deprivation, and constant maintenance of a loud, monotonous whining sound throughout the prison. The prisoner is forced to maintain the "stroika position" (spread-eagle) against the wall for up to twenty-four hours. Upon collapse, the prisoner is abused and forced to resume the position.

Threats: Prisoners are threatened with maiming, death, and rape of themselves or their families. Mock executions often are conducted, and prisoners are forced to witness the torture of their fellow prisoners.

Declarations: Individuals are forced to sign denunciations of their family, spouse, or political beliefs. This induces a sense of moral compromise.

Drugs: Victims are injected with harmless substances which they are told are toxic.

Nudity: Prisoners are forced to remain in a state of nudity in cold, damp, often insect-infested cells; or the prisoner is forced to share the cell with psychiatrically deranged mental patients.

PHARMACOLOGICAL TORTURE

Drug abuse: Prisoners are injected with depressant drugs (for example, haloperidol, aminazine, and triftazine) which lead to moodiness and depression. Other drugs which have been used (for example, scoline) can induce paralysis and inhibit breathing, and others (for example, apomorphine) may provoke vomiting. Injection of prisoners with drugs usually used to treat schizophrenia (for example, sulphazine) may lead to toxic inflammation of the liver, elevation of intraocular pressure, fluctuations of arterial pressure, tension and cramping of the muscles, stomach cramps, headaches, depression, and fever. . . .

THE DIFFICULTY OF CONTROLLING TORTURE

The application of torture by the state against individuals is a violation of such individuals' fundamental human rights as defined in various human rights instruments and arguably constitutes an international crime. Despite the existing legal proscriptions against torture, experience suggests that once torture is initiated, it becomes a self-perpetuating phenomenon and is difficult to control. Once individuals are labeled as being "outside the pale of humanity" and as deserving of ill-treatment, and once such individuals actually are subjected to torture and indict other innocent people, the process of torture becomes perpetuated and reinforced. The consequent "conspiracy scenario" is analyzed by Ruthven in the following terms:

[T]he varied and disparate manifestations of dissent born of evolutionary changes or contradictions in the social structure are perceived as the result of machinations by a "hidden enemy." The inquisitorial machinery with torture at its centre is established to "root" the enemy out. Denunciations are extracted under torture. Since most people faced with torture will confess to whatever is demanded of them (with the possible exception of the tested militants belonging to real underground organizations) the system becomes self-fulfilling and self-extending to the point where the initial aim of interrogation gives way to intimidation and ultimately to mass terror. Thus torture can become the means by which a relatively small and unrepresentative elite, such as a political party, a foreign-based regime, a local police or a military formation can obtain, monopolize or increase its political power. Unchecked, these tortured denunciations will attack every form of solidarity and group cohesion, resulting ultimately in a society of atomized individuals which has sometimes been defined as the end of totalitarian rule.[19]

19. Ruthven, *Torture: The Grand Conspiracy,* 292.

There seems to be little prospect for controlling the use of torture in the world so long as so many regimes are confronted by increasing economic and unemployment problems, by internal movements for ethnic and cultural autonomy, and by the strains of development. Faced with such problems, some regimes are likely to see "government by terror" as one approach to controlling domestic dissent and unrest. Nevertheless, ... two unique attempts [at controlling the use of torture in the world] deserv[e] analysis.

[Editors' note: The author next considers the 1975 UN Declaration on Torture (superseded in 1984 by the UN Draft Convention on Torture) and Amnesty International's proposals for codes of professional responsibility to control the use of torture, noting both the advantages and disadvantages of these approaches.]

CONCLUSION

Although torture is absolutely prohibited in virtually every comprehensive human rights instrument and thus can be considered as a fundamental human right, the practice of torture is widespread and used by governments of every political ideology in every geographic region in the world. Regimes appear to use torture as a tool to combat internal guerilla warfare, deter dissent and protest, and facilitate the implementation of controversial domestic policies.

Philosophically, human rights originate in the "human dignity of all peoples." However, the use of torture in the world suggests that individuals' enjoyment of certain universally accepted civil (human) rights generally is qualified by the exigencies facing political regimes. The greater the perceived insecurity and instability of a regime, the fewer fundamental civil (human) rights the regime is apt to permit individuals to enjoy.

Two international attempts to control the use of torture by governments [are under way at the present time]. The UN [Draft Convention on Torture] encourages governments to control the use of torture by affording torture victims certain civil and criminal remedies. The drafting and implementation of professional codes of ethics constitute an attempt to set forth professional norms of conduct in regard to the practice of torture which are to be enforced through the disciplinary processes of various professional associations.

The UN [Draft Convention on Torture] is unique in singling out the human right of freedom from torture for protection and in relying upon internal domestic legal processes rather than upon international avenues of redress to afford individuals protection from torture. The incremental strategy of selecting a particular "universal human right" for attention may prove to be a more effective approach for protecting and emphasizing the importance of human rights than has been the drafting of comprehensive human rights instruments. In addition, the [Draft Convention's] strategy of relying on domestic judicial processes for protecting individuals from torture recognizes that international implementation processes often are too time-consuming and technical to afford individuals meaningful protection of human rights, and that the protection of human rights essentially depends upon the domestic protections afforded to individuals.

However, the attempt to rely upon domestic remedies to control the use of torture may raise various problems of "proof," may involve difficulties in the application of the rather broad legal standards of "torture" and "other cruel, inhuman and degrading treatment or punishment," and may fail to recognize regimes' political control over the domestic legal process.

The codes of professional ethical conduct are based on the premise that nation-states cannot, it appears, be relied upon to protect individuals from torture. Domestically, some regimes will utilize torture to combat perceived internal threats while internationally most states' national security and diplomatic interests may dictate that they tolerate the use of torture by other governments. The professional codes of ethical conduct are an attempt to overcome states' unwillingness to combat the practice of torture in the world by placing an ethical obligation on various professionals to refrain from and, in some cases, protest against the use of torture by governments. The effectiveness of relying on professional codes of conduct to control the use of torture is limited by the conservatism of professional associations, the reluctance of associations to make political judgements [sic.], the limited scope of the professional codes of conduct, the confusion as to what a professional's ethical duty is in particular situations involving the use of torture, and, by some regimes, intimidation of and control over professional associations.

The efforts to control torture through both the

UN [Draft Convention on Torture] and through professional codes of ethical conduct are designed to be implemented in legal systems which are based on the due process of law which functions in free, democratic societies characterized by independent and responsible professionals. Any attempt to control the global use of torture through application of law or codes of ethical conduct ultimately is limited by the fact that, in many instances, torture is used as a conscious instrument of government "by terror" and the legal process and various professional groups have been shaped into instruments to legitimate and support governmental policies.

The problem of torture cannot be attacked in an isolated fashion, but must be viewed as being related to the general denial of human rights and general manipulation of the legal and governmental processes. At the same time, this discussion suggests that it is futile to attempt to protect individuals from torture through treaties and legal instruments when most governments systematically using torture might be categorized as "lawless."

QUESTIONS FOR REFLECTION AND DISCUSSION

1. On December 10, 1984, the UN General Assembly adopted and opened for signature the Convention Against Torture and Other Cruel, Inhuman or Degradiing Treatment or Punishment (A/Res/39/46, 39 U.N. GAOR Supp. [No. 51] at 197). Article 1 of the Convention defines "torture" to include the following six elements:

[1] any act [2] by which severe pain or suffering, whether physical or mental [3] is intentionally inflicted [4] by or at the instigation of a public official [5] on a person for such purposes as [5.1] obtaining from him or a third person information or confession, [5.2] punishing him for an act he has committed or is suspected of having committed, or [5.3] intimidating him or other persons. [6] It does not include pain or suffering arising only from, inherent in or incidental to, lawful sanctions to the extent consistent with standard minimum rules for the treatment of prisoners.

In assessing this definition, consider the following:

(a) Does "any act" encompass a related series of acts which together "intentionally inflict severe pain or suffering"? What difference would it have made had the drafters used the words "any systematic infliction of" instead of "any act by which"?

(b) Does the qualification of "severe" pain or suffering imply that torture is a question of degree, distinguishable from "cruel, inhuman or degrading treatment or punishment"? What standards should be applied or what variables should be used to establish "severe" pain or suffering?

(c) Does the fact that severe pain or suffering must be "intentionally inflicted" imply that there must be a specific intent to inflict severe pain or suffering? Or is it sufficient that the torturer know or have known that severe pain or suffering might result from her or his acts?

(d) Article 1 refers to the intention of state or governmental officials. Which ones? Lower as well as higher officials? Might low-level officials be insulated from responsibility if they have acted under orders? Might high-level officials be insulated from responsibility for the acts of their subordinates? What about vigilante groups composed of former state or governmental officials? Does the definition cover them?

(e) Is an "act" not torture if it does not serve one of the purposes listed in the fifth definitional element of Article 1? Is the enumeration of purposes exhaustive?

(f) The Standard Minimum Rules for the Treatment of Prisoners referred to in the sixth definitional element of Article 1 were adopted by the First United Nations Congress on the Prevention of Crime and the Treatment of Offenders on August 30, 1955. (See U.N. Doc. A/CONF./6/1, Annex I, A [1956].) These rules are open to interpretation by state officials, and their enforcement depends on the good faith of penal officials. How might these facts prove problematic relative to the definition of "torture"? Would repeated administrations of electric current for the purpose of killing a prisoner as punishment for a crime committed constitute torture? If so, does this mean that this form of capital punishment as practiced in the United States constitutes torture? What about other forms of capital punishment?

Does capital punishment without pain escape the definition of torture? What about the mental torture leading up to the killing, regardless of the chosen method?

2. Article 5 of the Universal Declaration of Human Rights states that no one "shall be subjected to torture or to cruel, inhuman or degrading treatment or punishment." Essentially the same provision is found in Article 7 of the UN Covenant on Civil and Political Rights, Article 3 of the European Convention for the Protection of Human Rights and Fundamental Freedoms, Article 5 of the American Convention on Human Rights, and Article 5 of the African Charter on Human and Peoples' Rights. Each of these provisions is deemed non-derogable. Is this desirable? Are there no instances when torture might be considered a regrettable but necessary procedure? Lippman cites the hypothetical case of an English Labor Minister who would permit the torturing of one known terrorist to save many innocent lives. Suppose that the terrorist had information that could help thwart a threatened detonation of a nuclear device. What then? Is torture a practice that should never be allowed under any circumstance? If not, how would you draw the line between the permissible and impermissible use of torture and who could you trust to draw it?

3. The Central Intelligence Agency of the United States has admitted to producing and distributing a secret manual that describes procedures for lethal bombing and torture activities that might assist guerrillas seeking to overthrow the Sandinista government of Nicaragua. Do you agree that the interests of the U.S. government in Central America warrant this type of instruction? If not, what kind of liability might the United States assume for this publication? Should victims of torture at the hands of those trained by the CIA be able to recover damages from the United States?

4. Do you share Lippman's conclusion that it is "futile to attempt to protect individuals from torture through treaties and legal instruments" when the governments who use torture are already outside the community of law-abiding nations? What about the cumulative effect of being identified as a torturing country, being condemned for your official acts, being forced to defend your acts by international agencies? Is it likely that, without this pressure, the acts of torture would be committed more widely, with more impunity, and with no hope for the tortured to find a forum where they can express their grievances? Consider the following observation of Professor Louis Henkin, "International Instruments for the Protection of Human Rights," in *Acta Juridica* (1979), 224–35 at 224:

> Rhetoric is important, . . . and even some hypocrisy may be tolerable as a first step. Acceptances of human rights in principle make respect for human rights the norm, violation illegitimate. It unleashes forces for compliance, forces both official and unofficial, internal and external.

5. RICHARD B. LILLICH *Civil Rights*

A decade ago this writer, surveying the development of international human rights law subsequent to the adoption of the U.N. Charter, observed that "the progress in the area of human rights has been almost exclusively in the direction of clarifying and codifying the substantive law norms. . . ." During the intervening years, which have seen considerable progress in the implementation area, this trend has continued apace, as exemplified by the recent adoption by the United Nations of the Convention on the Elimination of All Forms of Discrimination Against Women.[1] Yet, upon reflection, one may conclude that perhaps more codification than clarification has occurred. As Professors McDougal, Lasswell, and Chen conclude in their magnum opus, "[i]t is in the substantive definition of human rights that the greatest confusion and inadequacy pre-

1. Dec. 18, 1979, U.N.G.A. Res. 34/180 (XXXIV), 34 U.N. GAOR, Supp. (No. 46) 193, U.N. Doc. A/34/46 (1980).

vail. Little effort has been made to create a comprehensive map of the totality of human rights, and there has been little discussion of the detailed content of particular rights."[2]

This [essay], as its title indicates, is not intended to be a comprehensive map of all international human rights norms. Rather . . . it is basically a description *cum* commentary of those international norms which purport to guarantee and protect one bundle of rights: the civil rights of individuals. These rights, commonly considered to be the most basic and fundamental of all human rights, will be familiar to readers versed in United States constitutional law, for, as Professor Henkin has recalled:

Americans were prominent among the architects and builders of international human rights, and American constitutionalism was a principal inspiration and model for them. As a result, most of the Universal Declaration of Human Rights, and later the International Covenant on Civil and Political Rights, are in their essence American constitutional rights projected around the world.[3]

Since these rights find their expression in articles 3–18 of the Universal Declaration of Human Rights[4]—restated, supplemented, and occasionally modified by companion articles in the International Covenant on Civil and Political Rights[5]—for the sake of convenience they will be considered in the order they appear in the Universal Declaration.

Before beginning this survey, however, the human rights to be reviewed must be placed in proper juridical perspective. Specifically, what is their status under contemporary international law, and what restrictions may states impose upon their enjoyment? Unless these questions can be answered satisfactorily, human rights, no matter how nicely phrased, can have little real meaning in or effect upon the lives of individuals.

As to the first question, it now may be argued persuasively that substantial parts of the Universal Declaration, a U N General Assembly resolution adopted in 1948 without dissent and originally thought not to give rise to international legal obligations, have become, over the past third of a century, part of customary international law binding upon all states. This view, first advanced solely by legal scholars but subsequently supported by the statements of international conferences, by state practice, and even by court decisions,[6] now appears to have achieved widespread acceptance. Indeed the suggestion has even been made that the Universal Declaration has "the attributes of *jus cogens*," a statement that, in the opinion of this writer, goes too far if intended to imply that all rights enumerated in it have this character.[7] There is little doubt, however, that many of the human rights . . .—the prohibition of slavery being just one example— not only reflect customary international law but also partake of the character of *jus cogens*. This

---

2. Myres S. McDougal, Harold Lasswell, and Lung-chu Chen, *Human Rights and World Public Order: The Basic Policies of an International Law of Human Dignity* (New Haven, Conn.: Yale University Press, 1980), 64.

3. Louis Henkin, "Rights: American and Human," *Columbia Law Review* 79 (1979): 405, 415. See also *Message of the President Transmitting Four Treaties Pertaining to Human Rights*, S. Exec. Doc. No. 95-C D, E, and F, 95th Cong., 2d Sess. XI (1978):

> The International Covenant on Civil and Political Rights is, of the [four] treaties submitted, the most similar in conception to the United States Constitution and Bill of Rights. The rights guaranteed are those civil and political rights with which the United States and the western liberal democratic tradition have always been associated. The rights are primarily limitations upon the power of the State to impose its will upon the prople under its jurisdiction.

4. [See the Appendix.]
5. [See the Appendix.]
6. See, e.g., Filártiga v. Peña-Irala, 630 F.2d 876, 882 (2d Cir. 1980), where the Court of Appeals for the Second Circuit held that "the right to be free from torture . . . has become part of customary international law, *as evidenced and defined by the Universal Declaration of Human Rights. . . .*" (Emphasis added.) [For discussion of this important decision, see Reading 21, in Chapter 5 in this volume.]
7. Rosalyn Higgins, writing about human rights treaties but reasoning along lines applicable to the Universal Declaration as well, makes a similar point:

> [T]he suggestion has been made that human rights treaties have the character of *jus cogens*. There certainly exists a consensus that certain rights—the right to life, to freedom from slavery or torture— are so fundamental that no derogation may be made. And international human rights treaties undoubtedly contain elements that are binding as principles which are recognized by civilized States,

conclusion is particularly valid when the right in question appears in both the Universal Declaration and the Political Covenant. The latter, of course, is binding conventional law only between states parties to it, but many of its provisions now can be said to have helped create norms of customary international law—including one having *jus cogens* status[8]—binding even states which have yet to ratify it.[9] Dramatic evidence of this process at work may be found in the U.S. Memorial to the International Court of Justice in the *Case Concerning United States Diplomatic and Consular Staff in Teheran,*[10] where, after citing four articles of the Political Covenant (to which, ironically, Iran is a party but the United States is merely a signatory), the United States argued that Iran had violated not only conventional law but also "fundamental principles . . . of customary international law. . . ."

With respect to the second question, the restrictions which a state may impose upon an individual's internationally protected human rights come in two tiers, both of which must be kept in mind in determining the protection afforded by particular guarantees. On the first tier of restrictions, both the Universal Declaration and the Political Covenant contain provisions limiting the rights guaranteed therein. The former contains a general limitations clause, article 29(2), which provides that:

In the exercise of his rights and freedoms, everyone shall be subject only to such limitations as are determined by law solely for the purpose of securing due recognition and respect for the rights and freedoms of others and of meeting the just requirements of morality, public order and the general welfare in a democratic society.

In the Political Covenant, as Professor Higgins has pointed out, "[t]he references to the need for rights to be exercised in conformity with morality, public order, general welfare, etc., appear not as a general clause but as qualifications to specific freedoms."[11] The specific limitations (or, as she aptly terms them, "clawback" clauses[12]) in the Political Covenant relating to civil rights are contained in articles 12(3), 14(1), and 18(3). One can only endorse Professor Humphrey's warning that such limitations can be "highly dangerous (from the point of view of human rights). . . ."

On the second tier of restrictions which is relevant to the Political Covenant alone, article 4(1) thereof permits states parties to derogate from, i.e., suspend or breach, certain obligations "[i]n time of public emergency which threatens the life of the nation and the existence of which is officially proclaimed. . . ."[13] No derogation may be made, however, from the human rights contained in articles 6, 7, 8(1), 8(2), 11, 15, 16, and 18, evidence that at least some of these rights may have "attributes" of *jus cogens.*[14] Nevertheless, as

---

and not only as mutual treaty commitments. Some treaties may focus almost exclusively on such elements—such as the Genocide Convention—while others may cover a wide range of rights, not all of which may have for the present a status which is more than treaty-based. This being said, neither the wording of the various human rights instruments nor the practice thereunder leads to the view that all human rights are *jus cogens.*

Rosalyn Higgins, "Derogations Under Human Rights Treaties," *British Year Book of International Law* 48 (1976–77): 281, 282.

8. In seeking to determine what human rights protected by the Political Covenant have achieved *jus cogens* status, a good starting point is the list of rights which art. 4(2) makes nonderogable, i.e., rights which a state may not suspend even in time of war or national emergency.

9. There is ample language in the decisions of the International Court of Justice to support the late Judge Baxter's conclusion that [t]reaties that do not purport to be declaratory of customary international law at the time they enter into force may nevertheless with the passage of time pass into customary international law. Richard Baxter, "Treaties and Custom," *Recueil des Cours* 129 (1970–11): section 25, 57.

10. Memorial of the Government of the United States of America, Case Concerning United States Diplomatic and Consular Staff in Teheran, *International Court of Justice* (Jan., 1980), 3.

11. Higgins, "Derogations under Human Rights Treaties," 283.

12. By a "drawback" clause is meant one that permits, in normal circumstances, breach of an obligation for a specified number of public reasons. *Ibid.,* 281. It thus differs from a derogation clause, e.g., Article 4(1) of the Political Covenant, which allows suspension or breach of certain obligations in circumstances of war or public emergency. [See the Appendix, this volume.]

13. See generally, Joan Hartman, "Derogation from Human Rights Treaties in Public Emergencies," *Harvard International Law Journal* 22 (1981): 1.

14. Reservations to the Political Covenant, to the extent that they are directed to the rights guaranteed in these seven articles, presumably have no force or effect if these rights actually have acquired *jus cogens* status.

in the case of the limitation clauses discussed in the preceding paragraph, the fact that a wide variety of important rights—for example, the right to liberty and security of person guaranteed by article 9(1)—may be rendered temporarily "inoperative" by means of derogation is extremely troublesome from the human rights viewpoint. Certainly the existence of both tiers of restrictions—limitations and derogations—must be kept in mind when assessing the degree of protection actually afforded individuals by the language of articles 3–18 of the Universal Declaration.[15]

[Editors' note: The author next analyzes the civil rights of individuals as set forth in the Universal Declaration: rights to life, liberty, and security of person (Article 3); prohibition of slavery and servitude (Article 4); prohibition of torture and cruel, inhuman, or degrading treatment or punishment (Article 5); right to legal recognition (Article 6); rights to equality before the law and to nondiscrimination in its application (Article 7); right to a remedy (Article 8); prohibition of arbitrary arrest, detention or exile (Article 9); right to a fair trial (Article 10); presumption of innocence and prohibition of ex post facto laws (Article 11); right to privacy (Article 12); right to freedom of movement (Article 13); right to asylum (Article 14); right to a nationality (Article 15); right to marry and found a family (Article 16); right to own property (Article 17); and freedom of thought, conscience and religion (Article 18). Noting that these rights are set forth also in the International Covenant on Civil and Political Rights (1966), the European Convention on Human Rights and Fundamental Freedoms (1950), and the American Convention on Human Rights (1969), he points out their complexity and frequent ambiguity. He also opines that only the following rights may be considered part of customary international law: right to life; freedom from slavery and involuntary servitude; freedom from torture and cruel, inhuman, or degrading treatment or punishment; rights to equality before the law and to nondiscrimination in its application; freedom from arbitrary arrest and detention; presumption of innocence; and freedom of thought, conscience, and religion. He

concludes by emphasizing, inter alia, the international community's rank-ordering of these rights in terms of those that in the Political Covenant are made nonderogable, i.e., rights that may not be suspended by a state even in time of public emergency, declared or otherwise: right to life; freedom from torture and cruel, inhuman, or degrading treatment or punishment; freedom from slavery and involuntary servitude; freedom from debtor prison; freedom from ex post facto laws; and freedom of thought, conscience, and religion. The author's discussion makes clear that even basic procedural due process rights are seen to be only exceptionally a part of customary international law and nonderogable.]

RIGHTS TO EQUALITY BEFORE THE LAW AND TO NONDISCRIMINATION IN ITS APPLICATION (ARTICLE 7)

Equality before the law and nondiscrimination in its application are provided for by this article, which reads: "All are equal before the law and are entitled without any discrimination to equal protection of the law. All are entitled to equal protection against any discrimination in violation of this Declaration and against any incitement to such discrimination." Language almost identical with the first sentence of article 7 is found in the first sentence of article 26 of the Political Covenant; the second sentence of article 26, however, contains the following variation: "*In this respect*, the law shall prohibit any discrimination and guarantee to all persons equal and effective protection against discrimination on any ground. . . ." Language paralleling the first sentence of article 7 is found in article 24 of the American Convention, while the European Convention contains no directly corresponding provision.

Almost from the beginning, the words "equal protection of the law" caused confusion. According to one member of the Third Committee during debates on the draft Declaration, "it was not clear whether they meant that there should be laws which should be applied equally or that all were equally entitled to the protection of

15. [An issue] is raised by the use of the words "arbitrary" or "arbitrarily" throughout the Universal Declaration and the Political Covenant. . . . These words, it now seems clear, should be construed to prohibit not only "illegal" but also "unjust" acts. Thus, despite the fears of some observers, a state cannot impinge upon an individual's internationally protected human rights simply by enacting legislation making its acts legal on the domestic plane.

whatever laws existed." This lack of clarity, in the view of some observers, persists under the Political Covenant. Professor Robertson analyzes and evaluates the alternative interpretations as follows:

Broadly speaking, two quite different meanings seem possible: that the substantive provisions of the law should be the same for everyone; or that the application of the law should be equal for all without discrimination. The former interpretation would seem unreasonable; for example, in most countries women are not required to perform military service, while it is unnecessary that the law should prescribe maternity benefits for men. It would seem, therefore, that the meaning rather is to secure equality, without discrimination, in the application of the law, and this interpretation is borne out by the *travaux préparatoires.*[16]

He acknowledges that the second sentence of article 26, "if it stood alone, would constitute an important and far-reaching commitment and a general protection against discrimination," but points out that "in the Third Committee the words 'in this respect' were added at the beginning of this sentence . . . so that its scope is now limited to the general statement of equality and equal protection contained in the preceding sentence."[17]

This interpretation is consistent with the approach taken in article 2 of the Universal Declaration and article 2(1) of the Political Covenant, both of which mandate nondiscriminatory treatment, but only insofar as the rights set out in the respective human rights instrument are concerned. Articles 7 and 26, therefore, while specifically guaranteeing one important civil right to all persons on a nondiscriminatory basis, surely cannot be read to constitute a general norm of nondiscrimination invocable in other contexts. Properly limited, however, the right considered in this subsection probably now has become customary international law.

RIGHT TO A REMEDY (ARTICLE 8)

This unique article, added at the last minute by the Third Committee to fill a supposed lacuna in the draft Declaration, guarantees all persons "the right to an effective remedy by the competent national tribunals for acts violating the fundamental rights granted him *by the constitution or by law.*" Although, as one commentator has observed in an analogous context, "there is a certain anomaly in the right to a remedy itself being classed among the rights guaranteed,"[18] that fact has not prevented the inclusion of roughly similar provisions in article 2(3) of the Political Covenant, article 13 of the European Convention, and article 25 of the American Convention.

Since, as Professor Humphrey has remarked, "human rights without effective implementation are shadows without substance,"[19] there is no doubt that the right to a remedy is an extremely important one. For this reason, despite assertions that such a right was superfluous or would prove of little value, it has been included not only in the Universal Declaration and the Political Covenant, but, as indicated above, in the European Convention and American Convention as well. Its importance, however, depends greatly upon

---

16. Arthur H. Robertson, *Human Rights in the World* (Manchester, U.K.: Manchester University Press, 1972), 39, citing Annotation on the text of the Draft International Covenants on Human Rights, 10 U.N. GAOR, Annexes (Agenda Item 28, pt II) 1, 61 U.N. Doc. A/2929 (1955).

17. Ibid. "As a result, the phrase is, in the view of one expert, largely tautologous." Ibid., citing Egon Schwelb, "The International Convention on the Elimination of All Forms of Racial Discrimination," *International and Comparative Law Quarterly* 15 (1966): 996, 1019:

> The second sentence as amended . . . makes the article an accumulation of tautologies. It now says, *inter alia,* that the law shall prohibit any discrimination in respect of the entitlement not to be discriminated against. It says further that the law shall guarantee to all persons equal and effective protection against discrimination in respect of their entitlement to equal protection of the law. In other words: the second sentence has no normative content at all and the prohibition of "any discrimination" has, in fact, disappeared from the provision.

18. Francis G. Jacobs, *The European Convention on Human Rights* (Oxford: Oxford University Press, 1975), 215.

19. John Humphrey, "Report of the Rapporteur of the International Committee on Human Rights," in International Law Association, *Report of the Fifty-Third Conference* (Buenos Aires, 1968), 437, 457. His remarks echo the more poetic words of Justice Holmes: "Legal obligations that exist but cannot be enforced are ghosts that are seen in the law but are elusive to the grasp." The Western Maid, 257 U.S. 419, 433 (1922).

the scope of the "substantive" rights it is designed to protect. Here there is considerable variation in the language of the relevant articles.

The Universal Declaration, quoted above, guarantees an effective domestic remedy for acts which violate rights granted by the constitutions or laws of the various states. Thus, in contrast with article 7, whose reach extends only to acts in violation of the Universal Declaration, article 8's scope is potentially much broader. "It relates not to the rights granted under the Declaration," as Dr. Robinson notes, "but to those granted by the domestic constitution and domestic law. . . ."[20] Since the ambit of the rights granted by the latter generally is larger (at least on paper) than that of the rights enunciated in the Universal Declaration, the right to a remedy contemplated by article 8 may be regarded as a broad one indeed.

Unfortunately, both the Political Covenant and the European Convention are more restrictive in this regard. Effective remedies are guaranteed by article 2(3)(a) of the Political Covenant only to vindicate "rights or freedoms as herein recognized," i.e., recognized by the Political Covenant. Similarly, article 13 of the European Convention guarantees an effective remedy only for "rights and freedoms as set forth in this Convention. . . ." The American Convention, on the other hand, provides the person seeking relief the best of all possible worlds: article 25(1) combines the approaches of the Universal Declaration, Political Covenant, and European Convention, requiring states to accord prompt and effective relief "against acts that violate . . . fundamental rights recognized by the constitution or laws of the state concerned *or* by this Convention. . . ."

To date only article 13 of the European Convention has been interpreted and, in Professor Fawcett's words, its interpretation has revealed "a basic confusion of thought as to the real purpose and function of the Article."[21] Is article 13, he asks, "concerned with the international or the domestic implementation of the Convention, with the collective guarantee, or with internal remedies?"[22] Does the article, from the claim-

ant's perspective, mandate that an effective domestic remedy be in place ready to consider any alleged violation of the European Convention, or does it become applicable only after there has been a determination (by the Committee of Ministers, the European Court of Human Rights, or a domestic court applying the Convention as part of domestic law) that another, "substantive" article of the Convention actually has been violated? For textual and other reasons, Professor Fawcett leans away from the former ("domestic" or "internal") and toward the latter ("international" or "collective") view of the article. This view, which greatly minimizes the importance of the right to a remedy, has not been explicitly adopted by the European Court of Human Rights and hopefully will be rejected by the U N Human Rights Committee and the American Commission and Court of Human Rights when the issue arises under the Political Covenant and the American Convention, respectively. In any event, so much confusion exists about the scope of this right that it can be said with reasonable assurance that it is not part of customary international law.

PROHIBITION OF ARBITRARY ARREST, DETENTION OR EXILE (ARTICLE 9)

Article 3, it will be recalled, establishes not only the right to life, but also the right to liberty and security of person. The Political Covenant handles these rights in two articles, 6(1) and 9(1), the latter of which, in addition to guaranteeing "the right to liberty and security of person," provides, inter alia, "[n]o one shall be subjected to arbitrary arrest or detention." "Protection against arbitrary arrest and detention," Professor Jacobs rightly notes, "is clearly the central feature of any system of guarantees of the liberty of the individual."[23] Indeed, the drafters of the Universal Declaration considered the prohibition of arbitrary arrest and detention so important that, rather than treating it as just one liberty interest, they devoted a separate article to it, demonstrating their intention to establish it as an indepen-

---

20. Nehemiáh Robinson, *Universal Declaration of Human Rights* (New York: Institute of Jewish Affairs, 1958), 47.
21. James E. S. Fawcett, The Application of the European Convention on Human Rights, 232 (Oxford: Clarendon Press, 1969).
22. Ibid., 229.
23. Jacobs, *The European Convention on Human Rights*, 75.

dent human right. Thus, article 9 of the Universal Declaration provides that "[n]o one shall be subjected to arbitrary arrest, detention or exile."

The *travaux préparatoires*, revealing an understandable reluctance to define "arbitrary" and an enthusiastic endorsement of an amendment adding "exile" to the draft Declaration's proscription against "arbitrary arrest or detention," indicate that most members of the Third Committee were pleased with the article's "eloquent brevity" and content to leave it to the Political Covenant to spell out its general terms. The Political Covenant, in article 9, fulfills their expectations by elaborating in considerable detail the rights to be accorded a person who has been arrested or detained. Most of these rights also are protected by article 5 of the European Convention and article 7 of the American Convention in "substantially similar terms."

After the language quoted above, article 9(1) of the Political Covenant concludes with the following sentence: "No one shall be deprived of his liberty except on such grounds and in accordance with such procedure as are established by law." The purpose of this provision is to require states to spell out in legislation the grounds on which an individual may be deprived of his liberty and the procedures to be used. With the freedom of action of the executive branch of government thus restricted, Rector Dinstein observes, "[n]ot every policeman (or other state functionary) is entitled to decide at his discretion, and on his own responsibility, who can be arrested, why and how."[24] Nor is any detention allowed by law permissible, as a literal interpretation of the provision might suggest. Just as an arrest may not be arbitrary—defined as "unjust" and not merely "illegal"—so too must a detention not be arbitrary. The deprivation of liberty therefore must be not only in accordance with law, but also in conformity to the principles of justice.

The balance of article 9 defines certain guarantees applicable in case of any arrest or detention, plus certain special guarantees applicable when a person is arrested or detained on a criminal charge. Space dictates that these guarantees be listed rather than fully evaluated here. In the first, general category are the following:

Article 9(2). "Anyone who is arrested shall be informed, at the time of arrest, of the reasons for his arrest and shall be promptly informed of any charges against him."

Article 9(4). "Anyone who is deprived of his liberty by arrest or detention shall be entitled to take proceedings before a court, in order that that court may decide without delay on the lawfulness of his detention and order his release if the detention is not lawful."

Article 9(5). "Anyone who has been the victim of unlawful arrest or detention shall have an enforceable right to compensation."

In the second category—special guarantees applicable to persons arrested or detained on criminal charges—article 9(3) provides that such persons "be brought promptly before a judge" and thereafter "be entitled to trial within a reasonable time or to release." Additionally, it establishes a presumption that persons awaiting trial shall not be detained in custody; their release, however, may be made subject to guarantees of appearance, the most common of which presumably would be bail.

Interpretative guidance as to the meaning of most of the above provisions can be obtained from the nascent practice of the U N Human Rights Committee as well as the more developed practice of the European Court of Human Rights under article 5 of the European Convention. Given the differences in wording, however, the latter must be used with care. In any event, taking into account uncertainties about the contours and content of the prohibition of arbitrary arrest and detention, plus the fact that states may derogate therefrom under article 4(2) of the Political Covenant, it seems unlikely that little more than the basic core prohibition can be said to constitute part of customary international law at present.

RIGHT TO A FAIR TRIAL (ARTICLE 10)

This article, which along with its companion, article 11, guarantees individuals "the basic right to a fair trial [in] both civil and criminal matters," enunciates a very important right, for the implementation of all other rights depends upon the

---

24. Yoram Dinstein, "The Right to Life, Physical Integrity and Liberty, in *The International Bill of Rights: The Covenant on Civil and Political Rights*, ed. Louis Henkin (New York: Columbia University Press, 1981), 114, 130.

proper administration of justice. In its entirety, article 10 reads as follows: "Everyone is entitled in full equality to a fair and public hearing by an independent and impartial tribunal, in the determination of his rights and obligations and of any criminal charge against him." Two preliminary points should be made with respect to this language. First, it lumps together both criminal and civil proceedings, despite cogent arguments for their being treated separately, the potential for abuse of state power obviously being greater where the rights of an accused—as opposed to a mere party in civil lawsuit—are concerned. Second, it is so terse that it offers little help when applied to the facts of particular cases. Hence, here more than elsewhere, guidance as to the meaning of the right must be obtained from parallel provisions in subsequent international human rights instruments and the decisions of competent bodies interpreting them.

The requirements of a fair trial in criminal proceedings, the sole concern of this subsection, can be divided somewhat arbitrarily into four general categories: the character of the tribunal, the public nature of the hearing, the rights of the accused in the conduct of his defense and, lastly, a miscellaneous collection of other prescriptions.

The first category, the character of the tribunal, obviously is of prime importance. Article 10 requires tribunals to be "independent and impartial," as does article 14(1) of the Political Covenant and articles 6(1) and 8(1) of the European Convention and American Convention respectively. As Professor Harris has put it,

[t]hese are obvious and overlapping requirements. The primary meaning of "independent" is independence of other organs of government in the sense of the doctrine of the separation of powers: in particular, a judge must not be subject to the control or influence of the executive or the legislature. . . . The requirement that the court must be "impartial" needs little amplification. It is reflected in the "universally accepted doctrine" that no man may be a judge in his own cause

and is an obvious characteristic for a court to possess.[25]

Whether such independence and impartiality can be assured when a state resorts to ad hoc or special tribunals, as frequently occurs after revolutions or in national emergencies, is a doubtful proposition: for this reason, it is disappointing that article 10 does not speak directly to this point. In contrast, article 14(1) of the Political Covenant and article 8(1) of the American Convention add the requirement that the tribunal be "competent," a word which, according to the *travaux préparatoires* of the former, "was intended to ensure that all persons should be tried in courts whose jurisdiction had been previously established by law, and arbitrary action so avoided." Article 8(1) of the American Convention goes one step further, specifically stating that a trial must be conducted by a tribunal "previously established by law. . . ." Arguably, this requirement can be read into the "independent and impartial" language of the Universal Declaration.

The second category, the public nature of the hearing, also is of importance in protecting individuals from arbitrary proceedings. The drafters of article 10 of the Universal Declaration inserted the words "and public" between the words "fair" and "hearing" to insure the openness of trials, a procedure conducive to their fairness. Moreover, despite language in the *travaux préparatoires* that "[t]here were circumstances in which a secret trial might be acceptable," article 10 itself acknowledges no such exception. Article 14(1) of the Political Covenant, however, closely tracked by article 6(1) of the European Convention, contains a wide range of exceptions. Article 14(1) reads, inter alia, as follows: "The Press and the public may be excluded from all or part of a trial for reasons of morals, public order (*ordre public*) or national security in a democratic society, or when the interest of the private lives of the parties so requires, or to the extent strictly necessary in the opinion of the court in special circumstances

25. David J. Harris, "The Right to a Fair Trial in Criminal Proceedings as a Human Right, *International and Comparative Law Quarterly* 16 (1967): 352, 354–6. See also *The Application of the European Convention on Human Rights*, 156:

> The often fine distinction between independence and impartiality turns mainly, it seems, on that between the status of the tribunal determinable largely by objective tests and the subjective attitudes of its members, lay or legal. Independence is primarily freedom from control by, or subordination to, the executive power in the State; impartiality is rather absence in the members of the tribunal of personal interest in the issues to be determined by it, or some form of prejudice.

where publicity would prejudice the interests of justice. . . ." Such language, as Professor Fawcett remarks with respect to article 6(1) of the European Convention, is so broad that "it is doubtful whether the requirement of public hearing under the Convention is likely in practice to yield much protection."[26]

The rights of the accused in the conduct of his defense, the third category, presents the converse of the above. Rather than the Political Covenant undercutting a broad and unqualified right found in the Universal Declaration, here the Political Covenant spells out at length in article 14(3) just what rights an accused has in a criminal proceeding. In brief, they are the right to be informed promptly of the charge against him; the right to have adequate time and facilities to prepare a defense and to communicate with counsel; the right to be tried without undue delay; the right to be tried in his presence and to defend himself in person or through counsel; the right to *cross-examine* witnesses against him and to summon witnesses on his own behalf; the right to an interpreter; and the right not to be compelled to testify against himself. Roughly similar guarantees are found in article 6(3) of the European Convention and article 8(2) of the American Convention. As is apparent, they generally reflect the procedural due process rights developed by the U.S. Supreme Court from the fifth and fourteenth amendments to the U.S. Constitution.

The fourth and final category comprises a number of miscellaneous rights, none of which are set out in the Universal Declaration, which generally are thought to contribute to a fair trial in criminal proceedings. In the order in which they appear in article 14 of the Political Covenant, they are: the right of juveniles to be tried under special procedures; the right to appeal one's conviction and sentence; the right to compensation when one is convicted through a miscarriage of justice; and the right not to be subjected to double jeopardy. The fact that none of these rights is mentioned in the European Convention (and only three are guaranteed by the American Convention) suggests that they are part of conventional rather than customary international law, a status they are likely to retain until the Political Covenant becomes so widely accepted as to be generally norm-creating. Moreover, without the interpretative assistance of the Political Covenant, the right to a fair trial provided for in article 10 of the Universal Declaration seems too generally phrased to constitute a customary international law rule capable of application in concrete cases.

PRESUMPTION OF INNOCENCE AND PROHIBITION OF EX POST FACTO LAWS (ARTICLE 11)

This article, closely related to article 10 of the Universal Declaration, also is concerned with the rights of the accused in criminal proceedings. It establishes the presumption of innocence and proscribes ex post facto offenses. These important and distinct guarantees will be discussed separately.

Article 11(1) provides that "[e]veryone charged with a penal offence has the right to be presumed innocent until proven guilty according to law in a public trial at which he has had all the guarantees necessary for his defence." Since the latter part of this sentence is redundant, in view of the rights accorded accused by article 10, it was omitted when the language of article 11(1) was adopted, almost *in haec verba,* as article 14(2) of the Political Covenant. Language almost identical to article 11(1) is contained in articles 6(2) and 8(2) of the European Convention and American Convention, respectively. Thus, there is a unanimous consensus supporting the presumption of innocence in criminal proceedings; surely therefore it has become part of customary international law.

Little difficulty has been encountered so far in applying the principle under the European Convention, although, as Professor Jacobs cautions, it has a slightly different meaning in the civil law than it has at common law:

The principle of the presumption of innocence is reflected in English law in the rule placing the burden of proof on the prosecution. But it cannot be equated with that rule, to which there are in any event numerous exceptions. Under the inquisitorial system of criminal procedure found in many of the Contracting Parties [to the European Convention], it is for the court to elicit the truth in all cases. What the principle of the presumption of innocence requires here is first that the

---

26. Fawcett, *The Application of the European Convention on Human Rights,* 150.

court should not be predisposed to find the accused guilty, and second that it should at all times give the accused the benefit of the doubt, on the rule *in dubio pro reo*.[27]

While the principle thus concerns primarily the behavior of judges, the admissibility in evidence of prior convictions and the effect of pre-trial publicity have been alleged, so far unsuccessfully, to violate the right to be presumed innocent. Other such allegations can be anticipated as this right is tested under the Political Covenant and the American Convention.

Article 11(2), which proscribes ex post facto offenses, requires quoting in full. It states:

No one shall be held guilty of any penal offence on account of any act or omission which did not constitute a penal offence, under national or international law, at the time when it was committed. Nor shall a heavier penalty be imposed than the one that was applicable at the time the penal offence was committed.

Two points here are worth noting: first, the reference to international law, inserted "to exclude doubts as to the Nuremberg and Tokyo trials" and "to ensure that no one shall escape punishment for a criminal offence under international law by pleading that his act was legal under his own national law"; and, second, the extension, in the second sentence, of the nonretroactivity principle to increased penalties.

Article 15(1) of the Political Covenant, from which there may be no derogation according to article 4(2), closely follows article 11(2); thus it may be argued convincingly that customary international law now prohibits both ex post facto offenses and penalties. Moreover, article 15(1) adds a sentence designed to guarantee an accused the benefits of ex post faco legal reforms: "If, subsequent to the commission of the offence, provision is made by law for the imposition of a lighter penalty, the offender shall benefit thereby." Article 15(2) of the Political Covenant also adds an entirely new and arguably superfluous provision justifying past and authorizing future international war crimes trials: "Nothing in

this article shall prejudice the trial and punishment of any person for any act or omission which, at the time when it was committed, was criminal according to the general principles of law recognized by the community of nations." Articles 7 and 9 of the European Convention and American Convention, respectively, are based upon article 11(2) of the Universal Declaration and article 15 of the Political Covenant, albeit both contain one or more variations.

While the primary purpose of such ex post facto provisions is to prohibit retrospective penal legislation, a secondary purpose is to preclude "the courts from extending the scope of the criminal law by interpretation." Thus the European Commission, construing article 7 of the European Convention, noted that it "does not merely prohibit—except as provided in paragraph (2)—retroactive application of the criminal law to the detriment of the accused," but "also confirms, in a more general way, the principle of the statutory nature of offences and punishment . . . and prohibits, in particular, extension of the application of the criminal law *"in malam partem"* by analogy. . . ."[28] It further added that,

although it is not normally for the Commission to ascertain the proper interpretation of municipal law by national courts . . . , the case is otherwise in matters where the Convention expressly refers to municipal law, as it does in Article 7. . . . [U]nder Article 7 the application of a provision of municipal penal law to an act not covered by the provision in question directly results in a conflict with the Convention, so that the Commission can and must take cognisance of allegations and of such false interpretation of municipal law. . . .[29]

The above remarks, according to Castberg, "clearly keep the door open for preventing under Article 7 not only the application of criminal law by analogy, but also extensive interpretations."[30] Whether the U.N. Human Rights Committee, construing article 15 of the Political Covenant, or the Inter-American Commission on Human Rights, interpreting article 9 of the American

27. Jacobs, *The European Convention on Human Rights*, 113.
28. X v. Austria, (1965) Yearbook of the European Convention on Human Rights (European Court of Human Rights), 190, 198.
29. Ibid.
30. Fredde Castberg, *The European Convention on Human Rights* (Dobbs Ferry, N.Y.: Oceana Publications, 1974), 130.

Convention, take this approach too remains to be seen. The various proscriptions against ex post facto offenses certainly offer the three systems an opportunity to develop a similar body of restraints against retroactive judicial as well as legislative action.

QUESTIONS FOR REFLECTION AND DISCUSSION

1. Richard Lillich says that the civil and political rights of individuals are "commonly considered to be the most basic and fundamental of all human rights." Should they be? Why? Why not? Do you agree that they are the most basic and fundamental? If they are so basic and fundamental, why has the United States so far failed to become a party to the International Covenant on Civil and Political Rights (the "Political Covenant")?

2. Lillich notes the presence of "derogation" and "limitation" clauses in the Political Covenant and in analogous regional conventions, allowing states to derogate from or otherwise limit their obligations under these instruments. What is the difference between the two types of clauses? Why do they exist? Are they desirable? Do they not seriously undermine the effectiveness of the human rights instruments in question? From the standpoint of wanting to enhance such rights, which type is better? Why?

3. It is necessary, surely for states to be able to function effectively during public emergencies. But is it necessary that they be allowed to suspend or otherwise curtail human rights guarantees in the process? Note that some States—for example, Chile under Pinochet, the Philippines under Marcos—have for years operated under "states of emergency," with little or no regard for the civil and political rights of their peoples. Who defines "emergency" and what deference should be shown to the definition? A customary international law "doctrine of margin of appreciation" extends to states a certain margin or latitude in determining the existence of a public emergency. Is such a doctrine desirable?

4. As Lillich points out, certain civil and political rights are deemed "nonderogable." Which ones? Why? Is it clear which rights should be considered derogable and which should be considered nonderogable? Are some inherently less entitled to evasion than others? Why? Why not?

5. Lillich is at pains to identify which treaty-prescribed civil and political rights have become part of customary international law and which have not. Why? Is customary law less easily evaded than treaty law? What is the juridical effect of treaty law? Customary law?

6. Express exemptions to certain rights also indicate the manipulability of international human rights instruments. For example, while the prohibition against slavery and servitude may be said now to constitute *jus cogens* (i.e., a norm of fundamental world public policy from which no derogation is permitted), forced or compulsory labor is not so uniformly condemned. Indeed, according to Article 8(3) of the Political Covenant, the phrase "forced or compulsory labor" expressly does not preclude the performance of hard labor, and:

> (i) Any work or service, not referred to in [the performance of hard labor], normally required of a person who is under detention in consequence of a lawful order of a court, or of a person during conditional release from such detention; (ii) Any service of a military character and, in countries where conscientious objection is recognized, any national service required by law of conscientious objectors; (iii) Any service exacted in cases of emergency or calamity threatening the life or well-being of the community; (iv) Any work or service which forms part of normal civil obligations.

What difficulties might be encountered in restricting this preclusion? What constitutes an "emergency or calamity"? What are "normal civil obligations"?

7. While it is true that vague or overly broad words and phrases can be used to manipulate against particular human rights guarantees, might it not also be true that such words and phrases can allow penumbral rights to be protected? Consider, for example, the word "treatment" in Article 7 of the Political Covenant prohibiting "cruel, inhuman or degrading treatment or punishment." Decisions from the European Court of Human Rights (interpreting analogous language in the European Convention on Human Rights and Fundamental Free-

doms) have held allegations of brutality by prison officials or police officers, inadequate conditions of detention, and even discrimination on the basis of race to constitute "degrading treatment." Might not the term be expanded, additionally, beyond the boundaries of criminal law institutions into other state-sponsored facilities including hospitals, mental institutions, foster homes, and other centers of confinement? Would such an interpretation of "treatment" be desirable? Undesirable?

8. Rights cast at high levels of abstraction, such as "the right to life," also present problems. Does such a guarantee protect against, for example, capital punishment, voluntary euthanasia, or abortion?

9. Considering all the ways in which civil and political rights guarantees can be lawfully avoided and evaded, what is their status under contemporary international law?

6. JACK GREENBERG *Race, Sex, and Religious Discrimination in International Law*

A U.S. civil rights lawyer . . . surveying the international human rights vista experiences mixed feelings of despair (at how little can be achieved through employing international means) and déjà vu (at how international human rights resembles our domestic scene of the not too distant past). The U.S. law of race relations today is complex and rich, articulated in a superstructure of leading U.S. Supreme Court decisions, like *Brown v. Board of Education*,[1] which held unconstitutional racial segregation in education, and an infrastructure of thousands of high and low court pronouncements on what constitutes discrimination and what does not, as well as what are appropriate or necessary means of uprooting it. The explication in education alone continues in national legislation, such as Title VI of the Civil Rights Act of 1964, and in regulations of the Department of Education, secretarial decisions, administrative law judge determinations, state and local implementing legislation, and local school board rules. Similar proliferation of law, in its various modes of expression, is replicated in employment, health care, housing, voting, prison conditions, capital punishment, and almost every conceivable area of human activity. The most important legal issues, moreover, continue to change in form and substance.

Contrast this with the body of international human rights law. It is somewhat, but not a great deal, more detailed than basic U.S. constitutional texts. Confining ourselves for the moment to the Universal Declaration of Human Rights,[2] it con-

sists principally of declarations like those of article 1 ("All human beings are born free and equal in dignity and rights") and article 16 ("Men and women of full age, without any limitations due to race, nationality or religion, have the right to marry and to found a family"). The international covenants explicate these great principles somewhat, but as to detail only remotely resemble the corpus of U.S. civil rights law. A U.S. civil rights lawyer who would like to employ international human rights principles, for example, to assist black South Africans, Soviet Jews, or blacks in the United States must naturally wonder whether it is possible to convert the majestic international accords into concrete relief for victims of discrimination. The problem is partly one of means of implementation, but also one of the jurist's task of translating general principles into precise application. With this there has been scant experience in the international human rights domain. . . .

But if we look a quarter century back into U.S. law we find it was then little more developed than international human rights law today. Indeed, the U.S. law slightly over a century ago was not even nominally as advanced as the international documents we shall discuss. Only in 1868 did the fourteenth amendment pronounce that no state shall "deny to any person within its jurisdiction the equal protection of the laws." That provision and others of like purpose adopted after the Civil War were at best enforced in desultory fashion until the mid-twentieth century. Up to

1. 347 U.S. 483 (1954).
2. [See the Appendix.]

that time the country showed considerable disposition *against* according racial equality. Such landmark decisions as *Plessy v. Ferguson*[3] and the *Civil Rights Cases*,[4] which denied to blacks basic civil rights by restrictively interpreting the reconstruction amendments, were the norm. Great jurists like Holmes, Brandeis, and Stone joined in decisions denying rights which today the amendments are held to grant. . . .

The application, interpretation, and teaching of domestic human rights law developed in the United States when underlying political, economic, and social relations in the country changed. The new rules in turn permitted institutionalization of change and helped bring about further growth. Similarly, it seems not unreasonable to hope for change in international human rights doctrine and, particularly, in implementation as underlying conditions develop. As Professor Sohn has pointed out: "We must measure the accomplishments of the last thirty years not against utopian dreams but against the accomplishments of the last 3,000 years of recorded history."[5]

LEGAL AND POLICY CONSIDERATIONS

THE IMPORTANCE OF THE STRICTURES AGAINST DISCRIMINATION

Mere inspection of the basic international human rights documents demonstrates that racial, sexual, and religious discrimination are, certainly in terms of attention paid on the face of the agreements, the overarching human rights

concern of the international community. If one only considers the outlook of the United States, where coping with racial discrimination has been central to our constitutional development, and former colonial peoples' preoccupation with racial domination, it becomes clear why the U.N. Charter, the Universal Declaration, the international covenants, and the various conventions devote more attention to preventing discrimination than to any other single category of human rights. . . .

THE UNITED NATIONS CHARTER AND UNIVERSAL DECLARATION OF HUMAN RIGHTS

The basic provisions of international human rights law are the U.N. Charter and the Universal Declaration of Human Rights. Both ensure freedom from racial, sexual, and religious discrimination in a variety of ways.

Detailed explication of the general principles of the Charter and the Universal Declaration has been made in the International Covenant on Civil and Political Rights,[6] the International Covenant on Economic, Social, and Cultural Rights,[7] the International Convention on the Elimination of All Forms of Racial Discrimination,[8] and the Convention on the Elimination of All Forms of Discrimination Against Women,[9] while certain aspects have been provisionally defined in preliminary efforts to draft a Convention on the Elimination of All Forms of Religious Intolerance.[10] Other agreements deal with slavery,[11] genocide,[12] apartheid,[13] and various practices

---

3. 163 U.S. 537 (1896).
4. 109 U.S. 3 (1883).
5. Louis Sohn, "The Human Rights Law of the Charter," *Texas International Law Journal* 12 (1977):129–142 at 138.
6. [See the Appendix.]
7. [See the Appendix.]
8. Mar. 7, 1966, 660 U.N.T.S. 195.
9. U.N.G.A. Res 34/180 (XXXIV), 34 U.N. GAOR, Supp. (No. 46) 193, U.N. Doc. A/34/46 (1979).
10. U.N.G.A. Res. 36/55 (XXXVI), 36 U.N. GAOR, Suppl. (No. 51) 171, U.N. Doc. A/RES/36/55 (1981).
11. Slavery Convention, Sept. 25, 1926, 46 Stat. 2183, 60 L.N.T.S. 253; Protocol of Amendment to the Slavery Convention, Dec. 7, 1953, 212 U.N.T.S. 17; Supplementary Convention on the Abolition of Slavery, the Slave Trade, and Institutions and Practices Similar to Slavery, Sept. 7, 1956, 18 U.S.T. 3201, T.I.A.S. No. 6418, 266 U.N.T.S. 3; ILO Convention (No. 29) Concerning Forced or Compulsory Labour, June 10, 1930, 39 U.N.T.S. 55, reprinted in I. Brownlie, *Basic Documents on Human Rights*, 2d ed. (Oxford: Clarendon Press, 1981), 176; ILO Convention (No. 105) Concerning the Abolition of Forced Labor, June 25, 1957, 320 U.N.T.S. 291, reprinted in Brownlie, *Basic Documents on Human Rights*, 187.
12. Convention on the Prevention and Punishment of the Crime of Genocide, Dec. 9, 1948, 78 U.N.T.S. 277, reprinted in Brownlie, *Basic Documents on Human Rights*, 31.
13. International Convention on the Suppression and Punishment of the Crime of "Apartheid," Nov. 30, 1973, U.N.G.A. Res. 3068 (XXVIII), 28 U.N. GAOR, Supp. (No. 30) 75, U.N. Doc. A/9030 (1974), reprinted in Brownlie, *Basic Documents on Human Rights*, 164.

which are peculiar manifestations of discrimination. Specialized agencies, such as the International Labor Organization (ILO) and the United Nations Educational, Scientific, and Cultural Organization (UNESCO) have promulgated strictures against discrimination.[14] Regional, e.g., European[15] and inter-American,[16] and other applications of the same principles, e.g., the Helsinki Accords,[17] adopt the UN standards or formulate them somewhat differently. In these pages, however, we shall consider the substantive rules of only the principal documents, their applicability, and perhaps useful means of teaching about them.

UN Charter

The keystone international legal document, the UN Charter, makes clear at its outset the international community's basic commitment to equality. Its preamble asserts a reaffirmation of faith "in the equal rights of men and women. . . ." Among the purposes of the United Nations, it states, are "develop[ing] friendly relations among nations based on respect for the principle of equal rights and self-determination of peoples" and "promoting and encouraging respect for human rights and fundamental freedoms for all without distinction as to race, sex, language, or religion." "The United Nations shall place no restrictions on eligibility of men and women to participate in any capacity and under conditions of equality in its principal and subsidiary organs."

Among the powers of the General Assembly are initiating studies and making "recommendations for the purpose of . . . assisting in the realization of human rights and fundamental freedoms for all without distinction as to race, sex,

language, or religion." The United Nations shall "promote . . . universal respect for, and observance of, human rights and fundamental freedoms for all without distinction as to race, sex, language, or religion." Similarly, the Economic and Social Council "may make recommendations for the purpose of promoting respect for, and observance of, human rights and fundamental freedoms for all. Furthermore, the basic objectives of the international trusteeship system include assuring "equal treatment in social, economic, and commercial matters for all Members of the United Nations and their nationals, and also equal treatment for the latter in the administration of justice. . . ." In connection with apartheid in South Africa, this provision, and the feelings underlying it, have been the basis of a great deal of international expression and activity.

Universal Declaration

The Universal Declaration of Human Rights elaborates the Charter's equal rights prescriptions and, indeed, is suffused with the notion of equality. The preamble recognizes the inherent dignity and "the equal and inalienable rights of all members of the human family" as the "foundation of freedom, justice and peace in the world," and reaffirms "faith . . . in the equal rights of men and women." Ten of the thirty articles which constitute the International Bill of Human Rights are in one way or another explicitly concerned with equality, and others implicitly so. . . .

In addition to these numerous explicit references to equality, the concept is implicit in repeated references to "everyone" having the right to liberty, to effective remedies before competent tribunals, to freedom of movement, to nationality, and other rights. . . .

14. ILO Convention (No. 111) Concerning Discrimination in Respect of Employment and Occupation, June 4, 1958, reprinted in Brownlie, *Basic Documents on Human Rights*, 204; UNESCO Convention Against Discrimination in Education, Dec. 14, 1960, 429 U.N.T.S. 93, reprinted in Brownlie, *Basic Documents on Human Rights*, 234.

15. European Convention for the Protection of Human Rights and Fundamental Freedoms, Nov. 4, 1950, 213 U.N.T.S. 221, reprinted in Brownlie, *Basic Documents on Human Rights*, 242. See arts. 4, 9, 12, and 14.

16. See art. 43, Charter of the Organization of American States, 2 U.S.T. 2394, T.I.A.S. No. 2361, 119 U.N.T.S. 3; Protocol of Amendment, 21 U.S.T. 607, 721 U.N.T.S. 324; American Convention on Human Rights, Nov. 12, 1969, O.A.S.T.S. No. 36, reprinted in Brownlie, *Basic Documents on Human Rights*, 391.

17. See arts. 1(a) and 7 of the Final Act of the Conference on Security and Co-operation in Europe, signed Aug. 1, 1975, 73 Dept. State Bull. 323, 325 (1975), reprinted in Brownlie, *Basic Documents on Human Rights*, 320.

Enforceability of the Charter and the Universal Declaration

What is the legal effect of these equal rights provisions of the Charter and the Universal Declaration? That is a question of particular interest to U.S. lawyers because the Charter is the only one of the U.N. human rights instruments which the United States has ratified, and many scholars argue persuasively that the Universal Declaration has the force of customary international law because of its universal recognition. . . .

For the U.S. civil rights practitioner, the Charter's obligatory nature and the Universal Declaration's legal validity raise the question of the means by which they may be applied to particular instances of abuse. Of course . . . , states may raise the matter of non-observance by other states and may censure each other. And . . . international bodies established to implement the various conventions and covenants may receive and, in a variety of ways, respond to complaints. But are there more direct remedies capable of application to discrete cases utilizing legal means which are ordinarily employed within domestic legal orders? In a study of the relationship of the human rights provisions of the Charter to domestic legal orders of member states, Bernard Schlüter has concluded that "[s]elf execution of the human rights clauses is . . . a *possibility* in almost all civil law member states, the United States, the socialist countries and some Third World countries."[18] But, in an intricate analysis of particular provisions, potential modes of enforcement, legal doctrines in a variety of nations, and other factors, he seems to conclude no more than that "human rights clauses, or at least some of their parts, are likely to have some domestic legal effect in *many* states."[19]

There have been attempts to apply domestically the Universal Declaration or the Charter's human rights provisions. Those aspects which deal with racial discrimination, particularly, have been urged upon U.S. courts from shortly after the Charter's adoption to the present. The results have been uniformly discouraging, except to those who find hope in a fragment of affirmative dictum, the occasional less than conclusive scope of rejection, and the mere fact that the provisions have been advocated at all. . . .

The Charter and the Universal Declaration remain theoretically applicable to other issues which arise in U.S. courts, not only with regard to conditions in the United States, but with regard to situations in other countries which are claimed to be adjudicable in U.S. courts. Nevertheless, efforts to employ them have been unsuccessful. Professor Lillich has observed that while it is not often today that courts refer to efforts to employ the Charter and other international human rights doctrine as "tommyrot" or "junk and gobbledygook,"[20] cases regularly have been resolved "on as narrow and technical a basis as possible. As a consequence, the possibility for a legitimate, innovative role for United States domestic courts in the area of human rights has been ignored."[21] . . .

THE INTERNATIONAL COVENANTS AND THE RACIAL DISCRIMINATION CONVENTION

Just beneath the Charter and the Universal Declaration in importance are the two international covenants which unfold their general terms into some detail and provide means of implementation. The Economic Covenant entered into force 3 January 1976 and the Political Covenant entered into force 23 March 1976, both having been opened for signature ten years earlier. On 13 May 1968, the International Conference on Human Rights announced the Proclamation of Teheran which reiterated the basic precepts of both covenants, the Racial Discrimination Convention, and the Universal Declaration, and urged all peoples and governments to redouble their efforts to "provide for all human beings a life consonant with freedom and dignity and conducive to physical, mental, social and spiritual welfare."[22]

---

18. Bernard Schlüter, "The Domestic Status of the Human Rights Clauses of the United Nations Charter," *California Law Review* 61 (1973): 110, 114 (emphasis added).

19. Ibid., 162 (emphasis added).

20. Richard B. Lillich, "The Role of Domestic Courts in Promoting International Human Rights Norms, *New York Law School Law Review* 24 (1978): 153, 154.

21. Ibid., 176.

22. U.N. Doc.A/CONF.32/41 (1968).

Economic Covenant

The Economic Covenant recognizes that political and civil rights can be exercised effectively only under conditions of material, social, and cultural security. For example, if one is poor and illiterate, the right to vote is relatively uninformed, and power to persuade others in the political process relatively ineffective. A pauper charged with a crime cannot afford to employ effective counsel. For the poor, the right to own property, as asserted in the Universal Declaration, is as empty as the right to participate in the cultural life of the community, also affirmed in the Universal Declaration. Hence while the economic rights are asserted for their own sake and for the material security they would afford, they have been guaranteed also to give real meaning to civil and political rights.

Like the Charter and Universal Declaration, the Economic Covenant repeatedly asserts a right to racial, sexual, and religious equality. The preamble commences, "*Considering* that . . . recognition of the inherent dignity and of the equal and inalienable rights of all members of the human family is the foundation of freedom, justice and peace . . ." and the Covenant continues "the rights enunciated in the present Covenant will be exercised without discrimination of any kind as to race, colour, sex, language, religion, political or other opinion, national or social origin, property, birth or other status." The parties "undertake to ensure the equal right of men and women to the enjoyment of all economic, social and cultural rights" set forth in the Covenant. Fair and equal remuneration for work is assured and "in particular women [are] guaranteed conditions of work not inferior to those enjoyed by men, with equal pay for equal work."

Equal opportunity to be promoted is also assured. But this particular provision evokes, as did a provision in the Universal Declaration, the U.S. dispute over affirmative action: promotion is ensured "subject to no considerations other than those of *seniority* and *competence*." International human rights law is a long way from grappling with the details of implementation, but were it doing so, two contending camps would exist on this point of the Economic Covenant. One, like its counterparts among many U.S. labor unions, would argue that blacks (or other disadvantaged groups) are not entitled to compensation for past discrimination and must move from the end of the line into promotional opportunities, even if that long delays their rise to equality. The opposing group would argue the case of affirmative action advocates, that if conventional seniority rules result in perpetuating discrimination, they must be overruled. . . .

As with the Universal Declaration, various designated rights under the Economic Covenant shall be afforded "everyone," thereby prohibiting race, sex, and religion as criteria to be used to discriminate. For example, cultural life, the benefits resulting from scientific progress, and other gains of civilization must be afforded to "everyone."

Political Covenant

The Political Covenant also elaborates in various ways the prohibitions against racial, sexual, and religious discrimination. The parties undertake to ensure to all individuals the rights recognized in the Political Covenant "without distinction of any kind, such as race, colour, sex, language, religion, political or other opinion, national or social origin, property, birth or other status," the precise language also found in the Economic Covenant. Furthermore, "[t]he States Parties . . . undertake to ensure the equal right of men and women to the enjoyment of all civil and political rights. . . ." Even when the life of the nation is threatened by public emergency, although the parties may take steps derogating from certain obligations under the Political Covenant, such measures may "not involve discrimination solely on the ground of race, color, sex, language, religion or social origin." . . .

The Political Covenant contains all other relevant provisions. Article 8 forbids slavery. Article 14(1) states: "All persons shall be equal before the courts and tribunals." In the determination of criminal charges, "everyone shall be entitled to . . . minimum guarantees, in full equality." "Everyone shall have the right to recognition everywhere as a person before the law." "Everyone," the treaty continues, "shall have the right to freedom of thought, conscience and religion." Article 20 provides that "[a]ny advocacy of national, racial or religious hatred that constitutes incitement to discrimination, hostility or violence shall be prohibited by law," thereby raising serious issues under the First Amendment to the U.S. Constitution.

The states parties to the Political Covenant undertake to take "appropriate steps to ensure equality of rights and responsibilities of spouses as to marriage. . . ." "Each child shall have without any discrimination as to race, color, sex, language, religion, national or social origin, property or birth, the right to such measures of protection as required by his status as a minor. . . ." The factors mentioned in article 2, viz., race, color, sex, etc., may not bar persons from participating in public affairs. Adverting to U.S. constitutional language, the Political Covenant provides that "[a]ll persons are equal before the law and are entitled without any discrimination to the equal protection of the law." The treaty further provides that the law must prohibit and effectively protect against "discrimination on any ground such as race, color, sex, language, religion," and so forth. Ethnic, religious, and linguistic minorities are assured the right to enjoy their own culture, religion, and language.

The Racial Discrimination Convention

The Racial Discrimination Convention entered into force on January 4, 1969, well in advance of the international covenants. Although it largely repeats the discrimination provisions of the covenants, its existence as a separate instrument underscores the vast importance which the nations of the world place on non-discrimination. The preambular paragraphs of the Racial Discrimination Convention reiterate basic concepts of the Charter: "dignity and equality," "fundamental freedoms for all, without distinction as to race, sex, language or religion," "all human beings are born free and equal in dignity and rights," "all human beings are equal before the law and are entitled to equal protection of the law." Note, once again, the incorporation of language reminiscent of the fourteenth amendment to the U.S. Constitution.

Article I commences with a definition of racial discrimination as "any distinction, exclusion, restriction or preference based on race, color, descent, or national or ethnic origin which has the *purpose* or *effect* of nullifying or impairing the recognition, enjoyment or exercise, on an equal footing, of human rights . . ." (emphasis added). . . .

Article 1 of that Convention concludes by addressing affirmative action, referred to above several times:

Special measures taken for the sole purpose of securing adequate advancement of certain racial or ethnic groups . . . shall not be deemed racial discrimination, provided, however, that such measures do not, as a consequence, lead to the maintenance of separate rights for different racial groups and that they shall not be continued after the objectives for which they were taken have been achieved.

While this provision authorizes, but does not require, affirmative action, article 2(2) goes further:

States Parties *shall*, when the circumstances so warrant, take, in the social, economic, cultural and other fields, special and concrete measures to ensure the adequate development and protection of certain racial groups or individuals belonging to them, for the purpose of guaranteeing them the full and equal enjoyment of human rights and fundamental freedoms. (emphasis added)

However, such separate rights may not be continued after the objectives for which they were taken have been achieved.

The Racial Discrimination Convention not only condemns racial discrimination, but its states parties undertake to pursue, by all appropriate means, and without delay, a policy of eliminating it in all of its forms. The affirmative steps set forth in article 2 include repeal of laws and regulations which have the effect of creating or perpetuating discrimination, and prohibition by all appropriate means, including legislation, of racial discrimination by persons, groups, and organizations. . . .

Article 4 poses the contradiction between international human rights concepts and U.S. constitutional principles of free expression, even for groups which preach race hatred, which frequently arises. Article 4 provides that the parties to the Convention "condemn all propaganda and all organizations which are based on ideas or theories of superiority of one race or group of persons of one color or ethnic origin, or which attempt to justify or promote racial hatred. . . ." Parties shall declare it an offense punishable by law to disseminate "ideas based on racial superiority . . . as well as all acts of violence or incitement to such acts against any race or group of persons of another color or ethnic origin. . . ." In addition, they are required to "declare illegal and prohibit organizations, and also organized and all other propaganda activities, which promote and incite racial discrimination." . . .

The most comprehensive provision of the Racial Discrimination Convention is article 5. It provides that "States Parties undertake to prohibit and to eliminate racial discrimination in all its forms and to guarantee the right of everyone, without distinction as to race, color, or national or ethnic origin, to equality before the law, notably in the enjoyment of" a long catalog of rights. These include the "right to equal treatment before . . . tribunals," "[t]he right to security of person," and "[p]olitical rights." Other civil rights which the article includes are freedom of movement and residence, the right to leave any country, the right to nationality, the right to marriage, to own property, to inherit, to freedom of thought, conscience, and religion, to freedom of opinion and expression, and to peaceful assembly and association. Article 5 also lists "[e]conomic, social and cultural rights" whose enjoyment parties are to protect without discrimination, including the right to work, to form and join trade unions, to housing, public health, education, and training, and to participation in cultural activitiies. Finally, article 5 protects equal access to public accommodations. As Partsch has written,

[t]he unresolved question is whether the States Parties, in ratifying this treaty, become obligated to positively enact legislative measures which guarantee the rights listed in Article 5, or whether States Parties agree only to bar racial discrimination in the enjoyment of these rights to the extent that these rights are safeguarded by a particular State Party.[23]

To make these rights meaningful, article 6 requires states parties to assure everyone within their jurisdiction effective remedies against human rights violations and article 7 requires states parties to undertake affirmative measures of teaching and education to combat racial prejudice.

Enforceability

The Political Covenant, the Economic Covenant, and the Racial Discrimination Convention

are all in force. The United States has not ratified any of them, and the proposal of ratification which President Carter submitted to the Senate contains reservations providing that ratification would require no modification of U.S. law.[24] Ratification subject to such limitations, however, raises the question of why the United States, or any state making similar reservations, should ratify at all. In addition, there may be a question of whether such wholesale reservation is valid, or whether ratification subject to such reservation is valid. After all, the most oppressive and racist government could ratify any international human rights instrument if it contained reservations which would not require it to make any changes in its policies. Moreover, the United States proposes to make a declaration accompanying ratification which would deny to the treaties self-executing effect, so that they will not in and of themselves become effective as domestic law.

On the other hand, ratification would forbid regression which, in the United States, is unlikely anyway. Furthermore, while reservations could perhaps be repealed one by one, a step by step method of ratification does not seem to exist. Given the history of the United States' reluctance to join in international human rights compacts, ratification with wholesale reservations was apparently fastened upon as the most feasible political means of securing any U.S. acquiescence at all. . . .

Given the paucity of international enforcement and the practical limitations on effecting change through international bodies, the U N Commission on Human Rights Sub-Commission on Prevention of Discrimination and Protection of Minorities decided in 1977 "to consider, as a major part of its own contribution to the Decade for Action to Combat Racism and Racial Discrimination, ways and means of using domestic forums, including legislative forums, to help implement United Nations resolutions on racism, racial discrimination, *apartheid*, decolonization and self-determination and related matters." The report contains replies by a number of countries listing a variety of measures available in domestic forums.

23. Karl Josef Partsch, "Elimination of Racial Discrimination in the Enjoyment of Civil and Political Rights," *Texas International Law Journal* 14 (1979): 191, 193.
24. See Message of the President Transmitting Four Treaties Pertaining to Human Rights, S. Exec. Doc. No. 95-C, D, E, and F, 95th Cong., 2d sess. XI (1978).

The Committee on the Elimination of Racial Discrimination was established pursuant to article 8 of the Racial Discrimination Convention. Among the functions assigned to the Committee by the Convention is the review of reports which states parties to the Convention are required to submit on the measures they have taken to implement the Convention. The Committee has found that although many of the principles contained in the Racial Discrimination Convention are reflected in the constitution and laws of a great many countries, some countries have failed to adequately report on the measures they have adopted to give effect to the Convention's provisions because they have had no problems of racial discrimination. . . .

CONVENTION ON THE ELIMINATION OF ALL FORMS OF DISCRIMINATION AGAINST WOMEN

The most recent addition to the body of United Nations equal rights jurisprudence is the Discrimination Against Women Convention, opened for signature March 1, 1980. The states parties commenced by noting that the Charter and the Universal Declaration proclaim that "all human beings are born free and equal in dignity and rights," but that despite these instruments and various U.N. resolutions, discrimination against women continues. The Convention defines "discrimination against women" as "any distinction, exclusion or restriction made on the basis of sex which has the effect or purpose of impairing or nullifying the recognition, enjoyment or exercise by women, irrespective of their marital status, on a basis of equality of men and women, of human rights and fundamental freedoms."

The states parties agree to pursue immediately "all appropriate means" to eliminate all discrimination against women. They undertake, among other things, to "embody the principle of equality of men and women in their national constitutions," to "adopt appropriate legislation and other measures . . . prohibiting all discrimination against women," to "establish legal protection of the rights of women on an equal basis with men" through the country's national tribunals or other public institutions, as well as to "take all appropriate measures . . . to modify or abolish existing laws, regulations, customs and practices," which, in effect, discriminate against women.

Just as other international human rights agreements have, the Discrimination Against Women Convention addresses the affirmative action question. The "[a]doption by State Parties of temporary special measures aimed at accelerating *de facto* equality between men and women shall not be considered discrimination as defined in the Convention. . . ." These steps, it continues, will be discontinued when equality of opportunity and treatment have been achieved. But, special measures "aimed at protecting maternity shall not be considered discrimination."

To change "social and cultural patterns," states parties will take appropriate measures to eliminate all prejudices and practices which are grounded upon ideas of "inferiority or the superiority of either of the sexes. . . ." "States Parties shall take appropriate measures . . . to suppress all forms of traffic in women. . . ." Women must be assured the right of suffrage on equal terms with men and equal opportunity to represent their governments at the international level.

Discrimination against women in education must be eliminated and women must be provided "the same conditions for career . . . guidance, for access to studies," "the same curricula, the same examinations," "the same opportunities to benefit from scholarships," and the same opportunities to participate in sports activities. Moreover, nations must take steps to eliminate "any stereotyped concept of the roles of men and women" through education, reduce female drop-out rates and organize programs for females who have left school prematurely.

Since the right to work is "an inalienable right of all human beings," the states parties must strive to eliminate discrimination in the workplace by ensuring women the "same employment opportunities," "[t]he right to free choice of profession and employment," "equal remuneration," "social security," and "protection of health and . . . safety." Most importantly, in order to "prevent discrimination against women on the grounds of marriage or maternity," parties shall act to "prohibit, subject to the imposition of sanctions, dismissal on the grounds of pregnancy or of maternity leave and discrimination in dismissals on the basis of marital status," to "introduce maternity leave with pay . . . without loss of former employment, seniority or social allowances," and to "provide special protection to women during pregnancy in types of work proved to be harmful to them."

Women shall be treated equally with men in the economic world, with the same right to family benefits, bank loans, mortgages, and other forms of financial credit, and shall be accorded equality with men before the law and exercise a legal capacity identical to men. The parties shall ensure that women have the same rights as men "to enter into marriage," "freely to choose a spouse," and to acquire the "same rights and responsibilities during marriage and at its dissolution." Change of nationality by a husband during marriage shall not automatically change the nationality of the wife.

The Discrimination Against Women Convention came into force on September 3, 1981. Like all fundamental instruments written in general terms, it leaves unanswered many questions which will be resolved only when concrete applications are attempted. . . .

Declaration on Religious Discrimination

As with racial discrimination and women's rights, existing international accords secure the right to be free from religious discrimination. Nevertheless, a further, more detailed charter of religious equality has been adopted. On November 25, 1981, the General Assembly adopted the Declaration on the Elimination of All Forms of Intolerance and of Discrimination Based on Religion or Belief. The Declaration provides that everyone shall have the right to freedom of thought, conscience, and religion; that no one shall be subject to coercion which would impair his or her freedom to have a religion or belief of his or her choice; and that freedom to manifest one's religion or beliefs may be subject only to such limitations as are prescribed by law and are necessary to protect public safety, order, health, or morals, or the fundamental rights and freedoms of others.

The Religious Discrimination Declaration asserts also that parents shall have the right to organize family life in accordance with their religion or belief and that every child shall enjoy the right to have access to religious education and, conversely, no child may be compelled to receive religious teaching if it would be against the wishes of his or her parents. However, adopting a phrase which has currency in the U.S. law of

domestic relations, the Declaration states that "the best interests of the child" shall be the guiding principle in determining the kind of religious education the child receives.

The Declaration lists a number of freedoms, including the right to worship, to maintain charitable or humanitarian institutions, to acquire materials related to religious rights, to issue publications, to teach, to solicit financial contributions, to train leaders, to observe holidays, and to communicate with others regarding religion. It calls for national legislation which would enable persons to avail themselves of such freedoms. . . .

Interpretation and Applications of the Basic Instruments

We already have observed the scarcity of material bearing on the application and interpretation of the basic documents on equality, apart from scholarly exegesis. In this lies the greatest difficulty in understanding what the documents may require in particular ciircumstances. Of course, international agreements may be implemented differently from domestic law and some flesh may be observed on the bare bones of the texts by looking beyond judicial determinations or decisions by international bodies at, for example, unilateral censure by one government of another. But extrapolating from text alone has its limits. As any lawyer knows, general language, particularly that which deals with moral or social questions, is susceptible of various meanings which may change with circumstances. Witness the evolution in U.S. law from "separate but equal" to the prohibition of segregation to the development of questions arising from affirmative action.

Nevertheless, there are a few opinions which should be noted. Perhaps the most important is Judge Tanaka's dissenting opinion in the *South West Africa Cases (Second Phase)*.[25] In his conclusion he stated:

The principle of equality does not mean absolute equality, but recognizes relative equality, namely different treatment proportionate to concrete individual circumstances. Different treatment must not be given arbitrarily; it requires reasonableness, or must be in conformity with

25. (1966) I.C.J. 4.

justice, as in the treatment of minorities, different treatment of the sexes regarding public conveniences, etc. In these cases the differentiation is aimed at the protection of those concerned, and it is not detrimental and therefore against their will.[26]

Along with racial discrimination, discrimination on the basis of language is forbidden by the international guarantees. The *Belgian Linguistic Case*,[27] therefore, may illuminate other prohibitions of discrimination. While that case involved application of the European Convention on Human Rights and not the treaties discussed above, the European Convention does stem from the resolve of "European countries which are like-minded and have a common heritage of political traditions, ideals, freedom and the rule of law, to take the first steps for the collective enforcement of certain of the Rights stated in the Universal Declaration."[28]

Belgian law had divided the country into a Dutch-speaking region, Flanders, and a French-speaking area, Wallonia. Those who spoke French, but lived mainly in Dutch-speaking areas, were required to send their children to nearby schools where they were taught in Dutch. To attend French-speaking schools required travelling a considerable distance. A case was submitted to the European Commission on Human Rights from which it went to the European Court of Human Rights. The European Court held that distinctions based on language are illegal if they do not have objective and reasonable justification in relation to the aims and effects of the measures concerned. But, as in U.S. courts making constitutional decisions bearing on state legislation, considerable deference would be given to national authority. Accordingly, the Court held that dividing the country into linguistic regions did not violate the European Convention.

Yet, while the European Commission and Court are virtually unique as international bodies which have explicated judicially the elements of substantive international equal rights jurisprudence, they have not issued a great many decisions on the subject. Most have been decided on technical or procedural grounds.

Even though they rarely result in clearcut decisions, unilateral efforts at human rights implementation also deserve a brief review. Some involve governmental action, e.g., the Jackson–Vanik Amendments which restricted United States trade with the Soviet Union for the purpose of influencing Jewish emigration, or the Country Reports prepared by the U.S. State Department. . . .

[Editors' note: The author concludes by acknowledging the activities of nongovernmental organizations such as Helsinki Watch and the Lawyers Committee for Human Rights. He notes that "[t]here is good reason to believe that they have had some influence" but that "how much and under what circumstances is difficult to say."]

QUESTIONS FOR REFLECTION AND DISCUSSION

1. Given that both the International Covenant on Civil and Political Rights (the "Political Covenant") and the International Covenant on Economic, Social and Cultural Rights (the "Economic Covenant") expressly ensure freedom from racial, sexual, and religious discrimination, why has it been deemed necessary to have specific instruments (such as the International Convention on the Elimination of All Forms of Racial Discrimination, the Convention on the Elimination of All Forms of Discrimination Against Women, and the Draft Convention on the Elimination of All Forms of Religious Intolerance) to ensure the same freedom? Should not states be free to apply the principles expressed in the general instruments in their own way rather than being directed by provisions that may not be precisely tailored to a particular place and time?

26. Ibid., 311.
27. (1967) Yearbook of the European Convention on Human Rights (European Court of Human Rights), 594.
28. European Convention for the Protection of Human Rights and Fundamental Freedoms (see n. 14 above), preamble, para. 5.

2. The United States is party to none of the conventions mentioned in question 1. However, it is party to the UN Charter which, in several provisions, seeks to ensure freedom from racial, sexual, and religious discrimination. What would have been the obligation of the United States under international law as a party to the Charter if, in 1954, the U.S. Supreme Court were to have concluded that domestic constitutional law tolerated racial discrimination in our nation's public schools? Would the United States have owed a Charter-imposed obligation to the world community to correct the condition?

3. It has been suggested by human rights scholars McDougal, Lasswell, and Chen that the principles of racial equality and nondiscrimination may be considered part of international *jus cogens*, that is, part of a "newly emerged general norm of nondiscrimination which seeks to forbid all generic differentiations among people . . . for reasons irrelevant to capabilities and contribution" (M. McDougal, H. Lasswell, and L. Chen, *Human Rights and World Public Order: The Basic Policies of an International Law of Human Dignity* [New Haven, Conn.: Yale University Press, 1980], 738). Why, then, has the United States not become a party to any of the conventions mentioned in question 1? Also, is it reasonable to contend that principles of gender and religious equality and nondiscrimination likewise constitute international *jus cogens*? Is it not possible that some kinds of equality and nondiscrimination are more fundamental than others? If so, should it be thus?

4. South African apartheid is internationally condemned as a gross violation of the equal rights of the people of South Africa, and it is rejected by the United States. Yet the U.S. government hesitates to deal firmly with South Africa by, for example, assisting in South Africa's total economic isolation by imposing full-scale economic embargoes and boycotts. Some of the reasons given are national security interests in mineral resources and geo-strategic location, the ability to better influence policy by maintaining contacts, and the need to protect corporate investments. Are these and similar reasons persuasive? Can a country's national interests be measured against such a denial of life, liberty, and the pursuit of happiness? Are there arguments to be made that it is not in the national interest of the United States to support the apartheid regime regardless of any short-term economic or political benefit that might otherwise accrue?

5. Article 13(2)(c) of the Economic Covenant provides that "[h]igher education shall be made equally accessible to all, on the basis of *capacity.* . . ." (Emphasis added.) How might this language impinge on the controversy in the United States over quotas and affirmative action?

6. Greenberg observes that Article 4(1) of the Political Covenant prohibits discrimination "solely on the ground of race, color, sex, language, religion or social origin" even in respect of measures that, in situations of public emergency, derogate from certain obligations under the Political Covenant. How might the World War II Japanese relocation cases in the United States (e.g., *Korematsu v. United States*, 323 U.S. 214 [1944]) have been decided had this provision been applicable at the time? In an omitted discussion, Greenberg asks, "Were the Japanese-Americans evacuated from the West Coast *solely* because of ancestry or because of a belief that in case of invasion they would have aided the invaders?" Does Greenberg's question suggest that the word "solely" unreasonably undercuts the nondiscrimination guarantee? Would you recommend its deletion? Would your answer depend on whether the issue had to be decided in wartime or peacetime?

7. In *Washington v. Davis* (426 U.S. 229 [1978]), the U.S. Supreme Court held that mere discriminatory effect without the purpose of discriminating does not violate the Constitution. Might this case have been decided differently had the Racial Nondiscrimination Convention been in force in the United States at the time? If so, why?

8. Might Article 4 of the Racial Nondiscrimination Convention, requiring states parties "[to] declare illegal and prohibit organizations, and also organized and all other propaganda activities, which promote and incite racial discrimination," contradict First Amendment doctrine? How? Is there any reason why the Ku Klux Klans, Nazis, and similar racist groups should not be banished from, or otherwise severely restricted by, a democratic society that professes racial harmony as a matter of fundamental public policy?

9. Writes Kathleen Newland in *The Sisterhood of Man* (New York: W. W. Norton, 1979), 24:

> While political, economic, and civil relations are governed by laws made in accordance with some social ideals, the most basic contractual relationships between women and

men are left to the archaic, vague, and often contradictory mandates of custom, prejudice, and religion—even when these run contrary to stated ideals of equality.

What can be done to ensure that guarantees of sexual equality are more "real" than "cosmetic"?

10. In an omitted discussion, referring to the Convention on Nondiscrimination Against Women and the Declaration on Religious Nondiscrimination, Greenberg asks, "If a religion relegates women to a certain societal or familial status which otherwise would be deemed discrimination on the basis of sex, which convention governs?" How would you answer?

7. ANIMESH GHOSAL AND THOMAS M. CROWLEY *Refugees and Immigrants: A Human Rights Dilemma*

International law makes a distinction between ordinary migrants and political refugees. The United States—together with a few other countries—has had a long tradition of providing sanctuary to victims of political persecution, and the screening procedure for admitting refugees has been quite different from that used for ordinary "economic" migrants. Before the 1970 s, the number of people admitted into the U.S. as refugees was quite small in "normal" years; under the Immigration Act of 1965, six percent of the visas allotted were reserved for refugees, who were almost exclusively from communist countries or the Middle East. Abnormal influxes, such as the large number of Hungarian refugees after 1956 and Cuban refugees after 1959, could be handled by a special provision authorizing the attorney general to parole aliens into the United States in emergencies.

Since the mid-1970s, however, with a vast and sustained exodus from Indochina, the adequacy of the refugee law came under scrutiny. The ad hoc nature of the parole power, and a recognition of the vast numbers of refugees worldwide (estimated to be between thirteen and fourteen million) led to the Refugee Act of 1980,[1] raising the number of refugee preference slots from 17,400 to 50,000 per year. This law did not create the hoped-for order in processing refugee applications, however, since almost as soon as it went into effect, 120,000 Cuban "boat people" arrived in Florida when the Cuban government decided to allow (or force) their departure. At the same time, 15,000 Haitians landed in the U.S. torn between welcoming them and trying to stop them, the administration, after much confusion, decided to let them stay and labelled them "entrants" rather than refugees since, unlike legal refugees, they had not been screened and granted visas.

Public reaction to the influx has been hostile; according to a *Newsweek* poll, majorities of Democrats, Republicans, and independents agreed that the flow of refugees was harmful. The same poll showed a majority judging the refugees as fleeing economic hardship rather than political persecution. While it might appear easy to distinguish economic migrants from political refugees, a number of difficulties arise in the distinction, and the issue becomes even more complex if we examine the concept of "economic refugee."

THE RIGHT TO SANCTUARY

The 1967 Protocol Relating to the Status of Refugees,[2] to which the United States was a signa-

1. Public Law No. 96-212, 94 Stat. 102 (Mar. 17, 1980, codified in 8 U.S.C. §§1101–1254).
2. Protocol Relating to the Status of Refugees, opened for signature Jan. 31, 1967, and entered into force Oct. 4, 1967, 606 U.N.T.S. 268, reprinted in *Collection of International Instruments Concerning Refugees*, 2d ed. (Geneva: U.N. High Commissioner for Refugees, 1979), 40–44 (hereafter cited as *Collection*). This 1967 Protocol amended the Convention Relating to the Status of Refugees, adopted July 28, 1951, and entered into force Apr. 21, 1954, 189 U.N.T.S. 137 (1951).

tory, defines a refugee as a person who:

owing to a well-founded fear of being persecuted for reasons of race, religion, nationality, membership of a particular social group or political opinion, is outside the country of his nationality and is unable or, owing to such a fear, is unwilling to avail himself of the protection of that country; or who, not having a nationality and being outside the country of his former habitual residence, is unable or, owing to such fear, is unwilling to return to it.[3]

Those persons who are judged to fall under this definition are said to be "political refugees" as opposed to "ordinary migrants." The crucial phrase in the definition is "well-founded fear of being persecuted," which comprises both subjective states on the part of the refugee ("fear") and objective facts about the country from which the refugee is fleeing ("well-founded," "persecuted"). Definitions of these terms have been deliberately left vague so as to give a maximum of flexibility to those persons adjudicating refugee cases, yet certain types of situations in countries can be pointed to as the minimum required for the proper guarantee of human rights. Actions on the part of governments which fall below these minima would, in general, qualify affected persons from that country as political refugees. These basic minima include the following: (1) Persons must be secure from threats to life or freedom based on religion, nationality, political opinion or group membership. (2) Persons must be secure from serious discrimination which affects their political or civil rights. (3) Persons must be secure from such excesses as torture, cruel, inhuman or degrading treatment or punishment, arbitrary arrest or imprisonment, denial of a fair trial, or an invasion of the home, even if these practices are used in the enforcement of otherwise just laws. (4) Persons must be able to find and hold employment which is capable of sustaining basic human needs (food, clothing, shelter) and must be able to hold employment reasonably commensurate with their training.

It is this last minimum of human rights, specifically incorporated in two international accords and cited in a series of court cases involving refugees in Germany which raises the difficult distinction between "political" and "economic"

refugees. What distinction can be made between these two concepts, and can minima be set for "economic refugees" in a way analogous to the setting of minima for political refugees?

It must be noted that under the U N documents relating to refugees, the term "economic refugee" is difficult to define properly. Grahl-Madsen, perhaps the leading authority on refugee matters, labels the term "a misnomer [which] should be avoided."[4] This characterization of economic refugee is based on an analysis which sees economic factors as playing a role in deciding refugee status in that a person may be a victim of political persecution (and hence a refugee) when that persecution is carried out by means of economic policies. Such an individual is then simply a refugee in the sense of the U.N. definition. Someone fleeing a country for purely economic reasons to reach a country where there is a higher standard of living is an economic migrant, but not a refugee—thus the categories of political refugee and economic refugee. Under Grahl-Madsen's analysis, a person cannot present a "well-founded fear of being persecuted" solely on economic grounds.

This analysis finds support in the *U N Handbook on Procedures and Criteria for Determining Refugee Status*, wherein it is stated that, if he is motivated by economic considerations, a person is an economic migrant rather than a refugee. Yet the *Handbook* leaves open the possibility that "victims of general economic measures (i.e., those that are applied to the whole population without discrimination)" could be declared refugees, but that such a determination would "depend on the circumstances of the case," although some appeal to an underlying political motive seems necessary. It is those victims of general economic measures who could be considered refugees as persons who are persecuted not merely by economic means but for economic ends.

In detailing the economic minima which would qualify a person as a refugee, a distinction must be made at the outset between countries which are poor and remain poor despite the best efforts of their governments, and those countries which, while they would be poor naturally (perhaps because of lack of natural or human resources) are kept poor primarily through the ac-

3. 1967 Protocol, art. 1(3), *Collection*, 40.
4. See Atle Grahl-Madsen, *The Status of Refugees in International Law*, vol. 1 (Leyden: A. W. Sijthoff, 1966), 201–9.

tions or indifference of the government. Also, a reasonably healthy economy which is able to provide for its citizens can be impoverished by the actions of the government.

ANALYTICAL MODELS

Two further distinctions will be useful in this analysis: between anticipated and abrupt migration; between voluntary and involuntary migration, migration being defined in a general sense to cover any movement of persons from place to place.

Standard models of migration deal with what can be called anticipated migration, wherein the migrant person has planned the change in location and his choice is based on the sufficient attractiveness of the new country given all the cost factors of the move. Such migrants are not typically regarded as refugees at all, since their ability to plan and execute carefully their migration seems to mitigate against any persecution in their home country. They are seeking a better standard of living rather than fleeing either political or economic persecution. In contrast, abrupt migration involves a rapid, unplanned departure from the migrant's home country, often as the result of natural disasters (thus making them refugees in a common, nonlegal sense), but can also be the result of political or economic persecution. An example of such abrupt migration was the expulsion of ethnic Asians from Uganda, where some 50,000 were forced to leave the country within eighteen months. Thus as between anticipated and abrupt migration, anticipated migrants are in general not regarded as refugees of any kind or, if they are so regarded, it is as political refugees; abrupt migrants are indeed regarded as refugees but, again, of the political variety.

Voluntary versus involuntary migration raises a similar dichotomy. The involuntary migrant, who is the victim of natural or man-made circumstances, can easily be seen as a refugee of either the common or political type. The voluntary migrant is far more difficult to categorize. The fact of voluntariness does not necessarily point to a lack of persecution in the home coun-

try; it may mean no more than the lack of forceful expulsion. Yet the fact that the person could freely choose to leave his country does point to a level of political and civil liberties which must be taken into account in evaluating claims to refugee status. A voluntary refugee may also have had to leave his country illegally in order to escape conditions there, making his voluntary departure an indication of a lack of freedom in the country fled. If the conditions from which the person seeks refuge are severe enough, how voluntary is his departure (e.g., if he cannot feed or clothe himself, though he leaves of his own will, how "voluntary" has his departure been)? All these factors make the voluntary refugee particularly difficult to analyze.

The foregoing distinctions are typically presented with an analysis of "refugee" such as Grahl-Madsen's in mind, wherein only those fleeing political persecution can effectively qualify for refugee status. The remainder of this paper will seek to detail certain economic minima which should qualify a person for what will be termed politico-economic migrant status and would confer on the person the same rights and treatment of refugee status, but would be the result of economic measures taken by the government of his country of origin. An attempt will also be made to integrate this category of refugees into the existing categories and into the distinctions of anticipated from abrupt and voluntary from involuntary migrants.

The most fundamental economic minimum, as referred to in both the Universal Declaration of Human Rights and the International Covenant on Economic, Social and Cultural Rights[5] is the ability of workers to hold employment which can provide for themselves and their families a "decent living" which is "worthy of human dignity." Thus the employment must be able to supply the basic necessities of food, clothing, and shelter for the worker and his dependents. Clearly, if the economic policies of a government are such as to make the attainment of such employment impossible for the vast majority of the population, then the most basic of economic minima would be violated. This would be the case if the government either denied the worker any chance to be employed or kept him at a level where these basic needs could not be fulfilled.

5. [See the Appendix.]

COURT RULINGS

A series of cases decided in Germany involving persons who claimed refugee status on the basis of persecution which was of an economic nature[6] point to another minimum of economic human rights, that of the right of a person to hold employment which is "'suitable'' or "commensurate with his training and qualifications." Note that merely lowered or reduced pay has not been held to be sufficient to establish persecution; the pay given must be out of all reason to the nature of the work or to the level of education or training of the worker if refugee status is to be granted.

A second point brought out by the cases is the result which is typically reached when the economic hardship complained of is the result of a general policy of the government. Thus confiscation of land or property, if it is the result of a general policy of the government and the person affected is left with some other means of livelihood, does not constitute persecution in the requisite sense.

In sum, the findings of the German courts on those economic measures which will be construed as persecution are as follows:

(1) It is an established practice that economic proscription so severe as to deprive a person of all means of earning a livelihood . . . constitutes persecution in the sense of the Refugee Convention.

(2) Such proscription is deemed to exist in the case of systematic denial of employment. . . .

(3) It is also considered persecution if a person is denied all work which is "suitable" . . . or commensurate with his training or qualifications, or denied a "reasonable" . . . remuneration for his work. However, "economic disadvantages". . . , which term implies low or reduced pay, is not sufficient to constitute persecution. It is only if the pay is out of all reason that a person may claim refugeehood.

(4) Denial of opportunity for promotion is not considered persecution, nor is the denial of senior or better-paid jobs.

(5) Assignment to heavy or undesirable work does not *per se* constitute persecution, provided it is not grossly incommensurate with the person's skills.

(6) The fact that a person has to give up or abandon his private business is deemed not to constitute persecution, if this is the result of a general economic or fiscal policy (e.g., taxation), and the person concerned is allowed to earn his livelihood in some other way.

(7) Expropriation or confiscation of property (e.g., land, business) is also deemed not to constitute persecution, provided that it is carried out in pursuance of a general policy, and the person concerned is left with other means of livelihood.

(8) Measures aiming at an equitable or sensible apportioning of available housing space in short supply are deemed not to constitute persecution.[7]

POLITICAL AND ECONOMIC MINIMA

These economic minima, which are expanded from the fourth of the political minima already cited also match with two other political minima. The deprivation of any and all means of earning a livelihood directly involves the security of the person from threats to life, since the inability to hold any job means that the person cannot feed, clothe, house, and medically care for himself or his dependents. This minima is also related to the lack of pay that is reasonable. There is as well a relation to the freedom from discrimination in that confiscation of property or business must be the result of a general (not specific to that person) policy of the government which must leave the individual affected with an adequate means of livelihood. Thus as with the political minima, the economic minima can be listed so as to provide criteria for the adjudication of refugee claims. Those criteria, as formulated, would appear roughly as follows:

1. A politico-economic system which is the direct result of the actions of the central government and which denies a person or persons all means of earning a livelihood, so that the basic needs of life cannot be met, is in violation of those economic minima needed to maintain an adequate level of human rights. Persons who can show that they are seeking refuge from such conditions are eligible for status as politico-economic migrants and will be accorded the same status as those political refugees seeking refuge from immediate fear for their physical integrity.

2. A politico-economic system which discriminates against a person in such a way that he is denied reasonable employment which is com-

6. Grahl-Madsen, *Status of Refugees,* 201–8.
7. Ibid., 208–9.

mensurate with [his] skills and training has violated a basic economic human right. If a person can demonstrate flight from such conditions, he is eligible for the status of politico-economic migrant and will be accorded a status not greater than those fleeing discrimination which deprives them of political or civil rights, yet a higher status than that given to purely economic migrants.

3. Those victims of a general governmental policy who are *not* left with an appropriate means of earning a living can be considered politico-economic migrants as in 2 above.

4. Those persons who are seeking a better standard of living, but whose basic economic human rights are respected in their home country, will be classified as economic migrants who are not eligible for any kind of refugee status, but can apply for admission as regular immigrants.

5. Abrupt versus anticipated migration and involuntary versus voluntary migration should be used as weighting factors in individual cases and in an overall scheme of setting priorities for the admission of political refugees and politico-economic migrants. A possible solution might be to have those persons who have migrated abruptly or involuntarily be given a higher priority for admission than a person who, while fleeing the same sort of persecution, has been able to do so voluntarily or in an anticipated way, these latter persons having a somewhat higher burden of proof for granting of status than the former.

These criteria are not exhaustive, and can provide only a rough outline for what the standards might be for the admission of politico-economic migrants into a given country. What does emerge from these considerations is the extent to which certain economic human rights strike at the root of those concerns which informed the international documents on human rights and refugees. In particular, the need to have employment which is capable of providing the basic necessities of life parallels the most fundamental concern in the determination of standard political refugee status, i.e., whether the persecution complained of is such that it threatens the life or physical integrity of the person. Those persons who can show that, as the result of deliberate actions and policies of their government (not merely the natural conditions of the country), they suffer this type of persecution should be conferred a status which is second only to that of the person who flees because of a threat to his personal safety as a result of political persecution. Insofar as the

other economic rights can be seen to parallel the structure established for political rights, these persecuted persons should be accorded a status which is analogous to that given to other political refugees. Such a setting of priorities will have to be done by the individual country accepting the refugees, but the fundamental importance of economic human rights entails that such persecuted persons must be given an appropriately high status in admissions policies.

To conclude this section, an example of each of the categories of refugee will be presented, with an indication of how a person in each category would be handled under the foregoing analysis.

In the first category, suppose a certain ethnic minority is denied trading and other economic rights as a result of the government's policy of expelling an ethnic group deemed undesirable (e.g., Asians in Uganda). In such a case, the policy, though economic, is done for an overtly political motive and is directed only at the members of a certain ethnic group. Such persons are purely political refugees in accord with the 1951 Convention and 1967 Protocol, and can be granted such status irrespective of whether their departure was anticipated or abrupt (it is presumed that it was involuntary).

In the American context, one could compare the situation of upper- and middle-class Cubans who fled the Castro regime in 1959. It is clear, at one level, that such persons were fleeing Cuba for economic reasons: because of government policies, their livelihoods were threatened by seizure of their assets or by restrictions on their power to earn. Unlike the Asian Ugandans, Castro's policies were not aimed at a certain ethnic group. The policies implemented what might be seen as a mixed political and economic program which affected the entire country, yet had a more significant impact on the upper and middle classes. It is arguable that, given communist ideology, such policies were indeed aimed at these classes and that therefore they should qualify as political refugees because of membership in certain social groups. Such a position, combined with a clear preference for those fleeing communist countries in general, was the basis on which the United States accepted large numbers of these Cubans.

Under the preceding analysis, these Cubans would not have a clear claim to political refugee status and hence to asylum—certainly not as clear, for example, as the claims of officials of the former regime and probably not as clear as those of the Asian Ugandans. Certainly, any *individual* Cuban could make out a political asylum claim, but as a group these Cubans would seem to be economic migrants not entitled to politico-economic migrant status, even though they are not economic migrants in the purest sense.

Far more difficult cases are presented by Haitian and (to some extent) El Salvadoran asylum seekers. Their problems will be discussed below.

A second example might be a practicing physician in a certain country who desired to migrate to a more industrialized country where his skills will be better compensated. Such an individual is an economic migrant, even if the fact of his lower compensation is the result of a government policy (e.g., he is directed to work in a rural clinic rather than in a major hospital). Note that if he is forced to perform manual labor as a result of a policy aimed at eliminating certain professional classes, he may be eligible as either a political refugee if the policy affects only a certain class or as a politico-economic migrant if the policy of the government is an overall one which affects his class as well as others as part of a policy to enrich certain officials at the expense of the society. Whether his departure is abrupt or anticipated, voluntary or involuntary will in this latter case be weighted in considering his individual case.

What must be understood here is the clear case of a purely economic migrant and also how individual cases can move along a spectrum where more political factors enter the picture and where finally the person could be classified as a politico-economic migrant or even political refugee. Thus a doctor coming from the Dominican Republic for the sole purpose of attempting to earn more income by practicing in the United States would be a purely economic migrant, and would have to enter the country as any other immigrant. The conditions he is leaving are not the result of the policies of the government but rather of natural factors which keep the country poor. Yet a Vietnamese doctor who has been moved into a new economic zone might be able to claim asylum under the politico-economic migrant status (assuming he could not show pure political refugee status), although *one* reason for his wanting to come to America may be a desire for greater remuneration for his services. Determinative for the distinction between purely economic migrants

and politico-economic migrants is the set of factors concerning the government's role in the creation of the economic conditions which the individual is fleeing and how directly and individually those policies and conditions affect the person claiming asylum.

As the third example, a person is fleeing a country where he cannot hold any job or the job he holds is inadequate to provide the basic needs of life for himself or his family. Such conditions have existed for years as a result of the policies of his government, but he has only recently been able to leave the country. He has left voluntarily in that he was not expelled, but conditions in effect forced him to leave. He would be entitled to status as a politico-economic migrant and would have a priority slightly less than that of a purely political refugee fleeing for physical safety. The fact that he has left in an anticipated and voluntary way may raise his burden of proof over that of an involuntary or abrupt migrant, but the fact that he has been persecuted as a result of a general policy of his government is the determinative factor. His burden of proof will increase, and his priority will decline, as the persecution of which he complains moves toward the denial of suitable employment vis-à-vis his training and away from that employment necessary to sustain life.

This last example—that of the true politico-economic migrant—is starkly presented in the American context by the Haitian and, to a lesser extent, El Salvadoran refugees under the policy of the United States toward each group. Indeed the factual settings of these refugee groups present both the difficulties of applying the politico-economic migrant standard and cases where the category shows its usefulness and should be applied.

The Haitian problem dates from September 1963 and has continued for two deccades. The central issue has been the almost total denial of asylum claims made by Haitian refugees. The longstanding policy of the Department of State and the Immigration and Naturalization Service (I.N.S.) has been that Haitians are fleeing Haiti for purely economic reasons and thus are not political refugees. This contention has been held by both the Department of State and I.N.S. despite a vast amount of evidence as to the systematic persecutions of citizens and human rights violations which occur in Haiti. Judge James Lawrence King in *Haitian Refugee Center v. Civiletti*[8] devoted a large portion of his opinion to findings of fact concerning the amount and nature of persecution in Haiti and used such findings as a basis for enjoining the I.N.S. policy of summarily dismissing Haitians' asylum claims on the assumption that Haitians are merely economic migrants. Of particular importance is the discussion of the Haitians' status as politico-economic migrants (though this term was not used) in a section of Judge King's opinion entitled "Haitian Economics: The Economics of Repression," where he states:

The Duvalier family has maintained its rule by weakening its opposition. As the discussion above indicates, "opposition" is an all-inclusive term encompassing real, potential, and perhaps even imaginary enemies. Consequently, the efforts to weaken others have been wide-ranging, even random. Haiti's weak economy must be seen as part of this practice, its political implications understood. . . . The purpose of this discussion has been to show the degree to which Haitian economics is a function of the political system.

Indeed, the litigation situation in *Haitian Refugee Center* can be said to have arisen because of the failure of I.N.S. and the Department of State to take into account these factors, particularly the relationship between politics and the economy, in their asylum decisions. At the risk of oversimplification, it can be said that plantiffs in the case raised—and the court answered in the affirmative—the question of whether the Haitians were politico-economic migrants. Certainly Judge King did not use this term, yet his analysis points to precisely those elements which define this status.

The difficulties with the category of politico-economic migrant can be seen from this case. The drawing of distinctions between purely economic and purely political refugees is not always easy: the attempt to define clearly a third category depends not only on gathering a large set of facts about the social, political, and economic system of a given country, but also upon the task of interpreting these facts to determine how they interrelate. Crucial to this task is seeing causal connections between political structures and activities and economic consequences in order to see whether conditions are present that give rise to politico-economic emigration. That the task can be done is evidenced by Judge King's opinion. Whether it should be done is a matter of broad immigration and asylum policy. The benefits of this category—both in terms of analytical accuracy and as a tool for rational and humanitarian asylum policy—are well illustrated by the Haitian case. The Haitians are clearly more than merely economic migrants. The conditions in Haiti, particularly the political control of the economy and the oppressive practices of the Tonton Macoutes make it evident that much more than poverty is being fled. Yet the vast majority of Haitian refugees have engaged in no political activity in Haiti, and cannot be classified as being persecuted because of race, religion, nationality, membership in a social group, or holding certain political opinions (unless one counts "talking bad" about the government as a political opinion in the requisite sense). What is needed is a category between these two extremes, a category which can handle both conceptually and practically the situations of persons such as the Haitians. The case law has shown that such a category can be applied and that the equities of individual situations can be taken into account to prevent abuse. Such a category may well be needed to solve the evolving refugee problem caused by the civil war in El Salvador.

Given the expressed congressional and public desire for a more coherent refugee policy, a proper means by which to analyze and pass upon claims arising out of factual situations such as those presented by the Haitians is clearly a desirable step toward that goal.

[Editors' note: The authors next review the attitudes of five other countries "faced with significant refugee problems"—Canada, Honduras, Somalia, Pakistan, Thailand—toward the issues of political refugees and political-economic migrants.]

CONCLUSION

In comparing U.S. policy with that of these five nations, it is worthy of note that those nations with the most serious refugee problems (Somalia, Pakistan, and Thailand) have policies which are

8. 503 F. Supp. 442 (S.D. Fla. 1980).

not pronouncedly more restrictive than those of nations with far less serious migrant flows. Yet this apparent openness may be very deceptive. Masses of refugees, once present in a country, are nearly impossible to move. Thus what may appear to be an open migration policy may be nothing more than the inability of the government to effect any control over the flow.

In terms of specific comparisons, the Thai government has based repatriation on a perceived status of purely economic migration, and even the Canadian government may become less open to such migrants because of deteriorating economic conditions. Thus the status of politico-economic migrants is problematic for other nations on two levels. In the face of large refugee flows, to the extent some controls can be exercised, both purely economic and politico-economic migrants are likely to be excluded in an attempt to reduce overall numbers of refugees. To the extent that more control can be exercised, finer distinctions can be made among individual refugees, allowing for the full consideration of politico-economic claims. Thus in situations such as Somalia, Pakistan, and Thailand, where little or no control is possible, either all refugees will be admitted or an attempt will be made to make broad exclusions.

The second level is exemplified by the United States, Honduras, and Canada. Comparatively speaking, each country can control its refugee intake (though recent events in the United States show that such control can easily be lost), and thus the opportunity is present to make more refined distinctions. Yet domestic conditions may work restrictive effects similar to those caused by overwhelming flows of refugees. If the nation's economic and social service systems cannot—or will not—bear such an influx, economic and politico-economic migrants will be excluded. This will occur, as in the case of Canada and as proposed by some in the United States, in spite of the best of humanitarian intentions, for the simple reason that the people of that nation will demand that their own nationals be cared for properly first.

Thus both external pressures from large refugee flows and internal pressures from public opinion and unfavorable economic conditions may place restrictions on the admittance of would-be refugees. Other nations have already had to face situations in which such migrants, even where they can be clearly identified, have had to be excluded. The United States faces such choices presently, and the concept of politico-economic migrant discussed in this paper offers a rational basis for legislation and for discussion.

QUESTIONS FOR REFLECTION AND DISCUSSION

1. What is the theory behind not allowing "economic refugees" the same privileges as "political refugees"? How does one distinguish between the two? What criteria are appropriate for making the distinction?

2. Recently, Cubans, Haitians, and Southeast Asians have come to the United States as refugees in significant numbers. Two interests have collided: the desire to provide sanctuary to those wishing to leave their countries versus economic considerations such as welfare payments and an already high level of domestic unemployment. How should these considerations be balanced? How would you balance the right of a citizen to a standard of living adequate for the health and well-being of self and family (enshrined in Article 25 of the Universal Declaration of Human Rights) against the right set forth in the 1967 UN Declaration on Territorial Asylum declaring that no person shall be returned to any state where he or she may be subjected to persecution?

3. Historically, refugees have had no legal right to sanctuary, only the right to request sanctuary. In recent times, however, principles such as the right to territorial asylum and the right not to be returned (*non-refoulement*) to a country where there is a reasonable expectation of persecution have been asserted as the bases for extending legal rights to refugees. For example, Article 27 of the American Declaration on the Rights and Duties of Man states that "every person has the right, in case of pursuit not resulting from ordinary crimes, to seek and receive asylum in foreign territory, in accordance with the laws of each country and with international agreements." Analogously, Article 33 of the 1951 Convention Relating to the Status of Refugees states that "no contracting State shall expel or return

("refouler") a refugee in any manner whatsoever to the frontiers of territories where his life or freedom would be threatened on account of his race, religion, nationality, membership of a particular social group or political opinion." Which of these asserted rights—to asylum or to *non-refoulement*—appears stronger? That is, which might have greater binding effect on individual states?

4. Article 13 of the Universal Declaration of Human Rights recognizes the individual's right to emigrate. Article 49 of the American Declaration of the Rights and Duties of Man recognizes every person's right to change nationalities if another country is willing to accommodate him or her. Does the right to emigrate from one country create the right to be accepted in another?

5. In the Helsinki Accords, so-called Basket III rights include the reunification of family members by permitting emigration from the state of departure and immigration to the receiving state. Should a refugee seeking asylum and claiming *non-refoulement* consequently be allowed to bring the rest of her or his family into a country based on these asserted rights?

6. The Executive Branch and Congress are continuously reviewing refugee and immigration laws because they are constantly confronted with competing pressures to close the door behind the last entrant or to open the doors to all who seek protection. Thus the Carter administration overhauled the refugee policy of the United States with the Refugee Act of 1980 (Public Law No. 96-212, Sec. 201, 94 Stat. 102, 102–103 [1980] [codified in *United States Code*, vol. 8, sec. 1101(a)(42) [1982]), including incorporation of the UN definition of "refugee," that is, one who is outside her or his native or habitual country and is unwilling or unable to return because of a well-founded fear of persecution (see Article 1 of the Convention Relating to the Status of Refugees, July 28, 1951, 189 U.N.T.S. 137, and Protocol Relating to the Status of Refugees, Jan. 21, 1967, 19 U.S.T. 6223, T.I.A.S. No. 6577, 606 U.N.T.S. 267). While seeking to bring balance and fairness to a complicated issue, however, the Carter administration instead created controversy for the incoming Reagan administration, which soon undertook to manage a situation of increasing applications for admission to the United States resulting from the Carter administration's broad definition of "refugee" by deterring migration from Central and South America. As David Forsythe writes in "Congress and Human Rights in U.S. Foreign Policy: The Fate of General Legislation," *Human Rights Quarterly* 9 (1987): 382–404, at 398–99:

> First, [the Reagan administration] sought to make life in the United States, pending a determination of status, as unpleasant as possible. Claimants were no longer paroled into society but were detained—sometimes in difficult conditions. New detention facilities were constructed, and . . . one in Louisiana was located very far from urban centers— and from legal counsel that might assist the immigrants in defending their rights. Secondly, the Reagan administration instituted the policy of interdicting particularly Haitians before they could reach U.S. jurisdiction. The U.S. Coast Guard, with the permission of the Haitian government and with an official of that government on board, turned back Haitians before they could reach U.S. waters or shoreline, thus preventing them from making effective claims to refugee status in U.S. courts. The administration argued that an official from [the Immigration and Naturalization Service] on board was capable of making a sound determination at the time of interdiction. These and other policies were obviously intended to keep the number of successful claimants to an absolute minimum.
>
> In moving to reduce the number of refugees and asylees entering the United States, the Reagan administration was acting in conformity with the views of important members of Congress. Nevertheless, there were persistent criticisms that Haitians and others fleeing non-Communist situations were not being treated according to the intent of Congress when it passed the Refugee Act of 1980. State Department officials had invited this criticism in several ways. Some had testified honestly about the administration's policy. Said James N. Purcell of the Department's Bureau of Refugee Programs:

> If by unequal distribution [of refugees from second countries] that means we have fewer Africans or ones from the Western Hemisphere or the Near East than Indochinese, I think that is a matter of national interest. . . . While I think we have a uniform system, the application of that system has to vary by region depending on the politics and the requirements.

He also testified candidly that even when those fleeing Indochinese countries cited economic motivations, the State Department still treated them as victims of political persecution. He argued that their economic deprivation was class oriented, and hence political, and that they would be persecuted if sent back.

If you were a member of Congress responsible for drafting an immigration law, what provisions would you include regarding the qualifications necessary for refugee status, allowed number of entrants, return of refugees, and the incorporation of human rights standards into application and admission procedures? Would you be influenced by the words of Emma Lazarus (1849–1887) engraved in a tablet inside the pedestal of the Statue of Liberty: "Give me your tired, your poor / Your huddled masses yearning to breathe free / The wretched refuse of your teeming shore / Send these, the homeless, tempest-tost to me / I lift my lamp beside the golden door!"?

8. CHRISTIAN BAY *Human Rights on the Periphery: No Room in the Ark for the Yanomami?*

In 1992, there will [have passed] 500 years since the arrival of Columbus in the Americas. Perhaps there will be celebrations. Yet, for all the heralded achievements of the European civilizations, who transformed the territories on the continent into colonies and then into the new nations of the Americas, one should remember that the colonizers were resisted from the very beginning by the indigenous peoples and that they are still being resisted in some parts of the Americas, while in other parts these new nations have become the graveyards of once flourishing nations of indigenous peoples and cultures. And many of the indigenous peoples who have survived have been decimated by violence and disease and reduced to conditions of poverty and dependence. They are furthermore continually victimized by racial and ethnic prejudices and discrimination and this also when they seek to adopt the ways of the dominant culture.

Important human rights issues arise whenever people are oppressed or victimized, as happens disproportion[ately] to indigenous populations who have seldom or never been part of the new states, and whose habitats, both culturally and geographically, have tended to be far removed from the "corridors of power." In more than one sense, then, most of them may be considered peripheral peoples, reduced to subjection or dependency, whether the larger system surrounding them is mainly feudal or corporate-capitalist.

Some indigenous peoples are more peripheral than others, both geographically and culturally. In this paper I will discuss human rights and indigenous peoples in general, but with particular reference to one such people, probably the largest forest-dwelling indigenous people in South America: the Yanomami, a people whose survival is now in acute jeopardy.

The Yanomami (or Yanoama, or Yanomamo, etc.) probably number at least 8,000 in the State of Amazonas and the Federal Territory of Roraima in Brazil, near the border of Venezuela to the North, and another 10,000–14,000 in Venezuela. As technology, mobility, and population pressure have kept expanding economic activities and explorations in both countries, and missionary penetration as well, the Yanomami in both countries have in recent decades increasingly been victimized by intruders of many kinds, and menaced by powerful mining interests. Meanwhile, supporters of indigenous peoples in general, or of the Yanomami in particular, both in Brazil and Venezuela and abroad, have fought an uphill series of battles to achieve some protection for the Yanomami before it is irretrievably too late.

Good news from these battles ha[s] been scarce. Yet on March 9, 1982, what seemed like very good news—although it basically only meant recognizing the rights of the Yanomami—was announced. Brazil's Minister of State of the

Christian Bay, "Human Rights on the Periphery: No Room in the Ark for the Yanomami?" *Development Dialogue* 1–2 (1984): 23–41. Reprinted by permission the journal of the Dag Hammarskjöld Foundation.

Interior, Sr. Maria David Andreazza, on that date announced a plan to "interdict" a large continuous area, in fact some 7.7 million hectares, for the Yanomami, for "the preservation of their cultural patrimony." There was also mention of more extensive measures of support, to be administered by FUNAI (the National Foundation for the Indians) for their health, education and community development.

This implied promise is still on the books of Brazilian law; to this extent the Brazilian Yanomami are more fortunate than their Venezuelan cousins, who have no similar kind of theoretical protection for their supporters to refer to. But in Brazil there is still no definitive decree that would establish the promised park, let alone protect the lands from intruders. According to a recent (March 1983) estimate by Claudia Andujar, a leading Brazilian supporter of the Yanomami, there were at that time some 4,000 prospectors roaming around in what was supposed to be Yanomami territory.

To make matters worse, and indeed critical, it would seem, on November 10, 1983, a Presidential Decree was issued in Brasilia, to the effect that, in consultation with FUNAI, the National Department of Mineral Production will henceforth be granting mining concessions in Indian lands, when "necessary to the national security and national development," and perhaps to private corporations as well ("in exceptional cases"). Friends of Brazil's indigenous peoples were appalled, and protests came from many individuals and organizations, both Brazilian and foreign. The then Director of FUNAI, after extensive consultations, in the end exercised his legal veto, by way of refusing to countersign President Figueiredo's decree; whereupon the President dismissed the Director and appointed a new and perhaps a more pliable successor to the post. It remains to be seen whether it is still possible to reverse this catastrophic policy, which has made the prospects for the survival of Brazil's Yanomami bleaker than ever. . . .

In this paper I cannot address the pressing practical issue of what can and must be done to influence the governments of the two nations, both (and especially Brazil) laboring under heavy pressures of external debts, to find honorable, practical and immediate ways to protect the survival prospects of the Yanomami. This struggle

must be led from inside each country. I will attempt something else: to make the case that the Yanomami's cause represents the most urgent category of all present day human rights issues anywhere in the world, since not only individual lives but the lives of whole peoples are almost immediately at stake. The specific issue is whether we can tolerate the prospects of a "final solution" for the Yanomami. This is the moral issue. There is also the large existential issue: is a world without surviving indigenous peoples fit for survival for the rest of us? . . .

"Human rights" surely must mean the rights of all humans, and it may at first seem awkward to speak of the human rights of indigenous peoples. But I shall argue that survival is the most basic of all human rights, and that the menace to survival, even collective survival, is particularly extreme in the case of the Yanomami and other largely unacculturated indigenous peoples.

To pursue this argument I must first explicate my conception of human rights, and of the basis for the "natural" priorities that I find among categories of human rights. Next I develop my substantive case for insisting on the highest priority, as a human rights issue, for adequate protection of vulnerable peoples like the Yanomami against the mounting pressures that will soon destroy them, unless present trends can be reversed. In conclusion, I go beyond the human rights argument to develop not only moral but practical grounds for the urgent need to defend vulnerable peoples who live close to nature. Our own civilization has for too long proceeded to pursue the "conquest of nature" in heedless disregard for nature's limits; and it is time to confront and resist on a broad front the abuses of modern technology and the exploitive interests that these abuses serve. While for myself the moral grounds for defending indigenous rights come first, I mean to show that a viable future for our own "developed" nations and peoples requires a viable future for the indigenous peoples also, for their right to determine their own cultural development, and above all for their self-preservation.

Extrapolating from Maurice Cranston's classical discussion,[1] I shall assume that human rights are moral rights that are (1) universal, (2) paramount, and (3) practical. But I shall add two more definitional criteria, (4) human rights are entitlements that should (must) become incor-

---

1. Maurice Cranston, *What Are Human Rights?* (London: Bodley Head, 1973), 4–7, 21–4, 66–7.

porated in positive national and international law, as fully and as soon as possible; and (5) human rights cannot all be equally paramount: the ranking of relative urgency among categories of human rights must depend on (a) how basic is the level of *human need* which requires the enforcement of that right, and (b) how clearly and directly does a particular right bear on, and facilitate the meeting of, that kind of need? . . .

The conventional liberal wisdom asserts that the state exists for the sake of man, not man for the sake of the state. I mean to select and articulate a more precise interpretation of that affirmation: the highest-priority task of any legitimate state is to ensure, so far as possible, that all (universal) human needs are being met, with the *more* basic or urgent needs taking precedence over those that are less basic or less urgent. "Human needs" is in principle an empirical concept, but on a high level of abstraction. I shall take the term to refer to any and all requirements for (1) human survival, (2) physical security, health protection, (3) dignity, mental health, and (4) freedom—that is, individual and collective freedom of choice, within the social constraint stipulating that choices are entitled to protection only to the extent that they do not jeopardize the survival, health, dignity, or equally basic freedoms of choice for others.

To facilitate the needed cooperation between social scientists and political and legal professionals it is necessary to switch from needs-language to rights-language. My position is that the universal and supreme task for legitimate politics and law (legislation, administration, and adjudication) is to struggle for a world of secure human rights for all, with the more basic human rights taking precedence over those less basic.

Why are priorities among human rights required? Because some categories of needs *are* more important than others: say, the need for protection against torture compared to the need for vacations with pay.

Already in my definition of "human needs" I have suggested what I take to be the right order of priorities among human rights categories: survival rights must come first; then the right to protection from physical injury and disease; then the right to dignity, identity, conditions compatible with mental health; and finally, freedom rights, rights to individual choice and free development, within the limits of social constraints.

Why *these* priorities? Elsewhere I have argued that the top priority for survival rights, followed by those that protect our health and safety, is a matter of elementary common sense, in the realm of politics and law as it is in medicine. I concede that to attribute priority to dignity and related social rights over freedom rights is no longer a matter of common sense, especially in liberal-thinking societies; but this perspective has prevailed in the idealist mainstreams of philosophy from Plato to Hegel, and is today shared by Marxism and humanist psychology. Only the liberal-individualist philosophy that originated with Hobbes and Locke dissents, and constructs society on the basis of atomized, essentially unchanging, contractually oriented rather than socially rooted, individualists. . . .

Human rights are by definition universal, I have asserted. Does it still make sense to speak of *indigenous* human rights? I think it does. . . .

Not because they are indigenous peoples, but because they are human beings with indigenous cultures, and with unique ways of being human, should their defense and protection be a matter of the highest-priority concern for all people the world over who care about human rights, and for the media that undertake to keep us informed about international news.

Human rights are the rights of individual human beings everywhere. Does it nonetheless make sense to speak of *collective* human rights for indigenous peoples? I shall argue that it does, and also that these collective human rights must be distinguished sharply from corporate rights, which may be legal rights but cannot be human rights.

Every individual's survival is at stake when the destruction of a people is in progress. Likewise, every individual's health and dignity are at stake when ethnocide, the destruction of a human culture, is in progress, by way of destroying the natural habitat or the religious faith or the needed privacy of an indigenous people, for purposes of imposed "development," commercial exploitation, or "civilizing" religious instruction and conversion. Forced acculturation is declared public policy today in several Latin American countries: even the more humane statutes, comparatively speaking, assert that "integration" is the ultimate purpose of the state. In other words, the aim is the forced abandonment and destruction of ethnic and cultural identities, along with the "freedom" to compete for individual survival in the jungles of the city slums. This is not as bloody as outright genocide, but the result is the same: the extinction of yet another culturally distinct people. Ethnocide is like genocide on the installment plan.

Short of omnicide, the killing of all human beings, which today can be and possibly will be accomplished with a nuclear world war, I shall assume that outright genocide must be considered the ultimate crime against humanity. This is not only because we must consider it a worse crime to kill many persons than it is to kill one. With genocide, you kill the future, too, with all the aspirations, hopes, dreams, and insights that countless generations have built up, within a given culture. To face individual death is one thing; to face death for all your kin and for all that you care for is a horror of an entirely different magnitude.

Short of omnicide and short of genocide, ethnocide is also a monstrous crime, as it destroys the cultural dignity and identity of all members of a people, and very likely destroys their mental and physical health as well, as well as their unique world views and traditional knowledge, and it often terminates their ability or motivation to reproduce their own kind. The story has been repeated over and over again on the many "frontiers of development," in South America and elsewhere: once proud, self-reliant peoples have been reduced to a state of dependency on handouts and on alcohol and other drugs, with many men becoming beggars and many women prostitutes, and all becoming available for cheap labor under conditions approximating slavery. . . .

Can a collective human right to protection against ethnocide be in conflict with individual human rights to cultural choice? Do tribal elders, for example, have a moral right to forcibly prevent young members of their tribes from seeking outside contacts, or from moving away?

Undoubtedly, such conflicts frequently develop, and in principle I think the individual's right to choose how and where to live must prevail. But this requires that the choice must be possible—that a life within one's traditional community is still viable. If conditions of ethnocidal forced contact prevail, perhaps with the destruction of a people's means of subsistence to compound the crime, then neither the older traditionalists nor the younger members of a given community will have retained their most basic

right to choose, or preserve, a life with dignity among their own people.

Do indigenous individuals have a human right to reject certain traditional customs that they have come to find unacceptable, perhaps as a result of outside influence—for example, clitorectomy, as is still practiced in some African and Arab cultures, or infanticide? I should think yes, and perhaps even that they have a moral right to seek outside protection against such acts of violence if the community is effectively under a national jurisdiction for many other purposes; but I must stress that this poses an urgent challenge to anthropologists in collaboration with indigenous informants to account for the functions that such customs may have served, so that the possible damage from violations of traditions can be minimized.

There are many intricate theoretical issues involved in the analysis of human rights in the context of external threats to collective survival, once we take the position that genocide and ethnocide violate the most basic individual *and* collective human rights. Individuals singly *and* collectively have first of all a human right to life, to health, to dignity, and to freedom; as is well known in our society, too, individuals may suffer internal conflict, in that they may want to obey both personal inclinations and social responsibilities, even when the two would dictate opposite responses. People with such dilemmas may under some circumstances legitimately be ever so tenderly pushed, I should think, toward making the social choice. Perhaps elders in a community in danger of destruction are entitled to exert *some* pressure against youngsters taking off on their own, tempted by the anticipated glitter of far-away cities, in their perhaps media-influenced imagination.

But such pressures must stop short of physical violence, and cannot legitimately be continued for more than a couple of years past reaching adulthood, in my view; or for more than a couple of years past initial contact with outsiders. It is proclaimed in the Universal Declaration of Human Rights[2] that everyone "has the right to leave any country" (Article 13, 2); that must mean any reservation, or tribal territory, as well. However, I think this stipulation may be interpreted a bit more loosely in situations where an immediate choice to abandon a culture or a hab-

2. [See the Appendix.]

itat could contribute to foreclosing the opportunity to make the opposite choice even only a few years later.

The same Article also affirms everyone's right to "freedom of movement within the borders of each state" (Article 13, 1). This is not to be understood as an unrestricted freedom, however. It is in fact restricted by private property rights. In many countries landowners have a right to forbid anyone access to or across their territories.

A more reasonable arrangement obtains in other countries, including the Scandinavian, where landowners have no right to bar innocent passage or harmless recreation on their lands, excepting private gardens and fields under cultivation during the growing season. The right to move about freely is deemed more important than the right to block passage (neither can other innocent uses be blocked, such as picking wild berries or common wildflowers). In countries with endangered indigenous populations, on the other hand, there should be strict enforcement of a total ban on passage through their territories, except by invitations issued at *their* initiative.

Eventually, I believe, most of the now isolated or semi-isolated indigenous peoples will choose to integrate in some ways and to a degree with the larger society. But adequate time must be allowed for each people to make that choice and to determine freely how it will adjust, if that is the choice, in order to come to terms with life in the larger society. Prematurely enforced contacts again and again have destroyed, culturally and often physically also, vulnerable communities and the people whose roots were within them.

One final theoretical problem must be touched on: since human rights by definition are universal, in the sense of being in principle generalizable to all human beings, would it not be contradictory to speak of indigenous claims to extensive traditional lands as a category of human rights? This would indeed be contradictory. Claims to large land areas, whether individual or collective, cannot be validated as a human right. But for indigenous forest-dwelling peoples like the Yanomami, these claims should nonetheless be given the status of a legal right as well as a moral right, for these principal reasons:

1. Indigenous peoples have a moral right to keep all the lands that they need for their survival as peoples, at least for as long as they choose to support themselves in the traditional ways.

2. They have a human right to the means necessary to their survival.
3. They have a human right to exactly the same respect and legal protection for *their* property rights as any member of the larger society has for his or her property rights.

Moreover, as we shall see, there is much evidence that the indigenous peoples, for example in the Amazon Basin, have preserved their habitats as good custodians, while the people and interests that have driven so many of them out have been creating deserts where there were once healthy forests. But, whatever the force of this last justification for granting to indigenous peoples permanent title to their lands, this is a utilitarian justification, not a moral one rooted in their basic human needs, which is the end that, by my definition, human rights must serve.

One question remains: is it at all realistic today to engage in strenuous efforts to try to save the remaining, relatively unacculturated and unsubjugated, indigenous peoples from their destruction, in countries where they still exist? Or, as many would have us believe, is it impossible, too late, futile?

When conceived as a *general* principle there is in our civilization a wide agreement, I think, in support of the idea that all branches of the human family are equally human, and equally deserving of protection for their basic human rights; which means *more* deserving of assistance the more extreme their plight. Our mass media find it easier, to be sure, to empathize with well-known individual victims of human rights violations, for example with admirable persons like a Sakharov or a Walesa, but in my view a rational humanist must be even more deeply concerned when whole peoples are threatened with destruction. An analogy between politics and medicine may be useful: the medical staff in a good hospital do not worry equally about the health of every patient; instead, they provide for special care for those whose lives and health are in immediate or extreme danger.

The Kantian humanist premise is universal: each human life is to be treated as an end, never as a means. But are we today perhaps up against harsh historical realities that make the sanctity of human life a mere pipedream? Is the earth becoming too crowded, for one thing, to make universal human rights feasible; should we instead be struggling for the rights of Englishmen, or of Americans, or Canadians, or Latin Americans?

Garrett Hardin, the well-known Californian biologist, appears to think so: "Cherishing individual lives in the short run diminishes the number of lives in the long run . . . *the concept of the sanctity of life is counterproductive.* To achieve its goal the concept of the sanctity of life must give precedence to the concept of the sanctity of carrying capacity."[3] We must curtail food aid to Third World countries, Hardin has argued, unless they, or some of them, demonstrate that they can limit the growth of their populations. Otherwise, U. S. aid programs will lead to more mouths to feed, and over the coming decades the earth's soil and food resources will become progressively less and less adequate to feed the burgeoning Third World populations.[4]

As I have argued elsewhere, Hardin is right on one point: if we take for granted, as he does, the "Free World's" almost limitless freedom for individuals and corporations to engage in the accumulation of private wealth, by way of helping themselves to natural resources, and dumping their wastes, then we will indeed soon be approaching the limits to the earth's carrying capacity, and rising populations in any part of the world will speed us along on our perilous course. But we are not yet anywhere near the end of available food resources, and I find it utterly obscene to advocate cutting famine relief to the most needy peoples today, instead of trying to do something about our world's present maldistribution and waste (including the stupendous military waste of human and natural resources). Moreover, with increasing social welfare, as has been demonstrated in many parts of the world, birth rates soon tend to go down. However, Hardin is evidently a dogmatic liberal, for he chooses to recommend the sacrifice of the most basic human rights in much of the Third World for the convenience of affluent North Americans, whose present system of private-corporate enterprise is to be preserved, he insists, whatever the cost to other, relatively poor and powerless nations.

Let me pursue this issue one step further. While Hardin's argument about ecological limits

is valid and important as a long-term projection, he is radically wrong, I have concluded, about our immediate situation, and his proposed inhumane policies are unnecessary. But suppose that his stark diagnosis in truth had applied to our present situation; might it not then have been necessary to seize sparsely populated indigenous lands, at the cost of genocide, in order to help meet the nutritional requirements of more numerous populations?

Even in such a desperate, fortunately hypothetical situation, the case for seizing indigenous lands, especially in the Amazon Basin, would be very weak, as it turns out, for the ecological system that supports the rain forests turns out to be very fragile. There is mounting evidence that the soil and climatic conditions have radically deteriorated in the large areas of Brazilian rain forests that have already been turned over to ranch and pasture lands (for the principal purpose of exporting beef to First World markets). While the indigenous peoples of the Amazon have lived for thousands of years in harmony with nature, the European invaders' civilization, and especially with the use of our present-day technologies (agricultural, road-building, manufacturing and mining technologies), has produced not only rather empty savannahs where there had been forests teeming with life, but as well has produced large areas of almost lifeless deserts. . . .

Must the Amerindians of South America disappear? If their basic human rights do not impress the governments in this part of the world as important enough to stem the tide of ethnocide and genocide, can the same authorities now be made to see that they *need* these peoples to continue to protect their traditional lands from destruction? . . .

Of all the forces that the indigenous peoples of the Americas are up against, the constantly repeated and reaffirmed assumption, apparently shared by friend and foe and by the indifferent alike, to the effect that they are *doomed to disappear*, represents possibly the most intractable aspect of the massive menace to their future. It could become, even up to "the final solution" for

3. Garrett Hardin, "An Ecolate View of the Human Predicament," in *Global Resources: Perspectives and Alternatives*, ed. Clair N. McRostie (Baltimore: University Park Press, 1980), 49–71, at 57. (Hardin's italics.)

4. See Hardin, "Lifeboat Ethics: The Case Against Helping the Poor," *Psychology Today* 8 (Sept. 1974): 38–43, 123–26. Also see his excellent and important essay, "The Tragedy of the Commons," in his *Exploring New Ethics for Survival: The Voyage of the Spaceship Beagle* (Baltimore: Penguin, 1973), 250–64 (first published in 1968).

the last of the remaining native peoples, a cumulatively self-fulfilling prophecy.

The view that man's calling is to dominate nature, using the increasingly powerful tools of modern science and technology, has firm foundations in Western social and political thought of the last several centuries. "Only let the human race recover that right over nature which belongs to it by divine bequest," wrote Francis Bacon at the beginning of the seventeenth century, "and let power be given it; the exercise thereof will be governed by sound reason and true religion."[5] With the notable exception of Rousseau, the French Enlightenment embraced this faith in modern science and this view of Nature as the principal adversary, destined to be subjugated for the good of Mankind; and subsequent generations of liberals as well as Marxists have been following this lead. . . .

In truth there is a massive war going on today between technology and nature, and nature keeps on losing ground. This means that the human species keeps on losing ground, too, for we are rooted in nature and are a part of nature, even if most of us are no longer as directly embedded in nature and are not as immediately vulnerable as the still surviving, still relatively unsubjugated peoples, peoples like the Yanomami, who have lived in and have cared so well for their forest habitats for so many centuries. In sharp contrast with the commercial exploiters of our own civilization, the Yanomami have been responsible trustees of nature, for their own future generations, and have known how to keep their own numbers limited. Are they now to be denied a future?

We desperately need to call a halt to our civilization's continuing war against nature, or the whole human species will lose irretrievably. And the lines of defense must include and accentuate the battle for survival for the remaining largely unacculturated peoples, like those of the Amazon Basin. If they are destroyed, chances are that the rest of us will share their fate, without a very long respite, even if we are fortunate enough to avoid nuclear war. Pat Roy Mooney has shown, for example, that our civilization's increasingly artificial agriculture (i.e., it has come to depend on increasingly gene-standardized, high-yield crops of wheat, rice, corn, etc., which are increasingly vulnerable to blights on a catastrophic scale) now acutely endangers the future nutrition of billions, and he calls for international emergency measures to retrieve and protect the earth's rapidly dwindling diversity of germ plasm from plants on the growing Endangered Species lists, and especially from the natural relatives and ancestors to our principal foodcrop-producing plants.[6] In this way, too, we have at our peril kept turning our back on nature. An anonymous North American Indian has formulated this warning to us all, but with particular address to our industrial, scientific, and technological establishments! "When you have polluted the last river, when you have caught the very last fish, and when you have cut down the very last tree, it is too bad that then, and only then, will you realize that you cannot eat all your money in the bank."

QUESTIONS FOR REFLECTION AND DISCUSSION

1. The Yanomami in Brazil and Venezuela are of course not the only indigenous peoples threatened today. Others include the Miskitos in Nicaragua, the Kurds and Baluchis in Iran and Iraq, the Tamils in Sri Lanka, the Basques in Spain, and the Native Americans in the United States and Canada. Do such peoples have a right to self-determination? If so, what is the nature of that right? What responsibilities to ensure what measure of self-determination should be imposed upon national and provincial governments? Does or should your answers to these questions depend on whether the group is organized in such a way as to make it possible for their demands for self-determination to be effectively heard? Should some measure of self-determination be granted even when there is no armed struggle or threat of secession? If so, what kind or kinds?

2. When important business interests and "maximum growth" developmental policies

5. Quoted by William Leiss from Francis Bacon's *The New Organon.* See Leiss, *The Domination of Nature* (New York: Braziller, 1972), 50.
6. Pat Roy Mooney, "The Law of the Seed," *Development Dialogue* (Uppsala, Sweden: Dag Hammarskjöld Foundation, 1983), 1–2.

come into conflict with indigenous or other group rights, how is the conflict to be resolved? Do you agree that business firms should be expected to promote human rights? If so, according to what standards, how, and to what extent? Or do you believe that there is an unavoidable and irreconcilable conflict between the profit motive and the promotion of human rights? Do long-term nonmonetary gains compensate for possible short-term financial losses when promoting human rights?

3. If one were to conclude that the Yanomami and similarly situated groups are entitled to be left alone, would this imply that they would have no right to demand of national and provincial governments the affirmative use of economic and other resources to assist them in attaining higher levels of physical and material well-being? What if inaction might lead to the group's destruction?

4. Is it wise to place all responsibility for the protection of indigenous peoples on national governments? If so, what happens when there are not sufficient national resources to ensure the well-being of such peoples? Is it not then the responsibility of international institutions to step in? If so, how is such responsibility to be met without encroaching upon the prerogatives of state sovereignty?

5. To what degree should relationships between long-established colonizers and indigenous peoples be described as official racism? If discriminatory policies are extreme or if the degree of stigma associated with membership in the subordinated subculture is significant, does this not constitute a form of racism? What practical result might be gained for the Yanomami to describe Brazilian or Venezuelan governmental activity as racist?

6. Some writers describe the evolution of stereotypes between colonizer and colonized as a cycle of misunderstandings, communication breakdowns, and conflicts that arise when emotional images or habitual thinking becomes a substitute for knowledge. Consider the following account of the Dorobo by Andreas Fuglesang in ''The Myth of People's Ignorance'' (*Development Dialogue* 1–2 [1984]: 60–61 [footnotes omitted]):

> The Dorobo [of East Africa] are scattergroups comprised of persons dispersed by war, famine or natural disasters. They eke out a living on the periphery of the larger tribal societies, assimilating the language of their closest tribal neighbour. Of interest here is the image the settled farmers or the herders have developed of the Dorobo. Since the Dorobo do not farm or herd, their humanity is held in question by those who do. For the Masai, a Dorobo means a poor man because he does not own cattle; for the Kikuyu, because he does not own land. In the eyes of men, the Dorobo are women-like. In the eyes of the guardians of tribal morale, they are practisers [*sic*] of witch craft [*sic*]. In the eyes of the tribal establishment, they are considered devious, unreliable and conniving, as well as generally ignorant.
>
> The litany of traits ascribed to the Dorobo is common to the folklore of social outcasts in cultures the world over. The names of these subterranean creatures may vary—sirens, gnomes or trolls are but a few examples—but they belong to the no-man's-land between human beings and gods, devils and spirits.
>
> Evidently all societies have their barbarians, savages, poor people, workers . . . , or Dorobo. Whatever constitutes the responsible, moral, orderly, normal, progressive, knowledgeable and well-dressed citizen in a given society, these people are its opposite. Our world view is stuck in a dichotomy. Conceptually, it is a negative film without which we cannot process as positive image of ourselves.

''How,'' Fuglesang asks, ''are we to change this attitude and linguistic habit that so viciously labels other peoples as ignorant? Isn't the term ignorance just one culture's judgement on the knowledge of another culture?''

SELECT BIBLIOGRAPHY

Aga Khan, Sadruddin. *Study on Human Rights and Massive Exoduses.* UN Commission on Human Rights, 38th sess., 1981. Useful analysis of ''push factors,'' such as political upheaval, and ''pull factors,'' such as economic incentives, that often result in large-scale human rights violations, including those of refugees.

Bennett, Gordon. *Aboriginal Rights in International Law*. London: Royal Anthropological Institute of Great Britain and Survival International (Ireland), 1978. An analysis of the rights to which aboriginal peoples are entitled under current international law, and a critical evaluation of the prospects for successfully enforcing those rights.

Claude, Richard P., and Thomas Jabine, eds. "Statistical Issues in Human Rights" (Symposium). *Human Rights Quarterly* 8, no. 4 (1986). A technical assessment of the limits, uses and opportunities for improvement in the uses of statistics to report, analyze, and compare human rights internationally, with special reference to civil and political rights.

Commonwealth Group of Eminent Persons. *Mission to South Africa*. London: Penguin, 1986. A candid, unflattering statement of the wretched conditions of daily life faced by most South Africans. Also contains a description of the intransigence of the apartheid regime, its much vaunted reforms notwithstanding.

Fein, Helen. *Accounting for Genocide*. New York: The Free Press, 1979. An historical and sociological effort to explain the atrocious fact that, by 1945, two of every three Jews who had lived in Europe were dead.

Flanz, G. H. *Comparative Women's Rights and Political Participation in Europe*. Dobbs Ferry, N.Y.: Transnational Publishers, 1983. A multidisciplinary, country-by-country study of the sociopolitical status of women in all thirty-four European countries. In addition, traces a variety of women's political movements in Europe and includes an assessment of the United Nations Decade for Women (1976–1986).

Franck, Thomas M. *Human Rights in the Third World*. 3 vols. Dobbs Ferry, N.Y.: Oceana Publications, 1982. Documents and cases drawn from Third World experiences in constitution-drafting and decision-making regarding fair trial rights and equal protection, with materials on the effects of modernization of law on customary law.

Henkin, Louis, ed. *The International Bill of Rights: The Covenant on Civil and Political Rights*. New York: Columbia University Press, 1981. An authoritative guide to the provisions of the covenant. Topics include a description of the covenant as well as an examination of its meaning and interpretation.

Hevener, Natalie Kaufman. *International Law and the Status of Women*. Boulder, Colo.: Westview Press, 1983. A thorough documentary compilation of international norms on the status of women and data on the ratification of the relevant conventions on women's rights. Includes interpretive commentary.

Lillich, Richard B. *The Human Rights of Aliens*. Manchester: Manchester University Press, 1984. Pieces together the elements of a new body of international law bearing on the rights of aliens; also advances the thesis that the traditional authority of states over aliens has been eroded, insofar as international law previously tolerated abuses.

McKean, W. *Equality and Discrimination under International Law*. Oxford: Clarendon Press, 1983. Analyzes the principles involved in standards of equality as they are specified in international declarations and conventions. Also includes references to relevant judicial decisions.

Ramcharan, B. G., ed. *The Right to Life in International Law*. The Hague: Martinus Nijhoff Publishers, 1985. Legal scholars examine multiple aspects of the right to life and survival requirements, including the rights to development and peace, and international standards on genocide, arbitrary killing, and capital punishment.

Rodley, Nigel R. *The Treatment of Prisoners under International Law*. Oxford: Clarendon Press, 1986. Describes and examines the principles of international law that impose limits on governmental treatment of individuals deprived of their liberty.

Santa Cruz, Hernan. *Racial Discrimination*. rev. ed. New York: United Nations, 1977. A careful, comprehensive study of racial discrimination in the political, economic, social, and cultural spheres. This study was completed by a special rapporteur of the Sub-Commission on Prevention of Discrimination and Protection of Minorities.

"Security of the Person and Security of the State: Human Rights and Claims of National Security" (Symposium). *Yale Journal of World Public Order* 9 (Fall 1982). Analysis of how "national security" is used to derogate basic personal rights, with the U.S. Constitution and European human rights law as the backdrop.

Stover, Eric, and Elena O. Nightingale, eds. *The Breaking of Bodies and Minds: Torture, Psychiatric Abuse and the Health Professions*. New York: W. H. Freeman, 1985. An analysis of medical ethics and international human rights, with case studies from Chile, Paraguay, and the Soviet Union that illustrate the use for political purposes and abuse of health professionals by repressive regimes.

Swidler, Leonard, ed. *Religious Liberty and Human Rights*. Philadelphia: Temple University; Ecumenical

Press; New York: Hippocrene Books, Inc., 1986. Education for religious liberty, toleration and understanding is surveyed in six nations and among five major world religions.

Van Dyke, Vernon. *Human Rights, Ethnicity and Discrimination*. Westport, Conn.: Greenwood Press, 1985. A highly readable introduction to global problems of racial, linguistic, and religious discrimination; includes an analysis of the invidious treatment of indigenous peoples.

SELECT FILMOGRAPHY

Cambodia: Year Zero. American Friends Service Committee, producer. 1979. 60 min. color. The incredible story of Cambodia from 1975 to 1979. The brutality of the Pol Pot years is starkly portrayed, but within a sound historical and political context.

An Evening of Forbidden Books. PEN American Center, producer. U.S.A.: PEN, 1982. 60 min., b/w; VHS, 3/4-in. videotape. Selected readings by well-known authors from "forbidden books," those not allowed to be used or distributed in the United States at various times in recent history; includes a short history of book banning in America presented by Nat Hentoff.

Eyes of the Birds. Gabriel Auer, producer. France: Facets, 1982. 80 min., color, French (English subtitles); 16 mm. Dramatization of an International Red Cross delegation's visit to Libertad Prison in Uruguay, a so-called model prison in which the delegation discovers the effects of physical and psychological torture on prisoners.

The Forgotten Genocide. Michael Hagopian, producer. U.S.A.: Atlantic, 1976. 28 min., color; 16 mm. Story of the genocide of the Armenian people in 1915, with the intent of showing that such events do occur and threaten all humanity.

The Hooded Men. Canadian Broadcasting Corporation, producer. Canada: Facets, 1982. 60 min., color; 3/4 in., Beta, VHS videotape. Documentary examining torture in many countries, including Argentina, Nicaragua (pre-1981), Northern Ireland, and South Africa, through the eyes of a sensory deprivation researcher and former torturers and torture victims.

The Killing Fields. Roland Joffe, producer. U.S.A.: WHV, 1984. 142 min., color; Beta and VHS videotape. An uncompromising film about two men who find themselves caught up in the Khmer Rouge revolution in Cambodia. Based on a true story and starring Sam Waterston and Haing S. Ngor, the film presents a vivid portrait of modern-day genocide.

Land of Fear, Land of Courage. NBC News, producer. U.S.A.: CC Films, 1983. 60 min., color; videotape. Documentary filmed in South Africa, featuring Bishop Desmond Tutu, leader of the nonviolent struggle against apartheid, who discusses the time bomb of racial politics and the fears on both sides of the color-bar. Narrated by Edwin Newman.

The Migrants. Films, Inc., 1980. 52 min., color. Documents the plight of America's itinerant farm workers, which has improved very little since 1970.

Missing. Costa-Gavras, producer. U.S.A.: MCA, 1982. 122 min., color; Beta and VHS videotape. A young American journalist mysteriously disappears during a violent military coup in a South American country. When his wife (Sissy Spacek) and father (Jack Lemmon) attempt to find him, they are confronted with a deeply disturbing political discovery, the horrifying reality of the "disappeared." A 1982 Cannes Film Festival Award winner.

Prisoners of Conscience. Noel Fox, producer. U.K. Facets/Cinema Guild, 1980. 30 min., color; 16 mm. Film that illustrates the work of the human rights organization Amnesty International by tracing its efforts to achieve the release of two prisoners, a Russian and an Argentine. Follows the group's actions from the London research department to an adoption group working to obtain the prisoners' freedom.

Prisoner Without a Name, Cell Without a Number. Linda Yellin, producer. U.S.A.: Yellin, 1983. 100 min., color; videotape. Dramatization of the story of Jacobo Timerman, exiled Argentine newspaper editor, who was imprisoned and tortured by the military regime for being Jewish and for publishing editorials asking for an account of the "disappeared" in Argentina.

South Africa Belongs to Us. C. Austin, P. Chappell, and R. Weiss, producers. U.S.A.: Icarus/So. Africa Media/Ecufilm/Michigan Media, 1980. 57 min., color; 16 mm, videotape. Portrait of five Black women in South Africa, depicting their struggle for human dignity in the face of apartheid, for homes and food for their children, and for the liberation of the Black people; an in-depth focus on the economic and emotional burdens borne by Black women in South Africa.

Torture Victims Speak. Amnesty International/USA, producer. U.S.A.: Facets, 1984. 30 min., color; videotape. Three victims of torture—Alicia Portnoy of Argentina, Lee Shin-Bom of South Korea, and Reverend Simon Farisani of South Africa—speak of their experiences in this videotape produced at the Amnesty International/USA June 1984 meeting.

What Right Has a Child. United Nations, producer. Univ IL Films, 1968. 15 min., color; 16 mm. Classic film of children's art from around the world, with commentary by children talking about the Universal Declaration of Rights of the Child.

Your Neighbor's Son. J. F. Pederson and E. Stephensen, producers. Denmark: Facets, 1976. 55 min., color, Greek (English subtitles); 16 mm. Documents the training of Greek torturers under the military junta of the late 1960s. Dramatic reenactments are combined with interviews with former torturers, who recall their transformation from innocent recruits into merciless torturers, as well as with the testimony of victims and their families.

Z. Costa-Gavras, producer. U.S.A.: RCA-COL, 1969. 128 min., color; Beta and VHS videotape. An Oscar-winning foreign film based on actual events of political repression during the time of the Greek junta in the late 1960s. Reveals details of the political assassination of a deputy, ''Z,'' and the shocking aftermath of the crime. Stars Yves Montand, Irene Papas, and Jean-Louis Trintignant.

Chapter Three

Basic Human Needs, Security Rights, and Humane Governance

IN this chapter, we turn to a set of values—basic human needs, security rights, and humane governance—that concerns the right of individuals and groups to expect that governments, through domestic and international policy, will do something affirmative to bring about the realization of those values. In contrast to the preceding chapter, in which we were concerned with human rights conceived mainly in terms of the abstention of government ("freedoms from"), here we are concerned with human rights conceived mainly in terms of the intervention of government ("rights to").

Basic human needs encompass those "social goods" that are essential to human subsistence, for example, food, clothing, housing, medical care, and schooling. Public policies that affect these are critically important. Basic human needs imply the duty of governments to satisfy the welfare requirements involved, taking into account the constraints of limited resources and the vagaries of natural disasters such as droughts and floods.

Security rights refer to the rights of individuals and groups to enjoy reasonably reliable prospects of survival, for example, police protection and cultural preservation. They also refer to everyone's (including the unborn generations') need for a sustainable ecological balance, for self-determination, and for world peace.

Richard Falk has proposed the term *humane governance* in his call for a world order that can achieve essential human rights by transforming the political order as it now exists. His objective is to stimulate debate for the purpose of extending the boundaries of human rights beyond those set by the state system, with its operative code of sovereignty that narrows attention to carefully depicted national territorial limits.[1] Implicit in Article 28 of the Universal Declaration of Human Rights,[2] which proclaims that "[e]veryone is entitled to a social and international order in which the rights and freedoms set forth in this Declaration can be fully realized," humane governance refers to the right of individuals and groups to live in societies that realize or conscientiously attempt to realize the overarching values that inform this chapter. The term also draws attention to the duty of individuals, groups, governments, and institutions to assist the realization of these values both individually and cooperatively.

Of course, in our multicultural world the precise meaning of humane governance necessarily varies from country to country. The definition and enjoyment of human rights is directly related to the socioeconomic and political character of the societies in which they are exercised. The industrialized democracies of the "First World," for example, tend to stress the civil and political rights that serve their individualistic social orders. Socialist systems of the "Second World" seek a collectivist approach to human rights consonant with Marxist philosophy. The "Third World" of developing countries, which display a mix of ideological preferences and stages of economic growth (the oil-producing countries in contrast with, for example, impoverished Bangladesh or Chad), often demand greater attention to economic, social, and cultural rights, with an emphasis on group rights or "peoples' rights."

1. Richard A. Falk, *Human Rights and State Sovereignty* (New York: Holmes and Meier Publishers, 1981), 180–3.
2. See the Appendix.

One must understand, however, that these various categories of rights, while distinct, often display significant overlap and connection. For example, freedom of speech, perhaps the ultimate symbol of individualism, necessarily takes place in a group or social setting. The collective right to social and economic development is meaningless if it does not embody education rights for individuals. A people's cultural identity is preserved only if individuals are protected in their customary practices. In other words, the commonplace suggestion that traditional civil liberties are individual rights and that socioeconomic and cultural rights are collective rights breaks down when one analyzes the content of human rights. Categorizing rights as individual or collective is a useful first step in understanding their scope, and distinguishing between rights that are associated with political liberty on the one hand and socioeconomic equality on the other reflects ideological preferences that are real and significant.[3] However, in an increasingly interdependent and interpenetrating global community, any human rights orientation that seeks widespread legitimacy but that fails to recognize the essential interrelatedness of all human rights is likely to provoke widespread skepticism.[4]

The interrelatedness of individual and collective rights and of political liberty and economic equality—perhaps nowhere so evident as in the debate over appropriate goals for modernization in Third World countries[5]—is depicted in the basic needs/human rights approach to balanced human development proposed by Johan Galtung and Anders Wirak,[6] partially extrapolated in Table 1. The approach assumes that the purpose of development is to enhance the lives of "men and women everywhere" rather than "things, systems, and structures"[7] and, to that end, to serve the humane values of security, welfare, freedom, and identity.

Projected onto the national plane, the Galtung-Wirak approach points to the duty of governments to respect fundamental civil and political rights (the principal focus of the

3. See Warren Zimmerman, "Comparing the U.S. and U.S.S.R. on Social and Economic Issues," speech before a plenary session of the Helsinki follow-up meeting of the Conference on Security and Cooperation in Europe, Vienna, Dec. 12, 1986 (Washington, D.C.: U.S. Department of State, Office of Public Communication, Current Policy No. 95, 1987).

4. The interrelatedness of human rights of all categories becomes especially evident to policymakers intent upon practical and programmatic efforts to design or implement human rights policies. For example, in 1984, despite its propensity to stress political over economic rights, the United States Agency for International Development (A.I.D.) under the Reagan administration found it necessary to issue a "policy determination" that "[t]he developmental side of human rights activities of A.I.D. is an expressed recognition of the U.S. understanding that civil and political rights cannot be separated from economic policies and economic development" (U.S. Agency for International Development, *Policy Determination on Human Rights No. 12, September 1984*, Sec. II [Washington, D.C.: U.S.A.I.D., 1984]). Of course, the A.I.D. program during the Reagan years sought Third World development through free market economic policies and had as its goal programs and activities that would enhance the promotion of civil and political rights. But whatever one may think of that perspective, the statement makes clear that, in a development context, the promotion of human rights is closely interconnected with economic policy. Not clear is whether the economic policy that fuels the engine of economic growth meets basic human needs.

5. See, e.g., George W. Shepherd, Jr., and Ved P. Nanda, eds., *Human Rights and Third World Development* (Westport, Conn.: Greenwood Press, 1986). See also Amy Young-Anawaty, "Human Rights and the ACP-EEC Lome II Convention: Business as Usual at the EEC," *New York University Journal of International Law* 13, no. 1 (1980): 63–98; J. P. Pronk, "Human Rights and Development Aid," *International Commission of Jurists Review* 18 (1977): 33–9; David M. Trubek, "When Is an Omelet? What is an Egg? Some Thoughts on Economic Development and Human Rights in Latin America," *American Journal of International Law* 67, no. 5 (1973): 198–205.

6. See Johan Galtung and Anders Helge Wirak, "Human Needs, Human Rights and the Theories of Development," in *Indicators of Social and Economic Change and Their Applications*, Reports and Papers in Social Science No. 37 (Paris: UNESCO, 1976), 7–34 (hereafter cited as "Human Needs, Human Rights"). See also Johan Galtung and Anders Helge Wirak, "Human Needs and Human Rights—A Theoretical Approach," *Bulletin of Peace Proposals* 8 (1977): 251–8 (hereafter cited as "Theoretical Approach").

7. Galtung and Wirak, "Human Needs, Human Rights," 2, 8.

TABLE 1
THE GALTUNG-WIRAK MODEL OF BASIC NEEDS AND HUMAN RIGHTS AND THE
CORRESPONDING GOVERNMENT DUTIES TO PROVIDE GOODS AND SERVICES

VALUES	NEEDS/RIGHTS	GOODS/SERVICES
Security	Individual: Against attack	Personal security
	Collective: Against war and group destruction	Peace Self-determination
Welfare		
Physiological	Individual and collective	Food, water
Ecological	Climatic	Clothing, housing
	Somatic	Medical treatment
	Collective	Clean environment
Sociocultural	Self-expression, dialogue, preservation of group values	Schooling Cultural preservation
Freedom		
Mobility	Right to travel	Transportation
Exchange	Right to exchange information	Communication
Politics	Right to participate, to choose, to mobilize	Elections, parties, assembly, and meetings
Legal work	Rights of due process	Courts
	Right to work	Jobs
Identity		
Relation to self (individual needs)	Need of self-expression, creativity	Leisure
	Need for self-actualization to realize personal potential	Vacation
	Need for sense of purpose	Religion, ideology, culture
Relation to others (collective needs)	Need for affection, love, sex	Primary groups
	Need for association and support from others	Secondary groups

preceding chapter) and to provide needed goods and services to all on the basis of equality (the principal focus of this chapter). The current debate as to whether capitalism or socialism or some combination of the two affords the most promising route to the fulfillment of this duty as a function of national governance is sometimes broadly characterized as a contest between freedom and bread, the debate focuses on the issue of whether choices between freedom and bread must be made with a consequent imbalance in overall human development.[8]

Projected onto the international plane, particularly in relation to Third World development, the Galtung-Wirak approach raises key questions about the prospects for a world order rooted in mutual respect for the needs and rights of everyone and about patterns of interstate cooperation designed to promote self-reliant socioeconomic development as a means of preserving identity values that, as Galtung has observed, are based on the needs of people in their own societies. "Self-reliance," he writes, "implies reliance on one's own resources."[9] In short, the Galtung-Wirak approach begs us to seek ways to harness global

8. The jury is still out on this issue, as is perhaps best demonstrated by the extensive political-economy literature on the topic. See, e.g., Richard A. Falk, "Comparative Protection of Human Rights in Capitalist and Socialist Third World Countries," in Falk, *Human Rights and State Sovereignty*, 125–52; Paul Streeten, Shavid Javid Burki, Mahbul ul Hag, Norman Hicks, and Francis Stewart, *First Things First: Meeting Basic Needs in the Developing Countries* (Oxford: Oxford University Press, 1981); Tom J. Farer, "Policy Implications of the Possible Conflict Between Capitalist Development and Human Rights in Developing Countries," in *The Future of the Inter-American System*, ed. Tom J. Farer (New York: Praeger Publishers, 1979); Denis Goulet, *The Cruel Choice* (New York: Atheneum, 1977); Irma Adelman and Cynthia Morris, *Economic Growth and Social Equity in Developing Countries* (Stanford, Calif.: Stanford University Press, 1973).
9. Johan Galtung, *True Worlds* (New York: Free Press, 1980), 154.

cooperation for human development in order to minimize exploitative and dominance re-lationships among peoples and nations.

In addition to pointing up the essential interconnectedness of all human rights, the Gal-tung-Wirak approach encourages us to acknowledge that "rights are the means and that the satisfaction of needs is the end"[10] of holistic human development. "Like all other means-ends relations, the relationship is complicated,"[11] and the achievement of most needs/rights will require, especially in the developing Third World, integrated as well as enlightened and resolute responses on the national and international planes. Thus food, commonly conceived in the language of rights, becomes, in this new context, both an individual and collective physiological need. A clean environment, characteristically identified as, at the least, an individual right, becomes a collective ecological need. Self-determination and peace, almost always conceptualized in terms of rights, become collective needs for security against de-struction and war.

The first essay in this chapter, by David Lane, takes a thoughtful look at the construction of a social order intended to realize humane values under socialist governance. Lane looks at state socialism in practice and the importance it accords to accountability, freedom, and populist decision-making among human rights. Against Western critics who contend that the very nature of state socialism prevents its seriously considering civil and political rights, Lane argues that, though such rights will be delineated differently, state socialism can ar-ticulate and provide for them. Since the socialist state has many explicit affirmative duties toward its citizens, rights can be understood as the ability of citizens to cash in on the duties owed to them.[12] Against the champions of state socialism who contend that bourgeois civil and political rights are not their concern because such rights are predicated on class conflicts at odds with socialist ideas of solidarity, Lane again protests. In the first place, he notes, current socialist regimes have hardly rooted out class conflict; there remains an unequivocal need for civil and political rights to safeguard against the dangers of such conflict. Second, bearing in mind the omnipresence of the socialist state, the need for some legal redress against wrongful government action and neglect is clear. Underscoring the lessons of the Galtung-Wirak needs/rights approach, Lane concludes that the values of political freedom must be honored in order to meet welfare needs.

Rajni Kothari discusses the interrelation of human rights and development, bringing together in short compass the arguments of serious Third World thinkers who fear the cooptation of developing countries by industrialized ones in the process of modernization. The industrialization that has taken place depends heavily on the creation of Western in-dustrial enclaves by imported Western capital and know-how, and financing that indus-trialization has resulted in growing public debt burdens (as in Singapore, South Korea, Taiwan, and, more recently, Malaysia). Equally dangerous for dependent countries is the increased export of agricultural products, to the detriment of local populations who already are undernourished (as in the Philippines). An important response to these dependency patterns, Kothari suggests, is to insist that Third World development be unambiguously linked to the right of self-determination. Also, the right to development, to have any worth-while meaning, must be conceptualized in holistic—political as well as economic—terms

10. Galtung and Wirak, "Theoretical Approach," 258.
11. Ibid. See Philip Alston, "Making Space for New Human Rights: The Case of the Right to Devel-opment," *Harvard Human Rights Yearbook* 1 (1988): 3–40.
12. See, in this connection, Robert Dahl, "The Moscow Discourse: Fundamental Rights in a Democratic Order," *Government and Opposition* 15, no. 1 (1980): 3–30; Alice Erh-Soon Tay, "Marxism, Socialism and Human Rights," in *Human Rights*, ed. Eugene Kamenka and Alice Erh-Soon Tay (New York: St. Martin's Press, 1978); Belgrade Praxis Group "The Meaning of the Struggle for Civil and Human Rights," *Telos* 35 (1978): 186–91.

that take into account the full range of needs, rights, and governmental duties. Development, Kothari believes, must foster both freedom and bread.

The survival and welfare of human beings is tied at the most basic level to physiological needs common to everyone, such as nutritious food and clean water. Philip Alston's contribution highlights the anomalous status of the human right to food. While international law, as formally articulated, obligates states to take joint and separate action in the eradication of malnutrition and hunger, moral philosophers have for the most part failed to take this obligation into their accounting of the moral duties owed poor nations by rich nations (a conspicuous exception being Amartya Sen of Oxford University[13]). International economic and human rights law, perhaps because of the default of the philosophers, has been so narrowly construed as to result in the right to food's becoming a cruel hoax. International economic law, far from paying serious attention to the problems of world hunger, has tended to emphasize the smooth running of international commerce and the avoidance of conflict.[14] International human rights law, which the Western capital- and food-exporting countries tend to conceptualize in terms of civil and political rights, so far has found no place for the right to food among its categories of liberty. What famine relief aid has been given has tended to be extended as a matter of grace (ex gratia) and generally after the fact rather than in prevention. All this has a baleful effect, of course: the legitimacy not only of a claim to the right to food but of the entire system of international law tends to be undermined. Alston takes on these knotty issues, explores the nature and specifications of existing obligations, and hazards a prognosis for the future.

Like the right to food, the right to a clean environment is a specific human right addressed to basic welfare needs.[15] Henn-Juri Uibopuu discusses the individual's internationally guaranteed right to a clean environment. Anchored in the right to life and in the right to a standard of living adequate for health and well-being, as articulated in the Universal Declaration of Human Rights and the International Covenant on Economic, Social and Cultural Rights,[16] the right to a clean environment has more than a minimal biological content. However, national policy goals are not, and perhaps cannot be, equally respectful of the total human environment. For example, though the right to a clean environment requires, according to Uibopuu, that only the most minimal pollution be released into the biosphere, Third World countries are likely to purchase speedier development at the cost of environmental damage by, for example, choosing an industry-intensive agenda over a less ecologically damaging agricultural program (which, ironically, was the course taken by the present industrialized countries during the Industrial Revolution). Some countries are well situated to use safe modes of production, others are not. A country with valuable natural resources or other wealth can purchase hazardously produced items from elsewhere; another less-advantaged country may be forced to play host to multinational corporations that seek to avoid the more stringent environmental controls in wealthier countries.[17]

That some countries are saddled with environmental pollution (and other by-products of poverty) to the benefit of other countries more favorably situated in the international political

---

13. See Amartya Sen, *Poverty and Famine: An Essay on Entitlement and Deprivation* (Oxford: Oxford University Press, 1981).
14. See, e.g., M. G. Kaladharan Nayar, "Human Rights and Economic Development: The Legal Foundations," *Universal Human Rights* 2, no. 3 (1980): 55–81.
15. See, e.g., R. Michael M'Gonigle and Mark W. Zacher, *Pollution, Politics and International Law* (Berkeley, Calif.: University of California Press, 1979).
16. See the Appendix.
17. On this particular point, see Matthew Lippman, "Multi-national Corporations and Human Rights in the Third World," in Shepherd and Nanda, *Human Rights and Third World Development*, 249–72.

economy is a fact that must be evaluated in terms of human rights. Recalling Article 28 of the Universal Declaration of Human Rights (which proclaims that everyone is entitled to an "international order in which the rights and freedoms set forth in this Declaration can be fully realized"), a sense of global equity must be brought to bear, delineating not only rights but also obligations—both for citizens and for governments.

Such is the perspective advanced by the United Nations, with Third World endorsement, in the Declaration of the Establishment of a New International Economic Order.[18] The most important principles of the declaration are effective domestic control over natural resources, regulation of multinational corporate activities, just and equitable prices for primary commodities and other exports of developing countries, money and development finance reforms, market access for developing countries' products, and the strengthening of developing countries' scientific and technological capacities. Whether or not one finds these principles to be compatible with one's own "preferred world," they do prompt us to realize that ecologically sensitive global development must occur within the framework of an international political economy that is concerned as much with obligations as it is with rights.

The alternative, an anarchic international system unattentive to the total human environment, is the subject of a famous essay by the biologist Garrett Hardin. In "The Tragedy of the Commons,"[19] Hardin describes British cattle-grazing practices during the nineteenth century, wherein each cattle owner sought to maximize his individual well-being by adding to the total number of cattle on the finite grazing areas or "commons." A series of these uncoordinated decisions by the individual owners ultimately resulted in the demise of all of them because of the permanent destruction of the commons. In his analysis of this historical experience, Hardin extended the notion of the "commons" to include the open seas, the earth's atmosphere, and the space around the planet. His conclusion: that maximization of states' interests relative to the consumption of nonrenewable resources, environmental pollution, and population policy sorely requires some kind of global coordination that closely heeds the interrelation of rights and needs consistent with the collective security of all.

This compelling vision of the world as a commons and the perspective of global population of interconnected human beings should prompt us to think of human rights not only in terms of individual rights, such as the right to food and to personal security, but also in terms of collective rights such as a healthy environment or the equitable distribution of medical care. The needs of entire groups of people may also be connected to human rights.

Yoram Dinstein addresses the needs of entire groups in relation to what is perhaps the most widely accepted embodiment of group rights, namely, the right to self-determination,[20] which was proclaimed in 1966 in the international covenants on economic, social and cultural rights and on civil and political rights, and identified by Galtung and Wirak as a collective right designed to realize group security.[21] Dinstein asserts that all "peoples" are guaranteed this right, so that a "people" has the right to liberate itself from colonial rule or to separate itself from another nation not its own. However, it seldom is easy to define a "people." Some experts insist upon the "objective" criterion of a common history (lin-

18. May 1, 1974, U.N.G.A. Res. 3201 (S-VI), 6 (Special) U.N. GAOR, Supp. (No. 1) 3, U.N. Doc. A/9559 (1974). See also Programme of Action on the Establishment of the New International Economic Order, May 1, 1974, U.N.G.A. Res. 3202 (S-VI), 6 (Special) U.N. GAOR, Supp. (No. 1) 5, U.N. Doc. A/9559 (1974). In addition, see Report of the Secretary General, *The International Dimensions of the Right to Development as a Human Right*, U.N. Doc. E/CN.4/1334 (1979).
19. Garrett Hardin, "The Tragedy of the Commons," *Science* 162 (1968): 1243–8.
20. For an extensive, sensitive treatment of the right to self-determination, see Lung-chu Chen, "Self-Determination as a Human Right" in *Toward World Order and Human Dignity: Essays in Honor of Myres S. McDougal*, ed. W. Michael Reisman and Burns H. Weston (New York: Free Press, 1976).
21. See generally Galtung and Wirak, "Human Needs, Human Rights," 23–4.

guistic, religious, or territorial), while others insist upon the "subjective" criterion of a self-concept (i.e., some idea of what makes one a member of the group).

The often intractable problem of resolving competing self-determinist claims presents itself perhaps most acutely in the case that Dinstein describes: that of the Palestinian Arabs who, in the Israeli-occupied territories of the West Bank and Gaza and elsewhere in the Middle East, seek a state of their own. The UN General Assembly affirmed "the inalienable right of the Palestinian people in Palestine," including the rights of self-determination, independence, and sovereignty.[22] But the demographic transformation of the West Bank by an influx of Jewish settlers since 1967 has raised the question of whether self-determination refers in this instance to the territorial area, to the people in the area, or to the people previously in the area.

Speaking favorably of Palestinian Arab self-determination claims, Shawkey Zeidan writes:

> The right of Palestinians' self-determination is by now almost universally recognized in view of the severe deprivations of their human rights, their distinctive group identity, and their expressed desire to have a state of their own. Their principle or doctrine of self-determination has been discussed, analyzed, and debated at greath length in both academic and U.N. circles. . . .
>
> It is now universally recognized that the question of Palestine and the human rights of Palestinians constitute the core of the conflict. A durable and genuine peace requires the achievement of the legitimate Palestinian aspirations. . . .
>
> A peaceful resolution is possible, but moderation must be reciprocal. For the sake of a durable peace, Israel should reciprocate by indicating its willingness to withdraw from the territories it occupied in 1967. Acceptance by its neighbors, including the Palestinians, is in the last analysis the best guarantee of security in this imperfect world we all must live in and share.[23]

In contrast, the United Nations' support for Palestinian Arab self-determination is belittled by Michla Pomerance:

> Ignoring the complexities of the self-determination problem, the UN has proffered deceptively simple solutions and sham universality. Self-determination in the UN has become a matter of all or nothing, depending on how a group is labelled, subjectively, in relation to "colonialism," "racism," and "alien rule." Self-determination is viewed as an *absolute*, not a relative right—but only for favoured "selves." These are entitled [to] total independence and are encouraged to opt for it as the only proper solution. To others, self-determination is totally denied. The disfavoured have only obligations and no rights. To realize their rights, the favoured "selves" may freely use force and disturb international peace and security. In the new UN perspective too, democracy, human rights and representative government are either irrelevant or distinctly secondary to the right of self-determination.[24]

The intense—indeed, often vituperative—nature of this debate over conflicting Palestinian and Israeli claims suggests that self-determination, viewed as a collective human right, is not so much a remedy for a problem as it is a statement of the problem itself. Moreover,

---

22. Nov. 22, 1974, U.N.G.A. Res. 32/36 (XXIX), 32 U.N. GAOR, Supp. (No. 45) 172, U.N. Doc. A/9631 (1977).
23. Shawkey Zeidan, "A Human Rights Settlement: The West Bank and Gaza," in Shepherd and Nanda, *Human Rights and Third World Development*, 165–96, at 172 and 191.
24. Michla Pomerance, "Self-Determination Today: The Metamorphosis of an Ideal," *Israel Law Review* 19, no. 3–4 (1984): 310–39 at 338.

as is clear from the history of the Middle East, it is a problem that too often leads to bloodshed. Yoram Dinstein realizes this dilemma and without resolving it presents the enigmatic aphorism: "International law does not encourage civil wars, but it does not prohibit them either."

In the final essay in this chapter, Katarina Tomasevski approaches the ideal of a humane international order from a related but different angle: the right to peace, a collective security right in the Galtung-Wirak universe. Ironically, though often justified by a concern to prevent or limit the cruelties of war, arms trading and bomb stockpiling have enhanced the ability of governments to violate human rights in the most fundamental sense. Moreover, preparations for war earmark resources that could alleviate hunger and create jobs, and they make coercion and conscription a way of life much more often than not. Decisions shrouded in military secrecy under the figleaf of "national security" erode what potential exists for expanding constitutional democracy.

Of course, if what is done in fear of the possibility of war is bad, what is done in war itself is far worse. Wars are no longer local affairs; they typically engulf entire regions. Unconventional wars (guerrilla and terrorist), which are waged on behalf of many causes, deprive states of what was once their exclusive monopoly on belligerence. Venerable distinctions between combatants and civilians have been obliterated by new weapons and tactics. Wars of "liberation," characteristic of our century, inexorably conflict with the right to peace. And while important international institutions have been created, in the words of the Preamble to the UN Charter, "to save succeeding generations from the scourge of war," as well as numerous international treaties and resolutions that call for arms control and disarmament, still we have made insufficient progress to ensure the survival of the "commons." The Tomasevski essay takes on many of these disturbing facts and explores the nature and specifications of existing obligations in the name of the right to peace.

The history of the twentieth century offers clear instruction on the importance of peace. War in our time not only has killed millions of people, it also has killed the infant processes of democracy and human rights that affirm human dignity. We ask, How can peace be maintained? The first essential step in answering is the recognition that, as the Preamble to the Universal Declaration of Human Rights declares, "the inherent dignity of the equal and inalienable rights of all members of the human family is the foundation of freedom, justice and peace in the world."

9. DAVID LANE *Human Rights Under State Socialism*

Many critics, both liberal and Marxist, argue that the Western concept of rights is not (or should not be) applicable to the Soviet Union. There are three distinct types of criticism. First, that the doctrine of Marxism-Leninism is alien to the concept of human rights. Second, that individual rights are not defended because of the monistic structure of society. Only a pluralist society, it is argued, may secure rights for certain values (religious, ethnic), a monistic state abrogates individual and group rights. Furthermore, the totalitarian nature of Soviet society weakens the

independence of the individual from the state. Third, that the Russian heritage of orthodoxy and absolutism has continued into the modern period and provides no political supports to Western concepts of rights.

The first type of criticism is voiced by a school of thinkers within socialism who wish to jettison the liberal notions of human rights. Such socialists argue that traditional political rights are predicated on a capitalist society distinguished by possessive competitive individualism. Such rights as have developed under capitalism are based on the

Reprinted, with changes, from David Lane, "Human Rights under State Socialism," *Political Studies* 32 (1984): 349–68. Reprinted by permission.

assumption that there are conflicts of interest between right-holders and other members of society; this is at variance with the socialist ideal of community. A conflict of interests "presumed in the practice of rights could not arise [under socialism] and socialism . . . must involve not the revision but the abandonment of rights along with the institution of the state and its laws."[1] Insofar then as the state, acting on behalf of the working class, passes laws to protect and to enhance the interest of the working class, claims of individuals against the state are inimical to the interests of the working class and hence to the interests of society as a whole. This school would argue that "individual" rights have their intellectual and political *gravitas* in a bourgeois conception of society. Socialist society is based on a philosophy of fulfilling human need, not individual rights. Ruth A. Putnam argues that rights involve laws which require a state which for socialists is an "instrument of class repression." The legal codes in which rights are embedded are anathema to socialists—"Rights are the prized possessions of alienated persons."[2] This line of approach is endorsed further by writers such as Steven Lukes and L. Kolakowski who assert that Marxism (and particularly Marxism-Leninism) as a doctrine is alien to the concept of human rights.[3]

On the other hand, other contemporary writers, developing a more humanistic Marxism, and correctly in my view, have argued that human rights are an essential component of socialism. Shingo Shibata, Agnes Heller, and Tom Campbell[4] regard human rights as means to meet human needs; under socialism such rights are extended in form. While it is certainly true that the doctrine of inherent natural rights was regarded as being part of the democratic or bourgeois revolution, it would be incorrect to regard Marx and all of his followers to be indifferent to rights. It

forecloses the issue to dismiss "many peripheral variants of Marxism and to set aside all the intricate questions as to what may or may not be included in the list of human rights, to what extent their implementation depends on contingent historical conditions, etc."[5] The fact that Marx regarded human rights as emancipation of people in a social and economic sense does not imply the absence of rights under socialism in a legal and political one. Marxism has a humanistic human rights tradition as well as an authoritarian one. Marx and Lenin were opposed to sham rights which characterized capitalism and which favored the bourgeoisie. But this does not entail opposition to human rights as such. Political rights are a necessary complement to other social and economic rights and it is incorrect to regard Marxism as a philosophy indifferent to human rights. Marxism pays respect to individualistic human rights as part of the development of modern society; socialist rights should build on and extend such rights, rather than negate them. This is recognized even by the . . . leaders of the Soviet Union. . . .

Writers who deny the validity of rights under socialism adopt an ahistorical and abstract position. In an "ideal" communist society there would be no "state" in the sense of a ruling class stratum, but present-day societies are far away from such abstract formulations. One must also bear in mind the role of government as an administrative institution providing services and fulfilling public objectives. As officials may abuse their powers, the courts are needed to assert the prerogatives of citizens over misguided or wrongful actions by officials. . . . In seeking to explain the denial of human rights to many people by the actions of the Soviet and other governments, such critics have come to make such actions a principle of socialist action rather than a violation of socialist legality. Similarly, the argument is also uti-

---

1. Tom Campbell, *The Left and Rights: A Conceptual Analysis of the Idea of Socialist Rights* (London: Routledge & Kegan Paul, 1983), 7.
2. Ruth A. Putnam, "Rights of Persons and the Liberal Tradition," *Social Ends and Political Means*, ed. Ted Honderich (London: Routledge, 1976), 106. See also H. Klenner, "Jefferson and Ho Chi Minh: Shingo Shibata's Conception of Human Rights," *Social Praxis* 6, no. 1–2 (1979): 95–6.
3. Steven Lukes, "The Illusory Rhetoric of Human Rights," *The Times Higher Educational Supplement*, 30 January 1981; L. Kolakowski, "Marxism and Human Rights," *Daedalus* (Emory University Symposium 1983), esp. 6–7.
4. Shingo Shibata, "Fundamental Human Rights and Problems of Freedom: Marxism and the Contemporary Significance of the U.S. Declaration of Independence," *Social Praxis* 3, no. 3–4 (1975): 157–86; Agnes Heller, "The Declaration of Independence and the Principles of Socialism," *Social Praxis* 6, no. 1–2 (1979): 109–12; Campbell, *The Left and Rights* (see n. 1 above).
5. Kolakowski, "Marxism and Human Rights," 1.

lized by opponents of existing socialist states to label and condemn them as opposed to the concept of rights.

Such violations provide the basis for the second set of criticisms of rights under socialism. A sympathetic commentator on the USSR, Alice Erh-Soon Tay, regards the repression of Stalin's rule as being "based on sustained and systematic disregard of law and any respect for human dignity or human rights."[6] Such violations are not regarded as aberrations or exceptions but are generalized into a critique of socialist states. As Campbell has put it, they are conceived to illustrate that there is "something inherently antithetical between socialist theory and respect for individual rights. It may be no accident that governments expressing 'collectivist' doctrines appear to place less weight on freedom of speech, freedom of movement, and the right to take part in the selection of political authorities than those nations which regard themselves as liberal democracies. . . ."[7]

Western writers cite in support of this viewpoint the suppression of dissent. Contemporary dissenters in the Soviet Union are harassed by the police, independence of thought is denied and foreign travel, writing and residence is restricted. Chalidze and other dissidents have pointed to the ways that fundamental freedoms of speech, communication, person, association and movement are curtailed. But condemnation of the USSR must be tempered by the realization that human rights in all societies are infringed. The United States has used civil rights as an agency of its foreign policy to condemn the Soviet Union.

One must also consider whether the Western concept of human rights is not an ethnocentric one and whether the Soviet Union in some way compensates for the infringement of individual political rights against the state by the implementation of social ones. The denial of some rights to "dissidents" may not apply to other rights to other citizens. Deprivation of the political right to found a business enterprise and to trade on the market does not infringe the economic right of laborers to receive a just wage or the social right to permanent employment. . . .

The application to socialist states and particularly to the USSR of the doctrines of "human rights," as understood in the West and as expressed in the UN Declaration of Human Rights, has been questioned by cultural comparativists and they constitute the third approach mentioned above. Pollis and Schwab write: "only in the Western capitalist states, with a shared historical development and a common philosophic tradition does the concept of individual rights against and prior to the state exist. And only in these countries are political and civil rights implemented to a greater or lesser extent. Most non-Western states, frequently for a combination of cultural and ideological reasons and because of policy priorities set by the demands of economic development do not emphasise or attend to political and civil rights. On the other hand, socialist states seem to place greater emphasis on and have a better record with regard to economic rights than do Western democratic societies."[8]

Such writers, like those socialists who identify opposing liberal rights claims with bourgeois society, emphasize the interrelationship and interdependence between particular sets of human rights doctrines and the social, political and economic structures in which they are embedded. Hence human rights have a particularistic rather than a universalistic relevance. Philosophies of human rights adopted by Western states may be appropriate for them in respect of their concern with the rights of private property and to the rights to security which may be given to the individual in a pluralist society. They have their roots in the "particular experience of England, France and the United States." These may be contrasted with socialist societies in which economic, welfare and distributive rights are given more priority. The conceptual classification between individualistic and collectivist types of rights, which will be taken up later, may be summarized as follows:

Individualistic
Rights are possessed by individuals.
Rights are determined prior to, and opposed to, the state.

---

6. E. Kamenka and Alice Erh-Soon Tay, *Human Rights* (London: Edward Arnold, 1978), 109. For an earlier critique see John Lewis, "On Human Rights," in *Marxism and the Open Mind* (London: Routledge, 1957), 72.
7. Campbell, *The Left and Rights*, 2.
8. Adamantia Pollis and Peter Schwab, eds. "Introduction," in *Human Rights: Cultural and Ideological Perspectives* (New York: Praeger Publishers, 1980), xiii.

Rights are enforced through individual claims against the state.

Rights are observed through absence of interference by individuals and institutions.

Collectivist

Rights are held by groups or classes.

Rights are defined by, and activated through, the state.

Rights are enforced through administrative action.

Rights are achieved through positive actions by institutions and the state.

The comparativist approach, however, is not merely concerned with the conceptual differences outlined above, but seeks the origin of different approaches to rights in the traditional values, practices, and the ideographic features of specific societies. Many of the practices of the Soviet Union, it is pointed out, derive from an autocratic state in which Orthodoxy prevailed—rather than from Marxist political theory. Both the state structure of pre-1917 Russia and the traditions of the Orthodox Church gave no role to *individual* political rights. Individualism was a creed bound up with the Renaissance and Reformation, which had little influence on Tsarist Russia. Such ideas did not penetrate because of the isolation of Russia from Europe due to its size and inhospitable land mass. The integrative structures of Russia were more communal than individualistic. The traditional Russian *mir* or *obshchina* (commune) was essentially a collectivist body. The village assembly had powers of collective ownership of property given to it under the terms of the Emancipation of the Serfs in 1861. The Russian serf from being bound to the land, became bound to the commune. The American negro, by contrast, from being owned by one master was given his or her individual freedom. . . .

In my opinion, comparativists, such as Pollis and Schwab, take too deterministic a position. They ignore the heterogeneity of the Soviet political culture and the important role given by many Russian Marxists to conceptions of individual human and democratic rights. But this traditional background has undoubtedly influenced the evolution of the Soviet state. There was a symbiosis between traditional values and practices and those of the ideology guiding the Soviet state. The Soviet leaders had developmental goals. Priority was given to the provision of employment and also the fulfilment of life needs—for food, shelter, health and education. . . . The political rulers have been more concerned with industrialization, security and defense, and socialist norms of individual rights have been neglected and often infringed. There has been an unresolved tension between the salience of individual and collectivist rights.

Arguments, encountered above, claiming that rights are either inappropriate or even harmful to the integrity of a "socialist society" may be refuted on two counts. First, these arguments are often posed in terms of an abstract socialist society. The countries of Eastern Europe are not socialist in such an ideal sense: they have a state apparatus and considerable inadequacies in terms of the level of productive forces. At best they are transitional social formations. Second, rights-claims need not be restricted to the model of possessive competitive individualism associated with capitalism. Social and economic rights defined in the constitutions of state socialist societies have a corollary in the duties of agents of the state to provide certain facilities. Rights-claims by individuals then in existing societies may have the form of claims on officers of the state to implement rights of individuals. Officials may misuse their powers and they may be inert. Furthermore, interests in the political system (for instance, of a bureaucratic kind) may not be responsive to the legitimate rights-claims of citizens. Such claims do not imply antagonistic relations between state and citizen and are therefore quite legitimate under socialism and in a social formation between capitalism and communism.

Moving from Western conceptualizations about human rights under socialism to the study of rights in existing socialist states, one must emphasize the latent tension, mentioned above, between individual rights and class or collective rights.

In the Soviet Union and other state socialist societies the normative approach to rights may be studied in the context of the dominant ideology, and particularly in the Constitutions of these countries. In this respect we are concerned with what the political leadership of the dominant ruling class defines as legitimate rights. The extent to which these rights are implemented, or enjoyed by citizens, is a matter for empirical study and also for political and social analysis. . . .

The Declaration of the Rights of the Toiling and Exploited Peoples[9] has set the tone for Soviet declarations of rights. It did not, unlike other documents on rights, specify any rights of citizens against the state. It was a declaration of policy; it emphasized the role of class struggle in securing rights for the laboring classes (that is, peasants and workers).

In the first Constitution of the [Russian Soviet Federal Socialist Republic], published on 3 July 1918, the general principles of rights were articulated. These shared certain sentiments in common with the lists of rights declared as objectives in the American and French Revolutions. They included the "equality of all citizens before the law, irrespective of race or nationality" (Art. 22); the repression of national minorities or any attempts "in any way to limit their rights" (Art. 22) were illegal. The working classes were given "effective liberty of opinion," in the promotion of which were transferred to the workers and peasants "all the technical and material resources necessary for the publication of newspapers, pamphlets, books, and other printed matter." Their "unobstructed circulation throughout the country" was guaranteed (Art. 14). The workers were ensured "complete freedom of meeting" (Art. 15) and "full liberty of association" (Art. 16). To ensure "effective access to education, the RSFSR sets before itself the task of providing for the workers and poorer peasants a complete, universal and free education" (Art. 17). In addition, it reiterated the obligation on all citizens to work, the duty to perform a military service and to defend the Republic. Workers and peasants resident in Russia were given the right of citizenship of the Republic. Persecuted foreigners were given the right of asylum. . . . Leaving aside for one moment the fulfillment of the rights promised in the Constitution, the question arises how these provisions differ from constitutional rights proclaimed in the West.

First, rights in state socialist countries have been defined collectively not individually. In the seventeenth and eighteenth centur[ies], rights were conceived to inhere in persons, in individuals. These included freedom of the person, the right to political consultation through Parliament, freedom of conscience, and also important

economic rights for the individual to own property, to conduct economic enterprise unconstrained by the government. Broadly, such rights were secured in the English Revolution from 1640 to 1688, and the French in 1789; they were extended to America in 1776 and continued in the decolonization process of the twentieth century.

The Russian Revolution was a catalyst in the development of social and economic rights. This, of course, extended claims of social rights advocated by other socialist and pre-socialist thinkers, such as Tom Paine. Explicit rights to work, to social security, and to education have been proclaimed. In the economic sector individual rights to enterprise and to ownership of property were abolished; freedom from economic exploitation (in a Marxist sense of the production of exchange values) and rights to employment have been decreed; government ownership, control, and planning of the economy has been introduced. In addition, the individualist and "market" conception of political rights expressed through competition of political parties and interest groups has been replaced by the idea of a collective political interest articulated by one political party.

From the earliest days of the Revolution, the emancipation of men and women and the development of their human rights were regarded as being dependent on the interests of the working class, as expressed through the Communist Party and as activated by the government. In contrast, then, to Western states where rights are expressed as inalienable attributes of individuals, and are claims which the state cannot (or cannot lightly) override, human rights in the Soviet Union have been bound up with what the state can (or should) do to liberate the working class. In terms of the earlier discussion, needs were met by economic planning and social development rather than by the articulation of individual demands.

A second difference is that political rights in the West have been based on the notion of the equality of citizenship (for men if not for women). Inequalities of condition have been regarded by thinkers such as Locke, Rousseau and Mill as "artificial" creations of men, having no legiti-

9. Reprinted in James Bunyan and H. H. Fisher, *The Bolshevik Revolution* (Stanford, Cal.: Stanford University Press, 1934), 372–4. This was written by Lenin.

macy in the state of nature. . . . In Russia some such sentiments were expressed by liberal opponents of the autocracy, but the dominant political tradition up to 1917 was one of formal inequality of rights: people's status before the law was based on their rank or estate.

Uniquely of European countries, Russia did not experience the era of individual rights. The Tsarist autocracy was never broken by a liberal-democratic movement: individual freedoms of combination, of expression, were never achieved; there were restraints on individual ownership of land, on enterprise and on geographical mobility; religious toleration was not secured. The law classified people's rights in terms of their estate—not as possessions of any individual. The legal estates were only abolished in Russia in November 1917, and then members of different economic classes formally had different rights. Workers and peasants were recruited to the army. Constitutional rights were given to workers and employees, peasants and laboring cossacks. Businessmen, the clergy and "those who employ others for the sake of profit" did not enjoy civil rights and in the same category were criminals and those with disorders of the mind (Articles 64, 65).

Since the Russian Revolution, the content of rights claims in the West and in the USSR has changed. The "rights" extolled by thinkers of the eighteenth and nineteenth centuries were largely *political* rights. These have been extended during the twentieth century: de facto and increasingly de jure rights in Western states have covered social and economic matters. There has also been the recognition of group (particularly ethnic and gender) rights in addition to individual ones. Positive government action now is widely accepted in the West as a means to achieve individual and group rights of a social and economic kind. Despite the developments here which have occurred since the Second World War, there is still a strong residual belief that rights are about individual freedoms and that the government has a supportive, though essentially a limited, role in promoting rights. This view finds legitimation in the critique of Cranston[10] that the new social and economic rights are quite different in quality from the "inalienable" traditional political rights.

In the Soviet Union the approach to and emphasis on rights [are] different. The state (party and government) has played a dominant role in defining and implementing rights. Obligations and duties of the state to the citizen are specified and effectively limit individual action. (Planning secures the right of full employment but the absence of a market and the abolition of private property eliminates the rights of individual production and trade.) The Soviet state has always played a greater role in defining and implementing rights. Eighteenth- and nineteenth-century European thinkers articulated rights of individuals as individuals. Rights have been defined in post-1917 Russia *by* the government, not as claims *on* the government.

The emphasis on the duty of the individual to the state has greater salience in the USSR than in the West. . . . Unlike in Western liberal conceptions of rights where individuals are seen as having rights *qua* individuals to life and happiness, in the Soviet Union, these rights are limited by the present incumbents of political power when they are deemed to conflict with the state's role of safeguarding the collective interest.

The priority given to "the interests of the state or society" over the interests of the individuals is [seen] in the 1977 Constitution. Article 39 says: "Enjoyment by citizens of their rights and freedoms must not be to the detriment of the interests of society or the state, or infringe the rights of other citizens." Article 59 states: "Citizens' exercise of their rights and freedoms is inseparable from the performance of their duties and obligations. Citizens of the USSR are obliged to observe the Constitution of the USSR and the Soviet laws, comply with the standards of socialist conduct, and uphold the honor and dignity of Soviet citizenship." And Article 62 requires that "Citizens of the USSR are obliged to safeguard the interests of the Soviet state, and to enhance its power and prestige." The difference from Western liberal states is not just in the recognition of the limits of the individuals' rights. In no society are human rights absolute: homicide laws in Western states limit the right to life, as does antiterrorism legislation in respect of freedom of association. In state socialist society, not only are there far fewer restraints on the state's power to restrict individual rights but the state, through the "leading role" of the Party, may effectively define which individual rights are deemed to conflict

10. M. Cranston, "Human Rights, Real and Supposed," in *Political Theory and the Rights of Man*, ed. D. D. Raphael (London: Macmillan, 1967).

with the state's interests and in practice it is almost impossible to challenge the state's definition of illegitimate activity.

Soviet constitutional developments have also recognized individual rights. There is now less prominence given to class struggle and to the class basis of human emancipation and much more to individual rights. The scope of social and economic rights has been extended. The Constitutions of 1936 and 1977 explicitly define a wide range of "fundamental rights and duties of citizens." . . . The formal statements of rights are summarized in Table 1, which is divided into [categories of] economic, social and political rights.

Rights, however, have to be seen in a political context. Rights are claims on resources and values, and the definition and fulfilment of rights have to do with the distribution of power in society. The *individual* articulation of rights is circumscribed by the *collectivist* control claimed by the Communist Party. Article 6 of the Constitution declares:

The leading and guiding force of Soviet society and the nucleus of its political system, of all state organizations and public organisations, is the Communist Party. The CPSU exists for the people and serves the people. The Communist Party, armed with Marxism-Leninism, determines the general perspective of the foreign policy of the USSR, directs the great constructive work of the Soviet people, and imparts a planned, systematic and theoretically sustained character to their struggle for the victory of communism.

Similar sentiments may be found in the Constitution of other socialist states. . . .

Though group rights (for women, Blacks) are increasingly recognized in Western liberal states, the individual is the unit in which rights-claims are expressed. Under state socialism, the Communist Party (or analogous parties) is defined as the legitimate interpreter of the interests of the working class. . . . The role of the Party, as developed in the USSR, is likely to be a major impediment to the legitimacy of rights claims by individuals as practiced in Western liberal states. . . .

The lack of fulfilment of rights in the past history of the USSR has to be seen in the context of an unstable international political environment (civil and foreign wars) and with the absence of many of the preconditions for the evolution of certain rights. Elements of Marxist theory which are alien to bourgeois society (e.g. bourgeois class rights) were fused with traditional values and led to the imposition of a political system which placed little, if any, emphasis on individual human rights. This process is an episode in the evolution of the Soviet state and should not be conceived of as endemic to socialism. The extent and methods of the abrogation of individual rights under Stalin cannot be justified [ex post facto] even in terms of "nation-building" and economic growth. One should not gloss over, in the name of development, the unjustifiable breaches of civil rights, and the wrongdoings of the leadership and administration.

Richard P. Claude has pointed to some of the prerequisites for the implementation of human rights. To ensure constitutional limits on government, a "universalistic" and "secularized ideology of the rightful bases of political authority" is necessary; for civil liberties an ideological requisite is "acceptance of public-private person distinction in politico-economic discourse."[11] The Soviet Union has had none of these ideological underpinnings. Following the upheaval of revolution, civil war, the Second World War and the Cold War, there has been the absence of a secure legal system, there has been no generalized "support for a nonarbitrary, rationalized system of justice."[12] S. M. Lipset and Richard P. Claude have pointed to the conditions for a western-type democratic society. They include: an open class system, economic wealth, an egalitarian value system, a capitalist economy, widespread literacy, and high participation in voluntary organizations.[13] Pre-revolutionary Russia had none of these preconditions; the Soviet Union until relatively recently has had few of them and this list is still not fulfilled. Also, foreign powers were (and are) regarded by the Soviet leaders as threats to their internal security. . . .

The recent history of the Soviet Union and some of the socialist states of Eastern Europe illustrates that political subcultures are being created which are coming into conflict with the

11. Richard P. Claude, *Comparative Human Rights* (Baltimore: Johns Hopkins University Press, 1976), 40.
12. Claude, *Comparative Human Rights*.
13. S. M. Lipset, *Political Man* (London: Heinemann, 1963), 74–5.

TABLE 1
RIGHTS AS DEFINED IN THE 1936 AND 1977 SOVIET CONSTITUTIONS

1936 CONSTITUTION

Economic
Right to work, to "guaranteed employment." Right to own, as personal property, income and savings derived from work, to own a dwelling house and supplementary husbandry, articles of household and articles of personal use and convenience.
Right to inherit personal property.

Social
Right to rest and leisure, seven-hour day, annual vacations with pay, maintenance in old age, sickness or disability.
Education—free in all schools, in the native language.

Political
Rights of women on an equal footing with men "in all spheres of economic, cultural, government, political and social activity." Freedom of conscience, freedom of religious worship and freedom of anti-religious propaganda.
Freedom of speech, press, assembly, street processions and demonstrations. The right to unite in mass organizations. Right of inviolability of the person, of the homes of citizens and the privacy of correspondence.
Right of asylum to foreign citizens. Right to vote in elections, to nominate candidates through mass organizations and societies.

1977 CONSTITUTION

Economic
Socialist system ensures enlargement of the rights . . . and continuous improvement of living standards.
Rights to work, to choice of trade or profession.

Social
Right to housing.
Right to education, including teaching in native language. Right to cultural benefits. Right to freedom of scientific, technical and artistic work. Rights of authors, inventors and innovators protected.
Right to leisure and rest, working week of 41 hours, paid holidays, extension of social service and sport.
Health protection. Maintenance in old age, sickness or disability.

Political
Equality before law. Men and women have equal rights. Equality of rights of different races and nationalities.
Equality of rights of all citizens.
Right to participation in management and administration of the state, to vote and be elected to Soviets, to submit proposals to state bodies, to criticize shortcomings. Freedom of speech, press, assembly, meetings, street processions and demonstrations.
Right to asylum.
Right to associate in public organizations.
The right to profess any religion, to conduct religious worship.
Inviolability of the person, of the home. Right of privacy, of correspondence, telephone conversations and telegraphic communications.
Right to protection by state bodies.
Right to complain against actions of officials, state bodies and public bodies.

more traditional ones. . . . The traditional patterns of legitimacy, of the ideology of Stalinism, of central direction and control [are] being challenged by what Weber called the legal-rational. This involves a greater role being played by the legal system, by civil liberties and civil rights. Soviet legal theory has changed significantly since

the death of Stalin and has paralleled the conception of an all-people's state and developed socialism (*zrely sotsializm*). . . . As noted above, this is reflected by a greater concern for rights in the Constitution.

The reason for greater emphasis on legal norms is the growing differentiation of society.

Its advanced complexity, together with a more urbane and educated population, calls for a system of integration through exchange between various institutions and groups. Such exchanges, however, involve greater autonomy and 'rights-claims', on the one side, and a decline in the hegemony of the state apparatus, on the other. The scientific and cultural intelligentsia (of whom Sakharov and Medvedev are 'dissident' representatives) are a major force in this movement. The ideology of Marxism-Leninism may be utilized, at a normative level, to endorse and legitimize such claims. The values underpinning socialist states—at least under conditions of 'developed socialism'—provide a basis for claims to be made by aggrieved citizens and groups in defense of their rights. The salience of such values, however, has to be studied in the context of the evolution of particular individual states and their political cultures. One may contrast Poland and the USSR.

In Poland, the rise of the *Solidarity* movement epitomizes Polish claims for rights. It has widened and generalized the aspirations of other rights groups—The Workers' Defense Committee, Human Rights Committees. *Solidarity* was a mass movement embracing workers, intellectuals and peasants, including communists, non-communists and anti-communists. Prior to the assumption of military rule in December 1981, the rights to free assembly and collective bargaining had de facto been conceded by the government, claims for the right of 'free speech and press' and access to the radio and TV had been partly achieved. *Solidarity* campaigned publicly for the implementation of a wide range of rights: for the Church, for limitation of censorship and for the fulfilment of many other social rights—housing and health care. All these demands were in correspondence with rights defined in the Constitution. Concessions were obtained from the Polish government: not only were *Solidarity* and *Rural Solidarity* given official recognition, but the law on censorship, passed in July 1981, weakened central control over the media and excluded many items from it (e.g. textbooks, academic theses, Catholic Church publications, labor organizations' internal publications).

In the Soviet Union, on the other hand, there has been no such widespread civil rights movement. It is well known that a number of explicitly human rights groups have been founded: notably, the Initiative Group for the Defence of Human Rights in the USSR, the Human Rights Committee, the Moscow Branch of Amnesty International.[14] These groups advocate to various degrees the rights incorporated in the UN Universal Declaration of Human Rights; they are particularly concerned with freedom of the press, freedom of movement (both within and outside the USSR) and with the rights of various nationalities and religions. The movement, while qualitatively important, has been relatively isolated and on a very small scale. On admittedly inadequate data, Kowalewski estimates that the number of groups demonstrating rose from 6 in 1965 to 12 in 1976.[15] (These data should be regarded as an index rather than quantitative statements.) The movement is largely intellectual in composition. There is no involvement by rank and file communists. Similarly, the recent movement for workers' rights has had little support and has had only a small impact. The Association of Free Trade Unions of Workers in the Soviet Union (AFTU) was founded in 1979. Its Charter defines membership to be open to "any worker or employee whose rights and interests have been violated by administrative, governmental, party, or judicial agencies." AFTU activists were quickly apprehended: some were arrested and others sent to psychiatric hospitals. AFTU was followed by the Free Interprofessional Association of Workers (SMOT). Its leaders were harassed and arrested, and a similar fate has befallen other "rights" groups which have been set up in opposition to the authorities. It is difficult to gauge just how much support exists for these independent unions. But compared to Poland they are insignificant. . . .

The comparison between Poland and the USSR is impressive. Poland has had a history of greater assertiveness of rights against the government than [does] the USSR. Why is this the case?

The context in which rights may be articulated may be analyzed in terms of the legitimacy of the state and the strength of group cohesion (see Table 2). By "legitimacy" I refer here to sentiments of loyalty to the regime, to diffuse psychological orientations or supports. In the USSR legitimacy is strong: the Soviet state was secured

14. For a useful review see: David Kowalewski, "Human Rights Protest in the USSR: Statistical Trends for 1965–78," *Universal Human Rights* 2, no. 1 (Jan.–Mar. 1980): 5–29.
15. Kowalewski, "Human Rights Protest in the USSR," 18.

TABLE 2
INTERACTION OF FACTORS AFFECTING THE ARTICULATION OF RIGHTS

LEGITIMACY OF STATE

		Weak	Strong
INTERMEDIATE GROUP COHESION	*Weak*	(Spain)	USSR
	Strong	Poland	(USA)

by revolution, has fought and won a civil war and a world war. The "mobilization regime" was a peculiar mixture of industrial and social goals, traditional and charismatic authority (stemming from Tsarist Russia) and the evolving doctrine of Marxism-Leninism. In Poland, the state was created out of war and is associated with imposed Soviet rule. The Communist Party (PUWP) which has been the driving force and legitimating instrument of the Soviet mobilization system has not had widespread and deep support in Poland. The state has been weak. Poland has never had a strong charismatic leader comparable to the Tsar or Stalin. Traditional values manifested in nationalism and the Church have always been strong. The economic crises of the seventies and eighties further weakened its viability.

The "rights" which people may seek to articulate must be related to the strength of group cohesion because the expression of rights requires political organization. In the USSR, intermediate groups are weak: the Church has little popular following. The working class has no history of independent trade union activity. The peasants are effectively contained in collective farms. In areas where national and religious intermediate groups are stronger, outside the Russian heartland, there is greater support for Western notions of individual rights. The Western based "Soviet Area Audience and Opinion Unit" has found that Soviet citizens from the Baltic and Transcaucasion Republics "are more favourably disposed to *samizdat* than people from other areas of the USSR."[16] In Poland, intermediate groups—particularly the Church and intelligentsia—have a long history as independent forces continuing the traditions of the Polish nation. The manual working class has evolved with a trade union move-

ment in opposition to authority. The peasantry successfully resisted collectivization. Poland has a tradition of pluralism—if not of democratic government. Poland has always been greatly affected by European developments: it has had strong links with its neighbors Germany and Scandinavia. Its massive emigration between the Wars has in turn strengthened personal ties with Western Europe and the United States. Russia has no tradition of pluralism and has always been more isolated geographically and intellectually from the West. As illustrated in Table 2, the USSR has a strong state legitimacy and weak intermediate group cohesion. In Poland, the situation is reversed.

The dynamic of human rights in the USSR is to be found in "within system" changes rather than in the dissident movement. This is due not only to public sentiments, but to the power of the Soviet state. Rights claims articulated specifically against the state do not succeed. If individual rights are to be extended and secured they can only be achieved within—rather than against—existing institutions and procedures. In Poland, the state has been unable to meet the economic expectations of the population and has remained illegitimate; rights have been perceived to be claims on the state. The *Solidarity* movement in Poland, the Political Reform movement associated with Dubcek in Czechoslovakia in 1968, the emergence of "dissident" groups in the USSR, together with a tendency since Khrushchev towards greater legality by the political élites, and the claims of the 1977 Constitution, all point in different ways to the evolution of claims for civil rights under state socialism. It is true that the Reform Movement led to invasion, that *Solidarity*

16. *SAAOR Analysis Report*, 9–77, p. 10. Cited by E. Teague, *Radio Liberty Report*, RL 109/83 (Munich, 1983), 5.

was crushed, that the dissident movement has witnessed many infringements of rights. The significance of these developments is that they are indicative of claims on the guardians of political power, of assertions by individual and group interests which the authorities ignore at the cost of political stability and social solidarity. These tendencies seem to me to indicate that civil rights are by no means a dead issue either in Marxism or in the politics of the socialist states. They are, however, only the sharp end of rights-claims. In a less dramatic and less publicized form in the West, individual civil rights may be given greater recognition by process of law, by an awareness of the rights-claims of citizens requiring the officers of state to perform their constitutional duty. It is in the evolution of a more rational legal system which explicitly recognizes the duties of the state to meet rights, and the role of the individual in claiming them, that the realization of human

rights is likely to be achieved in the USSR. The articulation of such rights, however, lacks support in the traditional Russian political culture. . . . With the greater maturation of the society, and given relative international security, interest-demands are likely to increase. Such demands in the assertion of "rights" claims cannot be easily resolved in the fashion of an economic and political market exchange with the state, as in the West. The greater role of planning and of the government differentiates socialist societies from capitalist ones. Rights-claims should not be limited to the particular experience and model of Western capitalist states: this is an ethnocentric and mistaken approach. In both the Soviet Union and Poland, legitimacy is sought by the Party to define whose and which rights are fulfilled. This is a cardinal assumption on which the political system is organized and creates a fundamental dilemma for individual rights-claims.

QUESTIONS FOR REFLECTION AND DISCUSSION

1. David Lane contrasts individualist and collectivist conceptions of human rights. Is one conception better than the other? Which do you think would lead to the greatest good for the greatest number of people?

2. How do you respond to Lane's argument that rights claims against powerful socialist states are not appropriate since the state is all-powerful, and furthermore that the dynamic of the human rights movement in the USSR should be found within rather than outside or against the system? If human rights are to be secured "within—rather than against—existing institutions and procedures," what is the potential for abuse in the system? Or does Lane argue persuasively that the "dynamic" of the Soviet system in producing a rational legal system will effectively realize the human rights of individuals?

3. Writes Tom Campbell in *The Left and Rights: A Conceptual Analysis of the Idea of Socialist Rights* ([London: Routledge & Kegan Paul, 1983], 114–115) (footnotes omitted):

> It is in the light of [the] criterion of universality that socialism is often alleged to be an inadequate doctrine in that, it is argued, socialists are prepared to sacrifice important general rights of the individuals for the sake of the general welfare or the progress of society as a whole. Socialists, it is said, override free speech in the interests of political change, sacrifice the lives of those who represent the old order in times of social transition and, in general, withdraw human rights from those who oppose the policies of socialist governments.
>
> The short answer to such criticisms is that they are based on empirical generalizations about what happens in so-called socialist states more than on an examination of socialist theory. In addition to which, it can be pointed out that most of the rights in modern declarations of human rights, as they are adopted by governments, allow for such rights to be limited or suspended according to processes of law in times of national emergency. . . . This is, of course, to deny the absolute nature of human rights, a denial which can be said to be implicit in the most basic of all human rights, the right to life, which is often thought to be compatible with capital punishment. Clearly most, if not all, rights, with the possible exception of the right to a fair trial, may be forfeited for criminal behavior and some disorderly social situations are generally thought to justify the withdrawal or suspension of some human rights, such as the right to freedom of assembly, without calling into question that they are human rights.

Is the argument convincing that the derogation of human rights in times of emergency and the withdrawal of human rights in the presence of criminal conduct parallel socialism's operational, if not theoretical, approach to human rights?

4. What, if any, compromises in civil and in political rights should a socialist state be entitled to make to ensure the economic well-being of its people? To what extent, if at all, does economic well-being depend on the limitation of civil and political rights? By the same token, what, if any, compromises in economic and social rights should a capitalist state be entitled to make to ensure the political freedom of its people? To what extent, if at all, does political freedom depend on the limitation of economic and social rights?

5. In "Comparative Protection of Human Rights in Capitalist and Socialist Third World Countries" (*Human Rights Quarterly* 1, no. 2 [Apr.–June 1979], 5), Richard Falk speculates about some of the human rights difficulties that Third World countries face in choosing between capitalism and socialism:

> Surely, capitalism is not attractive, in general, from a human rights viewpoint for a Third World country. Its capital-intensive approach to development does not generally improve the relative or absolute poverty of the masses. The productive process, oriented around profits and foreign exchange earnings, tends to satisfy the cravings of the rich rather than the needs of the poor. In addition, when the masses are poor and excluded from the gains of the economy, as is the case in Third World capitalist countries (with some minor exceptions having special explanations), then a *structural* tendency to repress exists. There is no way to assure long-term stability in such a societal setting except by intimidating and repressing those who are victimized by it. Thus, while socialism cannot be preferred, given its record, capitalism is a recipe for doom, unless the country is exceptionally endowed with resources, including skills and leadership abilities, and even then, as the case of Iran illustrates, the results of a capitalist orientation may be national disaster.
>
> In effect, from an ideological perspective, socialism is the preferred system for a Third World country, but its record in practice is too poor at present to support the preference. From the viewpoint of human rights the prescriptive challenge is to reconstruct socialist practice so as to achieve greater overall protection of human rights, or alternatively, to comprehend at the level of theory the consistent betrayal in practice of socialist ideals.

Do you agree with Falk's analysis? Why? Why not?

7. Indira Gandhi once said that "it is not individuals who have rights but states." What arguments could you make for such a claim? Is the claim that the state is a substitute for the traditional communal group—hence the embodiment of the people—sufficient to justify the statement?

10. RAJNI KOTHARI *Human Rights as a North-South Issue*

PERSPECTIVE

The debate on human rights is in the throes of acute controversy. The controversy is not confined merely to the traditional dichotomy between civil and political rights on the one hand and economic, social and cultural rights on the other. The controversy has in fact deepened and closely draws on (a) the emerging redefinition of the development problématique as is reflected in the discussions on the New International Development Strategy, (b) the growing awareness of the centrality of the international dimension of development as found in the debate on the New International Economic Order, and (c) the increasing attention being given to the new thinking on alternative strategies of development and lifestyles.

These new considerations in the dialogue on development arise both from the practical constraints on resources and opportunities available

Reprinted, with changes, from Rajni Kothari, "Human Rights as a North-South Issue," *Bulletin of Peace Proposals* 11, no. 4 (1980): 331–8. Reprinted by permission.

for all-round development of the global community and the growing conviction that the prevailing patterns of development violate basic values and the capacity of human beings to realize their freedoms as well as the ability of a majority of nations to pursue freely their own paths of self-reliant development and cultural autonomy.

It is thus necessary to locate the issue of human rights in the emerging debate on development. That the main thrust of the human rights movement should be by reference to living conditions and the prospects for human freedom in the developing countries is, of course, obvious. But before examining the effect of the existing international order on the economic prospects of developing countries and on basic human rights and freedoms in these countries, it will be useful to locate the problem in the larger context of the development problématique laid out above.

THE DEVELOPMENT DEBATE

At the present time the development debate has entered a period of growing uncertainty. Development is not viewed any longer as a necessary progression from less to more and is instead focusing attention on structural, cultural and political factors. There has developed a growing critique of the earlier model of development based on a realization of the conceptual inadequacies of its basic premises. Thus there was an unrealistic conception of the world economy according to which growth in the industrialized countries was more or less automatically transmitted to Third World countries through the mechanisms of trade, technology transfer and development finance. Also most developing countries themselves seem to have paid less than adequate attention to the need for qualitative and structural changes in their societies, relying far too much on the logic of the GNP model whereby a certain course of growth and expansion would necessarily raise production and hence also living standards.

In point of fact, the very pursuit of such strategies has increased imbalances, disparities and absolute as well as relative poverty in the world. Similarly, it is widely recognized that there has been little progress in restructuring the existing international order. The present rules of the game continue to maintain the historical pattern of Northern command over world resources and a

disproportionately large consumption of these resources by industrialized countries—to the systematic detriment of living standards in developing countries.

The critique that emerged throughout the sixties and the seventies of such a pattern of development took many forms and has been articulated in a variety of ways—the Dependencia school pioneered by some Latin American thinkers, the Limits to Growth and Ecological schools, the Basic Needs school, the Self-Reliance school, and more strident than all these, the New International Economic Order school.

During this whole period, there has also emerged another comprehensive critique of development thinking which, while drawing upon the dependency, ecological, basic needs, self-reliance and NIEO streams in a more holistic framework, has focussed on the need to perceive poverty, inequity and oppression as essentially political and cultural tasks. This larger critique has not taken the form of a very specialized school like the others mentioned above. It has emerged from a variety of vantage points and is, of late, receiving attention by theoreticians, movements of dissent and even policy analysts in different parts of the world.

. . . On the other hand, the international status quo and its intellectual apologists have also been busy building new defenses for the old order. There has been a marked increase in the international efforts at coopting sources of challenge to domination and exploitation. One of the most important vehicles of this convergence has been militarization of developing societies.

Meanwhile, many of the concepts which originated in the developing world have also been coopted by the strategists of the present international order, as for example, the concepts of basic needs, self-reliance and alternative strategies of development. It is being done to ensure that developing countries take to a path of development that is less demanding of world resources and therefore less disruptive of the prevailing international structure.

Alongside militarization and certain new doctrines of international development strategy, there has of late emerged a new doctrine of containment, which arises out of the view that the standard of living and the lifestyle that have been achieved by the developed countries must be protected from any threat from the Third World, if need be by physical intervention in Third World regions. The new doctrine of containment that has emerged ranges over a variety of strategies, from a strident "resource diplomacy" and cooptation of new centers of power in the world to new doctrines of military preparedness against real or potential challenge from the Third World.

All of these trends pose a serious challenge to both liberal and egalitarian movements in the developing countries with the result that the prospects for human freedom and dignity seem more remote than ever before, and this without any certainty of improving the conditions of the people in large parts of the Third World.

Finally, there is also a growing sense of threat to cultural identity and civilizational values in Asia, in Africa and, though in a slightly different way, in Latin America, so that even the traditional defenses of poor societies seem to be crumbling before their eyes. Their technological know-hows are being eroded, their traditions of lifestyle and sharing of common heritage are being undermined, their religious and cosmological springs of survival and change are being destroyed. The political challenge involved in the development problématique of our times is therefore total. . . .

DEVELOPMENT AND HUMAN FREEDOM

The issue of freedom versus development (or unity or order) which has been posed time and again in human history has of late acquired urgent relevance—for the countries of the Third World, for the thinking on economic development (increasingly becoming one of the central issues in international relations), and for global policy in respect of the relationship between human rights and the achievement of a just world order. At long last, the technocratic view of global development (in which technology, unencumbered by politics, would remove poverty and inequity from the world) is giving place to one in which the diffusion of political rights and the capacity of various countries to achieve modes of development suited to their respective needs are seen as necessary concomitants of both a stable and a just world. This is a good time to re-examine certain assumptions about the relationship between democracy and development and to put the current debate on human rights in a proper global perspective.

THE ISSUE OF ECONOMIC DEVELOPMENT

The first of these assumptions, held steadfastly by a majority of theoreticians on development (especially in the North but also some in the South), is that a strong and centralized government with dictatorial powers is better able to embark on rapid economic development and take radical measures aimed at removal of poverty and inequity among the mass of the people. Evidence from a number of developing countries does not support this belief. Most of these countries present a picture of a high level of economic mismanagement accompanied by an increase in disparities and deterioration in the condition of the poorer sections of the people. Even where, either through the help of large-scale foreign corporate investment or through a process of internal exploitation by a local industrial and bureaucratic élite, high rates of economic growth have been achieved for a few years, the benefits of such growth have been cornered by a small élite. Practically no thought is given to initiating basic structural changes involving a better distribution of land or of incomes and employment, with the result that the condition of the ordinary people actually deteriorates.

The economic advantages of authoritarian regimes have always been illusory. Especially in culturally and demographically complex countries, it can turn out to be much worse as it ignores the need for involving different sectors and strata of the people in the productive process, which alone can generate the necessary demand for goods and services, and for undertaking reforms in the structure of economic relations, which alone can stimulate both an efficient system of production and an equitable system of distribution.

THE ISSUE OF STABILITY

The second assumption about the relationship between democracy and development is more political and has to be distinguished from the economic justification of authoritarianism. This is the widely held belief that democracy is unsuitable to developing societies as it brings large masses of people into the political process, raises expectations, and leads to unrest and instability. This is a belief held by a number of conservative thinkers in the West, especially in the United States, whose main concern is with sources of instability and conflict in the Third World which they think are likely to upset the fine balance on which the international system rests. They would rather put up with dictatorships that can maintain control and order and ensure compliance of the people than encourage a free and open competition for power which may, according to them, lead to rising expectations and class conflict. Apart from the low regard for freedom and dignity that is exhibited by these thinkers, they seem to underrate the possiblity of greater cohesion and stability that an open political process is likely to bring to societies so full of diversity and plurality of allegiance and identification.

THE REAL ISSUE

On the other hand, an end to authoritarianism without a concerted effort to eliminate the worst forms of human misery will not make sense in a large number of countries. The right to human dignity includes both political and economic rights. While an open polity is an essential prerequisite for carrying on the struggle for social justice by the deprived sections of the people, it is necessary also to recognize that the existence of democratic institutions does not by itself guarantee that the poor and the dispossessed will be able to fight for their basic economic and social rights. The two aspects—liberty and liberation—are intimately interwoven. The battle for human liberty is won only when the people themselves feel convinced of it and are prepared to wage it.

UNFORTUNATE DICHOTOMY

And the same is true of the removal of poverty. Our long experience with national planning, U.N. development decades, and external aid for raising standards of living of poor societies shows that while it is possible to build large infrastructures of capital and technology and promote expertise on all aspects of the development problem, they are by themselves incapable of removing the poverty of the masses. The removal of poverty is essentially a political problem: access to power and participation in the making of decisions. The dichotomy between political and socioeconomic rights is unfortunate and is based on a techno-

cratic and apolitical view of the development process. The "right to development" mentioned in a number of U.N. resolutions is not just an economic right. It is also a political right.

The points made above on the relationship between development and human rights become more salient when viewed in the larger framework of a changing global environment. It is the new economic and political framework of high capitalism, high technology and high militarism. It is a framework in which a growing inflationary spiral will greatly escalate the cost of essential raw materials, the cost of energy, and ultimately the cost of food itself, escalations that can only be controlled by rising unemployment. Internationally, this framework—whose basic featrues derive from an exploitative lifestyle which is fast spreading as a norm everywhere, including in the vast peripheries of the globe characterized by massive poverty, undernourishment and hunger—will entail a painful struggle over the distribution of world resources.

THE ISSUE OF LIFESTYLE

Here lies the crux of the matter. Crucial to the effect of an unjust international economic order on the economies of developing countries and the prospects for achieving an adequate standard of living in these countries is the whole question of lifestyle and the extent to which it tends to structure relationships between and within nations.

It is necessary to view the question of lifestyle as a fundamentally political issue, one that provides perhaps the most basic of all conflicts that inform today's world, the most important basis of stratification in the world—both internationally and domestically—and the most pertinent cause of the decline of human rights and fundamental freedoms in large parts of the world. It provides the greatest of all confrontations in the world, with the developed world wanting to maintain—and indeed enhance—the standard of living attained by [it] and the developing world seeking to achieve minimum living standards for its people.

SCENARIO OF CONFLICT

This involves three aspects of growing conflict. The first is the global structuring of the relationship between resources and human beings in which a minority of nations has, in pursuit of a parasitic and wasteful style of life, shored up a large part of world resources. The second aspect is the spread of the same style of life among the "modern" sector of the developing world which has produced deep divisions in these societies, both within each of them and between them severally.

The third aspect arises out of the first two and consists in the growing conflict over the access, distribution and control over world resources for maintaining and raising standards of consumption and lifestyle that have been achieved by the industrialized world and, through emulation and prompting, by the privileged strata of the developing countries. So powerful has been this model of a high-consumption lifestyle that it has undermined both the Liberal dream of expanding welfare for all and the Marxist dream of solidarity of the world proletariat ushering in an egalitarian, classless society. For, inherent in the maintenance of this lifestyle is access to and hence control over energy and industrial raw materials and this necessarily involves growing inequality—between rich and poor countries, between the tiny middle class and the large unorganized masses in the latter, and between the proletariat of the rich countries and the proletariat of the poor countries.

Growing Inequality

Inherent in such a pattern of inequality are many other distortions of our time—the conception of the global economic process as a homogeneous whole, the consequent need to turn formally independent countries into economic colonies, the strident safeguarding of differential advantages of the industrialized countries through all kinds of trade barriers and simultaneous pressure for assuring both the supply of commodities from the developing countries and markets therein for sophisticated consumer goods and gadgetry. For all this it becomes necessary to spread the culture of consumerism globally and at the same time contain and confine the capacities of newly industrializing countries within narrow technological limits; hence the crucial role of the multinationals. Above all, there is the increasingly global sweep of economic diplomacy for ensuring enough surpluses from the world

countryside for meeting the growing demand for resources of the metropolitan centers for maintaining their consumption levels. Given these powerful trends emanating from the existing international order, it is clear that the struggle for minimum living standards and human rights in the developing world is likely to be difficult and long drawn out.

Erosion

In fact, the struggle is running into new and deeper sands. The pursuit of rapacious lifestyles is not simply giving rise to structures of inequity and exploitation between and within societies and denial of basic necessities and fundamental human rights to the large majority of the world; it is also undermining the environment and the basic life support system. Indeed, the environmental erosion entailed in maintaining these lifestyles and concomitant modes of production, technology and land use and settlement patterns in various parts of the world is such that it is becoming increasingly difficult to provide for a *lasting* eradication of poverty and a *sustainable* improvement in the quality of life and levels of living of the world's poor and of future generations. The present patterns of development are so wasteful and destructive of natural resources—land, water and entire ecosystems—that they are producing an increasing and exponential growth in desertification, deforestation and soil degradation which are leading to an overall erosion of the productive process itself—and most of this in the developing countries.

THE NORTH-SOUTH ISSUE

The above analysis shows that central to the struggle for living standards as a basis for the achievement of human rights and fundamental freedoms is the issue of equity. It is an issue that permeates the relationsip between the North and the South, stratification within the South and stratification within the North (for there is growing evidence that under the impact of the crisis of world capitalism, and of unemployment and inflation in the industrialized countries, income disparities and the struggle for control over resources and opportunities is growing in the North as well).

Given this overall framework, it is clear that basic changes in the North are critical for overall structural change in the international order. While the point of departure of this paper is the developing world, it needs also to be stressed that basic changes in the developed world are necessary prerequisites for both (a) the sustainability of human development and survival of life itself [on] the planet and (b) the possibility of any stable and sustainable development of the developing countries which involves competition for the resources that have been in large part appropriated by the developed North. There is a crisis in the North too, arising out of the nature of the world system that it has created, and giving rise to a structural crisis in North-South relations.

TOWARD AN INTERNATIONAL FRAMEWORK FOR ALTERNATIVE DEVELOPMENT STRATEGIES AND LIFESTYLES

It is only in this context of a growing crisis in North-South relations that the concept of alternative development strategies and lifestyles acquires significance. It provides a framework for a more equitable, less wasteful, environmentally sound and socially responsible, self-reliant, decentralized and democratic mode of development—in both the North and the South and across the North-South divide. It needs to be added immediately that the prospects for alternative development and an austere and less wasteful and manipulated lifestyle in the North are not very bright unless an element of compulsion and inevitability is built into the process. This is where the pressure from the Third World for structural change in the global distribution of power and resources can help. Without this there is not much hope for the industrialized world or for dealing with the global economic crisis emanating from it.

Toward a New Ethics of Development

In a basic way, no doubt, the perspective of "alternative development" calls for a normative and philosophical reorientation—an alternative conception of the goals and objectives of development, an alternative vision of the future, an alternative system of values and attitudes, indeed an alternative cultural and intellectual paradigm. Such a paradigm should, among other things, emphasize restraint and self-control in economic behavior. It is useful to recall Gandhi's fundamental point that there can be no freedom or autonomy or self-reliance without a measure of self-control, without a capacity to control human greed and avarice and acquisitiveness, indeed without a measure of "sacrifice," in the here and now.

Gandhi put his finger on the most crucial dimension of moving towards a just social order when he called for a *limitation of wants* and warned his countrymen against falling prey to an industrial machine that not only reduces a majority of men to laboring slaves but also dictates what and how they should eat, wear, dress, sing and dance. Today his insights are even more relevant than when he lived. If men and women are to achieve freedom and dignity and a sense of wholeness, they ought to exercise self-control; autonomy without self-control degenerates into exploitation. If there is to be an end to exploitation and inequity and aggression in society and degradation and rampage and devastation of nature, the present norm of a high-consumption ethic must give place to one that both meets the minimum needs for all men and limits the needless expansion of wants that have no relationship to the basic requirements of body and mind.

Toward an Ethic of Collective Self-reliance

These are not merely ethical propositions. In a basic way they deal with the manner in which resources are to be distributed across regions. Nor again is this aspect limited merely to the relations between the developed and the developing countries. It applies no less to collective self-reliance among the developing countries which happen to be placed at different vantage points in their command over resources and skills and in their capacity to exercise leverage in North-South relations. This applies to the larger and more industrialized and technologically more advanced among the developing countries and above all to the OPEC [Organization of Petroleum Exporting Countries] countries. . . .

Such a closing of ranks is vital to the struggle for justice and human rights—it would be a mistake to expect that the world status quo will give up its position and control over resources and institutional structures. It is more likely that they would fight hard to safeguard their control over resources, markets, commodities and decision-making structures.

BACKLASH OF THE WORLD STATUS QUO

We have already spoken of the global sweep of economic diplomacy aimed at ensuring surpluses from the world countryside. Beyond this—and beyond the well-known re-cycling of excess resources from the richer and larger among the developing world by inducting them into the financial establishment of metropolitan centers—there will be other means of defense of the status quo. Important in this will be the threat of, and perhaps actual implementation of, military confrontation against the Third World—not just for securing oil suplies but indeed for halting the advance of and the collective solidarity of the Third World. Several documents emanating from the North, especially the U.S.A., point to the development of new doctrines of warfare aimed at the Third World.[1] Simultaneously, there are attempts at militarizing major centers of the Third World and at once making them further dependent on the industrialized countries and coopting them into the global power structure.

Within the developing countries too the maintenance of rapacious living standards of entrenched interests (especially of the urban middle class) will lead to further tightening of economic exploitation, social atrocities and political repression, not infrequently backed by military force. One can see a close tie-up between the resource cold war carried out by the centers of power in the North and the repressive regimes in the South leading to a situation of catastrophe—economic, political and social—in many of the developing countries.

The rise of repressive political structures may not be limited to the developing countries as the confrontation described here mounts. Indeed reports to the Trilateral Commission have already recommended the need for limiting the rights and freedom of citizens.[2] In short, it is a scenario of all-out confrontation by the haves of the world against the peoples of the world, in particular against the peoples of the Third World. The movement for human rights and fundamental freedoms has to be evolved, both conceptually and operationally, within this overall framework.

OVERVIEW: INTERNATIONAL AGENDA ON HUMAN RIGHTS

We can now recapitulate the analysis in the form of an agenda for discussion and further work. The issue of disparities in living and appropriate lifestyle and consequent impact on human rights and fundamental freedoms of men and women in the developing world needs to be dealt with at two levels: (a) at the level of re-orientation of values and preferences in the North and to the extent necessary in the South, and a restructuring of the relationship between the North and the South based on new thinking on development and a new leadership that is willing to implement these ideas; and (b) at the level of building a counterforce to the existing order, a counterforce that will compel "structural change"—in the North, in the South, and in the international order. Initiative for this will have in good part to come from the Third World. It will have to be based on:

(I) Collective Self-Reliance, its institutionalization at various levels, and a firm rejection of cooptation into the global power structure,

(II) the political movement towards a New International Economic Order,

(III) a meaningful adoption and implementation of a New International Development Strategy, and as part of all this and indeed only as part of this,

(IV) a well-thought-out international strategy for moving towards an alternative path to a better environment and life-

---

1. See, for instance, Guy J. Pauker, *Military Implications of a Possible World Order Crisis in the 1980s: A Project Air Force Report prepared for the United States Air Force* (Santa Monica: The Rand Corporation, 1977). For a detailed analysis of the new framework of containment through confrontation, see Rajni Kothari, "Towards a Just World." in *Toward a Just World Order*, ed. Richard Falk, Samuel S. Kim, and Saul H. Mendlovitz, vol. 1, 566–601 (Boulder, Colo.: Westview Press, 1982).

2. See, for instance, Michael S. Crozier, Samuel P. Huntington, and Joji Watanuki, *The Crisis of Democracy: Report on the Governability of Democracies to the Trilateral Commission* (New York: New York University Press, 1975).

style—globally, not just in the developing countries.

In conclusion, it may be stressed that the so-called energy crisis caused by the OPEC action in 1973 was an essential part of an overall strategy of global change. Indeed it was a turning point in North-South relations. There is need to devise new strategies of countering the continued dominance of the haves of the world. It is possible to do so, for perhaps for the first time in many decades the world establishment stands on a vulnerable basis—hence the call for "interdependence"—and the same applies to the rich and privileged strata within countries. There is an upsurge of consciousness and a growing assertion of the rights of the underprivileged in large parts of the world, and the situation is ripe for a major effort at structural transformation at various levels. What is needed is a collective effort for mobilizing this potential towards a movement for change, a clarity of vision that transcends old rhetoric and false categories, and a set of clear targets that are pursued with determination through a new "coalition of interests" that cuts across world regions and ideological barriers.

The "Right to Development"

Is it through such a movement of change that the defense of human rights and minimal standards of survival, dignity and self-realization can be renewed and revitalized. The "right to development" needs to be seen in such a comprehensive and holistic framework. It should cover both political rights of freedom of expression and association and economic rights of appropriate living standards and distributive justice. It should encompass both rights of states in the pursuit of national development and control of resources, and rights of individuals, cultural and ethnic groups and minorities. It should provide a deeper basis for human rights by ensuring a lasting and sustainable process of development, that is to say, it should not only entail protection of civil-political, socio-economic and cultural rights of diverse groups as integral parts of a social contract but also of sustainable patterns of development through a balance between nature, technology and human systems. And it should conceive all of this as part of a generalized process of liberation from both external and internal drives towards domination and subservience, exploitation and erosion, imperialism and anarchy.

Individual liberty—the traditional battle cry of human rights—can be achieved only in such a global process of liberation and in the larger context of a lasting unity of mankind based on international cooperation and world peace. In the absence of such a holistic perspective, human rights will remain a sectarian cause, ideologically sterile and politically controversial.

QUESTIONS FOR REFLECTION AND DISCUSSION

1. What does Rajni Kothari mean by a "holistic perspective" upon human rights? What elements does he envision as part of the balance of systems for which he argues? What problems do you see in constructing a "coalition of interests" that would "cut across world regions and ideological barriers"?

2. Julius Nyerere, ex-President of Tanzania, has commented: "Freedom and development are as completely linked as chickens and eggs. Without chickens, you get no eggs; and without eggs you soon have no chickens." He analogized: "Without freedom you get no development; and without development you soon lose your freedom." The inseparable interdependence of economic, social, and cultural rights with civil and political rights, as well as the inherent importance of such rights, has been repeatedly affirmed by the United Nations. Is this claimed interdependence valid?

3. It often is argued that it is necessary to restrict human rights for the sake of development. Is there any foundation to this contention? Should a trade-off be accepted as at least a possible necessity? How would Kothari answer these questions? Why?

4. In *Human Rights and Foreign Policy* ([Oxford: Pergamon Press, 1981], 19), Evan Luard observes that

human rights [for poor countries] begin with breakfast. What matters to them is that people should have enough to eat and to house and to clothe their families. The civil and political liberties to which Western countries attach such importance, therefore, are a luxury and an irrelevance which have little meaning for such countries.

How do you respond to this observation? How would Kothari? Is Luard contradicting the viewpoint expressed by Nyerere in question 2? Or is he talking about something else? If so, what?

5. In debate at the United Nations on the proposed new international economic order (NIEO), there has emerged a strongly held view that the establishment of an NIEO is an *essential* as opposed to an *important* element for the effective promotion and the full enjoyment of human rights and fundamental freedoms for all. That is, the establishment of a NIEO is seen by significant numbers of people to be indispensable for the exercise of all human rights. How does this viewpoint square with Kothari's? Is it consistent? Inconsistent? Is it likely to encourage the support of the Western countries for a "new international economic order"? What would Kothari say?

6. Kothari considers development to be a human right. Do you agree? Should development be considered a human right? If so, how do you define and operationalize it? Is it anything more than the achievement of all the economic, social, and cultural rights enumerated in, say, the Universal Declaration of Human Rights? If not, why speak of it as a separate human right? If so, what else might it be?

7. Kothari considers the "right to development" to be a political as well as an economic right? How is this possible? What does Kothari mean?

8. In 1977, during the period of martial law under President Ferdinand E. Marcos, Marcos said to the Board of Governors of the Asian Development Bank:

> In many Third World countries, there is great urgency today for national development to affirm and give real substance to our avowals in favor of human rights. Without any any concrete effort to provide for basic needs, and the minimum of human welfare, our commitment to human rights would become a farce. But we cannot procure our development at the expense of the rights of those whom we are, in the first place, pledged to liberate. There can be no trade-off between economic development and human rights.

Do you agree with this statement? Would Kothari? Considering its source, might you question its validity? Its political genuineness? What objectives might Marcos have been trying to serve by making the statement?

---

11. PHILIP ALSTON *International Law and the Right to Food*

INTRODUCTION

Few human rights have been endorsed with such frequency, unanimity or urgency as the right to food, yet probably no other human right has been as comprehensively and systematically violated on such a wide scale in recent decades. The importance of the relevant norms in international law is attested to by the fact that the right to freedom from hunger is the only human right which the framers of the two International Human Rights Covenants specifically termed "fundamental."[1] In addition, the right to food has been solemnly proclaimed by a succession of international conferences, in national constitutions, by governments and legislatures of all persuasions, and by many eminent and influential groups and individuals. Yet despite this impressive array of support for the right to food, no concerted effort has been made either to spell out in detail the implications of the relevant norm or to establish effective national and international machinery to promote compliance with existing international human rights obligations relating to food. While there is no shortage of reasons which have been proffered to justify this neglect, the magnitude of the continuing problems of hunger

1. [See the Appendix.]

Reprinted, with changes, from Philip Alston, "International Law and the Right to Food," in *Food as a Human Right*, ed. A. Eide, W. Eide, S. Goonatilake, J. Gussow & Omawale (Tokyo: United Nations University, 1984), 162–74. Copyright © 1984 by the United Nations University. Reprinted by permission.

and malnutrion in the world demands that urgent consideration be given to proposals which might help to bridge the gap between the rhetoric and reality and thereby contribute to realization of the right to food.

ARGUMENTS AGAINST RECOGNITION OF THE RIGHT TO FOOD

Before embarking upon an analysis of the existing international legal standards in this field it is useful to take note of the main arguments that have been used to justify the international community's failure to undertake any meaningful codification of norms relating to the right to food. Although the validity, or more appropriately the invalidity, of these arguments will not be explicitly considered in the present essay, it is necessary to keep them in mind when considering the feasibility (political as well as technical) of various proposals designed to overcome such objections to serious consideration of the right to food.

The first argument is, in essence, that such an exercise would be a waste of time since moral and humanitarian considerations alone will not move governments or other relevant actors to respect the right to food. In this view food is first and foremost a commodity which is traded annually for billions of dollars and its status as a human right is very much secondary to this fact. A sympathetic version of this ''realist'' thesis has been explained in the following terms by Haverberg:

In theory, moral considerations should play a significant role in policy decisions. In practice, however, such factors *per se* are not taken into account at the national planning level. . . . Nutrition cannot be sold to governments on humanitarian grounds. Since moral dicta and nutritional principles generally converge, the most that can be hoped for is that nutritional considerations will play a more dominant role in policy formulation, and thus moral issues while not explicitly addressed will be implicitly implied.[2]

The second argument is that the complexity of the issues involved in promoting realization of the right, and the absence of a universal consensus on either the causes of, or the solutions to, the problem, make it virtually impossible to establish effective machinery for implementation of the right to food. Thus, in the personal view of the Legal Counsel to the Food and Agriculture Organization (FAO), J. P. Dobbert, the right to food ''is not enforceable at the international level and only within very narrow contractual limits at the national level.''

The third argument, which is generally applied to economic, social and cultural human rights as a whole, is that civil and political rights are of prior importance and that economic rights such as the right to food are only likely to be realized once freedom has been attained by the peoples of the world. As Michael Novak, President Reagan's Ambassador to the UN Human Rights Commission has written:

Many in the world are indeed hungry. But there is a prior issue. Less than half the world—barely a third—is free. More than two-thirds is slave. . . . Hunger, or at least poverty, is the long-trend line of the human race. Such poverty did not begin with the present generation or with present-day economic systems. . . . If [President Carter] wishes to end hunger and poverty, let him first break the shackles of whole empires of the unfree.[3]

EXISTING INTERNATIONAL LEGAL STANDARDS RELATING TO THE RIGHT TO FOOD

. . . [T]he right to food has been situated in relation to the overall system which exists for the promotion and protection of human rights. In the present essay, consideration is given first to the range of right-to-food-related standards which have been adopted to date as part of international treaty law and then, more specifically, to the background and normative content of the single most important source—article 11 of the International Covenant on Economic, Social and Cultural Rights (ESCR Covenant).[4]

Other[s] . . . have noted the importance of article 25(1) of the Universal Declaration of Human

2. L. Haverberg, ''Individual Needs: Nutritional Guidelines for Policy?'' in *Food Policy: The Responsibility of the United States in the Life and Death Choices*, ed. Peter Brown and Henry Shue (New York: Free Press, 1977), 212.
3. Michael Novak, *The March of Defeat: Morality and Foreign Policy* (Washington, D.C.: Georgetown University Press, 1978), 38, 41–2.
4. [See the Appendix.]

Rights of 1948[5] which provides that "everyone has the right to a standard of living adequate for the health and well-being of himself and his family, including food." An analysis of article 11 of the ESCR Covenant should be seen not only against the background of that provision, but also of several other articles of the Universal Declaration. The most important of these are: (a) article 3 which provides that "everyone has the right to life"; (b) article 22 relating to the realization, through national efforts and international co-operation of economic, social and cultural rights; (c) article 28 which provides that "everyone is entitled to a social and international order in which the rights and freedoms set forth in this Declaration can be fully realized"; and (d) article 29(1) which states that "everyone has duties to the community."

Articles 28 and 29 . . . are of particular importance since they have no direct counterparts in the International Covenants which were intended to elaborate upon the provisions of the Universal Declaration. The other articles were taken up in the Covenants. The right to self-determination which is the first article in each of the two Covenants, is sometimes mistakenly neglected in the context of the right to food. It is clear that there is a strong incentive for states which are genuinely committed to achieving and maintaining their right to self-determination to ensure food self-reliance. In addition, however, it is also arguable that a government would be in violation of the right to self-determination if it permitted the exploitation of the country's food-producing capacity (natural resources) in the exclusive interests of a small part of the population or of foreign (public or private) corporate interests while a large number of the state's inhabitants were starving or malnourished.

Article 6 of the International Covenant on Civil and Political Rights,[6] which proclaims every human being's "inherent right to life," is also relevant to the right to food. This point was underlined in 1982 by the Human Rights Committee which was established to supervise states' compliance with their obligations under that Covenant. The Committee observed that the expression "inherent right to life" could not properly be interpreted in a restrictive manner and that protection of the right requires states to adopt positive measures rather than merely refraining from certain proscribed measures. More specifically, the Committee considered that it would be desirable for states parties to the Covenant "to take all possible measures to reduce infant mortality and to increase life expectancy, especially in adopting measures to eliminate malnutrition and epidemics."

Another important international law source of guarantees of the right to food is to be found in the four Geneva Conventions of 1949 and their two Protocols of 1977.[7] These instruments constitute the essence of modern international humanitarian law and they contain a number of provisions designed to ensure enjoyment of the right to food by both civilians and former combatants in time of war. Paradoxically, the relevant provisions are, in a number of respects, more detailed and comprehensive than those provisions of international law which govern realization of the right to food in peacetime.

None of the regional human rights instruments (the European Charter on Human Rights, the American Convention on Human Rights and the African Charter of Human and Peoples' Rights) contain any specific mention of the right to food. It appears that, in each case, the right to work and the right to social security are considered to be sufficiently comprehensive and to render specific provisions relating to food superflu-

---

5. [See the Appendix.]
6. [See the Appendix.]
7. [See Geneva Convention for the Amelioration of the Condition of the Wounded, and Sick in Armed Forces in the Field, Aug. 12, 1949, 75 U.N.T.S. 31; Geneva Convention for the Amelioration of the Condition of the Wounded, Sick and Shipwrecked Members of the Armed Forces at Sea, Aug. 12, 1949, 75 U.N.T.S. 85; Geneva Convention Relative to the Treatment of Prisoners of War, Aug. 12, 1949, 75 U.N.T.S. 135; Geneva Convention Relative to the Protection of Civilian Persons in Time of War, Aug. 12, 1949, 75 U.N.T.S. 287. See also Protocol Additional to the Geneva Conventions of 12 August 1949, and Relating to the Protection of Victims of International Armed Conflicts (Protocol I); and Protocol Additional to the Geneva Conventions of 12 August 1949, and Relating to the Protection of Victims of Non-International Armed Conflicts (Protocol II). For the texts of Protocols I and II, see Diplomatic Conference on the Reaffirmation and Development of International Humanitarian Law Applicable in Armed Conflicts, Final Act (1977), reprinted in *International Legal Materials*, Vol. 16 (1977) pp. 1391 & 1442.]

ous. The validity of this assumption would, however, appear to be questionable.

ARTICLE 11 OF THE ESCR COVENANT

The primary focus in the present analysis is on article 11 of the International Covenant on Economic, Social and Cultural Rights which proclaims the right to adequate food as well as the right to be free from hunger. Its pre-eminence among international right-to-food norms is due to the following factors: (a) it represents a codification of the earlier norm contained in the Universal Declaration of Human Rights; (b) its content was significantly shaped by the FAO; (c) it is more detailed and specific than most other relevant international legal norms; (d) 74 states (as [of] 1 September 1982) have formally accepted the obligation in international law to take steps to achieve progressively the full realization of the right; and (e) a mechanism has been established under the Covenant to monitor states parties' compliance with their obligations, including those relating to the right to food.

Article 11 of the Covenant states as follows:

1. The States Parties to the present Covenant recognize the right of everyone to an adequate standard of living for himself and his family, including adequate food, clothing and housing, and to the continuous improvement of living conditions. The States Parties will take appropriate steps to ensure the realization of this right, recognizing to this effect the essential importance of international co-operation based on free consent.
2. The States Parties to the present Covenant, recognizing the fundamental right of everyone to be free from hunger, shall take, individually and through international co-operation, the measures, including specific programmes, which are needed:
(a) To improve methods of production, conservation and distribution of food by making full use of technical and scientific knowledge, by disseminating knowledge of the principles of nutrition and by developing or reforming agrarian systems in such a way as to achieve the most efficient development and utilization of natural resources;
(b) Taking into account the problems of both food-importing and food-exporting countries, to ensure an equitable distribution of world food supplies in relation to need.

The importance of article 11 was recognized in the following terms by the FAO in its 1981 report on implementation of the Covenant:

It is . . . widely recognized that, by adopting the measures indicated in article 11.2 of the [Covenant], the international community would be in a position to eliminate completely the present state of chronic malnutrition and undernourishment and to mitigate considerably the effects of calamities.

Such an assessment assumes that the "measures indicated" in article 11 are rather clearer and more straightforward than most commentators have thought them to be. It thus becomes imperative to determine as far as possible, on the basis of both the preparatory work (*travaux préparatoires*) at the drafting stage, and by any other available materials, the precise normative content of the article.

. . . [A]rticle 11 was drafted in response to a specific proposal by FAO. Debate on the article in the Third Committee of the General Assembly was relatively brief and it could be said that the wording of the proposed article was subjected to less demanding analysis and scrutiny than that of almost any other article in the Covenant.

A LEGAL ANALYSIS OF ARTICLE 11

In order to make effective use of any norm of international human rights law it is necessary to establish: (a) its content; (b) the subjects or beneficiaries; (c) the objects or duty-holders; and (d) mechanisms to promote compliance. In the remainder of this [essay] the first three of these aspects will be examined with respect to article 11 of the Covenant.

THE CONTENT OF THE NORM

The "right to food" is in fact a shorthand expression encompassing two separate norms contained in article 11. The first, stated in paragraph 1, derives from the "right of everyone to an adequate standard of living for himself and his family, including adequate food" and can be termed the right to adequate food. The second, proclaimed in paragraph 2, is the "right of everyone to be free from hunger." In most analyses that have been undertaken to date the two have been treated as being synonymous, with a preference nevertheless being shown for the latter. It is submitted that, while on the one hand there is a significant difference between the two norms, with the first being much broader than the second, on the other hand the term "right to adequate food" is the appropriate overall one since there is no indication that paragraph 2 was intended by the drafters or by states which have ratified the Covenant to restrict or narrow the scope of the right proclaimed in paragraph 1.

The practical implications of taking, as the primary norm, the right to adequate food rather than the right to be free from hunger are significant. Whereas the former facilitates the adoption of a maximalist approach, the latter, which is more akin to a sub-norm, is able at least in theory to be satisfied by the adoption of policies designed to provide a minimum daily nutritional intake. While it may be appropriate to focus on freedom from hunger as a means by which to mobilize public support and as a starting point for national and international efforts, such an approach should be seen only as the first step towards realization of the primary norm which is the right to adequate food. In terms of quantity the notion of adequacy implies enough food to facilitate a normal, active existence rather than a minimum calorific package which does no more than prevent death by starvation. Moreover, in terms of quality the adequacy standard goes further than the freedom from hunger sub-norm in focusing on the cultural appropriateness of the food.

In essence article 11(2) is divided into sub-paragraphs dealing respectively with the national (article 11(2)(a)) and the international (article 11(2)(b)) dimensions of the right to food. The text of the latter, which requires that measures be taken to ensure an equitable distribution of world food supplies, is relatively straightforward although its precise implications are debatable. By contrast the former sub-paragraph is poorly drafted and confused despite the fact that it incorporates most of the keywords which should be in such a provision.

The principal objectives specified in article 11(2)(a) are: (a) to improve methods of food *production* with a view to promoting realization of the right to food; (b) to improve methods of food *conservation* with a view to promoting realization of the right to food; and (c) to improve methods of food *distribution* with a view to promoting realization of the right to food. In addition, the article lists other matters which, although presented as though they were only means for the achievement of the three main objectives, can be more

adequately characterized as secondary or complementary objectives. They are: (d) making full use of technical and scientific knowledge; (e) disseminating knowledge of the principles of nutrition; and (f) developing or reforming agrarian systems. Despite the absence of an appropriate comma, it seems safe to assume that the final phrase, "in such a way as to achieve the most efficient development and utilization of natural resources," applies to the paragraph in its entirety rather than only to objective (f).

Two points about article 11(2)(a) warrant particular emphasis. The first is that none of the individual objectives is relevant for its own sake but only insofar as it contributes to the realization of the overall normative end, which is ensuring the right of everyone to be free from hunger. Thus for example the Covenant cannot be interpreted as supporting increased food production or agrarian reform per se. This fundamental point has all too often been neglected or even contradicted in analyses to date of the right to food. The second point is that attempts to distill from article 11(2)(a) an ordered, detailed, operational approach to the right to food are misplaced given the lack of detail and the degree of confusion which characterize the provision.

Nevertheless, the broad content of the norm is relatively clear and, taken as it is, it is sufficient to enable a determination in some cases that particular acts, or omissions to act, are either in conformity or in conflict with the norm. But this is clearly not enough if the right to food is to be fully implemented. The question then is whether anything has been done to elaborate upon the provisions of the basic norm. Two possibilities warrant examination in this regard. The first is whether instruments adopted by various organs since the adoption of the Covenant in 1966 can be considered to have contributed to a codification of the norm. The most prominent candidate would be the Universal Declaration on the Eradication of Hunger and Malnutrition adopted by the World Food Conference and endorsed by the General Assembly in 1974. Yet while the Declaration does proclaim the "right to be free from hunger and malnutrition" it does not refer specifically either to article 25 of the Universal Declaration of Human Rights or to the Covenant. There is thus no stated intention of elaborating upon or interpreting the relevant provisions of the Covenant, and the content of the Declaration or similar instruments cannot be taken to constitute an authoritative interpretation of the norm.

The second potential means by which light could have been shed on the content of the norm is through the jurisprudence of the body charged with the supervision of states' compliance with their obligations under the Covenant. In practice, however, the Working Group established by the Economic and Social Council to assist it in this task has achieved nothing of any consequence in this respect.

THE SUBJECTS AND BENEFICIARIES OF THE RIGHT TO FOOD

The principal holders of the right to food under the terms of article 11 are individuals. The right of individuals is formulated in terms of "the right of everyone." Whereas sub-paragraph 2 uses only this phrase, the terminology used in sub-paragraph 1 is "the right of everyone . . . for himself and his family." The question which then arises is to what exactly is the individual entitled? In practical terms, the answer will depend on the circumstances of the individual and of his or her geographical location at a given time. From the present perspective the most important point is to recognize the need to develop, at the national level, a set of relevant legal norms which reflects and seeks to satisfy the state's international legal obligation to promote realization of the right of everyone to adequate food.

Another level at which one can identify a holder of the right to food is that of the state. Whether this is a collective right attaching directly to peoples or to states or whether it is rather an aggregation of the human rights of individuals which is articulated through the medium of the state, is an important theoretical question, but it is of limited practical relevance in the present context.

Article 11 does not specifically identify states as holders of the right to food. Nevertheless, by imposing duties upon states to act, "through international co-operation," the article implicitly vests rights in certain states as a corollary of the duty of all states to act. Moreover, in practical terms, the obligation of states parties "to ensure an equitable distribution of world food supplies

in relation to need" can only be operationalized on an inter-state basis. The shield (or the sword) of state sovereignty severely restricts the possibility of implementing such an obligation at any other level.

The question of which states might be entitled to make claims on the grounds that they are subjects of the right to food, can only be answered on the basis of an assessment of the overall availability of food at the national level by comparison with the aggregated needs of the state's inhabitants for adequate food. The closest the international community has come to making such a global assessment is the category of "most seriously affected countries" which were those which, in the wake of the 1972 oil-price rises, were deemed to be in need of emergency assistance to pay for minimum import requirements of food, fertilizers and industrial inputs. This categorization is effectively obsolete today. Other criteria would therefore need to be established in order to assess whether or not a particular country enjoys an equitable share of world food supplies in relation to need.

THE OBJECTS OR DUTY-HOLDERS OF THE NORM

In analyzing the duties relating to the right to food which derive from the relevant provisions of the Covenant four main categories can be distinguished. They are: (a) states in respect of their domestic duties; (b) states in respect of their external duties; (c) individuals; and (d) the international community.

Before seeking to establish the scope and nature of these duties it is useful to refer briefly to the approach to duties proposed by Henry Shue in his important work, *Basic Rights*.[8] . . . He suggests that three types of duties correlate with every basic right. As applied to what he terms a "subsistence right" such as the right to food, these are:

(a) Duties not to eliminate a person's only available means of subsistence—duties to *avoid* depriving.
(b) Duties to protect people against deprivation of the only available means of subsistence by other people—duties to *protect* from deprivation.

8. Henry Shue, *Basic Rights: Subsistence, Affluence and U.S. Foreign Policy* (Princeton, N.J.: Princeton University Press, 1980), 53.

(c) Duties to provide for the subsistence of those unable to provide for their own—duties to *aid* the deprived.

It is beyond the scope of this [essay] to analyze the consequences for various entities of applying such an approach to the duties which attach to the right to food. Nevertheless such an analysis will have to be undertaken sooner or later if the duties attaching to the right to food are to be [spelled] out and an appropriate system of accountability established. Such a system is an indispensable component of a comprehensive, balanced, practical and effective approach to the right to food.

States' Domestic Duties

In essence the domestic obligation of a state party to the Covenant is to take steps, to the maximum of its available resources with a view to achieving progressively the full realization of the right of everyone, without discrimination, to adequate food (articles 2(1), and 2, and 11(1)). . . . The key issue as regards states parties' domestic duties concerns the meaning of the obligation "to take steps." It is clear on the basis of the text both of article 2 and of articles 6–15 dealing with individual rights, that the phrase "to the maximum of its available resources" should not lead to the obligation being viewed exclusively as a matter of making appropriate budgetary allocations.

Although the Covenant does not contain any provision which is equivalent to article 2 of the International Covenant on Civil and Political Rights which specifically requires states to take "necessary" legislative and other measures, it is reasonable to assume on the basis of the *travaux préparatoires*, and of the practice of states in their reports under the Covenant that the "steps" required to be taken include the adoption of some type of legislative, executive and/or administrative measures oriented specifically towards realization of the right in question. The validity of such an emphasis on the role of law is also confirmed by the provisions of article 2(2) whereby states parties "undertake to guarantee" the exercise of the relevant rights without discrimination on certain grounds, article 3 by which states parties "undertake to ensure the equal right of men and women to the enjoyment" of the relevant rights, and article 4 whereby limitations on the enjoyment of rights are restricted to those

"determined by law." In addition, article 11(1) commits states parties to "take appropriate steps to *ensure* the realization of this right." [Emphasis Alston's.]

Insofar as a requirement to take legal or administrative measures can be deduced from the Covenant it does not amount to an obligation to ensure immediate realization. This is made abundantly clear by the use of the phrase "achieving progressively." Nevertheless, the leeway provided by this provision does not obviate the need to adopt at least rudimentary laws and for regulations and/or policy statements designed to establish appropriate policies and to form the basis on which progressive realization can be built. As an indication of good faith this could be expected to include the drawing up of a coherent, and as far as possible comprehensive, plan setting out the steps to be followed in seeking to realize progressively the right to food. Article 11(2) provides an indication of some of the matters which should be addressed in the context of specific legislative or administrative measures.

In contrast to states parties' obligations under the Civil and Political Rights Covenant, states parties to the other Covenant are not required to ensure that an effective remedy is available to any person whose economic rights, including the right to food, are violated. This would not of course preclude the adoption of such an approach in domestic law or in the context of a regional human rights arrangement.

Thus, despite the apparent vagueness of the domestic duties of states to implement the Covenant's provisions on the right to food their importance should not be underestimated. In addition to representing an international obligation on the basis of which they can be held accountable, politically as well as legally, states parties have also made a formal commitment against which their own peoples may assess their domestic policies.

States' External Duties

General Assembly resolutions 34/46, 35/179, and 36/133 have recognized that

in order fully to guarantee human rights and complete personal dignity, it is necessary to guarantee the right to (inter alia) . . . proper nourishment, through the adoption of measures at the national and international levels, including the establishment of the new international economic order.

Similarly food has figured prominently in various NIEO-related instruments such as the Programme of Action on the Establishment of a New International Economic Order.[9] This emphasis on the international dimensions of the right to food accurately reflects the approach adopted in the Covenant.

With respect to external duties states parties to the Covenant are obliged to take steps through international assistance and co-operation, especially economic and technical, to the maximum of their available resources with a view to achieving progressively the full realization of the right to food (article 2(1) and article 11). Although the potential beneficiaries of this provision are not specifically limited to states parties, the Covenant cannot readily be interpreted as vesting legal rights in non-states parties. States are also required to avoid depriving any people of [their] own means of subsistence (article 1(2)). The "essential importance of international co-operation" is further recognized in article 11(1), but it is stated to be "based on free consent." The significance of this qualification is open to debate. The *travaux préparatoires* do not enlighten us but the qualification was presumably inserted as a safety clause against any assumption that food-surplus states have an automatic responsibility to make transfers to food-deficit states. Nevertheless, "free consent" cannot reasonably be interpreted as nullifying the commitment to international co-operation (either in paragraph 1 or 2 of article 11) by rendering it entirely optional. Nor can it defeat the overall responsibility provided for in article 2. It should thus be taken as meaning that while an obligation to international co-operation exists, the form which such co-operation will take is to be determined in accordance with the free consent of the state concerned.

States parties to the Covenant also undertake to take measures "to ensure an equitable distribution of world food supplies in relation to need" and in so doing to take "into account the problems of both food-importing and food-exporting countries" (article 11(2)(b)). By applying the approach proposed by Henry Shue it is possible, in general terms, to arrive at the following list of duties which could be derived from this obligation.

Duties to avoid depriving

1. The duty to avoid international policies and practices which deprive other states of their means of subsistence or which promote an inequitable distribution of world food supplies.
2. The duty to mitigate national policies which have the effect of promoting an inequitable distribution of world food supplies.
3. The duty not to use food as an international sanction

Duties to protect from deprivation

4. The duty to ensure that international trade and aid policies and practices contribute as far as possible to the equitable distribution of world food supplies.
5. The duty to regulate the activities of domestically based entities (including transnational corporations and state trading enterprises) whose activities have, or might have, a significant impact on the distribution of world food supplies.

Duties to aid the deprived

6. The duty of food-surplus states to contribute to emergency buffer schemes and to assist in cases of internationally declared emergencies.
7. The duty to co-operate as far as possible with multilateral programs which are aimed at ensuring an equitable distribution of world food supplies.

It is clear, however, that such a list of duties is of limited practical value in the short term. What is required in the longer term is the transformation of these duties into a legally binding instrument which is presented as an elaboration of the general obligation laid out in article 11.

The Duties of Individuals

Before considering the question of the individual's duty to promote regulation of the right

---

9. Declaration on the Establishment of a New International Economic Order, May 1, 1974, U.N.G.A. Res. 3201 (S-VI), 6 (Special) U.N. GAOR, Supp. (No. 1) 3, U.N. Doc. A/9559 (1974). *See also* Programme of Action on the Establishment of the New International Economic Order, May 1, 1974, U.N.G.A. Res. 3202 (S-VI), 6 (Special) U.N. GAOR, Supp. (No. 1) 5, U.N. Doc. A/9559 (1974). In addition, see Report of the Secretary General, *The International Dimensions of the Right to Development as a Human Right*, U.N. Doc. E/CN. 4/1334 (1979).

to food, it must be noted that in human rights debates at the international level relatively little attention has been given to the overall question of the specific duties which may be considered to correlate to the rights [spelled] out in the International Bill of Human Rights. In general terms, however, the Preamble to each of the Covenants states that the individual does have "duties to other individuals and to the community to which he belongs [and] is under a responsibility to strive for the promotion and observance of the rights recognized" in the Covenant. In the context of the right to food this would seem to involve, as a minimum, a duty not to over-consume and not to waste food.

The range of individual duties could of course be further expanded in line with Shue's categories discussed above. In practice, the important point is that states parties to the Covenant are not only entitled, but are required, to give careful consideration to measures designed to promote the observance, on the part of individuals, of their relevant duties with respect to the right to food.

The Duties of the International Community

The duty to co-operate internationally is affirmed in general terms in articles 55 and 56 of the UN Charter and specifically in terms of the right to food in article 11 in conjunction with article 2 of the Covenant. To a large extent the

duties which can be attributed to the international community on the basis of the Covenant have been discussed above in relation to states' external duties. Further consideration, however, needs to be given to the duties relating to the right to food which can be attributed to the various food policies and operational agencies established by the international community. . . .

CONCLUSION

The foregoing survey of issues raised by the right to food provision of article 11 of the ESCR Covenant does not provide us with a particularly encouraging picture. Rather, it shows that while the basic norm is clearly enunciated, no amount of strict legal construction or interpretation of the subsidiary norms will suffice to produce a clear and widely acceptable framework within which the right to food could be effectively operationalized. As foreseen in article 23 of the Covenant, a convention spelling out the normative implications of the right to food is thus a fundamental prerequisite to effective action by states and by the international community towards operationalization of the right to food. Until such an exercise is undertaken the concept of a right to food as a human right will continue to be abused for rhetorical purposes while being ignored for all practical purposes.

QUESTIONS FOR REFLECTION AND DISCUSSION

1. As Philip Alston points out, economics and philosophy often are hard to distinguish when addressing questions such as the right to food. Is this an economic or moral problem? If it is both, what is the relationship between the two types of problems? Consider the following passage from John Rawls ("Social Unity and Primary Goods," in *Utilitarianism and Beyond*, ed. Amartya Sen and Bernard Williams [Cambridge: Cambridge University Press, 1985], 184–5), in which he discusses the relationship among primary goods (basic liberties, freedom of choice, shares of wealth, income, and self-respect) in economic utilitarianism:

> To an economist concerned with social justice and public policy an index of primary goods may seem merely *ad hoc* patchwork not amenable to theory. It is for this reason that I have tried to explain the philosophical background of such an index. For the economist's reaction is partly right: an index of primary goods does not belong to theory in the economist's sense. It belongs instead to a conception of justice which falls under the liberal alternative to the tradition of the one rational good. Thus the problem is not how to specify an accurate measure of some psychological or other attribute available only to science. Rather, it is a moral and practical problem. The use of primary goods is not a makeshift which better theory can replace, but a reasonable social practice which we try to design so as to achieve the workable agreement required for effective and willing social cooperation among citizens whose understanding of social utility rests on a con-

ception of justice. Economic theory is plainly indispensable in determining the more definite features of the practice of making interpersonal comparisons in the circumstances of a particular society. What is essential is to understand the problem against the appropriate philosophical background.

Do you agree with Rawls's formulation of the nature of the relationship between economics and philosophy? As it applies to the right to food?

2. Alston raises an interesting question concerning reciprocal rights over world resources. If Mexico, for instance, asserted a claim over food supplies originating in the United States, could the United States justify a claim over the oil in the Mexican wells? What arguments could be made for and against such reciprocal claims?

3. Is it justifiable to use food as a sanction, to punish behavior that violates the policies—particularly the clear policies—of the donor country? If so, when? In the past, the use of such a sanction has been for the most part ineffective. Would your answer be any different if it could be shown that the use of food as a sanction would positively influence oppressive regimes to move toward more democratic governance?

4. Alston raises the question of who is entitled to food, the individual or the state. Is this an important theoretical question? Why? Who do you think has a right to food?

5. Do you agree that the "right to life" should include the right to be free from hunger? Although perhaps sensible as a syntactical proposition, what legitimate difficulties could result from joining the two rights? Are any of these difficulties sufficient to weigh against the linkage of the two? What is lost by *not* linking the two rights together?

6. Do you agree with the critique that the right to food is only aspirational, that no practical norms can be developed in this area given the present geopolitical structure, and that the status quo therefore will continue indefinitely? Are Alston's arguments for the potential of human rights law to create new norms in this area convincing? Why? Why not?

12. HENN-JURI UIBOPUU *The Internationally Guaranteed Right of an Individual to a Clean Environment*

INTRODUCTION

Environmental disruption has only recently become the concern of almost all sectors of public life, both international and national. It was also a long time before jurists began to make contributions toward a worldwide solution of the problems of environmental protection, and it will take a long time to solve all the pending problems. We shall deal only with one sector of the spectrum of the newly-emerging international law of environmental protection: The status of the individual under this law. Nature preservation has focussed on fauna, flora and other features of man's surroundings and there already has been success in protecting them from destruction. But nowadays, it can be clearly stated, man himself has become the endangered species. It seems, therefore, legitimate to ask whether the individ-

ual already has obtained a special status under international environmental law, whatever this law may comprise and however elaborate its system may be. . . .

THE RIGHT OF AN INDIVIDUAL TO A SOUND ENVIRONMENT

The question whether individuals may enjoy special rights under international law has been thoroughly discussed in the past and an affirmative answer seems to be correct if we take into account the development of human rights after World War II. A repetition of all the manifold arguments in favor of this assertion is superfluous.

There also has been some discussion of the exact definition of "environment." Being origi-

Reprinted, with changes, from Henn-Juri Uibopuu, "The Internationally Guaranteed Right of an Individual to a Clean Environment," *Comparative Law Yearbook* 1 (1977): 101–20. Reprinted by permission of Kluwer Academic Publishers.

nally a French word used in the sense of "milieu naturel, que entoure l'homme," the notion of human environment provides the first logical connecting point for an assessment that the environment should serve human needs. If we accept that the protection of this environment by international legal norms is a newly emerging phenomenon, the legal status of the individual could or should be determined in one or another form. At first glance, there seem to be two possibilities: international environmental law in the making could have granted an individual special status, or the general law on human rights could have developed a special rule on such individual rights to a sound environment. Although a clear-cut division between these two claims seems impossible, it may be appropriate to analyze each separately.

The exact determination of the word "sound" will be made later in connection with an attempt at examining the scope of this alleged right of the individual.

International environmental law has emerged at the level of State-to-State claims. The cause célèbre, the *Trail Smelter Arbitration*,[1] clearly shows the elements of the "Law of Good Neighborliness": the prohibition of injurious deposition of deleterious pollutants in the territory of another State; the payment of compensation for past pollution damages; and the prescription of régimes which either prohibit the activity causing the harm or permit its continuation on a reduced scale. The act of contamination is considered here to violate the victim State's sovereign autonomy, and this sovereignty has hitherto remained the principal starting point in the "consideration of . . . state responsibility for conduct entailing extraterritorial environmental effects upon other states."[2]

After violation has been determined, a State whose territory is violated has the right to act on behalf of individuals under its jurisdiction and to collect compensation for them via diplomatic protection. This means that the individual has no special status under traditional international law. It is at the State's discretion to raise a claim on behalf of individuals. It might be feasible that a State may, for political or other reasons, not be willing to espouse claims of individuals in very small incidents of transnational pollution. On the other hand, the injured individual should have fulfilled two preconditions before diplomatic protection can be exercised on his behalf: he should have exhausted all his local remedies, and he should possess the nationality of the State exercising his diplomatic protection.

This traditional view would restrict claims of states on behalf of individuals to a State's own citizens. But some writers hold that the nationality test has become obsolete in cases of transnational pollution, since States in general act as if their own rights have been violated. If this were true, it would be a slight indication of an improvement in the status of individuals with regard to foreigners. Such claims based on the violation of rights of the State, however, would not fall under diplomatic protection.

The other precondition for diplomatic protection, the exhaustion of local remedies rule, has been overruled in some very special cases. Article XI of the Convention on International liability for Damage Caused by Space Objects[3] of 1971 leaves the victim of such activities the choice to call upon his own government or to forward a claim for reparation directly to the judicial or administrative organs of the state launching the space object. A comparable provision is contained in Article 3 of the Nordic Convention for the Protection of the Environment, concluded by Denmark, Finland, Norway and Sweden in 1974. . . .[4]

These cases are—from the point of view of the protection of the individual—unfortunately only exceptional. The system of newly emerging environmental law still consists of State-to-State claims.

The evolution of international environmental law has been described as having three steps. The first is characterized principally by reparation for

1. 3 R. *Int'l Arb. Awards*, 1911, 1938.
2. Gunter Handl, "Territorial Sovereignty and the Problem of Transnational Pollution," *American Journal of International Law* (1975): 50–76, at 54.
3. For the text, see *International Legal Materials* 10 (1971): 965.
4. For the text, see *International Legal Materials* 13 (1974): 591.

injuries caused, the second by treaty commitments, and the third by action on the international level amounting to a more or less permanent institutional cooperation. According to this, we already may have reached the second step and moved beyond the first phase providing for reparation for damage already caused. Some conventions on liability can be taken as evidence for this. International cooperation, such as within the United Nations Environmental Programme (UNEP), signals near entry into the third phase.

On the level of actors in the international arena, environmental law has not yet effectively penetrated into the sphere of individual rights. It is true that the Stockholm Declaration in Principle 1 states that:

Man has the fundamental right to freedom, equality and adequate conditions of life, in an environment of a quality that permits a life of dignity and well-being. . . .[5]

But, above all, this "common conviction" of the United Nations Conference on the Human Environment is not only highly vague and formulated in abstract terms, its sincerity also appears in a dubious light if we read that the solemn responsibility to protect and improve the environment for present and future generations is to be enacted by the elimination of policies of apartheid, racial segregation, discrimination, colonial and other forms of oppression and foreign domination. In Principle 21, moreover, the Stockholm Declaration takes three steps backwards to the doctrine of State sovereignty, declaring that States have the sovereign right to exploit their own resources pursuant to their environmental policies and have only the responsibility to ensure that activities within their jurisdiction or control do not cause environmental damage to other States or areas beyond the limit of their own jurisdiction. This Principle, referring to material damage done to another State, does not refer to

the territory of the polluting State and thus also not to its own inhabitants.

If the Stockholm Declaration is an expression of current international law, it may be disputed whether international environmental law has even reached stage two. Even if we take into account that the law concerning liability is developing toward "absolute" or "strict" liability for ultra-hazardous (abnormally dangerous) acts, this still presupposes that harm already has been done by transnational pollution. The second stage of the evolution of international environmental law, in which the individual could also have gained some proper rights, would be characterized by international action to prevent environmental disruption rather than by compensation after such damage has occurred.

HUMAN RIGHTS CONTAIN A SPECIFIC RIGHT OF AN INDIVIDUAL TO A CLEAN ENVIRONMENT

The development of the international protection of human rights in the last decades has shown some progress. This is especially true with regard to regional commitments such as the European Convention for the Protection of Human Rights and Fundamental Principles (European Convention on Human Rights) with its highly sophisticated enforcement machinery. . . .[6]

The most important improvement of the status of the individual through the protection of human rights is the entitlement to invoke rights not only versus other States (this protection might have been pursued on his behalf by the State of his nationality *qua* diplomatic protection) but also against his own State. A second improvement can be seen in the fact that for example, the UN International Covenant on Social, Economic and Cultural Rights[7] has gone beyond the traditional freedoms toward rights in which action of the State concerned is demanded. A

5. For the text, see *International Legal Materials* 11 (1972): 1461.
6. Done at Rome, Nov. 4, 1950. Entered into force, Sept. 3, 1953. Europ. T.S. No. 5. The European Convention is supplemented by eight protocols, five of which have entered into force: Protocol (No. I), done at Paris, March 20, 1952, entered into force, May 18, 1954, Europ. T.S. No. 9; Protocol (No. II), done at Strasbourg, May 6, 1963, entered into force, Sept. 21, 1970, Europ. T.S. No. 44; Protocol (No. III), done at Strasbourg, May 6, 1963, entered into force, Sept. 21, 1970, Europ. T.S. No. 45; Protocol (No. IV), done at Strasbourg, Sept. 16, 1963, entered into force, May 2, 1968, Europ. T.S. No. 46; Protocol (No. V), done at Strasbourg, Jan. 20, 1966, entered into force, Dec. 20, 1971, Europ. T.S. No. 55; Protocol (No. VI), done at Strasbourg, entered into force March 1, 1985, Europ. T.S. No. 114; Protocol (No. VII), done at Strasbourg, Nov. 22, 1984, Europ. T.S. No. 117; Protocol (No. VIII), done at Vienna, March 19, 1985, Europ. T.S. No. 118.
7. [See the Appendix.]

right to a clean environment could thus consist not only of a claim by an individual against an entity to refrain from some or other dangerous activities but also of a claim against an entity to act in a specific way, such as to provide him with some specific features in the form of a special standard indispensable for an adequate quality of life (e.g., clean air, fresh water etc.).

It is true that the drafters of the UN Universal Declaration of Human Rights[8] and of the European Convention on Human Rights have shown little concern with ecology. Only the UN International Covenant on Economic, Social and Cultural Rights refers in Article 12(1) to "environmental hygiene." We also have to take into account that the needs and aspirations of individuals are always conflicting to a certain extent. . . .

The inquiry of human rights as to a clean environment should start from the assumption that such a right exists under present international law as a specific legal norm. If this assertion cannot be proved, this right to a clean environment could, by analogy, be interpreted into some indisputable human rights, such as in particular the right to life.

The Right to a Clean Environment as a Specific Human Right

Article 12 of the UN Covenant on Economic, Social and Cultural Rights has specified Article 25 of the Universal Declaration on Human Rights which calls for a standard of living for everyone adequate for the health and well-being of himself and his family by: "(b) the improvement of all aspects of *environmental* and industrial hygiene . . ." (emphasis added). Whatever this notion of "environmental hygiene" may include, it is strictly still a provision of a Covenant only binding upon the parties to it and not a reflection of current international customary law. Embodied in an instrument devoted to social, cultural and economic rights, the lack of a precise definition is not surprising; and it may be argued that a clean environment for the individual is hereby

raised at the level of "social advance" but—nevertheless—confers some rights directly upon the individual. The further elaboration of this right depends largely on the willingness of the contracting States with regard to special measures in favor of the persons under their jurisdiction, but a complete non-observance of this provision certainly would amount to a violation of the Covenant. The matter of human environment is thus lifted from the exclusive sphere of state competences and made a matter of international concern in international conventional law. The difference to the treatment of the individual under general international environmental law is obvious, since here environmentally-harmful acts are considered if they are transnational but also if they have occurred within the boundaries of one State. Furthermore, it seems that the wording of Article 12(b) indicates not only that there is a duty to refrain from certain conduct or to pay compensation if this conduct has occurred. It also indicates that there is a duty on the contracting State to improve the living conditions of its inhabitants by special measures with regard to the human environment. . . .

The Right to Life Extended to a Right to a Clean Environment

All international instruments dealing with human rights include the "right to life" as a focal point of protection. This right is regarded so highly that it may not be derogated by a state even during public emergency. If it is true that such right to life is "meaningless as it guarantees (only) a meagre existence assuming no more than a brutish survival,"[9] then this right could at least be interpreted in the sense that it should offer protection against all kinds of threats to human life, including ecological dangers.

The more traditional contents of this right can be seen in the third sentence of Article 6(1) of the UN International Covenant on Civil and Political Rights:[10] "No one shall be arbitrarily deprived of his life." This phrase seems to refer more to the protection of the mere existence of the

---

8. [See the Appendix.]
9. L. F. E. Goldie, "A General View of International Environmental Law: A Survey of Capabilities, Trends and Limits," *Colloque 1973, La Protection de l'environnement et le droit international*, ed. Alexandre Kiss (Leyden: A. W. Sijthoff, 1975), 132–6.
10. [See the Appendix.]

human being, without pointing at any quality of life and well-being.

Declarations of international bodies may, on the other hand, serve as an indication of the emergence of an international consciousness for a more liberal interpretation of such right to life provisions. The Stockholm Declaration of the United Nations Conference on the Human Environment, for instance, proclaims in its preamble that both aspects of man's environment—the natural and the man-made—are essential to the enjoyment of his basic human rights, "even the right to life itself." Hence, in the future, his right to life may develop "ancillary claims for environmental protection and even enhancement."

The right to life can be regarded as a very typical individual right. If the notion of a "common shared environment" is understood in the sense that the basic values and prerequisites of man's life also comprise the international concern about his environmental quality, then the implementation of this right will lead to an internationally accepted and also guaranteed right of the individual to a clean environment *qua* his *right to life*. The law as it stands today, however, is far from clear in this respect. The trend towards a more comprehensive and liberal interpretation of the right to life, as including the right to a sound environment, is nevertheless so evident that it seems appropriate to pursue this point and propagate this approach. The duty of a lawyer after all is not only to show the existing law but also to make proposals for its future development. The right to life seems a good starting point for further development, if States fail to accept specific individual rights to environmental protection.

THE CHARACTER AND SCOPE OF THE ALLEGED RIGHT OF AN INDIVIDUAL TO A CLEAN ENVIRONMENT

After answering the question of the existence of the right of the individual to a clean environment—at least to a certain extent—in the positive, it is now necessary to determine the character and the potential scope of this right. The result of this inquiry will enable us to show the types of claims which could be based on this right and also the fora in which they could be pursued.

One observation already has been made: The right of an individual to a clean environment is formulated—wherever it exists—in highly vague

terms. It is an abstract formula, lacking precise definition. Only the right to life as a right to brutish existence can be regarded as an operative legal rule in the strict sense, since it constitutes a prohibition to deprive a person arbitrarily of his life. In all other cases, the right of an individual to something not exactly determined, such as a clean or sound or healthy environment, cannot be regarded as directly applicable. It is a prescription of an invitation addressed to the national legislator to enact implementing laws for protection or to issue standards for a tolerable impairment of the human environment. This phenomenon, however, is common to more or less all social, economic and cultural rights which depend in their implementation on many factors.

The factors which are pertinent to environmental law and its implementation are, first of all, objective. They belong to the natural environment, to resources, to climate and so on. Differences in the industrial development of States also play a decisive role in the implementation of environmental protection. A further factor may be the difference in the expectations of people, their characters and habitats.

Another distinction, which we propose hereinafter, could be between: (a) external factors, such as nature in all its forms; and (b) internal man-made factors, such as the means of production and consumer-goods, which man has produced from the raw materials of the universe. It is a harsh fact of life that the process of converting "nature" into "goods" has its own costs and brings danger to human welfare.

The interdependence of all these factors, and the unequal distribution of them among the world's people, leads us to a deplorable outlook for mankind. The ideal of equal environmental conditions for all human beings is an illusion and the determination of a uniform clean, sound, decent, healthy environment is therefore impossible. The scope and contents of the right of an individual to a clean environment will have to vary in accordance with natural preconditions, and, depending on goal values and strategies, according to the policies of the decision-makers. Furthermore, the different notions used in connection with human environment, such as clean, sound, healthy, etc., must not necessarily have the same meaning. An absolutely clean, pure environment is certainly impossible to achieve and could even be as harmful for human beings as, for instance, the drinking of chemically pure water, *aqua destillata*. The notion of "decent environment" might, on the other hand, be something less than a "pure and clean environment" and may represent a more realistic approach toward minimum standards "that are essential to the preservation of life at a realistic level or healthy existence. . . ."[11]

All these individual factors influence the potential scope of the individual's right and predetermine his types of claim under the right to a clean environment. They have to be taken into account when States on their municipal level enact legislation for environmental protection and issue standards of tolerable infringement. Principle 23 of the Stockholm Declaration reflects this assertion by referring to criteria agreed upon by the international community, nationally determined standards and the system of values prevailing in each country.

One doctrine should be further observed in any policy of forwarding claims: *ultra posse nemo tenetur*. Claims should be realistic; they should not deprive the State of its very essential economic means. The ecological equilibrium as a goal value also should not provide for the improvement of the situation of a social group to the detriment of another. This is valid for State-to-State relations as well as for claims of individuals or social groups within a State. The right of an individual always should have as an ultimate limitation the interests of the community.

EXTERNAL FACTORS DETERMINING THE SCOPE OF THE INDIVIDUAL'S RIGHT TO A CLEAN ENVIRONMENT

Variety of Nature

The variety of man's surroundings could lead to different realistic claims to his clean environment. The unequal distribution of natural resources and the sometimes artificial drawing of borders between political units has led to the establishment of States with different base values. The unequal distribution of population in the world, mostly striving for an easier way of producing goods from natural resources, has brought about overpopulation and waste of natural resources in some areas, while other areas are left more or less unspoil[ed]. The plea for an equally-

clean environment for all human beings is, furthermore, hampered by the fact that the notion of a "common shared environment" is far from being universally accepted and recognized. State sovereignty over natural resources, including the right of almost unrestricted exploitation, is only limited in so far as the territorial rights of other States are affected. On the other hand, some regions have special dangers for human beings such as endemic diseases.

The present state of man's natural surroundings can, however, be the object of improvement and, consequently, of his right to a clean environment. If such an improvement is not manageable, or within the budgetary limits of a State, man's claim can only be the preservation of the ecological status quo, the non-deterioration of his environment, which under some circumstances would be a desirable goal. With the introduction of the individual as an internationally-accepted protected person, such a right easily may be construed, since the law of good neighborliness has hitherto protected States at least from the injurious deposition of dangerous levels of deleterious pollutants from the territory of another State.

If the improvement of the ecological status quo is manageable and within the financial capacity of a State, the individual right could comprise a step-by-step amelioration of his living conditions. The external factors of nature can serve here as a guideline for reasonable claims, taking into account also community interests.

Differences in Development

Another decisive external factor for man's claims to a clean environment is the difference in the economic development of States. The different levels of industrialization and modernization go mostly hand-in-hand with the unequal distribution of natural wealth, but they also are a result of centuries-old accumulations of wealth and skill, as well as sometimes of colonial and other exploitation. The problems arising from this factual inequality are manifold. The most important one is the question of financial ability of States to undertake measures for environmental protection and ecological improvement. Such activities usually can be borne on a large scale only

11. W. Paul Gormley, *Human Rights and Environment: The Need for International Cooperation* (Leyden: A. W. Sijthoff, 1976), 88.

by wealthy States. The improvement of the living conditions of individuals in such States would only perpetuate the existing gap in socio-economic development between the "have's" and the "have-not's" and would "promote the freezing of the present international order."[12] It also involves the character of pollution, which is said to differ between developing and industrial countries. While developing States show a pollution of poverty, because of underdevelopment, industrial States produce affluent pollution.

The individual's right will have to take these facts into account. In industrial States it may be directed against damages which have occurred to man's environment; in underdeveloped States it may prevent damages caused by attempts of virulent economic expansion. There is, however, little hope that States which are faced with economic, energy and development crises will show great concern for ecological problems. Claims that States should refrain from polluting the environment at the cost of little or no economic growth are indeed unrealistic and all that the individual can hope for is a sound balance between economic and ecological needs.

The existence of different economic systems also may play a role in ecological policies. It seems at first glance that States with centrally-planned economies are in [a] better position to solve environmental problems than States with market economies. A central economic plan could more easily include all the necessary steps for the improvement of man's environment since considerations of profitability are of secondary importance. On the other hand, it may be the bureaucratic inefficiency, growing with the increase of administrative control agencies necessary for the implementation of such economic plans, which may hamper the improvement of the environment and the implementation of man's right to it.

INTERNAL FACTORS DETERMINING THE SCOPE OF THE INDIVIDUAL'S RIGHT TO A CLEAN ENVIRONMENT: THE WEIGHING OF VALUES

The scope of the right of an individual to a clean environment will not only depend on external objective factors but also on preferences which his State gives to environmental matters. States have to enact implementing laws and to issue standards in accordance with their ecological policies. In addition to the external factors, their policies will be influenced by various interest groups of their population. The character of the population also can play a role in this decision-making process. Some people may be satisfied with the existing ecological situation and make no claims for an improvement; other people may consider the same situation intolerable and demand environmental protection.

The problem of giving priority to a clean environment within the framework of human rights is most striking for developing countries. These States face a major challenge. They have to develop their economic macro-system to provide their population with a means for living, but simultaneously they have to avoid, as far as possible, the social costs of environmental degradation. If we take into account that these societies also are afflicted with widespread malnutrition and disease, high infant mortality, high illiteracy and endemic unemployment, then the scope of the right of an individual to a sound environment possibly could be only very restricted.

The issuing of ecological standards, which should give man protection from infringements upon his environment, can be regarded as a problem of the weighing of values. The justification of differing national environmental policies was accepted by the Organization for Economic Co-operation and Development (OECD) in its Guiding Principles on the Environment[13] also with regard to different social objectives and priorities attached to environmental protection.

The weighing of values also may play a role in situations in which the rights of individuals conflict with community interests. In such cases community interests certainly would have to prevail.

[Editors' note: The author next notes the fora available for environmental claims: the reporting system under the International Covenant on Economic, Social and Cultural Rights; the complaint machinery under the International Covenant on Civil and Political Rights and its Optional Protocol; and the arbitral and judicial tribunals constituted under the municipal law.]

12. Joao Augusto de Aranjo Castro, "Environment and Development: The Case of the Developing Countries," *International Organisation* 26 (1972): 401–16.
13. Adopted on Mar. 24–26, 1972. For the text, see *International Legal Materials* 11 (1972): 1172.

CONCLUSIONS

The internationally guaranteed right of an individual to a clean environment is still in its *statu nascendi*. It can be construed only by interpretation of vague terms in certain International Covenants or by extension of some recognized rights, such as the "right to life." It lacks a defined scope. it will be very difficult to determine universally acceptable standards of tolerable infringement of the human environment as long as natural and economic differences exist in the human biosphere. The implementing machinery of codified rights is also very poor; and the outlook for an internationally enforceable individual right is not very encouraging.

Still, it is necessary to develop the concept of this right further on a universal level. The most advanced functional system for the protection of human rights, the European Convention, cannot serve as a general model, since it may be argued that only the homogeneity of the parties to it and the level of economic development of its Member States have made this system possible. It even would seem unrealistic to suppose that the jurisdiction of the European Court of Human Rights can be extended to include rights of a non-judicial character, such as economic and social guarantees as pertains to the right to a clean environ-

ment. It may be appropriate to propagate within the framework of the United Nations a further codification of international environmental law, including the right of an individual to a sound environment. The confrontation of different social, political and economic systems within this organization, however, will not make this task easy. But only within the existing framework of an organization of this scope, may some modest compromises be attainable.

Environmental disruption is a danger to all human beings. The achievement of any "common shared environment" should be the goal of international cooperation; and the role of the individual in the struggle for it should not be underestimated. It is, nevertheless, true that the individual needs motivation for his active participation in this struggle, and such a motivation could be the improvement of his procedural status and the granting of special rights with regard to a clean environment. If environmental consciousness is raised and if the goal seems within grasp, the individual might try to influence decision-makers in his country to accept internationally guaranteed rights; if such action takes place all over the world, we may finally improve the existing environmental situation with effect for all mankind.

QUESTIONS FOR REFLECTION AND DISCUSSION

1. Why is Henn-Juri Uibopuu insistent upon finding an internationally guaranteed right of an individual to a clean environment? Who is entitled to a clean environment, the individual or society? Is it not enough that there be a group or people's right to a clean environment? If not, why not? In any event, does such a societal right exist?

2. Does Uibopuu say that the right to a clean environment is a justiciable or aspirational right? How does he assess the present geopolitical structure relative to the development of this right? Is he convincing about the potential of human rights law to create effective new norms in this area? In responding to these questions, consider the following extract from W. Paul Gormley (*Human Rights and Environment: The Need for International Cooperation* [Leyden: A. W. Sijthoff, 1976], 7) (footnotes omitted):

[The] factual data, tragically, seems endless. Daily press reports present equally grim statistics. Highway pollution is contaminating our rich farm lands and destroying much of the remaining animal life; species of plants and wildlife have [become], or are in danger of becoming[,] extinct. There is even the threat that the present level of artificial heating is helping to melt the polar ice caps. A mere change of one-half degree fahrenheit will result in melting ice raising the level of the oceans by two hundred feet, thereby flooding ten percent of the earth's land and inundating half of the world's major metropolitan centers, including New York and London. The fate of the Low Countries, especially The Netherlands, can only be surmised. Such Frankenstein-type prospects may not come to pass, in view of the fact that nature has the ability to "grow back" in devastated areas, as can be seen from the battlefields of World War Two. Yet, the fact remains, the world's growing population is polluting the previously untarnished Antarctic. Even some of man's dis[c]arded equipment and refu[s]e have been deposited on the moon. So severe is the spread of pollution that outer space has been threatened.

If existing command and enforcement structures are inadequate to the environmental challenge Gormley describes, what new kinds of norms, institutions, and procedures might be required? Might the right to an ecologically balanced environment necessitate the right of a person or society to resources that would permit maximum environmental protection? Would it be desirable to endow states—particularly economically disadvantaged states—with extraterritorial jurisdiction to prevent the spoiling of contiguous, hence potentially threatening, environments? Should people be required to emigrate to low-density population areas to alleviate ecological pressures?

3. Do you agree that the "right to life" should include the right to a clean environment? What, if anything, is gained by linking these two rights together? What, if anything, is lost by not linking them together?

4. Why might developing countries be hesitant to claim that a clean environment is a human right? Why might developed countries be more responsive to the same claim? Or is it the reverse? Consider again an extract from W. Paul Gormley (*Human Rights and Environment* [see question 2, above], 8) (footnotes omitted):

> The clash between the need to conserve resources and to preserve existing . . . life . . . must, regrettably, compete with the requirements of development. It is essential that this "head on clash" not be minimized, because of the interest of the world community in both [environmental] "protection" and [economic] "development." Admittedly, the pressure for rapid development is less significant in Western Europe and in North America. In Europe, greater emphasis is being placed on multinational organizations, especially by the Council of Europe, on the preservation of remaining species of wildlife and plants. Nevertheless, industrialized countries must rapidly exploit additional resources, from additional regions, merely to preserve their present positions (and the current standard of living of their peoples) to say nothing of a modest increase of their gross national product.

5. If developmental practices in developing countries threaten the environmental rights of developed countries, should the developed countries nonetheless be required to assume the cost of cleanup and repair? Why? Why not? Similarly, if environmental controls in developed countries inhibit the trade and growth of developing countries, hence the claimed right to development, should the developed countries be responsible for the financial difference? Why? Why not?

6. Many have observed that the gravest threat to the natural environment is nuclear war. Should individuals have a human right to be free of pollution of the land, sea, and atmosphere that nuclear weapons cause when tested or used?

13. YORAM DINSTEIN *Self-Determination and the Middle East Conflict*

SELF-DETERMINATION AS A COLLECTIVE HUMAN RIGHT

Self-determination must be perceived as an international human right. This is frequently hard to grasp inasmuch as self-determination can be exercised only by a people—namely, a group or a community—as distinct from an individual human being. However, international human rights are not monolithic, and a cardinal line of division has to be drawn between individual and collective human rights.

Individual human rights (for instance, free-

Reprinted, with changes, from Yoram Dinstein, "Self-Determination and the Middle East Conflict," in *Self-Determination: National, Regional and Global Dimensions*, ed. Y. Alexander and R. Friedlander (Boulder, Colo.: Westview Press, 1980), 243–58. Copyright © 1980 by Westview Press. Reprinted by permission.

dom of expression) are bestowed upon every single human being personally. Collective human rights are granted to human beings communally, that is to say, in conjunction with one another, within the ambit of a group: a people or a minority. Self-determination is just one among several collective human rights which are recognized nowadays under international law.

The reason why collective human rights in general, and self-determination in particular, are still human rights even though conferred on a group (a people in the case of self-determination) is that the group in question is not a corporate entity and does not possess a legal personality. Like all other human rights, collective human rights are accorded to human beings directly, without the interposition of the legal personality of a corporate entity, especially that of the state. The nature of these rights requires, however, that they shall be exercised jointly rather than severally.

SELF-DETERMINATION AS A RIGHT UNDER EXISTING INTERNATIONAL LAW

The right of self-determination is proclaimed in the two 1966 International Covenants on Human Rights: the one on Civil and Political Rights and the other on Economic, Social, and Cultural Rights.[1] Article 1(1), which is common to both covenants, states: "All people have the right of self-determination. By virtue of that right they freely determine their political status and freely pursue their economic, social and cultural development."

The covenants came into force only in 1976 and, as yet, are legally binding on less than one-third of the international community. Consequently, it is important to establish whether the right of self-determination has an independent existence, beyond the scope of the covenants, as an integral part of customary international law. There is, indeed, an influential school of thought that denies that self-determination is a legal right, with a corresponding duty, insofar as states not bound by the covenants are concerned. For non-

contracting parties, it is contended, self-determination is merely a political clarion call that they are under no obligation to heed. But the better view is that the right of self-determination has acquired, over the last decade or two, the lineaments of *lex lata*.

The political conception of self-determination for peoples has been gaining support since the days of the French Revolution, but particularly so from the end of the First World War. Although the Covenant of the League of Nations did not confirm it directly, one can detect the first burgeoning of the right within positive international law in the mandates system of the League. In the words of the International Court of Justice, in its judgment of 1962 in the South-West Africa cases: "The essential principles of the Mandates System consist chiefly in the recognition of certain rights of the peoples of the underdeveloped territories."[2]

Clearly, in the era of the League of Nations it was impossible to talk of a right of self-determination in the full sense of the term—not even within the confines of the mandates system—inasmuch as the authority to decide when a people was ripe for independence was given not to itself, but to external powers (the League and the mandatory state). Nevertheless, as was pointed out by the Hague Court in 1971, in its Advisory Opinion on the Namibia case: "It is self-evident that the 'trust' had to be exercised for the benefit of the peoples concerned, who were admitted to have interests of their own and to possess a potentiality for independent existence on the attainment of a certain stage of development."[3] The Court went on to say that "the ultimate objective of the sacred trust was the self-determination and independence of the peoples concerned," and it added: "Furthermore, the subsequent development of international law in regard to non-self-governing territories, as enshrined in the Charter of the United Nations, made the principle of self-determination applicable to all of them." More recently, in 1975 in the Western Sahara case, the Court took for granted the "principle of self-determination as a right of peoples."[4]

The right of self-determination of peoples is

1. [See the Appendix.]
2. South-West Africa Cases (Preliminary Objections), 1962 I.C.J. 319, 329.
3. Legal Consequences for States of the Continued Presence of South Africa in Namibia (South-West Africa) notwithstanding Security Council Resolution 276 [1970], 1971 I.C.J. 16, 28–9.
4. Advisory Opinion on Western Sahara, 1975 I.C.J. 12, 31.

mentioned in the Charter of the United Nations[5] in two places: in the list of the general purposes of the organization (Art. 1(2)) and in the provision relating to the specific purposes of the United Nations in the promotion of economic and social cooperation (Art. 55). Yet we must distinguish between a purpose that states merely have to strive to attain and a plain legal duty which must be discharged as such. It is preferable to regard the right of self-determination as derived not from the phraseology of the Charter, but from the practice of states after the establishment of the organization. This practice verifies the existence of the right of self-determination, and the "population explosion" that has occurred in the international community since the early 1960s eloquently testifies to it. . . .

Considering that customary international law in this area is fairly new and not very precise, the contours of the right of self-determination are somewhat blurred. Conventional international law, too, is not particularly helpful in removing doubts pertaining to the definition of self-determination, since the formula used in Art. 1(1) of the human rights covenants is quite laconic. If we take the statement "All peoples have the right of self-determination" as our guide, three expressions seem to require elaboration, i.e., "all," "peoples," and "self-determination." Let us proceed to ask (1) what is a "people"? (2) how comprehensive is the term "all"? and (3) what is the exact meaning of the phrase "self-determination"?

WHAT IS A "PEOPLE"?

It is necessary to differentiate between a people and a nation. A nation is easy to define as it consists of the entire citizen body of a state. All the nationals of the state form the nation. In each state there is one nation, and this is why the terms state and nation have become practically interchangeable. But within the compass of one state and one nation there can exist several peoples, large and small. Such a state is usually called "multinational," but what is actually meant is that the (one) nation comprises several peoples.

It is exceedingly difficult to define the term "people." There is no acid technical test which would enable us to determine whether a cluster of human beings constitutes a people. Even the number of the members of a group does not settle the issue: a people may consist of vast millions or of several scores of families (though, clearly, a single family or clan may not seriously claim to be a people).

Peoplehood must be seen as contingent on two separate elements, one objective and the other subjective. The objective element is that there has to exist an ethnic group linked by common history. The strength of the ethnic-historical link is admittedly a matter of contention. Frequently, it is suggested that the link must express itself, inter alia, in a common territory, religion, or language, but these requirements are unduly harsh. The vicissitudes of history are such that an ethnic group may lose its territory, split up into various religious factions, and speak in many different tongues. A period of trial and error serves as a crucible for the ethnic identity. If it does not disappear in time and space, its diverse mutations must be viewed with tolerance. In fact . . . , peoplehood is cemented by shared memories of common suffering. On the other hand, a random group of persons, lacking any common tradition, cannot be categorized as a people. When tens of thousands of men and women assemble temporarily (for example, to watch a football match) or associate for an extended campaign on behalf of a common cause (for instance, the women's liberation movement), they do not, thereby, turn themselves into a people.

Side by side with the objective element, there is also a subjective basis of peoplehood. It is not enough to have an ethnic link in the sense of past genealogy and history. It is essential to have a present ethos or state of mind. A people is both entitled and required to identify itself as such. Renan's famous reference to a *plébiscite de tous les jours*, in regard to the will to live together and to continue common traditions,[6] is very apposite indeed.

It follows that a people must itself delineate the purview of its common existence and settle criteria for belonging to the group. There is no place for a *Diktat* from outside in this respect: one people cannot decree that another group is not

---

5. [See the Appendix.]
6. Ernest Renan, "Qu'est-ce qu'une Nation?" in *Oeuvres complètes* (Paris: Calmann-Lévy, 1947), 1:887, 904.

entitled to peoplehood. Moreover, an individual cannot gate-crash and compel a people to admit him to its fold. The group has to make up its collective mind and resolve whether or not such an individual qualifies.

IS THE RIGHT OF SELF-DETERMINATION GRANTED TO ALL PEOPLES?

It is often argued that the right of self-determination does not embrace secession from an existing state and that it is, in fact, confined to the process of decolonization (particularly in Afro-Asia). But Art. 1(1) is very explicit on the subject: the right of self-determination is conferred on "all" peoples and not merely on some peoples in non-self-governing territories.

Under Art. 31(1) of the 1969 Vienna Convention on the Law of Treaties, the interpretation of treaties (and the human rights covenants are treaties) is governed by the basic rule that the "ordinary meaning" must be given to the terms of a treaty in their context.[7] This textual approach to the interpretation of treaties is based on numerous precedents in international jurisprudence, such as the advisory opinion on Competence of the General Assembly for the Admission of a State to the United Nations, in which the International Court of Justice stated (in 1950):

The Court considers it necessary to say that the first duty of a tribunal which is called upon to interpret and apply the provisions of a treaty, is to endeavour to give effect to them in their natural and ordinary meaning in the context in which they occur. If the relevant words in their natural and ordinary meaning make sense in their context, that is an end of the matter.[8]

The ordinary meaning of the term "all," in the context of the right of all peoples to self-determination, is that of entirety: each and every people is covered by the expression, irrespective of geographic or other considerations.

Nevertheless, it may be argued, perhaps, that the term "all" in Art. 1(1) is not as crystal clear as one may be led to believe and that, in fact, its meaning in the context is ambiguous. This is a doubtful argument at best, but in such a case Art. 32 of the Vienna Convention on the Law of Trea-

ties permits recourse to the preparatory work of the covenants (which, in any event, is allowed in order to confirm the meaning resulting from the application of the general rule of interpretation of treaties under Art. 31). However, even if we look into the preparatory work for Art. 1(1) of the covenants, there is no reason to conclude that the original intention of the framers of the clause incorporating the right of self-determination was other than what the text indicates on the face of it. . . .

The upshot of the matter is that the right of self-determination is accorded not only to peoples under colonial domination in Africa and Asia, but also to peoples living within independent Afro-Asian nations, as well as to those existing in Europe (for instance, in Scotland or the Ukraine) and in America. Just as a people under colonial domination [are] entitled to create a new state where none existed before, so can a people living within the framework of an extant state secede from it and establish [their] own independent country. This is precisely what was achieved by the Bengalis of East Pakistan when they created the new State of Bangladesh. This, too, is what was unsuccessfully attempted by the Ibos of East Nigeria when they tried to create a new state of Biafra.

Needless to say, when a people endeavor to secede from an existing state, the latter is not apt to accept calmly the prospect of its being carved up between several peoples, and it tends to resist the secession movement. Neither Pakistan nor Nigeria submitted gracefully to the scheme of its dismemberment. Modern international law prescribes a right (self-determination) which is loaded with political and psychological dynamite, but it does not have an answer to the question how that right is to be carried into effect. If a people insist on [their] right to secede, and the existing state refuses to acquiesce in the implementation of the right at its expense, the confrontation leads almost inevitably to civil war. International law does not encourage civil wars, but it does not prohibit them either. International law is simply indifferent to the phenomenon of civil wars, and in this negative sense may be said to permit them. This, of course, is an unfortunate state of affairs, especially at a time when an in-

---

7. Vienna Convention on the Law of Treaties, *United Nations Juridical Yearbook* (1969) 149.
8. Competence of the General Assembly for the Admission of a State to the United Nations, 1950 I.C.J. 4, 8.

terstate war is regarded as a crime against peace. But there has always been a gap between *lex lata* and *lex desiderata*.

It is noteworthy that the right of political self-determination is conferred on peoples everywhere, irrespective of the economic and social conditions in which they live. A people that sit by the fleshpots and enjoy the wealth of the land [are] still entitled to self-government in an independent state. But self-government implies the requirement that the seceding people [are] located in a well-defined territorial area in which [they] form a majority. When a people [are] dispersed all over a country—and constitute a minority in each of its parts—[their] secession would signify not (legitimate) self-government but (unjustifiable) domination of others.

WHAT IS THE MEANING OF SELF-DETERMINATION?

Self-determination is reflected, in the first place, in the determination of the self—the formulation of criteria for belonging to a people—and this is the subjective element in the definition of peoplehood. Self-determination also means that every people is entitled to determine freely its future course.

The right of self-determination has economic, social, and cultural connotations, but its quintessence is the political status of the people concerned. The thrust of self-determination is that a people—if [they] so will—[are] entitled to independence from foreign domination, i.e., [they] may establish a sovereign state in the territory in which [they] live and where [they] constitute a majority.

A complex question arises in terms of demarcating the region that has to be taken into consideration when one wants to determine whether a people demanding independence (and entitled to it in theory under the right of self-determination) may implement it in practice against the wishes of other peoples in the area. Frequently, the designation of the geographical boundaries of a region (which may be based on arbitrary yardsticks) predetermines the demographic question as to which people form a majority in it. The Ukrainians, for instance, are a distinct majority in the Ukraine, but a minority in the USSR as a whole. . . .

So far, we have proceeded on the assumption that there is an equal mark between self-determination and political independence (or statehood), but such is not the case. Independence is a right (where it is available) and not a duty. Even a people that constitute a sizable majority in a well-defined territorial area [are] entitled to waive political independence for economic and other reasons. Thus, the Puerto Rican people [have], time and again, freely chosen to decline independence. Instead, [they] ha[ve] opted for a special legal status (that of a commonwealth as distinct from a state) under the umbrella of the United States, with the island forgoing political rights for the sake of economic advantages. There is nothing inherently wrong in such a course of action, and Puerto Rico cannot be forced by others to assume independence against its will.

THE MIDDLE EAST CONFLICT

In Palestine, there are, and there have been for a very long time, two peoples: Jews and Arabs. It is often believed that the Jews, having been expelled from their homeland and scattered in the Diaspora many centuries ago, have returned to the Holy Land only since the dawn of Zionism late in the nineteenth century. But this is a misconception. At no time did the Jews completely cut off their umbilical cord to the Land of Israel. In fact, in the middle of the nineteenth century, several decades prior to the First Zionist Congress, Jews constituted a majority of the population in the city of Jerusalem and lived in fairly large numbers in other holy places throughout Palestine.

The demographic ratio between Arabs and Jews in Palestine has shifted over the years. Initially, the Arabs were in overall majority. Today the majority is Jewish. But the fundamental reality has not changed, and the land is shared by the two groups. It is the irony of fate that the respective positions of both are exceedingly similar in at least three ways.

1. There are more Jews outside Palestine than inside. There are also more Arabs outside Palestine than inside.

2. It is very difficult to answer the question: "Who is a Jew?" Is he a person who professes Judaism as a religion? Is he an offspring of the original twelve tribes? Is he a person who speaks Hebrew? All these are indubitably faulty criteria. By the same token, it is very difficult to answer

the question: "Who is an Arab?" Is he a person who professes Islam as a religion? Is he an off-spring of the original desert tribes of (Saudi) Arabia? Is he a person who speaks Arabic? None of these criteria is plausible.

3. There are many (especially Arabs) who deny that Jews in Palestine belong to a Jewish (as distinct from an Israeli) people. Again, there are many (especially Jews) who deny that Arabs in Palestine belong to a Palestinian Arab (as distinct from a Jordanian) people.

It is the tragedy of fate that Arabs and Jews apply to each other arbitrary yardsticks about what constitutes a people, refusing to concede one another's determination of self as sufficient or conclusive. There is no prospect of reconciliation in the Middle East unless and until both sides realize that neither lives in a vacuum and that both are entitled to self-determination. There is a Jewish people (or a part of the Jewish people) in Palestine, and there is an Arab people (or a part of the Arab people) in Palestine. Each must be free to determine its political fate. Neither can dictate to the other its decision. Since both have claims over the same country, and both want to proceed along separate paths, the only solution is partition of Palestine between them.

Such a position has been proposed time and again, and on each occasion it has been rejected by the Arabs within and without Palestine. The most famous instance is that of the Partition Resolution adopted by the [UN] General Assembly on 29 November 1947.[9] The Partition Resolution was hardly a matter of record when the Arab leadership in Palestine resolved to oppose it by force. At the outset (from 30 November 1947 to 14 May 1948), civil war raged in Palestine. But, with the establishment of the State of Israel on 15 May 1948, the regular armies of the neighboring Arab states resorted to an armed attack against the Jewish state. The war thus assumed an interstate character and became a crime against peace.

It is all too often alleged that Israel was created by the United Nations in the Partition Resolution.

But in fact, owing to Arab resistance, the resolution was washed by bloodshed. Israel emerged as an independent state from the throes of its war of independence. Subsequent to the Arab defeat in the battlefield, a different partition of Palestine was sanctioned by the armistice agreements of 1949.[10]

The 1949 partition of Palestine diverged from the 1947 plan devised by the General Assembly not merely in demarcation of boundaries, but also—and more conspicuously—in that only the Jewish state came into existence in Palestine. The counterpart Arab state was never launched into political orbit, not because the Jews objected (at the time they did not), but because the Palestinian Arabs themselves preferred to forgo the option of independence. Most of them, especially in the West Bank, cast their lot with Jordan. Others lived under Egyptian control in the Gaza Strip, and some chose to live in Israel.

For eighteen years, as long as the Palestinian Arabs in the West Bank and the Gaza Strip were free from Israeli interference and presumably (given the consent of Jordan and Egypt) could establish their own state in Palestine, they showed no inclination to proceed to do so. The idea of creating a third state between the desert and the sea, beside Jordan and Israel, was conceived after the 1967 Six-Day War, when the whole of Palestine had come under Israeli control and the complexion of the political scene had changed.

The so-called Six-Day War is actually in its eleventh year at the time of [this] writing. It has gone through a number of phases of both active hostilities and cease-fire. Some of the rounds of fighting are popularly referred to as separate wars (the War of Attrition and the Yom Kippur War), but they all are manifestations of the same on-going war. As long as the state of war continues, and even while the shooting is suspended, Israel is entitled to administer the territories that are under its "belligerent occupation." However, as pointed out by Oppenheim, whereas "the occupant . . . has a right of administration over the

9. General Assembly Resolution 181 (2) on the Future Government of Palestine, U.N. GAOR, 131. On the chain of events which led to the resolution and followed upon it, see Yoram Dinstein, "The United Nations and the Arab-Israel Conflict," in *The Arab-Israeli Conflict*, ed. John Norton Moore (Princeton, N.J.: Princeton University Press, 1974), 2:481, 482–3.
10. Egypt-Israel, General Armistice Agreement, 1949, *Kitvei Amana* 1, no. 1: 3; Lebanon-Israel, General Armistice Agreement, 1949, ibid., no. 2: 23; Jordan-Israel, General Armistice Agreement, 1949, ibid., no. 3: 37; Syria-Israel, General Armistice Agreement, 1949, ibid., no. 4: 49.

territory," "there is not an atom of sovereignty in the authority of the occupant."[11] This means that Israel has a right to *imperium* over, rather than *dominium* of, the occupied territories. Sovereignty is not transferred to the occupant, and Israel can only acquire title to any part of the occupied areas as a result of cession duly stipulated in a peace treaty.

By and large, Israel realizes that ultimately it will have to withdraw from the bulk of the West Bank as the price of peace. The interrelated conditions of peace, which Israel envisions, cover various contractual arrangements with the neighboring Arab countries guaranteeing secure and recognized boundaries for all parties. However, in the Israeli scheme of things, such arrangements do not include the establishment of an independent Arab country in the West Bank. Israel's objections to the creation of such a state are generated by actions taken and statements made by Palestinian Arabs in the last few years. Israel fears that the helm of the projected state, should it come into being, would soon fall into the irresponsible hands of military extremists and political adventurers with irredentist aspirations, and

that a new conflict would erupt before the ink was dry on the peace treaty terminating the present state of war.

The belligerents in the current Middle East conflict are sovereign states (Israel, on the one hand; Egypt, Syria, and Jordan, on the other), and it will be up to those parties to put an end to their war. The Palestine Arabs, as such, are not a belligerent party in this interstate war. The issue of in independent Palestinian Arab state did not trigger the war, when it started in 1967, and does not necessarily have to be dealt with in order to produce peace between the belligerent parties. It is a separate problem which could best be resolved against the backdrop of peace rather than in the context of war. . . .

In the final analysis, the only way to solve the Palestine problem is through compromise leading to peaceful coexistence of Arabs and Jews. After so many years of purposeless fighting, the Palestinian Arabs must begin to realize that only in the unimpassioned atmosphere of peace can it be expected that such a compromise will be reached. What they need is not a war of liberation but a peace of liberation.

QUESTIONS FOR REFLECTION AND DISCUSSION

1. In *Self-Determination and International Law* ([Hamden, Conn.: Archon Books, 1972], 192), U. O. Umozurike identifies the "basic characteristics" of self-determination as:

(1) government according to the will of the people; (2) the absence of internal or external domination; (3) the free pursuit of economic, social, and cultural development; (4) the enjoyment of fundamental human rights and equal treatment; and (5) the absence of discrimination on grounds of race, color, class, caste, creed or political conviction.

Given these standards, do you think many peoples enjoy full self-determination? Do peoples of color and other minorities in the United States?

2. Dinstein, a distinguished international lawyer, contends that in the area formerly called Palestine "there are, and there have been for a very long time, two peoples: Jews and Arabs"—each with an "incontrovertible right of self-detrmination" in the area. Do you agree? Compare the view of Henry Cattan, another distinguished international lawyer, in *Palestine and International Law: The Legal Aspects of the Arab-Israeli Conflict* ([London: Longman, 1973], 214) (footnotes omitted):

The right of the Palestinians to recover their homeland is a natural one. They and their forebears have been the inhabitants of Palestine since time immemorial. Their right to Palestine rests on law, on justice, on history and on plain common sense. A settled people who has always lived on its land and is suddenly and forcibly uprooted should not be required to justify its title in order to regain its homeland. The Palestinians have a right to exist no less than anyone else, and they have a right to live in their ancestral land. Who, save the biased cynic, would question their right to recover their homeland?

11. L. Oppenheim, "The Legal Relations between an Occupying Power and the Inhabitants," *Law Quarterly Review* 33 (1917):363–70, 64.

Turning to the Israelis, who are they? Excluding a small number of indigenous Jews who are Palestinians by birth and origin and whose number today does not exceed 100,000, the Israelis are a heterogeneous assemblage of alien Jews of different nationalities and places who left their own countries to come to Palestine to participate in the Zionist adventure of creating a Jewish state. On what basis then can Israel claim a right to exist in Palestine? On the basis of a flimsy and ridiculous historic claim of occupation of the country by doubtful ancestors some two thousand years ago? On the basis of promises which the Israelites claimed were made to them by the Almighty in the days of the Old Testament? On the basis of the iniquitous and illegal resolution of the General Assembly of the UN adopted in 1947 under improper pressures and in violation of the legitimate rights of the majority of the Palestinian population? On the basis of creation of a *fait accompli* by force and terror? On the basis of "humanitarian" grounds which are in no way humane? None of the grounds that have been urged in support of Israel's right to exist can resist an impartial examination, or invalidate or impair the right of the Palestinians to recover their homeland.

3. Is it possible to conclude from Dinstein's essay that, under the banner of "self-determination," the state of Israel may be imposing its own will on the Palestinian Arabs, in contravention of the Palestinian Arabs' right to self-determination? Asks Henry Cattan in *Palestine and International Law* (see question 2, above) at 214–15:

[F]or which State of Israel is the right to exist being claimed? Is it for the Jewish State which has been envisaged by the UN with its geographic boundaries and obligations towards its Palestinian Arab population as fixed in the resolution [181] of 29 November 1947? Or is it for the State of Israel which emerged in 1948, enlarged by its territorial conquests beyond the boundaries fixed in the partition resolution and forcibly emptied of its Arab population? Or is it for a new State of Israel enlarged further by some or all of the territories which it seized during its "defensive [Six-Day] war" of 5 June 1967?

4. Dinstein believes that the Palestinian Arabs displaced by the creation of the state of Israel have a right to self-determination in the West Bank and Gaza, now territories militarily occupied and administered by Israel. Consider once again the contrasting view of Henry Cattan in *Palestine and International Law* (see question 2, above) at 215–7 (footnotes omitted):

To the uninformed, the suggestion to leave to Israel the territories she occupied prior to 5 June 1967 and to the Palestinians the West Bank and the Gaza Strip appears on the face of it to achieve a compromise between the Israelis and the Palestinians by dividing Palestine between them. On closer examination, however, such a suggestion will be found to be completely unfair, unjust and illegal. . . .

Territorially, the proposal to allow Israel to retain the territories which she seized in 1948 and 1949 and to leave to the Palestinians the West Bank and the Gaza Strip means that Israel will be confined in its misappropriation of four-fifths of the territory of Palestine and *the Palestinians would be left with one-fifth of their homeland.* Is it conceivable or reasonable that a settlement of the Palestine Question could be achieved by restoring to the Palestinians a small part of their homeland? In giving to Israel 80% of the land of Palestine, such a proposal would even exceed in iniquity the UN partition plan of 1947 which allotted to the Jews 57%, and to the original inhabitants 43%, of the area of Palestine— and this at a time when Palestinians constituted two-thirds, and Jews only one-third, of the population. . . .

Legally, the proposal to abandon to Israel the territories which she occupied before 5 June 1967 violates the rights of the Palestinians and also condones aggression and injustice. Even before the UN resolution of 22 November 1974, which reaffirmed the rights of the Palestinians in Palestine, the legitimacy of Israel's acquisition of the territory allotted to the Jewish State under the resolution of 29 November 1947 was at best highly doubtful. What modern principle or precedent can be adduced to support the decision of a closely divided UN to confer on a primarily immigrant minority sovereignty over a land and dominion over the majority of its inhabitants? As to the territory forcibly seized by Israel in excess of that allotted by the partition resolution of 1947, no respectable jurist has seriously argued that the means employed in its acquisition could produce legal title. Arguably in both cases and undoubtedly in the latter, the status of Israel is that of a belligerent and wrongful occupier. Recognition of Israel's sovereignty over such territories is incompatible with international law, UN resolutions and the inalienable rights of the Palestinians. . . .

It is difficult to see how close those states which support Israel's right to exist can honestly deny to the Palestinians their own natural right to exist and to live in peace and freedom in their homeland. The question is not one of finding for them *a* homeland, or *some* homeland, but of recovering their *own*. The well-meaning people who suggest that the Palestinians should have a homeland either in the West Bank and the Gaza Strip or elsewhere outside their own, appear to be the victims of Israeli-Zionist propaganda which points to the vastness of the Arab world and insidiously suggests that the Palestinians should not grudge the Israelis their taking the small land of Palestine when they can live in some other corner of the Arab world. But the vast expanses of the Arab world—mostly arid desert—are not the usurped Palestinian homeland, and the Palestinians have neither the right nor the intention to live in any country other than their own, whether it be Transjordan, Syria, Saudi Arabia, or elsewhere.

What implications may be drawn from Cattan's analysis? Does it suggest the dismantling of the state of Israel? If so, does this mean or imply that the Jews who came to Palestine should or would be "thrown into the sea"? What about the possibility of one democratic state where Christian, Jew, and Moslem could live and work for peace and justice together?

5. As Dinstein correctly explains, the right to self-determination became a clarion call for the dismantling of colonial empires in the years following World War II. For quite some time, indeed, the principle was invoked almost exclusively with reference to the "advancement" of peoples in trust territories and to the development of "self-government" in colonial territories. Today, however, trust territories and colonial territories are few in number. Does this mean that, for the most part, the principle of self-determination has outlived its usefulness? Or does the principle of self-determination extend to noncolonial contexts also. If so, which ones? If not, why not? Is the problem of Palestinian self-determination a colonial or noncolonial problem?

6. One of the more painful reminders of the colonial era was the problem of self-determination in Namibia (or South West Africa), until 1989 under the grip of South Africa, which claimed the right to control the territory as a mandate established under the Treaty of Versailles following World War I. Despite the World Court's Advisory Opinion in *Legal Consequences for States of the Continued Presence of South Africa in Namibia (South West Africa)* (1971 I.C.J. 16), holding that South Africa's extension of apartheid to Namibia contravenes the UN Charter, and despite seemingly countless UN resolutions and other expressions of international outrage calling upon South Africa to cease its occupation of Namibia and to grant political independence to that territory, South Africa persisted. If you were a diplomat, what arguments based on human rights would you present to Pretoria to advance Namibian independence?

7. If, as Dinstein contends, both Arabs and Jews have an "incontrovertible right of self-determination" in Palestine, if there is no remedy in international law for such competing claims, and if neither side is willing to compromise, on what grounds can Dinstein say that the issue of an independent Palestinian state can best be resolved peacefully? Do events since 1989 point to any prospects for a peaceful resolution of this conflict?

8. Article 1 of the International Covenant on Civil and Political Rights and Article 1 of the International Covenant on Economic, Social and Cultural Rights both stipulate that "[a]ll peoples may, for their own ends, freely dispose of their natural wealth and resources" and that "[i]n no case may a people be deprived of its own means of subsistence." Does this mean that the principle of self-determination embraces *economic* self-determination as well as *political* self-determination? If so, what does it mean to speak of economic self-determination? What are the implications of such a concept?

9. If the principle of self-determination may be said to embrace economic self-determination, might it be envisaged in the context of the United Nations' global program for a "new international economic order" calling for, inter alia, "[f]ull permanent sovereignty of every State over its natural resources and all economic activities"? If so, might it not clash with Article 17 of the Universal Declaration of Human Rights guaranteeing "[e]veryone . . . the right to own property alone as well as in association with others"? How is a right to

economic self-determination to be reconciled with the right to property? What is the significance of the proviso in Article 1 of each of the above-mentioned covenants (see question 8) requiring that the free disposition of a people's natural wealth and resources must be "without prejudice to any obligations arising out of international economic co-operation, based upon the principle of mutual benefit, and international law"? What does this mean?

10. Does the right to self-determination embrace a general right of groups to secede from the states of which they are a part? Why? Why not?

14. KATARINA TOMASEVSKI *The Right to Peace*

WHY DO WE NEED A RIGHT TO PEACE?

War is by definition a means of violating human rights. Historically, the most massive violations of human rights have resulted from warfare. Yet, the jeopardy of human rights included in the notion of war is increasing in at least two respects. Firstly, we have become aware of the fact that preparations for waging war (whether offensive or defensive) represent the institutionalized violation of human rights: deprivations resulting from resource-allocation policies favoring military expenditure over welfare or agriculture can be substantiated nowadays by numerous data confirming that armaments and development are competing demands on public expenditures, and that favoring armaments entails not only economic, but social costs as well. Military preparations are generally founded on a state's right to enlist parts of its population into military service, thus depriving certain people of a considerable amount of their freedom while simultaneously teaching them to kill upon governmental orders. State security protection, encompassing loosely and widely defined military preparations, justifies the governmental power to: (a) withhold information not only from outsiders, but from its own population, thus depriving [citizens of] sufficient [information] to participate in decision-making, and, (b) to question people about their political attitudes. . . .

Secondly, warfare is becoming increasingly indiscriminate in:

Scope: It has become impossible today to name a war after a town or a river; when war breaks out, it imminently endangers whole regions or subcontinents.

Actors: States have lost their monopoly on waging war, and a host of non-state actors account for a large number of the armed conflicts (i.e. wars) we have today.

Targets: The civilian population will become the principal victim, not only the hostage of the contemporary arms race; irrespective of their methodologies or purported applications, all studies on the effects of future warfare point to civilians as the principal victims.

Weapon-systems: Soldiers no longer have the possibility to control weapons, once the trigger has been pulled, they just become a part of the complex and sophisticated war machinery.

Inclusiveness: There is hardly any part of the world or any aspect of societal life free from contemporary war preparations or the envisaged impacts of a future global war.

The conception of peace as a human right would undoubtedly help in raising public awareness that everyone has a stake in peace-keeping, widening public support for disarmament policy. Widening the scope of internationally proclaimed human rights by the inclusion of the rights to peace would theoretically pose no insurmountable problem. It has been accomplished recently, both by UN resolutions and scholarly treatises.[1] However, in terms of conceptualizing

1. Cf. Declaration on the Preparation of Societies for Life in Peace, Dec. 15, 1978, U.N.G.A. Res. 33/73 (it says in the first paragraph that "every nation and every human being . . . has the inherent right to life in peace"); and the series of articles on the right to peace in the *Bulletin of Peace Proposals* 11, no. 4 (1980) under the title, "The Right to Peace and Development" (P. Alston, "Peace as a Human Right"; S. P. Marks, "The Peace–Human Rights–Development Dialectics"; A. Lopatka, "The Right to Live in Peace as a Human Right"; and R. Bilder, "The Individual and the Right to Peace").

Reprinted, with changes, from Katarina Tomasevski, "The Right to Peace," *Current Research on Peace and Violence* 5, no. 1 (1982): 42–69. Reprinted by permission of the Tampere Research Institute.

such a right to peace, and especially assessing what would be its meaning as part of living law, not much progress has been made. . . .

It can be argued that peace is a supreme value of mankind and if not *the* supreme value cherished by international law, then certainly one of its supreme values. Thus, elaborating the notion of a human right to peace could be accorded a high priority. One line of reasoning in support of that is the scope and intensity of human rights violations occurring as a result of war, another one is the value of human life and the irreversibility of its loss. Both of them are recognized by contemporary international law, thereby establishing a preliminary framework for the right to peace.

PEACE AS THE SUPREME VALUE

The UN Charter proclaimed peace and security as the supreme values to be cherished, adding to them well-being and the promotion of human rights. Yet, some of the peace-promoting Charter provisions have never been implemented, such as the provision declaring that UN membership is open to peace-loving states and the one stating that contribution to international peace-keeping will be the principal criterion for electing non-permanent members of the Security Council.

The general prohibition of the use of armed force was envisaged as the cornerstone of the policy of international peace- and security-keeping. However, in spite of subsequent great achievements of the United Nations by the global process of decolonization, that process undermined protection of peace at all costs in favor of legitimizing the armed struggle for liberation and independence. As decolonization successfully expanded around the globe, the emergence of a hundred new members of the international community challenged the previously established hierarchy of the internationally promulgated values. One way of looking at it could [be] that—instead of a universal prohibition of the use of armed force—several categories of legitimate armed struggle emerged amounting to an international right of rebellion. Another way of evaluating the same development [w]ould stress the notion of

the necessity of redefining peace, following changes in the international community itself. Thus, peace came to be viewed not as mere avoidance of violent conflicts, but as a concept requiring elimination of the institutionalized violation of human rights and fundamental freedoms. Such a line of reasoning leads to the convergence of a policy promoting peace and fostering human rights; in short, the definition of peace would incorporate full respect for human rights (thus, combining the relationship between peace and human rights. . . .

Donald Keys writes: "The human condition is such that we routinely and systematically place active restraints on aggressive violence by human beings within every level of our societies, but we have yet to do so at the level of the world community. . . . [W]hat constitutes a justifiable means of achieving personal and national ends differs among countries and cultures."[2] Attitudes towards violence and consequent restraints on the use of violence are the basis of bitter disagreement in the international community. Whether discussing the use of armed force in relations between states, limits on the struggle of indigenous liberation movements or violent internal opposition to governmental policies, internationally accepted and implemented rules of conduct can seldom be found. A conclusion of David Gompert is worth quoting in this respect; he states: "As the legitimacy of many aspects of the post-war order became increasingly suspect, so did the presumed illegitimacy of effecting change by force."[3]

Yet, legitimacy of the use of force gives little comfort to those who become victims. The human, and deeply humane, aspiration to live in freedom from fear for one's life and well-being pleads for circumscribing the use of force at all levels, and bringing together the means to eliminate violence, thus leading towards the individual, national and international rights to peace.

How can this be established? Recent experience of the inability to enforce general prohibitions concerning violence—both internationally and internally—raises doubt upon the possibilities to work out universal solutions (such as an international treaty on the non-use of armed force in international relations, or stringent in-

2. Donald Keys, "The Neglected 'Software' Aspects of Disarmament," in *Disarmament: The Human Factor*, ed. Ervin Laszlo and Donald Keys (New York, Pergamon Press, 1981), 21.
3. David C. Gompert, "Constraints of Military Power: Lessons of the Past Decade," *Adelphi Papers*, no. 133 (London: International Institute for Strategic Studies, 1977), 4.

ternal legislation outlawing violence). Rather, the prevailing attitude today seems to be the examination of cases on their merits. It is accordingly advisable to see what is happening to prohibitions and/or justification of the use of force and violence on the international level, and on the other hand on national levels. Such an endeavor would result in a framework for analyzing the possibilities of a right to peace based not on its undoubtable desirability, but feasibility.

SHRINKING PROHIBITIONS CONCERNING THE USE OF ARMED FORCE

Even if we take the general prohibition of the use and/or threat of armed force (probably the most often-quoted Charter provision) for granted, there is still a wide margin for the use of armed force which has a dubious legal status. That margin is outlined by concepts such as "indirect aggression," "humanitarian intervention," "support for the struggle of national liberation movements," and the like. All of them could be called "limited war" for our purposes, as they originate in the principle of limited use of armed force (temporary, geographic or limited by purpose) and their main feature is that they are neither intended nor capable of jeopardizing territorial integrity or political independence of a state, even less of endangering international peace and security. That is exactly what makes them limited, and acceptable, or at least tolerable for the international community.

Imaginative doctrinal approaches came up with numerous theoretical constructions either defending such limited wars, or proving their illegality. Both approaches found support for their assertions in international legal rules. Yet, the larger part of it is found in soft law, as such cases are seldom brought to legal tribunals (if they are, pronouncement and verdicts never go as far as judging limited war as such).

It seems that a certain amount of permissiveness concerning the use of armed force is [inherent in] the contemporary state of affairs having on the one hand prohibition of the use of armed force, and on the other no dispute-settlement procedures that would be compulsory and efficient. Thus, the importance of limited war is seen as *justifiable self-help due to lack of [a] workable substitute*. Not only does its extensive use warn of its roots in the contemporary international legal

order and can no substantive change be envisaged, but it allows considerable *use* of armaments and methods of warfare.

The appropriate method for analyzing limited war seems to be first to find out how wide are the margins of justifiable use of armed force, and then to see what are the rules of waging such wars. The confused system of identifying and classifying armed conflicts—due to the lack of agreed-upon concepts ... —offers proof that limited war is *the* method of waging war and no serious attempt [to bring it] into the purview of international law is perceivable. Furthermore, it will be shown here that *the margins for waging limited wars are widening.*

To make things as simple as possible, it is best to stick to the chronological order of principles and norms pertaining to limited war. An analysis of UN documents should have precedence over regional and bilateral measures, as it is the only way to find out the trend that reflects the attitude of the international community as a whole.

The first step undertaken by the General Assembly is worth mentioning: by resolution 95(I) of 11 December 1946 it "*affirmed the principles of international law recognized by the Charter of the Nuremberg Tribunal and the judgement of the Tribunal.*" [Emphasis Tomasevski's.] They were supposed to reflect the established international law prohibitions concerning crimes against peace and security of mankind but it took four years till they appeared in condensed form. The International Law Commission, which was given the task of codifying them "as a matter of primary importance" did not get enough support to implement it. Confusion arose with respect to the fundamental question of whether those offenses are already a part of international law (and, if so, where are they to be found) or are they to be established by the complicated procedure of comprehensive analysis of international law sources. The result of the confusion was adoption of two different ways of dealing with the matter: one was a hasty adoption of the resolution confirming the Nuremberg principles, while another one consisted in encumbering the task of drafting a code of offenses against the peace and security of mankind by the International Law Commission. The task was assigned in November 1947, and its accomplishment is still uncertain.

The International Law Commission came up with the principles recognized by the Nuremberg Charter back in 1950 (however, the post-war enthusiasm faded away, and it was decided that the matter could wait till states gave comments). The international crimes falling within the purview of international law were grouped into three categories:

Crimes against peace: Planning, preparation, initiation or waging of a *war of aggression* or a war in violation of international treaties, agreements or assurances, including participation in a common plan or conspiracy with that aim.
War crimes: Violations of the laws or customs of war.
Crimes against humanity: Crimes against civilian population carried out in connection with crimes against peace and war crimes.

Those three categories of international crimes were upheld in all the later attempts [at] codification, but the scope of prohibitions included in defining specific punishable acts varied. For the purpose of analyzing what happened to prohibition of the use of armed force in limited wars, crimes against peace are the most relevant.

The underl[ying] idea of making international law prohibitions, aimed at preservation of peace and security, workable was the supremacy of the international law clause. Only acceptance of that principle would enable international law prohibitions to be applicable and enforceable universally. However, such a brave attempt aimed at changing the overriding sanctity of state sovereignty was flatly rejected, and international law was left to search for measures restricting state behavior that would be acceptable to states themselves. A difficult task indeed.

In spite of the fact that the Draft Code of Offences against Peace and Security of Mankind still circles around the General Assembly, being brought up as "urgent" and then dropped as "premature," it sheds some light upon the concept of aggression as *the* international crime against peace. The Draft suggests defining the crime of aggression as employment of armed force against another state, but excluding national and collective self-defense from the scope of the prohibition. The definition refers to acts of aggression, "including the employment by the authorities of a state of armed force against another state for any purpose other than national or collective self-defence." However, aside from the dangerous collective-defense escape

clause, the Draft offers an extensive enumeration of prohibions pertaining to limited war: . . .

4. The *organization,* or the encouragement of the organization, by the authorities of a state, *of armed bands* within its territory or any other territory for incursions into the territory of another state, or the *toleration* of the organization of such bands in its own territory, or the toleration of the use by such armed bands of its territory as a base of operation or as point of departure for incursions into the territory of another state, as well as direct participation in or support of such incursions.

5. The undertaking or encouragement by the authorities of a state of activities calculated to foment civil strife in another state, or the *toleration* by the authorities of a state of *organized activities calculated to foment civil strife* in another state.

6. The undertaking or encouragement by the authorities of a state of terrorist activities in another state, or the *toleration* by the authorities of a state of *organized activities calculated to carry out terrorist acts* in another state.[4]

Such a comprehensive prohibition was never repeated in any of the UN documents [on] this subject matter. If ever adopted, such a prohibition would be applicable to the larger part of contemporary limited wars: not only [does] it prohibit engagement of states in "incursions" into foreign territory, it forbids toleration of armed or terrorist groups within a state's jurisdiction.

The often quoted Declaration on Principles of International Law concerning Friendly Relations and Co-operation among States in Accordance with the Charter of the United Nations (General Assembly resolution 2625 (XXV) of 24 October 1970) contributed to the shrinking of prohibitions related to the use of armed force. Primarily, it introduced a two-level regulatory scheme for international relations: one level consisting of *principles* of international law (setting forth a sort of general guideline for mutual relations between states, and obligations of states towards the international community), and another one made up of specific international *obligations* assumed by states, which should be fulfilled in good faith. The regulation of the use of armed force—placed in the first group—thus consisted of enumerating "duties" of states, not obligations. The only two provisions retaining adherence to the so-called hard law are a statement that any war of aggres-

---

4. [Emphasis Tomasevski's.] *Yearbook of the International Law Commission, 1951,* Vol. II, and *1954,* Vol. II (New York: United Nations, 1951, 1954).

sion is a crime against peace, and [an]other one saying that a threat or use of force (against territorial integrity or political independence of any state) is a violation of international law.

The duties enumerated are the following:

1. Refraining from the threat or use of force for settling international issues.
2. Refraining from propagating wars of aggression.
3. Refraining from the threat or use of force to violate the existing international boundaries or demarcation lines.
4. Refraining from acts of reprisals involving the use of force.
5. Refraining from forcible deprivation of the right of self-determination of peoples.
6. Refraining from organizing, instigating, assisting or participating in civil strife or terrorist acts in another state, including acquiescence in the organization of such acts within the jurisdiction of a state.
7. Pursuing in good faith negotiations for the conclusion of a treaty on general and complete disarmament.

In comparison to the provisions of the Draft Code of Offences against the Peace and Security of Mankind, those duties are narrower in scope and weaker in legal force.

However, within the next two months another declaration was solemnly adopted, adding to the confusion already existing as to justifiable use of armed force. The Declaration on the Strengthening of International Security (General Assembly resolution 2734 (XXV) of 16 December 1970) repeated most of the provisions of the preceding Declaration, but added some new ones. Those particularly deserving attention call upon states to *render assistance to* "*the oppressed peoples in their legitimate struggle* in order to bring about the speedy elimination of colonialism or *any other form of external* domination,*" and reaffirm the international right of rebellion of peoples deprived of "their inalienable right to self-determination" by proclaiming their armed struggle to be legitimate. [Emphasis Tomasevski's.]

The period of the 1970s was thus marked by the impossibility of bringing into harmony the right to use armed force in order to achieve self-determination (coupled with the right to seek and obtain all forms of external assistance, meaning,

in short the engagement of foreign states), and the principle of securing territorial integrity and the existing boundaries of states.

The long-awaited Definition of Aggression is an illustrative example of the fuzzy state of the art concerning the prohibition of the use of armed force.[5] In its preamble the Definition says the following: "[It reaffirms] the duty of states not to use armed force to deprive peoples of their right to self-determination, freedom and independence, or to disrupt territorial integrity." What is the precise meaning of that provision is impossible to ascertain. In stating that armed force is not to be used to prevent the achievement of self-determination, it observes the rights of peoples, but then in the same sentence it turns to the contrary aim of preserving the territorial integrity of states (the assumption that self-determination can be implemented without touching upon the existing boundaries does not seem to be applicable at all).

In defining aggression the Definition sticks to the safe principle that aggression is the use of armed force by a state against another state, and gives examples of such uses that amount to aggression (invasion, armed attack, bombardment, blockade). When coming to the problem of wars waged by non-state actors, it adheres to a very limited prohibition: only the "sending by or on behalf of a state of armed bands, groups, irregulars or mercenaries (carrying out activities of considerable gravity) or its substantial involvement therein" could be treated as aggression. All other acts, however grave they may be, are left to the mercy of customary international law and possible UN justifications or condemnations.

Furthermore, there is an exception to any prohibition contained in the Definition of Aggression. And it is clear enough: "Nothing in this Definition . . . could in any way prejudice the right of self-determination . . . of peoples . . . particularly peoples under colonial and racist regimes and other forms of alien domination; nor the right of those peoples to struggle to that end and to seek and receive support." Briefly, prohibitions are applicable only to acts attributable to regular armed forces and in conditions of open and direct armed attack. Numerous possibilities of waging limited wars are left out and the strug-

---

5. Julius Stone wrote that ambiguities in the text of the Definition had been purposeful. Julius Stone, *Aggression and World Order: A Critique of United Nations Theories of Aggression* (Berkeley, Cal.: University of California Press, 1976).

gle for self-determination is exempted from the prohibitions.

International crimes against peace are thus limited to aggression, with authorization of governmental authorities and employment of regular armed forces.

It is important to note the consequent shrinking of the domain of state responsibility with respect to the use of armed force: what bases for state responsibility are actually left? Even if a case turned up for international adjudication, any court would have trouble in identifying international law norms pertaining to limited war. If such a case concerned implementation of the right of self-determination, all the novel regulation would speak of legitimacy of the use of armed force and of foreign assistance, while responsibility of the authorities preventing the implementation of the right of self-determination would be rather easier to prove. The case of Namibia could be taken as such an example.

Even in cases which seem to be easy to deal with, such as Afghanistan, one would encounter difficulties when applying the Definition of Aggression. The armed forces were employed therein "with the agreement of the receiving state," as the Definition states, and that is not aggression. (Yet, it could be argued that it is an aggression against the people.) However, peoples come into the purview of international norms if their right of self-determination is acknowledged within the United Nations. The right of self-determination of Afghans has been recognized as the basis for settling the "situation," but not as the basis for legitimate struggle. The General Assembly resolutions cautiously omitted the word "aggression," substituting a more neutral term "the continuing armed intervention"—not mentioning whose responsibility might be invoked—and referring to "all parties concerned" to seek the solution for the "situation" which made the General Assembly "gravely concerned." It would probably be easier to assess such warfare if international norms were precise. At least the pos-

sibility of pointing to the breach of an international obligation would be opened, and it would be possible to have some criteria applicable to the distinguishing between assistance to the oppressed peoples and outside intervention.

NATIONAL SECURITY IN JEOPARDY: CONFLICT-GENERATING ASPECTS OF FOSTERING HUMAN RIGHTS AND DEVELOPMENT

Just a brief repetition as an introduction: the principle enshrined in the international disarmament strategy is the "undiminished security of states at each stage of the disarmament process"; the other principle proclaimed is that disarmament must contribute to the development and enjoyment of human rights. If one turn[s] things around, the following question can be posed: what would be the effect of disarmament on internal security, that is, what consequences could it have for states with respect to the threat or use of force for preserving internal order? And, what machinery for settling internal conflicts generated by rising expectations do we have applicable in conditions of disarmament?

It has already been noted on numerous occasions that the UN Charter contains two concepts which are in conflict. According to one of them, the components of the world system are states, and the beneficiaries of international provisions should also be states. The second concept speaks of peoples and human beings, taking for granted that the beneficiaries of international policy-proposals—especially in the domain of development and human rights—are ultimately human beings. The same conflicting ideas are found in disarmament strategy: documents interchangeably refer to states and human beings, documents on the right to peace following the same pattern. . . .[6]

Back in 1948 the Universal Declaration of Human Rights proclaimed in its preamble the

---

6. The UN Commission on Human Rights proclaimed: "Everyone has the right to live in conditions of international peace and security and fully to enjoy human rights," in its Resolution 5 (XXXII) of 1976.

The difference in approach is evident in Eastern European literature. Upholding the concept according to which "human rights constitute a part of the rights a State [mind the capital "S"] awards to the individual . . . or even to the entire population," results in asserting that it is states who are entitled to a right to peace, and they might then extend such a right to their citizens.

A. Lopatka, "The Right to Live in Peace as a Human Right," *Bulletin of Peace Proposals* 11, no. 4 (1980): 362, et seq.

principle often invoked when it comes to balancing individual rights against rights of states. The Declaration stated: "it is essential, if man is not compelled to have recourse, as a last resort, to rebellion against tyranny and oppression, that human rights should be protected by the rule of law." If developed a step further, it seems to say that people have the right of rebellion if their rights are not protected. The meaning of "human rights protected by the rule of law" is the following: human rights should be guaranteed by internal law (proclaimed and enforceable) and individuals should have recourse to [an] internal procedure (accessible and effective) for safeguarding their rights. Such a procedure should lead to some international mechanism—after the internal remedies have been exhausted—which should, in its turn, be able to correct any governmental behavior inconsistent with international human rights standards. An obvious question emerges: what to do until all those "shoulds" are implemented? It seems that recourse to rebellion has to be granted as [an] ultimate means of self-help, and an analogy could be derived from the existence of the right of self-defense for states in international law. . . .

As [can be] illustrated by [a] review of humanitarian law norms, the right of rebellion is—by the criterion of the legal recognition of the rights of rebels—limited to struggle against colonialism, apartheid, racism and foreign occupation. Cases which could be subsumed under opposition to institutionalized violation of human rights (i.e. governmental policy negating human rights) cannot rely either on gaining international legitimacy or on safeguarding the rights of the people involved. The gap between the proclaming of human rights and guarantees which could surpass the obstacle posed by state sovereignty does not seem to diminish. Rights of states, whenever in conflict with individual rights, take precedence.[7]

However, as it took almost a century for . . . international law to eliminate "the bias of the system against revolutionary challenge,"[8] it can be said that human rights are being included in the international law domain at a much quicker pace. Suggestions aimed at restraining rights of states in favor of human rights guarantees, even at their implementation by force, are numerous. Suffice it here to quote two of them. One [notes] the emergence of a "recognition of universally prevailing human rights [which] resulted in support of internal resistance to structural violence,"[9] while the other goes even further, advocating adoption of an attitude which would in exceptional cases proclaim resort to armed force as an inference of democracy: "resort to coercive instruments by those seriously affected by social injustice, when due constitutional processes prove insensitive to their plights, must be tolerated [and] ought to be considered as part of the democratic process."[10]

It remains to be seen whether such suggestions find any support in the policy recommendations currently being adopted by the United Nations, which seek solutions to both human rights and development within a common disarmament-development strategy. Leaving aside simplistic assumptions that human rights will be automatically improved within a new international order, including the assertion that disarmament will release resources which will automatically advance development, thus eliminating causes of violence [inherent in] underdevelopment, one might look into the vision of life in peace in order to see what balance between individual and states' rights it envisages.

The UN Declaration on the Preparation of Societies for Life in Peace, considered as the first document proclaiming an individual right to peace, recognizes *"peace among nations* (as) mankind's paramount value," and proclaims that "every nation and every human being . . . has the

7. It should be kept in mind that human rights entered the realm of international law recently, and that they are not perceived as a legitimate international concern by a large group of states, primarily the Eastern European ones.
8. Richard A. Falk, *The International Law of Civil Strife* (Baltimore: Johns Hopkins University Press, 1971), 13.
9. V. A. Röling, "The Legal Status of Rebels and Rebellions," *Journal of Peace Research* 13, no. 2 (1976): 152.
10. Israel W. Charny, ed., *Strategies Against Violence: Design for Non-Violent Change* (Boulder, Colo.: Westview Press, 1978), 346.

inherent right to life in peace."[11] While reiterating obligations to respect rights of states in international relations and rights of peoples to self-determination, it says nothing about rights and obligations of states and peoples in internal relations, i.e. within states. The Declaration concludes that the "basic instrument of the maintenance of peace is the elimination of threats inherent in the arms race."

But we do have references to internal changes necessary for eliminating the "climate of fear and violence that erodes the quality of life." Those are found in the UN documents on crime prevention. The most important changes seem to be improving social conditions and enhancing the quality of life, ensuring greater security and protection of the rights and freedoms of all the people, and stable social conditions free from oppression and manipulation.

It does not seem possible to establish a governmental obligation which would secure an individual right to peace relying upon the sources we have. International sources would provide for a basis for speaking about an international right to peace pertaining to states (no matter how meager their chances of implementing such a right seem today). Internal measures which would lead towards an individual right to peace are a long way from possible international standards of proclamation and implementation. Yet, some support could be found in national laws establishing guarantees of fundamental human rights and individual freedoms, providing for public participation in decision-making, establishing the right and stipulating the right to conscientious objection to military service. However, internationally advocated policies of national development include proposals having (supposedly) direct bearing upon causes of internal disturbances. Furthermore, international standards-setting and cross-national comparisons of human rights implementation, and publicizing human rights violations should not be neglected as methods for fostering the promotion of human rights. Therefore, while it is safe to speak about [a] right to peace which would pertain to states nowadays, it is desirable to include the dimension of an individual right to peace, if merely as a sort of a distant goal of human rights and disarmament policy.

DISARMAMENT: RATIONAL APPROACH AND IRRATIONAL CONSTRAINTS

Numerous UN documents and expert studies reiterate the conclusion of disarmament being indispensable for the harmonious future development of the world, adding the assertion about the irrationality of the further development of armaments. If the world as a whole has already reached a tenfold overkill capacity, the argument goes, it does not make much sense to strive to increase it to a twelvefold overkill capacity. Yet, the notion of *sense* has to be used with utmost caution: what could be senseless for the world at large, could make a lot of sense for an individual country; what does not make any sense to an imaginary ordinary citizen makes a lot of sense for (a real) strategic planner who makes a living by developing worst-case scenarios.

There are [many] more arguments in favor of disarmament than just common sense. The latest UN Report on Disarmament and Development emphasizes its terms of reference as strengthening the socio-economic case for an empirically quantifiable and rationally imperative relationship between disarmament and development. What they attempt to say is that disarmament would not only relieve mankind from the constant fear of annihilation, but substantially increase availability of resources devoted to human development. Arms race and development cannot be treated as non-competitive: as resources are limited, their use for increasing armaments deprives public funds of resources for development or social welfare. Furthermore, as one aspect of the irrationality ascribed to the arms race develops from the conclusion that increasing armaments decrease[s] security, it ends up in realizing that strategic/military "sense" presents security requirements as requiring more and more armaments.

In spite of the injustice done to disarmament/development literature (attempting to persuade mankind that it would be much better off without

---

11. [Emphasis Tomasevski's.] Dec. 15, 1978, U.N.G.A. Res. 33/73. See also Stephen P. Marks, "The Peace–Human Rights–Development Dialectic," *Bulletin of Peace Proposals* 11, no. 4 (1980): 339–47.

the arms race) by posing the question whether all the rational arguments pleading for rechanneling resources from armament into development take sufficient account of the assertion that the arms race is irrational, it has to be brought up. . . . A futurologist, Hazel Henderson, found fault with the hierachical decision-making system in the world of today, placing decisions— which are as complex as they are dangerous— concerning war and peace in the hands of a few people. Such a hierarchy, she concludes, culminates in "the neat orderly world of the geo-political strategies, the war games with their erroneous concept that the world is operated upon by rational actors."[12]

Application of common sense to an analysis of circumstances hampering the process of disarmament . . . could [cause] consternation. The disarmament efforts started by negotiations among those having the largest arsenals. At the top of the hierarchy are the two great powers, others hardly being able to compete with respect to military hardware with either of them, let alone a combination of the two. Thus, the very leading military powers are empowered with a veto (not only in the Security Council, but extending to any disarmament negotiations) as to the use, deployment, development or elimination of the military potential. . . .

The untouchable position of the two great powers left alone, we can turn to other states to see what their position is in [the] armaments/disarmament process. They are primarily concerned with preserving their position [as] principal international actors, through the utilization of two powerful tools, one being the principle of sovereign equality and the other the prohibition of jeopardizing their integrity, independence and freedom in managing their internal affairs. The equality principle postulates undiminished security of all states throughout the process of disarmament. What is "undiminished security" is determined by each state: it is fully sovereign in assessing its needs for defense against external and internal security threats, equally sovereign in establishing what those threats are.

Accordingly, when estimating possibilities of having disarmament actually happen, we have to keep in mind that *dis*-arming is required from those who—by and large—owe their position to

arming. Little benefit can be derived from blaming the United Nations for not doing anything about disarmament, [it] cannot *do* anything, as [it was] not established for such purposes and [it does] not have the means required. . . .

This is the point where international law comes in: it reflects the exact scope and measure of restraint that states are willing to adhere to in the[ir] international relations and internal policies. . . . The overwhelming majority of documents advocating disarmament (belonging to the "soft" law domain) advocate conclusion of international agreements as *the* method of moving ahead towards the lofty goal of "general and complete disarmament under effective international control." . . . More often than not, such agreements are abundant with concepts containing such a degree of ambiguity to keep philologists busy.

If irrationality is included into analyzing the arms race, its preservation by strategic doctrines—such as deterrence—becomes easier to understand. The main point of deterrence is threatening "them" by annihilation, and thus preventing "them" from embarking upon annihilating "us." In order to justify increasing threats to them, the danger presented by them is outlined by worst-case scenarios. And, to make mutual threats credible, both the military capabilities and willingness to use them have to be demonstrated in a convincing way. As they are also using worst-case scenarios, the threat is being exaggerated to justify speeding up the arms race with the aim of keeping up with the competit[ion]. Accordingly, security is being preserved by increasing capabilities of annihilation.

Such strategic considerations, being converted into national policies while not restrained by international measures of control and disarmament, make all of humanity a single, helpless hostage. Yet, the contemporary peace movements are a sign of *the rebellion of the hostages.* Those whose rational argumentation did not affect the basically irrational reasoning of the highest levels in the decision-making pyramid demand not only a say in arming/disarming policies, but they require rational reasoning to be applied. Another valuable result of the peace movements that we are becoming aware of today is demanding peace as a right. . . .

12. Hazel Henderson, *The Politics of Reconceptualiztion* (New York: Doubleday, 1981), quoted in *Toronto Globe and Mail,* 14 July 1980, p. F8.

QUESTIONS FOR REFLECTION AND DISCUSSION

1. The 1978 UN Declaration on the Preparation of Societies for Life in Peace, cited by Tomasevski as "the first document proclaiming an individual right to peace," recognizes "peace among nations" as humankind's "paramount value." Do you agree that this is so? Why? Why not? Consider, in this connection, the following statement from Ruth Leger Sivard (*World Military and Social Expenditures, 1985* [Washington, D.C.: World Priorities, 1985], 5):

> The arms build-up has continued, at painful cost to the world community. . . . Violence is on the rise. There are more wars and more people killed in them. Four times as many deaths have occurred in the 40 years since World War II as in the 40 years preceding it. Increasingly the geopolitical designs of the major military powers are being worked out on the soil of other countries and with other people's lives. . . . In a world spending $800 billion a year for military programs, one adult in three cannot read and write, one person in four is hungry.

The 1978 Declaration goes on to proclaim that "every nation and every human being . . . has the inherent right to life in peace." Is there such a right? Does Tomasevski think so? If so, what is the evidence?

2. One of the principal purposes of the United Nations, according to Article 1(1) of the UN Charter, is "[t]o maintain international peace and security" and, to this end, "to bring about by peaceful means . . . adjustment or settlement of international disputes or situations which might lead to a breach of the peace." But, clearly, the United Nations has been unable to achieve these goals to any great degree. Why? In particular, why has the United Nations been generally unable to provide good offices, enquiry, mediation, conciliation, arbitration, adjudication, and other means of peaceful settlement for the resolution of interstate disputes? Might your answers to these questions affect your judgment about the existence or not of the right to peace? Why? Why not?

3. Irrespective of your answers to the foregoing questions, how might "peace" be defined? Johan Galtung, in "Nonterritorial Actors and the Problem of Peace" (*The Creation of a Just World Order: Preferred Worlds for the 1990s*, ed. Saul Mendlovitz [New York: The Free Press, 1975], 151–52), defines "peace" as the absence of "structural" as well as "direct" violence. Describing structural violence as "built into the social structure," Galtung writes:

> Everybody knows this structure from personal experience; it is found within and between countries; it is an embodiment of violence. This structure is reproduced in the agricultural, industrial, commercial, and administrative sectors of society in such a way that surplus is extracted from the lower levels and transferred upwards, making the higher levels richer at the expense of the lower levels, producing the famous "gaps" in development. The result is often highly differential morbidity and mortality rates between rich and poor countries, districts, and individuals.

Is it helpful or unhelpful to define "peace" in this way, as requiring not only the absence of hostilities (sometimes called "negative peace") but, as well, the presence of human dignity or social justice (sometimes called "positive peace")? Note, in this connection, the two Arabic words for "peace": *sulah*, meaning the end of hostilities or a truce, and *salaam*, meaning an enduring nonviolent relationship based on mutual respect. Is peace, in the sense of the absence of hostilities, possible without providing for mutual respect or otherwise restricting structural violence? Is it possible to speak of a right to peace without referring to both direct and structural violence? Why? Why not?

4. Are there economic barriers to peace? Who profits from a state of non-peace? Consider the question posed by John Somerville in *The Peace Revolution: Ethos and Social Process* ([Westport, Conn.: Greenwood Press, 1975], 150):

> What would be the probable effect of a law which provided that whenever the government waged war, and drafted the youth, all industry and capital would become public property for the duration, that private profit and private dividends would cease (be socialized), and all salaries would be limited to the scale of military pay? What proportion of the public would accept the moral principle that, if lives are drafted, property should also be drafted?

Can you think of any wars that would not have been waged if Somerville's moral principle had been accepted at the time? If so, should it be viewed as integral to the right to peace?

5. In *The Transformations of Man* ([New York: Harper & Brothers, 1956], 217–18), Lewis Mumford observes that "for the first time in history, man now begins to know his planet as a whole" and that "[t]he kind of person called for by the present situation is one capable of breaking through the boundaries of culture and history." Others, such as Samuel Kim, in *The Quest for a Just World Order* ([Boulder, Colo.: Westview Press, 1984], 55), observe that a "widening concentric circle of global consciousness accompanied by the refusal to accept the inevitability and legitimacy of global war, poverty, injustice, genocide, and eco-cide" is leading to one of the great transformations in the life of the species, one that will establish universally held values, such as the value of peace. Is the kind of person of which Mumford speaks in abundance in the world today? If so, what is the evidence? If not, what does this fact portend for the right to peace? Is the great transfuromation to which Kim refers a serious possibility without some cataclysmic conflict? If so, what is the evidence? If not, what does this fact portend for the right to peace?

SELECT BIBLIOGRAPHY

Alston, Philip, and Katarina Tomasevski. *The Right to Food*. The Hague: Martinus Nijhoff Publishers, 1984. Philosophical, policy-oriented and legal essays on the right to food, viewed as the most fundamental of the social and economic rights.

Crahan, Margaret E., ed. *Human Rights and Basic Needs in the Americas*. Washington, D.C.: Georgetown University Press, 1982. Uses case studies drawn from Latin America to test claims about political, military, and economic factors affecting basic needs and related U.S. policy.

Cristescu, Alfredo. *The Right to Self-Determination*. New York: United Nations, 1981. Historical and current development of self-determination analyzed by a special rapporteur of the Sub-Commission on the Prevention of Discrimination and Protection of Minorities.

Eide, Asborn, Wenche Barthe Eide, Susantha Goonatilake, Joan Gussow, and Omawale, et al., eds. *Food as a Human Right*. Toyko: United Nations University Press, 1984. Contains essays on the causes of hunger and discussions of the international norms used to evaluate the state's responsibility in helping its inhabitants gain a minimal right to food. Also investigates international efforts to promote structural changes consistent with food security.

Fitzgerald, Ross, ed. *Human Needs and Politics*. Rushcutters Bay, N.S.W.: Pergamon Press, 1977. A conceptual inquiry distinguishing wants and needs, and critical inquiry into the political implications of social science theories derived from Abraham Maslov's "hierarchy of human needs."

Galtung, Johan. *Human Needs as the Focus of the Social Sciences*. Oslo: University of Oslo Press, 1977. Offers a specific framework with normative and empirical implications for social science. Defines and clarifies concepts of "human needs" and argues that such needs should be the centerpiece of social research.

International Commission of Jurists. *Development, Human Rights and the Rule of Law*. Oxford: Pergamon Press, 1981. Collection of essays that defines "development" and "mal-development," as well as "human rights," in a global context emphasizing equally civil and political, and economic, social and cultural rights.

McCaffrey, St. C., and R. E. Lutz, eds. *Environmental Pollution and Individual Rights: An International Symposium*. Deventer, Netherlands: Kluves, 1978. Conference papers on the rights of individuals against acts of pollution. Includes twelve national reports on the kinds of individual and group actions available to citizens to redress environmental harms.

Pomerance, Michael. *Self-Determination in Law and Practice: The New Doctrine in the United Nations*. The Hague: Martinus Nijhoff Publishers, 1982. A critical analysis of United Nations politics on the right to self-determination. Argues that the imperative and immediate goal of self-determination for all peoples "under colonial or alien domination" too often applies the principles in an ad hoc and politically expedient way.

Ramcharan, B. G., ed. *The Right to Life in International Law*. The Hague: Martinus Nijhoff Publishers, 1985. Legal scholars examine multiple aspects of the right to life and survival requirements, including the rights to development and peace, and international standards on genocide, arbitrary killing, and capital punishment.

Shepherd, George W., Jr., and Ved P. Nanda, eds. *Human Rights and Third World Development*. Westport,

Conn.: Greenwood Press, 1985. A political science–oriented collection of essays, including several area studies, espousing the view that human rights and development concerns are not competing but complementary goals.

Shue, Henry. *Basic Rights, Subsistence, Affluence, and U.S. Foreign Policy.* Princeton, N.J.: Princeton University Press, 1980. A carefully argued brief for a universal human right to subsistence, combined with a systematic application of moral theory applied to U.S. foreign policy.

UNESCO. *Human Rights in Urban Areas.* Paris, 1983. Anecdotal and descriptive case studies emphasizing European, African, and Latin American experience with the marginalized urban poor, who are often unaware of their rights or made to feel unworthy to claim them.

Welch, Claude E., and Ronald I. Meltzer, eds. *Human Rights and Development in Africa: Domestic, Regional and International Dilemmas.* Albany, N.Y.: State University of New York Press, 1984. Political science–oriented essays on the realistic prospects for economic and political development in Africa, with attention to related human rights issues and problems.

Ziman, John, Paul Sieghart, and John Humphries. *The World of Science and the Rule of Law.* New York: Oxford University Press, 1986. Surveys the performance of thirty-five countries under the Helsinki Agreement in enforcing particular human rights crucial to the work of scientists.

SELECT FILMOGRAPHY

The Arab and the Israeli. Steve York, producer. U.S.A.: PBS Video, 1984. 60 min., color; videotape. Documentary on 1984 speaking tour of (expelled) Palestinian mayor Mohammed Milhem and Israeli Knesset member Mordechai Bar-On (former army officer and activist in the peace movement) who traveled to the United States to speak together publicly about mutual recognition and the dialogue for peace in the Middle East.

El Barco De La Paz. E. Katz, D. Halleck, and H. Kipnis, producers. U.S.A.: Fellowship Reconciliation, 1984. 28 min., color; ¾-in, VHS videotape. Documentary about the 1984 sailing of the Peace Ship to Nicaragua that was sponsored by Norway and Sweden to provide humanitarian aid and demonstrate the potential for nonviolent alternatives to the threat of war in Central America. Includes interviews with Nobel Peace Prize Laureates and Nicaraguan people to emphasize the importance of international attention to the issues of peace.

The Big Village. United Nations, producer. Barr/Univ IL Films, 1979. 25 min., color; 16 mm. A view of the relations between the "rich" and the "poor" nations from a Third World perspective. Questions why there are persistent inequities and how the resources and bounty of the earth can be shared.

Bottle Babies. Peter Krieg, producer. U.S.A.: New Time/Ecufilm, Michigan Media/CC Films, 1976. 26 min., color; 16 mm. Explores the alarming increase in malnutrition in Third World infants because of their consumption of imported powdered formula. Investigates one probable cause—the massive advertising campaigns of the multinational companies that sell these products.

Celso and Cora. Gary Kildea, producer. Australia: Philippine Resource, 1983. 109 min., color, Tagalog dialogue (English subtitles); 16 mm. Portrait of a young couple with children living in a squatter settlement in Manila. Follows their attempts to survive economically and as a family unit as they face daily life and confront the greater sociopolitical forces surrounding them.

The Face of Famine. Films, Inc., 1982. 75 min., color. Shows how enormous quantities of grain are used to feed livestock in the West and the repercussions of such a system on starving people all over the world.

For Export Only. Richter Productions, 1982. 112 min., color. Shows how products banned or restricted in the West, because of their danger to humans, are knowingly exported to the Third World by multinational corporations.

Hiroshima: A Document of the Atomic Bombing. Michigan Media, 1970. 28 min., color. One of the best documentations of the bomb's effects on Hiroshima.

Hiroshima-Nagasaki! August 1945. Museum of Modern Art Circulating Film Program, 1970. 17 min., b/w. Uses Japanese film withheld from the public for 20 years to show the results of the bombing.

The Palestinian People Do Have Rights. Icarus Films, 1979. 48 min., color. Presents a comprehensive examination of the Palestinian-Israeli conflict.

War, Human Rights and the Press. Robert MacNeil (Center for Communication), producer. New York: PBS, 1988. 60 min., color; VHS, ¾-in videotape. Six war correspondents discuss problems of reporting human rights news, e.g., atrocities in Afghanistan, Beirut, and Central and South America. Manipulation of the media is analyzed and the problems of "staged scenes" for television cameras.

The West Bank: Whose Promised Land? Esti Marpet, producer. U.S.A.: Electronic Arts, 1984. 30 min., color; videotape. A documentary that looks at the strained and often volatile day-to-day life of Israelis and Palestinians in the occupied West Bank. Residents of the region, Jewish and Arab, express a range of sentiments and political views on the status of the territory.

And Who Shall Feed This World? Films, Inc., 1975. 47 min., color. Does the United States have an obligation to provide food for the rest of the world? This film tries to answer that question.

ACTION

Chapter Four

International Approaches to Implementation

IN this chapter we consider international approaches to the implementation of human rights, first in terms of the United Nations; next in terms of the regional human rights regimes in Europe, the Americas, and Africa; and finally in terms of the thirty-five-country "Helsinki Process."

THE UNITED NATIONS

The United Nations is an international organization that seeks to foster friendly relations among nations, helps to maintain international peace and security, and works to facilitate economic, social, and cultural cooperation and development. Additionally, as set forth in Article 1 of its Charter, one of the United Nations' principal purposes is "[t]o achieve international co-operation . . . in promoting and encouraging respect for human rights and for fundamental freedoms for all without distinction as to race, sex, language, or religion."

The linkage of human rights with more familiar UN goals is no accident of the UN Charter. It reflects, rather, a connection that President Franklin D. Roosevelt saw between peace and freedom, between international security and human rights. In a message to Congress on January 26, 1941, Roosevelt enunciated "four freedoms": freedom of speech and expression, freedom of worship, freedom from want (meaning economic security), and freedom from fear (meaning a worldwide reduction of armaments and international peace).[1] These goals—especially in the wake of systematic genocide before and during World War II—were perceived as essential world concerns that mandated international cooperation and participation.

On the basis of this perception, the 1945 San Francisco conference that drafted the UN Charter sought not only to continue the struggle against tyranny begun during World War II, but, as well, to initiate the creation of effective norms, institutions, and procedures addressed to broadly defined human rights issues. The aim was not to fashion a world government; that would have been idealism run amok. The purpose was to achieve, step by step, a world community capable of securing the UN Charter's goals of peace and social justice—a golden-age image, perhaps, but one toward which, since the San Francisco conference, some ordered progress actually has been made.

Since 1945, the United Nations has taken three interrelated steps toward the advancement of human rights: (a) the formulation and definition of international norms of behavior regarding human rights; (b) the promotion of human rights through information, education, and training about human rights at all levels of social organization; and (c) the implemen-

1. Address to Congress by President Roosevelt, 87th Cong. Rec. 44 (1944), excerpted as "Four Human Freedoms," *Human Rights Quarterly* 6 (1984): 384–85. The most succinct statement connecting the global values of rights with international security was John F. Kennedy's maxim that "peace, in the last analysis, is a matter of human rights." Quoted in Arthur J. Goldberg, "Our Concern for Human Rights," *Congress Bi-Weekly* 32, no. 13 (Nov. 15, 1965): 8, at 9. The philosophy is elaborated in the context of a normative theory of world order explained by Samuel S. Kim, *The Quest for a Just World Order* (Boulder, Colo.: Westview Press, 1984).

tation of human rights norms through the design and creation of appropriate institutions and procedures. Each of these steps merits brief attention.

FORMULATING AND DEFINING HUMAN RIGHTS

The initial step of formulating and defining international human rights norms was taken soon after the United Nations was organized.[2] When the UN General Assembly first met in London in 1946, it transmitted to its Economic and Social Council a draft Declaration of Fundamental Human Rights and Freedoms "for reference to the Commission on Human Rights in its preparation of an international bill of rights."[3] In 1947, the UN Commission decided to apply the term "International Bill of Human Rights" to a declaration of human rights, a convention on human rights (to be called "The Covenant on Human Rights"), and measures of implementation. This decision led, in turn, to the adoption and proclamation of the Universal Declaration of Human Rights in December 1948 as the first of these projected instruments.[4] However, instead of one international covenant on human rights, there emerged, in 1966, two such covenants: the International Covenant on Economic, Social and Cultural Rights and the International Covenant on Civil and Political Rights.[5] Each contains a plan for international supervision of the rights it addresses and for resolution of complaints by one state against another. In addition, the Optional Protocol to the Political Covenant[6] provides important international machinery for dealing with claims from individuals regarding alleged state violations of the rights guaranteed in that covenant.

The drafting of human rights standards that are universally acceptable is necessarily an awesome task because the words used must be carefully chosen if, in our multicultural world, they are to be understood and taken seriously. In 1977, the late Allard K. Lowenstein, United States Representative to the UN Thirty-third Commission on Human Rights, paid tribute to Eleanor Roosevelt, who chaired the committee responsible for the drafting of the Universal Declaration of Human Rights. In arguing that "words matter," Lowenstein stated:

> Mrs. Roosevelt's . . . efforts to get agreement about what was meant by the words "human rights" . . . was the toughest semantic job of all, and the fact that that job eventually got done makes the complexities that still exist somehow more manageable. We have developed over thirty years' time a body of precedents and of common usages of words, and that is a formidable influence on what governments have to say they are trying to measure up to.[7]

Theodor Meron argues that by the 1980s, the drafting of human rights instruments had become somewhat haphazard.[8] In the early years of drafting the "International Bill of

2. For a succinct overview of the history of UN human rights formulation and definition, see Louis B. Sohn, "A Short History of United Nations Documents on Human Rights," *The United Nations and Human Rights*, 18th report (New York: Commission to Study the Organization of Peace, 1968), 39–186.
3. Feb. 16, 1946, ECOSOC Res. 1/5, U.N. Doc. E/CN/AC.1/3. The draft declaration is reproduced as Annex A of U.N. Doc E/CN.4/21. See John Humphrey, "The Universal Declaration of Human Rights: Its History, Impact and Juridical Character," in *Human Rights: Thirty Years After the Universal Declaration of Human Rights*, ed. B. G. Ramcharan (The Hague: Martinus Nijhoff Publishers, 1979), 21–40.
4. See the Appendix.
5. See the Appendix.
6. See the Appendix.
7. "Review of the U.N. 33d Commission on Human Rights," House Committee on Foreign Affairs, Subcommittee on Human Rights and International Organizations, *Hearing*, 95th Cong., 1st sess., May 19, 1977, 19.
8. Theodor Meron, *Human Rights Law-Making in the United Nations: A Critique of Instruments and Process* (Oxford: Oxford University Press, 1986), 278.

Rights," human rights standards were prepared with much deliberation. More recently, however, "[p]roblems of particular concern are the frequent lack of adequate research prior to the decision to initiate the law-making process, and inadequate supporting research throughout that process."[9] In his essay in this chapter, Tom J. Farer critically analyzes the "distance the U.N. has come in four decades," acknowledging many serious shortcomings as well as gains in its performance in advancing the cause of international human rights.

PROMOTING HUMAN RIGHTS

A second UN task is the promotion of human rights, by which is meant campaigns to "market" human rights, to increase knowledge about and public support for international human rights instruments such as the two covenants and the more specialized conventions and declarations promulgated in recent years. The United Nations' efforts to promote human rights include information exchanges, educational training courses, the establishment of human rights fellowships for scholars, programs of the United Nations University in Tokyo, and the advisory services of experts to aid member states with problems and issues in the field of human rights.[10] Additionally, the United Nations has undertaken special studies on apartheid, the "disappeared," freedom of religion, and freedom of movement across national boundaries—to mention but a few.

Particularly popular have been the worldwide and regional human rights conferences and seminars on diverse specialized topics, open to private individuals and organizations. Example topics are human rights in developing countries (Nicosia, 1968); the participation of women in the economic life of their states (Moscow, 1970); human rights and scientific and technological development (Vienna, 1972); women, equality, development, and peace (Copenhagen, 1980); and human rights teaching (Malta, 1987). Such conferences are important not only because they bring together interested private parties from throughout the world, but also, and more important, because they promote penetrating discussions of the deeper issues of injustice underlying human rights abuses. Scholars and other private persons in educational seminars are more free than governmentally instructed UN representatives to debate the information, research, and education needed to analyze the unjust conditions under which human rights are denied and to eradicate the root causes for their denial. In addition, such conferences, relying on widely accepted standards of human rights, can assess human rights progress from country to country. While it is true that no state technically is bound by an international human rights instrument until it has ratified or acceded to the instrument, still, in the sunlight of open international discussions, no state can escape scrutiny regarding its adherence to international human rights norms. In sum, human rights conferences attended by private persons only, when sponsored by the United Nations, can inform public opinion globally and thereby promote human rights standards as a basis for judging governments.

IMPLEMENTING HUMAN RIGHTS

In principle, international human rights conventions leave the task of directly enforcing their standards to the states parties to them, which are expected to enact the necessary legislation and other measures. But UN organs typically play a supervisory role in such implementation,

9. Ibid.
10. See, e.g., Evan Luard, "Promotion of Human Rights by UN Political Bodies," in *The International Protection of Human Rights*, ed. Evan Luard (New York: Frederick A. Praeger, 1967), 132–59.

and, as Farer suggests, they may be graded from "weak" to "strong" depending upon how directly and swiftly they respond to complaints.

The weakest, most indirect form of UN supervision of human rights is the requirement of government reporting, especially since, as in numerous human rights treaties, the requirement involves merely the ritual filing of reports with no questions asked. For example, states that are party to the International Convention on the Elimination of All Forms of Racial Discrimination[11] are obliged to report every two years to the UN Secretary-General on national measures taken to implement the agreement.[12] Detailed reporting requirements are contained as well in Part 4 of the International Covenant on Economic, Social and Cultural Rights. However, the delinquency rates for the states bound by these instruments are, unfortuately, all too high, suggesting that the procedure is regarded less seriously than was intended by the drafters.[13]

On the other hand, the promise of stronger UN supervision exists in the reporting systems that contain potential for specific legal accountability. One example is Article 40 of the International Covenant on Civil and Political Rights, which, when read in conjunction with Article 2, obliges the states parties to report the extent to which they have (a) adopted legislative or other measures to implement the rights recognized in the covenant, (b) ensured that persons whose rights and freedoms are violated have had access to effective remedies from competent judicial, administrative, or legislative authorities, and (c) guaranteed that competent authorities have enforced such remedies when granted. These reports are submitted to, and carefully scrutinized by, the Human Rights Committee set up under the covenant to supervise its implementation. The Committee has earned a positive reputation by becoming increasingly active in challenging governments in order to hold them to their commitments.[14]

This increasingly active role of the Human Rights Committee is consistent with the general trend of UN activity in the protection of human rights. As Farer points out, the role of the United Nations in the international protection of human rights has developed from that of a rudimentary receptacle for human rights complaints to that of a more active intermediary seeking to promote compliance with human rights norms and standards.

For example, upon becoming a party to the Optional Protocol to the International Covenant on Civil and Political Rights, which went into effect in 1978, any state party to the Political Covenant automatically recognizes the competence of the Human Rights Committee "to receive and consider communications from individuals . . . who claim to be victims of a violation by that State Party" (Article 1). While not empowered to supply a remedy directly, the Committee is empowered to demand of the accused state "written explanations or statements clarifying the matter and the remedy, if any, that may have been taken by that State" (Article 4(2)), thus offering some recourse to individuals whose rights have been violated.

Another example is the older "1503 Procedure," so-called because of UN Economic and Social Council Resolution 1503 of May 1970 that gave birth to it.[15] Involving "the entire

---

11. Mar. 7, 1966, 660 U.N.T.S. 195.
12. Ibid., art. 9.
13. See A. Glenn Mower, Jr., "Reports from State Parties," in *International Cooperation for Social Justice, Global and Regional Protection of Economic/Social Rights* (Westport, Conn.: Greenwood Press, 1985), 39–40. See also "The Reporting System," in Meron, *Human Rights Law-Making in the United Nations*, 237–40.
14. See, e.g., A. H. Robertson, "Individual Communications: The Optional Protocol," in *Human Rights in the World* (Manchester: Manchester University Press, 1982), 54–60.
15. Procedure for Dealing with Communications Relating to Violations of Human Rights and Fundamental Freedoms, May 27, 1970, ECOSOC Res. 1503 (XLVIII), 48 U.N. ESCOR, Supp. (No. 1A) 8, U.N. Doc. E/4832/Add. 1 (1970).

hierarchy of the UN's human rights organs"[16] (the General Assembly, the Economic and Social Council, the Commission on Human Rights, and its Sub-Commission on Prevention of Discrimination and Protection of Minorities), the procedure differs from that under the Optional Protocol in two important ways. First, it allows for communications from nongovernmental organizations and other interested groups as well as from individual victims and their representatives. Second, it is designed neither to expose publicly the states complained of nor to condemn offending states, but rather to consider situations of widespread, massive violations of human rights and to help the states concerned cease committing or allowing the commission of the violations in question.[17]

Though the United Nations' human rights oversight authority, even under the Optional Protocol, does not afford direct protection to victims of alleged violations, many people petition the United Nations with human rights complaints nevertheless. Since its founding, the United Nations has received myriad human rights complaints: between 1951 and 1971, it received 120,000 complaints from individuals and nongovernmental organizations, and in the 1980s petitions have averaged between 20,000 and 30,000 annually.[18]

The procedures for managing and processing these complaints are cumbersome, and they are explained by diverse factors, including the inability of states to reach agreement on how and even whether to protect human rights. Farer acknowledges the difficulties and shows how multiple UN organs are occasionally effective but more often are uncoordinated and ill-equipped to pressure an offending regime. The United Nations' perspectives and capabilities are generally long-term and indirect, so that direct, effective human rights protection remains an elusive goal. On the other hand, Farer does not hesitate to emphasize the positive UN record. He draws attention, for example, to successes in embarrassing such violators as Chile, Equatorial Guinea, and South Africa—successes, he explains, that are attributable to the occasional breaking down or rearranging of cliques of UN member states in ways that allow decision-making organs to act in concert. On balance, however, the United Nations, under current circumstances, is best at educating regimes about humane and cosmopolitan standards by dispensing or withholding its stamp of legitimacy relative to the human rights records of members.

Theo C. van Boven, Director of the UN Division of Human Rights from 1977 to 1982, has been unusually candid regarding obstacles to greater responsiveness of the United Nations on human rights matters.[19] According to van Boven, the Human Rights Commission members representing the interests of their governments have occasionally sidetracked complaints based on an alliance among members representing Third World military dictatorships, for example, Chile, Argentina, Paraguay, and Uruguay during the early 1980s. Also, East-

---

16. Dinah L. Shelton, "Individual Complaint Machinery Under the United Nations 1503 Procedure and the Optional Protocol to the International Covenant on Civil and Political Rights," in *Guide to International Human Rights Practice*, ed. Hurst Hannum (Philadelphia: University of Pennsylvania Press, 1984), 60.
17. Because of the confidentiality of the 1503 Procedure, its effectiveness is difficult to evaluate. Several close UN observers believe the actions taken under it are neither very strong nor uniform and effective. Antonio Cassesse, for example ("The Admissibility of Communication to the United Nations on Human Rights Violations," *Revue des Droits de l'Homme* 5 (1972): 375–97), believes that the secrecy surrounding 1503 Procedure activities of the UN Commission on Human Rights deprives various competent UN organs of valuable information on serious human rights violations. Theo C. van Boven ("A Peoples' Commission," in *People Matter: Views on International Human Rights Policy* ([Amsterdam: Meulenhoff Nederland, 1981], 59–67) writes that the 1503 Procedure at first appeared very promising, but the time consumed by its technicalities and the reluctance of the Human Rights Commission to act effectively turned high expectations to disappointment.
18. See Howard Tolley, Jr., *The U.N. Commission on Human Rights* (Boulder, Colo.: Westview Press, 1987), 125.
19. van Boven, *People Matter*, 40–84.

West rivalry often has resulted in inaction, as van Boven explains:

> It is . . . not to the credit of the United Nations that if one party raises an issue of concern, the other party that considers itself implicated counteracts by moving an issue that serves as a nuisance to the first party. It is in this manner that, for instance, the U.S.S.R. managed to block in the U.N. Commission on Human Rights any decision-making in the case of the Soviet scientist and human rights activist, Dr. [Andrei] Sakharov. Thus it happened when the United Kingdom moved a draft resolution concerning the fate of Dr. Sakharov, the U.S.S.R. made a counter move on human rights in Northern Ireland. Similarly, when the U.S.A. proposed U.N. action regarding the case of Dr. Sakharov, the U.S.S.R. retorted by proposing a draft resolution on indigenous people in the U.S.A. In fact, the result was that proposals and counter proposals neutralized each other because the majority of the membership of the Commission refused to take a stand on issues which they considered as being raised in the context of East-West confrontation. While we would readily agree that all these issues . . . involved matters of legitimate human rights concern, it is very doubtful whether the real human aspects of these issues are being served by raising them in the politicized context of East-West confrontation. Moreover, these types of actions tend to undermine the credibility and the reputation of the United Nations, but in reality the blame should be put on the political actors.[20]

van Boven's comments should not be taken to suggest a situation of gridlocked decision-making in the United Nations. According to Hans Thoolen, some of van Boven's constructive criticisms and suggestions have themselves met with success, for instance, the appointment of rapporteurs, special representatives, and subject-oriented working groups.[21] In recent years the United Nations has developed a few mechanisms to deal directly and sometimes immediately with particularly egregious types of human rights violations: "disappearances," arbitrary executions, and torture. UN Working Groups on these topics and individuals appointed as rapporteurs to assess specific human rights conditions have begun to issue outstanding and fearless reports that Nigel S. Rodley of Amnesty International says have effectively breached the UN "wall of resistance to action."[22] The development of the Working Group on Enforced and Involuntary Disappearances, the increasing reliance on special rapporteurs, "urgent messages," country visits, and reports "requiring immediate action" all involve innovations at the international level that Rodley describes in hopeful terms. Taken together, these mechanisms "represent an approximation of a United Nations habeas corpus; for they can act whenever there are reasonable grounds to fear violation of an individual's human rights entailing threat to life or limb."[23] Thus, while van Boven suggests, not incorrectly, that the United Nations is too often bogged down in red tape, Farer and Rodley show how the institution has occasionally risen above mere talk and taken appropriate action.

Outside the scope of Farer's essay but important to the cause of human rights is the work of the International Labor Organization (ILO). Created in 1919 as part of the League of Nations and becoming a specialized agency of the United Nations in 1946, the effectiveness of the ILO was recognized on its fiftieth anniversary when it was awarded the Nobel Peace Prize for "introducing reforms that have removed the most flagrant injustices in a great many countries." ILO activities include research and technical services as well as the for-

20. Ibid., 59, 67.
21. Hans Thoolen, "Introduction," in van Boven, *People Matter*, 5–12.
22. Nigel S. Rodley, "United Nations Action Procedures Against 'Disappearances,' Summary or Arbitrary Executions, and Torture," *Human Rights Quarterly* 8 (1986): 701.
23. Ibid., 700.

mulation of labor standards. It has gradually built up a body of more than 325 international conventions and recommendations that deal with such human rights topics as employment discrimination, migrant labor, the employment of the handicapped, child labor, social security, and equal pay for equal work. ILO standards prominently feature such basic trade union rights as freedom of association, the right to bargain collectively, and the right to strike.

To note but one example of UN norm-setting, ILO Recommendation Number 99 specifies guidelines and standards for the development of vocational rehabilitation services for the disabled.[24] It applies to all handicapped persons, whatever the origin or nature of their disability, and covers the essential features and scope of vocational rehabilitation, and the basic principles and methods of vocational guidance, training, and placement of the disabled. On the crucial question of job opportunities, the recommendation underscores the need to emphasize the aptitudes and working capacity of the disabled worker, on the theory that the handicapped deserve to be judged on their abilities rather than their disabilities.

The ILO uses its supervisory machinery to monitor governments' compliance with the ILO standards they have formally accepted. International publicity is one technique the ILO readily uses to urge governments to resolve their problems. Since 1964, the organization has documented more than fifteen hundred cases of progress by governments that have brought their laws and practices into conformity with ILO norms.[25]

REGIONAL SYSTEMS OF HUMAN RIGHTS IMPLEMENTATION

A strong argument can be made that the most promising prospects for human rights institution-building are at the regional rather than the global level. Support for this view lies in the "functional theories" developed to explain successful examples of international integration, such as the Council of Europe, organized in 1950. According to the functional integration theory, successful regional or international organizations initially perform relatively nonpolitical, technical activities that are mutually beneficial to all parties, for example, trade or defense. From this shared experience, people learn cooperative and extranational attitudes. Says one expert, Clovis C. Morrisson, Jr.:

> Gradually, an interlocking of extranational groups evolves. These groups perform more sophisticated, more widespread, more important tasks. Success in such endeavors produces "spillover" into other areas; that is, learned patterns of interaction, through success, encourage other such endeavors. National elites are slowly convinced of the importance of these groups and later on, so are the masses. . . . The integration reache[s] a high level of comprehensiveness, at which time final transfers of political and legal relationships can take place.[26]

---

24. ILO, *Basic Principles of Vocational Rehabilitation of the Disabled* (Geneva, Switzerland: International Labor Office, 1983).
25. ILO, *Freedom of Association: Digest of Decisions and Principles of the Committee on Freedom of Association of the Governing Body of the ILO* (Geneva, Switzerland: International Labor Office, 1988).
26. Clovis C. Morrisson, Jr., "The European Human Rights Convention System as a Functional Enterprise," *Universal Human Rights* 1 (Oct.–Dec. 1979), 81–92, at 82. See also, Ernst Haas, *Human Rights and International Action* (Stanford: Stanford University Press, 1970), and his "Turbulent Fields and the Theory of Regional Integration," *International Organization* 30 (Winter 1976): 173–213.

On the basis of this analysis, Morrisson concludes that "the European Human Rights Convention can be viewed . . . as a regional functional institution."

In their essay, Burns H. Weston, Robin Ann Lukes, and Kelly M. Hnatt write that the European Convention on Human Rights and Fundamental Freedoms[27] has given birth to the most effective and advanced international system for the interpretation and protection of human rights currently in existence. For example, the European Court has declared that the Austrian Government should pay damages to a criminal defendant who had been held too long before trial.[28] It has ruled that the United Kingdom violated the European Convention in forbidding the *London Sunday Times* from publishing an article on the thalidomide tragedy while civil litigation involving children whose birth defects were allegedly due to the drug was pending.[29] In addition, the European Court in Strasbourg has decided privacy cases involving abortion, telephonic eavesdropping, and homosexual activity. The court and the related Committee of Ministers of the Council of Europe have confirmed rulings of the German Constitutional Court that liberalization of abortion and the German wiretap laws did not violate the European Convention on Human Rights, but an Irish sodomy law of 1861 did violate human rights according to a ruling in 1988.[30]

Thus European human rights institutions have handed down binding supranational judicial decisions. Also, they have supplied a framework for effective multilateral diplomacy regarding human rights. For example, after a military coup in Greece in 1967, the Benelux and Nordic members of the Council of Europe produced a report condemning human rights abuses in that country. The report raised the specter of the expulsion of Greece from the Council, but, before that happened, Greece withdrew. In 1973, however, Greece was readmitted to the institutions of the European Convention and the Council of Europe after its government moved to comply with the council's conditions, including the lifting of a declared state of emergency, the release of all political detainees, the restoration of human rights, and the holding of elections under "a genuinely democratic constitution."[31] Such achievements in the resolution of human rights disputes reflect a high degree of regional integration, realistic implementation measures, and effective supranational institutional development.

Will the European example be followed elsewhere? Article 52 of the UN Charter encourages regional bodies within the UN system to make every effort to achieve pacific settlement of local disputes. Weston, Lukes, and Hnatt compare the institutionally developed but still fledgling Inter-American human rights system and the new, more weakly integrated African system with the relatively mature European system. Their essay analyzes the enforcement machinery of the three systems in terms of the scope of the rights proclaimed and the accessibility of the institutions charged with implementing them.

---

27. Nov. 4, 1950, E.T.S. No. 5.
28. Ringeisen v. Austria, 15 Eur. Ct. H.R. (ser. A) (1972) and 16 Eur. Ct. H.R. (ser. A) (1973).
29. Times Newspapers Ltd. v. United Kingdom, 30 Eur. Ct. H.R. (ser. A) (1979) and 38 Eur. Ct. H.R. (ser. A) (1981).
30. On the abortion issue, see Bruggeman and Scheuten v. Federal Republic of Germany, Application 5959175, Committee of Ministers, Resolution DH (78) 1 (adopted Mar. 17, 1978). On the wiretap issue, see Case of Klass and Others, 28 Eur. Ct. H.R. (ser. A) (1978). The right to respect for private life was the basis for a ruling favorable to David Norris, an Irish homosexual rights advocate; he contested nineteenth-century laws setting a maximum penalty of life imprisonment for homosexual acts, even if carried out in private between consenting adults. Norris v. Ireland. 38 Eur. Ct. H. R. (1988).
31. The Greek Case, European Commission of Human Rights, *Report of the Commission* adopted Nov. 5, 1969, Council of Europe, Doc. 15, 707/1 (1969), vol. 1, pt. 1 at 5–11; also Consultative Assembly of the Council of Europe, Res. 558, Jan. 22, 1974.

THE HELSINKI PROCESS

The final essay in this chapter, by A. H. Robertson, makes clear that the Final Act of the Conference on Security and Co-Operation in Europe (also known as the "Helsinki Agreement" or "Helsinki Accords")[32] is an unusual document that is not comparable to other regional instruments for the promotion and protection of human rights. Signed by the NATO countries and all the countries of Eastern Europe (except Albania) in Helsinki, Finland, on August 1, 1975, the Final Act was not intended to be a legally binding agreement. In addition, it does not add to the roster of legally binding human rights obligations. However, as Louis Henkin has argued, it "clearly precludes any suggestion that matters it deals with are within domestic jurisdiction and beyond the reach of appropriate inquiry and recourse."[33] Henkin concludes: "Gentlemen's agreements," such as the Helsinki Final Act, "and other non-binding political and moral undertakings are established instruments in international relations, and their violation brings important political and moral consequences."[34]

The political undertaking of the Helsinki Process involved recognition of the terms under which World War II was concluded, such as the postwar boundaries of Poland and Germany. The moral undertaking was the acknowledgment that fundamental standards of human rights are prominent in the foundation for durable peace. "In the field of human rights and fundamental freedoms," the Final Act (Principle I(a)(vii)) proclaims:

> The participating States will act in conformity with the purposes and principles of the Charter of the United Nations and with the Universal Declaration of Human Rights. They will also fulfill their obligations as set forth in the international declarations and agreements in this field, including inter alia the International Covenants on Human Rights by which they may be bound.

The Final Act legitimizes the principle that human rights protection is an essential ingredient of security and cooperation. Recognition of this principle is embodied in an agreement to continue the multilateral process initiated by the conference with follow-up meetings featuring the "thorough exchange of views" regarding the tasks defined by the Final Act (Principle I(b)(ii). On the other hand, the Final Act has no enforcement mechanisms. It provides only for periodic reviews of progress by representatives of the state signatories; thus it is long on promise and short on implementation. However, as Virginia Leary observes, this "vacuum" in implementation has been "filled by government spokesmen, intergovernmental organizations, parliamentary commissions, informal monitoring groups, and religious organizations, which have undertaken to investigate the implementation of the Final Act."[35]

Because Helsinki kindled new hopes and provoked human rights interest throughout the thirty-five countries involved—even *Pravda* and *Izvestia* published the text of the Final Act—it fostered monitoring groups to develop information on compliance with human rights standards. On May 12, 1977, the Russian physicist Yuri Orlov announced the formation of the Public Group to Promote Observation of the Helsinki Accords in the Soviet Union, commonly called the "Helsinki Watch Group." The Moscow group planned, among other things, to "accept directly from Soviet citizens written complaints of human rights violations"

32. Aug. 1, 1975, Dep't State Pub. No. 8826 (Gen'l For. Pol. ser. 298).
33. Louis Henkin, "Human Rights and 'Domestic Jurisdiction,'" in *Human Rights, International Law and the Helsinki Accord*, ed. Thomas Buergenthal (Montclair, N.Y.: Allanheld, Osmun/Universe Books, 1977), 21–40, at 29.
34. Ibid.
35. Virginia Leary, "The Implementation of the Human Rights Provisions of the Helsinki Final Act: A Preliminary Assessment, 1975–1977," in Buergenthal, *Human Rights, International Law*, 111–60, at 113.

and pledged to forward such complaints "to all Heads of States signatory to the Final Act and [to] inform the public at large of the substance of the complaints." Thereafter, such groups sprang up in the Soviet areas of the Ukraine, Lithuania, Armenia, and Georgia. Several other groups adopted the Helsinki principles in monitoring human rights violations, for instance, the Working Commission on Psychiatric Abuse and various religious committees for the defense of believers in the Soviet Union. In all cases, authorities responded by acts of persecution ranging from threats of violence and loss of employment to imprisonment, forced emigration, and incarceration in psychiatric hospitals.[36]

In the follow-up meetings in Belgrade and Madrid, the Soviet Union and other East European signatories to the Final Act generally took the view that discussion of specific cases and charges of human rights abuses constitutes interference in the domestic affairs of sovereign states. However, at the third review Conference on Security and Co-operation in Europe (CSCE) which opened in Vienna in 1986, the Soviet Union and its Warsaw Pact allies, after coming under concentrated and concerted attack for their human rights abuses, largely abandoned this tactic. They turned, instead, to a more activist strategy involving talk of a shift in their human rights policies consistent with the newly proclaimed "glasnost" or posture of "openness," and a counterattack against alleged instances of human rights violations in the West. On January 16, 1989, at the close of the Vienna Conference, thirty-five countries, including Canada, the United States, the Soviet Union, and all other European states exclusive of Albania, approved a new agreement for the further protection of human rights, including freedom of association, religion, travel, emigration, and special protection of individuals and organizations who monitor human rights conditions in the countries where they reside. The new CSCE agreement also called for better conditions for East-West business ventures, improved barter deals, and freer exchanges of enhanced economic statistics. Perhaps most importantly, however, for the first time since the Helsinki process began with the adoption of the Helsinki Accords in 1975, a formal CSCE mechanism was approved pursuant to which a signatory state must reply if another signatory state requests information about suspected abuses of human rights. Participating governments also were empowered to demand bilateral meetings to discuss such abuses and to notify the other CSCE states about such cases. All of which signaled a remarkable turn of events. As stated by British chief delegate Lawrence O'Keeffe, "[i]n essence, this [mechanism] is an embryo of a human rights court for all Europe. It's a new and different means of keeping up pressure."[37]

The process of constructing international human rights enforcement machinery is arduous and often frustrating for lack of swift results. Yet, there has been no lack of imaginative proposals for future institution-building, for example, the proposal to set up a UN Commissioner for Human Rights to deal with the most severe kinds of violations, those widely considered to be unacceptable and not subject to derogation.[38] Proponents of this idea argue that if the commissioner's role were limited to such glaring violations as executions without trial, it might be possible to obtain wide support for the office's establishment. Serious objections to the proposal boil down to the view that present-day international society simply has not matured enough to accept supranational enforcement institutions.

36. See David Kowalewski, "Human Rights Protest in the U.S.S.R.: Statistical Trends for 1965–1978," *Universal Human Rights* 2 (1980): 5–30. On Soviet crackdowns, see also Leary, "The Implementation of the Human Rights Provisions," 121–7; and Sidney Bloch and Peter Reddaway, *Psychiatric Terror: How Soviet Psychiatry Is Used to Suppress Dissent* (New York: Basic Books, 1977). See especially, *Basket III: Implementation of the Helsinki Accords*, vols. 2 and 3, Hearings before the Commission on Security and Cooperation in Europe (Washington, D.C.: U.S. Government Printing Office, 1977).
37. *Washington Post*, Jan. 16, 1989, p. A1, col. 6.
38. See Roger S. Clark, *A United Nations High Commissioner for Human Rights* (The Hague: Martinus Nijhoff Publishers, 1972).

Whether or not the objection to the proposal for UN Commissioner for Human Rights on grounds of practicality is persuasive, it calls attention to the need for realism in devising international human rights institutions that will be valid and effective.[39] The institutions must have sufficient regional or global support to gain acceptance by states and peoples and so the norms and mechanisms they create to implement human rights are perceived as correct and appropriate. To be effective, international institutions must be able to implement their objectives indirectly through education, dialogue, and supervision, and/or directly through diplomatic action and other measures—rarely through supranational directives. Of course, if we accept these standards of validity and effectiveness in assessing international implementation, we are met with the substantial challenge of directing responsible attention and constructive thought toward developing international human rights institutions in which people can believe and from which people can expect results.

15. TOM J. FARER *The United Nations and Human Rights: More Than a Whimper*

HUMAN RIGHTS IN THE PRE-CHARTER ERA

Until the Second World War, most legal scholars and governments affirmed the general proposition, albeit not in so many words, that international law did not impede the natural right of each equal sovereign to be monstrous to his or her subjects. Summary execution, torture, arbitrary arrest, and detention: These were legally significant events beyond national frontiers only if the victims of such official eccentricities were citizens of another state. In that case, international law treated them as the bearers not of personal rights but of rights belonging to their government and ultimately to the state for which it spoke. In effect, for the purposes of interstate relations, the individual was nothing more than a symbol and a capital asset. Assaults on his person carried out or acquiesced in by representatives of another state were deemed assaults on the dignity and material interests of his state, requiring compensation. . . .

In the ensuing decades, both through formal agreements and declarations evidencing the consensus necessary for customary law, states have bound themselves not to torture or summarily execute or enslave their citizens, or to convict them without due process of law or to dissolve their trade unions or to discriminate among them on the basis of race or religion or to do other things which today, as in the past, are the authors of despair. Many nations, going beyond declarations of self-restraint, have rallied with varying degrees of commitment behind the claim that the state had an affirmative obligation to protect its citizens from economic, social, and cultural impoverishment.

BUILDING A NORMATIVE FRAMEWORK

THE CHARTER

At its inception, the United Nations seemed destined to be the engine of human rights. Its

39. See J. S. Watson, "Legal Theory, Efficacy and Validity in the Development of Human Rights Norms in International Law," *University of Illinois Law Forum* 33 (1979): 609–41. Cf. Anthony D'Amato, "The Concept of Human Rights," *Columbia Law Review* 82 (1982): 1110–59.

Charter[1] announces the organization's purposes to include "promoting and encouraging respect for human rights and . . . fundamental freedoms for all without distinction as to race, sex, language, or religion." It mandates the General Assembly to "initiate studies and make recommendations for the purpose of . . . assisting in the realization of human rights." It authorizes the election of an Economic and Social Council which is in turn required to "set up commissions . . . for the promotion of human rights." And it embodies the pledge of all UN members "to take joint and separate action in cooperation with the Organization for the achievement of . . . universal respect for, and observance of, human rights."

To be sure, these provisions did not spring from a fierce, collective will to shatter the wall of national sovereignty wherever it sheltered some variety of oppression. John P. Humphrey, first Director of the Division of Human Rights at the United Nations, reports that, were it not for the efforts of a few deeply committed delegates and the representatives of some forty-two private organizations brought in as consultants by the United States, human rights would have received "only a passing reference."[2] While in the end they obviously did much better than that, their subordination in the organization's hierarchy of purposes is evident, above all in the Charter's authorization of UN enforcement action only in cases where it is required to prevent or terminate armed conflict between states. . . .

Events surrounding the adoption of the Charter and the resulting organization's early life contribute to one's impression of widespread ambivalence, if not to human rights per se, then certainly to the prospect of their enforcement through the medium of the United Nations. The Soviet Bloc quickly established the position to which it would thereafter cling, namely that UN activity should be confined to promulgating rights; enforcement, on the other hand, was a matter of purely domestic concern. But it was hardly alone in wishing to keep the United Nations out of the enforcement business. The once and (they apparently hoped) future colonial powers were hardly more enthusiastic at the prospect of UN "meddling" in their respective preserves.

It is, therefore, not surprising that both a joint initiative by Panama and Chile to include in the Charter articles guaranteeing specific human rights and a Panamanian proposal for a separate bill of rights were rejected as too controversial. Nor is it grounds for astonishment that at its very first session the Commission on Human Rights determined that "it had no power to take any action in regard to any complaints concerning human rights." Its immediate superior in the UN hierarchy, the Economic and Social Council, not only confirmed the Commission's noble act of self-denial but salted the self-inflicted wound by deciding that Commission members should not even review the original text of specific complaints by individuals lest, one supposes, the horrors recounted therein inspire second thoughts about the virtues of self-restraint.

THE INTERNATIONAL BILL OF RIGHTS

While some auguries for the future of the normative fledgling were ominous, others trembled with the promise of achievement. Aside from their considerable prominence in the Charter itself, human rights got an early boost from President Harry S. Truman when he addressed the closing session of the founding conference. "We have good reason," he told the delegates, "to expect the framing of an international bill of rights . . . that . . . will be as much a part of international life as our own Bill of Rights is a part of our Constitution," which, he might have added, also began life without one. As if inspired by the American president's vision, the Economic and Social Council (ECOSOC), having in early 1946 carried out its mandate to establish a Commission on Human Rights, made its first priority the drafting of an international bill of rights.

Led by Eleanor Roosevelt in her role as chairperson, the Commission went to work at a speed remarkable in comparison to the gait it would assume in later years when controversial issues of human rights begged for resolution. That the drafting task was destined for controversy quickly became apparent. As one could have predicted from the jousting over the Charter, the central point of conflict was whether or to what extent international concern for human rights should be

---

1. [See the Appendix.]
2. John P. Humphrey, "The U.N. Charter and the Universal Declaration of Human Rights," in *The International Protection of Human Rights*, ed. Evan Luard (New York: Frederick A. Praeger 1967), 39.

allowed to breach the wall of national sovereignty. No state seemed more determined to keep the wall intact than the organization's most powerful enthusiast for transnational liberation movements, the Union of Soviet Socialist Republics. When the first drafting stage culminated in the presentation to the General Assembly of the Universal Declaration on Human Rights,[3] the Soviet delegate declared it defective primarily because "a number of articles completely ignore the sovereign rights of democratic governments. . . . [T]he question of national sovereignty," he maintained, "is a matter of the greatest importance."[4] . . .

Delegates also tended to polarize over the relative emphasis between individual rights and community interests. If the proposed bill "did not stipulate the existence of the individual and his need for protection in his struggle against the State," declared the distinguished philosopher, Charles Malik, representing Lebanon, "the Commission would never achieve its intended purpose."[5] The Yugoslavian representative insisted that, on the contrary, the "new conditions of modern times [make the] common interest . . . more important than the individual interest."

In late 1947, facing the danger of impasse over political and ideological differences, the Commission agreed to divide the bill of rights into three parts: a declaration of principles that the General Assembly could adopt; a covenant rhetorically tied to the Declaration under which ratifying states would become subject to explicit legal obligations; and a separate agreement detailing enforcement machinery. . . .

Rejecting a Soviet proposal to postpone consideration until the following year, on 10 December 1948, the Assembly adopted the Universal Declaration by a vote of forty-eight to zero, with eight abstentions: South Africa, the Soviet Union, the Ukraine, Byelorussia, Czechoslovakia, Poland, Yugoslavia, and Saudi Arabia. When the vote was announced, Eleanor Roosevelt expressed the hope that the Declaration would be "the Magna Carta of all mankind."

Since, under the Charter, most General Assembly action has a nonbinding character, initially most scholars took the view that the Dec-

laration expressed moral values rather than legally binding norms. However, in part because it had passed without a negative vote, in larger part because many of its provisions subsequently found their way into formal international agreements or were incorporated in national constitutions, it has acquired a legal aura, the appearance of stating, if not having by its existence created, binding norms of state behavior.

The Declaration . . . was only the first step of the International Bill of Rights—a quickstep compared with the eighteen-year trudge which followed. Only through a further decoupling of the originally envisioned elements of the bill were the disputants finally able to resolve their often rancorous differences. The old polarities—human rights versus national sovereignty, individual liberty versus communal needs—continued to discourage consensus. The first seeded dispute primarily over two questions. One was whether economic, social, and cultural interests should be accorded the status of rights on a par with the traditional liberal values of free speech, religion, press, association, and so on. Despite Franklin Delano Roosevelt's inclusion in 1941 of "freedom from want" among the "four freedoms" for whose attainment the United States would face the risk of war, the Western allies as a group were inclined to answer "no." The Eastern Bloc, increasingly supplemented by newly independent states from the Third World, said "yes." The question of whether the covenant should follow the Declaration by recognizing explicitly a right to property structured a similar grouping of antagonists.

The drafters finally broke free from their impasse by agreeing as follows: First, there would be two covenants, one dealing with political and civil rights, the other with economic, social, and cultural rights. Second, insofar as implementing machinery was concerned, states could ratify either or both conventions and thereby assume no more onerous obligation than a periodic report.

In the case of the Covenant on Civil and Political Rights,[6] reports would cover "the measures [the states parties] have adopted which give effect to the rights recognized [therein] and . . . the

---

3. [See the Appendix.]
4. U.N. General Assembly, Official records, Part I. Plenary Meetings, Dec. 10, 1948, 923–4.
5. U.N. *Weekly Bulletin* 25 Feb. 1947, 170–71.
6. [See the Appendix.]

progress made in the enjoyment of those rights." These reports would be transmitted through the Secretary-General to an eighteen-person committee of experts elected under the Covenant and authorized to study and thereafter transmit the reports to the states parties and ECOSOC together with "such general comments as it may deem appropriate." (Article 40). Reports under the Covenant on Economic, Social and Cultural Rights[7] would enumerate "the measures . . . adopted and the progress made in achieving the observance of the rights recognized [therein]." (Article 16). They would be submitted to ECOSOC "for consideration in accordance with the provisions of the . . . Covenant"; and it in turn could transmit them to the Human Rights Commission "for study and general recommendations." (Article 19). Parties ratifying the Civil Covenant have the option under Article 41 of recognizing the jurisdiction of the Covenant's Human Rights Committee to hear complaints from other states that have also accepted this procedure. The Committee may hold hearings and promote friendly settlement. What it apparently cannot do is form an independent judgment about the merits of the complaint.

That power is reserved for cases, if any, arising under the so-called Optional Protocol to the Civil and Political Covenant.[8] States adhering to it recognize the Committee's authority to hear petitions from individual citizens alleging violations of their rights under the Covenant. After considering the petition "in the light of all written evidence made available to it by the individual and by the State Party concerned . . . [t]he Commitee shall forward its views to [them]." (Article 5). And then? The Protocol says only that "the Committee shall include in its annual report . . . a summary of its activities under the . . . Protocol." (Article 6). . . .

These flabby and for the most part optional instruments of compliance gentled the opposition of those numerous governments hostile to external assessment of their domestic behavior. The statement of substantive norms also eases anxiety, since it gives to states a considerable margin of discretion. . . .

Some flexibility in the interpretation and enforcement of most rights is, of course, essential, if for no reason other than to assure their availability to all groups in society and to maintain

that degree of public order without which no right is secure. Everyone cannot exercise the right of assembly in the same place at the same time. If the government cannot referee, private power will be imperious and freedom correspondingly reduced. While governments must, therefore, have a margin of discretion, where its exercise is essentially unmonitored, a limited discretion readily deteriorates into license. . . .

THE HUMAN RIGHTS MACHINERY: FORM

While enthusiasts for the International Bill of Rights were suffering through its prolonged gestation, the member states of the United Nations, rather than invoking that process as an excuse for avoiding initiatives certain to attract the conflicts of interest and ideology delaying the bill's delivery, moved forward (gingerly, to be sure) under the authority of the Charter and the banner of the Declaration. Its relevant activities over the years fall into three distinct categories: Defining and clarifying the rights of individuals (standard-setting); studying particular human rights or human rights in particular places and recommending measures for their fuller realization (subdivided by some writers into "promotional" and "protective" functions); providing assistance directly to victims of human rights delinquencies (the humanitarian function).

Humanitarian Assistance

[Direct aid] has had without doubt the most tangible and far ranging impact on human rights in our time; yet it is the least controversial. Indeed, it often skips the minds of people when they talk about the human rights activities of the United Nations (or disparage the absence thereof). The two most indisputably effective and important instruments of direct assistance are the International Childrens Emergency Fund (UNICEF) and the High Commissioner for Refugees (UNHCR).

Observers of the UNICEF and High Commissioner operations are uniformly impressed by their leanness and by the energy and commitment of those who administer them. Their

7. [See the Appendix.]
8. [See the Appendix.]

achievements alone would support the claim that, with all its institutional constraints, the United Nations has managed to play an important role in the defense of human rights.

A lush variety of organs work to carry out the United Nations' other tasks in the field of human rights. A recently published diagram of the relevant bodies [see Figure 1] unfocuses the eye with its complex mix of boxes, circles, and lines representing and connecting councils, commissions, sub-commissions, committees, special committees, working groups, divisions, centers, offices, and special rapporteurs. . . .

The General Assembly reigns, of course, at the apex of the institutional pyramid, with plenary authority to create subsidiaries for any purpose enumerated or implied in the Charter (used, for example, to establish the Office of the High Commissioner for Refugees in 1951 and the successive committees on apartheid beginning with the Special Committee of 1962), and [is] free to act either through those subsidiaries or directly on any human rights issue that engages the concern of its members. Within the institutional framework created by the Charter, the Economic and Social Council (ECOSOC) serves, subject to the ultimate authority of the General Assembly, as the principal organ of the United Nations concerned with human rights.

Articles 62 through 66 of the Charter authorize the Council to "make recommendations for the purpose of promoting respect for, and observance of, human rights and fundamental freedoms for all," to "prepare draft conventions for submission to the General Assembly," to call international conferences, to coordinate the activities of the specialized agencies, to obtain reports both from them and from member states on the steps taken to give effect to its own recommendations and to recommendations on matters falling within its competence made by the General Assembly and to perform "such other functions as may be assigned to it by the General Assembly." The Council is a quintessentially political body, its fifty-four members, elected by the General Assembly on the basis of so-called "equitable geographical distribution," being formal representatives of UN member states.

Equally political in its forms as in its functions is the Commission on Human Rights established by ECOSOC in 1946 to serve as the organization's principal locus for human rights activity, whatever it might be. Politicization of the Commission seems to have been a second thought, albeit one which came ever so quickly after the first. At its first session in 1946, ECOSOC appointed in their individual capacity nine members to serve as the nucleus of a larger body. The Nuclear Commission, as it was called, quickly issued a report recommending that "all members of the Commission on Human Rights should serve as nongovernmental representatives." Meeting later in 1946, the Council rejected this proposal, deciding instead that the Commission should consist of one representative from each of eighteen members of the United Nations selected by the Council. . . .

In the performance of its several functions, to be discussed below, the Commission has frequently employed working groups and special rapporteurs. As of January 1987, eight of the former were conducting studies on topics as diverse as human rights in South Africa, enforced or involuntary disappearances, the right to development, and rights of the child. Meanwhile a clutch of special rapporteurs were working to enlighten the Commission on such issues as torture, summary or arbitrary executions, and human rights in El Salvador, Iran, Chile, and Afghanistan (oxymorons all).

An additional flock of working groups and rapporteurs indirectly services the Commission through its principal subsidiary, the Sub-Commission on the Prevention of Discrimination and the Protection of Minorities. Although in theory the twenty-six members of the Sub-Commission are elected as independent experts, in part because they must be nominated by states (in practice almost invariably their own state), many are no less instruments of their respective governments than their counterparts on the parent body. But at least until very recently, enough members have actually satisfied the formal requisites of independence and expertise to make this child considerably more adventurous and scrupulous than its parent. It presently employs working groups on communications concerning consistent patterns of gross violation of human rights, on slavery, and on indigenous populations, and special rapporteurs on topics including states of siege, the death penalty, and the right to leave and return to one's own country. . . .

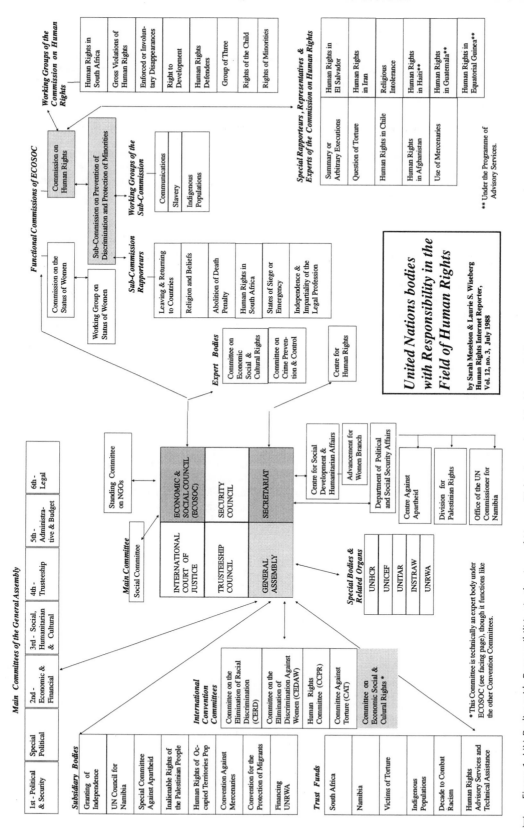

Figure 1 UN Bodies with Responsibilities in the Area of Human Rights (reproduced in *Human Rights Internet Reporter* 11 [Dec. 1985]: 21–22; reprinted with permission)

Article 28 of the Covenant on Civil and Political Rights provides for the establishment of an eighteen-member committee composed of nationals of states parties to the Covenant elected by the parties from a list of nominees presented by them to the Secretary-General. It follows from my earlier discussion of the covenant system that, with respect to those countries that have only ratified the Covenant, the Committee's role is to consider the reports which the parties are required to submit concerning the measures they have taken to give effects to the rights enumerated in the Covenant. The same Committee hears interstate and individual complaints against states that have expressed acceptance of Committee jurisdiction in such cases under Article 41 of the Covenant and the Protocol respectively.

The Committee has been functioning since 1977. Although the Covenant gives it a legal basis independent of the Charter, because the Covenant makes the Secretary-General an integral part both of election and reporting procedures and because the Committee is dependent on the United Nations for logistical support, it is regarded as a body functioning within the general framework of the UN system.

THE HUMAN RIGHTS MACHINERY: PRAXIS

It is a commonplace of scholarship to find three phases in UN human rights activities during which the organization's main focus was, in turn, standard-setting (conventions and declarations), promotion (advisory services, broad studies, and an incipient reporting system), and protection (establishment of procedures for assessing information received from private persons and groups concerning possible gross violations and reporting thereon to the general membership, fact-finding in certain cases where member states allege grave violations, and efforts to mitigate or terminate violations in particular cases). "Since 1977," according to two scholars who seem to endorse this temporal ordering of UN activity, "a fourth stage has . . . emerged, which emphasizes the structural and economic aspects of human rights issues."[9]

Like all scholarly efforts to order the confused

scrum of life, these phases correspond only roughly to actual events within the UN system. For instance, the fact that the so-called fourth stage (also referred to commonly as the recognition of "third generation rights") manifests itself to a large extent in proposed declarations and similar efforts at norm generation, nicely illustrates the overlapping, indeed cumulative character of these phases. The phases themselves illustrate something else. They certainly are not the expression of some ineluctable logic of sequence.

Of course one had to begin with standards of some sort. But implicit in the Nuremberg indictments was the proposition that at least with respect to the right to life and freedom from torture, there already were standards. And as for other rights essential to even the slimmest conception of human dignity, surely they were stated with sufficient clarity in the Universal Declaration to allow their immediate use for assessing the behavior of member states.

Nor is it possible to argue that years of technical assistance and general studies were a necessary condition of effective or evenhanded efforts to protect human rights. Violations of those like the right to life whose centrality is universally conceded—as evidenced, for example, by provisions in the principal covenants and conventions making them nonderogable—are readily identifiable in any and every context. Governments have not been in doubt about the content of their obligations. Protective activity, such as it has been, came last and late because a large proportion of member-state governments, while unwilling to insist on a plenary discretion in the choice of means for their various ends, were hardly less reluctant to subject themselves to whatever constraints arise from the risk of exposure.

Viewed only as an institution engaged in standard-setting, the United Nations presents a handsome profile. Usually by very large majorities approaching unanimity, the General Assembly has approved declarations and conventions broadly elaborating the core rights of human dignity. Its subordinate body, ECOSOC, has, for instance, gone beyond condemning slavery to identifying and prohibiting slavery-like practices such as debt bondage which are not unknown in the contem-

9. Egon Schwelb and Philip Alston, "The Principal Institutions and Other Bodies Founded Under the Charter," in *The International Dimensions of Human Rights*, ed. Karel Vasak (Westport, Conn.: Greenwood Press for UNESCO, 1982), 2:231, 250–1.

porary world. And in spelling out the rights of women, the General Assembly itself has cut right across the grain of custom in more than a few member states. However, when one views, as I now will, its efforts to protect the actual exercise of enumerated rights, something less engaging meets the eye.

THE PROBLEMATICS OF PROTECTION

By examining the actions and omissions of the Commission and the Sub-Commission and their interactions with ECOSOC and the General Assembly over the course of four decades, one can acquire a fair picture of the organization's present capacity for protective activity. Scrutiny of the Committee of Experts under the Covenant reinforces the impression thus gained. Attributing any capacity at all to the United Nations requires a certain leap of faith in the efficacy of exposure by a credible fact finder. For other than the unusual case where human rights violations produce a threat to or breach of the peace, thus providing the jurisdictional conditions for mandatory sanctions under Chapter 7 of the Charter, exposure is the principal weapon in the UN armory.

[Editors' note: The author next recounts the experience of the Inter-American Commission in Human Rights in respect of the "weapon" of exposure, concluding that its record is better than UN organs in this regard.]

The organs of the United Nations concerned with human rights, above all the Commission together with its institutional superiors, particularly ECOSOC, have evinced neither a comparable enthusiasm for the protective mission nor a comparable capacity for impartial judgment. As early as January 1947, when the members of the Commission on Human Rights gathered for their first regular session, the United Nations had already received a large number of letters containing allegations of human rights violations. In effect, the Commission was being petitioned for assistance in obtaining the redress of grievances against member states.

As I pointed out earlier, it responded to this initial opportunity to define some protective role by concluding that it had none. In the words of the report of that first session summarizing the Commission's reaction to individual communications: "The Commission recognizes that it has no power to take any action in regard to any complaints concerning human rights."[10] In what seemed an effort to avoid even inadvertent pressure on governments accused of human rights violations, it also decided that communications containing such allegations would not be circulated to the individual members even on a confidential basis. Rather they would receive, but only in private meetings, a confidential list containing only a brief, presumably sanitized indication of the substance of these dangerous, if not positively offensive, epistles. . . .

For more than twenty years thereafter, the Commission remained an instrument of nonprotection lounging under the protective wing of the Council. As proof of its existence, it summoned the energy to draft soaring standards and issue occasional reports of a comfortably general character. Yet, despite its fierce commitment to inoffensiveness, the Commission could not always manage to match the Council's reticence. In 1950, it requested establishment of a system of annual human rights reports by member states. The Council responded by returning the proposal for further study. And there it might have remained had not the United States taken up the matter in 1953 apparently as a counterweight to its concurrent declaration that it would not become a party to any human rights treaty. United States support produced a prodding resolution addressed by the General Assembly to the Council. The latter body, moving with all its deliberate speed, managed in only three years to adopt an operative resolution. Since the very making of a report, much less its content, was effectively left to the discretion of states, the reporting process was not calculated to roil any of the world's chancelleries. And with one exception it did not. . . .

The beginning of the end of the doctrine of impotence was signalled in 1965 when the Committee of Twenty-Four summoned ECOSOC's attention to information concerning violation of human rights in southern Africa submitted by petitioners to the Committee. As if awakened thereby from a long dream of sleep, ECOSOC responded immediately by inviting the Commission to consider as a matter of importance and urgency the question of the violation of human rights, including policies of racial discrimination

10. E/259 (1947) paras. 21, 22.

and segregation and of apartheid in all countries, with particular reference to colonial and other dependent countries and territories, and to submit its recommendations on measures to halt those violations.

In their valuable survey of human rights institutions under the Charter, Schwelb and Alston summarize the successive actions of the General Assembly, ECOSOC, the Commission, and the Sub-Commission which during the period 1966 to 1971, fashioned the machinery for human rights protection which has operated without fundamental change since then.[11] The principal components of its normative framework are Commission Resolution 8 (XXIII) of 1967 and ECOSOC Resolutions 1235 of 1967 and 1503 of 1970. In Resolution 8 the Commission added an agenda item on the "Question of Violations" and in a marked expansion of Sub-Commission jurisdiction beyond the problems of minorities, directed it to bring to the attention of the Commission any situation which it has reasonable cause to believe reveals "a consistent pattern of violations . . . [and] to prepare . . . a report containing information on violations of human rights and fundamental freedoms from all available sources." Under its resolution the Commission could chose to initiate "a thorough study" of the described situations which it said were exemplified by apartheid in South Africa and racial discrimination in Southern Rhodesia.

In Resolution 1235, adopted on 6 June 1967, ECOSOC welcomed the Commission's decision and declared the Commission's and the Sub-Commission's right "to examine information relevant to gross violations of fundamental rights and fundamental freedoms" contained in the individual communications [which], under the Council's successive edicts, had been screened from Commission review since 1947.

These steps left in their wake uncertainty about the way in which communications would be handled and employed and about the willingness of the Sub-Commission, Commission, and Council actually to study, much less publicize, human rights violations ocurring outside southern Africa. Sensitivity on the latter point surfaced during the debate preceding adoption of Resolution 1235, expressed in the form of objections (from representatives of the United Kingdom, the Philippines, and Tanzania) to the idea

even of studies being made without the target state's consent and in the successful amendment pressed by the Soviet Union and Afro-Asian states making racial discrimination the primary point of concern. Continued sensitivity about publicizing the contents of private communications became apparent when some governments objected to use by Sub-Commission experts of such communications as evidence in reports under 1235 describing human rights violations by named states.

While efforts by the Eastern bloc and most Afro-Asian states to impose a narrow focus as a matter of principle continued to be defeated by narrow margins, in practice the Commission advanced beyond the southern African heartland, and the territories occupied by Israel during the 1967 Middle East War, with studied caution. Moreover, the procedures finaly adopted for handling private communications eased the concerns animating advocates of the narrow focus. Authorized by ECOSOC resolution 1503 (XLVIII) of 1970 ("Procedure for dealing with communications relating to violations of human rights and fundamental freedoms") and elaborated by the Sub-Commission in 1971, they operate in the following manner.

Personnel of the Human Rights Centre (formerly the Human Rights Division) prepare summaries of the thousands of communications received annually alleging violations of human rights and forward them to a five-member Working Group of the Sub-Commission. The Working Group convenes for two weeks each summer, just prior to the annual four-week meeting of the Sub-Commission, and decides whether communications concerning a particular government, considered in light of that government's response, if any, "appear to reveal a consistent pattern of gross and reliably attested violations of human rights and fundamental freedoms." All communications satisfying that criterion, in the opinion of a majority of the Working Group (which must have the usual geographic balance), are placed on the Sub-Commission's agenda. The Working Group's meetings are closed and its decisions confidential.

Since neither the secretariat nor the Working Group inform correspondents that their letters or petitions are being considered, the latter, if they are to supplement their original communication

---

11. See Schwelb and Alston, "The Principal Institutions," 272–3.

at all, must do so blindly, that is without any knowledge either of the Working Group's initial reaction or of the contents of a government's response. The Working Group could, but apparently does not, alleviate this difficulty—indeed, one could argue, this fundamental unfairness in its procedures—by exercising its discretion to seek additional information. Exclusion of correspondents and petitioners continues through all stages of the 1503 procedure.

Nothing in the resolution establishing it or in Sub-Commission practice suggests that the Working Group has discretion not to forward communications which meet the criterion. The Sub-Commission, however, has acted as if it bears no comparable obligation to the Commission. For reasons known only to it, since its review of 1503 communications also is confidential, it has postponed forwarding cases despite access to evidence of gross violations that would have satisfied fact finders afflicted with even the slightest degree of impartiality. Resolution 1503 explicitly authorizes the Sub-Commission to take into account not only the communications brought before it by the Working Group and the replies of governments but also "other available information." Perhaps taking a cue from its parent, the Working Group is reliably reported to have behaved in at least one case as if it too had a plenary discretion to decide what situations should move on through the process.

Cases forwarded by the Sub-Commission must then pass successfully through the Commission's own five-member Working Group before arriving at last on the Commission's agenda. The Commission is empowered under 1503 to respond in a variety of ways. It may, in effect, dismiss the case (technically it terminates consideration) either by finding that gross violations have not been committed or, apparently, for any other reason it deems satisfactory. Or it may keep the case on its agenda for further consideration at a later session (a minimum delay of one year). Or it may decide to initiate a "thorough study" of the situation, with or without the consent of the concerned government. Or, with the consent of the relevant government, it may investigate the situation through the medium of an ad hoc committee of "independent persons whose competence and impartiality is beyond question."

As an alternative, however, it could break out of the constraints of 1503. Drawing on its authority under Resolution 1235, it can appoint an ad hoc working group or a special rapporteur to study the situation, prepare a report and draft recommendations which the Commission can debate publicly, adopt, and forward to ECOSOC. Strenuous efforts by governments facing indictments to bar public debate, much less action, concerning situations being considered under 1503 have, unfortunately, succeeded in some cases.

"Action" Under 1235 and 1503

At the time of its adoption, Resolution 1503 was widely seen by scholars and activists as a step beyond 1235 in the development of protective machinery. This perception probably stemmed from the fact that, while initiatives under 1235 lie entirely in the hands of member states and hence are inevitably governed by political criteria, 1503 gave the power of initiative for the first time to individuals and NGOs [nongovernmental organizations]. Under it, they could trigger action, even if only the action of confronting unpleasant facts of international life. To many, this seemed an enormously valuable precedent, a breach in the citadel of the mutual-protection society, one that could be progressively enlarged. Perhaps in the long run it will turn out that the optimists were right. But to this point, 1235 has shown greater promise. What can nevertheless be said for Resolution 1503 proceedings is that at least they have ceased to be a bottomless receptacle for petitions of the desperate. . . .

Although, as I have already suggested, the Sub-Commission can hardly be accused of carrying out its tasks with reckless zeal, since 1973 it has forwarded for Commission consideration a substantial number of cases. And they have included regimes aligned with both the United States and the Soviet Union as well as some relatively unaligned in global politics. Howard Tolley, a leading authority on the Commission and Sub-Commission, estimates a referral rate of six to eight cases a year. From 1978, when the Commission began naming countries that had been the subject of "decisions" (without indicating the nature of the decision), to 1984, twenty-eight countries have been so identified. But in no case to date has the Commission exercised its power to undertake a thorough study or to seek the consent of a delinquent state for the creation of an investigating committee. The closest it has come is in the case of Equitorial Guinea, another of the great abattoirs of our time. Despite a record of atrocities dating back to the dictator Macias' accession to power in 1968, the case bobbed about in the great sea of 1503 until 1979. Then, in the face of Macias' rejection even of secret contacts with a personal representative of the Secretary-General, the Commission authorized disclosure of the 1503 materials. When, shortly thereafter, Macias was overthrown, the Commission invoked not 1503 but 1235 to justify appointing a special rapporteur who thereafter compiled what amounted to a mere historic account of the regime's crimes.

While the Commission has done little to vitalize the 1503 procedure, it has not entirely abjured a protective function. But, as already suggested, it has acted, either expressly or implicitly, pursuant to the grant of authority under 1235 and/or ad hoc request for action from the General Assembly or ECOSOC. The brutal overthrow of the democratically-elected government of Salvador Allende in Chile stimulated the first serious rights-protecting initiative of the Commission— and, indeed, of the UN system as a whole—unrelated to conditions in colonial territories, Israeli-occupied territories, and South Africa. Thomas Franck, in his useful and provocative study of the United Nations, *Nation Against Nation*, describes the system's variegated response:

On March 1, 1974, the Commission . . . [authorized] its chairman to address a cable to the Chilean military authorities expressing the members' concern for the protection of the lives of political prisoners and calling for strict observance of the principles of the United Nations Charter and the International Covenants on Human Rights. ECOSOC, by consensus, quickly seconded that demand. Next, the Sub-Commission . . . called for a "study" of Chilean human rights violations, and the General Assembly— charging the Chilean junta with "gross and massive violations," including "the practice of torture" and operating "concentration camps"— demanded the immediate release of all political prisoners and safe conduct out of the country for those who desired it.

In the spring of 1975 the Human Rights Commission set up a working group of five members to inquire into these charges. Although the working group was refused admission to Chiile, it was able to report to the 1975 Assembly, which, in

turn, expressed "its *profound distress* at the constant flagrant violations of human rights, including the institutionalized practice of torture, cruel, inhuman or degrading treatment or punishment, arbitrary arrest, detention and exile." . . . The vote on this resolution was 95 to 11, with 23 abstentions. The United States, Canada, and all of Western Europe voted for its adoption.[12]

Since then the Commission has exercised the right to investigate on its own motion notorious cases of gross violations and to consider such cases in public proceedings. Investigations have been carried out by ad hoc working groups or individual rapporteurs. (In the Bolivian case, he was called a "special envoy.") The subjects of such procedures have included Bolivia, El Salvador, Guatemala, Poland, Afghanistan, and Iran. The Commission has even been moved to criticize a state's human rights record without benefit of an extensive prior investigation. In a 1983 resolution on the situation in Kampuchea following, paradoxically, Vietnam's overthrow of Pol Pot's genocidal regime, the Commission condemned "the persistent occurrence of gross and flagrant violations of human rights" in that country. Presumably most members were more inflamed by Vietnam's invasion of a fellow Third World state than by the suffering of the population that had survived Pol Pot. Most of the public action succeeded inconclusive confidential processing under 1503. Examples are El Salvador, Guatemala, Bolivia, Afghanistan, and Iran.

The Sub-Commission has also asserted the authority to make public recommendations for action even in cases being simultaneously considered under 1503. Tolley records five cases where the confidentiality requirement was thereby avoided: Uganda, Bolivia, Paraguay, Afghanistan, and Iran.[13]

The United Nations is now a participant, however ambivalent, in the defense of human rights. That is indisputable. Equally indisputable is its discriminatory attitude toward enforcement and its refusal in all cases other than Rhodesia and South Africa to recommend sanctions. Nor is there much sympathy among its members for unauthorized humanitarian intervention.

Being weak and vulnerable states, most members see themselves only as objects of intervention. Moreover, being former colonies or de facto

12. Thomas Franck, *Nation Against Nation* (Oxford: Oxford University Press, 1985), 234–5.
13. Howard Tolley, Jr., "The Concealed Crack in the Citadel: The United Nations Commission on Human Rights' Response to Confidential Communications," *Human Rights Quarterly* 6 (Nov. 1984): 422, 442.

dependencies of powerful states, most recall the many occasions in the past when the words humanitarian intervention served as a fig leaf for the crass thrust of imperial interests. Anxious to build walls of precedent behind which to shelter, they have condemned interventions even by other Third World states against irredeemably barbarous regimes. In 1971, for instance, when India attacked the armed forces of West Pakistan (as it then was) who were busily engaged in a campaign of extermination against all Hindus in East Pakistan and educated Bengali Muslims, the General Assembly, by a vote of 104 in favor to eleven against (with ten abstentions) called for an immediate cease fire and, in effect for the withdrawal of Indian troops, despite the predictable consequences for the population of East Pakistan.

THE FUTURE OF UN ENFORCEMENT ACTIVITIES?

The trajectory of political and social development within and among nations will determine the form and vigor of UN-sponsored activity. Predicting that trajectory is work more for the seer than the analyst. One thing that can be said with confidence of its accuracy is that human rights enforcement will remain highly politicized and therefore intensely controversial. How could it be otherwise? As Stanley Hoffman noted shortly after the inauguration of Jimmy Carter, "[t]he issue of human rights, by definition, breeds confrontation. Raising the issue touches on the very foundations of a regime, on its sources and exercise of power, on its links to its citizens or subjects. It is a dangerous issue. . . ."[14] But the history of the last forty years suggests that, absent a nuclear holocaust, it will remain an unavoidable one.

It certainly seems to be fixed on the agenda of superpower diplomacy. Reluctantly planted there by Nixon and Kissinger, it has now survived through another two and one-half administrations. Its durability has been confirmed by its easy transit from Carter to Reagan, presidents otherwise so different in ideology and style. Events have also confirmed its capacity to complicate negotiations over issues central to humanity's future.

In his address to the Soviet people following the summit talks in Iceland, General Secretary Gorbachev described U.S. insistence on discussing human rights issues as an effort to insinuate intractable ideological differences into the discussion of nuclear arms control and disarmament. While the General Secretary congratulated himself for, as he saw it, warding off this diversion, President Reagan's spokesmen celebrated the President's success in forcing reference to the issue.

Communist leaders are by no means alone in seeing efforts to enforce primarily political and civil rights as a form of ideological assault by the advanced capitalist democracies rather than as the promotion of universal shared values. So many Third World regimes, spread right across the ideological spectrum, reacting at best ambivalently and often with outright hostility to Carter's initiatives (despite his readiness, at least rhetorically, to treat freedom from want on a par with political and civil freedoms) did persuade more than a few observers that human rights were just a provincial product of the Western liberal tradition with poor prospects in the global market of ideas. The outlook is particularly bleak, they argue, in those many parts of the world where, unlike Latin America or possibly India, indigenous concepts of political legitimacy survived the era of Western imperial domination. . . .

The idea of human rights—today, in fact, a not always comfortable coalition of liberal and socialist ideologies—may have been born in the West, but it has made its venue global. Its champions these days are not invariably the high-tech capitalist democracies. . . .

I think it is fair to say that, except during the Carter years, not one of the large Western democracies (as opposed to the Dutch and the Swedes) has been a leader in the United Nations or regional fora either in efforts to strengthen the machinery of human rights protection or to marshall pressure against non-communist villains. France, for example, was among the last members of the Council of Europe to adhere to the treaty provisions granting individuals the right to petition for enforcement of their rights under the European Human Rights Convention. Throughout the history of the United Nations, the British government has looked with little sympathy on efforts to strengthen the enforcement machinery. And the United States, during the Reagan era, has often stood virtually alone in opposing condem-

---

14. Stanley Hoffman, "The Hell of Good Intentions," *Foreign Policy* 29 (1977–78): 8.

nation of Chile, South Africa, and other delinquents with whom we share, among other things, secret intelligence.

By contrast, a small number of Third World states have sometimes been in the vanguard of human rights defense. In the OAS [Organization of American States], for example, Barbados, Mexico, and Venezuela were prominent among those members attempting, after the coming of Reagan, to maintain the institutional momentum achieved during the Carter years. . . .

Despite all the horror that surrounds us, I believe, as I said at the outset, that we are in a new era. At its outset, we had the Word, the Universal Declaration. In the past four decades it has acquired a little flesh. Within its means, means so conspicuously limited by the fact that material sanctions and incentives remain at the discretionary disposition of powerful states, the United

Nations organization has helped. Historical perspective eases the pull of cynicism. Having won a revolution in the name of man's inalienable rights, the Founding Fathers of the United States incorporated slavery into the new nation's constitutional foundations. Seventy-six years passed before formal emancipation. And another century passed before blacks in the United States could enjoy the full rights of citizenship.

The distance the United Nations has come in four decades is one ground for optimism about where it will go in the next four. Another is the effort so many governments have made to restrain its forward progress and to evade its primitive machinery of enforcement. By their acts they have recognized the influence the idea of human rights has acquired over the minds of their subjects. Hypocrisy continues to offer credible evidence of the possibility of virtue.

QUESTIONS FOR REFLECTION AND DISCUSSION

1. Is the UN human rights system described by Tom Farer the optimum system that could be conceived for the promotion and protection of human rights on the global plane? The optimum system that is *possible*? What are its strengths? Weaknesses? What realistic improvements might be made? What is Farer's opinion?

2. Farer notes the wide array of human rights treaties that have emanated from the UN. Has all this law-making been useful? Effective? Can you think of any human rights abuses that should be the subject of additional UN law-making? Or is all this prescriptive activity just a waste of time? Why? Why not?

3. Despite the United Nations' long-term contribution to the promotion of human rights through the preparation and adoption of standard-setting treaties that, by definition, are intended to be binding, widespread violations of even the most fundamental human rights continue more or less unabated. To minimize damage to its already fragile authority and prestige, might it not be better for the United Nations to propose, instead, model laws that, optionally, could later be enacted into national legislation? Indeed, might not a model laws approach to the promotion of human rights serve the cause of human rights more effectively at the local level precisely because it would not necessitate ratification procedures and because it could be adapted to local idiosyncracies?

4. For that matter, is there anything to prevent the incorporation into local law of the substantive provisions of UN-adopted human rights treaties? On September 2, 1986, the City Council of Burlington, Iowa, adopted an ordinance adding the substantive provisions of the UN International Convention on the Elimination of All Forms of Racial Discrimination to the City's governing law. The *Burlington Hawkeye* reported that "[t]he idea of turning international conventions into local ordinances proposes an end run around the recalcitrant [US] Senate. Widespread adoption by localities will constitute a national endorsement which the Senate will be under pressure to recognize" ("City Shows Local Issues Have Global Roots," *Burlington Hawkeye*, Sept. 21, 1986). It quoted Professor Burns Weston, who helped to inspire the movement, as saying that "[t]his will force judges in local jurisdictions to pay attention to international justice. . . . [It is] a case of thinking globally and acting locally." Would the United Nations be well advised to reconsider the uses to which its many proposed or minimally ratified human rights treaties might be put?

5. What is the role of the UN Commission on Human Rights? Of the Sub-Commission on Prevention of Discrimination and Protection of Minorities? Are these organs effective? How, if at all, might they be improved?

6. As Farer points out, Resolution 1503 of the UN Economic and Social Council and the Optional Protocol to the International Covenant on Civil and Political Rights each make it possible for private parties to petition the UN human rights system directly. Is this a good thing? Are the two procedures effective? Equally effective? How, if at all, do they differ? How, if at all, might each be improved?

7. A drawback of ECOSOC Resolution 1503 is that the petitioner must show the existence of "a consistent pattern of gross and reliably attested violations of human rights and fundamental freedoms." Thus, "non-gross" violations or isolated human rights violations do not give rise to admissible petitions. Is this a desirable state of affairs? Why? Why not?

8. Individuals petitioning against the actions of their own governments may have difficulty securing proper documentation of their grievances. Also, they may have difficulty transmitting their documented communications to the appropriate UN bodies authorized to receive them. For these reasons, it is important that nongovernmental organizations such as Amnesty International be allowed to petition on behalf of individuals unable to do so effectively for themselves. Why, then, are nongovernmental organizations not permitted to petition the Human Rights Committee under the Optional Protocol? Would it be desirable to liberalize the Optional Protocol procedures?

9. Might it be a good idea to extend formal UN participation to human rights nongovernmental organizations? If so, what might that formal status be and what might be the consequences of formalizing that status?

10. A key feature of all the UN petition procedures is the requirement that the petitioner have exhausted her or his domestic remedies. Is this a good thing? A bad thing? Why?

11. Several international human rights instruments, such as the International Covenant on Economic, Social, and Cultural Rights, rely primarily or exclusively on countries' reports to such UN agencies as the International Labor Organization (ILO) and the United Nations Educational, Scientific and Cultural Organization (UNESCO) as their means of ensuring compliance with human rights principles and standards. Are reportorial means of enforcement effective in redressing human rights violations? What problems might they pose? What advantages, if any?

12. Well over a decade ago, Costa Rica proposed the appointment of a UN High Commissioner for Human Rights. This proposal was never acted upon. Why? Should it have been? Why? Why not?

13. At one time or another the establishment of two new subcommissions of the UN Commission on Human Rights has been proposed, one for the promotion of human rights and the other for the protection of such rights. (See, e.g., U.N. Doc. E/CN.4/L.1324 [1976].) Is this a good idea? Why? Why not?

14. An important unofficial conference of experts known as the Assembly for Human Rights, which met in Montreal in March 1968, concluded that the Commission on Human Rights has "a status which is not commensurate with the important responsibilities entrusted to it" and proposed that it should be given the same standing as the Economic and Social Council. (See Montreal Statement of the Assembly of Human Rights, presented to the UN Conference on Human Rights in Teheran, 1968.) Do you agree with this proposal? Considering that it probably would require amending the UN Charter, would it be feasible? Others have suggested the establishment of new machinery, including an organization for the promotion of human rights (the "United Nations Agency for Human Rights") as a subordinate UN body with a human rights council as its main organ. (See, e.g., Sohn, "U.N. Machinery for Implementing Human Rights," *American Journal of International Law* 62 [1968], 909.) Is this a useful suggestion? A feasible one? What might be some of the problems involved? Some of the advantages?

15. An international criminal court under UN auspices has been frequently suggested. (See, e.g., the Draft Statute for an International Criminal Court prepared under the auspices of the UN Commission on International Criminal Jurisdiction in 1953, 9 U.N. GAOR, Supp. [No. 12] Annex 23, U.N. Doc. A/2645 [1954].) Though so far not acted upon, is the idea a good one? If so, what kinds of cases might come before it? Should any violation of an internationally recognized human right be within its jurisdiction? Or only severe violations of truly fundamental rights, such as "crimes against humanity"? Would an international criminal code effectively contribute to the enforcement of international human rights? What difficulties might be entailed in formulating such a code?

16. Though the enforcement of international human rights at the global level often may be problematic, are there constraints that prevent states from disregarding human rights principles and standards whenever they please? If so, what are they?

17. On balance, has the United Nations done a good or a bad job in promoting human rights? In protecting human rights? What are your reasons for concluding as you do? What does Farer say?

16. BURNS H. WESTON, ROBIN ANN LUKES, AND KELLY M. HNATT *Regional Human Rights Regimes: A Comparison and Appraisal*

INTRODUCTION

For Americans at least, active concern for human rights on the international plane is demonstrated perhaps most conspicuously in the promotion and protection of human rights through the United Nations and its allied agencies—apart, that is, from the promotion and protection of human rights through United States foreign policy and the work of such nongovernmental organizations as Amnesty International. Supplementing this globally-oriented human rights activity, however, are international human rights regimes operating regionally in Western Europe, the Americas, Africa and the Middle East. Concededly, Asia is not yet represented,[1] and only the first three of the represented regions have gone so far as to create enforcement mechanisms within the framework of a human rights charter, as evidenced by the European Convention for the Protection of Human Rights and Fundamental Freedoms[2] and the European Social Charter,[3] the

1. Asia has done relatively little to establish regional human rights institutions. As one commentator has observed:

> Asia is a conglomeration of countries with radically different social structures, and diverse religious, philosophical, and cultural traditions; their political ideologies, legal systems, and degrees of economic development vary greatly; and, above all, there is no shared historical past even from the times of colonialism. Most research on human rights problems in Asia has, therefore, been national rather than regional.

Hiroko Yamane, "Asia and Human Rights," in Karel Vasak, *International Dimensions of Human Rights*, 2 (Westport, Conn.: Greenwood Press, 1982), 651.

On the other hand, the United Nations has encouraged the Asian region, so far unsuccessfully to begin some sort of human rights initiative and certain nongovernmental organizations have provided some stimulus by holding conferences to discuss regional human rights issues. In addition, the Standing Committee of Lawasia (a professional association of Asian and Western Pacific lawyers) is working to secure the ratification of the two United Nations human rights covenants and to establish a Center for Human Rights in the region. For recent discussion regarding these developments, see generally Yamane, "Approaches to Human Rights in Asia," in *International Enforcement of Human Rights*, ed. Rudolf Bernhardt and J. Jolowicz (Berlin: Springer-Verlag, 1987), 99.

2. European Convention for the Protection of Human Rights and Fundamental Freedoms, Nov. 4, 1950, E.T.S. No. 5 (entered into force, Sept. 3, 1953) (hereafter, European Convention). Eight protocols supplement the European Convention, six of which have entered into force: Protocol (No. I), Mar. 20, 1952, E.T.S. No. 9 (entered into force, May 18, 1954) (hereafter, Protocol I); Protocol (No. II), May 6, 1963, E.T.S. No. 44 (entered into force, Sept. 21, 1970) (hereafter, Protocol II); Protocol (No. III), May 6, 1963, E.T.S. No. 45 (entered into force, Sept. 21, 1970); Protocol (No. IV), Sept. 16, 1963, E.T.S. No. 46 (entered into force, May 2, 1968) (hereafter, Protocol IV); Protocol (No. V), Jan. 20, 1966, E.T.S. No. 55 (entered into force, Dec. 20, 1971); Protocol (No. VI), E.T.S. No. 114 (entered into force, Mar. 1, 1985); Protocol (No. VII), Nov. 22, 1984, E.T.S. No. 117; Protocol (No. VIII), Mar. 19, 1985, E.T.S. No. 118.

3. European Social Charter, Oct. 18, 1961, E.T.S. No. 35 (entered into force, Feb. 26, 1965) (hereafter, European Social Charter).

Reprinted, with changes, from Burns H. Weston, Robin Ann Lukes, and Kelly M. Hnatt, "Regional Human Rights Regimes: A Comparison and Appraisal," *Vanderbilt Journal of Transnational Law* 20, no. 4 (1987): 585–637. Reprinted by permission.

American Convention on Human Rights[4] and the Banjul (African) Charter on Human and Peoples' Rights.[5] The Permanent Arab Commission on Human Rights, founded by the Council of the League of Arab States in September 1968[6] but since then understandably preoccupied by the rights of Palestinian Arabs in and to the Israeli-occupied territories, has yet to bring a proposed Arab Convention on Human Rights to successful conclusion, and so far has tended to function more in terms of the promotion than the protection of human rights. Nevertheless, the regional development of human rights norms, institutions and procedures is likely to grow. Already an important dynamic of international human rights law and policy, it is, in any event, here to stay. . . .

THE ORIGINS AND STRUCTURES OF THE REGIONAL HUMAN RIGHTS REGIMES

THE EUROPEAN REGIME

The European human rights regime began following the entry into force, in September 1953, of the European Convention for the Protection of Human Rights and Fundamental Freedoms (European Convention). The first regional human rights regime created, it was developed deliberately to safeguard against the revival of aggressive and repressive dictatorships by ensuring "the collective enforcement of certain of the rights stated in the Universal Declaration [of Human Rights]."[7] It was thought that "[i]f the dictators had built their empire by suppressing individual freedoms, then an effective system for the protection of human rights would constitute a bulwark against any recrudescence of dictatorship."[8]

Thus, pursuant to the European Convention, a series of additional protocols and the European Social Charter (whose drafting began immediately after the European Convention entered into force), the Council of Europe (Council), led by a liberal-socialist coalition and believing that European institutions and values favored human rights, ha[ve] sought to guarantee a broad range of both "first generation" (civil and political) and "second generation" (economic, social and cultural) rights. Believing also that their relations were strong enough to withstand a human rights regime based on reciprocal scrutiny, they have done so through a combination of adjudicative and reportorial procedures within the framework of the Council of Europe, including a commission, a court of human rights and certain of the administrative and parliamentary organs of the Council—all located in Strasbourg, France.

The European Convention

Together with its first and fourth additional protocols, the European Convention, in force and effect relative to all twenty-one Member States of the Council of Europe, addresses primarily civil and political rights and freedoms.[9] A broad non-discrimination provision supplements these declared rights and freedoms and secures their enjoyment "without discrimination on any ground such as sex, race, colour, language, religion, political or other opinion, national or social origin, association with a national minority, property,

4. American Convention on Human Rights, No. 22, 1969, O.A.S.T.S. No. 36, at 1, O.A.S. Off. Rec. OEA/Ser. L/V/II.23 doc. 21 rev. 6 (1979), reprinted in 9 I.L.M. 673 (1970) (entered into force, July 18, 1978) (hereafter, American Convention).
5. Banjul Charter on Human and Peoples' Rights, June 28, 1981, O.A.U. Doc. CAB/LEG/67/3/Rev. 5 (1981), reprinted in 21 I.L.M. 58 (1982) (entered into force, Oct. 21, 1986) (hereafter, African Charter).
6. See Council of the Arab League, Res. 2443/48, Sept. 3, 1968.
7. A. Roberston, *Human Rights in the World*, 2d ed. (Manchester, U.K.: Manchester University Press, 1982), 82.
8. Ibid., 80.
9. European Convention (see n. 2, above), art. 2 (the right to life); art. 3 (the right to humane treatment); art. 4 (freedom from slavery and involuntary servitude); art. 5 (the right to personal liberty and security); art. 6 (the right to a fair trial); art. 7 (freedom from ex post facto laws); art. 8 (the right to privacy); art. 9 (freedom of thought, conscience and religion); art. 10 (freedom of expression); art. 11 (freedom of assembly and association); art. 12 (the right to marriage and family); and art. 13 (the right to legal protection). Protocol I: art. 1 (the right to personal property); art. 2 (the right to free choice of education); and art. 3 (the right to free elections). Protocol IV: art. 1 (freedom from debtor prison); art. 2 (the right to free movement and residence); art. 3 (freedom from national territorial expulsion); and art. 4 (freedom from the collective expulsion of aliens). . . .

birth or other status." Also, to guarantee these rights and freedoms, the Convention establishes two primary organs—the European Commission of Human Rights (European Commission) and the European Court of Human Rights (European Court)—and, in addition, frequently relies on the Council's Committee of Ministers.

The European Commission is elected by the Committee of Ministers of the Council of Europe and presently consists of twenty-one members (no two from the same state), each serving for a six-year term. The Commission's jurisdiction extends to inter-state applications automatically, without the express consent of the States Parties involved, and to petitions by any person, group of individuals or nongovernmental organization (NGO) claiming to be the victim of a violation by a State Party to the European Convention, provided that the respondent State Party has made a declaration recognizing the Commission's competence to receive such petitions.[10]

The Commission's duties are to determine the admissibility of applications, to ascertain the facts concerning an application properly before the Commission and to attempt "to secure a friendly settlement." If the Commission cannot secure a friendly settlement, the European Convention directs it to report the facts and its opinion of the case to the Council's Committee of Ministers and, optionally, to make recommendations to the Committee. Alternatively, the Commission may bring suit before the European Court of Human Rights provided, however, that the respondent State Party has formally recognized the Court's compulsory jurisdiction.

The European Court—elected by the Consultative Assembly of the Council of Europe for a renewable term of nine years and, like the Commission, also consisting of twenty-one members (no two from the same state), all "of high moral character and . . . recognized competence"—has jurisdiction only over States Parties that have consented to the Court's jurisdiction explicitly. As of early 1987, twenty of the twenty-one members of the Council had accepted the Court's compulsory jurisdiction. For consideration of each case brought before it, the Court sits as a "cham-

ber" of only seven judges, six of whom the President of the Court chooses by lot before the opening of each case and the seventh of whom is a concerned state national or other person sitting in ex officio capacity chosen by the concerned State Party.

The Court is directed to interpret and apply the European Convention whenever cases are brought to it by the Commission or by a State Party. Significantly, however, individuals have no official standing before the Court; thus, to ensure fairness, the Commission has relied increasingly on the input of individual complainants in its representation of their cases before the Court, and the Court, in turn, has made it possible for counsel to represent individuals if the individuals so desire. In addition, although a judgment of the Court is both final and binding, the Court is not responsible for its execution. Indeed, the Court lacks the capacity to execute a judgment. Instead, the Court is directed to transmit a judgment to the Committee of Ministers which, in turn, "shall supervise its execution."

Finally, the Committee of Ministers, though not a creature of the European Convention and composed of persons who, unlike the members of the Commission and Court, serve not in their individual capacity but as governmental representatives, also plays a major role in the promotion and protection of human rights under the European Convention and its additional protocols. Indeed, as one commentator has suggested, the Committee is the "ultimate guarantor of human rights under the [European] Convention."[11] Absent the referral of an application to the Court by the Commission or a concerned State Party, the Committee is responsible for deciding whether a breach of the European Convention has occurred. Additionally, as indicated, the Committee is the sole organ within the framework of the European human rights system with the power to execute judgments, and in this capacity the Committee often has passed resolutions requiring states to remedy proven violations. It has not yet actually imposed, however, the most serious sanction: expulsion from the Council of Europe.

10. . . . As of this writing, twenty of the twenty-one States Parties had formally recognized the competence of the Commission to receive individual applications. . . .

11. Kevin Boyle, "Practice and Procedure on Individual Applications Under the European Convention on Human Rights," in *Guide to International Human Rights Practice*, ed. Hurst Hannum (Philadelphia: University of Pennsylvania Press, 1984), 135.

The European Social Charter

The European human rights regime so far described, an adjudicative process available only for applications and petitions claiming violations of civil and political rights, is available for complaints brought pursuant to the European Convention for the Protection of Human Rights and Fundamental Freedoms (European Convention). By contrast, economic, social and cultural rights—so-called second generation rights—are left to be promoted and protected elsewhere, under the European Social Charter (Charter) and primarily by reportorial means.

Under the Charter, in force and effect relative to fourteen of the twenty-one Member States of the Council of Europe, the States Parties undertake to consider the economic, social and cultural rights enumerated therein[12] "as a declaration of aims which [they] will pursue by all appropriate means" and to submit biennial progress reports to the Council's Secretary-General concerning those substantive provisions "as they have accepted." A Committee of Experts, consisting of not more than seven members nominated by the States Parties and appointed by the Council's Committee of Ministers "from a list of independent experts of the highest integrity and of recognized competence in international social questions," examines the reports that the Secretary-General has received. A subcommittee of the Governmental Social Committee then considers both the reports of the States Parties and the conclusions of the Committee of Experts, and the Secretary-General submits the conclusions of the Committee of Experts to the Council's Consultative Assembly. Ultimately, however, similar to its enforcement powers under the European Con-

vention relative to civil and political rights, the Committee of Ministers is responsible for the promotion and protection of the economic, social and cultural rights that the Charter enumerates. Article 29 of the Charter provides that "the Committee of Ministers may, on the basis of the report of the Sub-committee, and after consultation with the Consultative Assembly, make to each Contracting Party any necessary recommendations."

THE INTER-AMERICAN REGIME

In 1948, concurrent with its establishment of the Organization of American States (OAS), the Ninth International Conference of American states adopted the American Declaration on the Rights and Duties of Man,[13] an instrument similar to, but coming a full seven months before, the Universal Declaration of Human Rights.[14] Subsequently, in 1959, the Fifth Meeting of Consultation of Ministers of Foreign Affairs created—under the auspices and within the framework of the OAS, by means of a political resolution—the Inter-American Commission on Human Rights, which since has undertaken important investigative activities concerning human rights in the Americas. Finally, in 1969, the Inter-American Specialized Conference on Human Rights, at a meeting in San José, Costa Rica, adopted the American Convention on Human Rights (American Convention) which, among other things, committed the previously established OAS Inter-American Commission on Human Rights to the implementation of the Convention. The American Convention, also known as the Pact of San José, entered into force on July 18, 1978, when

---

12. European Social Charter (see n. 3, above), II, art. 1 (the right to work); art. 2 (the right to just conditions of work); art. 3 (the right to safe and healthy working conditions); art. 4 (the right to a fair remuneration); art. 5 (the right to organize); art. 6 (the right to bargain collectively); art. 7 (the right of [employed] children and young persons to protection); art. 8 (the right of employed women to protection); art. 9 (the right to vocational guidance); art. 10 (the right to vocational training); art. 11 (the right to protection of health); art. 12 (the right to social security); art. 13 (the right to social and medical assistance); art. 14 (the right to benefit from social welfare services); art. 15 (the right of physically or mentally disabled persons to vocational training, rehabilitation, and social resettlement); art. 16 (the right of the family to social, legal, and economic protection); art. 17 (the right of mothers to social and economic protection); art. 18 (the right to engage in a gainful occupation in the territory of other contracting parties); and art. 19 (the right of migrant workers and their families to protection and assistance).

In addition, Protocol I (see n. 2, above), art. 2, states that "[n]o person shall be denied the right to education."

13. OAS Res. XXX, adopted by the Ninth International Conference of American States (Mar. 30–May 2, 1948), Bogotá, O.A.S. Off. Rec. OEA/Ser.L/V/1.4 Rev. (1965).

14. [See the Appendix.]

Grenada became the eleventh State Party to the treaty,[15] thus setting into motion a regional human rights regime comparable to the one already evolving in Europe.

Like the European Convention, the American Convention gurantees a wide range of civil and political rights.[16] Also, like the European Convention, a broad non-discrimination provision supplements these guarantees by ensuring the free and full exercise of the enumerated rights and freedoms "without any discrimination for reasons of race, color, sex, language, religion, political or other opinion, national or social origin, economic status, birth, or any other social condition." Additionally, reminiscent of the European Social Charter but without comparable detail, the American Convention obligates the States Parties to achieve progressively "the full realization of the rights implicit in the economic, social, educational, scientific, and cultural stan-

dards set forth in the Charter of the Organization of American States."[17]

Also like the European Convention, the American Convention provides for two specialized—and comparable—enforcement mechanisms: the above-mentioned, preexisting Inter-American Commission on Human Rights, headquartered at the OAS in Washington, D.C.; and an Inter-American Court of Human Rights, situated in San José, Costa Rica. Each is accorded "competence with respect to matters relating to the fulfillment of the commitments made by the States Parties to [the American] Convention." In addition, resembling the functions of the Committee of Ministers of the Council of Europe within the European human rights regime, the General Assembly of the OAS plays an important role.

The Inter-American Commission on Human Rights, composed of seven members (no two from the same state) elected in their personal ca-

15. As of this writing, twenty of the thirty-two OAS Member States have ratified the American Convention. . . .

16. American Convention (see n. 4, above), art. 3 (the right to juridical personality); art. 4 (the right to life); art. 5 (the right to humane treatment); art. 6 (freedom from slavery and involuntary servitude); art. 7 (the right to personal liberty); art. 8 (the right to a fair trial); art. 9 (freedom from ex post facto laws); art. 10 (the right to compensation for miscarriage of justice); art. 11 (the right to privacy); art. 12 (freedom of conscience and religion); art. 13 (freedom of thought and expression); art. 14 (the right of reply); art. 15 (the right of assembly); art. 16 (freedom of association); art. 17 (rights of the family); art. 18 (the right to name); art. 19 (rights of the child); art. 20 (the right to nationality); art. 21 (the right to property); art. 22 (freedom of movement and residence); art. 23 (the right to participate in government); art. 24 (the right to equal protection before the law); and art. 25 (the right to judicial protection). . . .

17. American Convention (see n. 4, above), art. 26. The OAS Charter referred to is the 1948 Charter as amended by the Protocol of Buenos Aires in 1967. See Charter of the Organization of American States, Apr. 30, 1948, 2 U.S.T. 2394, T.I.A.S. No. 2367, 119 U.N.T.S. 3 (hereafter, OAS Charter), and Protocol of Amendment, Feb. 27, 1967, 21 U.S.T. 607, T.I.A.S. No. 6847 (hereafter, Protocol of Amendment).

The economic, social, educational, scientific and cultural "standards" of the OAS Charter are detailed in Chapters VII–IX thereof. The economic "standards" include increase in the per capita national product; equitable distribution of national income; adequate and equitable systems of taxation; modernization of rural life in accordance with equitable and efficient land-tenure systems; accelerated and diversified industrialization; stability in domestic pricing; fair wages, employment opportunities, and acceptable working conditions; rapid eradication of illiteracy and expansion of educational opportunities; extension and application of modern medical science; proper nutrition; adequate housing; healthful urban conditions; promotion of socially responsible private enterprise; and expansion and diversification of exports (OAS Charter, art. 31). The social "standards" include a nondiscriminatory right to material well-being and spiritual development; a right to work; a right to collective bargaining; fair and efficient systems and procedures for economic consultation and collaboration; operation of socially responsible systems of public administration, banking and credit, enterprise, and distribution and sales; incorporation and increasing participation in society of the marginal sectors of the population; recognition of the importance of labor unions, cooperatives, and professional and community associations; development of an efficient social security policy; and adequate legal aid for all persons (OAS Charter, art. 43). The educational, scientific and cultural "standards" include encouragement of education, science, and culture in development plans; Member State cooperation in meeting educational needs, promoting scientific research, encouraging technological progress, and preserving and enriching the cultural heritage of their peoples; ensuring the effective exercise of the right to education; and giving special attention to the eradication of illiteracy and the strengthening of adult and vocational educational systems (OAS Charter, arts. 45–48). . . .

pacities by the Member States of the OAS General Assembly for a one-time renewable term of four years, has a dual role, one as an organ of the American Convention and the other, an older role, as an organ of the OAS, with the OAS Charter and the American Declaration as its normative instruments. Thomas Buergenthal, former President of the Inter-American Court of Human Rights, on which he still sits, comments on this dual role:

As [an O.A.S.] Charter organ, the Commission has jurisdiction over all O.A.S. Member States, whether or not they have ratified the Convention; as a Convention organ, its jurisdiction extends only to the States Parties to the Convention. Here its jurisdiction is more specific and its powers more extensive. The powers of the Commission as Charter organ lack precision, which is just as well, for the ambiguities about the scope of its powers gave it greater flexibility to deal imaginatively with gross violations of human rights prior to the entry into force of the Convention. It retains that flexibility in dealing with states that have not ratified it and in responding to emergency situations involving large-scale human rights abuses in the region.[18]

In any event, under the American Convention the main function of the Inter-American Commission is to "promote respect for and defense of human rights." This purpose is to be accomplished, according to the American Convention, by developing awareness of human rights, making recommendations to OAS Member States, preparing studies or reports, requesting information from OAS Member States, responding to and advising OAS Member States on matters relating to human rights and submitting annual reports to the OAS General Assembly. Also, it is to be accomplished by taking action on petitions and other communications, a function the Convention details at some length. Like the European Commission, the American Commission is directed to determine the admissibility of individual (private) petitions, to undertake fact-finding and attempt friendly settlements, to report to the OAS Secretary General as well as to the parties involved, *for publication*, about the facts and the solution reached if it achieves a friendly settlement

and, if it fails to achieve a friendly settlement, to prepare a confidential report and, optionally, to tender proposals and recommendations and submit cases to the Inter-American Court of Human Rights. In addition, the Commission is charged to receive and review annual reports from the States Parties so as to monitor progress relative to economic, social and cultural rights.

The Inter-American Court, like the Commission, consists of seven members (no two from the same state) elected in individual capacity, for a renewable term of six years, by the States Parties to the Convention "from among jurists of the highest moral authority and . . . recognized competence in the field of human rights." It is directed to interpret and apply the American Convention in both contentious and advisory jurisdiction. In exercising its contentious jurisdiction, however, which may result in an order for compensatory damages, permanent or temporary injunctive relief, or both, the Court is accessible only to the Inter-American Commission and to those State Parties to the American Convention that, like their European counterparts, have expressly recognized such jurisdiction.[19] As in the European human rights regime, individuals have no formal standing before the Court— they have standing only before the Commission, which alone may file an individual's case with the Court, provided the Commission has completed its proceedings applicable to the case. Also, as in Europe, and notwithstanding that all judgments rendered pursuant to the Court's contentious jurisdiction are "final and not subject to appeal," the Court lacks the power to enforce its judgments and preliminary rulings; instead, it must rely mainly on the OAS General Assembly (just as the European Court must rely on the Council of Europe's Committee of Ministers). In exercising its advisory jurisdiction, on the other hand, the Court is open not only to the States Parties to the Convention and to the Inter-American Commission, but also to all Member States of the OAS (including non-States Parties to the Convention, such as the United States) and to the OAS and all its organs as well (including, obviously, the Commission).

Finally, the OAS General Assembly, though a

---

18. Thomas Buergenthal, "Human Rights in the Americas: View from the Inter-American Court," *Connecticut Journal of International Law* 2 (1987): 303, 306–7.

19. American Convention (see n. 4, above), art. 61(1). As of this writing, ten of the nineteen States Parties to the American Convention have accepted the Court's contentious jurisdiction. . . .

creature of the OAS Charter and not the American Convention, also plays an important role in the promotion and protection of human rights under the American Convention. To quote Judge Buergenthal: "The Assembly is the principal organ of the [O.A.S.] whose human rights powers have their source both in the O.A.S. Charter and in the [American] Convention."[20] The annual reports that the Court must submit to the General Assembly, specifying "in particular, the cases in which a state has not complied with its [the Court's] judgment, making any pertinent recommendations," thus take on added significance. The General Assembly's freedom to discuss the matter and to adopt whatever OAS sanctions it deems appropriate at least partially mitigates the Court's incapacity to enforce its judgments and rulings.

Thus, the core structure of the Inter-American human rights system is similar to that of its European counterpart. Some significant differences exist, however, and four stand out in particular.

First, reminiscent of the American Declaration on the Rights and Duties of Man, albeit with little apparent practical significance, the American Convention, unlike the European Convention, details individual duties as well as individual rights. Thus article 32 (entitled "Relationship Between Duties and Rights") reads:

1. Every person has responsibilities to his family, his community, and mankind.
2. The rights of each person are limited by the rights of others, by the security of all, and by the just demands of the general welfare, in a democratic society.

Comparable obligation language exists also in the African Charter on Human and Peoples' Rights.

Second, relative to individual petitions and complaints by one State Party against another, the American Convention reverses the approach taken under the European Convention. Whereas Europe utilizes a mandatory inter-state complaint and optional individual petition procedure, the Americas utilize an optional inter-state complaint and mandatory individual petition procedure. In contrast to the European Commission of Human Rights, the Inter-American Commission on Human Rights has authority to consider inter-state complaints only if both of the States Parties, in addition to ratifying the Convention, have for-

mally recognized the competence of the Commission to receive and review such complaints. On the other hand, the Commission may accept a private individual petition against any state simply on the basis of the respondent state being a party to the American Convention. In addition, unlike the European Convention, the American Convention does not limit the right to file individual petitions only to victims of violations, leaving the process open to almost everyone.

Third, and as already noted, the Inter-American Court of Human Rights has advisory as well as contentious jurisdiction, whereas the European Court, while also possessed of advisory jurisdiction, is more constricted in this respect. The Inter-American Court's advisory jurisdiction, defined in article 64 of the American Convention, is extensive. . . . Until recently the Inter-American Court has decided all cases referred to it pursuant to its advisory jurisdiction.

Finally, both the Inter-American Commission and the Inter-American Court (but especially the Commission) operate beyond as well as within the framework of the American Convention. The Commission is as much an organ of the OAS Charter as it is of the American Convention, with powers and procedures that differ significantly depending on the source of the Commission's authority, particularly in relation to human rights petitions and communications. The Court, while primarily an organ of the Convention, nonetheless has jurisdiction to interpret human rights provisions of treaties other than the American Convention, including the human rights provisions of the OAS Charter.

THE AFRICAN REGIME

In 1981, following twenty years of pleas by the United Nations Commission on Human Rights, interested states, nongovernmental organizations and others, adopted at the Eighteenth Assembly of Heads of State and Government of the OAU the African Charter on Human and Peoples' Rights, formally known as "the Banjul Charter on Human and Peoples' Rights." The Charter entered into force on October 21, 1986, and, as of this writing, thirty-one of the fifty OAU Member States have ratified it.

20. Thomas Buergenthal, "Implementation in the Inter-American Human Rights System," in Bernhardt and Jolowicz, *International Enforcement of Human Rights*, 58.

Like its European and Inter-American counterparts, the African Charter provides for both "first generation" (civil and political) rights[21] and "second generation" (economic, social, and cultural) rights.[22] Also resembling its European and Inter-American predecessors, it ensures the enjoyment of the rights and freedoms that the Charter recognizes and guarantees "without distinction of any kind such as race, ethnic group, color, sex, language, religion, political or any other opinion, national and social origin, fortune, birth, or other status." In addition, reminiscent of, but going beyond the American Declaration on the Rights and Duties of Man and the American Convention, it details individual duties as well as individual rights—to the family, society, the state, and the international African community.

In contrast to its European and Inter-American counterparts, however—indeed, going distinctively beyond them—the African Charter recognizes the rights of "peoples," or so-called third generation or solidarity rights, to wit: the right of all peoples to equality without "domination of a people by another"; the right of all peoples to existence and self-determination; the right of all peoples to freely dispose of "their wealth and natural resources"; the right of all peoples to their economic, social and cultural development, including "equal enjoyment of the common heritage of mankind"[23]; the right of all peoples to national and international peace and security; and the right of all peoples to "a general satisfactory environment favorable to their development." The States Parties to the Charter undertake to promote and ensure, through "teaching, education and publication," respect for and understanding of these rights and freedoms together with the first and second generation rights and freedoms that the Charter enumerates.

Similarities and differences with the European and American human rights regimes are evident also in the enforcement mechanisms and procedures that the African Charter embraces for the purpose of promoting and protecting the rights and freedoms it recognizes and guarantees. In contrast to its European and Inter-American counterparts, for example, it does not provide for a court of human rights. Commentators have stated that African customs and traditions favor mediation, conciliation and consensus over the adversarial and adjudicative procedures common to Western legal systems. Like its European and American counterparts, however, it does provide for the establishment of a commission. Known as the "African Commission on Human and Peoples' Rights," it exists within the framework of the OAU and consists of eleven members (no two from the same state) elected in their personal capacities by the OAU Assembly of Heads of State and Government for a renewable term of six years. Its purpose is "to promote human and peoples' rights and ensure their protection in Africa."

To these ends, the Commission is authorized to promote human and peoples' rights by various informational, educational, prescriptive and cooperative means; to ensure their protection pursuant to the Charter (in its contentious jurisdiction); to interpret the Charter at the request of a State Party, an institution of the OAU or an African organization recognized by the OAU (in its advisory capacity); and to "[p]erform any other tasks which may be entrusted to it by the [OAU] Assembly of Heads of State and Government."

21. African Charter (see n. 5, above), art. 3 (the right to equal protection before the law); art. 4 (the right to life); art. 5 (the right to humane treatment, including freedom from slavery); art. 6 (the right to personal liberty and security); art. 7 (the right to a fair trial, legal protection, and freedom from ex post facto laws); art. 8 (freedom of conscience and religion); art. 9 (the right to information and freedom of expression); art. 10 (the right to free association); art. 11 (the right to assembly); art. 12 (freedom of movement and residence, freedom from national territorial expulsion, and freedom from the collective expulsion of non-nationals); art. 13 (the right to participate in government and free elections and of equal access to public property and services); art. 14 (the right to property); and art. 18 (the right to marriage and family). Notably absent from the foregoing list of rights is the right to privacy. Probably this is due to African customs and traditions that see human identity more in group than individual terms. . . .

22. African Charter (see n. 5, above), art. 15 (the right to work); art. 16 (the right to physical and mental health); art. 17 (the right to education and to cultural participation); and art. 18 (the right to family assistance and to protection of women, children, the aged, and disabled). . . .

23. . . . The term "common heritage of mankind," originally used in conjunction with the resources of the deep seabed, is now understood to embrace shared Earth-space resources; scientific, technical, and other information and progress; and cultural traditions, sites and monuments. See Burns H. Weston, "Human Rights," *Encyclopaedia Britannica*, 15th ed., 20:714, 717. [Reprinted as Reading No. 1. in Chapter 1 above.]

Additionally, in its contentious jurisdiction, the Commission may resort "to any appropriate method of investigation" and receive, investigate, report on and make recommendations concerning both inter-state complaints of alleged violations of the Charter and private (individual) "communications" of alleged violations of the Charter, the latter being in no way limited to victims of violations. Legally competent to preside over both public and private human rights complaints, the African Commission is thus comparable to its European and Inter-American counterparts. However, because this legal competency is conditional almost entirely on the concerned states being parties to the African Charter, the African Commission also is distinctive. Whereas the European regime favors a mandatory inter-state complaint and optional individual petition procedure and the American regime favors an optional inter-state complaint and mandatory individual petition procedure, the African regime opts for a mandatory approach in both instances.

The African Commission is distinctive, finally, in yet another way—again, it seems, as a consequence of African customs and traditions. Like the European and Inter-American Commissions, the African Commission, after determining an application to be admissible, is expected, in its contentious jurisdiction, to undertake fact-finding, attempt an amicable settlement, prepare a report, and, generally in its discretion, make recommendations (to the OAU Assembly of Heads of State and Government). Beyond these procedural steps, however, in the absence of a human rights court to which it might make further appeals and through which enforceable decisions might be rendered, the Commission (and, therefore, the concerned state and private parties) has little recourse. As a consequence its emphasis is on mediation, conciliation and consensus as opposed to adversarial processes. In contrast to its European and Inter-American counterparts, the African Commission is expected to function more in a reportorial than an adjudicative fashion.

All of this suggests, of course, that the African Commission may prove less effective than its European and Inter-American counterparts in guarding against and correcting human rights abuses. The principle of state sovereignty or domestic jurisdiction is not easily surmounted even under the best of circumstances. On the other hand, given the African Commission's deliberate creation as an organ of the OAU and its consequent intended close relationship to the OAU Assembly of Heads of State and Government (analogous to the European Commission's affiliation with the Committee of Ministers of the Council of Europe and the Inter-American Commission's ties to the General Assembly of the OAS), the case reports it must submit to the OAU Assembly and the periodic activity reports it must likewise submit naturally could take on added significance. With the OAU Assembly free to adopt whatever sanctions it deems appropriate, the African Commission's relatively limited capacity to act on its findings could be at least partially mitigated. Of course, given the inexperience of the African regime, it remains to be seen how the Commission and the OAU Assembly will act.

THE EFFECTIVENESS OF THE REGIONAL REGIMES

From a humanistic standpoint, the European, Inter-American and African human rights regimes hold out great promise. However favorably or unfavorably they may compare to some ideal human rights system or to each other, the rights they recognize, the institutions they establish and the procedures they prescribe add up to an assault on the global state sovereignty system that is of truly historic proportions. International relations, it seems, are at long last beginning to be conducted, in theory and on the regional plane at least, as if people—not only states—really mattered.

But how good is the promise in fact? How effective are the three regional regimes in actuality, or how effective might they realistically be, in safeguarding the human rights they are designed to promote and protect?

[Editors' note: The authors proceed to consider these questions, first, "from the standpoint of the accessibility of each regime to those persons whose rights are alleged to be violated" and, second, "from the standpoint of the admissibility of the human rights grievances brought for judgment." Regarding the first issue, the authors conclude that the European human rights regime is superior because it is more established and better known, ergo accessible, and also because it exists in a social and political environment that favors restricting governmental abuse. The authors note, however, that the institution of the one-site study in the Inter-American system helps to alleviate that system's inadequacies and that the granting of standing to non-victims, especially nongovernmental organizations, helps to overcome the system's inherent weaknesses. Regarding the second issue, the authors conclude that each human rights regime suffers from limitations in their jurisdiction over states and private parties, in the rights they recognize, in the curtailing derogation and "clawback" clauses they allow, and, to a lesser extent, in the rules of procedure they impose, arguing that while these rules seem not to impede the effective handling of legitimate human rights grievances for the most part, the generality and vagueness of the procedural terminology allow for potential manipulation in our "Kafkaesque world."]

CONCLUSION

Once the three regional regimes declare a human rights grievance admissible, the initial procedures followed are quite similar, particularly insofar as individual and other private petitions are concerned. Each commission conducts fact-finding and attempts to achieve a friendly settlement. If the attempts at friendly settlement are successful, each commission then prepares a report stating the facts and its findings for submission to the states concerned and to the regional organs designated by each governing instrument—to the Committee of Ministers and the Secretary General of the Council of Europe in the case of the European regime, to the OAS Secretary General in the case of the Inter-American regime and to the OAU Assembly of Heads of State and Government in the case of the African regime. If the commissions are unable to reach a friendly settlement, then, in the case of the European regime, the commission prepares and submits a similar report to the concerned states and the Committee of Ministers, with the right to make such "proposals" as the European Commission sees fit. In the case of the Inter-American regime, the Commission submits a similar report to the concerned states only, with the right to make such "proposals and recommendations" as the Inter-American Commission sees fit. And in the case of the African regime, the Commission submits a similar report again to the states concerned and to the OAU Assembly of Heads of State and Government, but this time with the right to make such "recommendations" as the African Commission deems useful. Additionally, under the European and Inter-American regimes, but not under the African regime (for lack of an appropriate tribunal), the states concerned and the respective commissions may refer a case to their respective regional courts for final adjudication and disposition. Under the European system, alternatively, the Committee of Ministers may consider and decide the case.

It is not the purpose of this [essay] to appraise each regional regime's efficiency in dealing with these grievance procedures—in processing the applications and in implementing the decisions reached relative to them. Of course, a thorough empirical study along these lines is very much in order. If bureaucratic or other inefficiency significantly marks the process of handling interstate complaints and private petitions, then certainly the effectiveness of the human rights regime in handling human rights grievances will be open to serious question. But in exploring these issues we are limited by the infancy of the African regime and by the relative inexperience of the Inter-American regime under the American Convention; also, in general, by a dearth of readily available probative data.

Still, by way of conclusion, some general statistical data drawn from the experience of the oldest of the regional human rights regimes—the European—may prove insightful even though [they] lack clarity in a number of respects. Of the 34,015 private petitions filed with the European Commission during the period 1973 to 1986 (supplementing 18 inter-state complaints filed with the Commission during the same period), the Commission registered only 12,327 (or about one-third) and declared only 492 of these to be admissible. Later rejecting eight on the merits, the Commission reported to the Committee of Ministers in 310 of these 492 cases. In addition, as of January 1, 1986, the European Court had heard 109 cases, one of them an inter-state case.

On the basis of th[ese] data, one surely can say that the European regime has been genuinely recepptive to processing human rights grievances, both private and inter-state—so receptive, indeed, that it now suffers in effectiveness from an "unprecedented" backlog of cases such that "the time presently needed . . . to examine an [individual] application as to its admissibility and merits is often more than five years."[24] In addition, however, it seems fair to conclude that the European regime has been either extraordinarily diligent in winnowing out defective claims or, mindful of its statist origins, unduly conservative in defining valid ones. Possibly it has been both. In any event, bearing in mind that statist imperatives often tend to outweigh the values of human dignity even in modern-day Europe, 492 admissible claims out of 34,015 filed and 12,327 registered over a thirteen-year period (or about 1% and 4% respectively) seems not an impressive record from a progressive point of view. On the other hand, informed commentators have said that the European regime has significantly affected the promotion and protection of human rights in the European context—by upholding the rights of individuals, by influencing States Parties and by providing a model upon which the other two regional systems could draw.

Likewise, one may congratulate the Inter-American regime for its efforts to promote and protect rights. While its statistical data [are] difficult to secure, informed observers conclude that it has been by and large successful in pressing states to protect individual rights and in influencing countries to change patterns of abuses. Former President of the Inter-American Commission Tom Farer explains the Commission's subtle yet important influence in Argentina:

In the Argentine case the Commission's very presence seemed to have opened doors and wndows hitherto closed primarily to the Argentine people themselves. The press suddenly discovered the problem of the disappeared. A few judges began, albeit very cautiously, to probe behind official assurances and to question the comprehensiveness and intensity of restrictions on personal freedom.[25]

One must note, however, that Farer is speaking of the Commission in its capacity as an organ of the OAS as opposed to the American Convention. And on this critical distinction, former President of the Inter-American Court, Judge Buergenthal,

writing in 1987, had the following to say:

The entry into force of the American Convention has permitted the existence side-by-side of the juridically more formal Convention system with that of the more flexible [OAS] Charter-based system, giving the Commission and Court many more institutional tools for dealing with human rights violations than are available in other human rights systems. The individual petition machinery of the inter-American system has been a complete failure. Individual cases appear to get lost in a system that is geared to large-scale violations. In part that is due to the fact that the Commission treats individual petitions under the Convention in much the same way as those that come in under the Declaration. By blurring the juridical differences that exist between these two types of petitions, the Commission has failed to take advantage of the greater powers it has under the Convention to dispose of complaints.[26]

Buergenthal added: "The petition system consequently still operates as it did before the Convention entered into force, which may explain, but certainly not excuse, the fact that no contentious case has as yet been referred to the Court by the Commission."[27]

Thus, the regional human rights regimes, including the African regime which has only recently come into operation, undergo a continuous process of criticism and refinement, appraisal and recommendation. Many commentators have suggested normative, institutional and procedural adjustments necessary to make the three regional regimes more effective—for example: *in the case of the European regime*, placing individual petitions on the same mandatory footing as inter-state complaints, permitting access to non-victims representatives as well as to victims and merging the European Commission and Court; *in the case of the Inter-American regime*, placing inter-state complaints on the same mandatory footing as individual petitions and exploiting the full authority of the Inter-American Commission under the American Convention; *in the case of the African regime*, creating a court, narrowing the derogation clauses of the African Charter and de-politicizing

---

24. European Commission of Human Rights, Council of Europe, Survey of Activities and Statistics 2 (Strasbourg: Council of Europe, 1986). In the face of this situation, brought about in part by a failure to secure "an adequate increase of staff in the budget for 1987," the European Commission was forced to cancel two of the four additional week-long sessions it had hoped to add in 1987 to its normal five two-week sessions to address the backlog problem. Ibid.
25. Tom J. Farer, "OAS at the Crossroads: Human Rights," *Iowa Law Review* 72 (1987): 401, 402.
26. Buergenthal, *Implementation*, 75.
27. Ibid. As of this writing, three contentious cases are before the Inter-American Court.

the activities of the African Commission; *in the case of both the European and Inter-American regimes*, raising the standing of individuals at the court level, expending more energy to urge Member States to accept the full extent of the jurisdiction of the commissions and the courts, and narrowing the interpretation of the derogation clauses in both of the conventions; and *in the case of all three regimes*, raising the requirements for the promotion and protection of economic, social and cultural rights.

Hopefully the international legal community will act on these recommendations without delay especially those that seek to enhance accessibility and reduce the problems of admissibility. Though "[d]ecent, pluralistic societies cannot be built in a day,"[28] the regional promotion and protection of human rights [are] perhaps the most effective vehicle for advancing the cause of human dignity worldwide. They deserve, therefore, maximum responsible attention and encouragement.

QUESTIONS FOR REFLECTION AND DISCUSSION

1. Burns Weston et al. suggest that the regional approach to human rights protection offers opportunities for the effective enforcement of human rights sometimes not available on the global level. Why? What are they?

2. At around the time of its founding, the United Nations questioned the development of regional human rights regimes. Why might it have done so? What role, if any, should the United Nations now play in the development of regional human rights regimes? Might it assist in the development of regional implementation machinery in the Middle East and Asia? If so, how? What factors are or might be impeding the establishment of human rights regimes in these regions at the present time?

3. How do the European, Inter-American, and African human rights regimes differ? How different are they in their origins and what effect did their different origins have in their definition and development? What surrounding conditions or factors have given them shape and how?

4. What are the strengths of the three regional human rights regimes? What are their weaknesses? What factors contribute to the effectiveness of each? To the weakness of each? What steps should be taken to increase their effectiveness? What steps are realistic?

5. The on-site study technique, by which human rights commissions and working groups investigate alleged human rights abuses on or near location, has been important in the Inter-American system. Why might this be the case? Why, as it happens, has it not been utilized in the European context? Might it be a useful procedure under the African Charter? Is it likely to be used in the African context? Why? Why not?

6. Currently, the European and American human rights conventions do not include definitions of, and protective enforcement mechanisms for, economic, social, and cultural rights. Should these rights be protected and refined using the mechanisms already established for the protection and refinement of civil and political rights? Why? Why not? What are the most effective means for the protection of "second generation" or, for that matter, "third generation" rights? How does the African system proceed in this regard?

7. What do the "duties" outlined in the American Declaration and the African Charter entail? Why are duties not included in the European Convention? Should they be? How are duties enforced? If you conclusion is that they are unenforceable, then why were they included?

8. As Weston et al. observe, the right of individual petition is available automatically under the American Convention (Art. 44), but only against states making a declaration to this effect under the European Convention (Art. 25). They note also that, under the American Convention (Art. 45), state-to-state complaints may be presented only if the states involved have made declarations recognizing such competence but that, under the European Convention (Art. 24), such competence is conferred automatically. Why do the two conventions take reversed positions as to these two enforcement techniques? Why does the later African

---

28. Tom J. Farer, *Grand Strategy of the United States in Latin America* (New Brunswick, N.J.: Transaction Books, 1988) 174.

Charter (Arts. 47–48 and 55–56) assume an automatic approach in each instance? Is the automatic approach, which surely should generate more business, therefore the better of the two?

9. Weston et al. make the point that neither the European nor the American human rights convention allows the individual direct access to the courts. Asks Frederic L. Kirgis, Jr. (*International Organizations in Their Legal Setting* [St. Paul, Minn.: West Publishing Co., 1977], 912): "Given the willingness of states that become parties to the American Convention to subject themselves to individual petitions submitted to the Inter-American Commission, why should they balk at giving individuals standing [i.e., legal competence] to refer cases to the Court after an adverse Commission decision?" Why, indeed? In fact, why should not the individual have standing in international law generally?

10. Article 53 of the European Convention provides that the states parties will "undertake to abide by the decision of the [European] Court in any case to which they are parties." Article 68(1) of the American Convention says essentially the same thing relative to the Inter-American Court. The fact is, however, that the European and Inter-American courts are reduced to reliance upon voluntary compliance or international pressures to achieve the implementation of their decisions. Does this fact reduce the effectiveness of the European and Inter-American courts? Their stature? How does the United States Supreme Court enforce its judgments?

11. Why has the United States not become a party to the American Convention? Is it likely ever to become a party? If so, what preconditions will be required? If not, why not?

17. A. H. ROBERTSON *The Helsinki Agreement and Human Rights*

This [essay] will consider the provisions concerning human rights in the Helsinki Agreement of 1975 and the developments to which they have given rise. . . .

THE FINAL ACT OF THE HELSINKI CONFERENCE

The Conference on Security and Cooperation in Europe was formally opened at Helsinki on July 3, 1973; continued at Geneva from September 18, 1973, to July 21, 1975; and concluded at Helsinki on August 1, 1975. The 35 participants included all the states of Eastern and Western Europe, except Albania, and also the United States and Canada. The Holy See and the three "ministates" of Liechtenstein, Monaco, and San Marino participated on a basis of equality with the U.S. and the U.S.S.R.

The final Helsinki session was attended by the heads of state or of government of nearly all the participating States including President Valéry Giscard d'Estaing, Chancellor Helmut Schmidt, Premier Leonid Brezhnev, Prime Minister Harold Wilson, and President Gerald Ford. The final agreement, which was signed on August 1, 1975, included four sections relating to questions of security in Europe; cooperation in the fields of economics, science and technology, and the environment; cooperation in humanitarian and other fields; and the "follow-up" to the conference.

One should note at the outset that the final act of the conference is not a treaty, but a declaration of intentions. The Helsinki final act does not use the standard formulation for a treaty. Rather it states, "The High Representatives of the participating States have solemnly adopted the following." It then continues, "The participating States will respect each other's sovereign equality . . ."; "The participating States regard as inviolable all one another's frontiers . . ."; "The participating States will respect the territorial integrity of each of the participating States"; and so on. . . .

The fact that it is not a treaty does not mean that the Helsinki final act is unimportant. But a failure to understand that it is something less than a treaty and does not establish legal obligations would lead to confusion—perhaps even to acrimony. Most people would agree that the final act sets out moral, and no doubt political, obligations of states, but these obligations are not binding in international law. As a result, it is inaccurate, from a legal point of view, to speak of the "Helsinki Agreement." But since this expression has come into common use and is more manageable than the "Final Act of the Conference on Security and Cooperation in Europe," there is no harm in adopting it, so long as it is understood that the word "Agreement" is used in its popular, not legal, sense.

The second point to be noted is that the final act is concerned principally with international security and relations between states. For various reasons it was impossible to conclude a peace treaty after the end of World War II. During the period of the Cold War it was evident that formulation of a mutually satisfactory definition of relations between East and West remained an impossibility. But after some years of "détente" and of the new "Ostpolitik" of Chancellor Willi Brandt, the agreement between the two Germanies and the admission of both to the United Nations, some new arrangements for "peaceful coexistence" between East and West finally seemed possible. For years the Soviet Union had been seeking recognition by the other powers of its western frontiers as established after the end of the war, and Brezhnev had made this recognition a central issue of his foreign policy. After much hesitation the Western powers agreed to the holding of a Conference on Security and Cooperation in Europe, even though many people in the West feared that, while the Soviet Union had much to gain from the recognition of its frontiers, there was little that the Western powers were likely to receive in return. They had no territorial claims to make (except for the Germans, who knew in advance that the reunification of Germany was not to be expected), and they recognized that any fundamental political changes in the Eastern countries in the direction of liberalization were to be excluded. Nonetheless, the Western nations tried to obtain certain modest concessions in regard to freedom of movement and of information between East and West. Such concessions, it was thought, might be the beginning of a gradual liberalization of authoritarian regimes.

The third preliminary point concerns the human rights provisions of the final act. Since the latter act deals with relations between and interests of states, the provisions concerning human rights do not seek to protect the individual as such. The interests of individuals are rather subordinated to reasons of state. The final act does not follow the method of the Universal Declaration or of the U.N. covenants in providing that "everyone has the right to" a number of fundamental rights and freedoms. Rather, it provides that "the participating States will respect human rights and fundamental freedoms." Thus, in accordance with the whole philosophy of the final act, it is the action of states which is envisaged rather than the situation or behavior of individuals as such.

The first three sections of the actual text of the final act are commonly known as three "baskets." It is widely believed that the third basket contains the provisions concerned with human rights, but this assumption is a mistake. More important to a consideration of human rights is Basket One, which begins with a "Declaration on Principles Guiding Relations Between Participating States." This declaration sets out ten fundamental principles:

1. Sovereign equality and respect for the rights inherent in sovereignty.
2. Refraining from the threat or use of force.
3. Inviolability of frontiers.
4. Territorial integrity of states.
5. Peaceful settlement of disputes.
6. Non-intervention in internal affairs.
7. Respect for human rights and fundamental freedoms, including freedom of thought, conscience, religion, or belief.
8. Equal rights and self-determination of peoples.
9. Cooperation among states.
10. Fulfilment in good faith of obligations under international law.

Each of these principles is explained in some detail in the final act. It is perhaps significant that the principle concerning human rights and fundamental freedoms has an eight-paragraph explanatory text. This text . . . makes four principal points. First, "the participating States will respect human rights and fundamental freedoms"; freedom of thought, conscience, religion or belief are mentioned specifically. Second, the participating states promise to "promote and encourage the effective exercise of civil, political, economic, social, cultural, and other rights and freedoms." It is important to note that while this affirmative statement relates to human rights and fundamental freedoms in general, it does not specify expressly those rights and freedoms to which it applies, except for freedom of thought, conscience, religion or belief. It is significant that the very widely drawn reference to "civil, political, economic, social, cultural and other rights and freedoms" is preceded by the words "promote and encourage." Thus the participating states agree to a considerably weaker statement than would be a promise to "respect" these rights and freedoms. It recalls Articles 1(3) and 55 of the U N Charter, which by speaking of "promoting and encouraging respect" for human rights and fundamental freedoms contain an expression of intention for the future without an immediate obligation.

The third principal point to note in the text is that it contains a statement that the participating states will respect the rights of national minorities; the text thus recalls Article 27 of the Covenant on Civil and Political Rights. The fourth point is that there are two references in the text to the human rights work of the United Nations. The sixth paragraph—which states that the participating states will endeavor "jointly and separately, including in cooperation with the United Nations, to promote universal and effective respect" for these rights and freedoms—substantially repeats Article 56 of the charter. Finally, in the eighth paragraph, the participating states assert that they "will act in accordance with the purposes and principles of the Charter of the United Nations and with the Universal Declaration of Human Rights." This paragraph refers specifically to the states' "*obligations* as set forth in the international declarations and agreements in this field, including *inter alia* the International Covenants on Human Rights, by which they may be bound."

To summarize, then, it is evident that the "Declaration on Principles Guiding Relations Between Participating States" includes respect for human rights among its basic principles, alongside such other principles as the inviolability of frontiers, the peaceful settlement of disputes, and refraining from the use or threat of force. The seventh principle in the final act is wide in scope, because its second paragraph refers to the effective exercise of all categories of rights and freedoms, but it is also limited in effect because (like the Charter itself) it contains expressions of intention to "promote" and "encourage" rather than affirmative statements of a determination to "respect" human rights. In addition, some of its provisions would appear to be tautologous, as reaffirming existing obligations. However, this is not a criticism, since the constant reaffirmation of the obligation to respect human rights may help to impress that obligation more indelibly in the conscience of both governments and the general public.

It is now time to examine the third basket. (It is not necessary for the purpose of this essay to consider Basket Two, which sets out a series of measures relating to commercial exchanges, industrial cooperation, science and technology, and the environment.) The contents of Basket Three can be summarized briefly. Entitled "Cooperation in Humanitarian and Other Fields," Basket Three contains four sections. The first relates to "human contacts" and deals inter alia with reunification of families, marriages between citizens of different states, travel, tourism, meetings of young people, and sports activities. The second section—which would be of great importance for the future if effectively implemented—concerns the free flow of information. The participating states "make it their aim to facilitate the freer and wider dissemination of information of all kinds" and set out a number of steps to be taken for this purpose relating severally to oral, printed, filmed and broadcast information. The steps to be taken include measures "to facilitate the improvement of the dissemination on their territory of newspapers and printed publications . . . from the other participating States" and measures "to improve the conditions under which journalists from one . . . State exercise their profession in another." Finally, Basket Three contains two short sections about cooperation and exchanges in the fields of culture and education.

POST-HELSINKI DEVELOPMENTS

The signature of the Final Act of the Conference on Security and Cooperation in Europe was much more widely acclaimed and its contents more widely publicized in the East than in the West. This fact is not surprising. The Soviet Union had a greater interest in the successful conclusion of the conference, because the final act constituted an official acceptance by the West of the territorial acquisitions of the USSR during World

War II. What had been agreed by three powers at Yalta—and a good deal more than that—had now been accepted as permanent 30 years later by the whole of Europe, plus the United States and Canada. This was a real achievement for Soviet diplomacy. . . .

The publicity given to the final act led many people to believe that its provisions on human rights would be implemented and that an era of liberalization was about to begin. The well informed knew that all the East European states also had ratified the U.N. covenants and thus accepted binding obligations in international law to respect human rights. With these two significant developments, it was hardly surprising that politically conscious individuals began to expect their governments to allow a freer flow of information and greater liberty of expression—even if they were not so foolhardy as to expect the right to form a political opposition.

The most striking example of this new spirit was in Czechoslovakia; there nearly 500 intellectuals and others subscribed early in 1977 to a human rights manifesto which they called "Charter 77." The manifesto takes as its point of departure the ratification by Czechoslovakia and the publication in the "Czechoslovak Register of Laws" on October 13, 1976, of the two U.N. Covenants on Human Rights and the reaffirmation of the covenants in the final act of the Helsinki Conference. "Charter 77" welcomes accession to those agreements but also continues: "Their publication, however, serves as a powerful reminder of the extent to which basic human rights in our country exist, regrettably, on paper alone." A series of examples [is] then given of various rights which have been proclaimed and protected by the covenants but, in fact, are systematically violated in Czechoslovakia. These rights include freedom of expression, freedom of information, freedom of religion, freedom of association, the right to form trade unions, the right to privacy, and the right to emigrate freely.

"Charter 77" is not an organization and expressly states that it does not form the basis for a political opposition. Rather, its subscribers seek to conduct a constructive dialogue with the political and state authorities, just as many nongovernmental organizations do in democratic countries. The signatories authorized three of their number to act as spokesmen; the first of these was Jan Patocka.

The repressive measures taken against the signatories of "Charter 77" have been widely reported in the press. . . . Eleven signatories of the charter, all ousted members of the Central Committee of the Czechoslovak Communist Party, . . . appealed to other European communist parties to protest against this repression, insisting that the government's actions gravely discredit socialism not only in Czechoslovakia but in the whole of Europe.

"Charter 77" has, in fact, evoked considerable support in other Eastern European countries. In Yugoslavia, Milovan Djilas, a former leader of the Communist Party, . . . appealed to West European communist parties to support the charter and the movement for human rights not only in Czechoslovakia but also in his own country where, he [said], on a proportional basis there are as many political prisoners as in the Soviet Union. Repercussions also have been observed in East Germany, in Poland, and in Romania, where the writer Paul Goma, who led the movement for the observance of the Helsinki provision, was arrested.

But the most important reaction to the Helsinki Agreement was no doubt that in the Soviet Union itself. A committee under the chairmanship of Yuri Orlov was established to supervise its application; the detention of Alexander Ginzberg . . . led to the signature of a manifesto by 248 supporters; and Andrei Sakharov, who formed the Soviet Committee on Human Rights nearly ten years ago, . . . continued his struggle in unprecedented fashion, including an American television interview, a personal letter to President Carter, and a letter to all the heads of State or of government who signed the final act. President Carter replied to Sakharov's letter, "You may be assured that the American people and our government will maintain their firm engagement to promote respect for human rights not only in our country but also abroad." Vladimir Boukovsky, who was exiled from the Soviet Union in December 1976 after serving 12 years in prison, in an exchange for the Chilean communist leader Luis Corvalan, was received by President Carter in February 1977 and testified to a Congressional committee that none of the human rights provisions of the Helsinki Agreement [were] being respected in the U.S.S.R. In February 1977, Andrei Amalrik, a dissident historian exiled in 1976, solicited an interview with President Giscard d'Estaing of France which was refused, but Amalrik spoke to the press in Paris as a representative of the committee on the application of the Helsinki Agreement.

Similar developments continued in 1978. Yuri Orlov, after a trial from which all Western observers and Andrei Sakharov were excluded, was condemned to seven years in a labor camp and five years' exile. This led to a protest from 500 nuclear physicists at the European Organization for Nuclear Research in Geneva, calling for a suspension of collaboration with the Soviet Union until he should be liberated. Another human rights worker, Anatoli Shcharansky, suffered prolonged detention awaiting trial on a charge of treason, for which he risked the death penalty.

This brief—and necessarily incomplete—summary of . . . well-known developments paints the broad outlines of a picture of the contemporary scene and shows that the Helsinki Agreement—or, more specifically, its human rights provisions—[has] had an effect. In Eastern Europe the impact has surpassed the expectations of some of its authors; in the communist world, reaction to the agreement highlights the fact that its human rights principles remain largely a dead letter in those countries. What is new is that the Helsinki texts have been widely publicized in Eastern European countries and that this publicity has given new courage to those who are prepared to fight for their rights.

Still another new factor is the reaction to the agreement in the West, particularly that of the President of the United States. The Soviet Union has retorted that this Western reaction constitutes an improper interference in its internal affairs, which in itself is contrary to the Helsinki Agreement . . . , [a] point of view [that] cannot and should not be dismissed out of hand. The sixth principle in the "Declaration on Principles Guiding Relations Between Participating States" . . . concerns non-intervention in internal affairs. This principle states in part:

The participating States will refrain from any intervention, direct or indirect, individual or collective, in the internal or external affairs falling within the domestic jurisdiction of another participating State, regardless of their mutual relations.

Therefore, it is necessary to ask whether acts such as President Carter's letter to Andrei Sakharov [or] the testimony of Vladimir Boukovsky before a Congressional committee . . . constitute an "intervention, direct or indirect . . . in the internal . . . affairs falling within the domestic jurisdiction" of the Soviet Union.[1] This evokes the question . . . of the repeated attempts of Western and other states to introduce a procedure that would permit the U N Commission to consider complaints of violation of human rights and the equally repeated objection of the USSR that such action would violate Article 2, Paragraph 7, of the charter, which prohibits the United Nations from intervening "in matters which are essentially within the domestic jurisdiction of any State."

The problem of the meaning and effect of this provision of the U N Charter is as old as the United Nations itself. Since the same problem arises in relation to the Helsinki Agreement, it seems appropriate to summarize the issues involved at this point. . . .

Until 1945 international law considered that the manner in which a state treated its own nationals was, except in very unusual circumstances when humanitarian intervention was permitted, a question within its own jurisdiction and competence and one with which other states had no right to intervene. To illustrate this attitude, the late René Cassin often cited Goebbels's address to the Council of the League of Nations in which the latter asserted that the way in which the German government treated certain categories of German citizens was the concern of the German government alone. However morally reprehensible Goebbels's attitude may have been, it could be justified legally at the time.

Since that time, however, the legal position has changed. Matters in which states have accepted obligations in international law have ceased to be questions solely within their domestic jurisdiction. The unfettered rule of national sovereignty no longer applies. Other states that have accepted such obligations have a legitimate interest in seeing that the common undertakings are respected. The mere fact that these undertakings may relate to the maintenance by a state of the human rights of its own citizens does

---

1. An American proposal to the UN Commission on Human Rights requesting that the Soviet government provide information "about recent reports of arrests and detention in the U.S.S.R. of persons who have been active in the cause of promoting human rights" had to be withdrawn in the face of a countermotion by Bulgaria not to discuss the American proposal.

not justify a derogation from the fundamental rule of international law: *Pacta sunt servanda*. This reasoning provides the legal basis for President Carter's statement to the United Nations on March 17, 1977, in which he said:

The search for peace and justice means also respect for human dignity. All the signatories of the U N Charter have pledged themselves to observe and respect basic human rights. Thus, no member of the United Nations can claim that mistreatment of its citizens is solely its own business. Equally, no member can avoid its responsibilities to react and to speak when torture or unwarranted deprivation of freedom occurs in any part of the world.

The same basic argument applies in relation to the final act of the Helsinki conference. Although this agreement is not a treaty enshrining obligations under international law, it does contain firm expressions of intention to which particular solemnity was attached in an essentially political context. Consequently, each participating state is entitled to expect that every other participant will honor its word.

QUESTIONS FOR REFLECTION AND DISCUSSION

1. The Helsinki Final Act is not a treaty. How, then, can it be said to have any binding force and effect? Would it be any more effective if it had been made a treaty in the first place?

2. The U.S. Congress responded to the signing of the Helsinki Final Act by establishing the U.S. Commission on Security and Cooperation in Europe (CSCE Commission). (See Foreign Relations Authorization Act, 22 U.S.C. Sec. 3001–8 [1976].) The United States was, in fact, the only signatory state to establish an official governmental body to implement provisions of the Final Act (although subsequently the United States and other states did create private oversight groups: "Helsinki Monitors"). In any event, the Foreign Relations Authorization Act directed the Commission to (a) monitor the acts of the signatories which reflect compliance with, or violations of, the Final Act, with special regard to provisions bearing upon cooperation in humanitarian fields, and (b) monitor and encourage the development of programs and activities of the U.S. government and private organizations with a view to expanding East-West economic cooperation and cultural interchange. What reasons might explain why the United States is the only signatory of the Helsinki Final Act to have established an active and viable governmental oversight body?

3. Since its establishment in 1976, the CSCE Commission has become one of the two principal congressional bodies concerned with human rights, the other being the House Subcommittee on Human Rights and International Organizations (established initially to oversee the work of the United Nations following U.S. ratification of the UN Charter). Each body has had an important hand in shaping U.S. human rights foreign policy, but the influence of the CSCE Commission over the years is understood to have been greater than that of the House subcommittee. Writes Margaret Galey in "Congress, Foreign Policy and Human Rights Ten Years After Helsinki" (*Human Rights Quarterly* 7 [1985], 334–72, at 371):

> While the Carter and Reagan Administrations have implemented human rights policy differently—the former using public diplomacy and the latter quiet diplomacy, the CSCE Commission and the Subcommittee have made a difference in United States foreign policy by raising human rights concerns, airing the issues, and seeking influence on Administration [policy]. . . .
>
> The CSCE Commission . . . has coordinated human rights policy over the last eight years with the Executive Branch. . . . As for the Subcommittee, it has always had less influence on Administration policy.

What might explain the CSCE Commission's influential role in shaping US human rights policy—indeed, a role more influential than that of the older House Subcommittee on Human Rights and International Organizations?

4. Is resort to a highly politicized mechanism like the Helsinki process more desirable or less desirable than utilizing the human rights machinery of the United Nations? What does an agreement such as the Helsinki Final Act permit that the more institutionalized UN procedures do not, and vice versa?

5. In 1980, in response to the Soviet invasion of Afghanistan and under pressure from their governments, the national Olympic committees (NOCs) of many Western and Western-aligned countries boycotted the Moscow Olympic Games. They did so on the theory that one should not participate in the Olympic Games, which are aimed at the promotion of world peace, in a country that recently committed an aggressive act. All this took place, however, in the context of the 1975 Helsinki Final Act which contains in its "Third Basket," relative to cooperation in humanitarian and other fields, a provision on international sporting contacts:

> In order to expand existing links and co-operation in the field of sport the participating States will encourage contacts and exchanges of this kind, including sports meetings and competitions of all sorts, on the basis of the established international rules, regulations and practice.

How is the boycott of the 1980 Moscow Olympic Games to be assessed from the point of view of the Helsinki Final Act? In "The Boycott of the 1980 Moscow Olympic Games and Detente" (*Essays on Human Rights in the Helsinki Process*, ed. A. Bloed and P. Van Dijk [1985] 181–201, at 197), Rob Siekmann ponders this question:

> In my view, the appeal of the American and other governments to boycott the Games is in conflict with the paragraph on sport, which implies that the participating States will not discourage any contacts in the field of sport. However, I do consider that the appeal was totally justified as a reaction to "Afghanistan," a violation of almost the entire Decalogue [of "principles guiding relations between participating States"] and, unlike the non-implementation of the paragraph on sport, a violation of international law. . . . [Yet] it is submitted here that only reasons of principle relating to sport can be a justification for a sport boycott, at least from the perspective of the sporting world. Racial discrimination in sport is an example of this type of reason. In the case under discussion, the NOCs need only have considered whether the Olympic Games could take place normally as a sporting event and an opportunity for young sportsmen of the world to meet in a spirit of better understanding between each other and of friendship, notwithstanding "Afghanistan." Personally, I would have answered this question affirmatively.

In Siekmann's view, was the boycott a violation of the Helsinki Final Act? Of international law? Of international morality? What is your view? Should sports be a part of the struggle over international human rights? Why? Why not?

7. Before Secretary Gorbachev established his "glasnost" policy, the Reagan administration continuously charged that the Soviet Union was not to be trusted because it was a mendacious state, a breaker of treaties, a nation run by "unprincipled thugs" who believe that legal promises are like fences—made to be climbed. In support of this viewpoint, the Reagan administration alleged Soviet violations of, among other things, the Helsinki Final Act. Did such allegations support a valid argument? Why? Why not?

SELECT BIBLIOGRAPHY

Bloed, A. and Pieter Van Dijk, eds. *Essays on Human Rights in the Helsinki Process*. Boston: Kluever Inc., 1985. Essays written by the Dutch Helsinki Group examine the status of the "Third Basket" concerning human rights at the conclusion of the Madrid talks (1980–83).

Buergenthal, Thomas A., ed. *Human Rights, International Law and the Helsinki Accord*. Montclair, N.Y.: Allanheld Osman/Universe Books, 1977. Essays produced by a conference concerned with such questions as the nature of the obligations undertaken by the Helsinki signatories, the problem of "domestic jurisdiction," and the effect of the accord on the concept of "self-determination."

Buergenthal, Thomas A., Robert Norris, and Dinah Shelton-Kehl. *Protecting Human Rights in the Americas*. Strasbourg: Engel, 1982. A systematic review of the human rights provisions of the Inter-American instruments and a detailed analysis of the institutions (in San José, Costa Rica) designed to implement the norms adopted by the Inter-American regional system.

Cassesse, Antonio, ed. *UN Law/Fundamental Rights*. Alphen van den Rijn, Netherlands: Sijthoff and Noordhoff, 1979. A wide-ranging collection of articles on such topics as the Third World's response to human rights violations, multinational corporations, and nongovernmental organizations as participants in the development of international norms.

Haas, Ernest B. *Human Rights and International Action: The Case of Freedom of Association.* Stanford, Calif.: Stanford University Press, 1970. Examines cases brought before the International Labor Organization to assess, by the standards of "functional" theory, the impact the UN machinery has on the evolution of a world consensus on human rights.

Hannum, Hurst, ed. *Guide to International Human Rights Practice.* Philadelphia: University of Pennsylvania Press, 1984. An introduction to human rights procedures for the international law generalist, surveying the practice of human rights from the lodging of complaints by individuals to institutional standards setting and protection.

Joyce, J. A. *The New Politics of Human Rights.* London: Macmillan, 1978. Describes the new international law and international organizations that seek to impose limits on the treatment of individuals deprived of their liberty; focuses on international politics affecting specific cases (Chile under Pinochet, decolonization in North Africa) and issues (science and technology, the right to peace).

Kavass, Igor I., Jacqueline P. Granier, and Mary Frances Dominick, eds. *Human Rights, European Politics and the Helsinki Accord: The Documentary Evolution of the Conference on Security and Cooperation in Europe, 1973–75.* 3 vols. Buffalo: Hein and Co., 1981. A selective collection of the discussion and working papers leading to the Helsinki Accords, including some verbatim records of speeches and debates; assembled at Vanderbilt University School of Law.

LeBlanc, L. T. *The OAS and the Promotion and Protection of Human Rights.* The Hague: Martinus Nijhoff Publishers, 1977. Analyzes and describes the origins and organization of the Inter-American Commission on Human Rights and offers several case studies of the Commission's work in Brazil, Chile, Cuba, and the Dominican Republic.

Lerner, Nathan. *The UN Convention on the Elimination of All Forms of Racial Discrimination.* 2d ed. Alphan van den Rijn, Netherlands: Sijthoff and Noordhoff, 1980. A concise commentary on the convention, and a ten-year review of the UN Committee on the Elimination of Racial Discrimination and the techniques it used to scrutinize the progress of states parties.

Ramcharan, B. G. *Humanitarian Good Offices in International Law.* The Hague: Martinus Nijhoff Publishers, 1983. The legal, organizational and conceptual bases for the UN Secretary-General to play a "good office" role (i.e., the cooperative rendering of services) in human rights cases, such as were involved with Indochinese "boat people" and American hostages in Iran, are explored.

Ramcharan, B. G., ed. *International Law and Fact-Finding in the Field of Human Rights.* The Hague: Martinus Nijhoff Publishers, 1982. A practitioner's guide to the technical issues, principles, and problems involved in compiling information about human rights violations; treats fact-finding by both international governmental and nongovernmental organizations.

Robertson, A. H. *Human Rights in the World: An Introduction to the Study of the International Protection of Human Rights.* 2d ed. Manchester: Manchester University Press, 1982. A beginner's introduction to international concern for human rights and the international and regional organizations that seek to protect them, written by the former Director of Human Rights of the Council of Europe (1962–73).

The United Nations and Human Rights. New York: United Nations Office of Public Information, 1984. A descriptive survey of the more than fifty detailed declarations and conventions dealing with human rights and the numerous UN organs that currently devote time and resources to human rights questions.

van Boven, Theo. C. *People Matter.* Amsterdam: Menlankoff, 1982. The poignant views on international human rights policy of the one-time director of the United Nations Division of Human Rights (1977–82), pressured from his position by an "unholy alliance" of dictatorial governments, left and right.

Zuijdwijk, T. J. M. *Petitioning the United Nations. A Study in Human Rights.* New York: St. Martins Press, 1982. A historical description and analysis of the changing UN institutions and procedures open to individual and nongovernmental organization petitioners invoking international human rights law.

SELECT FILMOGRAPHY

Namibia: A Trust Betrayed. United Nations, producer. UN IL Films, 1974. 27 min., color; 16 mm. Namibia (previously known as South West Africa), rather than progressing toward independence, has been swallowed up into South Africa in defiance of the United Nations and the International Court of

Justice. Despite the termination of its mandate, South Africa refuses to relinquish the mineral-rich country. The South African system of apartheid has been applied in the territory, where ninety percent of the population is black.

A Worker's World. 20 min.; VHS. (Available on loan from the ILO office, 1750 New York Avenue NW, Suite 330, Washington, D.C. 20006, attention Technical Information Office.) The International Labor Organization, one of twelve Specialized Agencies related to the United Nations, is ordinarily concerned with social justice. The film explains the work of the ILO, including the development and enforcement of ILO conventions.

Chapter Five

National Approaches to Implementation

THE implementation of human rights is a responsibility of individual nations as well as of international institutions. Anchored in the many human rights treaties to which states have become party, in customary state practice, and in the general principles of law recognized by the world's different legal systems, it is a responsibility that is made explicit in the UN Charter.[1] According to Articles 55 and 56 of the Charter, all UN member states "pledge themselves to take joint and separate action in cooperation with the [United Nations]" to promote "universal respect for, and observance of, human rights and fundamental freedoms for all without distinction as to race, sex, language or religion."

One significant way in which this state responsibility for the promotion and protection of human rights is exercised is by the adoption of international human rights principles and standards in the national constitutions and basic laws that fix the structure of governments. Over one-third of all nations, especially those emerging from colonialism after World War II, have modeled their fundamental rights provisions on the Universal Declaration of Human Rights,[2] proclaimed by the UN General Assembly in 1948 as a "foundation for justice and peace in the world."[3] International human rights principles and standards thus have become not only a matter of constitutional obligation but, as well, a matter of increasingly universal expectation—a consequence that, over time, makes the goal of worldwide humane governance more than a utopian dream.

The new Philippines Constitution, promulgated on February 4, 1987, with the plebiscite support of 78% of Filipino voters, is a recent, much celebrated example of a government charter influenced by internationally articulated human rights principles and standards.[4] Drafted in an open assembly of diverse political parties and groups and replacing the constitution discredited by Ferdinand Marcos, under whose rule human rights abuses had become notorious and widespread,[5] the new constitution is noteworthy for its emphasis on civil liberties and principles of social justice drawn explicitly from internationally prescribed human rights instruments. Indeed, in the true spirit of Articles 55 and 56 of the UN Charter, the new constitution straightforwardly proclaims that the promotion of human rights is constitutionally required. "All educational institutions," it commands, "shall include the

---

1. See the Appendix.
2. See the Appendix.
3. See Egon Schwelb, "The Influence of the Universal Declaration of Human Rights on International and National Law," *Proceedings of 53d Annual Meeting of the American Society of International Law* (1959): 217–29 at 222–3; and *UN Seminar on the Experience of Different Countries in the Implementation of International Standards of Human Rights*, June 20–July 1, 1983, ST/HR/SER.A/15. See also John Humphrey, "The Universal Declaration of Human Rights: Its History, Impact and Juridical Character," in *Human Rights: Thirty Years after the Universal Declaration*, ed. B. G. Ramcharan (The Hague: Martinus Nijhoff Publishers, 1979), 21–40; and B. G. Ramcharan, "The Role of Regional, National and Local Institutions: Future Perspectives," in ibid., 233–48.
4. The Constitution of the Republic of the Philippines, adopted by plebiscite in February 1987. The constitution, as adopted by The [Filipino] Constitutional Commission of 1986 on October 12, 1986, is reproduced in Albert P. Blaustein and Gisbert H. Flanz, eds., *Constitutions of the Countries of the World* (Dobbs Ferry, N.Y.: Oceana Publications, 1986), Philippines Supplement.
5. See Richard P. Claude, "The Philippines," in *International Handbook of Human Rights*, ed. Jack Donnelly and Rhoda Howard (Boulder, Colo.: Westview Press, 1987), 279–99.

study of the Constitution . . . [and] shall . . . foster love of humanity, respect for human rights . . . and teach the rights and duties of citizenship."[6]

After 1971, when President Marcos declared martial law, habeas corpus and civil liberties were suspended in the Philippines on the theory that more rapid social and economic advances could be made in a "disciplined society." During the Marcos years, which lasted until Corazon Aquino displaced Marcos in 1986, government data on social indicators were frequently suspect, tending to justify martial law because of rigged statistics alleging year-by-year improvements in housing, education, health, and other basic needs.[7] To countermand such self-serving government fraud, the new constitution guarantees not only conventional freedoms of speech, press, and association but also the "right to information on matters of public concern," including access to "government research data used as the basis for policy development. . . ."[8] Nongovernmental groups monitoring policy thus are empowered to keep tabs on the government.

In addition, the Philippine Bill of Rights contains strong protective provisions against authoritarian rule and the abuses of personal security that were characteristic of the Marcos regime. It strictly prohibits arbitrary arrest by the military in the absence of a lawful court order.[9] Secret detention centers, which were widely used for torture-interrogation during the 1970s, are outlawed.[10] "Torture, force, violence, threat, intimidation or other means which violates the free will [of] any person under criminal investigation" is prohibited.[11] Also banned is the use of "physical, psychological or degrading or inadequate penal facilities under sub-human conditions,"[12] and the national legislature is instructed to provide for penal and civil sanctions for human rights offenders as well as "compensation and rehabilitation of victims of torture or similar practices, and of their families. . . ."[13]

Another section of the new constitution is devoted to social justice "to enhance the inalienable right to dignity."[14] Several provisions deal with land distribution and labor policy, agrarian and natural resource reforms, problems of the urban poor and housing, education, women, indigenous peoples, and "the people's right to health."[15] Health care is to be promoted through a comprehensive program that "shall make essential goods and social services available to all citizens at affordable cost, . . . with priority for the needs of the disadvantaged, sick, elderly, disabled, women and children."[16]

6. The Constitution of the Republic of the Philippines (see n. 4, above), art. 14, sec. 3(1)(2).
7. See Michael L. Tan, *The State of the Nation's Health* (Manila: Health Action Information Network, 1986), 6.
8. Constitution of the Republic of the Philippines, art. 3, sec. 7.
9. Ibid., art. 3, sec. 1.
10. Ibid., art. 3, sec. 2.
11. Ibid., art. 3, sec. 3.
12. Ibid., art. 3, sec. 12(2)(4).
13. Ibid., art. 3, sec. 19(1)(2). In the foregoing and related provisions, the Philippines Constitution became the first national charter to address fully all of Amnesty International's "12-Point Program for the Prevention of Torture" adopted by Amnesty International in October 1983 as part of its Campaign for the Abolition of Torture: (1) official condemnation of torture; (2) limits on incommunicado detention; (3) no secret detention; (4) safeguards during interrogation and custody; (5) independent investigation of reports of torture; (6) no use of statements extracted under torture; (7) prohibition of torture in law; (8) prosecution of alleged torturers; (9) training procedures; (10) compensation and rehabilitation; (11) international response mechanisms; and (12) ratification of international instruments. See Amnesty International, *Torture in the 80's* (London: Amnesty International Publications, 1984), 249–51.
14. Constitution of the Republic of the Philippines, art. 13, sec. 1.
15. Ibid., art. 13, sec. 3–14.
16. Ibid., art. 13, sec. 11.

Thus, the new Filipino constitution is explicit in its commitment to the implementation of human rights. "The State shall promote social justice in all phases of national development," it proclaims.[17] "The State values the dignity of every human person and guarantees full respect for human rights."[18] And to these ends, in addition to guaranteeing a broad spectrum of civil, political, economic, social, and cultural rights, the new constitution establishes a permanent Commission on Human Rights authorized to investigate complaints, to visit jails and prisons, to make recommendations to the Congress, and to organize a program of research and education so as "to enhance respect for the primacy of human rights."[19] In addition, in a novel provision, the Commission is ordered to "monitor the Philippine Government's compliance with international treaty obligations on human rights."[20]

The adoption of international human rights principles and standards in national constitutions and basic laws is of course only one way in which states exercise their responsibility for the promotion and protection of human rights. The effort to promote and protect human rights has become a permanent fixture of modern-day diplomacy and foreign policy as well. Indeed, in such countries as Canada, the Netherlands, Norway, and the United States, the promotion of international human rights has become the province not only of foreign policy-makers but also of legislators dealing with foreign assistance programs. Additionally, albeit still on a limited scale, international human rights are sought to be implemented by way of litigation in domestic courts. The essays in this chapter consider the national implementation of human rights in terms of the conduct of foreign policy generally, unilateral humanitarian intervention, legislative implementation, and judicial enforcement.

FOREIGN POLICY

Before the election of President Carter in 1976, public discussion of human rights in Ferdinand Marcos's Philippines was suspect, as was all political talk. With the advent of Carter's human rights rhetoric in U.S.-Filipino diplomacy during the martial law years of the late 1970s, however, Filipinos became newly emboldened to question their government. As one attorney in Manila stated in 1977, "[s]ince so much can now be said and done in the name of 'human rights' which was previously forbidden, it is not surprising that there is much curiosity about these human rights."[21] Indeed, widespread concern about abuses of human rights was one of the decisive factors that finally tumbled the Marcos tyranny in 1986. There is thus good reason to believe that, during the Marcos years, the Carter administration's concern for human rights in the Philippines (and elsewhere) helped to make talk of human rights in the Philippines legitimate.

Verbal behavior in politics does seem to bring about small but significant changes. This is a point Richard Claude stressed in a 1979 essay wherein he argued that American diplomacy should be used to criticize the repressive practices of the Marcos regime.[22] Of course,

---

17. Ibid., art. 2, sec. 10.
18. Ibid., art. 2, sec. 11.
19. Ibid., art. 13, sec. 17(1)–(6).
20. Ibid., art. 13, sec. 17(7).
21. Richard P. Claude, "Human Rights in the Philippines and U.S. Responsibility," in *Human Rights and U.S. Foreign Policy: Principles and Applications,* ed. Peter G. Brown and Douglas MacLean (Lexington, Mass.: Lexington Books, 1979), 247.
22. Ibid., 229–54.

it is difficult to demonstrate that diplomacy that relies on "human rights talk" and raises popular expectations has any but indirect consequences. Evan Luard, however, a British political scientist with diplomatic experience in pressing for human rights, is more sanguine. In his wide-ranging essay in this chapter, he argues that, by relying on diplomacy to nudge regimes toward human rights compliance, there always is the possibility of direct as well as indirect positive consequences. Changes may be induced even within the government itself when officials who favor a more humane policy (partly because of its foreign policy effects) prevail to some extent over those who favor a repressive policy (some Filipino torturers under the repressive Marcos regime faced military disciplinary action, for example). Even if these direct effects are minimal and symbolic, Luard avers that "it is the international climate as a whole which will be altered by expressions of concern in such matters." Hopefully, the expectations that are placed on all members of the international community are slowly changed.

Luard's analysis of human rights diplomacy is taken a step further by R. J. Vincent, who argues that, in addition to the indirect and more obvious consequences of placing diplomacy in service to human rights, "[t]here is also a deeper sense in which human rights have arrived in foreign policy than that which observes the presence in foreign offices of desks bearing that title.[23] Vincent continues:

> Human rights now play a part in the decision about the legitimacy of a state (and of other actors and institutions) in international society, about whether what it is or what it does is sanctioned or authorized by law or right. It's not now enough for a state to be, and to be recognized as, sovereign. Nor is it enough for it to be a nation-state in accordance with the principle of self-determination. It must also act domestically, in such a way as not to offend against the basic rights of individuals and groups within its territory.[24]

Self-styled realists, on the other hand, dismiss interest in human rights worldwide as a short-term fad. William F. Buckley, Jr., for one, has called the promotion of human rights through foreign policy a kind of naive evangelism bound to founder on the rocks of international political realities,[25] although such skepticism seems belied by the long-term commitments that some governments clearly have made to institutionalize their human rights programs. As the American Association for the International Commission of Jurists has noted approvingly:

> In the United States, the office of Assistant Secretary of State for Human Rights and Humanitarian Affairs was established by an Act of Congress in 1974 and given responsibility for human rights that cannot be overridden by other officials with area responsibilities. In 1986, France created the office of Secretary of State for Human Rights, a ministerial post attached to the Prime Minister, with responsibility for both foreign and domestic human rights policy. Together with the Consultative Committee on Human

23. R. J. Vincent, *Human Rights and International Relations* (Cambridge: Cambridge University Press, 1986), 130. See also Tom J. Farer, ed., *Toward a Humanitarian Diplomacy* (New York: New York University Press, 1980); Natalie Kaufman Hevener, *The Dynamics of Human Rights in U.S. Foreign Policy* (New Brunswick, N.J.: Transaction Books, 1981); and David D. Newsom, *The Diplomacy of Human Rights* (Lanham, Md.: University Press of America, 1986).
24. Vincent, *Human Rights and International Relations*, 130.
25. William F. Buckley, Jr., "Human Rights and Foreign Policy: A Proposal," *Foreign Affairs* 58 (1980): 775–96. Cf. Michael Novak, *Human Rights and the New Realism, Strategic Thinking in a New Age* (New York: Freedom House, 1987). See also House Committee on Foreign Affairs, Subcommittee on Human Rights and International Organizations, *Hearings: Status of U.S. Human Rights Policy (1987)* 100th Cong., 1st sess., 1987.

Rights created in 1984 and attached to the Foreign Ministry, France has given institutional support and a political base for the development of human rights policy.[26]

Yet is it not true that shaping foreign policy often is made difficult by the inevitable tension between, on the one hand, demand for the independence of nations and, on the other hand, demand for the expansion of freedom and democracy? Noninterference can, in effect, be the equivalent of tolerating oppression; urging freedom and human rights upon others can create international tension.

Whether this dilemma is real or only apparent is a topic of ongoing debate in the United States and elsewhere, and the outcome is by no means clear. Former Secretary of State Henry A. Kissinger, who dominated foreign policy in the Nixon and Ford administrations, regularly argued against linking human rights issues with foreign policy decisions.[27] Kissinger said he supported human rights but that American commitments abroad had to be based not primarily upon moral judgments but upon a realistic assessment of national security priorities. According to Kissinger, neither public threats against violator-regimes nor "grandstand" condemnations of one country by another are likely to produce significant human rights gains. Moreover, neither the fact-finding machinery nor the criteria for judgment have been established whereby one country can confidently condemn another on human rights grounds. Human rights, Kissinger maintained, should be factored into foreign policy, if at all, by means of "quiet diplomacy."

The philosopher Henry Shue has criticized the Kissinger perspective and chastized the Reagan administration for lack of even-handed diplomacy in support of human rights:

> The bizarre notion has been promulgated by the Reagan administration that each government should be allowed to pick and choose among established human rights its own favorites and attend exclusively to those favored rights. This attempt at selective enforcement of human rights is authorized by a formal policy memorandum adopted by the Department of State on October 27, 1981, which states: "'Human rights'—meaning political rights and civil liberties—conveys what is ultimately at issue in a contest with the Soviet bloc. The fundamental distinction is our respective attitudes toward freedom. . . . We should move away from 'human rights' as a term, and begin to speak of 'individual rights,' 'political rights,' 'civil liberties.'"
>
> Such a narrowing of human rights to political rights and civil liberties would omit rights to physical security like the rights against torture and "disappearance" that are explicitly listed in the laws controlling U.S. foreign assistance. It also dismisses the third general category of internationally recognized human rights, the right to fulfillment of vital needs such as food, shelter, health care, and education. The supposition seems to be that a nation can simply focus upon the rights that are "at issue in a contest" with its principal adversary and relegate all the other rights to the periphery.[28]

According to Shue, the Reagan administration's selective use of diplomatic tools to ignore human rights violations among friendly authoritarian regimes was short-sighted and risked

---

26. American Association for the International Commission of Jurists, *Human Rights and Foreign Policy, The Role of Government, 1985 and 1986* (New York: American Association for the International Commission of Jurists, 1987), 11–12.

27. See Hugh M. Arnold, "Henry Kissinger and Human Rights," *Universal Human Rights* 2 (1980): 57–71.

28. Henry Shue, "Playing Hardball with Human Rights," *Report from the Center for Philosophy and Public Policy* 3, no. 4 (College Park, Md.: University of Maryland Center for Philosophy and Public Policy, 1983), 9–11, at 9. An expanded version of this article is "In the American Tradition, Rights Remain Unalienable," *The Center Magazine* 17, no. 1 (Santa Barbara, Calif.: Center for the Study of Democratic Institutions, 1984): 1–6, 17–34 (discussion).

long-term adverse consequences. By associating itself with repressive regimes, the United States eventually loses friends and support. "[I]t is not easy to cultivate the favor of the violators without incurring the hatred of the violated, who in many cases are likely to form the next government whenever it comes. . . . This is not a moral argument—it is an appeal to national interest—but it is highly relevant for those self-styled realists who want us to deal with the world as it really is."[29]

Luard considers these and related issues. His essay reprinted here, in an abridged form, has been circulated and read widely in the foreign ministries of the world's major capitals.

HUMANITARIAN INTERVENTION

In 1979, during the last year of the Carter administration and shortly before he was to be nominated by President Reagan for the position of Assistant Secretary of State for Human Rights, Ernest W. Lefever testified before Congress to the effect that President Carter's diplomatic preachments addressed to various dictators were demonstrably counterproductive to American interests.[30] Asserting a "realist perspective," he said: "It is clear that a score of allies have been unhappy with a policy they regard as arrogant and unfairly applied."[31] For example, "[the military regimes in] Brazil, Argentina, Uruguay, and Guatemala have been alienated to the point where they have refused military assistance from Washington. And Brazil has served notice that it wishes to withdraw from its Security Assistance Agreement of 25 years standing."[32] Lefever concluded that "[t]his alienation of allies gives aid and comfort to Moscow," and that such intervention in the internal affairs of other countries is often inappropriate[33]—a position, it may be noted, that until recently marked Soviet international human rights policy.

If mere diplomatic preachment about human rights is controversial, then surely overt state involvement in the internal affairs of another country for human rights purposes—in the form, say, of military deployments or aid cut-offs—will be widely debated also. In his thoughtful essay, Jack Donnelly presents strong arguments against foreign intervention, no matter how attractively wrapped in the language of humanitarianism. Still, he cautiously draws a line between intervention, which he condemns, and the assertion of bilateral influence in foreign affairs in pursuit of human rights objectives, which he applauds. He calls for a strategy of "positive non-intervention," that is, a program that would require "non-involvement with regimes guilty of massive violations of human rights." Thus he does not associate himself with the Lefever position that aid cut-offs are too costly to the United States in its relations with military dictators.

A U.S. policy dissociating the United States from the Argentine military dictatorship of the 1970s was vindicated after that regime was replaced in 1983 by the democratic government of President Raul Alfonsin. Strongly supportive of human rights, the newly elected government brought many high-ranking military leaders to criminal trial and meted out prison terms to military officers found by the Argentine judiciary to have violated human rights.[34] In addition, President Alfonsin explicitly announced that the foreign policy of a

29. Shue, "Playing Hardball with Human Rights," 11.
30. See Senate Committee on Foreign Relations, Subcommittee on International Organizations, *Hearings: Human Rights and U.S. Foreign Policy*, 96th Cong., 1st sess., 1979, 216–40.
31. Ibid., 223.
32. Ibid., 223.
33. Ibid., 224.
34. Americas Watch, *Truth and Partial Justice in Argentina* (New York: Americas Watch, 1987), 25–60.

democratic Argentina would include the promotion of international human rights as a priority objective. In this light, the Argentine experience appears to support Donnelly's—not Lefever's—analysis of the consequences of bilateral aid cut-offs as sanctions for human rights violations.

Of course, neither the Soviet intervention in Afghanistan (1979) nor that of the United States in Grenada (1983)—the first claimed to be in response to an official "invitation," the second claimed to be a "rescue mission," and each justified on human rights grounds— shows much respect for Donnelly's noninterventionist viewpoint (or, for that matter, Lefever's). Each does, however, help to make Donnelly's case that unilateral armed intervention, humanitarian no less than Machiavellian, is fraught with the potential for abuse and replete with negative implications for peace and world order. Such, at any rate, was the conclusion of the UN General Assembly in both instances, notwithstanding the Soviet Union's and the United States' efforts to clothe their actions in human rights rhetoric.[35]

In any event, when talking about the unilateral use of superpower force at least, it is well to be skeptical of the sincerity of those who invoke the doctrine of humanitarian intervention, a point of view strongly endorsed by Wil D. Verwey, a Dutch professor of international law, and shared by many others.[36] Verwey argues that such action, when not authorized by the United Nations, presumptively "reflects, in essence, power politics on a hegemonial basis, not a legal right of any kind."[37] He proposes, instead, that any state or group of states using the label "humanitarian intervention" to justify the use of armed force should be prepared to submit evidence to the UN that meets seven conditions or tests of international legality: (1) that the intervening state has a "relative disinterest" in the situation, in the sense that its overriding concern is the protection of human rights; (2) that there is an emergency situation in which fundamental human rights of a nonpolitical nature are being violated or are about to be violated on a massive scale; (3) that only a last-resort armed action can save the actual or potential victims; (4) that there is not enough time to await action by the United Nations or UN action has proved ineffectual; (5) that the impact on the authority structure of the target state will be minimal; (6) that military action is proportional to the requirements of the rescue mission; and (7) that the action does not threaten to incur more human losses than it seeks to prevent.[38]

Many commentators have pointed out that in a world made up of countries pledged to the objectives of the UN Charter, caution, restraint, and skepticism are called for in response to any effort to excuse the use of armed force in the name of human rights. As Thomas Franck and Nigel Rodley have observed, with irony, "nothing would be a more foolish

---

35. The Soviet Union's arguments pleading self-defense and invoking humanitarian intervention were explicitly rejected by the UN General Assembly in U.N.G.A. Res. A/Res.Es. 6/2, Jan. 14, 1980. Similarly, the United States' arguments pleading self-defense and invoking human rights concerns did not prevent the General Assembly from denouncing U.S. intervention in Grenada as violative of international law. See U.N.G.A. Res. 38/7, Nov. 2, 1983.
36. See Wil D. Verwey, "Humanitarian Intervention," in *The Current Legal Regulation of the Use of Force*, ed. Antonio Cassese (Dordrecht, Netherlands: Martinus Nijhoff Publishers, 1986), 57–78. See also Michael J. Bayzler, "Reexamining the Doctrine of Humanitarian Intervention in Light of the Atrocities in Kampuchea and Ethiopia," *Stanford Journal of International Law* 23 (1987): 547–619; Richard B. Lillich, "Forcible Self-Help by States to Protect Human Rights," *Iowa Law Review* 53 (1967): 325–51; John Norton Moore, "The Control of Foreign Intervention in Internal Conflict," *Virginia Journal of International Law* 9 (1969): 205–342. See generally Richard B. Lillich, ed., *Humanitarian Intervention and the United Nations* (Charlottesville, Va.: University Press of Virginia, 1973); John Norton Moore, ed., *Law and Civil War in the Modern World* (Baltimore, Md.: Johns Hopkins University Press, 1974); Fernando R. Teson, *Humanitarian Intervention: An Inquiry into Law and Morality* (Ardsley-on-Hudson, N.Y.: Transnational Publishers, 1987); Ann Van Wynen Thomas and A. J. Thomas, Jr., *Non-Intervention: The Law and Its Import in the Americas* (Dallas, Tex.: Southern Methodist University Press, 1956).
37. Verwey, "Humanitarian Intervention," 70.
38. Ibid., 74–75.

footnote to man's [sic] demise than that his [sic] final destruction was occasioned by a war to ensure human rights."[39]

LEGISLATIVE IMPLEMENTATION OF HUMAN RIGHTS

In *Liberal America and the Third World*, Robert Packenham shows how, since the 1940s, the United States has sought to use foreign aid legislation to achieve various social and political aims in the recipient countries, for example, free enterprise and trade unionism.[40] More recently, these aims have come to include the promotion of "internationally recognized human rights." Beginning in the 1970s, Congress sought to influence overseas development policy by attaching several human rights amendments to the Foreign Assistance Act of 1961, for example, in Section 116 (also known as the "Harkin Amendment"):

> No assistance may be provided . . . to the government of any country which engages in a consistent pattern of gross violations of internationally recognized human rights, including torture or cruel, inhuman, or degrading treatment or punishment, prolonged detention without charges, causing the disappearance of persons by the abduction and clandestine detention of those persons or other flagrant denial of the right to life, liberty, and the security of person, unless such assistance will directly benefit the needy people in the country.[41]

But Congress did not limit itself to restrictions on development aid for roads, schools, hospital construction projects, and the like. It restricted foreign military assistance as well, seeking, in Section 502B of the Foreign Assistance Act,[42] to cut off arms and military aid to any country engaging in "a consistent pattern of gross violations of human rights . . . unless the President certifies in writing . . . that extraordinary circumstances exist warranting provision of such assistance (see. 502c(i)).

In his essay, David P. Forsythe studies the multiple legislative efforts made by the U.S. Congress to influence foreign aid and foreign policy since 1973. Categorizing such legislation and assessing Congress's effectiveness in influencing the conduct of foreign affairs, he concludes that the legislative branch has lacked "the attention span, the will power, and the consensus for effective oversight that would implement the original congressional intent."

Effectively carried out or not, these legislative developments in the United States during the 1970s and 1980s have spurred a lively debate over the linking of foreign aid with human rights standards. Supporting the view that the link is essential are the arguments that (a) since its inception, U.S. foreign aid has been viewed not as international charity but as a tool of foreign policy associated with specific goals consistent with U.S. values;[43] (b) to be

---

39. Thomas M. Franck and Nigel S. Rodley, "After Bangladesh: The Law of Humanitarian Intervention by Military Force," *American Journal of International Law* 67 (1973): 275–305, at 300.
40. Robert Packenham, *Liberal America and the Third World* (Princeton, N.J.: Princeton University Press, 1973).
41. 22 U.S.C. §2151 (1982).
42. 22 U.S.C. §2304 (1982).
43. See, e.g., Tom Harkin, "Human Rights and Foreign Aid: Forging an Unbreakable Link," in Brown and MacLean, *Human Rights and U.S. Foreign Policy*, 15–26. See also Cyrus Vance, "Law Day Speech at the University of Georgia School of Law," *Department of State Bulletin* (Apr. 30, 1977); Sandy Vogelgesang, *American Dream–Global Nightmare: The Dilemma of U.S. Human Rights Policy* (New York: W. W. Norton, 1980).

durable, a foreign policy must reflect the values of its constituent people;[44] and (c) a country that annually appropriates billions of dollars to more than eighty countries cannot deny a sense of purpose or be blind to the consequences of its aid.[45] Additionally, linkage strategy is seen to associate U.S. human rights policy with that of like-minded countries. Canada, Norway, and the Netherlands all link their programs of foreign aid with the human rights record of recipient countries.[46] In all of these countries, the term "conditionality" has been added to the jargon of international politics, with legislators debating the merits of making financial and military aid to governments conditional on their respect for human rights.

Whatever the justification for conditional legislation, however, the debate over the appropriate place for ethical considerations in implementing foreign aid policy has the allure of an impressionist painting. From a distance we can discern the features of the painting quite clearly, but when we move closer to analyze the component elements, the image dissolves and we wonder why it seemed so clear. The analogy seems to characterize the approaches of Carter and Reagan to integrating human rights into their foreign policy. According to David Carleton and Michael Stohl, if one moves from the human rights rhetoric of these two administrations to the empirical details of the implementation of their policy, some of the most apparent differences blur.[47] While the rhetoric contrasts sharply from the Carter administration to the Reagan administration, a careful analysis of the respective aid distribution programs leads to the conclusion that, in policy implementation, the two administrations were remarkably similar. Both leaned heavily on the exception clauses in the human rights statutes and neither "acted in accordance with the established human rights package."[48] Forsythe's essay describes similar findings.

JUDICIAL ENFORCEMENT OF HUMAN RIGHTS

In the United States, the judiciary's role in implementing international human rights principles and standards has been cast as a very minor part. A case decided in 1952 by the Supreme Court of California, *Sei Fujii v. State of California*,[49] propounded the doctrine that the human rights provisions of the UN Charter, though informed by the Universal Declaration of Human Rights and constituting the elements of a binding treaty, were nevertheless not "self-executing"—that is, they "do not purport to impose legal obligations on the in-

44. For opinion in the United States, see Susan Welch and David P. Forsythe, "Foreign Policy Attitudes of American Human Rights Supporters," *Human Rights Quarterly* (1983): 491–509. For opinion in aid-recipient countries, see House Committee of Foriegn Affairs, Subcommittee on Human Rights and International Organizations, *Hearings: Implementation of Congressionally Mandated Human Rights Provisions*, 97th Cong., 1st sess., 1981, 1:29–34.
45. Henry Shue, *Basic Rights: Subsistence, Affluence, and U.S. Foreign Policy* (Princeton, N.J.: Princeton University Press, 1980).
46. Robert Matthews and Cranford Pratt, "Human Rights and Foreign Policy: Principles and Canadian Practice," *Human Rights Quarterly* 7 (1985): 159–88; Norwegian Institute of Human Rights, *Human Rights in Developing Countries: A Yearbook on Countries Receiving Norwegian Aid* (Olso: Norwegian University Press, 1986); Peter R. Baehr, "Concern for Development Aid and Fundamental Human Rights: The Dilemma as Faced by the Netherlands," *Human Rights Quarterly* 4 (1982): 3–52; Antonio Cassese, ed., *Parliamentary Control over Foreign Policy-Making* (Germantown, Md.: Sijthoff and Noordhoff, 1980).
47. David Carleton and Michael Stohl, "The Foreign Policy of Human Rights: Rhetoric and Reality from Jimmy Carter to Ronald Reagan," *Human Rights Quarterly* 7 (1985): 205–22.
48. Ibid., 227. See Note, "Human Rights Issues in United States foreign policy," *Harvard Human Rights Yearbook* 1 (1988): 179–297.
49. 38 Cal.2d 718, 242 P.2d 617 (1952).

dividual member nations or to create rights in private persons."[50] Technically this precedent was binding only on the courts of California, and for this and other reasons litigants in later years[51] made efforts to invoke the UN Charter and the Universal Declaration of Human Rights to challenge such national actions as the United States' involvement in the Vietnam war[52] and U.S. support "aiding the forces of racial repression in Southern Africa."[53] However, as Richard Lillich has thoroughly documented, such efforts in state and federal courts, while well intentioned, unfortunately have proved abortive.[54] Yet Lillich's evaluation is tempered with hope:

> To date the cases that have been litigated before the United States courts have not been winners, at least in the traditional sense, but they have achieved the not inconsiderable result of calling increased attention to the issue of implementing international human rights law. At the very least, they have raised the consciousness of lawyers, judges, government officials and the general public—both in the United States and abroad—to the existence and, perhaps more importantly, to the potential of this body of law. Human rights advocates should continue to use the courts not only to seek relief or establish useful precedent, but also to marshal public opinion against governments, including that of the United States, which violate human rights.[55]

In 1979, a landmark civil suit filed in Brooklyn against a former Paraguayan police official succeeded where previous cases had failed, and thus revealed the potential in U.S. courts for international human rights law. Richard P. Claude describes the development and outcome of the case in the concluding essay in this chapter. In *Filártiga v. Peña-Irala,*[56] a federal district court judge ruled that the family of a sixteen-year-old Paraguayan youth who had been tortured and murdered in Paraguay was entitled to $10.4 million in damages from a former Paraguayan police official who had later moved to New York. The decision rested on the Alien Tort Claims Act of 1789.[57] Lawyers at the Center for Constitutional Rights in New York City represented members of the deceased youth's family in New York and claimed that the act gave U.S. courts jurisdiction to hear claims stemming from injuries inflicted abroad if the wrongdoer later was found in the United States. In 1980, a federal court of appeals panel in Manhattan accepted that argument and permitted the survivors of Joelito Filártiga to sue former Police Chief Américo Peña, then living in Brooklyn. In awarding the damages in 1984, Judge Eugene H. Nickerson ruled in part that the acts of torture described in the case were "so monstrous as to make Peña an outlaw around the globe" under the tenets of customary international law.

---

50. 38 Cal. 2d at 722; 242 P. 2d. at 620–621. The California Supreme Court reversed the state District Court of Appeals insofar as the district court had based its decision on the UN Charter and the Universal Declaration of Human Rights. However, it proceeded to hold the Alien Land Law invalid on the ground that it violated the equal protection clause of the Fourteenth Amendment to the U.S. Constitution.
51. Cf., masterful survey by Bert B. Lockwood, Jr., "The United Nations Charter and United States Civil Rights Litigation: 1946–1955," *Iowa Law Review,* 69, no. 4 (1984), 901–56.
52. See, e.g., Mitchell v. United States, 386 U.S. 972 (1967).
53. See, e.g., New York Times Co. v. City of New York, Commission on Human Rights, 41 N.Y. 2d 345; 361 N.E. 2d 63 (1977).
54. Richard B. Lillich, "The Role of Domestic Courts in Promoting International Human Rights Norms," *New York Law School Law Review* 24 (1978): 153–78. For an annotation and comparative review of nearly one thousand human rights cases decided by the superior courts of thirty countries, see Paul Sieghart, *The International Law of Human Rights* (Oxford: Oxford University Press, 1983).
55. Lillich, "The Role of Domestic Courts," 177.
56. Filártiga v. Peña-Irala, 630 F.2d 876 (2d Cr., 1980).
57. 28 U.S.C. §1350 (1976).

Filártiga v. Peña-Irala marks the first time that the U.S. courts ventured into an area traditionally reserved for the executive and legislative branches of government, branches that often are too constrained by political interests to take effective action in halting or remedying human rights violations. The case is of more than academic interest because it foreshadows similar suits against torturers and death-squad members from Argentina,[58] the Philippines,[59] and elsewhere who have sought refuge in the United States. It provides a glimpse of a world community in which states establish themselves as advocates and defenders of universal human rights principles in the objective atmosphere of their court rooms.

18. EVAN LUARD *Human Rights and Foreign Policy*

INTRODUCTION

There has probably never been a time when there was so much concern about human rights questions as there is today. Because the world is so much smaller, we are all today more conscious of the human rights violations that occur in other parts of the world and more determined to do something about them. There is a widespread sentiment that this concern should not simply be voiced by ordinary citizens, or by non-governmental organizations such as UN [Associations] and Amnesty [International groups], but should be expressed in the foreign policy of governments. Foreign policies, in other words, should not just be concerned with the promotion of narrow, national self-interest but with remedying the injustices suffered by many in other countries living under tyrannical and inhumane governments. If government policies reflect the deep concern of their citizens on this issue, the means available to governments, and to governments alone, can be brought into play and help to influence the policies being pursued by other governments towards their own populations, and to end, or at least reduce, the grievous violations of rights which many continue to suffer. . . .

There is nothing new in concern among governments about human rights matters. Questions concerning freedom, the right to a fair trial, the rule of law, freedom from torture or arbitrary imprisonment, the right of assembly, freedom of speech and so on, all these have been the stuff of politics within states almost since states began.

Even concern about the enjoyment of such rights in *other* states goes back two centuries at least, to the beginning of the agitation over slavery and the slave trade in the late eighteenth century. The question of the role of human rights issues in foreign policy has been discussed for well over a century (for example, in the controversy over Gladstone's famous Midlothian campaign, when he challenged the response of the Disraeli government to Turkish atrocities in Bosnia and Bulgaria). . . .

The desire of a government to play an active role in this field, however, encounters immediate difficulties. Its concern to make an issue of human-rights violations in some other country may conflict with other important foreign policy aims. . . . Any government that seeks to commit itself to such a policy is bound to find itself faced by difficult choices and to encounter serious constraints which appear to limit its freedom of action. It must be one of our purposes in this essay to examine how serious these constraints really are.

FOREIGN POLICY CONSTRAINTS ON HUMAN RIGHTS POLICY

What then is the nature of the constraints?

First, all governments need to have dealings with almost every other government of the world, whether it approves of them or not, on many diverse questions. It must deal with them over the welfare of its own nationals resident in

---

58. See Alfredo Forti and Debora Benchoam v. Carlos Guillermo Suarez-Mason, 672 F. Supp. 1531 (U.S.D.C., No. Cal. 1987), resulting in a $21 million award to the plaintiffs.
59. See José Sison v. Ferdinand Marcos, Civil No. 86-0 58-A (9th Cir., 1987).

that country, or trading there; over commercial and other matters between the two states; over many practical problems affecting both states; over any aid program it may be implementing; and over many wider issues affecting the international community as a whole. It will deal with them both bilaterally and in the [United Nations] and other international organizations. Such dealings are designed (as Winston Churchill said about the act of recognition) "not to confer a compliment but to secure a convenience." An active campaign designed to denounce the domestic policies of such a government will inevitably arouse deep resentment and will complicate dealings on any practical matter between the two states. It may endanger commercial or other prospects and the securing of government contracts. It will certainly damage political goodwill (about which our embassies abroad are often mainly concerned). And since it will not necessarily bring any improvement in the human rights situation in the country concerned in any case, it is understandable that many governments are reluctant to stick their necks out on such issues (and are nearly always advised by their representatives on the spot not to do so).

In some cases there may be more special reasons why it is believed inadvisable to antagonize the other government concerned. That state may be considered important for strategic reasons, may even be an ally, so that to engage in criticisms which might endanger the government's position may be held to be highly undesirable on defense grounds. . . . Or the state concerned may be an important commercial partner. . . . It may be an important supplier of raw materials: as South Africa is to all Western countries. It may be a financially powerful state which could make its displeasure felt in the foreign exchange markets, a consideration which some believe to have virtually silenced criticism of Saudi Arabia and other oil-producing states in recent years. Finally, it may be a great power with which negotiations on many delicate subjects, including vital strategic issues, are being undertaken: thus, for example, the conclusion of a [Strategic Arms Limitation Talks, SALT] agreement with the Soviet Union was regarded by some as so important as to deter too outspoken criticisms of [its] human rights policies by the United States.

A third kind of argument that can be used against attempts to undertake an active human rights policy is that it is contrary to the rules of diplomatic intercourse. The tradition that each state exercises full sovereignty within its own territory and that other states therefore should not interfere in such matters is firmly established and is said to reduce the danger of conflict among states through mutual interference. This rule, it is sometimes held, precludes any criticism of the actions of other governments within their own countries. International bodies, such critics claim, are equally debarred from interfering in such matters: Article 2(7) of the U N Charter states that nothing in the Charter "shall authorize the United Nations to intervene in matters which are essentially within the domestic jurisdiction of any state." . . . If every government began criticizing and commenting on all action of every other government in every part of the world, even undertaken within their own territories, offering perhaps conflicting advice, the conduct of international affairs would, under this view, become impossible. Is it not far wiser, it is asked, to maintain the traditional rules on this question and so reduce the possible areas of conflict?

Finally, the fourth type of argument often used against governments taking too active a role on these matters is that such efforts are in any case ineffectual: they will have no influence. They are thus a waste of energy, resources, and political capital. The type of government that engages in this oppression of basic human freedoms, it is said, is often already intensely insecure in its internal position and is unlikely to be deterred from its policies by outside criticism. Indeed for such a government it may be a point of honor to ignore all criticisms to demonstrate its own dependence and its unwillingness to be deterred. . . . Outside condemnation might, by attracting publicity to the affair, even cause a government to behave more toughly than would otherwise be the case, to show that it cannot be intimidated. Finally, it is argued that overt criticisms on such questions, by alienating the government concerned, may in fact serve to *reduce* the influence of outside governments which make them, and make it less likely that they can have any useful impact in similar situations in the future.

The force and influence of all these different arguments should not be underestimated by those who are concerned about human-rights questions. All of them may be challenged: and we will in the next section look at the weaknesses of some of them. But they are none of them altogether irrational. And the important point is that, whether or not they are true, they are *believed* by many governments and so deter attempts at least by governments to pursue an active policy in this field (none of the arguments of course apply to activity by unofficial organizations). The objections are ones that therefore have to be considered carefully. . . .

HOW IMPORTANT ARE THESE CONSTRAINTS?

The first argument we described suggested that, because governments have to deal with each other all the time on a wide variety of issues, they cannot risk exacerbating their relations by injecting controversial issues of human rights policy which will inevitably cause grave offense and may even fatally damage relations in every field, so endangering other important ends or policy.

It is of course the case the [a] government [is] at all times obliged to deal on a day-to-day basis with many governments whether or not it approves of them, on a large number of different and mainly uncontroversial issues. Most of these relations will continue whatever posture one government may adopt on human rights issues. The argument we described has force only if it is assumed that expressions of concern by one government on human rights questions will totally prejudice the conduct of normal business with the government that is criticized. But there is little evidence for this assumption. It is unreasonable to expect that relations will be totally unaffected. But the *degree* to which relations are damaged will depend partly on other factors governing the relationship between the two states, and it will depend even more on the manner in which the issue is raised. If the complaints made are aired in a polemical and highly political style, or are pursued obsessively and to the exclusion of all other questions, the relationship may indeed be seriously damaged. If, on the other hand, the complaint made is raised in the proper forum, in reasonable terms, and is consistent with the policy pursued on similar matters towards other states, this need not be the case. If the issue has been raised first on a confidential basis, and without publicity, the government concerned will be given notice in advance that the matter is one which genuinely arouses strong feelings and will be less surprised if it is subsequently raised in a public forum. Similarly if the charges made are specific, factual and backed by firm evidence,

rather than vague and generalized, it will have less justification for any belief or accusation that they are inspired by malice or political prejudice. Perhaps the most important condition is that of consistency. If Western governments (as in the early cold war years) denounce only human-rights violations in Eastern Europe, but ignore those of their allies in the West; if communist states denounce the situation in Chile or Northern Ireland, but say nothing of that in Cuba or Ethiopia, they cannot expect to be treated as unbiased in such campaigns.

The fact that human rights issues have already in the last few years become so much the normal stuff of international politics has reduced the danger that any expression of concern on such matters can be used by other governments as a justification [for] breaking off or damaging relations. Not only Western countries but many developing states as well have become increasingly active over such issues and play a growing role in the international bodies responsible. . . . No individual government can any longer insulate itself altogether from this change in the international climate. Even the Soviet Union today submits to questioning on its domestic policies in the [UN] Human Rights Committee (which supervises the implementation of the Covenant on Civil and Political Rights). [The Soviet Union] and nearly all other states gladly participate elsewhere in the discussion of the human rights policies of [the] South African, Chilean and Israeli governments, and rightly reject any attempt by the governments of those countries to claim immunity on the grounds of domestic sovereignty. It is thus almost universally recognized that serious violations of human rights are a matter of concern to the international community as a whole and, while the states accused will doubtless continue to protest when other governments criticize their record, it is less and less likely that inter-state relations will be fatally damaged because one state dares to criticize the performance of another in this field, so long as it does so in the appropriate matter. . . .

The second objection to an active policy on human rights which we described concerned the special difficulty which arises when human rights violations occur in states which have a particular importance, whether diplomatic, strategic or commercial. Thus it is argued that, even if Western governments can afford to be outspoken in condemning a remote and insignificant state in Africa or Asia whose goodwill is unimportant, they should be less uninhibited in their public criticism of states which are their close allies, or which have the power of life or death for their economies, or even those [with] which they are negotiating over important strategic questions.

The first thing to be said about this is that if this is the objection to an active human-rights policy, such a policy can still be pursued towards the great majority of states, which do not fall into any of these categories. But even in the other cases, the argument is open to challenge. It is, for example, often the case that where there is a special relationship with a particular country of this kind, it is a reciprocal one: the government being criticized may attach quite as much importance to that relationship as the one that is doing the criticizing. In these circumstances even though the former may be resentful of criticism, it will have in practice no alternative but to accept it and will be most unlikely to take actions that are seriously damaging to its partners. . . . The fact is that such regimes usually (as in all these cases) have nowhere else to go. They are tied firmly into their existing alliances, both by a strong ideological conviction and by prudent self-interest. . . . It might rather be argued that the fact that such countries are allies gives . . . states both a greater right and a greater incentive in seeking to bring about the changes in such regimes which alone can make them acceptable and durable partners. . . .

It is thus far less the case than is often suggested that governments must constantly maintain a prudent silence about the policies of other states which are important to them. Provided, once more, criticisms are raised in a reasonable and unpolemical manner, reactions are unlikely to be so drastic as it [is] occasionally suggested. . . . The fact is that governments today have come to expect comment on human rights affairs by other states; and there is no evidence that they will wantonly sacrifice the relations that are most important to them by overreacting to expressions of concern which, however unwelcome to them, can never be a fatal threat to their vital interests.

The reason that governments generally refrain from speaking out on such questions is because it is inconvenient to do so, not because it is fatally damaging. It is not believed to be worthwhile to create difficulties in relations with important states for ends that are regarded, by most officials and by many ministers, as only marginal in importance. How far a government will in practice go in criticizing a friendly or politically important state about its human rights policies depends usually on the degree to which public opinion at home demands it, rather than on the absolute scale of [the foreign state's] atrocities. . . .

The third difficulty we noted against making human rights considerations a prominent element in foreign policy was that the pursuit of human rights aims by governments (as against unofficial organizations) is contrary to the traditional rules of diplomatic intercouse forbidding interference in internal affairs. Here the simple answer is that the rules of diplomatic intercourse change all the time, and have changed quite dramatically in the last thirty or forty years. Such a change was already manifested in the UN Charter, in which provision was explicitly made for the discussion of human rights matters in the organization, and in its Commission on Human Rights in particular. This has been reinforced by the subsequent establishment of regional organizations devoted to the same subject.[1] . . . And it is shown above all in the current practices of states, many of which (not all developed countries) continually make clear the importance they attach to the conduct of other governments in this respect.

Nor are these arguments overcome by referring to traditional conceptions of "sovereignty" or to Article 2(7) of the UN Charter already quoted.[2] For definitions of the sovereign rights of states, or of what is "essentially within the domestic jurisdiction" of a state, as the Charter puts it, are continually evolving. So is the definition of "intervene" in that context. Today there are few states that consider it inadmissible for another government to express concern about human rights issues *in general*, while many accept that this carries with it the implication that governments must sometimes express concern about the human rights situation in particular states. International law has never been a static and inflexible body of rules. And it is perhaps in this particular area that it has evolved most rapidly in recent years.

The final argument we noted against a government playing too active a role in this field was that such policies are anyway ineffective. Few

1. [See Reading 16 in Chapter 4 in this volume.]
2. [See the Appendix.]

governments are influenced by public expressions of concern on such matters, it is said, and may only be incited to worse excesses. But this argument is contrary to the facts. There are a considerable number of cases where international pressures, including public expressions of concern by other governments, have led to significant improvements in the human rights policies of particular states. . . .

But this criticism anyway misconceives the effect that is ultimately to be expected from the actions of government in this field. For few realistic observers expect that, because one or two governments begin to state their concern about the human rights situation in a particular state (say Uganda or Equatorial Guinea), the government of that country is suddenly going to reverse all its policies and become all at once a model of virtue. In the short term, little may happen. But there may be a number of indirect effects. First the government under attack, whether or not it undergoes a change of heart, may be gradually brought to realize that there are significant external costs to the type of policy it is pursuing. At least its foreign office, which is usually most aware of foreign criticisms, may become an influence within the government machine for a reform of policy. Secondly, human rights campaigners within the country concerned may be given new hope and encouragement, and redouble their own efforts to secure reforms. Changes may be induced within the government itself, with those favoring a more liberal policy (partly because of its foreign-policy effects) prevailing over those furthering repressive policies (as occurred for a time in South Korea). But above all, it is the international climate as a whole which will be altered by expressions of concern on such matters. The expectations that are placed on all members of the international community are slowly changed. New norms of the behavior to be expected from civilized governments are established. Regional organizations, that may have previously been ineffective in this field, may become more active. It is this wider effect, the slowest and most indirect of all, which may nonetheless ultimately be the most important in reducing the scale of human rights violations. For ultimately it will affect the expectations and attitudes of all: even those of future governments which might otherwise be tempted towards tyrannical policies.

Thus none of the arguments that have been put forward against an active human rights policy are convincing. This does not mean that the arguments should be discounted altogether. It must be accepted that there are real difficulties for any government in carrying out a firm and consistent human rights policy. It will on occasion appear to conflict with other foreign-policy aims, whether it is accommodation with a superpower, the cultivation of relations with an influential third world country, or even the maximizing of exports. What is suggested here is not that such choices never have to be made. It is that the conflict is not as acute as is often made out. Relative frankness on human rights issues is normally compatible with the achievement of other foreign-policy goals. Equally important, even where a direct choice has to be made, the human rights objective, in a world where very serious human rights violations still occur, ought in many cases to prevail (put differently, there are costs in not responding to human-rights violations). But this requires courage among governments. . . .

To make such a policy successful . . . requires consistency and toughness. No foreign-policy objective can be achieved without a price. The saving of lives elsewhere, the prevention of torture and other violations of essential liberties, may be a goal for which it is sometimes worth paying such a price.

THE ENDS OF HUMAN RIGHTS POLICY

If it is accepted that the concern that is now widely felt over human rights should be reflected in foreign policy, what are the precise objectives such a policy should try to achieve, and how should it set about achieving them?

The first distinction to be made is between the general and the particular. Policy will be concerned in part to secure *general* recognition of the importance of human rights all over the world and to define precisely what are the rights that all governments should protect. And in part policy will be concerned with preventing or deterring *particular* violations of rights in individual countries in all parts of the world. Both of these have their part to play and neither can be ignored. Unless general principles are clearly laid down and widely publicized, governments cannot even know what is expected of them, nor is there a standard by which to judge their policies. Conversely, there is no value in establishing general principles in abstract form, unless a real attempt is also made to ensure that they are observed in practice. Until recently most of the energies of the international community were devoted to the former task. And it could be said that there now exists a fairly broad set of general statements of principle, setting out the main rights which the international community demands should be protected. The latter task—ensuring that these principles are observed—is by far the more difficult, partly for the reasons we have considered in the previous section. But it is to this that the world community needs to devote the greatest attention today.

Let us first seek to suggest briefly the main objectives to be pursued by governments in this field, before going on to look at the way they can best be attained. The first aim of any government that is deeply concerned in these issues, I would suggest, is to ensure that human rights concerns remain constantly at the top, or near the top, of the international agenda. The easiest policy to pursue in this field is to remain silent. . . . But if the [concerns are] as important as many people believe, and if governments can have an influence that other groups cannot, then it is essential that governments, as well as unofficial organizations, continue to make human rights an important international issue and ensure that they are publicly discussed. And if, as I have suggested, it is the entire climate of international opinion which has most influence in determining the policies pursued by governments, it is essential that those governments which are concerned on such questions continually raise it to the forefront of attention in order to influence the attitudes and expectations of others.

A second important aim of human rights policy must be to ensure that the minimum standards of human rights which civilized states expect to see observed are satisfactorily defined. Here a considerable amount of progress has already been made by the international bodies responsible over the last thirty or forty years. The essential standards governments should observe were first laid down, in somewhat general terms, in the Universal Declaration of Human Rights, formulated more than forty years ago and endorsed by almost the entire international community. . . . One of the continuing aims of governments working in this field is to clarify and amplify this code, particularly by extending it in certain specialized areas.

A third aim of policy must be to ensure that better machinery exists to try to see that the new codes are complied with. It is of no value laying down general principles if these principles continue to be flouted by large numbers of governments, including many that have in theory subscribed to these documents. It is generally accepted that the UN bodies responsible should now move on from legislation to the process often described as "implementation": ensuring that governments adequately conform with the good intentions which they have professed. Improvement of the machinery to achieve this is by no means easy, because of the resistances that exist among large parts of the membership to granting the UN effective powers in this field. This results partly from a general sensitivity about sovereignty, a reluctance to see any interference by international bodies in domestic matters. And it results partly from the fact that many governments have skeletons in their own cupboards and recognize that if more effective machinery were created it could well be applied against themselves.

The fourth and most important aim of human-rights policy must be to bring direct influence on governments all over the world so that the grave violation of human rights which today are unhappily still only too common are less likely to occur. As we have seen, this is both the most important and the most difficult task. Governments are often as indifferent to the representations of individual governments as to the recommendations of international bodies. Often they may believe that their own survival depends on the continuation of policies of repression, that they face a "security" problem which requires that "subversive" forces should be suppressed. In these circumstances, even if they recognize that serious violations of human rights are occurring, they may feel that these are the inevitable cost of maintaining power, or bringing a disturbed situation under control. . . .

This is not an exclusive list of the human-rights aims which a . . . government concerned with such matters will wish to pursue. But it probably includes the main objectives that governments will have in mind. Let us now go on therefore to consider the more difficult question, what are the *means* by which such objectives can best be achieved?

THE MEANS OF HUMAN RIGHTS POLICY

The first of the aims I have mentioned—ensuring that human rights remains near the top of the international agenda—is perhaps the easiest to achieve. No government has any reason to feel inhibited from declaring in general terms its concern on this question. . . . It is . . . essential that . . . governments . . . show their support for that general objective and . . . make clear the importance they too attach to performance in this field. Only if . . . states are being judged, by their friends as well as by their opponents, partly on the basis of their performance in this respect, is their behavior likely to be influenced. Only if the importance which civilized states attach to the preservation of elementary human rights, even in poor states, is continually reaffirmed, will the necessary international climate be established and the attitude of governments and populations alike be gradually transformed. . . .

The second general aim we mentioned was to carry forward the process of defining and elaborating the responsibilities of states in assuring the protection of human rights. Here the means required to achieve this are well established and no revolutionary changes are needed. Since any convention or other instrument in this field must, if it is to have any influence, reflect the views of the international community generally, it can only emerge from a process of international negotiation as at present. There may be room for improving the procedures used for this purpose. . . . There is a case for asking the International Law Commission . . . to be more closely involved in the process in the future. . . . Since it is balanced by nationality, like all UN bodies, it reflects as well as they do the varying national approaches to such questions. But [it] will not be so influenced by narrowly political factors as purely intergovernmental bodies sometimes are. . . .

The third objective we named for a constructive human rights policy was the improvement of the international machinery which at present exists for promoting and protecting such rights. Foreign policy concerning human rights must be partly a policy for improving this machinery.

[Editors' note: The author next critiques the human rights machinery of the United Nations and of the emerging regional human rights regimes, the focus of Readings 15 and 16, respectively.]

We come now to the final objective which we defined: action by individual governments to bring about improvements in the human rights situation elsewhere.

What are the means available to an individual government in pursuing this aim? What steps can it take to influence a situation that exists in other countries and to persuade another government to mend its ways?

The following are the main types of action which a government can take to influence other states on such matters, in ascending order of urgency:

(a) confidential representations to the government concerned
(b) joint representations made with other governments
(c) public statements of concern in parliament or elsewhere
(d) support for calls in such bodies as the UN Commission on Human Rights for investigation of the situation
(e) direct initiation of such action in international bodies
(f) cancellation or postponement of ministerial visits
(g) restraints on cultural and sporting contacts
(g) embargoes on arms sales
(i) reduction in aid programs
(j) withdrawal of an Ambassador
(k) a cessation of all aid
(l) the breaking of diplomatic relations
(m) trading sanctions

This list is not necessarily exhaustive. There are additional gradations that could be introduced at different levels. But it probably includes the main type of response open to governments in dealing with such questions. . . .

If action on these lines by outside states is to be effective, there are a number of conditions that need to be fulfilled. First, the policy must be pursued consistently, regardless of political prejudice or diplomatic convenience. This will sometimes involve difficult and unwelcome choices, both for governments and even more for diplomats. At present our diplomats abroad, perhaps because they are dealing on a day-to-day basis with a particular set of rulers, tend to become gradually committed to the existing regime and acquire a marked reluctance to take any steps which may be unwelcome to them. Equally, they are most unwilling to have contacts with groups or organizations that are regarded by those authorities as "subversive." . . . But the effect of this policy is questionable even so far as . . . material interests are concerned; for it means that when a government is overthrown—a not uncommon occurrence in recent times—we are known as the friend of the displaced and discredited regime and are distrusted by the incoming government with which we will in addition have had no previous contacts. But such a policy is even more damaging to our aims in the field of human rights, because it prevents our diplomats from having any contacts with those forces that may be doing most to promote respect for human rights, contacts which may be of great importance to their morale. . . .

So an important condition of an effective human rights policy (and also perhaps a condition of effective diplomacy) is the establishment of contacts with as broad a section of the population as possible, including political opponents of the government. But there is a corollary for this need for contacts (and one that may be more welcome to foreign office establishments). This is that, even where the human rights record of a government is appalling, there is every disadvantage in a total severing of relations. This in practice provides the worst of all worlds. Not only is all hope of influencing the regime in question lost, but an isolated regime often becomes still more brutal than before. Equally serious, all opportunity for showing moral support for opposition groups, or influencing the situation in any other way, is also abandoned. By washing our hands of the situation we may feel we are keeping our souls pure. But in practice we condemn the population under pressure to isolation, and ourselves to impotence. We salve our own consciences but abdicate responsibility. . . .

The case for maintaining contacts, however oppressive the government, and however alienated its population, has always been accepted in relation to such countries as South Africa and the Soviet Union, both serious human-rights offenders. It has been generally agreed in those cases that the promotion of contacts provides at least a chance to influence the climate of opinion within those countries, and give support to those forces that are working for change. The same considerations apply equally elsewhere. There is a strong case for deliberately fostering contacts with countries where human rights are being seriously violated. Certain kinds of contact are of particular value in this type of situation. It is, for example, especially important to maintain links with professional, academic and religious groups which are often doing something to keep the spirit of freedom alive. . . .

Our aid program too can sometimes be used far more constructively than by simply cutting it off in mid-stream when human rights violations occur. In general aid should not be provided to governments, in the form of large prestige products which may redound to their glory, but direct to the people. Small-scale assistance can be given, independently of the regime in power, to church groups and others running projects in the field to help those most in need. . . . It should go primarily to educational and agricultural projects, or small-scale co-operatives, that will make the biggest contribution in creating employment and meeting basic needs, rather than in large-scale dams, roads, steel mills, which bring little direct benefit to most of the population. Where aid is given in this way, and is providing direct benefit to the people, it should not be cut off because of human rights violations, except possibly in the most exceptional circumstances. It is wrong and illogical that the people of a country, already suffering under an oppressive regime, should be penalized further to punish the sins of their rulers. Moreover, aid programs may provide a means, however marginal, of influencing the situation through the many direct contacts which result: once it is cut off all chance of influence is lost and the direct contacts with the population are destroyed.

On the other hand, the halting of arms supplies and other kinds of military assistance should be one of the first steps taken once it is established that serious human rights violations are occurring. [As is evident], such assistance is directly used, or may be so used, by the government in its oppression of its population. Yet, nevertheless, it can reasonably be claimed by the recipient government as a mark of friendship and approval. There is thus a need for regular reappraisal of all such programs to ensure that the human-rights policy of recipient states is satisfactory. Such a policy needs, moreover, to be fully co-ordinated among different organs of the government so that the defense sales section of the Ministry of Defense is not busily peddling arms to a government that may be regarded with disapproval by political departments. . . . The breaking off of trade relations is the most serious step of all that can be taken. . . . It will therefore only be considered in the most extreme cases. . . .

On the other hand, investment in a country with a bad record could be prevented or at least discouraged at a much earlier stage. Many believe that this should already have occurred in the case of . . . investment in South Africa. The breaking off of diplomatic relations should be at least equally rare. If, as has been argued, there is always some value in maintaining contacts, it is nearly always best to retain diplomatic representation in some form (especially since, once broken, diplomatic relations cannot be restored without appearing to grant a mark of approval). If a gesture is required, the withdrawal of an Ambassador, while retaining the rest of the staff, has the necessary symbolic effect without destroying communications altogether.

It is in any case wrong to believe that the most drastic step is always the most influential. Sometimes the most effective weapon is direct representations to the government concerned. Visiting ministers, even if they have arrived for some other purpose—to negotiate a trade agreement or discuss civil aviation affairs—can take the opportunity to make clear the concern caused in their own country by reports of serious human-rights violations, and the obstacle these place in the way of continued co-operation: the minister approached may then use his own influence within the government machine to bring about changes in policies. Visiting foreign ministers should be particularly ready to take up such questions; and even when at home they can express their concern, either about a particular incident or a general situation, to the Ambassador of the state in question. At present, because the basic philosophy of foreign offices is always business as usual, such representations are relatively rare. This allows the erring government to feel that there are few serious political costs to [its] misdemeanors. But direct representations of this sort can be of special influence. Many governments may be prepared to ride out a critical report or two by Amnesty International. But if made to feel that the whole texture of their international relationships [is] being affected, they may be more willing to consider seriously radical changes in policy.

Representations on such matters (which will normally be unpublicized, though the wisdom of letting it be known that such a question has been breached can be considered in particular cases) of course carry far greater weight if they come from several governments together rather than from one. This also reduces the political costs of taking action and lessens the problem of *locus standi*, that is, the right of governments to intervene in matters in which their own nationals are not directly concerned (though since Britain and France already in 1863 had no hesitation in sending notes protesting againt Russia's treatment of its Polish subjects, there is perhaps no good reason for states to be overconcerned about this question today). In serious cases, therefore, there are good grounds for joining with other like-minded governments in voicing concern and expressing the hope that the situation will shortly be improved. There is certainly a case for far more frequent joint initiatives of this sort than has occurred in the past (they are at present very rare indeed), for they are perhaps more likely to give a government serious reason to re-think its policies than any representations made on a unilateral basis. The EEC [European Economic Community] has at least once taken such a step (in relation to a Latin American country) but could with advantage do so more often.

A final way in which governments can influence such questions, at least indirectly, is by giving assistance to the many unofficial organizations that are active in this field. These non-governmental organizations are indeed in some ways more effective on this subject than governments. They are able to speak, and certainly to publish, their concern more freely than governments usually do. They are less likely to be accused of political bias, or a desire to score points off a political opponent. And they are more likely to be accepted as reflecting and representing the opinions of ordinary people everywhere. For this reason one of the most useful things that governments can do is to provide assistance for such groups. Financial assistance would not usually be welcomed by them, since they would feel that their independence could be prejudiced, or at least that this might be believed. But there can be regular exchanges of information and ideas, a pooling of knowledge about the situation in particular states; joint seminars or other activities to educate the public; and co-operation in international human rights bodies. . . .

One thing that is certainly necessary if outside governments and human rights organizations are to be more successful in the future is that a greater degree of information should be made available to the public about the situation that exists in different countries all over the world. At present, though most educated people have a vague idea of what is happening in individual countries, impressions are generally very unclear, based on stray newspaper reports rather than reliable and systematically compiled evidence. In practice the degree of concern that is felt about each situation depends almost entirely on how far it happens to have been high-lighted by the press and television. . . .

If outside opinions, including outside governments, are able to play a more effective role in preventing . . . outrages [from] occurring. . . , it is essential that they should be equipped with more objective information about the situation that exists all over the world, and the relative scale of the violations that are occurring. As we have seen, governments usually only take action when their own public opinion is aroused; and a better informed public opinion would do much to stimulate more effective action by governments. The most useful action that could be taken by human rights organizations—perhaps Amnesty [International] or the so-called human rights network working together—would be the publication of an annual survey of the human rights situation in every country in the world (or at the very least all those where human rights are being seriously violated), with some indication of the gravity of the situation in each place. . . . It would magnify many times the value of the periodic reports at present issued about individual countries, because it would present a comprehensive picture of the world situation so far as human rights violations are concerned: it would give people an idea of the *relative* seriousness of the problems in different countries of the world; and it would serve to remind people of the *continuing* problems existing in countries that had not perhaps been reported on individually for some years. It would not only be of assistance to all unofficial organizations and individual workers in this field. It would assist governments— and not only in this country—in showing them where they should best direct their own efforts without being accused of political partiality.

CONCLUSIONS

We have now examined the problems that occur for governments in seeking to express in their policies the concern that is felt among their populations about human rights violations elsewhere. When all that is involved is the passing of resolutions and the drafting of conventions, these problems are not great. There may be differences of view between governments about the type of machinery to be established, and the standards to be laid down; but these are not acute political issues and receive little publicity. The difficult problems occur when it is necessary to move on from that process to seeking to influence the conduct of governments in relation to their own populations in their own territories. It is at this stage that many governments feel constrained to pull their punches: because of the danger, in their own eyes, of prejudicing their relations with the governments in question or damaging particular national interests. The natural instinct of nearly all governments, and even more of diplomats, is to maintain smooth working relations with whatever authorities they have to deal, and to avoid injecting into these delicate political issues such as human rights problems. These attitudes derive partly from the narrow way in which national interests are conceived by many. The wider and more long-term national interests—in bringing about a world in which fewer people are killed, tortured or imprisoned without reason and more enjoy basic freedoms, including the freedom to have a say in the way they are governed; even the less noble one of securing the gratitude of future governments once the oppressive regime has been overthrown, while at the same time winning some respect for demonstrating concern on these questions— these count for little against the immediate aim of not offending existing governments (perhaps a little human rights training for diplomats, or at least intensive briefing on the question before each foreign posting, would be a help; there is little in the current training of diplomats to lead them to take much interest in this subject). Only if these wider aims come to play a much larger role than they have in the past would governments begin to become more active in the protection of human rights elsewhere. . . .

QUESTIONS FOR REFLECTION AND DISCUSSION

1. Evan Luard writes of a significantly increased foreign policy interest in human rights in recent years. What accounts for this increased interest? Luard suggests that it is explained, at least in part, by an increased world awareness and concern for what happens in a moralistic sense. Are there more pragmatic reasons? If so, what are they?

2. Most internationally recognized human rights, it is fair to say, are of Western origin. This is particularly true of civil and political rights. Accordingly, one might reasonably question whether it is appropriate for a Western human rights foreign policy to expect that these rights should be applicable to, or imposed upon, countries with radically different socio-economic and political foundations, conditions, and persuasions, for instance, Third World countries. What is your judgment?

3. Luard outlines a number of arguments against an active human rights foreign policy. What are they? Which, if any, is the most persuasive to you? To a government? Can you think of any others?

4. To what extent should one be concerned about being too aggressive in the pursuit of a human rights policy? How might the following passage, omitted from the Luard essay, affect your answer:

> [T]he Western campaigns on behalf of dissidents in the Soviet Union do not in fact alter Soviet policy on that question and only make it difficult for the Soviet Government to make the concessions which it might otherwise be willing to grant and so intensify the possibility that harsh penalties may be imposed as a demonstration that that government cannot be deflected from its chosen course by outside criticism.

5. Is it appropriate for a foreign policy to embrace military sanctions in defense of human rights? Economic sanctions? Diplomatic sanctions? Which? When? Where? How? Why?

6. What criteria do you think a government uses when deciding upon foreign policy alternatives in the area of human rights? Is it possible that a government might shy away from an active human rights policy because of the impact such a policy might have upon essentially unrelated foreign policy concerns? For example, when the United States is critical of Soviet human rights practices, do the United States and the Soviet Union then find it difficult or impossible to deal with one another in other realms, such as arms control and disarmament? If so, to what extent should this be allowed to happen? Is it better to sacrifice concern for human rights on the altar of stable international relations or is it better to risk tension in international relations in favor of the promotion and protection of human rights? Which? When? Where? How? Why?

7. Luard identifies a variety of different actions that governments can take to influence other States on human rights matters:

(a) confidential representations to the government concerned
(b) joint representations made with other governments
(c) public statements of concern in parliament or elsewhere
(d) support for calls in such bodies as the UN Commission on Human Rights for investigation of the situation
(e) direct initiation of such action in international bodies
(f) cancellation or postponement of ministerial visits
(g) restraints on cultural and sporting contacts
(h) embargoes on arms sales
(i) reduction in aid programs
(j) withdrawal of an ambassador
(k) a cessation of all aid
(l) the breaking of diplomatic relations
(m) trading sanctions

Which of these actions do you believe is the most easily instituted? The most influential? The most disadvantageous? Would any have been adequate to prevent or stop the slaughter of more than six million Jews in Nazi Germany? Of more than a million Cambodians during the Pol Pot Khmer Rouge Regime in the mid-1970s? Of the recent massive deaths in Ethiopia under the rule of Colonel Mengistu Haile Mariam? Note that Luard does not list a show of armed force or military sanctions. Why?

8. Luard notes that his list of human rights aims is not an exclusive one. What other goals might one identify?

19. JACK DONNELLY *Humanitarian Intervention and American Foreign Policy: Law, Morality, and Politics*

INTERVENTION, NONINTERVENTION AND INTERNATIONAL LAW

The essence of intervention is foreign involvement in the internal affairs of a country; violation—short of war—of the rights of sovereignty; infringement of the political independence of a state. Maintaining the useful linguistic distinction between "interfere" and "intervene," "intervention" can be defined as dictatorial interference in the internal affairs of another state involving the use or threat of force, or substantially debilitating economic coercion.[1]

Thus defined, intervention is illegal on its face.[2] If states can be presumed to be morally legitimate, intervention is also prima facie immoral.[3] In many cases, though, it is anything but impolitic, and thus intervention remains a pervasive element of contemporary international relations, despite the clear conflict with legal and moral norms.

These norms, however, continue to have considerable force and significance. Even intervening powers accept the principle of nonintervention and generally do conform to it in practice. Furthermore, interveners usually go to great lengths to obtain an "invitation;" barring this, they strain for some other argument to show that they are not really "intervening." The very transparency of such justifications attests to the powerful normative force of the principle of nonintervention.

The tension between general norm and particular action becomes particularly interesting, and revealing, where considerations of self-interest recede and the intervention receives a principled justification in terms of giving priority to competing values. These "hard cases," which today arise most frequently with regard to international human rights, present us with conflicting intuitions and principles.

On the one hand, internationally recognized human rights primarily address the way a state treats its own citizens. On its face, this is a purely internal affair. On the other hand, concern for the human rights of foreign nationals has a solid moral foundation and has become a part of many national foreign policies and the activities of numerous international organizations. But while acting on this concern is likely to conflict with the principle of nonintervention, the priority of nonintervention is hardly unquestionable; particularly in cases of gross and persistent systematic violations of human rights, we are pulled strongly in both directions.

The alleged "humanitarian intervention" exception to the general rule of nonintervention seeks to resolve this conflict in favor of action. I shall argue, however, that a radical doctrine of nonintervention is, despite its flaws, preferable to the principle of humanitarian intervention; international law does not recognize humanitarian intervention, and considerations of policy

---

1. Compare Wolfgang Friedmann's definition: "dictatorial interference in the domestic or foreign affairs of another state which impairs that state's independence." "Intervention and International Law," in *Intervention in International Politics*, ed. Louis G. M. Jaquet (The Hague: Martinus Nijhoff Publishers, 1971), 40.

2. There is no serious dispute over the prima facie illegality of intervention; nonintervention is simply the other side of the coin of sovereignty. Disagreements arise only over delineating the scope of activities that are to be considered intervention, and the alleged exceptions to the general rule. For a thorough discussion of the principle of nonintervention, see R. J. Vincent, *Non-Intervention and International Order* (Princeton, N.J.: Princeton University Press, 1971); Nicholas Greenwood Onuf, "The Principle of Nonintervention, the United Nations, and the International System," *International Organization* 25 (Spring 1971): 209–27.

3. The strongest recent case for this presumption is Michael Walzer, *Just and Unjust Wars* (New York: Basic Books, 1977), especially chapters 4 and 6. See also Michael Walzer, "The Moral Standing of States," *Philosophy and Public Affairs* 9 (Spring 1980): 209–29; the critiques of Walzer's position by Charles R. Beitz, David Luban, and Gerald Doppelt, *Philosophy and Public Affairs* 9 (Summer 1980): 385–403.

Reprinted, with changes, from Jack Donnelly, "Humanitarian Intervention and American Foreign Policy: Law, Morality and Politics," *Journal of International Affairs* 37 (1984): 311–28. Copyright © 1984 by the Journal of International Affairs. Reprinted by permission.

strongly counsel against recognition in the future. Furthermore, arguments for humanitarian intervention misconstrue the nature of the interaction of law, morality and policy. In contrast, the doctrine of nonintervention—and traditional international law in general—captures the essence of this interaction and thus plays an important role in helping to establish and maintain at least minimal standards of international order and justice.

DEFINING HUMANITARIAN INTERVENTION

Humanitarian intervention, in the strict sense, must be distinguished from rescue missions on behalf of one's own nationals threatened or held captive in a foreign country. . . . Whether justified or unjustified, rescue missions raise issues quite different from those raised by humanitarian intervention. Special ties to the victims in an internationalized dispute also exclude many other alleged instances of humanitarian intervention. . . .

Numerous other alleged examples involve merely verbal protest, usually through diplomatic channels. This is "intervention" only in an excessively broad sense of the term. While the governments to whom such protests are addressed regularly respond with charges of intervention, such polemical uses must be resisted if "intervention" is to be distinguished from "influence" or "interference," and if "humanitarian intervention" is to retain its substantive interest. Still other instances probably should be excluded since they are responses to a single outrage rather than a pattern of gross and pervasive abuse, or an extraordinarily grave single act of similar magnitude.

Summarizing such restrictions, all of which accept the arguments of interveners at face value, "humanitarian intervention" can be defined as intervention (in the narrow sense of coercive in-

| | *Provocation* | |
	"Genocide"*	Other violations
Military	1	3
Response		
Non-military	2	4

* "Genocide" is used here fairly loosely to mean massive human rights violations including arbitrary official killings of a significant fraction of a given population, or an identifiable target group within that population.

Figure 1. Matrix of Human Rights Violations and Responses

terference in the internal affairs of another state) in order to remedy mass and flagrant violations of the basic human rights of foreign nationals by their government. Unless otherwise noted, this essay shall discuss only unilateral humanitarian intervention;[4] actions by international organizations, although included in the definition, are likely to be particularly rare, given the current authority of international organizations. They raise somewhat different political, legal and moral issues.

Even in this relatively narrow sense, humanitarian intervention may involve a great variety of responses to a wide range of human rights violations. Four broad types can be identified. These categories represent only rough divisions of a continuous field, rather than the rigid boxes [shown in Figure 1]. Examples of each type—setting aside the problem of the very questionable motives of the interveners—would be: (1) The Indian invasion of East Pakistan/Bangladesh; (2) American trade sanctions against Amin's Uganda; (3) U.S. involvement in the Spanish-American War; and (4) U.S. economic subversion of the Allende regime in Chile. I shall concentrate on Types 1 and 2 (military and non-military responses to human rights violations of genocidal proportions), which are the most frequently discussed cases and, given the severity of the human rights violations involved, are most likely to be justified.

INTERNATIONAL LAW AND HUMANITARIAN INTERVENTION

Is humanitarian intervention, thus defined, permissible under international law? . . . The central place of the principle of nonintervention in traditional international law hardly needs emphasis; sovereignty is the foundation of international law and nonintervention is simply another way of expressing the correlative duty to respect the sovereignty of other states. The contemporary UN Charter system in no way alters this. Article 2(7) states: "Nothing in the present Charter shall authorize the United Nations to intervene in matters which are essentially within the domestic jurisdiction of any state . . ." and nowhere is it even hinted that unilateral intervention is sanctioned. More recent documents, such as the Declaration on Principles of International Law Concerning Friendly Relations and Co-operation Among States, also reaffirm sovereignty and nonintervention in the strongest terms.[5] Therefore, proponents of the doctrine of humanitarian intervention must show it to be a recognized exception to the general rule.

The standard arguments for the legality of humanitarian intervention rely heavily on examples intended to establish that humanitarian intervention was an accepted practice of the European great powers. But not only do most of these examples involve rescue missions, self-interested or hypocritical actions against Turkey, or mere diplomatic protest, they even fail to satisfy the standards by the defenders of humanitarian intervention.[6] In particular, few if any of these examples meet the requirement of disinterestedness.

Even a casual student of history ought to be shocked, or at least amused, by the notion that nineteenth-century Europe was the classic locus for the development of the practice of humanitarian intervention; such arguments generally rely on accepting the self-serving justifications of interveners at face value. Fortunately, we can forego a ponderous examination of individual cases here. . . . The real issue is whether such cases establish humanitarian intervention as a principle of customary international law; that is, whether there is a clear pattern of state practice coupled with the belief that such practice is the law (*opinio juris et necessitatis*). The simple fact is that instances of genuine humanitarian intervention—which certainly number no more than a

---

4. "Unilateral" actions are those undertaken without the sanction of a higher international authority, whether done alone or in concert with other states.

5. [For UN Charter, see Appendix. Declaration on Principles of International Law Concerning Friendly Relations and Cooperation Among States in Accordance with the Charter of the U.N. Oct. 24, 1970, U.N.G.A. Res. 2625 (XXV), 25 U.N. GAOR, Supp. (No. 28) 121 U.N. Doc A/8028 (1971).

* "Genocide" is used here fairly loosely to mean massive human rights violations including arbitrary official killings of a significant fraction of a given population, or an identifiable target group within that population.

6. Such standards typically require severe human rights violations (including widespread arbitrary killings), exhaustion of other remedies, disinterestedness, proportionality, and cooperation with relevant international organizations. See, for example, Richard B. Lillich, "Forceable Self-Help under International Law," *Naval War College Review* 22 (1970), 60–61.

dozen or two—were extraordinarily rare exceptions. In fact, states generally ignored atrocities of equal or greater magnitude.

As a right, rather than an obligation, the intervener would have considerable liberty to choose when, where, how, and even whether to exercise this "right." Nonetheless, the extreme rarity of its exercise, and the obvious considerations of self-interest in most cases where the right was claimed, clearly show that humanitarian intervention was not the prevailing practice. Furthermore, there is no evidence that it was widely accepted by states as a principle of customary international law. . . .

Post-Charter practice is, if anything, less supportive of (unilateral military) humanitarian intervention. For example, the alleged humanitarian motives of the Soviet Union in Hungary or the United States in Vietnam have met with well-deserved and nearly universal ridicule. In the Dominican Republic, even the U.S. government could muster only the weakest of arguments for a rescue mission, before falling back on the geopolitical-ideological formulations of the Johnson Doctrine; the Soviets used the similar principle of "socialist internationalism" to explain their invasion of Czechoslovakia. Humanitarian motives probably played an important part for at least some of those involved in the post-independence turmoil in the Congo, but the original Belgian intervention was at best a rescue mission with a very large dose of self-interest, while later "interventions" were at the invitation, or at least with the consent, of the generally recognized government, and thus not intervention (coercive interference).

The seventies did produce two major instances of intervention with apparently genuine humanitarian motives—in Bangladesh and in Uganda—but even here self-interest was at least as important a motive. Both cases have been well-studied elsewhere, but it is nonetheless useful to recall the essential elements of the more recent case—the Uganda of Idi Amin.

The heinous nature of Amin's rule is beyond dispute. The human rights records of a handful of post-war regimes have been worse, but Amin's barbarism, his penchant for international notoriety, and the absence of major countervailing ideological, strategic or economic concerns, made Uganda an ideal situation for humanitarian intervention, and thus a useful test case. Not only was there no humanitarian intervention throughout most of Amin's reign, there was considerable resistance, especially among African and Islamic countries, even to admit that this was a legitimate issue of international concern. Some countries, including the United States, did eventually adopt trade sanctions, but these came only after several years, hundreds of thousands of deaths, gross ethnic discrimination, and wholesale violations of the full range of internationally recognized human rights. Several widely publicized provocations involving British and American nationals seem to have been necessary to inspire even this response, which was restricted largely to modest Western economic sanctions. And the Tanzanian invasion that ultimately toppled Amin came only after an armed Ugandan attack. . . .

Humanitarian concerns certainly played a major part in president Julius Nyerere's decision to intervene and the invasion clearly imposed severe economic hardships on Tanzania. Nonetheless, self-interest explains at least the timing of the intervention and the long-standing animosity between the two countries—which in 1972 had escalated to Tanzanian support for an exile invasion of Uganda—certainly suggests self-interest as a leading motive. Furthermore, Tanzania's reluctance to admit its participation and its use of self-defense arguments at the July 1979 Organization of African Unity summit clearly suggest that Nyerere perceived the doctrine of humanitarian intervention to be an exceedingly questionable basis for action. It should also be noted that the decision to leave several thousand troops in Uganda well after the final elimination of Amin's forces clearly violates the standards proposed by the defenders of humanitarian intervention. "As much as one would like to agree to such an action against Amin, the Tanzanian action clearly failed to meet the doctrine's legal standards."[7] Even if the ouster of Amin were to count as an example of genuine humanitarian intervention, the general legal doctrine would not be significantly stronger: a single case of action every decade or two, in the face of literally dozens of instances of inaction, in no way establishes humanitarian intervention as state practice. "At

7. Farooq Hassan, "Realpolitik in International Law: After Tanzanian-Ugandan Conflict 'Humanitarian Intervention' Reexamined," *Willamette Law Review* 17 (Fall 1981): 859–912, at 912.

most, the rare case justifies itself and no more: even then, the claim is tenuous."[8]

More modest arguments for humanitarian intervention seek to show only that it is not unambiguously illegal. For example, Richard Lillich argues that even if the UN Charter requires the renunciation of unilateral intervention, this does not imply the enthronement of a principle of absolute nonintervention; rather, as the remainder of the Charter clearly indicates, it demands the creation of alternative collective mechanisms. Since these have not been effectively established, Lillich says, unilateral humanitarian intervention has therefore become justifiable.[9] This assumes, however, that there was a right to humanitarian intervention that was conditionally renounced in 1945. There was not.

To show that the Charter is implicitly compatible with humanitarian intervention, it must be established that mass and flagrant violations of human rights are not essentially matters of domestic jurisdiction and that the unilateral exercise of force to remedy such violations is permissible. In other words, paragraphs 7 and 4 of Article 2 of the Charter must be shown not to apply.

Article 2(4) clearly prohibits military intervention: "All members shall refrain in their international relations from the threat or use of force against the territorial integrity or political independence of any state, or in any other manner inconsistent with the Purposes of the United Nations." While "promoting and encouraging respect for human rights" is listed in Article 1(3) as one of the major purposes of the Charter, another Purpose—the first one listed, in fact—is "to maintain international peace and security . . . and to bring about by peaceful means, and in conformity with the principles of justice and international law, adjustment or settlement of disputes." Unilateral military intervention, whatever its motive, is not peaceful settlement or adjustment, and thus is inconsistent with the first Purpose of the Charter. Even if the Purposes are not listed in order of importance, the Charter's complete silence on enforcing human rights clearly suggests the priority of the unambiguous prohibition of armed force.

The reference to territorial integrity or political independence does not permit humanitarian intervention either. The *travaux préparatoires* clearly indicate that this phrase was added at the request of the smaller states in order to strengthen the prohibition on the use of force, rather than to allow an exception to the general rule. In addition, if the human rights violation is sufficient to justify a military response, it is hard to imagine a remedy short of toppling the regime in power, which would seem to be intervention. A double effect argument might show that this would not be essentially a violation of political independence—but only at the cost of opening a pandora's box of deceptive, self-justifying arguments. In any case, military intervention is a clear violation of a state's territorial integrity.

Turning from military to nonmilitary responses, domestic jurisdiction is the primary legal barrier to nonmilitary humanitarian intervention. International human rights are undeniably a matter of legitimate international concern. There are fairly clear international human rights standards, especially the Universal Declaration of Human Rights and the International Human Rights Covenants.[10] This does not make the human rights practices of states a matter of international jurisdiction, however, let alone a fit subject for unilateral intervention by other states.

The Charter references to human rights are weak, and extremely general. Besides Article 1(3) and the Preamble's expression of determination "to reaffirm faith in fundamental human rights," the only other major substantive references to human rights are in Article 55, where the promotion of "universal respect for, and observance of, human rights and fundamental freedoms" is reaffirmed, and in Article 56, where members "pledge themselves to take joint and separate action in co-operation with the Organization" for this purpose. No powers of coercive enforcement are granted, either explicitly or implicitly—let alone a right to unilateral intervention.

The major international human rights documents since 1945 also create only weak obligations backed by enforcement mechanisms that

---

8. H. Scott Fairley, "State Actors, Humanitarian Intervention, and International Law: Reopening Pandora's Box," *Georgia Journal of International and Comparative Law* 10 (Winter 1980): 29–63, 32, 63.

9. Richard B. Lillich, "Humanitarian Intervention: A Reply to Ian Brownlie and a Plea for Constructive Alternatives," in *Law and Civil War in the Modern World*, ed. John Norton Moore (Baltimore: Johns Hopkins University Press, 1974), 229–251, 250.

10. [See the Appendix.]

implicitly rule out humanitarian intervention. The Universal Declaration of Human Rights is explicitly only a standard of achievement; it never broaches the issue of enforcement. Even considering that the Declaration has now achieved something of the status of customary international law, its silence on enforcement remains beyond question. The International Covenant on Civil and Political Rights gives treaty status to a similar, but more thoroughly elaborated, list of human rights, but intervention is implicitly ruled out by the Covenant's enforcement provisions, which call for periodic reporting and optional procedures for the investigation of complaints. The International Covenant on Economic, Social and Cultural Rights is even weaker.

The existence of even the most precise international standards implies nothing about their enforcement; even a legal obligation need not be attached to an effective mechanism of coercive enforcement. This is especially true in international law, where obligations are voluntarily assumed by sovereign states, which are not only quite free to accept obligations lacking coercive enforcement, but in fact tend to restrict their obligations to those without even effective international monitoring. If human rights violations threaten international peace and security, collective UN action is perhaps legally warranted. There is, however, no basis for holding that unilateral enforcement of human rights standards through humanitarian intervention is permitted under international law; neither custom nor treaty recognizes humanitarian intervention.

MORALITY, FOREIGN POLICY, AND HUMANITARIAN INTERVENTION

Morality provides the strongest justification for humanitarian intervention: simply because atrocious violations of human rights take place overseas hardly seems sufficient to justify turning one's back. "Surely to require a state to sit back and watch the slaughter of innocent people in order to avoid violating blanket prohibitions against the use of force is to stress blackletter at the expense of far more important values," and is "a classic example of throwing the baby out with the bathwater."[11] Even Michael Walzer, who presents the strongest moral argument for nonintervention, allows intervention in response to human rights violations that shock the moral conscience of mankind.[12] In addition, most legal critics of humanitarian intervention admit the moral attractions of the doctrine as well.

Such arguments rest heavily on the notion of an international community. In effect, humanitarian intervention is viewed as a mechanism for enforcing very minimal compliance with communal standards of decency and human dignity. The moral basis of nonintervention, however, is the equally plausible notion that separate national communities deserve moral respect from outsiders. Mass and flagrant violations of human rights bring the national and international communities into conflict.

Nonintervention rests on the right of self-determination: how a people is ruled, and by whom, is largely up to its own free decision. Humanitarian intervention rests on the presumption that a genocidal regime does not have the consent of the people, so that the general rule of nonintervention does not apply. Such an argument, however, confuses the injustice of a regime with the right of others to remedy that injustice.

Violation of A's right by B in no way entails a right of C to enforce A's right; simply because a wrong is committed, we cannot assume that anyone has a right to rectify it—let alone a third party. If a people has a right to be ruled by a government that respects basic human rights, a nation under the domination of a genocidal tyrant has a right to revolt; this view, which lies at the heart of the Lockean/contractarian natural rights tradition, is widely accepted. Foreign actors, however, would seem to lack similar authority to overthrow a tyrant.

Genocidal tyranny certainly represents a fundamental breakdown in the national community, strengthening the case for remedial international action. The international community, however, is no less fragmented, disrupted, or unable to act effectively to ensure respect for basic human rights. International human rights are implemented almost entirely through national means, and coercive enforcement occurs through unilateral national action—if it occurs at all.

The demise—or stillbirth—of international

---

11. Lillich, "Forcible Self-Help," 344, 347.
12. Walzer, *Just and Unjust Wars*, 101–8.

enforcement machinery gives individual states no right to act for the community as a whole. At best, the intervener can claim to be acting for the community by default. But while this argument may have a certain rough-and-ready appeal, it hardly establishes either legal or moral authority for unilateral intervention and the vigilantism it implies has serious practical and moral drawbacks. Nonetheless, massive human rights violations continue to cry out for remedial action.

Humanitarian intervention thus seems to present a genuine moral dilemma in which important and well-established principles conflict so fundamentally that reasonable [persons] of good will may disagree on how that conflict is to be resolved. Policy considerations, however, clearly suggest that it should not be sanctioned as a general norm. Furthermore, arguments for humanitarian intervention seem to ignore the political environment of international law and the decisive interaction of law, morality and politics in the operation of legal norms.

Collective humanitarian intervention by the United Nations is controversial enough, given the force of Article 2(7), the clear, although perhaps diminishing, political and ideological bias of the Organization on human rights matters, and the discriminatory effects of power, alliances and ideology on UN decision-making. Nonetheless, the veto, combined with the extreme reluctance of most states to permit the United Nations to use armed force, probably would insure minimum abuse of an explicit norm authorizing Type 1 (see [Figure 1]) humanitarian intervention by the United Nations.

Practical considerations, however, suggest though that even Types 2 and 4 humanitarian intervention by the United Nations probably ought not to be allowed. Nonmilitary UN intervention would be subject to much greater abuse, both because such measures can be undertaken by the General Assembly alone and because the lower costs of action is likely to reduce the stringency of the standards applied. Logical consistency might make it hard to disallow nonmilitary measures where military ones are permissible, although consistency here probably would be more of a vice than a virtue. But whatever the status of collective measures, unilateral humanitarian intervention of all types must be resisted.

Lillich argues that "it is a realistic assumption that no state with the capabilities to act will allow its own nationals and the nationals of other states to be killed or injured abroad."[13] If this were true, at least the concerns over discrimination would be largely eliminated. The assumption, however, is outrageously unrealistic. Most major post-war instances of genocidal violations of human rights have met with inaction, for reasons ranging from "security interests" to simple lack of interest. In the last fifteen years, the most prominent examples include the cycle of barbarous atrocities in Burundi and Rwanda, the decimation of Cambodia under Pol Pot and his successors, the death of at least ten percent of the population of East Timor in the struggle against incorporation by Indonesia, and the systematic killings of Indians in Guatemala. Unless even massive killings overseas are "brought home" in a very concrete way *and* competing security, political or economic interests are absent, potential situations of humanitarian intervention have been met with inaction.

When will states act? Necessary conditions seem to include very low prospects of successful retaliation or loss of benefits, the absence of Cold War concerns (which alter at least the perceived costs or benefits of action), and an unusually high level of popular interest in the situation. In practice, this implies restricting humanitarian intervention to actions against weak, notorious and particularly peripheral countries, especially pariah regimes in relatively insignificant countries. As Farooq Hassan notes, "the doctrine has never been invoked against any of the European nations" and has been supported by "no author of any consequence from Asia or Africa."[14] Furthermore, unless there are also clear and considerable selfish national interests to be furthered, "humanitarian" intervention almost certainly will not take place, a point underscored by the recent examples of Bangladesh, Uganda and the Central African Empire/Republic. While some might hold that even this is better than nothing at all, the systematic discrimination implicit in any practical system of humanitarian intervention at best greatly reduces its attraction. . . .

Intervention is a serious enough problem without offering great powers a fine-sounding cover for self-interested schemes. For example, John Norton Moore advocates "more responsive

---

13. Lillich, "Forcible Self-Help," 344–45.
14. Hassan, "Realpolitik in International Law," 862.

normative standards" of intervention.[15] While he has in mind greater responsiveness to international community standards, in practice exceptions to the principle of nonintervention are likely to be made in reply to the self-interested demands of individual states. In a world where the major demands on international law made by states are for exceptions, and formulations that allow the unchecked pursuit of national interests, "responsiveness" is that last thing we need in normative standards governing intervention.

There are no objective standards to which we can appeal in seeking to justify humanitarian intervention. As has been widely noted, structural features of contemporary international relations and domestic politics greatly encourage or facilitate self-interested intervention. Of particular importance is the absence of effective international authority over decisions to intervene. Therefore, priority ought to be given to minimizing opportunities for intervention, rather than creating doctrines certain to be abused to justify self-interested actions. . . .

Even if we restrict ourselves to a crude measure of human rights performance such as arbitrary killings, we face serious difficulties. Both absolute and per capita killings certainly must be taken into account, but establishing even a rough threshold presents major problems. Furthermore, simple numbers alone tell only part of the story; of equal importance are the duration and the trend, and the degree of government involvement. Judgments of trend and official complicity, however, are especially subject to partisan manipulation.

For most rights other than the right to life, the interpretative problems become effectively unmanageable. For example, popular consent is crucial to the moral justification of nonintervention, and the right to popular participation in government is among the least controversial of internationally recognized human rights, at least when it is stated in very general terms. But what counts as satisfying or violating this right is a matter of intense dispute, with seemingly unavoidable ideological overtones; "the people" is a notoriously elusive body, and its will tends to be divined by potential interveners largely on the basis of controversial ideological presuppositions.

And the selective blindness induced by one's own interests and ideology, and the selective paranoia engendered by the presence of the interests and ideologies of one's opponents, and the irresistible conclusion is that a doctrine of humanitarian intervention would, in practice, become "simply a cloak of legality for the use of brute force," used primarily against "weak neighbors whose civilizations are held in contempt and under circumstances that have more to do with self-interest of the 'liberators' than the 'liberated.'"[16]

Traditional international law, however, largely avoids these practical problems, by assuring that (customary) international law reflects (only) genuine communal norms. State practice provides a behavioral test, while *opinio juris* is a test of a principle's prescriptive force; when both are satisfied, we can say with considerable assurance that the legal principle in question reflects the considered views of the community of nations. Such consensus greatly diminishes the potential for abuse.

Arguments for humanitarian intervention—and numerous other proposals based on the view that the current level of international community and cooperation is dismally low and that the substance of the current international legal consensus is sadly deficient—are essentially moral or "legislative" proposals for altering international law by reversing the traditional relationship between law, state practice and the sense of obligation. Such new "legal" principles aim to transform rather than reflect practice, and create rather than codify a sense of obligation. They try to use international law to validate and promote values far in advance of those currently in fact accepted by states.

The noble aims of such legal idealism, however, are subverted by precisely the moral "defects" they attempt to reform. "Advanced" values may suit a community that has reached an appropriate level of political, emotional, intellectual and institutional development. In practice, however, the current "corruption" of real states and the absence of effective international authorities to restrain them virtually guarantee pervasive abuse of a principle of humanitarian intervention. Therefore, establishing such a principle is likely to produce a worse situation, as defined by

---

15. John Norton Moore, "Introduction," *Law and Civil War: "Comments," Proceedings of the 61st Annual Meeting of the American Society of International Law* (1967) 76.
16. Hassan, "Realpolitik in International Law," 862.

the values being promoted. These values may even be corroded through pervasive cynical abuse.

The legalization of humanitarian intervention is almost certain to face the fate of other attempts to legislate morality, namely, evasion at best. Law, whether domestic or international, can hold a community to standards which it generally accepts and respects, but by which individuals occasionally find it hard to abide. It also can help to protect the community against outlaws and provide some assurance to individuals who comply that others will not be allowed to use this compliance to unfair advantage. Law cannot, however, make the majority of people or states better than they truly want to be; it must take its subjects as they are, in the sense of the best that they are willing to become.

Individuals and states alike certainly need to be exhorted to adhere to higher standards of behavior, but this is primarily the task of morality. Law can serve such a hortatory function, effectively, only if it is but a few steps ahead of its subjects. Traditional international law—including the prohibition of humanitarian intervention—begins from, and insists on remaining constrained by, this fundamental political fact. In the area of human rights, the vast bulk of states in every area of the world simply are unwilling to accept more than a rather vague commitment to international human rights standards, whether because of distrust of international enforcement, disagreements over the meaning and implications of the standards, or simple cynicism in the profession of adherence to these standards. For these reasons, humanitarian intervention is precluded as a principle of international law.

The most prominent cost in this refusal to push too far beyond the existing international consensus is, as the moral arguments for humanitarian intervention suggest, the seeming sacrifice of justice to power. But would the legalization of unilateral humanitarian intervention promote justice? Almost certainly not. Instead, self-interest would be promoted and the name of justice cruelly abused.

If justice is truly to be served by international law, the way the principles of international law are likely to be served by states must be taken into account. Traditional international law—but not the legal idealism of proposals for humanitarian intervention—meets this basic requirement. In international law, questions of justice are both moral and political questions; international law is in many ways the intersection of international morality and politics, and both must be accommodated. Arguments for humanitarian intervention try to capture law for morality alone. But neither law nor morality is well served when politics is excluded.

INFLUENCE WITHOUT INTERVENTION: RESPONDING TO HUMAN RIGHTS VIOLATIONS

"Nonintervention" means only the renunciation of "intervention," in the strict sense of coercive interference. International human rights, however, are an appropriate subject for the exercise of international *influence*. Inaction in the face of massive human rights violations is not only morally inappropriate, it is in no way required by international law.

For example, diplomatic protests, as well as not-so-diplomatic public denunciations, are unquestionably permitted. Talk may be cheap, but rarely is it free, especially given the sensitivity of most governments to charges of human rights abuses; even discreet diplomatic protests may provoke retaliation in a variety of forms. Furthermore, mere words are not necessarily powerless to produce practical change, especially if the human rights violations in question are easily remedied and they are not perceived to be important to the survival of the regime—or if the protesting country has considerable moral or material influence.

Material influence, however, raises the question of coercion. Recall that Article 2(4) prohibits "the threat or use of force." The meaning of "force" here is controversial, but in view of the increasing importance of economic issues in international relations and the consequently greater opportunities for dictatorial interference without armed force entering into the picture, it seems to me best to read it to cover extreme forms of economic coercion. Therefore, I have included "substantially debilitating economic coercion" in my definition of intervention. This, however, requires that we distinguish legitimate economic influence from illegitimate (interventionary) economic coercion.

On the one hand, no country is under an obligation to trade with a particular country (or on particular terms), except for voluntary treaty commitments. Likewise, there is no obligation to give foreign aid to any particular recipients, again barring treaties to the contrary. On the other hand, some countries are so dependent on a single source of trade or aid that manipulating this dependence can be as coercive as the threat or use of armed force; in some cases, the economic threat is even more credible. Therefore, the right of a country to arrange its trade and aid as it sees fit may clash with its obligation not to intervene in the internal affairs of another country.

As a general rule, this conflict can be resolved in favor of the right of states to order their international economic relations as they see fit. Human rights are a legitimate concern of national foreign policy, in pursuit of which otherwise acceptable instruments of foreign policy—including foreign economic affairs—usually may be used.

The vast majority of bilateral economic relations are not essential to the economic well-being of either party. Furthermore, alternative (although not necessarily as rewarding) buyers and sellers almost always are available. Therefore, only in the rarest cases would even a complete cessation of trade or aid have more than a minor or short-run impact, and even then trade or aid could be gradually phased out to provide an acceptable cushion. In other words, breaking economic relations will almost always fall below the threshold of intervention.

But why bother, if the impact really will be so limited? There are numerous moral reasons for action: for example, the moral force of major human rights violations demands that all legitimate options be pursued, barring strong countervailing considerations; material complicity can be eliminated; and, at minimum, a significant moral statement is made. Furthermore, such measures may have a substantial practical impact, particularly if sanctions are imposed by several countries.

If all major trade or aid partners sever their ties to a genocidal regime, the cumulative impact is likely to be equivalent to humanitarian intervention—but without an intervener. Each individual action is justifiable, but the cumulative impact would be a boycott equivalent in effect to international Type 2 humanitarian intervention. Particularly if the range of trading partners is considerable, or if no alternative partners present themselves, these measures can be presumed to reflect international public opinion and to represent a genuine, if uninstitutionalized, mechanism for the collective enforcement of community standards. Boycotts are especially attractive because the potential for partisan abuse is very low: since there are considerable economic incentives to cheat on a boycott, substantial compliance would signal true international consensus, while self-interested boycotts will fail, with the costs borne primarily by the boycotters.

These arguments for an economic boycott can be extended to political noninvolvement as well. Even international public opinion is not entirely without force. Furthermore, some countries are able to exercise considerable political influence, particularly in the relatively frequent cases where oppressive regimes depend heavily on not only economic, but political, support from a major power.

Therefore, a strategy of what can be called "positive nonintervention"—thorough noninvolvement with regimes guilty of massive violations of human rights—shows considerable promise; at worst it would eliminate complicity in international human rights violations and preclude some of the more blatant political manipulations of human rights concerns. In fact, "positive" nonintervention may represent the best possible basis for an active, effective international human rights policy that combines high moral and legal standards with a substantial degree of political realism. This is particularly true if we interpret "positive" nonintervention as an obligation, rather than as a right, or if it should become the core of a country's international human rights policy, rather than just a sporadically exercised option. . . .

POSITIVE NONINTERVENTION: A NEW BASIS FOR U.S. HUMAN RIGHTS POLICY

More often than not, American influence has been used, or left unused, so as to contribute to the stagnation or deterioration of human rights conditions abroad. As a rule, human rights concerns have given way in American foreign policy to perceived ideological, security and economic interests. Far too often, the United States has refused to act decisively against human rights violators with whom it has close ties (e.g., South Africa), has embraced regimes with dismal human rights records (e.g., the Philippines), and on occasion has even overthrown a regime with a relatively good human rights record in order to install an oppressive dictatorship (e.g., Guatemala). Former President Carter raised some (largely unfulfilled) hopes for change in this pattern, but under the [succeeding] administration the United States returned, with a vengeance, to the traditional subordination of international human rights concerns to even minor or imaginary countervailing interests.

Perhaps the most troubling feature of American policy has been the use of alleged human rights concerns to camouflage self-interested interventions. For example, human rights rhetoric was used during the ideologically and economically motivated subversion of the Allende regime, to pursue Cold War policies against the Soviet Union, and to justify the not-so-covert war against Nicaragua—at the same time that the human rights practices of El Salvador, which certainly are worse than Nicaragua's, are cynically recertified as acceptable. Sadly, a plausible case can be made that the greatest contribution the United States might make to human rights in Latin America, and in many other places as well, would be to end its involvement.

"Positive" human rights nonintervention would represent an important new departure for American policy, by combining moral, legal and political considerations into a relatively coherent, and potentially effective, policy. By taking massive violations of human rights, wherever they occur, to be a particularly powerful prima facie argument for positive nonintervention—i.e., for at least the gradual phasing out of all relations with the human rights–violating regime—practical opportunities for improving human rights practices abroad would be maximized, while opportunities for partisan manipulation of human rights concerns and the language of human rights would be minimized.

History shows, in the First, Second and Third Worlds alike, that a people's human rights will be secure against serious abuse by their government only if they *take* their rights and then aggressively defend them; if human rights are merely given, they will soon be lost or taken back. Therefore, active reformist involvement, of the type pursued in El Salvador today, probably is fundamentally misguided as a human rights strategy, even if the American effort is sincerely dedicated to human rights.

At minimum, interest and power are required for successful action to improve human rights

conditions. Since these usually are present in sufficient quantity only at the national level, regimes guilty of mass and flagrant violations of human rights should be left to the people of that country, who alone can secure the enjoyment of their rights. For those concerned about American interests, it should also be noted that a regime which respects human rights is likely to be relatively secure against both internal and external subversion.

Surprisingly little can be done to aid in the struggle against an oppressive regime: such action is almost certain to count as illegal intervention, and thus will be hard to accept in the first place. Even delivering support to insurgents is likely to be difficult. At home, there is likely to be little interest, on the part of governments, elites and the masses alike, and any such interest is almost always sporadic and easily submerged to a vast array of material and ideological concerns; at best, political support is usually available only for weak measures. Furthermore, it is exceedingly unlikely that the rare improvements that might be achieved can be maintained through external action, if only because of the difficulty of action at a distance.

Foreign states, however, can contribute significantly to the maintenance or establishment of an oppressive regime: for example, foreign support for a government can have a major, even decisive, impact on that government's fortunes and survival, particularly in countries with low social and political mobilization. This is especially true as the task of propping up an already established regime is a relatively easy one, given the power of inertia and the advantages of incumbency. Furthermore, assistance can be relatively easily delivered, and, in the American case, considerations of self-interest are much more likely to seem to be satisfied by involvement, which should make even vigorous action relatively palatable in political terms.

Whatever occasions for improving human rights conditions might be sacrificed by a policy of positive nonintervention, therefore, are outnumbered several times over by the interventionist abuses that would be avoided. It must be stressed, though, that positive nonintervention implies aggressive action on behalf of human rights, as well as significant changes in American foreign policy.

Perhaps the most important change would be the virtual elimination of "human rights" arguments for direct support of major human rights violators. Such a change could be expected to have a significant positive impact in light of the ease with which arguments of the alleged progress of a regime, or that it is the lesser of two evils, have been manipulated for partisan advantage. Subversion and similar direct assaults on authority structures also would be largely ruled out. At the very least, such distasteful and easily misused practices could be minimized.

Positive nonintervention would not be without costs. These costs sometimes even will be sufficient to override the general rule of noninvolvement. International human rights goals are only one part of a foreign policy, and it is generally agreed that in the conflict between important "self-interested" national goals and the goal of improved human rights conditions abroad, self-interest usually should take priority. We should not forget, though, that such countervailing concerns tend to be systematically overemphasized and misperceived; at the very least, we must demand that these countervailing "objective" interests be subjected to the same sort of careful, even cynical, scrutiny that human rights concerns regularly receive.

By beginning with a policy of non-support for major human rights violators, the burden of proof would be shifted to those claiming competing "national interests." As a result, these interests would have to be more clearly specified, and the ways in which they deserve priority made clearer and more explicit; today, almost any claim of "national interest" tends to be treated as a virtually conclusive argument for jettisoning competing human rights concerns. Under a doctrine of positive nonintervention, human rights goals, rather than being lost in the shuffle and bustle, would be placed, initially, at the head of the list. At the very least, this would help to clarify the true nature and substance of our policy and actions; it might even reduce the frequency with which human rights concerns are sacrificed.

Certainly there is a substantial element of optimism involved in proposing that positive nonintervention become the basis of American international human rights policy. For example, such a policy would require abandoning the long-standing American tendency to view issues in the Third World through the distorting lens of largely irrelevant Cold War concerns. The prospects for such changes are, admittedly, not very good today.

It also must be admitted that third party intervention, whether in support of or opposed to the established government, is likely to complicate matters considerably, where it does not fundamentally recast the nature of the problem. As was noted above, the moral foundation of nonintervention is self-determination. Therefore, third party intervention raises the issue of violations of self-determination and provides a plausible moral basis for counter-intervention. But while counter-intervention may restore some sort of political balance, it almost certainly will not leave the target country unaffected or unchanged. Furthermore, arguments for counter-intervention are easily abused and at best amount to retaliatory lawlessness. Nonintervention may still be the preferable course in such as case, but it is only the lesser evil.

Finally, let me stress that the argument for positive nonintervention sketched here has been oversimplified, underdeveloped, and probably even overdrawn, in the interest of provoking thought and discussion. Nonetheless, positive human rights nonintervention seems to me to represent a constructive fusion of moral, legal and political considerations and to provide the basis for a policy that is defensible in absolute terms, or at least far less flawed than its major competitors. Furthermore, it illustrates the capacity of traditional international law to accommodate new and important moral concerns—if the political will to do so truly exists among states. Positive nonintervention also suggests that traditional international law provides better guidance in incorporating moral concerns into an effective and defensible foreign policy than either the "realism" of those who would totally abandon the pursuit of international human rights, or the idealism of those who would treat international law as a primarily moral, rather than political, creature. In other words, traditional international law may provide the model for the integration of morality and politics many people seek in American foreign policy.

QUESTIONS FOR REFLECTION AND DISCUSSION

1. What constitutes unilateral humanitarian intervention? A speech in the United Nations critical of another country's mistreatment of its own or other citizens? A transboundary

radio or television broadcast for the same purpose? A recall of an ambassador or a termination of diplomatic relations in protest of a country's mistreatment of its own or other citizens? A trade embargo or a deployment of armed force for the same purpose? One writer once stated that "intervention may be anything from a speech of Lord Palmerston's in the House of Commons to the partition of Poland" (P. H. Winfield, "The History of Intervention in International Law," *British Yearbook of International Law* 3 [1922–23]: 130–49, at 130). Would Donnelly agree? How does he define the concept of unilateral humanitarian intervention? Is his definition broad? Restrictive? Too broad? Too restrictive?

2. Assuming that the international law doctrine of unilateral humanitarian intervention means, at a minimum, the right of State A to use force against State B for the purpose of protecting the inhabitants of State B from inhumane treatment by State B, what factors should State A be required to take into account when seeking to justify a right to unilateral humanitarian intervention? In this connection, consider the following passage omitted from the Donnelly essay:

> While there have been major advances in recent years in human rights fact-finding, even the facts are subject to considerable uncertainty and partisan abuse. Consider, for example, the problems of information gathering in communist countries, of the systematic American underreporting of the victims of state terror in El Salvador. And where the facts are not in dispute, there is usually a fatal problem of standards: what counts as a sufficiently high level of human rights violations to justify unilateral humanitarian intervention?

3. What constitutes lawful unilateral humanitarian intervention? Unlawful unilateral humanitarian intervention? What criteria might help to distinguish between the two? What does Donnelly think? Does he believe that unilateral humanitarian intervention is never permissible morally? Legally? Sometimes permissible morally? Legally? Why? Why not?

4. Reconsider question 3 in light of Article 2(3) of the UN Charter, which requires that "[a]ll Members shall settle their international disputes by peaceful means in such a manner that international peace and security, and justice, are not endangered"; also Article 2(4), requiring that "[a]ll Members shall refrain in their international relations from the threat or use of force against the territorial integrity or political independence of any state, or in any other manner inconsistent with the Purposes of the United Nations." Among the purposes of the United Nations is "friendly relations among nations based on respect for the principle of equal rights and self-determination of peoples" (Art. 1(2)) and "international co-operation in solving international problems of an economic, social, cultural, or humanitarian character, and in promoting and encouraging respect for human rights and for fundamental freedoms . . . (Art. 1 (3)). Are these UN Charter provisions compatible with unilateral humanitarian intervention? Incompatible?

5. Reconsider question 3 in light of the following provisions of the Charter of the Organization of American States, to which countries as diverse as Chile, Nicaragua, and the United States are party and theoretically bound:

> *Article 18.* No state or group of States has the right to intervene, directly or indirectly, for any reason whatever, in the internal or external affairs of any other State. The foregoing principle prohibits not only armed force but also any other form of interference or attempted threat against the personality of the State or against its political, economic, and cultural elements.
>
> *Article 20.* The territory of a State is inviolable; it may not be the object, even temporarily, of military occupation or of other measures of force taken by another State, directly or indirectly, on any grounds whatever.
>
> *Article 21.* The American States bind themselves in their international relations not to have recourse to the use of force, except in the case of self-defense in accordance with existing treaties or in fulfillment thereof.

Is unilateral humanitarian intervention never permissible among the member states of the OAS?

6. Can any case be made in support of a right to unilateral humanitarian intervention? If so, what are the arguments and how does one guard against humanitarian rationales being used by stronger nations to justify attacks upon weaker nations, as the Soviet Union may be said to have done in Hungary (1956), Czechoslovakia (1968), and Afghanistan

(1979), and as the United States may be said to have done in the Dominican Republic (1965) and Grenada (1983). If not, how, in the face of an extremely fragile UN Security Council, is it possible to prevent or stop atrocities such as the slaughter of more than a million Cambodians during the Pol Pot Khmer Rouge Regime in the mid-1970s, the apparently intentional death-by-starvation of a similar number of Ethiopians during 1984–85, or the continuing physical and psychological degradation of more than two million blacks in South Africa?

7. Clearly, Donnelly is not enamored of unilateral humanitarian intervention even if it can be said to be sometimes permissible either morally or legally. But what does he recommend in the alternative? Is his support of unilateral "positive nonintervention" anything more than unilateral humanitarian intervention by another name? What is the difference, if any, between the two? Suppose State A were to protest State B's human rights practices by withdrawing developmental assistance or trade privileges upon which State B depended, resulting in a significant deterioration of State B's economy. Would this constitute unilateral "positive nonintervention" or unilateral humanitarian intervention? What would Donnelly say? Either way, would it be legally permissible? In "American Intervention in Cuba and the Rule of Law" (*Ohio State Law Journal* 22 [Summer 1961]: 546–85), Richard Falk argues that the Eisenhower administration's withdrawal of Cuba's preferential sugar import quota to the United States, ostensibly in protest of Cuba's human rights practices, amounted to unlawful unilateral intervention since Cuba's economy was then dependent on the U.S. market. Frank Dawson and Burns Weston make the same point in "*Banco Nacional de Cuba v. Sabbatino:* New Wine in Old Bottles" (*University of Chicago Law Review* 31 [1963]: 63–102, at 94). Would Donnelly agree?

20. DAVID P. FORSYTHE *Congress and Human Rights in U.S. Foreign Policy: The Fate of General Legislation*

INTRODUCTION

Students of human rights and U.S. foreign policy know well that between 1973 and the end of the first Reagan administration the U.S. Congress placed a raft of human rights laws on the books. The present author categorizes the legislation as hortatory, general, country-specific, and function-specific. The focus here is on the general legislation. The hortatory acts have faded into political oblivion, whether they be parts of laws or nonbinding portions of congressional resolutions. That is precisely why they are labeled hortatory. By contrast, the country-specific and function-specific laws have received great attention, so much so that their fate requires separate analysis.

This essay argues the following about general legislation: Congress as a whole cannot usually give effective oversight to this legislation because the votes are not there to force the executive to follow the letter—or indeed sometimes even the spirit—of the laws adopted. When the executive disagrees with Congress on human rights it is only rarely that the Congress become sufficiently concerned about the fate of general legislation to compel the executive to implement the law. The actions of the first Reagan administration show especially clearly the executive's systematic disregard for congressional intent in much general human rights legislation, as well as Congress's inability to alter executive policy on general matters. Absent specific legislation, U.S. foreign policy would still be characterized by the Imperial Presidency.

SECURITY ASSISTANCE

Section 502B of the Foreign Assistance Act of 1961, as amended, reads in part that "no security assistance may be provided to any country the government of which engages in a consistent pattern of gross violations of internationally re-

Reprinted, with changes, from David P. Forsythe, "Congress and Human Rights in U.S. Foreign Policy: The Fate of General Legislation," *Human Rights Quarterly* 9 (1987): 382–404. Copyright © 1987 by Johns Hopkins University Press. Reprinted by permission.

cognized human rights . . . unless the President certifies in writing to the [Congress] that extraordinary circumstances exist warranting provision of such assistance. . . ."[1] The law further provides that if the President certifies extraordinary circumstances, "the Congress may at any time thereafter adopt a joint resolution terminating, restricting, or continuing security assistance for such country."[2] Among other provisions, section 502B states that "licenses may not be issued under the Export Administration Act of 1979 for the export of crime control and detection instruments and equipment"[3] to a gross violator of human rights unless the President certifies the need otherwise. Section 502B, offered in 1974 as a sense of the Congress resolution,[4] was made binding in 1978.[5]

The Carter administration was the first to have the responsibility for implementing section 502B as law, and it is now evident that it paid some attention to this statute—much more so than the preceding Republican administration when the section was not so clear or so clearly binding. The Carter administration never formally named a gross violator nor formally certified extraordinary circumstances, and even within the State Department it was not completely clear how section 502B affected executive decisions. To some participants in the Department, it seemed that the section was applied to twelve countries: Argentina, Bolivia, El Salvador, Guatemala, Haiti, Nicaragua, Paraguay, Uruguay, the Philippines, South Korea, Iran, and Zaire. The latter four seemed to fit the category of extraordinary circumstances; security assistance was actually terminated to the first eight.

It also seemed clear that the bowels of the State Department bureaucracy, especially the geographical bureaus, did not want to implement this statute. It *is* clear that the higher officials, while they might give some attention to the statute, would not implement the letter of the law by publicly naming those engaged in a consistent pattern of gross violations or going through the formal process of certifying exceptions.

There were also times when section 502B was largely ignored. Indonesia's security assistance was never restricted, yet its government held thousands of political prisoners for long periods and engaged in protracted brutal actions in East Timor. The Carter administration recommended increased military assistance to El Salvador in 1980 and early 1981 at a time when gross violations of human rights were pronounced and undenied. At approximately this same time the administration sought increased military sales and the transfer of military equipment to Guatemala, despite the continuation of massive violations of human rights.

These actions by the Carter administration went without effective challenge in the Congress, except concerning Guatemala. Hearings were held on human rights in Indonesia and East Timor but the only congressional action that forced a change in executive policy was a denial of proposed military items to Guatemala in 1980 for 1981.

On the subject of the transfer of crime control equipment, including items that might be used for torture and mistreatment as well as general repression, information is classified by the government. Interviews in Washington indicate that the Carter administration did seek to implement this provision. The State Department through the Human Rights and Humanitarian Affairs Bureau (HA) did have a list of countries in this regard, and did engage in conflict, particularly with the Department of Commerce, in order to restrict certain sales to certain countries. U.S. companies and the Department of Commerce wanted the transfers; they thought human rights restrictions were an idealistic interference in business practices that would result in a loss of trade to competitors. Yet HA and top officials in the Carter administration sometimes prevailed in blocking such transfers on the basis of part of section 502B. The confidential reports sent to Congress seemed to satisfy those few members of Congress and staff persons who tracked these events.

The Reagan administration changed policy drastically concerning security assistance. It wanted to increase security assistance to countries that were anti-communist, and hence it refused to consider reducing security assistance or

---

1. 22 U.S.C. § 2304(a)(2) (1982).
2. Ibid. § 2304(c)(4)(A).
3. Ibid. § 2304(a)(2).
4. Foreign Assistance Act of 1974, Public Law No. 93-559, sec. 46, 88 Stat. 1795, 1815 (1974) (adding § 502B to the Foreign Assistance Act of 1961) (later amended).
5. International Security Assistance Act of 1978, Public Law No. 95-384, sec. 6, 92 Stat. 730, 731 (1978) (codified as amended at 22 U.S.C. § 2304(a) (1982)).

sales because of human rights considerations. In so doing the Reagan administration ignored the spirit and letter of section 502B. It held two fundamental views in this regard. First, the United States faced a clear and present danger from the Soviet Union and its allies and proxies; the United States should respond with more, not less, security assistance. Second, repressive allies of the United States, by definition, were better than communists because they would eventually move toward democracy; therefore they did not engage in a consistent pattern of gross violations of human rights. This view, called by some the Kirkpatrick thesis on dictatorships and double standards, has in fact been Reagan policy with regard to most of section 502B. It was articulated consistently by Elliott Abrams, the Assistant Secretary of State for Human Rights and Humanitarian Affairs during the first Reagan administration.[6]

No security assistance was cut, much less terminated, by the Reagan administration for human rights reasons during the 1981–1984 period. Indeed, security assistance was up some 300 percent by 1984, compared to 1980.

Congress, it can be noted, approved this increase in security assistance and as a body did not object to the Reagan administration's burial of the core provisions of section 502B. There were critics, however, of the administration's treatment of this and other human rights statutes. These critics were found mainly in House committees or subcommittees dealing with foreign affairs, and among private groups. But with the exception of certain Latin American countries, the administration got in general the security assistance it wanted. The Congress did use country-specific legislation to limit or block military assistance or sales to Chile and for a time to Argentina, El Salvador, and Guatemala. A number of members of Congress or their staff persons indicated in interviews in 1986, however, that the core of 502B was a dead letter as far as its direct influences on policy was concerned.

The Reagan administration did, by contrast, seek to implement the part of section 502B dealing with crime control equipment. In this respect the Reagan administration was similar to the Carter administration. In fact, Reagan's human rights team may have exceeded Carter's in vigor and effectiveness, although it is difficult to know since the overall picture remains classified. Interviews toward the end of the first Reagan administration indicated that in a given year Reagan's people at the Department of State blocked more crime control equipment in the name of human rights than Carter's staff. . . .

Under the Reagan administration, however, several controversial transfers were approved, to be rolled back under negative publicity. Shock batons, said to be for cattle control but obviously used by police forces against persons, were approved for both South Africa and South Korea. And equipment that could be used for torture was approved for export to all NATO countries, including Turkey where torture was a fact admitted even by the administration. These approvals were variously attributed to insensitivity by the Department of Commerce, laxness by the Department of State, or other causes. Congress played a role, along with the press, in successfully pressuring the executive to change these specific approvals. Congressional sources of both parties seemed satisfied with the Reagan administration's overall record on this particular part of section 502B.

ECONOMIC ASSISTANCE

The Harkin Amendment, section 116 of the Foreign Assistance Act of 1961, as amended, prohibits economic assistance to "the government of any country which engages in a consistent pattern of gross violations of internationally recognized human rights . . . unless such assistance will directly benefit the needy people in such country."[7] This ban was extended to the Food for Peace program[8] and to U.S. insurance for Amer-

6. See Jeane Kirkpatrick, "Dictatorships and Double Standards, "*Commentary* 68 (Nov. 1979): 34–45. Her thesis has actually been around for some time. See, e.g., Henry Kissinger, "Continuity and Change in American Foreign Policy," in *Human Rights and World Order,* ed. Abdul Aziz Said (New Brunswick, N.J.: Transaction Books, 1978). See also Abrams's speech to World Jewish Congress, New York City, an. 19, 1982 (text furnished to the author by Mr. Abrams). See further Charles Maechling, Jr., "Human Rights Dehumanized," *Foreign Policy* no. 52 (Fall 1983): 124. Mr. Abrams critiques Mr. Maechling but does not refer to the statements quoted here, in *Foreign Policy* no. 53 (Winter 1983–84): 173–74.
7. 22 U.S.C. § 2151n(a) (1982).
8. 7 U.S.C. § 1712 (1982).

ican investors abroad.[9] Congress gave itself the authority by joint resolution to override an executive decision on these matters.[10]

Section 116, signed into law in 1974, was not given much attention during the Kissinger years. The Carter administration altered this state of affairs. The so-called Christopher Committee, named after Deputy Secretary of State Warren Christopher, was created and functioned actively to coordinate assistance policy across departmental lines. Human rights was one of the factors taken into account in the decision to provide a certain amount of economic aid. Section 116 was thus brought to bear on U.S. policy, and the Carter administration occasionally reduced some aid levels because of a consistent pattern of gross violations of internationally recognized human rights. The administration did not make these decisions public. Moreover, the Agency for International Development (AID), an independent agency but tied closely to the State Department, tried to honor the wording of section 116 concerning "needy people." If the view is correct that most AID programs are for "needy people" or meeting basic human needs (BHN), nevertheless some AID activity is directed to promoting national economic growth in a more general sense. During the Carter administration AID altered some of this latter activity to conform with the intent of section 116. About a half-dozen other countries received special scrutiny from the Carter team concerning P.L. 480, the Food for Peace program, because of serious human rights problems. The Reagan administration altered State Department policy regarding section 116, but not so much AID policy. It was clear from the public and private record that the Reagan administration was as reluctant to manipulate economic as security assistance in the name of human rights. Said Assistant Secretary Abrams in 1983, "[W]e are reluctant to use economic aid as tools for our [human rights] policy." The Christopher Committee was effectively disbanded, despite a congressional resolution urging its continuation. A lower ranking coordinating committee met periodically. Occasional memoranda were circulated on the subject of human rights and economic aid, but the entire subject

was downgraded. HA, like the rest of Reagan's State Department, did not want to restrict economic aid for human rights reasons. The administration was prepared to restrict aid to some leftist regimes—e.g., Nicaragua, which had its aid terminated on the second day of the Reagan administration. Sometimes human rights and sometimes strategic concerns were cited as the reason for such restrictions. . . .

The Agency for International Development, for its part, continued to alter some of its programs to deny general development aid to certain gross violators and continued to monitor closely P.L. 480 programs in a handful of nations where food might be denied to some on political grounds. Other aid to those regimes continued when they met basic human needs. It was rare for HA to challenge AID decisions on these matters. Since most AID programs were seen as essentially BHN programs, the programs and countries so affected were few.

Some members of Congress did focus on one action by the Reagan administration related to section 116. In 1983 the administration, at a time of civil unrest in Chile related to repression by the Pinochet regime, signed an agreement with that government permitting future insurance for American investors under the Overseas Private Investment Corporation (OPIC). The administration did not at this time certify progress on human rights as required by other congressional legislation, but it moved ahead with the OPIC general agreement anyway. The propriety of this action was challenged by several representatives. Administration spokespersons argued that the signed agreement did not violate section 116 because no specific OPIC contracts had been signed. Concerned members of Congress argued that the general agreement was the wrong signal to send to Chile, given its continuing violations of human rights.[11] At the time of [this] writing, no specific OPIC contracts had been concluded with Pinochet's Chile.

Another part of section 116 was implemented by AID during the Reagan administration. Congress, not the executive, initiated the idea of a positive use of economic aid linked to human rights. In 1981 Congress made available $1.5 mil-

9. 22 U.S.C. § 2199(i) (1982).

10. 22 U.S.C. § 2151n(b) (1982).

11. House Committee on Foreign Affairs, Subcommittees on Human Rights and International Organizations and on Western Hemisphere Affairs, *Hearings: Human Rights in Argentina, Chile, Paraguay, and Uruguay,* 98th Cong., 1st sess.; October 4 and 21, 1983, especially at 171–74.

lion for the promotion of civil and political rights in developing countries, provided that the money was not used to influence any election.[12] In 1984 that sum was expanded to just over $3 million, again on congressional initiative.[13] AID willingly implemented this small program, approving a variety of projects such as providing human rights materials to libraries, helping to train monitors for elections, and helping to pay the costs of human rights seminars for lawyers. Privately some AID officials noted the difficulty of finding projects that could be safely executed in authoritarian developing countires where working for civil and political rights could be seen by the ruling authorities as subversive activity.

Private studies have concluded that [amounts of] both security and economic assistance during the Carter and Reagan years were largely maintained at consistent levels. They were not adjusted to any great extent for human rights or other reasons.

MULTILATERAL BANKS

In the International Financial Assistance Act (IFI Act) of 1977, Congress instructed the executive via section 701 to use its "voice and vote" in international financial institutions (IFIs) "to channel assistance toward countries other than those whose governments engage in . . . a consistent pattern of gross violations of internationally recognized human rights . . . unless such assistance is directed specifically to programs which serve the basic human needs of the citizens of such country."[14] This language was always controversial, for when proposed first in 1976 and then again in 1977 it was opposed by the executive as an unwise restriction on executive authority and a politicization of the multilateral banks. After 1980 the language became the focal point for a long-running debate between the Reagan administration and its critics concerning human rights.

The forum for much of this debate was the

Subcommittee on International Development Institutions and Finance of the House Committee on Banking, Finance and Urban Affairs. There were several reasons why this should be the place for general debate on the human rights policy of the Reagan administration. The language of the IFI Act was similar to other human rights legislation, containing the phrase "consistent pattern of gross violations of internationally recognized human rights." More importantly, there were personnel reasons fueling the debate. On the Subcommittee on International Development Institutions, both the chair and the ranking minority member were interested in human rights, possessed of formidable intellectual powers, and critical of Reagan policy. The chair was Jerry Patterson, Democrat from California. The ranking Republican was Jim Leach, Republican from Iowa. They were more informed, active, and critical during the 1981–84 period than others who could have used their positions to stimulate debate or legislation but did not. . . .

On the Senate side there was no focal point for human rights debate. Republicans held the majority after 1980 and were somewhat reluctant to criticize the policies of a Republican president—with exceptions. There was no human rights subcommittee. Therefore, much oversight of general human rights legislation was attempted by the House, especially by the Subcommittee on International Development Institutions.

The Carter administration, despite having opposed the 1977 IFI legislation, gave some attention to its provisions on human rights during the 1978–1980 period. It certainly did not emphasize this legislation. It did abstain or vote against a number of loan proposals in the IFIs on human rights grounds, and the list of targeted states included right wing allies. . . . All loans to these states were eventually approved. It is evident that the United States did not pressure its voting partners to block these loans. Hence the Carter delegation could go on record as voting a concern for human rights without really interfering with

---

12. International Security and Development Cooperation Act of 1981, Public Law No. 97–113, sec. 306, 95 Stat. 1519, 1533 (1981) (amending sec. 116(e) of the Foreign Assistance Act of 1961) (codified at 22 U.S.C. § 2151n(e) (1982)).

13. Public Law No. 95-118, sec. 701, 91 Stat. 1067, 1069–70 (1977) (codified as amended at 22 U.S.C. § 262d(a), (f) (1982)).

14. Department of State Authorization Act, Public Law No. 98-164, sec. 1002(a)(1), 97 Stat. 1017, 1052 (1983) (codified at 22 U.S.C. § 2151n(e)(1) (Supp. III 1985)).

IFI programs. Nevertheless it could at least be said that the Carter administration did not [flout] the IFI Act.

The same could not be said for the Reagan administration. In 1981 that administration began to change U.S. policy in the multilateral banks by voting for loans to right wing allies while voting against loans to certain left wing developing countries. Moreover, it did so initially without providing Congress with what the latter thought was the adequate consultation called for in the law. The two actions together produced a vigorous response from Patterson's subcommittee and eventually some revision of the 1977 legislation.

It is useful at the outset of this analysis to have a clear picture of the changes made by the Reagan administration in U.S. voting in the multilateral banks. . . . Rhetoric aside, it is clear that the Kirkpatrick thesis on dictatorships and double standards progressively became U.S. policy in the IFIs.

In 1983 there was a joint hearing before Patterson's subcommittee and the Subcommittee on Africa of the House Committee of Foreign Affairs. The chair of the latter subcommittee was Representative Howard Wolpe, Democrat from Michigan. The following exchange occurred with Assistant Secretary Abrams:

> Chairman Wolpe: Let me ask you this. Do you believe that Angola is, in the language of the statute [section 701] . . . a gross violator of human rights?
> Mr. Abrams: I have never formed an opinion about that.
> Chairman Wolpe: More importantly, nor has your own Human Rights Bureau.
> Mr. Abrams: We don't actually form opinions about that question because it is not a useful way to spend our time.[15]

In more guarded moments, administration officials argued that improvements interrupted a consistent pattern of violations. This prompted Representative Leach on more than one occasion to remark that one could still have a consistent pattern of gross violations even if there were some improvements. "It is as if one were to argue in the days of Nazi Germany that the closing of Dachau and Auschwitz, while leaving Buchenwald open, would represent sufficient 'improvement' to warrant a legal determination that a 'consistent pattern' of gross violations no longer existed."[16]

Patterson, Wolpe, Leach, and other members of Congress stressed the logic and legislative history of the law. These individuals were joined by various human rights groups which testified in opposition to administration policy. In 1983 they persuaded Congress to drop the word "consistent" from the IFI Act. The intention was to signal the administration to stop using the "improvement doctrine" to justify continued assistance, especially in the IFIs, to those right wing governments with a pattern of gross violations of human rights. As Chairman Patterson said in testimony, "The deletion clarifies and strengthens, rather than drastically changes congressional intents and helps clear up ambiguities which have dogged efforts to encourage even-handed enforcement of Section 701."[17] But the administration continued its double standard of supporting loans to right wing regimes while voting against loans to leftists. One might force an administration to change its tactical arguments, but one could not by legislation force an administration to alter a deeply held view of the world.

Toward the end of the first Reagan administration there appeared to be some confusion in U.S. policy in the IFIs, at least with regard to Chile. In 1984 and 1985 in a context of considerable public debate, the administration first voted for a loan to Chile in the InterAmerican Development Bank, despite a clear pattern of violations of fundamental human rights by the Pinochet dictatorship. Later the administration abstained on another vote, with a spokesperson indicating human rights reasons. Shortly thereafter the administration indicated further support

---

15. House Committee on Banking, Finance and Urban Affairs, Subcommittee on International Development Institutions and Finance, and House Committee on Foreign Affairs, Subcommittee on Africa, *Hearing: Human Rights Policies at the Multilateral Development Banks,* 98th Cong., 1st sess., June 22, 1983, 85.

16. House Committee on Banking, Finance and Urban Affairs, *Report 98–178,* 98th Cong., 1st sess., May 16, 1983, 27.

17. House Subcommittee on Human and International Organizations, House Committee on Foreign Affairs, *Hearings: Review of U.S. Human Rights Policy,* 98th Cong., 1st sess., 3 Mar., 28 Jun., 21 Sept., 1983, 140.

for the Pinochet regime in several ways, thus calling into question the reason for the abstention. Policy thus seemed confused, although one could ṇot discount the possibility that an effort by HA to emphasize human rights violations might have been reversed by others in Washington.

It should be noted that the critics of the administration were in a weak bargaining position regarding section 701. They could try to shut off funding to the IFIs, but this would tend to throw the baby out with the bathwater. Most of the critics were liberals who supported the multilateral development banks as a good way to help developing countries. They did not want to cripple the banks or hurt the lesser developed countries by cutting off funds over Reagan's human rights policies. Hence the leverage of the critics was limited, as they admitted publicly, and as Reagan officials perceived all along. . . .

With regard to implementation of section 701 of the IFI Act, one can say that the Carter and Reagan administrations, especially their Treasury Departments, disliked the provisions on human rights. The Carter team did not flagrantly violate the law but rather used its vote in the IFIs to signal concern about the human rights situation in a balanced list of countries, without interfering with the loans. The Reagan team basically ignored the law, except when it used human rights as a weapon against a leftist regime.

The fate of section 701 was the same as that of 502B and 116. While all of this general legislation mildly influenced the Carter administration, which was predisposed to do something about human rights, it failed to influence the Reagan administration. The core problem was that any general legislation could be avoided by the executive with specious arguments. . . . As one Carter official from the HA Bureau remarked in an interview, only partially in jest, "We used the straight face test. If you could go up on the Hill and testify and keep a straight face while making your arguments, you could probably get away with it. If your argument was so silly you couldn't keep a straight face, your policy was in trouble."

Congress as a body did not want to substitute its wisdom for the executive's on security assistance; it did not want to cut BHN aid over human rights; and it did not want to reduce the U.S. con-

tribution to the multilateral banks. The last two points pertained especially to liberals, who were the chief critics of Reagan's human rights policies. Unless Congress resorted to supplemental country-specific legislation, its general enactments on human rights could be ignored or violated by the executive—and they were by the Reagan administration. The two exceptions were the provision of 502B regarding crime control equipment and AID deliberations concerning what was a BHN program under section 116. The situation regarding sections 502B, 116, and 701 was summed up by Aryeh Neier of Americas Watch, in testimony in 1983:

> It seems sort of foolish to have to say "and we meant it" with respect to various legislation. Even so, there may have to be legislation that says "and we meant it." That is, if the administration seems to flout guidelines in the law as to U.S. programs, then the Congress simply has to have outright prohibitions and not merely discretionary determinations by the administration.[18]

[Editors' note: The author next analyzes United States refugee policy (see Reading 7 in Chapter 2 in this volume) and United States policy toward communist emigration." He concludes that Congress was too fragmented to pressure the executive to provide fair and nonideological treatment to persons seeking refugee status in the United States. He concludes also that Congress was more united in pressing for reasonable emigration from communist countries, particularly Romania.]

EXPORT-IMPORT FINANCING

Brief mention can be made of the rapid rise, limited use, and rapid decline of the idea that the U.S. Export-Import (Ex-Im) Bank should be a tool in the fight to promote human rights in U.S. foreign policy. Congress authorized the President to deny Ex-Im credits to human rights violators where the U.S. national interest would be so advanced.[19] In such cases, foreign parties could not obtain an Ex-Im loan to purchase goods or services from American companies.

The early form of this authorization was supported in principle by the Carter administration, but that administration never saw economic

---

18. *Hearings: Human Rights in Argentina, Chile, Paraguay, and Uruguay* (see n. 11 above), 134.
19. 12 U.S.C. § 635(b)(1)(B) (1982).

sanctions as a major weapon in the struggle to protect human rights abroad. Its support for UN economic sanctions on Rhodesia was the major exception that proved the basic rule. It had to be pushed by Congress into a coffee embargo on Uganda. The Carter team denied or delayed Ex-Im credits to only four countries (Argentina, Chile, South Africa, Uruguay).

It is not surprising that Ex-Im loans ceased to be even a limited tool for the attempted protection of human rights during the Reagan administration. In an era of U.S. trade imbalances and growing concern about the U.S. ability to compete successfully in world markets, there was little inclination in Washington to restrict U.S. exports in the name of human rights. Indeed, in congressional hearings on the Ex-Im Bank during the first Reagan administration, human rights was a subject of no consequence whatsoever. Needless to say, the administration did not act under the authorization granted to it to link Ex-Im loans with human rights. Only on the subject of South Africa was there a continuing desire in the Congress to prevent Ex-Im credits in the name of human rights. Congress required the executive to certify that agencies and companies benefiting from Ex-Im loans were making progress in implementing the Sullivan Principles designed to end racial segregation in South Africa's economy. This "Evans Amendment" had some symbolic importance, but it affected a very small part of the South African economy and was overshadowed by the subsequent congressional move toward general economic sanctions.

CONCLUSIONS

Congress has passed general legislation on human rights, but it has lacked—as a general body—the attention span, the will power, and the consensus for effective oversight that would implement the original congressional intent. On security assistance it may be that most members of Congress came to accept the executive's argument, repeated by different administrations, that the public naming of a gross violator of internationally recognized human rights was not a good idea in U.S. foreign policy. On economic assistance it was difficult to focus on human rights violations if some U.S. aid was reaching the most needy people in a foreign society. On indirect aid via multilateral institutions, concerned members of Congress had little leverage; most who were concerned about human rights were also concerned about development aid to lesser developed countries. How could they pressure the executive to link human rights to loans without cutting off the money for loans? . . . There was not . . . interest in using the U.S. Export-Import Bank for human rights purposes, except in South Africa.

It was one thing to pass general laws in favor of human rights. It was another thing to get the executive to give them serious attention. It was, in fact, difficult to get Congress as a body to engage in oversight of what it had originally legislated, although specialized subcommittees on the House side made a serious effort in a number of cases.

QUESTIONS FOR REFLECTION AND DISCUSSION

1. Traditionally, in the United States, the making and shaping of international human rights policy has been done by the executive branch, with help from the legislative and judicial branches. Why, in recent years, has Congress asserted itself in this realm? Is that a desirable departure from tradition? Why? Why not?

2. David Forsythe identifies several ways in which Congress has made itself felt in the making and shaping of U.S. international human rights policy. Which has been the most effective? The least effective? Why?

3. Forsythe describes the response of the Carter and Reagan administrations to the international human rights initiatives taken by Congress in recent years. In terms of promoting and protecting international human rights, which administration has the best record? The worst? Is either very good? Why? Why not?

4. As is apparent from Forsythe's essay, both the Carter and the Reagan administrations manipulated congressional human rights policy to suit their particular conveniences and purposes (although, it appears, the latter more than the former). Should the executive branch ever be permitted to distort or ignore congressional intent in this regard? If so, under what circumstances? If not, why not?

5. Is it fair to identify a particular administration as tolerating human rights violations when it seeks to circumvent congressional intent relative to the promotion and protection of international human rights? Other than for Machiavellian reasons, why might a particular administration be less than vigorous in the defense of international human rights policy as congressionally defined? Might there be economic or security factors that could operate to retard the advancement of human rights through foreign policy even in the presence of the best of intentions? If so, what might they be and how should they be factored into the balance of relevant considerations? What costs might be involved?

6. In discussing the Reagan administration's reasons for refusing to consider reduced security assistance or sales because of human rights considerations, Forsythe mentions "the Kirkpatrick thesis on dictatorships and double standards," that is, the view that anticommunist dictatorships allied with the United States are more likely than communist regimes to move eventually toward democracy and that therefore the United States should respond with more, not less, security assistance to such countries, given the clear and present danger of the Soviet Union and its allies. Do you agree with the Kirkpatrick thesis? Why? Why not? Is there any evidence that her thesis may have historical validity? What about now democratic Portugal and Spain, not so long ago fascist Portugal and Spain?

7. Should the manipulation of United States' foreign aid be used to promote human rights? Does not such a policy smack of "cultural imperialism"? In the absence of a centralized world authority capable and willing to support the struggle for human rights, is there any alternative?

8. Food aid may be one of the most important tools available to the United States to influence the human rights policies of other countries. Is food aid used in this way? Why? Why not? Should it be? Why? Why not?

21. RICHARD P. CLAUDE *The Case of Joelito Filártiga in the Courts*

This case study details the humanitarian work and adversities befalling the family of Dr. Joel Filártiga and the torture-murder of Joelito, his seventeen-year-old son. The essay describes and analyzes Dr. Filártiga's legal vindication through civil litigation in the United States. Filed in 1979, *Filártiga v. Peña-Irala*[1] has helped to set United States judicial policy on a course of reform. It has made clear that abusers of internationally defined human rights from other countries who find themselves in the United States can be held liable for damages. . . .

THE POLITICS OF PUBLIC HEALTH IN PARAGUAY

"My clinic is called the 'Clinic of Hope,' and our praxis is hope," Dr. Joel Filártiga stated in 1982. He was referring to El Sanatorio la Esperanza, which he founded and operates. It is the largest private health clinic for the poor in Paraguay. This clinic serves between 32,000 and 37,000 *campesinos* (peasants) in the central great valley and surrounding mountains around Ybycuí. From a tobacco-producing family, Joel Holden Filártiga Ferreira chose to work in the rural area centered at Ybycuí because, in his words, "there was no doctor there to serve the people.". . .

In its report on *Health Conditions in the Americas, 1977–1980,* the Pan American Health Organization profiles Paraguay as a country characterized by problems of undernourishment and malnourishment, a high incidence of parasitic and infectious communicable diseases, diseases preventable by vaccination, tuberculosis, Chagas' disease, leprosy, and accidents and violent acts— maladies of extreme poverty, bad sanitation, and neglect. . . . By any measure, the health situation in Paraguay is unsatisfactory because public financing of health services is insufficient to meet

1. Filártiga v. Peña-Irala, 630 F.2d 876 (2d Cir. 1980).

Reprinted, with changes, from Richard P. Claude, "The Case of Joelito Filártiga and the 'Clinic of Hope,'" *Human Rights Quarterly* 5 (1983): 275–95. Copyright © 1983 by Johns Hopkins University Press. Reprinted by permission.

current needs, and because existing health establishments are unable to provide total population coverage. In short, the Paraguayan politics of public health yield bleak prospects for [improvement].

The chief hospital serving the needs of the rural poor in Ybycuí is El Sanatorio la Esperanza, the Clinic of Hope, founded by Dr. Joel Filártiga in 1960. Dr. Filártiga says the facility:

has become my life, an expression of my philosophy. I believe that all people have a basic human right to medical care and, given the reality that all but a handful of doctors refuse to leave the comforts of the cities to practice medicine in the countryside, it was the only decision I could make and still retain my integrity.[2]

La Esperanza receives no government aid. It operates on the basis of Dr. Filártiga's volunteer work, with the assistance of his wife, Nidia, acting as nurse and with the part-time help of their three daughters. Until his death in 1976, Joel, Jr., who was then a high school student, acted as a driver and chauffeur at the Clinic. Patients often pay for medical services by stacking wood or by giving such goods as vegetables and chickens. Since the tragic day when the Filártigas' son was murdered, no charges have been levied on Thursdays as a way of honoring Joelito's memory. As this income is not sufficient to meet the expenses of the Clinic, fundraising is done internationally by the sale of Dr. Filártiga's artwork—which primarily consists of pen and ink drawings designed to symbolize human anguish connected with political irresponsibility.

Dr. Filártiga's art involves a combination of expressionism and surrealism described by the Asunción newspaper *La Tribuna* as "the pure and unmasked encounter with psychic pain." The work is in the manner of the Mexican muralists Orozco and Siquieros. It speaks of the poverty and powerlessness of the peasants through such symbols as prison bars, ballot boxes with no slot, broken guitars, and the suffering faces of peasants. His sketches are exhibited in Europe, throughout Latin America, and in the United States. They are found in private collections as well as galleries and museums worldwide. The artist says that he has dedicated both his medicine and his art to the poor. But he says, "this com-

bination of endeavors is seen as political because (in Paraguay) the structure of society inclines many to take advantage of the poor in order to get more profit." Filártiga also says: "To do the opposite—to try to take what those people have to return it to the poor—it's a matter that's seen as subversive."

In December 1975 and for two months thereafter, Dr. Filártiga went on a fundraising tour in Mexico and the United States. During the tour, he spoke about mindless repression of the peasants and harsh conditions of the rural poor in Paraguay. He noted that his art "is not designed to be beautiful but it is supposed to be true." He asked for donations from the sale of his art for the Clinic of Hope. . . .

While Dr. Filártiga was away from Paraguay in early 1976 an event developed with fateful results for the Filártiga family. A group of Paraguayan guerrillas initially organized in Argentina, the *Organización Político-Militar* (O.P.M.) surprised authorities by its successful infiltration through the border town of Posdas, Argentina. In March and April, confrontations between O.P.M. guerrilas and the Paraguayan police involved several shootouts with losses of life on both sides. A wave of ferocious repression resulted in hundreds of people being detained. . . .

Speaking of events in 1976 and writing in the Jesuit magazine *America,* Alberto Cabral stated, "in mid-March, when the police first began receiving reports about the O.P.M., they were still attempting to gather information and identify their targets. Because of Dr. Filártiga's notoriety as an outspoken critic of the regime, he and his family immediately came under suspicion." Cabral concluded that Filártiga's exhibition and lecture tour through California and Mexico in 1976 fueled government suspicion. "Furthermore, the family's frequent trips to visit Mrs. Filártiga's mother in Posadas, Argentina—the point from which guerrilla reinforcements reportedly were infiltrating—contributed toward making the Filártigas prime suspects."[3]

THE KILLING OF JOELITO

When a society such as Paraguay becomes politicized, nothing is neutral. Thus Dr. Joel Filár-

2. Quoted by Michele Burgess, "Physician Artist is the Schweitzer of Paraguay," *Maryknoll* (September 1978), 8–10, 9.
3. Alberto Cabral (pseudonym for Richard Alan White), "Political Murder in Paraguay," *America* (Apr. 23, 1977), 376–78 at 377.

tiga's artwork, his clinic, his lecture tours, his work with the poor—all became suspect. Américo Peña-Irala, a neighbor of the Filártigas and police inspector of Asunción, took action. Whether Peña was cleared by the Chief of the Secret Police, Pastor Coronel, and the Paraguayan Minister of the Interior, Sabino Agosto Mantanaro, to kidnap the son of Dr. Filártiga remains a disputed matter. In any event, the kidnapping of Joelito was planned to take place while Dr. and Mrs. Filártiga were eighty miles away at La Esperanza, the clinic in Ybycuí. Supposedly, the scheme was designed to obtain information from Joelito regarding Dr. Filártiga in order to convict the physician of sedition.

Late during the night of 29 March 1976, Américo Peña and three other police officials kidnapped Joelito from the Filártiga home in Asunción and took him to the police station (*comisaria*). There they tortured Joelito brutally for one and one-half hours as they questioned him about his father's activities. The entire torture and interrogation session was tape recorded. However, no evidence against Dr. Filártiga was obtained; instead the recording carried Joelito's voice pleading, "I do not know anything. Why are you doing this to me?"

Peña and the three other police beat and whipped the youth severely over his entire body. They also resorted to the use of high voltage electric shocks administered to Joelito through his fingertips and through a wire inserted in his penis. The electric shocks were ultimately increased to such a frequency and intensity that Joelito died of cardiac arrest. In the face of his unexpected death, Peña and the other officers panicked and attempted to disguise their deed by severing Joelito's major arteries so that the body could not be embalmed and thus would require quick burial.

Paraguayan law excuses from punishment a "crime of passion" by a husband who kills another caught in adultery with his wife. To bring the killing of Joelito under this shield, the four policemen took the body to Peña's own house (which was only two doors down the street from the Filártiga residence in Asunción). The police inspector supervised the placing of the corpse into the bed of the seventeen-year-old daughter—Rosario Villalba—of Peña's mistress, Juana B. Villalba. Peña then contacted Rosario's husband,

Hugo Duarte, and told him to come to the Peña residence immediately. Pleading a toothache, Duarte left his work as a night clerk and arrived home only to be beaten by Peña and the other police. He was forced to agree to a fabricated story to the effect that he had found Joelito in bed with his wife and killed him in a fit of passion. Duarte was then arrested, and Dr. Hernán Molines, the Coroner, made out a false medical report supportive of the "crime of passion" theory. Judge Diógenes Martinez, who was later assigned to try the case, arrived at the house to legalize the falsified death certificate.

Four hours after Joelito was quietly kidnapped from the Filártiga house, his twenty-year-old sister, Dolly, was awakened at her home by two uniformed police officers from a nearby police station. She was taken to Peña's house, where she was shown the whipped, slashed, and electric shocked corpse of her brother. In Dolly's testimony:

They told me to be as quiet as possible because it was dawn. They also asked me to take away the body of my brother as soon as possible and bury it. To which I answered them that they should let me think; that I didn't know what to do. In my desperation, I ran to the street, and I met Peña in the hall of the house. I asked him, "sir what have you done to my brother?" He answered me, "shut up. Here you have what you have been looking for and deserved."[4]

Rosario, the supposed adultress, was arrested as a material witness, but released on 7 April 1976. She then sent a note to Dr. Filártiga saying that she wished to speak to him, but before a meeting could be arranged, she disappeared. Rosario Villalba has not been found since that time, although a Filártiga cousin, Juan Alberto Filártiga, attempted to locate her. He too has subsequently disappeared.

Dr. Joel Filártiga requested and obtained an independent autopsy from three prominent Paraguayan physicians. They concluded that Joelito was whipped and beaten in the commonly known execution style used by police and that he died of cardiac arrest caused by electric shocks. "I thought the most important thing was to document the facts," Dr. Filártiga said. As part of the documentation, he took many photographs of the corpse.

Paraguayan law allows a private party, on

---

4. Transcript of hearings before Magistrate John L. Caden, Feb. 12, 1982, Filártiga v. Peña-Irala, Civil Case No. 79-917 (E.D.N.Y.), at 15–16.

leave of the court, to proceed with a criminal suit in conjunction with the state, but with his/her own lawyer and witnesses. The Filártigas brought such a suit to challenge the government's version of Joelito's death—the "crime of passion" theory. When Dr. Filártiga's attorney, Horacio Galeano Peronne, asked that key police officers be summoned, the lawyer was arrested. He was taken to the central police headquarters where he was caged and shackled to a wall. Inspector Peña arrived on the occasion, 30 September 1976, and threatened to kill Galeano Perrone as well as members of the Filártiga family and friends if they continued to press the lawsuit against him. Harassment tactics were used further to reinforce the threat. Dr. Filártiga was threatened with a loss of his medical license. Anonymous phone calls were frequent and frightening. Mrs. Filártiga and her daughter were detained in jail for one day. Attorney Galeano Perrone was disbarred. Finally, a Paraguayan court denied the Filártiga request to file the suit.

Even though the Paraguayan legal process failed, the process of affecting public opinion did not. Before Joelito's funeral, the family decided upon the unusual step of displaying the nude, wrecked body of the deceased for public viewing. The outpouring of local sympathy for the Filártigas was substantial, with two thousand people attending the funeral. Five thousand color duplicates of a photo of Joelito's tortured corpse were circulated in Paraguay and abroad. Pictures and documentation of the crime were sent to Amnesty International in London. Human rights groups worldwide took an interest in the case. The U.S. Embassy sponsored a widely publicized exhibition of Dr. Filártiga's art at the Paraguayan-American Cultural Center. Asunción newspapers carried a photograph of the September 1976 affair, portraying Ambassador George Landau shaking hands with Dr. Filártiga. The exhibit was dedicated to Joelito's memory.

THE FILÁRTIGAS' SEARCH FOR JUSTICE

By late 1977, the case of the politically motivated torture-murder of Joelito Filártiga had become a major international human rights issue. Under a barrage of criticism for human rights violations in Paraguay, reinforced by suspension of international loans to the country and protests by U.S. Ambassador Robert White, General Stroessner "retired" Inspector Peña from the police. Shortly thereafter, on 21 July 1978, Américo Peña, his mistress Juana B. Villalba, their son and her niece, using their real names, entered the United States. They claimed to be tourists en route to visit Disney World, but instead they went to Brooklyn, New York. There they lived until exiled Paraguayans and human rights groups, primarily the Council on Hemispheric Affairs, discovered Peña's whereabouts. As a result, the U.S. Immigration and Naturalization Service arrested Peña and those with him, and charged him with overstaying their three-month visa.

Upon arraignment the day after their arrest, Peña, his mistress, son, and niece requested immediate voluntary deportation, and they were ordered deported within five days. But the Immigration and Naturalization Service obtained an order from U.S. District Court Judge Eugene H. Nickerson staying the deportation order to allow further investigation of Peña's activities while in the United States. Dolly Filártiga, living in Washington, D.C., at the time and seeking political asylum in the United States, was joined by her father—then in New York—in an effort to use [the] U.S. legal process to question Peña. As a result of the request to hold Peña, Judge Nickerson issued a temporary stay of the deportation order to allow the defendants to secure an attorney, to permit questioning by the Filártigas, and to give the Immigration and Naturalization Service an opportunity to review the circumstances surrounding Peña's entry to the United States.

The Filártigas sought legal representation from Michael Maggio—an immigration attorney in Washington, working in conjunction with the Center for Constitutional Rights in New York. The legal strategy was the creation of Center lawyers Peter Weiss, Rhonda Copelon, and Jose Antonio Lugo. They intervened in the deportation proceeding to file a ten million dollar civil suit against Américo Peña under the antique terms of a little-used provision of the Judiciary Act of 1789. That law, the Alien Tort Statute, now codified as Title 28 of the United States Code, Section 1350, provides: "The district courts shall have original jurisdiction of any civil action by an alien for a tort only, committed in violation of the law of nations or a treaty of the United States."[5]

---

5. 28 U.S.C. §1350 (1976).

Peña's lawyers filed a motion to dismiss the Filártigas' alien tort action, denying that torture is a tort (personal wrong) in violation of the law of nations (international law). Peña claimed that the proper forum for such a hearing was Paraguay (invoking the doctrine of *forum non conveniens*) and describing as "mind-boggling" the notion that in the name of human rights a United States court could hold a man in custody on a civil matter. Américo Peña's attorney, Murray D. Brochin, said that there were no grounds to detain his client further and that the suit was simply an attempt to "propagandize against conditions in Paraguay." Peña's defense of *forum non conveniens* became more persuasive when, just before Judge Nickerson was to rule on the motion, the Paraguayan Supreme Court suddenly and unexpectedly reversed the lower court's ruling denying the Filártigas standing to bring their criminal action. The timing of the court action in Asunción, the circumstances surrounding it, and the ruling itself led to changes that it was politically inspired. In fact, the Filártiga suit was later dismissed in Paraguay.

After Judge Nickerson's stay was granted, a flurry of newspaper articles publicized the case. Some journalists questioned Américo Peña's connections in the United States and Paraguay. The *New York Times* reported on Paraguayan government activities in the United States, as alleged by a Paraguayan refugee in New York. Gilberto Olmedo-Sanchez claimed that he had been the object of death threats from Paraguayan government agents in New York who were angered by his role in identifying Peña in Brooklyn. The Council on Hemispheric Affairs issued a press release suggesting that there was something faulty about the granting of a visa to Peña in the first place and that the responsible U.S. Consul Officer, William Finnigan, should be queried. The *Atlanta Constitution* and the *Los Angeles Times* focused on questionable activity by U.S. officials in Paraguay. For example, Richard Alan White, a historian of Paraguay, presented this argument in a *Times* opinion editorial:

Peña is a suspected figure in a prostitution ring operating in the New York area. During the past several years, hundreds of young females, the majority from the rural Paraguayan town of Caraguatay, have entered the United States under visas that may have been obtained illegally from the U.S. consulate in Asunción. . . . These women are induced into prostitution upon their arrival in New York by the Paraguayan ringleaders. In Paraguay, it is generally understood that Peña was among the privileged officials who shared in the profits from international prostitution and narcotics smuggling.[6]

Despite newspaper and television coverage of the Peña case and related sensational issues, and notwithstanding Carter Administration policy designed to promote international human rights, Judge Nickerson finally ruled in Peña's favor.[7] He held [that] precedent constrained him to interpret the jurisdiction provisions of the Alien Tort Statute so as to preclude consideration of a foreign country's treatment of its own citizens. The ruling rested on recent cases dealing, not with human rights, but with unrelated claims. Nevertheless, the district court postponed Peña's deportation while the Filártigas unsuccessfully petitioned the United States Supreme Court for a stay of the deportation order. When the high court did not oblige, Judge Nickerson granted the motion to dismiss the case on 14 May 1979, acknowledging the strength of Peña's argument but leaving the door open for appeal.

The Filártigas filed notice that they would seek a review of Judge Nickerson's decision in the Second Circuit Court of Appeals. That court was quickly apprised that a number of *amicus curiae* briefs would be filed supporting the Filártiga position. They would challenge as anachronistic the perception that problems arising under the international law of human rights may not be dealt with by domestic courts.

Political scientists in the United States long ago discarded the notion that the judicial process is devoid of all politics. Although the charge is seldom heard in the United States—as it is in Paraguay—that the judiciary lacks independence, nevertheless it is generally conceded that in the United States subtler political considerations, involving no improprieties, are often at work. For example, the litigant in civil suits in the United States who enjoys the assistance (in the form of supporting briefs) of government and private groups has a significant advantage. International concern for the plight of the Filártigas translated into the filing of numerous briefs from agencies

6. Richard Alan White, "In New York a Key Paraguayan Murder Suspect Faces U.S. Justice," *Los Angeles Times*, 15 April 1979, part V, p. 3, col. 3–4.
7. Memorandum and order, Filártiga v. Peña, Civil Case No. 79-917 (E.D.N.Y., 15 May 1979).

of government, prestigious human rights groups, and respected scholars. As appellants, the Filártigas were aided by an impressive array of attorneys from the Center for Constitutional Rights, the Department of Justice, the Department of State, Amnesty International, the International Human Rights Law Group, the Council on Hemispheric Affairs, the Washington Office on Latin America, the International League of Human Rights, and the Lawyers Committee for International Human Rights.

Moreover, the Filártigas submitted to the court of appeals the affidavits of several legal scholars to support the view that the law of nations prohibits torture. Richard Falk of Princeton University averred that "it is now beyond reasonable doubt that torture of a person held in detention that results in severe harm or death is a violation of the law of nations." Thomas Franck of New York University offered the argument that torture has now been rejected by virtually all nations, although it was once commonly used to extract confessions. Richard Lillich of the University of Virginia detailed the sources of authority for the proposition that officially perpetrated torture is a "violation of international law." Myres McDougal of Yale University stated that it has long been recognized that such internationally defined offenses as torture "virtually affect relations between states."

Argument in *Filártiga v. Peña-Irala* took place

before Chief Justice Feinberg and Circuit Judges Kaufman and Kearse. Their historic decision came down on 30 June 1980. They unanimously held that officially sanctioned torture is a violation of international law. They therefore found that the Alien Tort Statute provided a basis for the exercise of federal jurisdiction in the wrongful death action brought by the Paraguayan plaintiffs against the Paraguayan defendant.

Because Judge Nickerson in the trial court had dismissed the Filártiga suit for lack of subject-matter jurisdiction, the threshold question for the court of appeals was whether the conduct alleged by the appellants violated the law of nations.[8] In his skillfully composed opinion, Judge Kaufman acknowledged the relevance to that question of the views of leading jurists and scholars.[9] He noted that torture has been consistently condemned by numerous international treaties,[10] including the American Convention of Human Rights,[11] the International Covenant on Civil and Political Rights,[12] and the Universal Declaration of Human Rights.[13] Torture is also renounced as an inhuman act in the Declaration on the Protection of All Persons from Being Subject to Torture.[14] In that resolution of the United Nations General Assembly, torture is defined as "any act by which severe pain and suffering, whether physical or mental, is intentionally inflicted by or at the instigation of a public official on a person for such purposes as intimidating him or other

---

8. Filártiga, 630 F.2d at 880. The opinion of the court stated:

   [W]e conclude that official torture is now prohibited by the law of nations. The prohibition is clear and unambiguous, and admits of no distinction between treatment of aliens and citizens. . . . [I]nternational law confers fundamental rights upon all people vis-à-vis their own governments. While the ultimate scope of those rights will be a subject for continuing refinement and elaboration, we hold that the right to be free from torture is now among them. (630 F.2d at 884–85)

9. Ibid., 883.
10. The court included Article 55 of the United Nations Charter in its analysis of treaties. The Charter is described by Judge Kaufman as a treaty binding the United States, and it provides:

   With a view to the creation of conditions of stability and well-being which are necessary for peaceful and friendly relations among nations . . . the United Nations shall promote . . . universal respect for, and observance of human rights and fundamental freedoms for all without distinctions as to race, sex, language or religion.

Moreover, according to Article 56, all members of the United Nations "pledge themselves to take joint and separate action in cooperation with the Organization for the achievement of the purposes set forth in Article 55" (630 F.2d at 881).
11. Art. 5, signed Nov. 22, 1969, entered into force July 18, 1979, O.A.S.T.S. No. 36, at 1; O.A.S. Doc. OEA/Ser.K/XVI/1.1, doc. 65 rev. 1 corr. 1 (1970); reprinted in Inter-American Commission on Human Rights, *Handbook of Existing Rules Pertaining to Human Rights*, O.A.S. Doc. OEA/Ser.L/V/II.50, doc. 6 at 27 (1980).
12. [See the Appendix.]
13.]See the Appendix.]
14. Adopted Dec. 9, 1975; U.N.G.A. Res. 3452 (XXX), 30 U.N. GAOR Supp. (No. 34), U.N. Doc. A/10034 (1975).

persons." It also calls for redress and compensation for torture victims "in accordance with national law." Judge Kaufman approvingly noted that these declarations are supposed to specify the obligations of member nations under the Charter of the United Nations.[15]

The United Nations Charter is a treaty to which both the United States and Paraguay adhere. Nevertheless, the court did not rely on the Charter to bring the Filártiga complaint within the treaty provision of the Alien Tort Statute. Rather, the court relied on the Charter and clarifying declarations as evidence of an expression of the evolving law of nations. The court acknowledged that "there is no universal agreement as to the precise extent of the 'human rights and fundamental freedoms' guaranteed to all by the Charter," but "there is at present no dissent from the view that the guarantees include, at a bare minimum, the right to be free from torture." The court ruled further: "This prohibition has become part of customary international law, as evidenced and defined by the Universal Declaration of Human Rights."[16]

Having found human rights in customary international law, the court was positioned to broaden the reading previously given to the Alien Tort Statute in cases concerning a state's treatment of its own citizens. These cases, which had inhibited Judge Nickerson, involved commercial matters, not human rights. Such cases involving theft and fraud, while lamentable, did not satisfy the jurisdiction requirements of the Alien Tort Statute, but torture has been elevated to an offense against all humanity and a violation of customary international law which is a changing and evolving facet of the law of nations.

In the final paragraph of his opinion, Judge Kaufman employed memorable language which sensitively characterized the impetus behind the modern evolution of customary international law:

From the ashes of the Second World War arose the United Nations Organization, amid hopes that an era of peace and cooperation had at last begun.

Though many of these aspirations have remained elusive goals, that circumstance cannot diminish the true progress that has been made. In the modern age, humanitarian and practical considerations have combined to lead the nations of the world to recognize that respect for fundamental human rights is in their individual and collective interest. Among the rights universally proclaimed by all nations, as we have noted, is the right to be free of physical torture. Indeed, for purposes of civil liability, the torturer has become—like the pirate and slave trader before him—*hostis humani generis,* an enemy of all mankind.[17]

Since the court of appeals found that jurisdiction [could] properly be exercised over the Filártigas' claim, the action was remanded for further proceedings in the district court. But the defendant made no court appearance, and Peña's New York lawyers withdrew when their legal bill remained unpaid. In June 1981, Judge Nickerson entered a default judgment for the Filártigas. In February 1982, hearings to assess damages and to examine the ten million dollar claim of the Filártigas were held before Magistrate John Caden.

In these hearings, four medical experts—physicians and psychologists—presented affidavits on the effects of torture on family survivors. For example, Dr. Frederico Allodi concluded:

... both Dolly and Dr. Joel Filártiga complain of and manifest psychological and psychosomatic disturbances that affect their physical and mental health, their familiar, social and occupational performance in a severe and profound manner and will, most probably, affect them for many years to come. It is also my considered opinion that their symptoms of physical and psychological ill health are compatible, in every way, with those manifested by individuals who were subjected to similar experiences, either directly or affecting the persons of close relatives in their Latin American countries in the past decade. It is finally my conclusion that those health and behavioral disturbances are intimately and causally related to the experiences they both underwent as close relatives of a victim of violence and as subjects of the profoundly distressing involvement in a

---

15. Filártiga, 630 F.2d at 883.
16. Filártiga, 630 F.2d at 882.
17. Filártiga, 630 F.2d at 890. The opinion cited with approval The Paquette Habana (175 U.S. 677, 700 [1900]), commenting that "courts must interpret international law not as it was in 1789, but as it has evolved and exists among the law of nations of the world today (630 F.2d at 881). Cf. Banco Nacional de Cuba v. Sabbatino, 376 U.S. 398 (1964).

police and legal investigation of the death of their relative, Joel Filártiga.[18]

A Canadian psychiatrist, Dr. Allodi is the author of "The Psychiatric Effects in Children and Families of Victims of Political Persecution and Torture." In his sworn statement in the Filártiga case, Dr. Allodi concluded that damages awarded to Dolly and Dr. Joel Filártiga could not achieve *restitutio ad integrum*—that is, they could not "make the victims whole"—but "symbolic and material compensation will help return to them a sense of trust in the justice and safety of the world, self-esteem and internal calm that is essential for the amelioration of the . . . symptoms of physical and psychological ill health." Similar conclusions were presented by Dr. Ana Deutsch, an Argentine political exile and a member of a medical group investigating the medical and psychological consequences of torture.

In the 1982 hearings, Dolly Filártiga and Dr. Joel Filártiga also testified. They offered poignant statements on the personal consequences for each of them resulting from Peña's outrageous acts. Dolly Filártiga testified that she had planned to study medicine, but after what had happened, "I think I will not be prepared to handle more pain." Dr. Filártiga described the three occasions of his own past tortures at the hands of Paraguayan authorities, which he had provoked by bringing free health care and anti-government political views to his rural patients.

The next witness was Jacobo Timerman, author of *Prisoner Without a Name, Cell Without a Number*.[19] He said that in the Filártiga case, "torture is on trial." He testified regarding its effects on the victim and on society at large. Timerman argued that once you have been tortured, torture is with you forever and that there is nothing you can do about it: "the moment you are tortured, and the days after torture, and the years after torture, they have changed your human condition. It is a biological change. . . . Your feelings are different." The wrong done is the most destructive imaginable, because "in the loneliness of the tortured man, . . . there is nothing, nothing is left to you; not your body, not your mind, not your imagination, and not your dreams, absolutely nothing." When torture is incorporated into a society, you have changed . . . civilization."

Former U.S. Ambassador to Paraguay Robert White was also called to offer his reflections on conditions in Paraguay. He testified that political torture is so "institutionalized" in Paraguay that "perfectly normal people get up and go to their jobs and their work is torture." Asked whether the Filártigas could get justice in Paraguay, the Ambassador answered simply, "No, it's impossible." In reply to the question of whether international opinion provided the Filártigas some protection in Paraguay, he said, "the only thing Paraguay responds to are international pressures." Ambassador White was further queried, "What role do you think the existence of civil remedies for the victims of torture, as we are here in this court for, might play in the overall effort to stop torture?" In a telling reply, Robert White testified:

I think one example might illustrate this. After the case was decided in favor of Dr. Filártiga [by the Court of Appeals], one of the people closest to General Stroessner told me that I just had to do everything possible to get this decision reversed. They don't really understand the inde-

---

18. Affidavit of Dr. Frederico Allodi (Filártiga v. Peña, Civil Case No. 79-917 [E.D.N.Y. 1982] at 2). In an accompanying affidavit by Dr. Glenn Randall and Dr. Jose Quiroga (respectively the San Francisco and Los Angeles chairmen of Amnesty International Medical Groups), the expert findings state, "it is evident that members of the Filártiga family are also victims of Joelito's torture and have suffered heavily. As victims they suffer in ways similar to the victim but not as a result of physical torture. Their suffering is psychological . . . more difficult to treat and less evident initially" than physical problems. Affidavits of Dr. Glenn Randall and Dr. Jose Quiroga (Filártiga v. Peña, Civil Case No. 79-917 [E.D.N.Y. 1982] at 8). Randall and Quiroga conclude:

In summary, the whole family has suffered since 1976 following Joelito's death. From what we know, the suffering is characterized by recollection of traumatic events, disintegration of family ties, both biographically and emotionally, feelings of guilt, multiple somatic complaints, reduced involvement with the external world, feelings of estrangement with other people, loss of interest in previously enjoyed social activities, sleep disorders and nightmares. These symptoms present in multiple members of the Filártiga family constitute the psychiatric diagnosis of Post-traumatic Stress Disorder. (Ibid., 15)

19. Jacobo Timerman, *Prisoner without a Name, Cell without a Number* (New York: Knopf, 1981).

pendence of our court system here. And he stressed to me that no Paraguayan government figure would feel free to travel to the United States if this judgment was upheld because, you know, they would feel that they would be liable to arrest for just being in any state in the United States.[20]

On 12 January 1984, Judge Nickerson announced a total judgment against Peña and for the plaintiffs. Taking standards of punitive damages into account, it amounted to $10,385,364—the largest damage amount ever assessed against a Paraguayan national.

CONCLUSION

The Filártiga episode in Paraguay and later litigation in the United States are important for many reasons. First, the heroic example of the Filártiga family in undertaking humanitarian efforts on behalf of the public health needs of the poor involves a consciousness-raising process. It has had a salutory effect upon the Ybycuí peasantry. They and the residents of Asunción have been educated by Dr. Filártiga's example, and that of his family, to their human rights and to the prospects for their solidarity. Dr. Filártiga said: "After Joelito died, a peasant told me—'You may not understand, Doctor, what is happening to you, because you are too close to it. But we do understand. Your son was killed, not because he was the son of Filártiga, but because he was the son of one serving us, the poor people. The punishment is not just for you, but it is also for us the poor.'"

Second, the example of the Filártiga family in "telling the world" of their human rights complaint demonstrates the efficacy of international public opinion. The painful and hazardous process of building international contact and cooperation with human rights groups helped the Filártigas in their task of "making the world understand." The work of diverse groups was effective in explaining events in Paraguay. Such groups as Amnesty International, the International Commission of Jurists, the Council on Hemispheric Affairs, the Paraguayan Commission for the Defense of Human Rights, the International League for Human Rights, and the Inter-American Commission for Human Rights all

helped in the mobilization of shame. In the light of the reports of such groups, Dr. Filártiga said that the family was consoled by the lesson that "the dead count when they leave a testimony." He said that reports of such organizations have impressed upon Paraguayans the lesson that "the torturers are seen as criminals publicly judged."

Third, the court of appeals decision represents a victory, not only for the Filártiga family but also for the many governmental and nongovernmental organizations which lent their fact-finding skills to scrutinize the problem of institutionalized torture in Paraguay and elsewhere. Such groups are sustained by an occasional moral victory. Several of them joined efforts in the multiple friend of the court briefs presenting research and analysis that discernibly influenced the judgment of the court of appeals. Having succeeded in this landmark case, human rights nongovernmental organizations have become alert to and watchful for "progeny cases" which might benefit by the Filártiga principles.

Fourth, the ruling in *Filártiga v. Peña* "that deliberate torture perpetrated under color of official authority violates universally accepted norms of the international law of human rights regardless of the nationality of the parties" is a significant contribution to the growing weight of authority focusing on international standards of basic human rights. In this, the United States is by no means alone. In the period 1948 to 1973, the constitutions or other important laws of over 75 states either expressly referred to or clearly borrowed from the Universal Declaration of Human Rights. The Declaration has also been relied upon in a number of cases in domestic courts of various nations. In *Filártiga v. Peña*, the United States joined a growing number of countries whose courts have recognized that international law transcends sovereign boundaries to protect individuals from their own government officials.

Finally, *Filártiga v. Peña* should have an important impact on the prospects for international human rights enforcement. International law and its implementation [are] based upon a horizontal power structure with no central enforcing authority. Compliance is the result of any given state's internal motivation, desire for accommodation, need for reciprocity with other states, and—in the words of Thomas Jefferson—its "decent respect for the opinion of mankind." Where

20. Transcript of hearings before Magistrate John L. Caden (see n. 4, above), 78–79.

the United States is concerned, the *Filártiga* ruling means that those who flagrantly disregard accepted norms of the international law of human rights should not expect refuge from justice in the United States and that, in appropriate cases, the doors of United States courts are open to the persecuted who find themselves shut out of their homeland. As if welcoming the opportunity to place the United States on the right side of social justice, Judge Kaufman concluded the *Filártiga v. Peña* opinion thus: "Our holding today giving effect to a jurisdictional provision enacted by our First Congress, is a small but important step in the fulfillment of the ageless dream to free all people from brutal violence." The unanimous Court of Appeals for the Second Circuit found that torture is a violation of international law, and the district court applied this rule to the allegations made by the Filártigas. Thus the issue was crystallized as one of the progressive applications of international law in general and of the application of international law by national courts in particular. This development cannot help but encourage those such as Dr. Filártiga who courageously reject establishment-serving myths and frauds and those human rights groups which seek to widen the scope of protection for the individual against the abuse of power.

QUESTIONS FOR REFLECTION AND DISCUSSION

1. In *The Paquette Habana* (175 U.S. 677 [1900]), the Supreme Court stated that

where there is no treaty, and no controlling executive or legislative act or judicial decision, resort must be had to the customs and usages of civilized nations; and, as evidence of these, to the works of jurists and commentators, who by years of labor, research and experience, have made themselves peculiarly well acquainted with the subjects of which they treat. [These works] are trustworthy evidence of what the law really is.

From the standpoint of the interrelation of national and international law in the United States, what is significant about the *Filártiga* case?

2. Judge Irving R. Kaufman's opinion in *Filártiga* included the following statement:

[A]lthough there is no universal agreement as to the precise extent of the "human rights and fundamental freedoms" guaranteed to all by the [UN] Charter, there is at present no dissent from the view that the guaranties include, at a bare minimum, the right to be free from torture. This prohibition has become part of customary law, as evidenced and defined by the Universal Declaration of Human Rights . . . which states, in the plainest of terms, "no one shall be subjected to torture." The General Assembly has declared that the Charter precepts embodied in this Universal Declaration "constitute basic principles of international law" . . . (630 F. 2d at 882)

This statement is significant. Why?

3. Is the Court's finding in *Filártiga* that torture violates customary international law consistent with the requirement that custom, to be law, must be accepted as law? Amnesty International consistently reports that torture is employed under color of authority in many countries, including countries with legislation prohibiting torture. Do these numerous violations undermine the court's finding that torture violates customary international law? If a state agrees "in principle" that torture is contrary to international law, does that constitute state practice for purposes of determining the existence or not of international custom accepted as law? Why? Why not? See, on the one hand, James S. Watson, "Legal Theory, Efficacy and Validity in the Development of Human Rights Norms in International Law," *University of Illinois Law Forum* 3 (1979): 609–41, and Eric Lane, "Demanding Human Rights: A Change in the World Legal Order," *Hofstra Law Review* 6 (1978): 269–95. On the other hand, see Lowell F. Schechter, "The Views of 'Charterists' and 'Skeptics' on Human Rights in the World Legal Order," *Hofstra Law Review* 9 (1981): 357–98, and Louis B. Sohn, "The International Law of Human Rights," *Hofstra Law Review* 9 (1981): 347–56.

4. The Alien Torts Claims Act (28 U.S.C. § 1350) provides that "[t]he district courts shall have original jurisdiction of any civil action by an alien for a tort only, committed in violation of the law of nations. . . ." Assuming the *Filártiga* court was correct in deciding that torture violates customary international law, and thus the law of nations, might there

be other conduct that courts would find similarly violative of the law of nations? The *Filártiga* opinion suggests that "the ultimate scope of those [international human] rights will be a subject for continuing refinement and elaboration (630 F. 2d at 885).

Relying in part on the *Filártiga* analysis, in *Forti v. Suarez-Mason* (672 F.Supp. 1531 [N.D. Cal. 1987]), the court determined that two additional alleged acts constitute violations of the law of nations for purposes of jurisdiction under the Alien Tort Claims Act. Judge Jensen held that causing "prolonged arbitrary detention and summary execution" violates obligatory and definable international customary law norms and thus denied motions to dismiss on these counts. However, Judge Jensen dismissed two other counts—causing "disappearances" and "cruel and inhuman punishment"—for failure to state claims upon which relief could be granted, reasoning that the legal standards to apply to determine if violations existed were not clearly defined or accepted. What factors should a court use in determining whether or not a customary international human rights norm clearly exists? Quoting *Filártiga*, Judge Jensen replied that it is "only where the nations of the world have demonstrated that the wrong is of mutual, and not merely several, concern, by means of express international accords" (630 F.2d at 888). Applying this criterion, was Judge Jensen correct in dismissing the "disappearances" and "cruel and inhuman punishment" claims? Note that Judge Jensen further observed that the "courts are not to prejudge the scope of the issues that the nations of the world may deem important to their interrelationships, and thus to their common good." Which way does this observation cut?

5. In 1984, four years after *Filártiga*, the UN General Assembly adopted and opened for signature the Convention Against Torture and Other Cruel, Inhuman or Degrading Treatment (U.N. Res. A/39/46, 39 U.N. GAOR, Supp. [No. 51], 197, U.N. Doc. A/39/708 [1984]). Since this convention was considered necessary, does that fact raise doubts as to whether torture (and other cruel, inhuman, or degrading treatment) had been prohibited by customary international law at the time *Filártiga* was decided?

6. After *Filártiga* was decided, the defendant, Peña-Irala, was deported to Paraguay, a default judgment was granted, and damages were assessed to cover the expenses of the plaintiffs plus punitive damages of $5 million to each plaintiff. These damage awards were not enforced. Does this fact undermine the significance of the decision?

7. Assuming that *Filártiga* was correctly decided, how might a U.S. court, operating under the Alien Tort Claims Act that made *Filártiga* possible, decide a claim against an individual (or group of individuals) acting without state authority or under color of state authority accused of torture (or terrorism)? See *Hanoch Tel-Oren v. Libyan Arab Republic*, 726 F.2d 774 (D.C. Cir. 1984), *cert. denied* 470 U.S., 1003 (1985).

8. The act of state doctrine is a rule of judicial deference that prohibits judging the validity of a foreign act of state so as to avoid embarrassing the executive branch in its conduct of foreign policy. The doctrine of sovereign immunity, which permits domestic courts to decline jurisdiction because of the sovereign status of a defendant state, serves much the same purpose. So, too, does the so-called political questions doctrine, pursuant to which the judiciary finds a question to be constitutionally allocated to one or both of the other "political" branches of the government. How might a domestic court surmount these barriers to justiciability to enable adjudication of human rights cases brought against foreign states? How should domestic courts draw the line between foreign policy and international human rights law? The Alien Tort Claims Act that was the basis of the *Filártiga* case affords one answer. Can you think of any others?

9. In *Sei Fujii v. California* (217 P.2d 481 [1950]), mentioned in the introduction to this chapter, a California District Court of Appeals held invalid a state statute forbidding aliens not eligible for citizenship to "acquire, possess, enjoy, use, cultivate, occupy, and transfer" real property on the grounds that the statute conflicted with the UN Charter and the Universal Declaration of Human Rights. On appeal, the California Supreme Court held the statute invalid under the Fourteenth Amendment but expressly rejected the lower court's view that the UN Charter's provisions on human rights had become the "supreme law of the land" (38 Cal.2d 713, 242 P.2d 617 [1952]). Chief Justice Gibson, referring to UN Charter Articles 1(3), 55, and 56, stated, in part:

> The fundamental provisions in the charter pledging cooperation in promoting observance of fundamental freedoms lack the mandatory quality and definitiveness which would indicate an intent to create justiciable rights in private persons immediately upon rati-

fication. Instead, they are framed as a promise of future action by the member nations. (38 Cal.2d at 724, 242 P.2d at 621–22)

What legal obligations, whether or not "self-executing," actually are imposed by Articles 1(3), 55, and 56? If a case raising the question of whether or not these provisions are "self-executing" came before the U.S. Supreme Court, which so far has not happened, how do you think the Supreme Court would rule? Would it make any difference what type of alleged human rights violation was at issue?

10. What is the proper role of domestic courts in the struggle for internationally guaranteed human rights? Consider the assertions of Richard A. Falk (*The Role of Domestic Courts in the International Legal Order* [Syracuse, N.Y.: Syracuse University Press, 1964], xi–xii):

> Two sets of considerations dominate my interpretation of the proper role for domestic courts to play. First, international law exists in a social system that possesses weak central institutions. As a result, international tribunals are not consistently or conveniently available to resolve most disputes involving questions of international law. Domestic courts can help to overcome this structural weakness in the international legal system. Also, since no international institution is endowed with legislative competence, it is difficult to change old rules in response to changes in the composition and character of international society. If international law is to develop into a universal basis of order, then it is necessary that divergent attitudes toward the content of law be treated with respect. The older states must put forth a special effort to broaden international law enough to make it compatible with the values of socialist and anticolonial states. It is of no value to insist upon the old rules developed when all of the active international actors accepted *laissez-faire* economics at home and imperialism abroad. Domestic courts in the older states can help adapt international law to the modern world by developing principles that express tolerance for diverse social and economic systems.
>
> Second, domestic courts must struggle to become their own masters in international law cases. The executive must not be allowed, and must certainly not be invited, to control outcome of judicial proceedings by alleging the precedence of foreign policy considerations. The courts are not good vehicles for the promotion of foreign policy; moreover, the independence of courts from national political control is essential if international legal order is to be upheld and developed. A legal tradition depends upon the autonomy of its method and the saliency of its governing principles. Only an independent judiciary can establish a tradition.

Do you agree with Falk? Is his proposal realistic? Why? Why not? Do not international human rights guarantees rest upon such a precarious basis that proposals such as this one must be seen as absolutely necessary, however realistic or unrealistic?

SELECT BIBLIOGRAPHY

Brown, Peter, and Douglas MacLean, eds. *Human Rights and U.S. Foreign Policy.* Lexington, Mass.: Lexington Books, 1979. Multiauthor analytical essays evaluating the Carter administration's human rights policies, including case studies on Korea, the Philippines, and Iran.

Farer, Tom J. *The Grand Strategy of the United States in Latin America.* New Brunswick, N.J.: Transaction Books, 1988. Critically examines U.S. policy, which the author believes too often misunderstands Latin American internal political dynamics; also criticizes formalistic approaches to human rights.

Farer, Tom J., ed. *Toward a Humanitarian Diplomacy: A Primer for Policy.* New York: New York University Press, 1980. Essays in "moral diplomacy" addressed to the potential influence of the United States in global affairs because of its economic and technological power.

Fowler, Michael Ross. *Thinking About Human Rights: Contending Approaches to Human Rights in U.S. Foreign Policy.* Lanham, Md.: University Press of America, 1987. Analytical and critical assessment of the premises and underlying assumptions of four major schools of thought regarding human rights as a component of U.S. foreign policy.

Hannum, Hurst, ed. *Guide to International Human Rights Practice.* Philadelphia: University of Pennsylvania Press, 1984. An introduction to human rights procedures for the international law generalist, surveying the practice of human rights from the lodging of complaints by individuals to institutional standards setting and protection.

Hassan, Farooq. "A Conflict of Philosophies: The *Filártiga* Jurisprudence." *International and Comparative Law Quarterly* 32 (1983): 250–58. A critique of human rights law-making, which allegedly ignores the role of consent in international law.

Kommers, Donald P., and Gilburt D. Loescher, eds. *Human Rights and American Foreign Policy.* Notre Dame, Ind.: Notre Dame University Press, 1979. Examines conflicting ideologies linked to human rights, describing the human rights foreign policy objectives of the Carter administration and critically assessing priorities in American foreign policy.

Lillich, Richard B. *U.S. Ratification of the Human Rights Treaties with or without Reservations?* Charlottesville, Va.: University Press of Virginia, 1981. Essays by legal experts in response to President Carter's transmission of four human rights treaties to the Senate for ratification but with the reservation that each be non-self-executing, hence unenforceable in U.S. courts.

Newberg, Paula R. *The Politics of Human Rights.* New York: New York University Press, 1981. Essays addressing the universalization of an acceptable core of human rights, and issues of human rights and basic needs in U.S. foreign aid policy.

Newson, David D. *The Diplomacy of Human Rights.* Lanham, Md: University Press of America for the Institute for the Studies of Diplomacy of Georgetown University, 1986. Multiple authors explore the foundations of human rights diplomacy, followed by nine case studies including Indonesia, Iran, Korea, Romania, South Africa, and the Soviet Union.

Novak, Michael. *Human Rights and the New Realism: Strategic Thinking in a New Age.* Lanham, Md.: Freedom House, 1986. Neoconservative analysis of the relationship of human rights to strategic thinking, connecting human rights issues to conflicts between the Soviet Union and Western liberal democracies.

Owen, David. *Human Rights.* London: Jonathan Cape, 1978. One-time British Ambassador to the United State advances the case for an active British policy in support of human rights, with special reference to apartheid, world poverty, world peace, and the United Nations.

Shue, Henry. *Basic Rights, Subsistence, Affluence, and U.S. Foreign Policy.* Princeton, N.J.: Princeton University Press, 1980. A carefully argued brief for a universal human right to subsistence, combined with a systematic application of moral theory to U.S. foreign policy.

Vincent, R. J., ed. *Foreign Policy and Human Rights Issues and Responses.* New York: Cambridge University Press, in association with the Royal Institute of International Affairs, 1986. A review of human rights issues involving South Africa, the Soviet Union, the Palestinians, and Northern Ireland, as well as analyses of U.S. and European diplomacy and Third World perspectives.

Vogelgesang, Sandy. *American Dream, Global Nightmare: The Dilemma of U.S. Human Rights Policy.* New York: Norton, 1981. Explores the interconnections between diplomacy, U.S. domestic politics, and international economics as background for an analysis of human rights diplomacy, its limits and possibilities, from the vantage point of the Carter administration.

Wiarda, Howard, ed. *Human Rights and U.S. Human Rights Policy.* Washington, D.C.: American Enterprise Institute for Public Policy Research, 1982. Conservative theoretical approaches to human rights (Kirkpatrick, Novak, Schifter) and some perspectives on the influences affecting the Reagan administration's policy on human rights.

SELECT FILMOGRAPHY

Americas in Transition. Obie Benz, producer. USA: Icarus/Michigan Media 1982. 29 min., color; 16 mm. Examines the roots of military dictatorships in various Latin American countries and their effects on citizens; also looks at some attempts at democracy, the influences of communism, and the role of the U.S. foreign policy in the region. Narrated by Ed Asner.

El Salvador: Another Vietnam. Michigan Media, 1981. 53 min., color. Examines the civil war in El Salvador in light of the Reagan administration's decision to "draw the line" against "communist interference" in Central America.

Human Rights. Close-Up Educational Media, 1987. 60 min.; VHS, Beta, 3/4-in videotape. Hodding Carter, Former Assistant Secretary of State for Public Affairs under President Jimmy Carter, argues that human rights remain a vital concern in world affairs and should remain a concern of foreign policy. Includes discussion of the Reagan administration and Amnesty International.

The Politics of Torture. ABC News, producer. USA: Ecufilm, 1978. 50 min., color; 16 mm. With examples from Iran, the Philippines, and Chile, explores U.S. foreign policy in fulfilling a highly publicized promise to promote human rights and raises questions regarding the role of the government and corporations in supporting these regimes.

Salvador. Oliver Stone, producer. USA: VES, 1985. 123 min., color; Beta, VHS videotape. Based on American photojournalist Richard Boyle's experiences in El Salvador, starring James Woods as Boyle. Dramatizes the murderous strife and questions the American government's willingness to prop fascist regimes so long as they promote American interests.

To Sing Our Own Song. BBC, producer. Great Britain: Films Inc., 1982. 50 min., color; 16 mm, videotape. Documentary on resistance to the Marcos regime in the Philippines; focuses on Jose Diokno, active in the opposition, who is critical of U.S. foreign policy and U.S. support for what he believed was a repressive government.

Unfinished Business. Steven Okazaki, producer. USA: Couchette, 1984. 60 min., color; 16 mm. Documentary about three men of Japanese ancestry who refused to go to internment camps in 1942 and were convicted and imprisoned for violating U.S. Executive Order 9066; their personal stories and their efforts, through the courts, to overturn the original convictions are interwoven with archival footage of the camps.

Chapter Six

Nongovernmental Organization, Corporate and Individual Approaches to Implementation

ADDRESSING the enforcement of human rights, Louis Henkin has written that it was "the early assumption [of the founders of the United Nations] that states might be prepared to scrutinize other states and be scrutinized by them."[1] This optimism has not stood the test of time, however. There is a discernible lack of commitment on the part of many governments to protect human rights in their own countries or through international institutions at the global level. Except for the Netherlands and the Scandinavian countries, which consistently champion the cause of human rights, there has been little "horizontal" enforcement of the sort suggested by Henkin. Instead, we have become familiar with the grass-roots defense of human rights by individuals and private groups.

On any given day, the news media carry stories about individual heroics on behalf of human rights—by the antiwar Salvadoran "co-madres" anguished over the "disappearance" of their loved ones, by South Korean dissidents protesting press censorship and police abuse, by black South Africans striking to protest abysmal working conditions, by Tibetan monks demonstrating against Chinese interference with cherished customs, and so forth. Occasionally, given adequate publicity and fanfare, such actions earn the attention and good will of groups that seek to win support for the struggle for human rights by conferring distinguished human rights awards, groups such as the Martin Luther King, Jr., Foundation, The Carter-Menil Human Rights Foundation, the Robert F. Kennedy Memorial Fund, and the International League for Human Rights. The symbolism involved in these awards lends credibility and strength to individual initiatives. When Soviet physicist Andrei Sakharov and Argentine humanist Adolfo Perez Esquivel speak up against government abuses, their voices are enhanced by their status as Nobel laureates. Indeed, the recent willingness of the Nobel Committee to award the Peace Prize to such persons for their courageous work in defense of human rights not only "says volumes about the intimate connection between the advancement of important human values and the establishment of peaceful societies"[2] but also speaks of the important role that private individuals and groups can play in pursuit of human rights on the international plane. It is significant, writes Lynn H. Miller,

> that several Nobel awards have gone to private individuals or organizations whose efforts often have run directly counter to the practices of governments or important political parties. In a world where such recognition is possible, governments and their spokesmen no longer are without effective gadflies from within their societies to push them toward the fuller enhancement of the rights of human beings.[3]

Among the most conspicuous nongovernmental human rights organizations to which Miller refers is, of course, Amnesty International, recipient of the Nobel Peace Prize in 1977.

---

1. Louis Henkin, *The Rights of Man Today* (Boulder, Colo.: Westview Press, 1980), 94.
2. Lynn H. Miller, *Global Order: Values and Power in International Relations* (Boulder, Colo.: Westview Press, 1985), 173.
3. Ibid.

HUMAN RIGHTS NGOS

By and large, nongovernmental organizations (NGOs) have been significant catalysts in the promotion and protection of internationally recognized human rights. To sustain pressure for human rights, such groups have come to be essential. In trying to influence governments to rectify human rights violations, NGOs characteristically fight an uphill battle in which human rights often are sacrificed by government officials to realpolitik—the need for economic markets, favoring military allies, or preserving entrenched elites. Jerome J. Shestack compares the NGOs dedicated to the human rights struggle to the mythical Sisyphus who resolutely pushed a weighty stone up a steep mountain: "[T]he pinnacle may never be reached. Still, while traveling the upward road, obstructions are overcome; the path is made smoother for others."[4] Like Sisyphus, the NGOs do what they must. The struggle itself takes on a symbolic meaning, enhancing human dignity. "[W]hen all is said and done, there is no other human course to pursue."[5]

Human rights NGOs are private associations of individuals concerned with the promotion and protection or implementation of one or more internationally recognized human rights. Amnesty International probably the most famous such group, has more than 500,000 members in more than 150 countries. Amnesty International seeks the release of persons detained arbitrarily—because of their beliefs, for example—provided such persons have not used or advocated violence. The group terms these people "prisoners of conscience."[6]

Not all human rights NGOs are international in membership or universal in scope. But among those comparable with Amnesty International are the International Commission of Jurists (headquartered in Geneva), the International Federation of Human Rights (Federation International des Droits de l'Homme, Paris), the International League for Human Rights (New York), and the Minority Rights Group (London).[7] These four groups are international in that they have a contributing membership base and affiliates from throughout the world. The International Committee of the Red Cross, deriving its international status from its unique role as guardian of the Geneva Conventions on humanitarian law dealing with wartime conditions,[8] is a special case because its membership is wholly Swiss.

The international human rights NGOs have special "consultative status" with the United Nations. They have direct access to the UN Commission on Human Rights, its Sub-Commission on the Prevention of Discrimination and Protection of Minorities, the International Labor Organization, and the United Nations Educational, Scientific and Cultural Organization (UNESCO). Whenever the item, "Violations of Human Rights," is taken up by the

---

4. Jerome J. Shestack, "Sisyphus Endures: The International Human Rights NGO," *New York Law School Law Review* (1978): 89–123, at 90.
5. Ibid., 89.
6. See Harry M. Scoble and Laurie S. Wiseberg, "Human Rights and Amnesty International," *Annals of the American Academy of Political and Social Science* 413 (1974): 11–26. *See also* James Frederick Green, "NGOs," in *Human Rights and World Order*, ed. Abdul Aziz Said (New Brunswick, N.J.: Transaction Books, 1978); Roger S. Clark, "The International League for Human Rights and South Africa, 1945–1957: The Human Rights NGO as Catalyst in the International Legal Process," *Human Rights Quarterly* 3, no. 4 (1981): 101–36.
7. The Minority Rights Group develops information on oppressed ethnic, linguistic, and religious groups worldwide, e.g., Koreans in Japan, Tamils in Sri Lanka, and the religious Baha'i of Iran. Individual reports are occasionally compiled and published in paperback volumes for use in British universities and elsewhere. Regarding the world's minorities, see Georgina Ashworth, ed., *World Minorities*, vol. 2 (Middlesex, U.K.: Quartermaine House, 1973).
8. See David P. Forsythe, "The Red Cross as a Transnational Movement: Conserving and Changing the Nation-State System," *International Organization* 30, no. 4 (1976): 607–30.

UN Commission on Human Rights, the most courageous and outspoken champions of human rights usually are the representatives of the NGOs.

A special category of private human rights activity is the work of professional organizations whose membership and concerns transcend national boundaries.[9] In recent years, international professional associations have established human rights units or committees to support colleagues who, despite political pressure, follow professional ethical standards or who speak out critically about public policy. Lawyers, having a stake in the rule of law, were among the first to organize international collegial support. The Committee on International Human Rights of the American Bar Association's Section on Individual Rights and Responsibilities publishes "network mailings," urging lawyers to write letters of support for their counterparts overseas. When Dr. Vu Quoc Thong, former Dean of the University of Saigon Law School, was forbidden by the new Vietnamese government to practice law and was barred from emigrating, attorneys wrote on his behalf to the Ministry of Justice of the Socialist Republic of Vietnam.

Such international action is spreading among the professions. PEN, an international association of poets, playwrights, essayists, editors, and novelists, pledges support for writers silenced by repressive governments and focuses attention on their plight by mobilizing assistance, dispatching letters to officials, and occasionally sending representatives to foreign capitals to obtain information on imprisoned writers. A comparable London-based group is "Article 19," which takes its name from the provision of the Universal Declaration of Human Rights that proclaims "the right to freedom of opinion and expression [which includes] freedom to hold opinions without interference and to seek, receive and impart information and ideas through any media and regardless of frontiers."[10]

Scientists, too, have acted collectively for international human rights. The Human Rights Committee of the National Academy of Sciences (Washington, D.C.) has taken up the cause of Soviet and Chilean dissident scientists. The Science and Human Rights Program of the American Association for the Advancement of Science has issued reports on the abuse of South African health workers and Latin American technicians. In Europe, the International Council of Scientific Unions (Paris) has a committee on the "Safeguard of the Pursuit of Science," which documents cases of scientists who have been seriously restricted in the pursuit or communication of their research. In addition, Physicians for Human Rights (Boston) gained attention when it sent Dr. John Constable, the Harvard Medical School burn specialist, to Chile to attend Rodrigo Rojas and Carmen Quintana after police in Santiago tried to incinerate them for engaging in a protest demonstration against the Pinochet regime. Physicians for Human Rights also has issued reports on the use of tear gas by the South Korean police and on the use of shotguns in Panama for crowd control.

The largest number of human rights NGOs are domestically oriented groups, the first such group being the French League for Human Rights, established in 1902. With the support of the great French writer, Victor Hugo, the league was organized in reaction to the Dreyfus case and attendant French anti-Semitism. The French example was imitated by other domestically based groups in Western Europe and by the American Civil Liberties Union (ACLU) in the United States. The ACLU grew out of the National Bureau of Civil Liberties, which was organized in 1919 to oppose arbitrary deportations of both naturalized citizens and disfavored aliens. The European leagues and the ACLU followed similar patterns of growth. While formed in response to specific situations of conflict, they soon pursued a

---

9. See Union of International Associations, *The Future of Transnational Associations from the Standpoint of a New World Order* (Brussels, 1977). See also Robert O. Keohane, *Transnational Relations and World Politics* (Cambridge, Mass.: Harvard University Press, 1972).
10. See the Appendix.

broad range of activities in defense of individual civil liberties and in expanding democratic governance.

Another category of human rights organizations comprises "solidarity groups," which focus on human rights in a particular foreign country. There are, throughout Western Europe and North America, scores of groups that monitor human rights problems in the Soviet Union and various Eastern European countries. Examples include the Help and Action Committee (headquartered in Hericy, France), which publishes an "urgent action" newsletter to stimulate letters of protest to the USSR and Eastern Europe, and the Information Centre for Polish Affairs (London), which periodically publishes the "Uncensored Poland News Bulletin."

Two political scientists, Harry Scoble and Laurie Wiseberg, have studied human rights NGOs extensively and published numerous profiles and analyses of them. They have concluded that NGOs perform six functions: (a) information gathering, evaluation, and dissemination; (b) advocacy; (c) developing human rights norms and "lobbying"; (d) legal aid and/or humanitarian relief; (e) building solidarity; and (f) moral condemnation and praise.[11]

INFORMATION PROCESSING

The chief function of human rights NGOs is the processing of information, since few governments or other agencies undertake the job. This activity is directed to two ends: educating people about the extent of their rights and disseminating information about rights violations.

The goal of educating people about their rights stems from a basic notion that seems self-evident but is fundamentally important: people have a right to know their rights. The right to know one's rights is unique among human rights because it encompasses both a substantive rule and a method of implementation. We need to know our rights in order to assert and defend them.[12] In the Declaration of Principles of the Helsinki Accords,[13] the thirty-five signatory countries confirmed (in Article 7) "the right of the individual to know and act upon his [sic] rights and duties. . . ." Perhaps the best analysis of this proclaimed right is that of Vratislav Pechota, a Czech scholar, who defines the right to know as

an individual's freedom to seek, receive, impart, publish and distribute information and ideas about civil, political, economic, social and cultural rights, both those guaranteed

---

11. See Harry M. Scoble and Laurie S. Wiseberg, "The Importance and Functions of Human Rights Organizations," unpublished paper (Cambridge, Mass., Human Rights Internet, 1980), 11–12. See also Jan Egeland and Thomas Kerks, eds., *Third World Organizational Development: A Comparison of NGO Strategies* (Geneva: Henry Dunant Institute, 1987). The NGO functions identified by Scoble and Wiseberg are similar to, though not coextensive with, the seven "decision functions" identified by Yale scholars Harold Lasswell and Myres McDougal as cutting across the formal institutions of executive, legislative, and judicial decision-making that work to transform political demands into normative realities: intelligence, promotion, prescription, invocation, application, appraisal, and termination. See Harold D. Lasswell and Myres S. McDougal, "Criteria for a Theory About Law," *Southern California Law Review* 44 (1971): 362–94.
12. J. Paul Martin of the Columbia University Center for Human Rights has written that "students need to be prepared to use international human rights standards to make discriminating and . . . objective judgments with regard to the political and economic affairs of their own and other countries." "Human Rights—Education for What?", *Human Rights Quarterly* 9 (1987): 414–22, at 415. An example of an NGO-produced educational publication for mass distribution is, Uganda Human Rights Activists Organization, *Know Your Rights*, ser. 1 (Kampala, 1986).
13. Final Act of the Conference on Security and Co-operation in Europe, Aug. 1, 1975, Department of State Publication No. 8826 (General Foreign Policy Series 298).

by national constitutions and laws, and those proclaimed in the Universal Declaration of Human Rights and other pertinent international instruments.[14]

To realize this right, one must be free to

> seek assistance from public officials, non-governmental organizations and institutions, private attorneys and other experts to elucidate the exact meaning and purport of these documents. Perhaps freedom to organize and participate in civil educational programs should also be protected under this concept.[15]

Manifestly, if individuals have the right (and need) to receive information about their rights, then appropriate groups must be protected in their efforts to provide such information.

The dissemination of information about rights includes publishing reports about rights violations, an activity that involves, as well, gathering and evaluating information. Getting the facts straight and analyzing them carefully is an especially serious matter in the human rights field because lives, personal and organizational integrity, and the legitimacy of regimes are all at stake. As David Weissbrodt and James McCarthy have emphasized, "to inspire corrective efforts by governments, human rights organizations must demonstrate that their factual statements are true and thus constitute a reliable basis for remedial governmental policy."[16] Otherwise, the reports, newsletters, press releases, and "action alerts" that human rights NGOs typically disseminate to stimulate governmental action and upon which the news media rely to document abuses simply will not be believed, and access to the corridors of power and to the media will be denied them.

Because the reliability of the NGOs disseminating human rights information depends upon their careful gathering and evaluation of information, the accuracy and credibility—hence integrity—of NGO fact-finding missions must be ensured. To this end, procedural rules, the "Minimal Rules of Procedure for International Human Rights Fact-Finding Missions," were agreed to at a meeting of the International Law Association in Belgrade in 1980.[17] The adoption of such rules reflects widespread agreement that the documentation of human rights violations can be strengthened and made less haphazard by the use of more nearly uniform standards for collecting information.[18] As it is, the reports of human rights groups often cannot be readily compared because of the variation in information-gathering, evaluation, and reporting techniques.

ADVOCACY

Advocacy, in the case of human rights NGOs, means actively espousing the claims of persons whose rights have allegedly been violated and is, of course, of particular interest to lawyers.

---

14. Vratislav Pechota, *The Right to Know One's Human Rights: A Road Toward Individual Freedom* (New York: The Jacob Blaustein Institute for the Advancement of Human Rights, 1983), 6.
15. Ibid., 7.
16. David Weissbrodt and James McCarthy, "Fact-finding by International Human Rights Organizations," *Virginia Journal of International Law* 22 (Fall 1981): 1–89, at 5–6.
17. See "Draft Minimal Rules of Procedure for International Human Rights Fact-Finding Missions," *Report of the Subcommittee on Equal Application of Human Rights Laws and Principles of the International Committee on Human Rights* (London: International Law Association, 1982).
18. See Hans Thoolen and Berth Verstappen, *Human Rights Missions: A Study of the Fact-Finding Practice of Non-Governmental Organizations* (Dordrecht, Netherlands: Martinus Nijhoff Publishers, 1986). See also Randy B. Reiter, M. V. Zunzunegui, and José Quiroga, "Guidelines for Field Reporting of Basic Human Rights Violations," *Human Rights Quarterly* 8, no. 4 (1986): 628–53 (part of a symposium, "Statistical Issues in the Field of Human Rights").

In 1978, the American Bar Association published a report in which former Congressman Allard K. Lowenstein urged American lawyers to be creative in developing effective responses to the racist institution of South African apartheid:

> The notion that government should do everything is objectionable to all of us. . . . People have an obligation to do a lot more. And in the forefront of such people ought to be lawyers. In South Africa, the bar is at the forefront of trying to figure out ways that people's rights, as limited as they are in the laws of South Africa, at least can be fought for by lawyers who every day risk their careers and their security to take on these cases; some American lawyers are trying to help in South Africa. But there is so much more that can be done—person to person, lawyer to lawyer—in implementing what governments can do and in making those concerns of citizens around the world something that is shared by people who have a common purpose and common humanity.[19]

But it is not only lawyers who engage in human rights advocacy. NGOs do as well, as demonstrated by the early example of the Anti-Slavery Society, founded in Great Britain in 1823.[20] Advocacy also means recommending or otherwise seeking to provoke, in an essentially educational mode, specific policy choices in keeping with preferred values. Today, the Anti-Slavery Society actively advocates policies and programs directed against child labor abuse and related problems. It also joins with other groups, such as Survival International, to plead the cause of the Yanomami Indians in Brazil and other indigenous peoples,[21] a daunting task particularly when the media are uninterested, the public indifferent, and the authorities uncaring. In such a case, the NGO's challenge is to highlight an issue sufficiently to give it political salience.

Advocacy encompasses many functions: education, espousal, persuasion, public exposure, criticism. In chronically difficult situations, such as South African apartheid, advocacy may mean carefully orchestrated and persuasive trade and commercial policies. Even if such campaigns do not presage the end of apartheid, they illustrate the cost to South Africa of its uncivilized practice of depriving blacks of their human rights.

DEVELOPING HUMAN RIGHTS NORMS AND INFLUENCING POLICY

NGOs frequently are instrumental in the development and drafting of human rights norms and in the implementation of public policy. Influencing policy, or "lobbying," is closely akin to advocacy, but the latter is primarily educational while lobbying is designed to provoke specific policy responses by targeting decision-makers who can influence policy to remedy particular human rights violations. For instance, in 1987, Survival International USA secured an agreement with the World Bank to consult on Third World lending activities such as dams and roads in wilderness areas where the projects would predictably affect indigenous peoples and their right to survival and to political, economic, and cultural self-determination.

19. Allard K. Lowenstein, "Keynote Address," in *International Human Rights Law and Practice: The Roles of the United Nations, the Private Sector, the Government, and Their Lawyers,* rev. ed. ed. James C. Tuttle (Philadelphia: America Bar Association, 1977). See also Ralston Deffenbaugh, Jr., "The Southern Africa Project for the Lawyers' Committee for Civil Rights under Law," in *Global Human Rights: Public Policies, Comparative Measures, and NGO Strategies,* ed. Ved P. Nanda, James R. Scarritt, and George W. Shepherd, Jr. (Boulder, Colo.: Westview Press, 1981), 289–304; George W. Shepherd, Jr., "Transnational Development of Human Rights: The Third World Crucible," in ibid., 213–18.
20. The success of the Anti-Slavery Society lay principally in its making people aware of the evils of systematic abuse (illustrating, parenthetically, the educational aspects of the advocacy role).
21. See Reading 8 in Chapter 2 in this volume.

A well-known example of NGO involvement in the development of international human rights norms was the drafting of the Universal Declaration of Human Rights. "The representatives of NGOs may have been influential in the drafting process as much for their personal expertise and prestige," writes David Weissbrodt, "as for the importance of their organizations."[22] Generalizing from this experience, Weissbrodt continues:

> By their presence in drafting sessions and by their individual contacts with national delegates or UN staff, NGO representatives can have even more impact than their more formal interventions in open sessions. Most diplomatic experts and staff are eager for the ideas and information which thoughtful and knowledgeable NGO representatives could provide to great advantage. Amnesty International has been credited with raising world consciousness about torture and assisting with the adoption of the UN Declaration on the Protection of All Persons from being Subjected to Torture and Other Cruel, Inhuman or Degrading Treatment or Punishment. Amnesty International and the International Commission of Jurists have taken an active part in the preparation of the draft principles on the rights of detainees and of the draft convention against torture.
>
> Similarly, eight NGOs joined in 1979 in urging the Sub-Commission on the Protection of Minorities and Prevention of Discrimination to establish a new mechanism for encouraging nations to ratify the principal human rights treaties. The Sub-Commission established a working group to inquire about progress toward ratification and to offer advice to states encountering obstacles.[23]

"It is clear," Weissbrodt concludes, "that international NGOs provide one way by which individuals may become actively involved in the day-to-day protection of human rights. These organizations achieve so very much with their minimal resources that it is possible to foresee that they could do far more if there were adequate support."[24]

It is not only at the international level, however, that human rights NGOs are active in the defense of internationally guaranteed human rights. Their presence is felt, too, at the national level. The Washington Office on Latin America, for example, headquartered on Capitol Hill, was influential in urging that U.S. foreign development aid to repressive South American regimes be cut off. According to Professor Lars Schoultz, the Washington Office on Latin America, along with the (Quaker) Friends Committee on National Legislation, played a key role in the enactment of Section 116 of the U.S. Foreign Assistance Act (the so-called Harkin Amendment),[25] which restricts economic aid to regimes in gross violation of internationally defined human rights.[26]

LEGAL, MEDICAL, AND HUMANITARIAN ASSISTANCE

Human rights violations, particularly "gross violations," often impose harsh legal and medical burdens on their victims. Hence, legal aid and medical assistance, commonly uncertain and/or unavailable in countries accused of violations, become important NGO functions.

22. David Weissbrodt, "The Contributions of International Nongovernmental Organizations to the Protection of Human Rights," in *Human Rights in International Law: Legal and Policy Issues*, ed. Theodor Meron (Oxford: Clarendon Press, 1984), 403–38, at 429.
23. Ibid.
24. Ibid.
25. See Lars Schoultz, *Human Rights and United States Policy Toward Latin America* (Princeton, N.J.: Princeton University Press, 1981), 196. See also Ray Philip, Jr., and J. Sherrod Taylor, "The Role of Non-Governmental Agencies in Implementing Human Rights in Latin America," *Georgia Journal of International and Comparative Law* 7 (1977 suppl.), 477–506.
26. See Reading 20 in Chapter 5 in this volume.

Legal aid on behalf of human rights causes takes many forms. Some groups, such as the Lawyers Committee for Human Rights (New York), rely on cooperating attorneys whom they engage for legal defense. The Center for Constitutional Rights (New York) provided co-counsel in the case of *Filártiga v. Peña-Irala*[27] and the International Human Rights Law Group (Washington, D.C.) supplied an amicus curiae brief. The Law Group also has sent legally trained foreign observers to public trials, as in the political trial of the Yugoslav poet Vlado Gotovac. Legal assistance has been provided in other situations, such as the inquest into the circumstances surrounding the death of Steven Biko, the black civil rights worker who the South African government claimed, to the disbelief of foreign legal observers, had "died accidentally" while in prison. Finally, domestic legal aid groups have done exemplary and sustained work in many Third World countries, for example, the Free Legal Assistance Group, several of whose members lost their lives in the Philippines during the late 1970s, and the Legal Aid Institute of Indonesia, whose founder, Adnan Buyung Nasution, has suffered much governmental harassment.

Medical assistance often is of critical importance to persons victimized by torture, cruel, inhumane treatment and punishment, and other egregious human rights deprivations. The International Committee of the Red Cross is well known for its humanitarian assistance to victims of "man-made" as well as natural disasters, giving medical supplies, blankets, clothing, food, and shelter to countless thousands. Its work is paralleled by that of the World Council of Churches, Physicians for Human Rights, CARE, Catholic Relief Services, Caritas, and numerous other organizations concerned with human rights and humanitarian assistance on a global scale. But medical work done to assist legal investigations, that is, forensic medicine, is a uniquely pertinent contribution. In 1984, the *American Journal of Forensic Medicine and Pathology* published a special symposium issue on human rights and forensic medicine[28] that recounted, among other things, the work of Dr. Clyde C. Snow and his Argentine team who identified the remains and determined the cause of death of persons who "disappeared" in Argentina between 1976 and 1983.[29] The work of Dr. Snow and his associates proved conclusive in the convictions, by Argentine criminal courts, of some of the persons accused of the deaths in question.[30]

BUILDING SOLIDARITY

Building solidarity is an NGO function that involves, but goes beyond, all the activities associated with the four functions already elaborated. Political scientist George Shepherd, Jr., has analyzed this function in detail in a study of anti-apartheid politics. Fundamentally integral to such politics, according to Shepherd, is "liberation aid," by which he means

27. 630 F.2d 876 (2d Cir. 1980). For a discussion of this case, see Reading 21 in Chapter 5 in this volume.
28. See "Special Symposium on Human Rights and the Forensic Scientists," ed. Luke G. Tedischi; and Clyde C. Snow, Lowell J. Levine, Leslie Lukash, Christian Orrego, and Eric Stover, "The Investigation of the Human Remains of the 'Disappeared' in Argentina," *American Journal of Forensic Medicine and Pathology* 5, no. 4 (1984): 297–300. See also John Ziman, Paul Sieghart, and John Humphrey, *The World of Science and the Rule of Law: A Study of the Observance and Violations of the Human Rights of Scientists in the Participating States of the Helsinki Accords* (Oxford: Oxford University Press, 1986).
29. The majority of the deaths occurred during 1976–78 in the course of the government's "dirty war" against subversives, but such killings continued until 1983. See Snow et al., "The Investigation of the Human Remains," 297.
30. An example of a domestic medical group supplying human rights survivors with important services is the Philippine Action Group Concerning Torture (PACT), a private health group that offers medical services to torture victims and their families, often for Post-Traumatic Distress Disorder.

commitment to the political struggle.[31] "Its central theme is transnational political support from one group to another across national boundaries to achieve a common objective, the realization of human rights by those who are oppressed."[32] In the anti-apartheid struggle, the building of solidarity has encompassed campaigns for divestment, disinvestment, documentation of human rights violations in South Africa, and humanitarian assistance to victims of apartheid. Similarly, when the Argentine Institute for Human Rights sent its newly formed team of forensic doctors to the Philippines in 1987, it was engaging not only in a generous process of technology transfer to the Philippines, for identification of the remains of the missing from the Marcos years, but also in a genuine act of transnational solidarity, acknowledged as such by the Medical Action Group of the Philippines and the Filipino Families of Victims of Involuntary Disappearances (FIND).[33]

MORAL CONDEMNATION AND PRAISE

In the eighteenth century, Thomas Jefferson based his case for independence from colonial subjugation upon "a decent respect for the opinion of mankind." Much of the work of human rights NGOs, which have no enforcement authority and so must rely on moral outrage to mobilize shame, involves the effort to appeal to that sense of injustice that resonates among human beings everywhere in the face of repression. Since even the most tyrannical regimes avoid admitting their criminality, they are sensitive, to a greater or lesser extent, to moral condemnation. As Scoble and Wiseberg have observed:

> While one may become a cynic in the face of the fact that most national elites mouth adherence to human rights standards and hypocritically violate those same rights which they profess to defend, there may nonetheless be a positive aspect to this blatant hypocrisy. The more the rhetoric is repeated, the more genuflections to the International Bill of Human Rights, the costlier it becomes for elites to violate the rights of people. It is costlier in two respects. First, because hypocrisy undermines the legitimacy of the regime in the eyes of its own people, resistance to oppression is fortified. Secondly, when the legitimacy of the regime is called into question internationally, the government at least risks sanctioning by other states or by inter-governmental organizations. While governments are loath to employ sanctions against offenders, particularly where they perceive economic or national security interests, the possibility of such enforcement increases as elites increasingly profess their commitment to human rights.[34]

Human rights NGOs not only morally condemn gross violators of human rights, they also occasionally praise governments for acts and policies that demonstrate a genuine respect for human dignity. For example, when Argentine President Raul Alfonsin announced that high-ranking military officials involved in human rights transgressions would be brought to criminal trial, his government was widely praised by human rights NGOs for setting an

31. George Shepherd, Jr., *Anti-Apartheid: Transnational Conflict and Western Policy in the Liberation of South Africa* (Westport, Conn.: Greenwood Press, 1977), 120.
32. Ibid.
33. See Richard P. Claude, Eric Stover, and June P. Lopez, *Health Professionals and Human Rights in the Philippines* (Washington, D.C.: American Association for the Advancement of Science, 1987), 49–52.
34. Scoble and Wiseberg, "The Importance and Functions of Human Rights Organizations," 1–20. See also Robert A. Friedlander, "Human Rights Theory and NGO Practice: Where Do We Go from Here?" in Nanda, Scarritt, and Shepherd, *Global Human Rights*, 212–28; and Art Blaser, "Assessing Human Rights: The NGO Contribution," ibid., 261–88.

important precedent.[35] On the other hand, perhaps demonstrating the power of withholding praise (as opposed to threatening moral condemnation), human rights NGOs were initially cautious when Andrei Sakharov was released from his internal exile in Gorky in 1986. The renowned physicist and political dissident expressed appreciation and praise for the government's action, but human rights NGOs were uncertain whether most or all Soviet political prisoners would be freed. After 1987, as it happened, hundreds of others confined in Soviet prisons, gulags, and psychiatric wards were released by the government.

In the first essay in this chapter, Richard N. Dean details the work of many NGOs concerned with human rights abuses in the USSR and concludes that there are many things that NGOs do or can do better than states (or the media). Governments tend to be fickle in their attention to human rights. NGOs, on the other hand, with their persistent harping on the mistreatment of dissidents, supply continuous support and solidarity, helping to galvanize human rights movements that might otherwise languish in the face of antagonistic authorities. Regarding the Soviet Union, at any rate, Western NGOs were able to see to it that dissidents were not forgotten, and their efforts, according to Dean, generated a degree of accountability on the part of the Soviet regime that otherwise would not have been forthcoming. Largely written before the fast-moving events associated with the Gorbachev policies of *glasnost* ("public openness") and *perestroika* ("restructuring") that have begun to result in some human rights improvements in the USSR, Dean's essay nonetheless emphasizes that continued NGO pressure on the Soviet Union is needed to sustain and expand the progress made. The essay should be read with special attention to the analysis of the functions and strategies of NGOs in the Western world to bring about human rights improvements in the Soviet Union.

In addition to human rights NGOs, the work and impact of business enterprises, for example, foreign (often multinational) corporations in South Africa, must also be taken into account. Though most multinational corporations operating in South Africa "really had not given the topic of international human rights a lot of thought," notes J. Frederick Truitt, "until forced to it by organizations as diverse as the American Friends Service Committee, Resist, the Interfaith Center for Corporate Responsibility, and the Institute for Sport and Social Analysis,"[36] still the business community cannot escape the challenge of human rights wherever it may arise, or at least not in southern Africa. In 1978, a UN report documented the extent of foreign trade and assistance to South Africa and Namibia and asserted that multinational corporations "are building up South Africa's economy so that it will be better able to resist challenges to apartheid from the international community."[37] It concluded that "a complete withdrawal of economic interests and the reversing of economic relationships are the minimum pressures required to bring about drastic change."[38] In other words, as another kind of NGO, the business enterprise has important responsibilities in the area of human rights.

In the second essay in this chapter, Mary C. Gosiger focuses on private American financial involvement in South Africa. She assesses the divestment campaign that "has swept the United States," reviewing government, university, and corporate actions. Her analysis should stimulate the reader to question whether, in a world that aspires to global human rights, financial institutions should conduct business with repressive regimes as mere profit seekers

---

35. See Americas Watch, *Truth and Partial Justice in Argentina* (New York, 1987), 1.
36. J. Frederick Truitt, "The Improbable Alliance: Human Rights, Prosperity and International Business," *Worldview* 23 (May 1980): 24–27, at 24.
37. E/CN.4/Sub/2/383/ Rev. 1 (1978), para. 289.
38. Ibid., para. 302. See Philip Alston, "International Trade as an Instrument of Positive Human Rights Policy," *Human Rights Quarterly* 4, no. 2 (1982): 155–83.

or whether, in contrast, they have an affirmative duty to act as responsible agents of progressive social change.

Finally, it should be noted that the individual has an important role to play in redressing human rights injustices; for, if individuals do not join the human rights struggle, governments and other social institutions will succeed in their disregard of simple human respect. Happily, history is replete with examples of such opposition (today called "activism"), whether by individuals or by groups of individual "dissidents." The heroic action of Andrei Sakharov in founding the human rights movement in the Soviet Union, for example, ranks him with such historic figures as Thomas Paine and Martin Luther King, Jr. Each of these defiant dissidents was a dauntless proponent of the human spirit in the face of serious repression. Each, at great personal risk and cost, was successful in pursuing human rights goals thought by opponents and adherents alike to stand for revolutionary ideas.

In the last essay, Jordan Paust, an international lawyer, looks at the right to armed resistance and revolution, the ultimate sanction against tyrannical government and human rights abuse. Exploring both the nature and scope of the right so as to clarify a theory of legitimate resistance, he argues that two standards must be met to justify its invocation: first, the resistance or revolution must be taken up on the authority and in the interest of the majority of the people, not simply an aggrieved minority; second, it must be taken up against a state that oppresses its citizenry by political or economic means. For international human rights purposes, Paust looks for guidance to the preamble of the Universal Declaration of Human Rights:

> It is essential, if man is not to be compelled to have recourse, as a last resort, to rebellion against tyranny and oppression, that human rights should be protected by the rule of law.

Exploring the limits of permissibility beyond the Universal Declaration, in the UN Charter and other international normative sources, Paust concludes that a majority of a people is free to resist or revolt against the government when that majority no longer participates in its own destiny or when its future has been essentially coopted by an elite few. It is thus on the basis of a denial of the fundamental right of self-determination that a viable theory of legitimate resistance and armed revolution may be mounted. The issue remaining, of course, concerns the criteria by which to judge whether the right to self-determination has been violated.

Whatever the criteria that apply, the fact is that the peoples of the world, regardless of differences in cultural traditions and institutional practices, increasingly are demanding to participate in the shaping of the world in which they live.[39] Their demands stem from the enduring elements of most of the world's great religions and philosophies. However, what used to be a dream of uncertain promise now is emerging as a necessary reality of world order, and it can safely be predicted that the contemporary global human rights movement will continue to gain in strength. For the foreseeable future, that sinewy strength will derive substantially from individual and nongovernmental actions undertaken on behalf of all who suffer at the hands of oppressive and repressive governments and societies.

---

39. See Henry J. Steiner, "Political Participation as a Human Right," *Harvard Human Rights Yearbook* 1 (1988): 77–134.

22. RICHARD N. DEAN *Nongovernmental Organizations: The Foundation of Western Support for the Human Rights Movement in the Soviet Union*

PREFACE

Since 1985 when this essay was originally written,[1] the first signs have begun to appear of what may prove to be a period of great reform in Soviet political, economic and social life. Mikhail Gorbachev's policy of *glasnost* has encouraged open debate in the press on [a] wide spectrum of issues. Mr. Gorbachev has publicly denounced the abuses of power of the Stalinist period. Long-suppressed films and books are emerging. The Soviet press even reports disputes among members of the Communist Party elite, as the ouster of Boris Yeltsin from his position as the head of the Moscow Communist Party indicated. More and more Soviets are being allowed to travel abroad, a policy which may eventually erode Soviet resistance to relaxing their emigration policy.

Even Mr. Gorbachev's economic policies may have far-reaching consequences for human rights issues. Those policies promise extensive reforms, including the requirement that Soviet enterprises be "self-financing" and that such enterprises may be liquidated if they are not profitable. For the first time since the 1920s, foreigners are permitted to invest directly in Soviet enterprises and own up to 49% of such enterprises under the new Soviet joint venture legislation. Both of these economic reforms have market economy overtones and, at this point, one can only speculate on the impact such reforms, if fully implemented, may have not only on the Soviet economic system but also on Soviet political and social life.

Perhaps not so surprisingly, it appears that the "non-governmental organizations" (whose activities in support of the human rights movement in the Soviet Union are the subject of this [essay] do not appear to have had a direct impact on the shaping of Mr. Gorbachev's policies. The return of the Sakharovs from Gorky to Moscow in late 1986, the release of over 200 dissidents and permission granted to prominent Jewish refuseniks to emigrate from the Soviet Union are actions which Mr. Gorbachev has endorsed; however, the reasons for his support remain unclear. There is little doubt that Mr. Gorbachev is attempting to improve the Soviet human rights record to enhance the image of the Soviet Union in the West, and the Western press has responded with much media coverage and guarded enthusiasm. Mr. Gorbachev also seems to believe that at least limited democratization is necessary to implement his economic reforms. These two factors seem to explain Mr. Gorbachev's "human rights initiatives" more effectively than does the thesis that he is responding to Western pressure through the activities of NGOs. His harsh responses during the December 1987 summit meetings to journalists' questions on human rights issues seem to confirm the continued existence of Soviet intransigence in the face of direct Western criticism and pressure.

However, one must not discount the indirect impact that NGOs have had on the shaping of Mr. Gorbachev''s *glasnost* policy. The very fact that Mr. Gorbachev has chosen to act in very specific ways, such as in the case of the Sakharovs and the release of other dissidents, is a tribute to the efforts of the NGOs in holding Western attention to the problems faced by those particular Soviet human rights activists. Without the perseverance and sustained commitment of certain NGOs to publicizing and building support for these dissidents, one doubts whether such individuals would have been beneficiaries of Mr. Gorbachev's *glasnost* policy. In addition, even the fact that Mr. Gorbachev believed that the inclusion of such human rights "concessions" in his *glasnost* policy was necessary is a tribute to the commitment of NGOs in insisting that human rights issues remain among the critical issues in U.S.-Soviet relations.

Most observers of the Soviet system agree that any democratic reform in the Soviet Union is far more likely to result primarily from the interplay of domestic political, social and economic forces

---

1. The analysis here borrows in part from an earlier article by the author, "Contacts with the West: The Dissidents' View of Western Support for the Human Rights Movement in the Soviet Union," *Universal Human Rights* 2, no. 1 (Jan.–Mar. 1980): 47–65.

Prepared for this volume by Richard N. Dean.

rather than from outside pressures. Recognition of this fact, particularly that NGO contributions will almost always be indirect, is important in shaping the most effective future strategies for NGOs. There is little doubt that NGOs will continue to play a significant role. The Western press should be able to gain greater access to participants in the human rights movement in the Soviet Union now that *glasnost* is in place. Opportunities to publicize human rights problems should increase and, at the same time, if Soviet-American relations improve, opportunities for NGOs to influence positively the treatment of human rights activists in the Soviet Union may also increase. Recent Soviet intolerance of organized protests, whether by Crimean Tatars or Soviet Jews, demonstrates that *glasnost* has limits and the uncertainty about Mr. Gorbachev's hold on power, as a result of the recent well-publicized debates within the Kremlin leadership over the pace of economic reform, indicates that NGOs will be needed also to perform their "traditional" roles, as described in this essay.

BACKGROUND

The 1970s witnessed the growth of widespread support in the West for the fledgling Soviet human rights movement. Such support emanated from individuals of various political viewpoints, national and international organizations, governmental agencies and both the print and broadcast media. The detente of the early 1970s laid the groundwork for growing Western awareness of human rights problems in the Soviet Union as dissidents who had so long been denied access to the West suddenly had opportunities to grant interviews, hold press conferences and have their views and proposals for reform published in the West. Westerners were reading and hearing about restrictive Soviet emigration policies, the arrests and persecution of Soviet writers, scholars and scientists and the horrible application of psychiatric treatment to dissidents. The Helsinki Final Act of 1975 became a highly-publicized source of human rights guidelines and spawned a variety of "monitoring groups" in the Soviet Union and the United States, which sought to review their respective governments' implementation of those guidelines. President Jimmy Carter adopted a policy of overt support for persecuted peoples worldwide and was successful in obtaining legislation which made U.S. foreign aid in part dependent upon the human rights record of recipient nations. The Soviet authorities' inhumane and abusive treatment of such brilliant figures as Alexander Solzhenitsyn and Andrei Sakharov outraged Westerners, and the "show trials" of Anatoli Shcharansky, Yuri Orlov and Vladimir Bukovsky exposed for the world's review the repressive and brutal nature of Soviet totalitarianism. Access to the West was so broad that the dissidents even advised the West how to support their activities and debated among themselves (in the Western press) the appropriate nature and extent of such support.

As U.S.-Soviet relations worsened and the Soviet authorities became more successful in repressing dissident activities, by the early 1980s Western attention to the problems of Soviet human rights activists had waned. No longer were the dissidents front page news in major Western newspapers. President Carter's human rights initiatives were blunted and, following his defeat in the 1980 election [by] Ronald Reagan, virtually halted. Issues of international security and the arms race increasingly preoccupied Western politicians. In only a few years, what had appeared to be broad Western support for the Soviet human rights movement had dwindled. Increasingly, Western non-governmental organizations have taken on a more significant role in maintaining and building such support. The "NGOs", as such organizations are typically referred to, have emerged as the foundation for Western support and appear to be the key to broadening such support over the next few decades. For the purpose of this [essay], the term "NGO" refers simply to non-governmental (i.e., private) organizations which have an interest in, and a commitment to, the protection and promotion of human rights on an international level.

THE NEW IMPORTANCE OF NGOS

There are several reasons for the increased significance of NGOs in marshalling Western support for the Soviet human rights movement. First, NGOs are better suited than the media or governmental organizations to provide consistent, long-term support for Soviet human rights activists. NGOs have succeeded in building constituencies in the West that are concerned about particular issues within the Soviet human rights movement and therefore are able to commit personnel and finances in an organized fashion. The allocation of such resources tends to reflect longer-term commitments by such organizations, which tend to be less influenced by the vagaries of politics and media interests. The successes and failures, the achievements and disappointments of Soviet human rights activists over the last twenty years underscore the need for perseverance. Neither the press nor governmental organizations are institutionally capable of such consistency and perseverance. The attention of the Western media waxes and wanes depending on available information and their judgement about the newsworthiness of the plight of Soviet dissidents. The main elements of the Western newspaper and broadcast media are certainly an important, though inconsistent, source of publicity for the dissidents. One cannot look to the media, however, for the foresight, strategy and commitment necessary to sustain and build Western support for Soviet human rights activists. NGOs, particularly organizations which focus on particular aspects of the Soviet human rights movement such as religious persecution, emigration and psychiatric abuses, also have the benefit of narrowly-focused agendas. Governmental organizations constantly face agendas which require the resolution of competing claims, which are influenced by political and economic pressures, and which are frequently dominated by urgent circumstances. Such an environment has not generally permitted such organizations to devote sufficient time and resources to building consistent Western support for Soviet human rights concerns. Public diplomacy on human rights issues between East and West in such forums as the Helsinki review conferences has degenerated into exchanges of accusations and allegations among nations. In such forums human rights issues are seldom addressed on their merits, but rather become an opportunity for political "chest-beating" in the perpetual debate over which political system, Soviet or American, is more advanced, humane and democratic.

NGOs are also better able to monitor and respond to the many and varied forms of human rights activism that have emerged in the Soviet Union. The post-Stalin human rights movement in the Soviet Union was driven principally by concern for civil and political rights. As the movement grew, however, its concerns broadened to include economic, social and cultural rights.[2] Certain activists, for example, advocated independent trade unions; others, particularly after the adoption of the Helsinki Final Act, sought to reunite families and increase cultural exchange. It was therefore inevitable that, as the human rights movement broadened its agenda, more Western NGOs with diverse and specialized concerns, including labor unions and cultural organizations, have become involved.

A second development has also contributed to the emergence of NGOs as the foundation of Western support. The deterioration in U.S.-Soviet relations commencing in the mid-1970s had two important consequences for Western support of the Soviet human rights movement. First, the increase in international tensions, particularly the arms race, has diverted attention from Soviet human rights activists. At the height of detente, the media devoted far more attention to Soviet human rights issues. With the Soviet invasion of Afghanistan, the crushing of the Polish Solidarity movement, the breakdown in arms control negotiations in Europe, the shooting down of the Korean Air Lines commercial flight, and the debate over President Reagan's Strategic Arms Initiative ("Star Wars"), human rights concerns have received less coverage. The second consequence has been more subtle, though equally important. Contacts between Western journalists and Soviet dissidents were plentiful in the early to mid-1970s. Andrei Sakharov's regular interviews with the Western press in his Moscow apartment are the best example of how easily and widely information was disseminated about the activities of dissidents. By 1980, however, such contacts had been almost completely eliminated by the KGB's widespread arrests of dissident leaders. Ironically, the loss of such contacts has been best symbolized by the exile in 1980 of Sakharov and his wife, Yelena Bonner, to Gorky, a city off-limits to foreigners. Since 1980 the Soviets have also adopted new postal practices which have restricted the flow of letters, other written materials

---

2. Two excellent sources for the history and development of the human rights movement in the USSR are L. Alexeyeva, *Soviet Dissent: Contemporary Movements for National, Religious, and Human Rights* (Middletown, Wesleyan University Press, 1985) and J. Rubenstein, *Soviet Dissidents: Their Struggle for Human Rights*, 2d ed. (Boston: Beacon Press, 1980).

and packages to and from the Soviet Union. In 1982 the Soviets drastically reduced the number of long distance telephone lines between the Soviet Union and the West. It is no longer possible to make a direct telephone call; all calls must be placed through operators with often several hours' delay. Beginning in 1984 new legislation was also implemented imposing penalties on Soviet citizens who transport or provide overnight accommodation to foreigners without official permission. Without direct access to dissidents, the media has been forced to depend more and more on the contacts and investigative efforts of NGOs.

Finally, there is a certain institutional logic to the growing prominence of NGOs. Issues spawn organizations. The NGOs have quite logically emerged as more significant as the issues relating to the Soviet human rights movement generally and Western support in particular became better known and more focused.

THE IDENTITY OF THE NGOS

The combination of great attention in the West to the Soviet human rights movement in the 1970s and the breadth and diversity of the issues raised by Soviet human rights activists attracted the attention of a great number and variety of NGOs which, in turn, led to the formation of other NGOs. These NGOs fall into three broad categories: (1) general human rights organizations; (2) organizations specifically devoted to Soviet human rights issues; and (3) professional organizations whose activities may include attention to certain human rights issues. A complete listing of these organizations is beyond the scope of this [essay]. Only a representative sample is described in this section to provide a sense of the range of activities conducted by such NGOs.

The best known NGO among the first type of organization is probably Amnesty International, a London-based organization whose purpose is to secure the release of prisoners of conscience throughout the world, to improve prison conditions in accordance with U N standards and to provide support and encouragement to the fam-

ilies of political prisoners. Amnesty has contributed significantly to Western awareness of human rights issues in the Soviet Union. Its documentation of the confinement and treatment of dissidents in Soviet prisons, labor camps and psychiatric wards has been a key means of publicizing the plight of political prisoners in the Soviet Union.[3] In addition to its investigative efforts, Amnesty attempts to assist dissidents primarily through local chapters, which disseminate information and conduct letter-writing campaigns, issue press releases and promote awareness of the cases of individual Soviet dissidents.

Performing a more specialized information dissemination function is Human Rights Internet.[4] HRI compiles, synthesizes and publishes bimonthly reports which summarize human rights issues on a country-by-country basis throughout the world. HRI's reports reprint articles, summarize scholarly and journalistic articles and list bibliographic information disseminated about Soviet dissidents. Such reports include information about developments in Soviet policy and the activities of Western NGOs, politicians and scholars concerning the Soviet human rights movement. Such reports serve as a convenient and valuable source of information on current Soviet human rights issues.

Since human rights problems also involve legal questions, NGOs whose membership consists primarily of attorneys concerned about international human rights problems have also played a significant role in the support of Soviet human rights activists. The Lawyers Committee for International Human Rights has prepared petitions seeking review by the United Nations Human Rights Commission of the treatment of dissidents such as Andrei Sakharov and Yuri Orlov. The International Human Rights Law Group, an organization of lawyers which has focused on the procedural protections afforded to individuals under national laws, recently conducted a symposium of more than 30 international law experts to evaluate the procedural irregularities in the Soviet government's prosecution, conviction and imprisonment of dissident Yosif Begun.[5] The International League for Human Rights established a formal bond with the Soviet Human Rights Committee, an organiza-

---

3. See, e.g., Amnesty International, *Prisoners of Conscience in the U.S.S.R.: Their Treatment and Conditions,* 2d ed. (London, 1980).
4. HRI publishes the *Human Rights Internet Reporter* four times a year from the Harvard Law School.
5. The symposium was held in January, 1984, in Washington, D.C.

tion founded in Moscow in 1970 by Andrei Sakharov, Valery Chalidze and other prominent dissidents.

The second type of NGOs are those organizations concerned specifically with human rights issues in the Soviet Union. These organizations span a variety of concerns, including political, social, religious and cultural. Among the best known is the U.S. Helsinki Watch Committee, founded following the adoption of the Helsinki Final Act of 1975 to monitor its implementation by the signatory nations. This Committee is the American counterpart of the Helsinki monitoring committees which were founded in Moscow, the Ukraine, Georgia, Lithuania and Armenia and has been an important source of information not only about violations of Soviet obligations under the Final Act, but also about the brutal persecution to which the leaders of the five Soviet Helsinki monitoring groups have been subjected. For example, the U.S. Helsinki Watch Committee recently published a report entitled *Ten Years Later: Violations of the Helsinki Accords*, which reported on the compliance of the Soviet Union and Eastern Europe with the Final Act.[6] The report details the persecution of the Helsinki "monitors," 70 of whom are either currently in prison or have served prison terms in the last decade. The report also itemizes specific Soviet violations of the Final Act in the areas of freedom of expression, contacts with foreigners, freedom of movement (including cross-border family visits and emigration), freedom of religion and minority and ethnic rights.

While concern for the implementation of the Final Act was the reason for the creation of the U.S. Helsinki Watch Committee, more specific cultural and religious concerns have led to the formation of other NGOs in this second category. The best known is the National Conference for Soviet Jewry (NCSJ), founded in 1973, which seeks to assist Soviet Jews who desire to emigrate from the Soviet Union in their efforts to live without fear of persecution or discrimination. The NCSJ has become the major coordinating agency for American activity in support of Soviet Jews. The organization works through many national agencies and over 200 local affiliated councils,

federations and committees throughout the United States. Another similar organization is CREED, the Christian Rescue Effort for the Emancipation of Dissidents, which was organized to provide assistance and to intercede on behalf of individuals who are imprisoned, refused emigration or suffer other persecution for their religious faith. Both the NCSJ and CREED work through U.S. government agencies to apply pressure on Soviet authorities to release prisoners and minimize persecution. The NCSJ maintains a policy research and development program at its Washington, D.C., office through which it provides information to U.S. politicians and attempts to influence American policy towards the USSR.

Other NGOs in this second category include organizations founded directly by dissidents who were evicted from the Soviet Union or had their Soviet citizenship revoked while traveling abroad. Best known in this group is the Russian Fund to Aid Political Prisoners, founded by Alexander Solzhenitsyn in Switzerland in 1974. This organization has raised funds in the West which have been distributed in the Soviet Union to provide aid chiefly to the families of imprisoned dissidents. Another such organization is Khronika Press, based in New York, which is the U.S. publisher of the *Chronicle of Human Rights*. Since 1973 the *Chronicle* has been one of the most thorough and accurate sources of information in the West about the Soviet human rights movement, particularly about the persecution of individual dissidents.

The third general type of NGO involved in Western support of the Soviet human rights movement are large professional organizations which have focused on issues raised by Soviet activists that are related to their professional interests. The most well-known example is the World Psychiatric Association (WPA) which investigated, challenged and ultimately censured Soviet psychiatrists for their participation in brutal treatment regimes for dissidents, including the use of mind-altering and extremely painful drugs, shock therapy, straitjackets and indefinite hospitalization.[7] The American Bar Association has from time to time protested the persecution of

6. A Helsinki Watch Report published by the U.S. Helsinki Watch Commission (New York and Washington, 1985).
7. See, generally, S. Bloch and P. Reddaway, *Psychiatric Terror: How Soviet Psychiatry Is Used to Suppress Dissent* (New York: Basic Books, 1977); P. Reddaway, "Political Abuse of Psychiatry in the USSR: The Effectiveness of World Pressures", in *Russia* (Silver Spring, Md.: Foundation for Soviet Studies, 1984), 21. See also Eric Stover and Elena O. Nightingale, eds., *The Breaking of Bodies and Minds* (New York: W. H. Freeman, 1985).

Soviet lawyers and the organization's mandate may extend to challenging violations of Soviet civil and criminal procedural laws which frequently occur when the Soviet authorities arrest and imprison dissidents. Various Western scientific and policy organizations such as the Trilateral Commission and organizations as varied as the World Postal Union (WPU) and the AFL-CIO have been involved either directly or indirectly in supporting the efforts of Soviet human rights activists. The WPU has provided a forum for protests against Soviet failure to comply with international postal regulations regarding the delivery, confiscation and opening of mail. In July 1984 the WPU openly censored the Soviets and adopted new proposals in an effort to force the Soviets to comply with international postal practices. The support of the AFL-CIO has been more direct; it has long supported the work of Alexander Solzhenitsyn and sponsored a series of lectures by him in the United States about Soviet repression and Western responses.

THE CONTRIBUTION OF THE NGOS

The most important contribution of the Western NGOs to the support of Soviet human rights activists is publicity. With the crumbling of detente in the late 1970s and the attention of the media focused on the arms race, terrorism and other international issues in recent years, the NGOs have become the most significant source of information about Soviet human rights activists. Continued Western support of such activists has depended to great extent on the consistent efforts of the NGOs to build awareness in the West of the persecution of dissidents and repressive nature of Soviet civil rights law and practice. This function has taken on special significance with the reduction in Soviet sources of information as a result of the Soviet authorities' comprehensive crackdown on dissent over the last several years. The Helsinki monitoring groups in the Soviet Union have been decimated; their members, many of whom had direct access to Western correspondents in the 1970s, have been either imprisoned or forced underground. Even the *Chronicle of Human Rights*, the most comprehensive printed source of information since 1973, has not been published since 1982.

The publicity generated by the NGOs in support of Soviet dissidents takes several forms. Primarily, the information focuses on the initiatives taken by such activists and the repressive responses of the Soviet authorities. The U.S. Helsinki Watch Committee has carefully monitored and reported the harassment, arrests and imprisonment of members of the five Soviet Helsinki monitoring groups. Amnesty International and the NCSJ also direct the efforts of their local chapters to familiarize themselves with the cases of particular dissidents. For example, the U.S. Helsinki Watch Committee has reported a minor change in the Soviet penal code which increased punishment for prisoners for "malicious disobedience of the administration of corrective labor institutions."[8] Such legislation granted the Soviet authorities discretion to extend the sentences of prisoners up to three years for minor disciplinary infractions. The Committee then explained how such a change may permit Soviet authorities to keep political prisoners imprisoned indefinitely, despite the expiration of their original prison sentences, and cited 35 cases during 1982–83 in which the sentences of political prisoners had been extended on the authority of this legislation. Amnesty International and the U.S. Helsinki Watch Committee have both reported extensively on the conditions of Soviet prisons at which political prisoners are known to be held and on the harsh treatment of such prisoners, including the denial of food, visits and mail and the use of solitary confinement and other brutal punishments.

Such publicity has important benefits for Soviet human rights activists. First, individual dissidents and refuseniks are not forgotten. How easily the Soviet authorities could send an activist not only to prison or exile, but also to obscurity, were it not for the efforts of NGOs to publicize the plight of these victims. Second, such publicity mobilizes public sentiment and, in certain circumstances, action. Even though the instances are rare in which such publicity has been directly linked to altering the tactics or policies of the Soviet authorities in their treatment of dissidents, it is easy to overlook the fact that such publicity continues to have a significant impact on U.S. foreign policy. Indeed, the "human rights" issue was apparently high on President Ronald Reagan's agenda for his discussions with Secretary-General Mikhail Gorbachev in November, 1985

8. *Ten Years Later* (see n. 6, above), 225–26.

and was featured as one of the topics for the "pre-summit" held in October 1986 in Reykjavik, Iceland. Although U.S. politicians, particularly those of a conservative leaning, have used for their own political purposes allegations about Soviet human rights violations, such self-serving uses should not obscure the value of NGO investigations and analyses in providing evidence to support such allegations. The recent release of Anatoli Shcharansky is a tribute to the perseverance of the NCSJ and other NGOs which consistently kept his plight, including his poor health and allegations of mistreatment by prison officials, before Western politicians and the media for more than eight years.[9]

Such publicity also builds credibility for the dissidents in the West. The international reputations of such organizations as Amnesty International, the World Psychiatric Association and the International Commission of Jurists, each of which, among many other highly regarded organizations, has publicized Soviet repression, have made the claims of the Soviet human rights activists much more believable in Western eyes, which, in turn, has led to greater support for their cause.

Equally important for the cause of human rights in the USSR is that, as the credibility in the West of Soviet human rights activists has increased, Western respect for the Soviet government, because of its repressive policies and its inability to handle internal disagreement without violence, has diminished. Standard Soviet diatribes about dissidents being Western spies, warmongers, drug-dealers and mental incompetents are viewed in the West as absurd tantrums by an inept government. Soviet politicians and scholars trumpet that their system of government is the most democratic the world has ever known. Few in the West would agree, in large part because of NGO revelations about the decidedly undemocratic way in which dissidents are treated. Even the highly publicized Soviet peace movement and its progeny, the "nuclear freeze" movement, have suffered in the West. Nothing could have so undermined Western perceptions of Soviet sincerity in these movements as the arrest in Moscow in 1982 of the members of the Soviet independent peace movement, the Group to Establish Trust Between the USSR and the USA. Indeed, the repressive nature of the Soviet political system remains in the eyes of many Westerners a major impediment to establishing consistent, peaceful and cooperative relations with the Soviet Union.

The dissidents themselves, even though they are divided over what means of Western support for their cause is most appropriate, have unanimously affirmed the crucial importance of publicity. Andrei Sakharov's statement before the AFL-CIO in 1977 merits lengthy quotation:

> First of all, I wish to discuss the issue of communications, which is critical for the human rights struggle in the USSR and for my public activity. The only weapon in our struggle is publicity, the open and free world. . . . During this era of detente and a broadening struggle for human rights, communications with the West, receipt in the West of information about human rights violations and the effective, conscientious utilization of such information have become crucial. Successful cooperation in the struggle for human rights is possible only if we energetically combat the shameless measures adopted by the Soviet authorities to sever our channels of communication. . . .
>
> What actions do we expect from you? Assistance in initiating a major campaign in the press and in Congress against violations of the freedom of exchange of information. Support for intergovernmental negotiations on this issue. Measures to enhance the effectiveness of broadcasts to the Soviet Union and Eastern Europe. . . . Promotion of unhindered international television broadcasts from communication satellites.[10]

The dissidents are unanimous in their belief that world public opinion, mobilized by the Western press, serves as a significant restraining force on Soviet abuses of human rights. One aspect of this is the dissidents' contention that the pressure of world public opinion has led either to the release or to the better treatment of a number of political prisoners, among them Zhores

---

9. Shcharansky's recent biography contains numerous references to the efforts of the NCSJ, such as arranging meetings for Shcharansky's wife with U.S. government officials and members of the media and in initiating the formation in October 1977 of the Ad Hoc Commission on Justice for Anatoly Shcharansky in Washington, D.C. M. Gilbert, *Shcharansky: Hero of Our Time* (London: Macmillan, 1986), 218, 224, 352.

10. Andrei Sakharov, "Soviet Workers, the AFL-CIO and Human Rights," speech reprinted in *A Chronicle of Human Rights* 28 (1977).

Medvedev and Valentin Moroz. Another aspect of this is the dissidents' belief that public opinion shields them from even harsher reprisals from the government. According to Anatoli Shcharansky, during the 1970s the Soviet government tolerated a certain level of dissidence because "to take more direct measures against us would be to return to the days of Stalin and that they don't want. They are interested in Western public opinion and in detente and in good economic relations, and most of the present leaders are the very men who survived Stalin. World opinion is what keeps us going, what keeps us alive."[11]

Not only does publicity about dissident activities serve to mobilize Western public opinion, but it also provides information to the Soviet people as a means of enlisting support and of promoting unity among the dissidents. Yuri Galanskov has explained the importance of this function:

The Western press, and especially the Western radio stations [Radio Liberty, Voice of America, Deutsche Welle] broadcasting in Russia publicize the arbitrariness and acts of crude coercion by Soviet official personnel, and thus force the state bodies and officials to take action. In this way the Western press and radio are fulfilling the tasks of what is at present lacking in Russia, an organized opposition, and thereby stimulating our national development.[12]

In addition to publicity, the NGOs have contributed action. As indicated above, publicity generated by NGO activities is clearly an important source of information in shaping U.S. policy, both for the White House and Congress. However, NGOs have also successfully taken direct action in support of their cause. The best example [is] the lobbying activities of the NCSJ in influencing U.S. policy to pressure the Soviets to ease restrictions on Jewish emigration. Such NCSJ pressure has been consistent over the last decade and enjoyed its most dramatic victory in the passage by Congress of Jackson-Vanik Amendment to the Trade Act of 1974, which conditioned the granting of certain trade benefits to the Soviet Union on Soviet willingness to ease emigration restrictions. As a result of the continuing efforts of the NCSJ, the Jackson-Vanik Amendment re-

mains law and has been an important factor in emphasizing the great value the United States has attached to support for the dissidents. In this case, such support has probably worked to the commercial disadvantage of the United States because the Jackson-Vanik Amendment has certainly hindered the development of the U.S.-Soviet trade.

The effect of NGO actions on Soviet policy and practice regarding dissidents is more difficult to judge. The Jackson-Vanik Amendment has certainly been a clear indication to the Soviets of U.S. concern about human rights issues. While the Amendment has not achieved a dramatic shift in Soviet emigration policy, there is some evidence that at times when the Soviets are interested in creating a positive impression in the West, such as prior to an important round of diplomatic meetings, to the proposed submission of the SALT II arms control treaty to the U.S. Senate, and to Congressional hearings about extending certain trade benefits to the USSR, they have temporarily eased emigration restrictions, permitting more Jews to leave for the West. In connection with the November 1985 summit meeting much publicity was devoted to Soviet plans to permit a number of their citizens to emigrate to the West to be reunited with their spouses.

While NGO actions do not appear to have directly resulted in new Soviet legislation or policies improving the treatment of dissidents, there are examples in which such action has yielded results in individual cases. The dissidents have recognized the effectiveness of such effort, particularly the personal intervention of Amnesty International officials. Vladimir Bukovsky attributes his release in 1965 from confinement in a psychiatric hospital to a personal visit to the hospital director by a member of the Amnesty International who threatened to bring the matter before an international tribunal.[13] The personal petition of the assistant director of the British Section of Amnesty International before the Minister of Internal Affairs is reputed to have prompted the transfer of Sergei Kovalev to a Leningrad prison so that he could receive proper medical care.[14]

NGO action to combat Soviet use of psychi-

---

11. *Time,* Feb. 21, 1977, 22.
12. Quoted in P. Reddaway, *Uncensored Russia* (New York: McGraw-Hill, 1972), 225.
13. "Vladimir Bukovsky: Remarks to the American Psychiatric Association," *A Chronicle of Human Rights* 26 (1977): 55–56.
14. "Kovalev Receives Treatment," *Samizdat Bulletin* 50 (1977).

atric measures against dissidents has yielded more dramatic results. The Soviet authorities used psychiatric measures to punish dissidents prior to the beginning of the post-Stalin human rights movement in the mid-1960s. However, by 1970 the evidence indicated that a significant number of dissidents were being committed to psychiatric hospitals and subjected to harsh, brutal treatment. Vladimir Bukovsky, a dissident who himself had endured two separate confinements in Soviet psychiatric hospitals, began accumulating evidence of Soviet psychiatric repression which he had sent to the World Psychiatric Association in 1971. Although the WPA did not act on Bukovsky's submission then, after examining additional evidence presented by the Working Commission to Investigate the Use of Psychiatry for Political Purposes, Moscow-based dissident organization, the WPA in 1977 narrowly passed a resolution censuring the USSR. The WPA also established a review committee to investigate individual cases of abuse submitted by its members. The Soviet authorities harshly criticized the action of the WPA and, as international scrutiny and pressure increased over the next few years, the Soviets sought to cover up their actions, leading to the further humiliation of Soviet psychiatrists in world public opinion and outrage from Western medical professionals. By 1981, the Soviets had arrested the entire leadership of the Working Commission and Soviet psychiatrists had refused to cooperate with their Western colleagues in any review of their diagnostic techniques and procedures. Increasing pressure to expel the Soviets from the WPA built from 1981 [to 1983]. During that period, the Soviets dramatically shifted their tactics and invited Western psychiatric practices in an effort to avoid expulsion. By January 1983, however, the Soviets had apparently concluded that such efforts would be unsuccessful and, only seven months before the next WPA meeting, the Soviet society resigned to avoid expulsion.

The example of the WPA is instructive in understanding the vital role NGOs can play in supporting Soviet human rights activists. There is no doubt that the actions of the WPA, coupled with the pressures of world public opinion, were effective in preventing the escalation of psychiatric abuse in the USSR and in at least forestalling its acceptance as a repressive technique in Eastern Europe. Moreover, it appears that such support may have actually reduced the number of dissidents confined to psychiatric hospitals.

There are several reasons for the effectiveness of Western action, spearheaded by the WPA, in these circumstances. First, as an internationally-renowned professional organization, the WPA gave the dissidents broad public exposure and their claims worldwide credibility. Second, the WPA focused on a specific, circumscribed abuse—the use of psychiatric measures and techniques—about which its member societies were experts. Their revelations of Soviet psychiatric practices therefore were authoritative and convincing. The Soviets had no substantive defense, particularly since no Soviet diagnosis of a dissident as mentally ill has ever been confirmed by a reputable Western psychiatrist. Third, the attack on Soviet psychiatry hit a particularly sensitive Soviet nerve. The Soviets have always been concerned about their prestige and acceptance in the international community. An attack led by medical peers on the competence, independence and morality of an important segment of their medical profession forced the Soviets to alter their tactics and apparently to rely less on psychiatric means in repressing dissent. This development also suggests a fourth reason for the success of the WPA's actions. As Peter Reddaway, one of the leading analysts of the Soviet human rights movement, has noted, the Soviet authorities do not need psychiatric abuse to accomplish the repression of dissent.[15]

AN EVALUATION: SUGGESTIONS FOR FUTURE NGO SUPPORT

While there is no doubt that the importance of NGOs in marshalling Western support for the Soviet human rights movement has increased over the last several years, certain weaknesses remain in the approaches and activities of these organizations. The NGOs remain a fragmented array of groups whose activities and strategies are seldom coordinated and [are] often guided by little more than urgent reactions to Soviet persecution of individual dissidents. Little attention, if any, is given to broader strategies and planning for the future. NGO strategies also tend, despite the diversity of the organizations involved, to be

15. Reddaway, "Political Abuse of Psychiatry in the USSR," 21.

remarkably similar. Press releases, press conferences and interviews, letters of support to dissidents, of protest to Soviet authorities and international organizations, and of concern to Western politicians, lobbying efforts in the West and personal contacts in the West and the Soviet Union, cover the range of NGO activities. The success of such activities is difficult to measure. From a U.S. policy perspective, these activities would appear to have been successful to the extent that they are seen as encouraging or at least affirming the Reagan Administration's commitment to promoting democratic reform in the USSR. From the perspective of effecting change in the USSR, however, the results are less encouraging. A few isolated battles have been won—dissidents freed, exchanged, exiled from the USSR or, perhaps, not as harshly treated as they otherwise might have been. The fundamental Soviet policy of intolerance toward any form of political dissent has remained unaltered. It is at this level that NGO activities should be carefully reviewed with a view to developing new strategies and activities to affect Soviet actions.

First, NGOs should study and understand the significance of the broader historical and political stage on which Soviet human rights activists perform their tragic drama. The last twenty years have proved that effecting change in a well-entrenched, totalitarian political and social system is a long-term commitment. Such a commitment must include an understanding that support for the dissidents is inextricably linked to the broader (and more difficult) issue of supporting democratic reform in the Soviet political system. The task is made more difficult by Russian and Soviet history. The democratic reforms sought by the dissidents have never characterized, with few, short-lived exceptions, either Russian or Soviet politics. Soviet political philosophy assumes that rights are granted (and therefore may be revoked) by the state; rights are not inherent in or innate to human beings, as they are believed to be in the Western tradition. Moreover, in Russian and Soviet political and social thought individual rights and expression have always been subsumed to the "collective." With such a philosophical foundation, it is not surprising that dissidents are persecuted for harming the interests of the Soviet State and its people or that Soviet leaders do not fully understand Western support for the cause of such dissidents. Such a historical, political and philosophical tradition with its roots in over six hundred years of Russian and Soviet history defies simple and quick solutions. NGOs committed to the democratization of the Soviet political system must begin by understanding, and imparting to their constituencies, not only this background but also the necessity of a commitment to gradual, incremental change. . . .

The education of the NGOs should also include a better understanding of East-West relations. Regrettably, many of the factors which may contribute to the reform of the Soviet political system are beyond the control of the NGOs (and, indeed, of the West) and may only be indirectly influenced by them. For example, hindsight now demonstrates that the great upsurge in human rights activism in the 1970s rode a wave of Western support made possible by detente. It is important to remind oneself that, if the goal is to aid dissidents and promote democratic reforms, one must be in a position to exert some influence on the Soviet system. During the 1970s Western support was more successful in protecting some dissidents from imprisonment, lightening the punishment of others and shaping American and international public opinion than has been the case in the 1980s because U.S.-Soviet relations were much better during the former period. Since the Soviet Union "closed up" and reduced contacts with the West in response to worsening East-West political relations, Western influence has done little to deter Soviet persecution of dissidents.

The development of effective, long-term strategies by NGOs will require a better understanding not only of the historical, philosophical and political context of human rights issues, but also of the Soviet political system itself. One cannot apply Western political assumptions to the human rights problems in the Soviet Union and hope to have much impact. This part of the background education of NGOs should include attention to such perplexing questions as: why the Soviet authorities have reacted so violently to all forms of dissent, even avowedly non-political forms such as freedom of worship for the small groups of Soviet Pentecostals and Jehovah's Witnesses; what forms of protest or dissent have been successful in the Soviet Union; what tactics have the Soviet authorities adopted to suppress dissent and why were those tactics chosen over other possibilities; why are the Soviet authorities so sensitive to world public opinion and what opportunities exist, such as the initiatives of the

WPA, to influence Soviet actions based on such sensitivity; what political, cultural or social groups within the USSR may be influenced by Western contacts.

Second, there should be greater coherence and unity among the NGOs. Such efforts are particularly important because successful action by one NGO, whether in influencing the release of a political prisoner or merely in obtaining information about the arrest of another dissident, is important to other NGOs. Unified action is likely to yield better results in generating Western support since the opportunity would exist to elicit participation from many more and diverse constituencies in the West. Commitment to greater unity is also likely to be mutually encouraging to NGO leaders and to foster the development of longer-term and broader-based strategies for supporting dissidents and effecting change in the Soviet political system. Such coherence and unity can be most effectively achieved by efforts to build links among the various NGOs through informal exchanges of information, conferences, and regular meetings. Such links might eventually develop into a broadly-representative coordinating organization which would serve as the focal point for exchanging information, promoting Western support and formulating tactics and strategy.

Third, the long-term effectiveness of the NGOs is likely to depend upon their ability to broaden their base of support in the West. To a certain extent, greater communication and unity among the NGOs will begin this process. However, there are additional strategic steps which NGOs should take, such as linking the cause of human rights in the Soviet Union to other issues in U.S.-Soviet relations and building ties with highly-regarded professional and other organizations whose members could tie their professional expertise and interests to specific human rights issues. Regarding issue-based linking, NGOs should broaden their appeals beyond publicizing the plight of individual dissidents (although there is no question that this is a critical function) to focusing on the relationship between human rights issues and such well-known issues in U.S.-Soviet relations as arms limitation and disarmament, trade and commerce and cultural exchange. With respect to arms limitation and disarmament, NGOs should be marshalling evidence in attempts to demonstrate a causal relationship between a more politically open society and a less aggressive leadership. Such an argument is premised on the theory that in a more democratic society the political leadership is more accountable to domestic political issues and, ultimately, to its constituency. A related approach is to discuss the arms race in terms of mutual, national mistrust and to argue that such trust will never develop permanently until the Soviet political system becomes more democratic, i.e., at least until dissident political views are permitted and reported to the public (even if not heeded by the leadership). One of the most critical substantive issues in arms control negotiations, verification (in all its many applications), traces its roots to problems of mistrust between the United States and the Soviet Union.

NGOs need to approach trade and commerce and cultural exchange issues with creativity. Links between these issues and human rights issues have largely been negative. For example, the Jackson-Vanik Amendment led to a severe reduction in U.S.-Soviet trade. Countless scientific symposiums, cultural performances and other artistic and technical exchange opportunities have been foregone by Americans as a protest to Soviet persecution of human rights activists. The point here is not to suggest that the Jackson-Vanik Amendment was ill-advised or that such scientific and cultural embargoes are wrong, but merely to suggest that insufficient effort has been devoted to the positive impact increased contacts with the Soviets through trade and cultural exchange may have on the treatment of dissidents and even, more optimistically, on the reformation of Soviet society itself. Such inquiries by the NGOs should be made in the context of important trends in the world such as the extraordinary advances in communications technology and the popularization of computer technology. Efforts by the Soviet authorities to restrict access to photocopying machines and printing presses will soon seem to be ridiculously futile endeavors as dissidents are able to obtain greater access to high-speed communications networks and data processing facilities.[16] The impact of high technology development on the human rights movement could be profound in that dissidents will have a greater access not only to the West but also to each other.

16. For a good discussion of this topic, see, generally, D. Shanor, *Behind the Lines: The Private War Against Soviet Censorship* (New York: St. Martin's Press, 1985).

NGOs should examine whether such developments may be enhanced by better U.S.-Soviet relations, shaped in part by increased trade and cultural exchange. Such efforts, of course, must be tempered by national security considerations, but nonetheless should provide fruitful areas for study by NGOs. In addition, where possible, NGOs should develop and publicize the links between increased trade and a more open economic and political system for Western businessmen and between more meaningful cultural and scientific exchange and greater artistic freedoms in the Soviet Union for Western artists and scientists.

Building links to other prestigious and influential organizations should be another effective method by which NGOs can broaden their base of support. The importance of this approach is enhanced by its close relationship to issues that affect Soviet national prestige, such as medical, scientific and cultural expertise, credibility and honors. The activities of the WPA in response to Soviet psychiatric abuses most clearly demonstrate the significance of this relationship and the success an internationally renowned organization may have in this area. NGOs should cultivate relationships with international organizations in which the Soviets participate and also with organizations having ties to the Soviet Union, but which are not primarily human rights–oriented. The U.N. Human Rights Committee, created under the U.N. Covenant on Civil and Political Rights to review compliance by parties to the Covenant, is the type of international organization whose proceedings NGOs should closely monitor and whose delegates NGOs should regularly brief regarding developments in the Soviet human rights movement. Regrettably, since the United States is not a party to the Covenant, it does not have a representative on the Human Rights Committee. However, Western concerns about the persecution of dissidents are articulated by representatives of Western countries which are signatories and the Soviet representative on the Committee must respond in that forum to such concerns.

The NGOs should also cultivate relationships with national organizations, which in the United States would include the American Bar Association, the American Medical Association and various scientific and technical groups. Domestic organizations in the West are not likely to be as effective as international organizations in exploiting Soviet national prestige. However, censure of Soviet actions by the American Bar Association would certainly be a newsworthy event in the United States and would increase awareness of the plight of dissidents and build wider support for their cause. Such relationships with national organizations also have a potentially more significant value over a longer period of time. Increasingly, such organizations are developing ties to their Soviet professional counterparts. For example, under the auspices of the ABA, U.S. lawyers are offered opportunities to tour the Soviet Union and meet with Soviet lawyers and judges. As such ties develop, more opportunities will arise for discussions about human rights problems, either informally or in joint panel discussions or other meetings. While such discussions are not likely to yield immediate results, Soviet professionals appear to be gaining influence in Soviet society. Such contacts may one day result in better treatment for dissidents and even reforms in the Soviet legal and political system. The ascendancy of Mikhail Gorbachev to power may even accelerate this process. . . . His emphasis on economic efficiency may result in this younger, better educated and more sophisticated professional class gaining influence much more rapidly than would have been the case under earlier regimes.

Fourth, the NGOs should gain greater sophistication about how to effect authentic and lasting improvement in the treatment of Soviet human rights activists. Such a perspective will certainly require the NGOs to educate themselves about the Russian and Soviet political, historical and social context of the human rights movement, to build stronger links among themselves and develop more unified, coherent and longer-term strategies, and to build a broader base of support by linking human rights concerns with important political, economic and social issues and with influential international and Western organizations. In addition, however, the development of such sophistication will involve a better understanding of the relative effectiveness of overt pressure, subtle diplomatic influence or personal contacts in influencing both Soviet and American policy.

For example, the relationship between improved East-West reactions and influence on Soviet policy provides an important springboard for NGO investigation. It has been too easy for NGOs to choose one of the two extreme positions. NGOs

tend to advocate either no contact with the Soviets on a commercial, social or political level as
a protest for Soviet persecution of dissidents or
enhanced, widespread contacts with apparent
blindness to Soviet human rights violations.
NGOs should be willing to examine and propose
intermediate positions and to seek greater sophistication in understanding when public pressure on the Soviet authorities is likely to be successful and when private diplomatic initiatives
might more effectively accomplish the goal.

From a Soviet perspective, the Western approach to Soviet human rights issues has been
consistently negative. The Soviets have been criticized and condemned, not, of course, without
some justification. However, the NGOs have the

opportunity to influence positively these issues by
approaching them in a more constructive fashion.
Far too little Western attention has been given to
human rights issues which the Soviets have handled well. Little effort has been made in the West
to define the areas in which Soviet and Western
human rights theories and practice are in accord.
Finally, no attempts have been made to bring together in a non-politicized forum Soviet and
Western experts on human rights issues to discuss
the differences in Soviet and Western perspectives on such issues and to study ways of reducing
conflict and handling these issues more constructively. Such initiatives are challenges to well-in-
formed and forward-looking NGOs.

QUESTIONS FOR REFLECTION AND DISCUSSION

1. Why are human rights NGOs important actors in the international human rights movement? What purpose or purposes do they serve? Are they more effective than states or
international organizations in promoting and protecting human rights? What are their comparative advantages? Their comparative weaknesses?

2. Human rights NGOs have published much information on Soviet human rights policies, in particular the treatment of Soviet dissidents—suggesting, perhaps, that a primary
purpose and function of human rights NGOs, in the Soviet Union at least, is to stimulate
sympathetic human rights action by others, for example, professional associations, trade
unions, scientific organizations, educational institutions, and church groups. What does
Dean have to say about NGOs' effectiveness in the Soviet Union in this regard? Might human
rights NGOs be more effective in other countries? Less effective? Why?

3. Which category of human rights NGOs identified by Dean has contributed most to
the human rights movement in the Soviet Union? What characteristics of this category make
the NGOs effective?

4. On numerous occasions, the KGB has cracked down on Soviet human rights groups
and their connections to the West, imprisoning their leaders or banishing them to internal
exile (for example, Andrei Sakharov). In *Human Rights and Foreign Policy* (Oxford: Pergamon
Press, 1981), British scholar-diplomat Evan Luard suggests that Western human rights NGOs
are in part responsible for this state of affairs. He writes:

> [T]he Western campaigns on behalf of dissidents in the Soviet Union do not in fact alter
> Soviet policy on that question and only make it difficult for the Soviet Government to
> make the concessions which it might otherwise be willing to grant and so intensify the
> possibility that harsh penalties may be imposed as a demonstration that the government
> cannot be deflected from its chosen course by outside criticism. (p. 6)

How, if at all, does Richard Dean deal with this observation?

6. Often it is difficult for a human rights NGO to resolve whether it is useful or not to
take action on a particular country or issue. As David Weissbrodt observes in "The Contribution of International Nongovernmental Organizations to the Protection of Human
Rights" (*Human Rights in International Law*, ed. Theodor Meron [Oxford: Clarendon Press,
1984], 403–29, at 409), a human rights NGO must answer several key questions before
this issue can be determined:

> Might intervention help or hurt the victims? What sort of intervention would be most
> effective? Have interventions with this country or with respect to this type of problem
> been successful in the past? Are the officials of the country receptive to initiatives from

outsiders? Are the facts sufficiently well established to permit diplomatic intervention or publicity? Which NGO would be most effective in raising the issue?

How would one answer these questions in the context of the Soviet Union? How does Dean?

7. Should the role of human rights NGOs be strengthened? If so, how? If not, why not? What does Dean say?

8. For maximum effectiveness in promoting and protecting human rights in the Soviet Union, is it better for Western human rights NGOs to concentrate on influencing Soviet domestic policy or the foreign policies of their respective countries? Why? Suppose the target country were one other than the Soviet Union, say, Chile, Indonesia, Iran, or South Africa? Would your answer be different? Why? Why not?

23. MARY C. GOSIGER *Strategies for Divestment from U.S. Companies and Financial Institutions Doing Business with or in South Africa*

INTRODUCTION

South Africa is the only country in the world with a system of legalized racism. With a population of 29 million, consisting of 4.5 million whites (Afrikaners and English-speakers), 20.9 million Africans (blacks), 2.6 million Coloureds (mixed race), and 821,000 Indians (Asian in origin), only the whites, comprising 16 percent of the population, enjoy full rights of citizenship. The apartheid system is inherently separate and unequal. For instance, Africans are not permitted to vote, to move freely, or to live and work where they choose. They are denied freedom of speech, press and association, and often lack access to the legal system. In addition vast disparities exist between whites and blacks in the areas of wages, education, and health care. These are but a few of the realities of apartheid.

In today's highly interdependent international arena, South Africa does not operate in isolation. United States financial involvement in South Africa is extensive, totaling over $14 billion, including bank loans, direct investment, and shareholdings. In 1979, United States investment accounted for 20 percent of total foreign investment in South Africa. In 1983, American financial institutions accounted for 26 percent of all loans made to South Africa. As of March 1984, United States banks had $4.6 billion in outstanding loans to South Africa. By 1984, direct investments by United States corporations totaled $2.3 billion. Approximately 350 United States companies conduct business in South Africa. In addition, there is extensive United States indirect investment; that is, in 1982 the United States held about $7.6 billion in South African companies' securities, three times the amount of direct investment.

In response to the atrocities of apartheid, and extensive United States financial involvement in South Africa, a massive divestment campaign has swept the United States. Most often targeted by this campaign are state and local governments and universities. Their responses to these pressures have varied in their attempts to resolve a number of complex issues.

The most intensely debated issue stems from differing views as to the role United States firms and financial institutions can and should play in South Africa. Some proponents of divestment believe that extensive financial involvement provides United States firms leverage to promote change in the apartheid structure. Supporters of this position argue for a policy of selective divestment as a way to pressure companies to embark on specific courses of action and to subscribe to certain codes of conduct. Other divestment proponents believe that any United States financial presence in South Africa bolsters the apartheid regime. Supporters of this position urge a policy of complete divestment to pressure United States companies to disinvest from South Africa.[1] Despite the polarity of their underlying assumptions, both approaches are based on the belief that United States companies and financial insti-

1. Divestment refers to the withdrawal of stocks, by private and public investors, from United States companies or financial institutions operating with or in South Africa which fail to meet specific criteria. Disinvestment refers to the financial and physical withdrawal of all United States companies from South Africa.

tutions should not conduct business with or in South Africa as mere profit seekers, but have an affirmative duty to act as responsible social agents. Thus, divestment is a way to pressure United States firms to promote change in South Africa, albeit through different channels.

Summarized below are state and local government and university divestment actions. Following is an evaluation of the most common strategies adopted by those states, cities, and universities that have taken divestment action with respect to South Africa. These include: divestment from banks making loans or having outstanding loans to the South African Government; divestment from companies that sell strategic products or services to the South African Government; divestment from companies that do not adhere in some form to the Sullivan Principles; and complete divestment. An evaluation of these strategies reveals that in some instances United States companies operating in South Africa can play a progressive role in promoting change and that in other instances United States companies directly support, perpetuate, and strengthen the apartheid system. Different divestment strategies will work in different circumstances depending on many factors:

Any attempt to use firms to promote change in South Africa must recognize that different firms utilize different technologies, have different relationships with the South African government, employ different numbers of white and black workers, and produce different products. Consequently, different firms have different interests, different constituencies, different opportunities, different degrees of influence, and different degrees of susceptibility to pressure.[2]

Thus, a responsible and effective divestment policy should acknowledge the various roles United States companies and financial institutions can and do play in South Africa, and accordingly adopt selective and flexible divestment strategies which address the complexities of apartheid and United States financial involvement in that system.

STATE AND LOCAL ACTION/PUBLIC FUND DIVESTMENT

Although targeted by the anti-apartheid campaign in the early 1970s, most state and local governments have begun to enact divestment measures only in the past few years. Divestment actions by state and local governments are important for two reasons. First, because these entities are responsible for large financial holdings, divestment of these funds has a greater impact on South Africa than action by universities or churches. Second, divestment action by state and local governments forces public debate about how Americans can help end apartheid.

Since 1976, eleven states, thirty-six cities, four counties, and one United States territory (Virgin Islands) have enacted legislation restricting public fund investment and/or purchasing related to South Africa. These measures mandate divestment of approximately $5 billion from United States companies and banks involved in South Africa.

UNIVERSITY ACTION

University campuses became the target of divestment campaigns in the wake of the 1976 Soweto uprising. As student groups in the United States joined forces with the student protesters of South Africa, campus activism led to significant divestment actions. By 1982, over thirty colleges and universities had divested more than $100,000,000 from banks and corporations conducting business in South Africa. In 1985 antiapartheid demonstrations again swept the nation's campuses in response to more violence and repression in South Africa.

Despite student activism, many trustees of universities and colleges have opposed total divestiture. Fiscally conservative trustees fear increased transaction costs, losses due to the purchase of high risk stocks in a South Africa-free universe, and loss of endowments from corporate donors and alumni connected with companies affiliated with South Africa. However, with the recent sweep of student demonstrations, many colleges and universities have succumbed to increasing pressure to reevaluate their existing investment policies. The American Committee on Africa estimates that fifty-five universities and colleges have partly or fully divested $320,000,000 of South African-related assets, and that close to thirty of these schools have made the decision since April 1985.

---

2. Jonathan Leape, Bo Baskin, and Stefan Underhill, eds., *Business in the Shadow of Apartheid: U.S. Firms in South Africa* (Lexington, Mass.: D.C. Heath, 1985), xxxii–xxxiii.

BANKS MAKING LOANS OR HAVING OUTSTANDING LOANS TO THE SOUTH AFRICAN GOVERNMENT

As previously noted, United States banks had $4.6 billion in outstanding loans to South Africa as of March 1984. In recent years, more than 125 United States banks have made loans to the South African Government or private borrowers doing business in South Africa. Divestment policies that prohibit the investment of funds in banks that make loans or have outstanding loans to the South African Government are premised on one or both of the following rationales: first, such loans are vital to the stability of the South African economy and thus directly assist and support the maintenance of apartheid; second, direct loans to the South African Government provide the United States with an interest in maintaining the status quo in South Africa by tying the health of the United States economy to the South African Government's ability to pay its debts.

South Africa does in fact rely heavily on foreign loans for the stability of its economy. This reliance results in part from its chronic trade and payment imbalances. An increase in imports and a marked decline in gold prices resulted in a balance of payments deficit in 1981. In response, the South African Government dramatically increased its borrowing. In 1981 alone, it borrowed $479 million. By early 1982, South Africa's debt was approximately 13 percent of its gross domestic product as compared to 6 percent in 1980. Such extensive reliance on foreign loans shows that pressure on United States banks to cease making new loans to South Africa and not to renew existing ones as they mature is an effective means to destabilize the South African economy.

Recent developments have borne out this conclusion. In July 1985, Chase Manhattan Bank became the first large United States bank to refuse to renew its short-term loans to the South African Government, with Bank of America quickly following. This led other United States banks to do the same. The decision of United States and other foreign banks not to renew short-term loans prompted a massive demand for United States currency that the South African Reserve Bank could not supply. As a result, South Africa began to lose approximately $1 billion per month in short-term credit, which precipitated a drop in value of the South African rand to an all-time low of 35 United States cents on 27 August 1985.

The Government responded that day by suspending the foreign exchange and stock markets. Then, in early September, the South African Government announced what Finance Minister Barend de Plessis termed a "'comprehensive policy strategy'—a unilateral moratorium on the repayment of principal on foreign loans." Such action by a major trading nation is the first of its kind. This series of events substantiates the realities that the South African economy is severely dependent on foreign loans for its stability, and that the ability of the South African Government to pay its debts has a direct impact on the United States banking system.

However, whether destabilization of the South African economy will force the South African Government either to grant rights to blacks or to reinforce the status quo is not yet known. In any event, destabilization weakens the economic strength of the apartheid regime, providing an incentive to the government to renegotiate its apartheid policies to maintain its position in the Western community. It also alleviates United States culpability in supporting the repressive policies of apartheid through direct monetary support.

COMPANIES THAT SELL STRATEGIC PRODUCTS OR SERVICES TO THE SOUTH AFRICAN GOVERNMENT

Investment policies that require divestment from United States companies that sell strategic products or services to the South African Government are based on the assumption that such operations directly perpetuate apartheid: first, by providing the enforcement apparatus necessary to administer apartheid; and second, by strengthening the economic and military sufficiency of the Afrikaner regime, leaving South Africa less dependent on international trade and insulating the government from international pressure.

United States companies make vital contributions to strategic sectors of the South African economy. For example, United States corporations control 70 percent of the computer market, 33 percent of the automotive market, and 44 percent of the petroleum producers market.

Despite the sophistication of the South African economy, its consumer market is not large enough to warrant the large expenditures on research and development necessary to produce complex mainframe computers. As a result, South Africa is dependent on United States computers. Not only have United States computer companies spurred the economic growth of the country, but some have directly assisted in the administering of apartheid. For example, Control Data Corporation sold equipment to the South African police in violation of United States Commerce Department regulations. I.B.M. has sold computers to the South African Department of Interior which uses a computerized population registry to implement the Pass Laws, a bulwark of the apartheid structure.

United States companies also directly support apartheid by providing transportation to the forces responsible for carrying out and maintaining the status quo. Currently the Ford Motor Company and General Motors manufacture cars and trucks used by the police and military.

Petroleum is the one natural resource that South Africa does not possess. Therefore, the South African Government has declared petroleum to be a strategic product because of its critical importance to the functioning of the economy. Major United States oil companies such as Exxon, Texaco, Mobil, and Standard Oil of California have supplied oil to the South African Government, helping it withstand an OPEC [Organization of Petroleum Exporting Countries] embargo. United States companies not only provide vast amounts of petroleum to the South African Government, but in addition Fluor Corporation of California, under contract with the South African Coal, Oil, and Gas Corporation, provided $4.2 billion worth of coal-to-oil conversion plants, helping South Africa achieve energy self-sufficiency.

The significant role that United States companies play in supplying the South African Government with strategic products and services places them in direct support of apartheid. Investment strategies requiring divestment under these circumstances discourage United States firms from directly strengthening the apartheid regime. Although a cutoff of advanced United States technology would serve to alleviate United States culpability in the perpetuation of apartheid, it would not hasten its end if South Africa is able to purchase these necessities from alternative markets.

In recent years, however, international action has severely restricted foreign trade and investment with and in South Africa. In 1973, the Arab members of OPEC placed an embargo on oil sales to South Africa. In 1977, the United Nations Security Council imposed a mandatory embargo on military sales to South Africa. Individual nations that have restricted trade and/or new investment include Norway, Canada, Sweden, Denmark, France, Japan, and the United States. These actions taken together reveal a worldwide hesitancy to provide direct support to the apartheid regime of South Africa.

The South African Government claims that it can survive these international economic pressures, proudly pointing to the facts that it was able to withstand the OPEC oil embargo, and that in response to the United Nations arms embargo South Africa increased its military self-sufficiency from 50 percent in 1977 to 95 percent today. However, South Africa did not attain these achievements on its own. From the beginning of the oil embargo in 1973 until 1979, Iran provided 87 percent of South Africa's oil imports in violation of the boycott. Fluor Corporation's construction of coal-to-oil conversion plants greatly enhanced South Africa's self-sufficiency in this vital area. France violated the arms embargo and supplied South Africa with military equipment. In addition, although South Africa was able successfully to develop its own arms industry, this has not been true in other strategic sectors such as computers. . . .

Thus, a concerted effort by international communities to isolate South Africa in areas of strategic importance could have a devastating effect on the Afrikaner regime's ability to run the economy. Furthermore, as the situation in South Africa has become increasingly inflamed resulting in greater financial risk, many transnational companies may be wary about making new investments in South Africa. Were the United States to withdraw from specific strategic markets, inflicting a further blow to the declining economic climate, it would provide additional disincentive to foreign companies to invest new funds in South Africa.

DIVESTMENT FROM COMPANIES THAT DO NOT ADHERE TO THE SULLIVAN PRINCIPLES

The Reverend Leon Sullivan, a black Philadelphia minister and member of the Board of Directors of General Motors, developed the Sullivan

Principles in 1977. The Principles establish a voluntary code of conduct for United States companies operating in South Africa.[3] A large number of divestment policies require divestiture from companies that are nonsignatories to the Sullivan Principles, or have not received an appropriate performance rating for compliance with the Principles.[4] This strategy is based on the belief that United States companies can be a progressive force for change in bringing about the peaceful abolition of apartheid.[5] This theory is based on three contentions: first, the Principles serve to improve the quality of life of black workers working

for American corporations, both on the job and outside the work environment; second, through moral leadership, American companies serve as a model for other businesses; third, "economic growth . . . is the ultimate liberating force," in that such growth requires increasing the involvement of blacks into South Africa's political and economic systems.

In reality, speculation varies as to the potential success of the Sullivan Principles in helping bring about nonviolent change in South Africa. Cumulatively the statistics appear impressive. Yet in some instances these statistics exaggerate the

---

3. "The Sullivan Principles and American Companies in South Africa," *Proxy Issues Report* (Washington, D.C.: Investor Responsibility Research Center, 1984), C-2. The Principles were amplified in 1984, in response to the slow progress of change in South Africa. The Principles are:

1. Non-segregation of the races in all eating, comfort and work facilities.
2. Equal and fair employment practices for all employees.
3. Equal pay for all employees doing equal or comparable work for the same period of time.
4. Initiation of and development of training programs that will prepare, in substantial numbers, blacks and other non-whites for supervisory, administrative, clerical and technical jobs.
5. Increasing the number of blacks and other non-whites in management and supervisory positions.
6. Improving the quality of employees' lives outside the work environment in such areas as housing, transportation, schooling, recreation and health facilities.

1984 Amplification, Increased Dimensions of Activities Outside the Workplace.

· Use influence and support the unrestricted rights of black businesses to locate in the urban areas of the nation.
· Influence other companies in South Africa to follow the standards of equal rights principles.
· Support the freedom of mobility of black workers to seek employment opportunities wherever they exist, and make possible provisions for adequate housing facilities of employees within the proximity of workers' employment.
· Support the recision of all apartheid laws.

"Sullivan Principles," *The CTC Reporter*, 19 (Spring 1985): 33.
4. Arthur D. Little Inc. rates signatories to the Principles on their performance. The rating system consists of the following categories: I—Making good progress; II—Making progress; III—Needs to become more active; IV—Endorsers of the principles that have few or no employees; V—New signatory; VI—(Discontinued in 1984); VII—Signatory with headquarters outside the United States. "The Sullivan Principles" (see n. 3, above), C-10.
5. Three of the most vocal supporters of the Sullivan Principles are the signatory companies, the South African business community, and the Reagan Administration. Signatory companies have consistently asserted that they constitute a progressive force for change in South Africa. . . . The Reagan Administration has advocated strongly a policy of "constructive engagement" and peaceful change through diplomatic channels. . . . In September 1985, President Reagan issued an Executive Order imposing a series of sanctions against South Africa. This action did not represent a change in administration policy, but was merely a means of preempting a stronger sanctions bill which had already passed in the House of Representatives and was pending before the Senate. It was expected that a veto by Reagan, would easily be overridden by the necessary two-thirds vote. Reagan's order banned the sale of computers to South African security agencies; *"proposed* a ban of the import of the Krugerrand, the South African gold coin, *subject* to consultation with United States trading partners" (emphasis added); barred *most* loans to the South African government; and prohibited the export of *most* nuclear technology. . . . When Secretary of State Shultz spoke before the World Affairs Council in February 1984, he reiterated a frequently expressed administration view that "a process of change has indeed begun" and that "economic development is a powerful change for social and political evolution." . . . He further praised United States companies for their role in bringing about this change, urged voluntary adoption of the Sullivan Principles, and denounced disinvestment and economic sanctions. . . . It should be noted that between 1981 and 1983, the Reagan administration approved the export of more than $28.3 million in military technology to South Africa, while similar exports had totaled only $18.6 million over the prior thirty years. . . .

benefits to black employees. Furthermore, these statistics do not reflect the practices of individual companies, which vary significantly. There is also disagreement over the potential impact the Sullivan Principles can have for the majority of South Africa's blacks. Finally, the Sullivan Principles contain two weaknesses. First, they fail to recognize that United States companies operating in South Africa must abide by South African law. Second, the Principles, at least in the past, have generally limited themselves to workplace reforms and have not addressed the basic structures of apartheid.

Signatory companies' collective performance in implementing the Principles reveal both successes and failures in improving the lot of their black employees. Reliance on the Sullivan Principles rating system should be tempered by the fact that there is no truly independent assessment or accounting in rating companies' compliance with the Sullivan Principles. Arthur D. Little Inc., which reports on compliance, does no on-site inspection or verification. They simply compile their report based upon information supplied by the companies. Moreover, the employees and/or their representatives have no vote in the process. As for Principle I (nonsegregation of the races in all eating, comfort, and work facilities), Arthur D. Little's *Eighth Report* (1984) asserts, "All of the reporting units stated that they have achieved complete *de facto* non-segregation of their facilities." However, the Report provides no supporting evidence to assess the accuracy of this claim. The Report also states that all of the signatory companies are in compliance with Principle 3 (equal pay for all employees doing equal or comparable work for the same period of time) and have been since 1981. Yet this means little when in most companies the lowest pay grades are almost exclusively filled by blacks. However, the signatory companies have made some significant strides in the area of wages. Since 1980 the average annual pay increases at signatory companies has been 16 percent for whites as compared to 20 percent for blacks. In addition, the Principles require that signatories pay their lowest paid employees at least 30 percent more than the minimum established level. In 1983, 90 percent of reporting companies fulfilled this obligation.

As for Principle 4 (initiation and development of training programs that will prepare blacks, Coloureds, and Asians in substantial numbers for supervisory, administrative, clerical, and technical jobs), signatory companies contributed $3,603,841 in 1982 to black employee education and training programs, increasing to $6,012,408 in 1983. Yet the success of Principle 4 in actually improving the positions of black employees depends on Principle 5 (increasing the number of Blacks, Coloureds, and Asians in management and supervisory positions). The *Eighth Report* revealed that white workers hold 95 percent of the managerial positions and 61 percent of the supervisory positions, as compared to 2 percent and 21 percent, respectively, for blacks.

Principle 6 requires signatory companies to improve the quality of employees' lives outside the work environment in such areas as housing, transportation, schooling, recreation, and health facilities. In the years from 1978 to 1983 signatories spent $78,540,000 in the areas of education and training, health and welfare, and black entrepreneurship, with significant increases from 1980 on. In 1983 alone, the amount totalled $22,418,000. Yet these model schools, housing projects, and black businesses continue to operate within the segregated system of apartheid. Therefore, while collectively these figures show a dedication on the part of signatory companies to improve the lives of their black employees, in some instances, the figures belie the actual extent of improvement.

Companies initially do not decide to operate in South Africa to be agents for structural change. Rather they choose to do business in a foreign country because of the favorable business climate it offers. For instance, in 1983 South African investment returns for manufacturing were 43 percent higher than average returns elsewhere in the world and mining returns were 82 percent higher. South Africa provides three economic incentives for conducting business in the country. First, South Africa provides cheap labor which allows companies to avoid the high cost of organized labor. Second, easy access to raw materials enables companies to avoid high shipping costs. Third, South Africa provides cheap goods available for trade. This is not to say that companies once operating in South Africa do not strive to eradicate racial injustice, many do. This has become increasingly so as anti-apartheid campaigns gain force on the homefront.

The difficulty in any selective divestment strategy lies in determining which companies are agents for structural change and which support the apartheid regime. The mere fact that a company is a Sullivan signatory does not guarantee the former. Arthur D. Little's *Seventh Report* (25 October 1983) revealed that of the 108 out of 120 signatories that completed the rating questionnaire, twenty-nine rated in the top category ("making good progress"), thirty-eight rated in the second category ("making progress") and forty-one rated in the third category ("needs to become more active"). Thus, over half of the signatories either failed to complete the questionnaire or did not meet the basic requirements. According to the *Eighth Report* (1984), more than one-fourth of the 126 signatories received the lowest possible rating.

Furthermore, the fact that a company receives a high rating in complying with the Sullivan Principles does not necessarily mean that it is dedicated to promoting change. For instance, under Principle 2 signatory companies are called upon to "[s]upport the elimination of discrimination against the rights of blacks to form or belong to government registered and unregistered unions and acknowledge generally the rights of blacks to form their own unions or be represented by trade unions which already exist." It has been persuasively demonstrated that "trade unions promise to be a major force in the dismantling of apartheid and the creation of a democratic society in South Africa." Nevertheless, a number of highly rated Sullivan signatories have resisted attempts of blacks to engage in collective bargaining and have obstructed unionization of the workforce itself. Such companies include I.B.M., Motorola, and Colgate-Palmolive.

In contrast, a number of other United States signatories have taken steps to promote black trade unions. In the late 1970s, the Kellogg Company became the second company in South Africa to sign a formal agreement recognizing a black trade union. In 1980, the Ford Motor Company was the first company in South Africa to permit full-time black shop stewards in its factories. This is merely one example demonstrating the varying degrees of commitment by signatory companies to the Sullivan Principles. While all companies operate in South Africa because of its favorable economic climate some United States firms adhere to the Principles with a determined effort to reform the system. For others, adoption of the Sullivan Principles is merely a means of promoting a better image at home to diffuse the rapidly growing divestment movement.

A frequent controversy surrounding the Sullivan Principles centers on the number of blacks that they affect. Advocates on one side of the issue point to the fact that while black workers account for over 80 percent of South Africa's workforce, all United States companies operating in South Africa employ less than 1 percent of the black workforce, and signatory companies employ only 0.4 percent. Thus it is argued that even if the Principles were fully implemented they would affect an insignificant number of workers, and, therefore, the Principles are ineffective in helping bring about peaceful change. This position underestimates the spheres of influence outside the workplace, and does not take into account the example signatories set for other firms operating in South Africa. Proponents on the other side of the issue point out that most of the major United States employers in South Africa have signed the Principles, and 74 percent of the workers employed by United States companies are with Sullivan signatories. Supporters on this side assume that because the majority of blacks employed by United States companies are employed by signatory companies, United States companies may make sweeping reform for blacks in South Africa. This position exaggerates the scope of United States companies' influence and activities.

In balance, the Sullivan Principles do require United States companies to exert action and influence where tenable. United States companies have in fact moved beyond mere workplace reforms under Principle 6. Furthermore, the 1984 Amplification calls on United States companies to support the recision of all apartheid laws, as discussed below. It should be remembered that any major reform must come from within South Africa itself. United States companies operating in South Africa can only weaken the rigid boundaries of apartheid, thereby opening the channels for internal change.

When a company decides to operate in South Africa, it also decides to adhere to South African laws. "[I]ts immigrant company employees must live and abide by the residence, employment, and social laws of apartheid. Its native South African employees must . . . obey the rigid pass laws and residence laws and procedures for plant workers." In addition, United States companies pay taxes to the South African government. Furthermore, there are several laws which require United States companies operating in South Africa to support directly the apartheid regime: the National Key Points Act and the Petroleum Products Act.

The National Key Points Act empowers the Minister of Defense to designate any business operating in South Africa a key point industry. The Act requires "key" industries to provide security in cooperation with the South African Defense Force in the case of what the government determines to be "civil unrest." The Government offers companies designated as "key" industries financial incentives to buy weapons and to train company security guards. These provisions have been applied to a number of United States corporations of strategic importance to the apartheid regime. Because designation as a key industry is classified, it is not known whether any of these provisions were triggered in 1985 under the Emergency Laws. The Petroleum Products Act of 1966 and 1967 requires oil companies to refrain from imposing any conditions on the sale of their oil. This Act makes remaining in South Africa conditional upon corporate willingness to sell to the government, including the military and police, upon government demand. Such laws make the operation of affected United States companies far more detrimental to South African blacks than beneficial, no matter what their practices in the workplace.

Another frequent criticism of the Sullivan Principles is that they confine themselves almost entirely to workplace reforms, raising no objections to the fundamental structure of apartheid. As a result, black workers leave Sullivan plants at the end of the day to return to a segregated society where they are relegated to the status of noncitizens. It thus is argued that the potential contribution of the Principles in bringing about significant change is severely limited in that they make no demand for political change. While this analysis accurately reflects the scope of the Principles in the past, the 1984 Amplification calls for a frontal attack on apartheid. Although the Amplification does not require active opposition but rather the use of "influence" and "support" it realistically confronts the scope of United States companies' abilities to change apartheid. Given that United States companies are bound by the laws they seek to repeal, it is probable that the government would not long tolerate active opposition. Furthermore, given the vast amounts of capital that United States companies provide to the South African economy, the range of their "influence" and "support" may be wide, and the effects significant.

In conclusion, an effective divestment strategy should not use the Sullivan Principles to label companies as either agents of apartheid or advocates for peaceful change. First, United States companies that are signatories to the Sullivan Principles engage in a variety of practices in their operations in South Africa. Some strive to improve the lot of black workers both in and out of the workplace, while others merely use the Principles as a shield to fend off public pressure. Second, although the Principles do prescribe a code of conduct calling on signatory companies to contribute to peaceful change, their potential for bringing about significant reform is, in some instances, limited by the actualities of operating in South Africa. Third, the fact that a company is not a signatory to the Principles is not conclusive that the company support apartheid or is not concerned with bringing about change in South Africa. For instance, newspapers and airlines have few employees in the country and have few or no direct dealings with the South African Government. It thus is not worth their time and effort to subscribe to the Principles where their prospects for promoting change are minimal. In other instances, companies may follow the Sullivan Principles or other similar code of conduct, while not subscribing to the Principles themselves. Thus, a responsible investment policy should not use the Sullivan Principles as a blanket rule for divestment, but should look to the individual practices of the companies to determine which companies are an effective force in bringing about a peaceful change, and which companies operate in South Africa merely to make a profit, irrespective of the realities of apartheid and the support they lend it. The Sullivan Principles should be but one source to look at in making this determination.

DIVESTMENT FROM ALL UNITED STATES COMPANIES DOING BUSINESS IN SOUTH AFRICA

A policy of complete divestment from United States companies operating in South Africa is based on the belief that any United States financial presence in South Africa both economically and morally supports apartheid. This position is based on the following contentions: first, United States companies are incapable of bringing about significant change; second, economic growth has not led to the attainment of civil and political rights for the black majority; and third, complete United States divestment would have a crippling effect on the apartheid regime and, thus, force it to reform its policies.

A blanket rule of complete divestment ignores the impact that United States companies could have in reforming apartheid. As previously stated, some United States companies provide little or no support to the South African Government, while at the same time making significant strides in promoting the equality of blacks. A policy of complete divestment urging complete United States disinvestment would deny blacks a force for progressive change. Furthermore, it appears that United States companies are more influenced by pressures to adopt specific policies and practices in their operations than they are to pressures urging complete withdrawal. It is doubtful that many companies would withdraw from South Africa without significant economic instability in South Africa itself.

Past decades of economic growth belie the assertion that continued economic development results in an increased involvement of blacks into South Africa's political system. The removal of blacks from the mainstream of social, economic, and political life is deeply rooted in South Africa's history. Cheap black labor has been integral to South Africa's economic development. It therefore is doubtful that the South African Government will change the very system that has allowed it to prosper, that is, apartheid.

Events in recent years support the proposition that despite economic growth, South African whites will not relinquish their favored position. The government has intensified its repressive policies in the areas of pass laws, migratory labor practices, and political dissidents. The Internal Security Act of 1982, denying black civil, political, and legal rights, clearly shows that the white minority is politically and ideologically entrenched in support of apartheid. At the same time, the government has granted limited rights to a slight majority of urban blacks, granting them access to more skilled jobs, better educational opportunities and greater freedom of movement. However, these benefits are limited only to the number of blacks needed to maintain the growing economy. It thus appears that the South African Government is creating two classes of blacks, driving a wedge between a small class of urban employed blacks and the vast majority of blacks located within the homelands, where ingress and egress is controlled, and where the economic misery goes largely unseen. "[T]hese measures taken as a whole indicate that apartheid is not being dismantled in the face of industrial growth but is being made a more efficient instrument of that growth."

As expanded economic growth has not lessened the repressive measures of apartheid, proponents of complete divestment argue that economic disinvestment would. If United States companies were to disinvest from South Africa, the probable economic impact would be staggering. A cut-off in United States direct investment would deprive the government of a range of strategic products and services, critical technology, and vital capital. It would also have devastating effect on South Africa's manufacturing operations and other industries that rely on imported machine tools, plants and machinery, electronic equipment, computers, and chemicals to maintain both regular production lines and industrial expansion. Production would be seriously disrupted, costs would escalate, and there would be considerable economic dislocation. The loss of tax revenues from United States companies would further disrupt the South African economy. Thus, investment policies which encourage complete disinvestment from South Africa through divesting from all companies conducting business in South Africa attempt to weaken and isolate the apartheid regime, and thus, bring about its ultimate destruction.

However, the state of South Africa's economy, whether growth or decline, is not responsible for the perpetuation of apartheid. Rather apartheid stems from the religious, social, and moral beliefs of the Afrikaners. The continued repression of blacks in the face of economic growth reveals the strength of the Afrikaners' convictions. In past periods of economic instability, racial turmoil, and violence, the practice of the South African Government has been to strengthen and reinforce its theory of separate development.

With few exceptions, the Afrikaners remain convinced that the benefits of maintaining their power and privilege through minority rule and apartheid far outweigh the costs. Thus, the central concern of white South Africans, and Afrikaners in particular, has been and still is that of how best to maintain their position as conditions continually change within and around South Africa.[6]

It is doubtful, therefore, that complete United States disinvestment would induce the Afrikaners to renegotiate their positions and policies on apartheid.

CONCLUSION

The divestment campaign, combined with increased economic instability, has had a marked effect on United States financial involvement in South Africa. Only eleven new United States businesses have moved into South Africa while twenty to thirty companies have withdrawn from the country since 1980. A number of others have either reduced their operations in South Africa or pledged not to expand their existing ones. An increasing number of United States companies are subscribing to codes of conduct aimed at eliminating racial inequality.[7] Of even greater consequence, the divestment movement has discouraged incalculable new investment. Thus, the divestment campaign met with considerable success in discouraging United States companies from providing vast amounts of capital to the apartheid system.

That the United States divestment movement is having a marked effect on United States operations in South Africa is evidenced by Pretoria's reaction to the movement. On 3 March 1985, the South African Government announced the creation of a special post "to coordinate action against overseas campaigns for divestment from South Africa." The government has also financed extensive lobbying in the United States, forming two corporate committees to lobby against pending state and city divestment legislation. It has also supplied legislators with letters and articles opposing divestment and provided trips to South Africa for legislators and newspaper editors. It has sponsored investment conferences and placed advertisements about progress and change in United States journals and newspapers. These actions taken together demonstrate a real fear by

the South African Government of the impact that United States divestment can have on the support of the apartheid regime by United States companies.

The South African Government has also recently instituted a number of internal changes to redeem itself in the eyes of the world community. These "reforms," however, are merely cosmetic, making no attempt to dismantle the foundations of apartheid. For example, the recision in April 1985 of laws which prohibited interracial marriage and sex has little effect because blacks and whites are legally required to reside in separate areas. The "reform" constitution of 1983 was nothing more than "an attempt by the Nationalist [P]arty leadership to curb and contain pressures for change by buying off . . . the [Asian and Coloured] population." Over 80 percent of the Indian and Coloured population boycotted the elections for their respective parliaments, exposing the touted reform as a sham, totally rejected by the people whom it was intended to pacify. Another example of cosmetic reform came in September 1985, when the government announced that it would grant citizenship to blacks, who although assigned to the four "independent" homelands, reside in urban areas of the country. "Citizenship" for South African blacks has little significance when they are denied any voice or participation in the political system. Furthermore, this grant of citizenship has no effect on those blacks confined to their "tribal" homeland, nor does it attack the homelands policy itself. It is important to expose these "reforms" for what they really are, that is, an attempt by the South African Government to represent the illusion of progress and change to the outside world in order to diffuse the rapidly growing divestment movement while making no changes in the apartheid structure.

In conclusion, the divestment movement has enjoyed considerable success in urging United States businesses to play an active role in bringing about the collapse of apartheid. It is important that these pressures not be lifted in the face of cosmetic reform by the South African Government. Yet divestment pressures should recognize the varying roles United States firms can and do

6. Leape et al., *Business in the Shadow of Apartheid*, xvii.
7. In 1977, when Leon Sullivan first announced the Sullivan Principles, there were 12 signatory companies. By 1984, the number had risen to 121. For current data, see "Unified List of U.S. Companies Doing Business in South Africa and Namibia," available from the American Committee on Africa, 198 Broadway, New York, NY 10038.

play in South Africa, and thus urge support, pressure, example, and withdrawal where appropriate. In short, "To see that U.S. firms can retard progress, to see that they can also promote progress, and, amid the complexity and ambiguity of South Africa, to be able to tell the difference is the challenge of understanding business in the shadow of apartheid."[8]

QUESTIONS FOR REFLECTION AND DISCUSSION

1. Should corporations and other business enterprises be involved in promoting and protecting internationally guaranteed human rights or should they stick to that for which they are established—producing goods and services and making profits? Why? Why not?

2. Do corporations and other business enterprises have any comparative advantages relative to other entities or groups in promoting and protecting internationally guaranteed human rights? If so, what are they? If not, why not?

3. Have corporations and other business enterprises been effective in safeguarding and enhancing the rights of blacks and "coloureds" in South Africa? What does Mary Gosiger say?

4. It often is argued that U.S. corporations and other business enterprises in South Africa should remain in that country to help improve the lives of black South Africans and attempt to influence the South African government on important human rights issues. Is such an approach workable? Desirable? Should not U.S. firms withdraw from South Africa altogether? The report of the Study Commission on U.S. Policy Toward Southern Africa (*South Africa: Time Running Out* [Berkeley, Calif.: University of California Press, 1981], 418–19) makes three recommendations:

> First, U.S. corporations and financial institutions operating in South Africa should commit themselves to a policy of nonexpansion and those businesses not already there should not enter the country. Second, a generous proportion of corporate resources—determined in accordance with a specific "social development expenditure standard"—should be set aside to improve the lives of black South Africans. Third, U.S. companies that have not yet subscribed to the Sullivan Principles should do so, and compliance should be effectively monitored.

Do you agree with these recommendations? Why? Why not? Bearing in mind that these recommendations were made in 1981, do you think the Study Commission would make the same recommendations today?

5. Have the Sullivan Principles served the purposes for which they were designed or have they served, instead, as an excuse for companies to remain in South Africa? Do you agree with the Communications Task Group of the Sullivan Signatory Companies (*Meeting the Mandate for Change* [New York: Industry Support Unit, 1984], 22) that "the signatories believe that their continued presence in South Africa can do more to improve the status of blacks than withdrawal?" Or is this assertion a smokescreen to justify continued presence and profiteering in South Africa? Whatever your answer, what is your evidence?

6. Which of the Sullivan Principles do you believe has had the greatest positive effect? The least positive effect? In each case, why?

7. Aside from adhering to the Sullivan Principles, what other strategies might be used by corporations and other business enterprises in South Africa to advance human rights there? Is there anything else the business world might do?

8. Relative to the promotion and protection of human rights in South Africa, is corporate divestment or disinvestment the more effective strategy? Are there other strategies that might prove more effective? If so, what are they?

9. According to Gosiger, which divestment strategy is the most effective? The least effective? Why? How might divestment strategies be strengthened?

10. Should the human rights role of corporations and other business enterprises be strengthened? In South Africa? In other countries? If so, how? If not, why not?

---

8. Leape, et al., *Business,* xxxvi.

24. JORDAN J. PAUST *The Human Right to Participate in Armed Revolution and Related Forms of Social Violence: Testing the Limits of Permissibility*

This country, with its institutions, belongs to the people who inhabit it. Whenever they shall grow weary of the existing government, they can exercise their constitutional right of amending, or their revolutionary right to dismember or overthrow it. [1]

These are the words not of a twentieth-century revolutionary or even an eighteenth-century founder of our Republic, but of a nineteenth-century Republican President at the beginning of a long and destructive civil war in the United States. What Abraham Lincoln recognized was the fundamental democratic precept that authority comes ultimately from the people of the United States, and that with this authority there is retained a "revolutionary right to dismember or overthrow" any governmental institution that is unresponsive to the needs and wishes of the people.

The right of revolution recognized by President Lincoln has, of course, an early foundation in our history. Both the Declaration of Independence (1776) and the Declaration of the Causes and Necessity of Taking Up Arms (1775) contain recognitions of this right, and several state constitutions within the United States consistently recognized the right of the people "to reform, alter, or abolish government" at their convenience. Indeed, our Republic was founded on revolution. As Justice Black has recognized:

Thomas Jefferson was not disclaiming a belief in the "right of revolution" when he wrote the Declaration of Independence. And Patrick Henry was certainly not disclaiming such a belief when he declared in impassioned words that have come on down through the years: "Give me liberty or give me death." This country's freedom was won by men who, whether they believed in it or not, certainly practiced revolution in the Revolutionary War. [2]

The American Revolution served as a precursor for numerous others in the Americas, Europe, and elsewhere, even into the twentieth century. Today, it is common to recognize that all peoples have a right to self-determination and, as a necessary concomitant of national self-determination, a right to engage in revolution. Yet, it is not as widely understood that, under international law, there are limits to the permissibility of armed revolution and the participation of individuals in revolutionary social violence.

The purpose of this [essay] is to clarify the nature and scope of the right of revolution. In doing so, it will be necessary to identify the relationship between the right of revolution and the international legal precepts of authority, self-determination, and more general norms of human rights. With these interrelations in mind, one can also identify and clarify relevant legal constraints on armed revolution and the participation of individuals in such a process. . . .

GENERAL LEGAL POLICIES AT STAKE

NATURAL LAW, AUTHORITY OF THE PEOPLE, AND THE AMERICAN REVOLUTION

Early in our history, we appealed to natural law and the "rights of man" to affirm the right of revolution. Two historic declarations provide an inventory of the forms of oppression thought to justify armed revolution. Our Declaration of Independence proclaimed to the world the expectation that all governments are properly con-

1. Abraham Lincoln, "First Inaugural Address" (Mar. 4, 1861), in *Lincoln's Stories and Speeches,* ed. Edward F. Allen (New York: Books, Inc., 1920), 212; American Communication Ass'n v. Douds, 339 U.S. 382, 440, n.12 (1950) (also quoting Lincoln's 1848 speech before the House of Representatives).
   In this article, the right of "revolution" refers to the right fundamentally to change a governmental structure or process within a particular nation-state, thus including the right to replace governmental elites or overthrow a particular government. . . .
2. *In re* Anastaplo, 366 U.S. 82, 113 (1961) (Black, J., dissenting) (citing Zechariah Chafee, *Free Speech in the United States* (Cambridge: Harvard University Press, 1964), 178). See also American Communication Ass'n v. Douds, 339 U.S. 382, 439–40 and n.12 (1950) (quoting Adams, Jefferson, Clay, and others).

Reprinted, with changes, from Jordan J. Paust, "The Human Right to Participate in Armed Revolution and Related Forms of Social Violence: Testing the Limits of Permissibility," *Emory Law Journal* 32 (1983): 545–81. Reprinted by permission.

stituted in order "to secure" the inalienable rights of man, that governments derive "their just powers from the consent of the governed," and that "it is the Right of the People to alter or abolish" any form of government which "becomes destructive of these ends." More specifically, the American people denounced the King of England as a tyrant who was "unfit to be the ruler of a free People" because, among other things, he invaded "the rights of the people," dissolved representative governmental bodies, obstructed the administration of justice, failed to control the depredations of the military, and engaged in numerous other strategies of tyranny and oppression. . . .

Since the dawn of our constitutional history, the Supreme Court has consistently recognized that the primary source of authority in the United States is the people of the United States. As the Court early declared, "their will alone is to decide." Thus, necessarily, any criterion of permissibility under United States domestic law must ultimately be compatible with the will of the people of the United States. The "authority of the people" is *the* peremptory criterion; and, under domestic law, their will alone is to decide.

For this reason, the right of revolution is in the nation as a whole and is not a right of some minority of an identifiable people. In Locke's view, the right of revolution was a right of the majority of a community. This view was shared by many of the founders of our Republic as well as many others, and is reflected in early state constitutions. It formed the basis, moreover, for President Lincoln's distinction between a permissible exercise of the "revolutionary right" of the people to dismember or overthrow a government and the claim of only a part of that people to secede from the Union. Such a claimed right of secession, involving the use of force, and other claims by individuals or minorities of the right to engage in the use of violence in self-defense against political oppression raise different issues, some of which are beyond the scope of this [essay]. Revolution as such, however, is a right of the people.

In view of the above, one can also recognize the propriety of a claim by the government, when representing the authority of the people, to regulate certain forms of revolutionary violence or, when reasonably necessary, "incitement to vio-

lence" engaged in by a minority of the people of the United States and without their general approval. Indeed, several Supreme Court cases document the permissibility of such a claim, although a few others seem to go too far. If, however, the right of revolutionary violence is engaged in by the predominant majority of the people, or with their general approval, the government (or a part of thereof) would necessarily lack authority, and governmental controls of such violence or incitements to violence would be impermissible. Thus, for example, it would be constitutionally improper to allege that "incitement to violence" is always a justification for governmental suppression of such conduct even if violence is imminent. Permissibility does not hinge upon violence as such, but ultimately upon the peremptory criterion of authority—i.e., the will of the people generally shared in the community. . . .

In summary, numerous cases either affirm or are consistent with a distinction between permissible forms of violence approved by the authority of the people and unlawful violence, especially violence engaged in contrary to the authority of the people. Perhaps in recognition of such a distinction, Justice Black has stated:

> Since the beginning of history there have been governments that have engaged in practices against the people so bad, so cruel, so unjust and so destructive of the individual dignity of men and women that the "right of revolution" was all the people had left to free themselves. . . . I venture the suggestion that there are countless multitudes in this country, and all over the world, who would join [the] belief in the right of the people to resist by force tyrannical governments like those.[3]

As the next section demonstrates, there are apparently "countless multitudes . . . all over the world" who would recognize the permissibility of such a right of revolution by a people.

PERMISSIBILITY UNDER INTERNATIONAL LAW

It is doubtful whether Justice Black had in mind specific portions of the Universal Declaration of Human Rights when he recognized the seemingly wide approval of a general right of rev-

---

3. *In re* Anastaplo, 366 U.S. 82, 113 (Black, J., dissenting). See also American Communication Ass'n v. Douds, 339 U.S. at 439–40 and n.12 (Jackson, J., concurring in part and dissenting in part).

olution, but he could have. The preamble to the Universal Declaration declares, for instance, that "it is essential, if man is not to be compelled to have recourse, as a last resort, to rebellion against tyranny and oppression, that human rights should be protected by the rule of law."[4] As one commentator has noted, the preamble to the Universal Declaration actually supports the right of revolution or rebellion, and it reflects the growth of acceptance of that right at least from the time of the American Declaration of Independence, an acceptance so pervasive as to allow text writers to conclude that "the right of a people to revolt against tyranny is now a recognized principle of international law."

Indeed, prior to the American and French Revolutions of the eighteenth century, the right of revolution had been accepted in several human societies. Scholars have identified related expectations, for example, among the early Greeks and Romans; in Germanic folk law; among naturalist theorists such as Thomas Aquinas in medieval Western Europe; and in the writings of early international scholars such as Grotius and Vattel. . . .

Today, the right of revolution is an important international precept and a part of available strategies for the assurance both of the authority of the people as the lawful basis of any government and of the process of national self-determination. Under international law, the permissibility of armed revolution is necessarily interrelated with legal precepts of authority and self-determination, as well as with more specific sets of human rights. For example, the right to change a governmental structure is necessarily interrelated with the question of the legitimacy of that structure in terms of the accepted standard of authority in international law and with the precept of self-determination, both of which are interrelated and are also interconnected with the human rights of individuals to participate in the political processes of their society.

As recognized in numerous international instruments and by the International Court of Justice, all peoples have the right to self-determination and, by virtue of that right, to freely determine their political status.[5] Similarly it is recognized "that the application of the right of self-determination requires a free and genuine expression of the will of the peoples concerned."[6] As noted elsewhere, a state that complies with the principle of self-determination is one possessed of a government representing each and every person—the whole people—belonging to its territory. Political self-determination, in fact, is a dynamic process involving the genuine, full and freely expressed will of a given people, that is, a dynamic aggregate will of individuals. The "will of the people" is actually the dynamic outcome of such a process and reflects an equal and aggregate participation by individuals and groups in a process of authority.

Furthermore, there is a significant consistency among the precept of self-determination, the human right to individual participation in the political process, and the only standard of authority recognized in international law. That consistency is evident in documented expectations of the international community concerning the sharing and shaping of political power through a process involving a relatively full, free, and equal participation by individuals who are the members of a given nation-state. Indeed, self-determination and human rights both demand that the only legitimate basis of the authority of any government is the dynamic process of self-determination and authority noted above.

The first two paragraphs of Article 21 of the Universal Declaration of Human Rights recognize the rights of every person "to take part in" the governmental processes of one's country and to "equal access to public service." The more significant content of Article 21, however, is set forth in paragraph 3 that states: "The will of the people shall be the basis of the authority of government; this will shall be expressed in periodic and genuine elections which shall be held by secret vote or by equivalent free voting procedures." A legitimate government, the Universal Declaration affirms, is one in which the "will of the people" is the basis of authority. The authority of a government exists lawfully on no other basis, in no other form. Indeed, the only

---

4. [See the Appendix.]
5. Western Sahara Advisory Opinion, 1975 I.C.J. 12, 31–33, 36 (citing several international instruments including the authoritative Declaration on Principles of International Law, U.N. G.A. Res. 2625, 25 U.N. GAOR Supp. (No. 28) at 121, U.N. Doc. A/8028 (1970)). . . .
6. Western Sahara Advisory Opinion (see n. 5, above), 32, para. 55. See also ibid. at 33, paras. 58–59. . . . See generally UN Charter (in the Appendix), art. 76, para. b ("self-government" related to "the freely expressed wishes of the peoples concerned").

specific formal reference to the concept of authority that one finds among all of the major international legal documents is the reference to the authority of the people of a given community.[7]

Many interrelated norms from the Universal Declaration, when taken together, tend to confirm the clear and unswerving criterion of authority contained in the third paragraph of Article 21. The Universal Declaration affirms the fundamental expectations that all human beings are born free and equal in dignity and rights (Article 1); that everyone is entitled to all the rights and freedoms set forth without distinction of any kind, for example, without distinctions on the basis of race, sex, political or other opinion (Article 2); that everyone has the right to recognition as a person (Article 7); and that all are equal before the law and are entitled to equal protection (Article 7).[8] When one considers how individuals acting within a political process are to exercise their rights to take part in governmental processes and to obtain equal access to public service in a manner that is consistent with the rights of each and every person to equality, dignity, and the equal protection and enjoyment of law, it seems clear that participation should be on the basis of one person, one voice. Stated differently, an equally weighted "will" of each individual conjoined in a so-called "will of the people" or common expression is the only formula that allows equal individual participation in a political process. Having this in mind, it is understandable why Article 21 contains other references to what one might term the related aspects of a process of authority. There is a great deal of illuminating consistency within the Article.

As mentioned, paragraphs 1 and 2 of the Article proclaim a right "to take part" and a right of "access" for each and every person, and these are supplemented especially by Articles 1 and 2 of the Declaration as well as by the overall purpose of the instrument. What is of further significance with regard to a process of authority and the standard of authority recognized in paragraph 3 of Article 21 is the fact that the third paragraph also contains related and fairly precise exemplifying language. Not only is the "will of the people" to be the basis of the authority of any given government, but "this will shall be expressed" in free and periodic elections held on the basis of "universal and equal suffrage." Thus, one has an example of the interconnections between the exercise of individual rights of equal participation in the political process and an outcome of a political process that allows a relatively full, free, and equal participation—the aggregate will of individual participants.

From the above it is evident that the people of a given community have the right to alter, abolish, or overthrow any form of government that becomes destructive of the process of self-determination and the right of individual participation. Such a government, of course, would also lack authority and, as a government representing merely some minority of the political participants, it could be overthrown by the majority in an effort to ensure authoritative government, political self-determination, and the human rights of all members of the community equally and freely to participate. . . .

Although the process of authority is dynamic and individuals might engage in violence with the approval of the people, the right of revolution is not a right of only some minority of the people or to be utilized in an effort to oppress the authority of the people. Indeed, in view of the many interrelated international legal precepts noted above, an oppression of the authority of the people is a form of political slavery that is not only violative of human rights but also constitutes a treason against humanity.

THE CONCEPT OF REVOLUTION AND CRITERIA OF PERMISSIBILITY

When one considers further the use of the concept of revolution in American legal history, one is struck by the fact that many conceptual

---

7. See, e.g., Universal Declaration of Human Rights (in the Appendix), art. 21, para. 3 (everyone has right to a government which conforms to the will of the people).

8. These recognitions of right are, to a degree, also expressly recognized in the United Nations Charter. The preamble to the Charter, which is as relevant as the articles of a treaty to its meaning, reaffirms both the "dignity and worth of the human person" and the "equal rights of men and women." UN Charter (in the Appendix), art. 1, para. 3, art. 55, para. c (adds the expectation that human rights and fundamental freedoms shall be implemented "without distinction as to race, sex, language, or religion"). See also M. McDougal, H. Lasswell, and L. Chen, *Human Rights and World Public Order: The Basic Policies of an International Law of Human Dignity* (New Haven, Conn.: Yale University Press, 1980), 709 (recognizing that these and other rights are interrelated for purposes of aggregate protection of the right to political participation).

categorizations have been utilized. The right of revolution has been described variously as "the great and fundamental right of every people to change their institutions at will"; a "legal right" of the people; "the reserved right" of a people; "an original right" of the people; a "natural right"; "a most sacred right"; "an indubitable, inalienable, and indefeasible right" of the community; and a "revolutionary right."

Perhaps some of these are useful, but they seem merely to supplement the general points noted above that this right is that of the people, it is their right to change their institutions at will, and the peremptory criterion of permissibility remains the authority of the people. Even the United States Supreme Court has added little to clarify the criteria or the policies at stake in differing social contexts.

Although some have recognized that armed revolution is a form of "self-defense" for an oppressed people and others seek to limit the right of revolution to cases of a reasonably necessary defense against political oppression, the principles of necessity and proportionality should apply only to the strategies of violence utilized during revolution and are not needed for the justification of a revolution. Indeed, according to Lincoln, Jefferson, and so many of the founders, revolution is justified whenever the people generally so desire. Furthermore, no limitation on the right of the people to engage in revolution is consistent with the precepts of authority and self-determination addressed above. In this sense, the early recognition by the Supreme Court that there "can be no limitation on the power of the people of the United States" is certainly consistent with both domestic and international standards of authority as well as the correlative principle of self-determination.

The "necessity" test endorsed by some writers might actually relate to another question, the question of when a defense of right arises because of oppression of an individual's right to participate in the political process. It might be argued that an individual or group has a right to use strategies of violence when reasonably necessary and proportionate to the effectuation of a human right to participate. If so, such a use of violence is not to be engaged in to deny participation by others or to oppress others politically, and such

a use of violence might not have as its aim the achievement of an authoritative revolution by the people as a whole. Nevertheless, permissible revolution might be stimulated by such a strategy, and governmental elites that deny a relatively full and free sharing of power might themselves be denied some form of participation temporarily in order to effectuate the fuller and freer sharing and shaping of power by all participants.

It is important to reiterate here that the right of revolution as such is not vested in some minority of an identifiable society. Violence as a right of political failures is incompatible with any objective conception of self-determination of a people and contravenes domestic and international standards of authority as well as the human right of other persons to participate.

Professor Charles Black has identified a related question—whether disobedience of state laws is compatible with the authority of a federal constitutive process.[9] Professor Black argues that a revolutionary movement using massive "civil disobedience" mounted against "the very structure of state power" is not necessarily unconstitutional or "incompatible with federal allegiance." He also suggests that we are not "bound to hold up the wax hand of the effigy of state law" in such a circumstance where state power "cannot and will not fulfill its basic obligations to federal law and human justice." Thus, he argues that certain forms of revolutionary activity can result in revolutionary change within a part of the overall constitutive process and that a higher, overall authority reflected in "federal law and human justice" can provide a useful criterion for choice about permissibility. Actually, as Black notes, such a movement within a federal union can be supported by federal authority and constitute "a mere claim of legal right, asserted against what only seems to be law." Others seem to agree that such a claim is permissible and go so far as to suggest that it is not a claim to engage in civil "disobedience," but is actually an appeal to supreme federal law within a federal union. It is, at least, a claim to disobey one set of putative laws under a claim of deference to another. . . .

One of the more involved contextual approaches to the ethics of revolution generally is that offered by the philosopher Herbert Marcuse.[10] Marcuse noted that "[v]iolence *per se* has

9. See Charles Black, "The Problem of the Compatibility of Civil Disobedience with American Institutions of Government," *Texas Law Review* 43 (1965): 492–525.
10. Herbert Marcuse, "Ethics and Revolution," in *Revolution and the Rule of Law,* ed. Edward Kent (Englewood Cliffs, N.J.: Prentice Hall, 1971). This is, of course, a different focus than one addressing the legality of revolution.

never been made a revolutionary value by the leaders of historical revolutions." What should be considered, he argued, are the goals sought to be achieved and predictable social outcomes. Rational criteria can aid in what he termed an "historical calculus" of the "chances of a future society as against the chances of the existing society with respect to human progress." For Marcuse, a rational historical calculus:

must, on the one side, take into account the sacrifices exacted from the living generations on behalf of the established society, the established law and order, the number of victims made in defense of this society in war and peace, in the struggle for existence, individual and national. The calculus would further have to take into account the intellectual and material resources available to the society and the manner in which they are actually used with respect to their full capacity of satisfying vital human needs and pacifying the struggle for existence. On the other side, the historical calculus would have to project the chances of the contesting revolutionary movement of improving the prevailing conditions, namely, whether the revolutionary plan or program demonstrates the technical, material, and mental possibility of reducing the sacrifices and the number of victims.

At the same time, Marcuse was quick to identify a peremptory limit to revolutionary "means." As he explained:

No matter how rationally one may justify revolutionary means in terms of the demonstrable chance of obtaining freedom and happiness for future generations, and thereby justify violating existing rights and liberties and life itself, there are forms of violence and suppression which no revolutionary situation can justify because they negate the very end for which the revolution is a means. Such are arbitrary violence, cruelty, and indiscriminate terror.

From a legal perspective, Marcuse's statement about the means of violence is equally relevant. Under international law, including the law of human rights, there are certain forms of violence

that are impermissible per se. Included here are strategies and tactics of arbitrary violence, cruelty, and indiscriminate terror. International law also prohibits the use of violence against certain targets, and permissible uses of force are conditioned generally by the principles of necessity and proportionality. . . .

CONCLUSION

Here, an effort has been made to identify and clarify the nature and scope of the right to revolution in both United States domestic and international law. As noted, the right of revolution is a right of the people. It is to be exercised in accordance with a peremptory precept of authority documentable in both United States constitutional and international law, the will of the people expressed through a dynamic process involving an aggregate will of individuals. Revolution is actually one of the strategies available to a people for the securing of authority, national self-determination and a relatively free and equal enjoyment of the human right of all persons to participate in the political processes of their society.

With regard to the separate question of the legality of various means of furthering revolution, numerous sets of domestic and international law already proscribe certain forms of social violence. For example, international law, including human rights law, prohibits tactics of arbitrary violence, cruelty, and indiscriminate terror; the targeting of certain persons (such as children) and certain things; and generally any unnecessary death, injury, or suffering. . . .

Finally, those who are rightly concerned about the evils of any form of violence and the threat that domestic violence can pose to human dignity and international peace might also consider the warning of former President John F. Kennedy: "[T]hose who make peaceful evolution impossible make violent revolution inevitable."[11]

QUESTIONS FOR REFLECTION AND DISCUSSION

1. Why might the Jordan Paust essay be the last in this book? Is it that violence on the part of individuals is the ultimate weapon of the disenfranchised or otherwise marginalized?

11. Address by John F. Kennedy at Punta del Este, quoted in *The Law of Dissent and Riots*, ed. M. C. Bassiouni (Springfield, Ill.: Thomas, 1971). President Kennedy also declared, "Is not peace, in the last analysis, basically a matter of human rights?" Address by John F. Kennedy at American University (June 10, 1963), quoted in McDougal et al., *Human Rights and World Public Order*, 236, n. 229.

Or is it that private violence—particularly revolutionary private violence—never should be used in the first instance or in an early stage of political struggle? Perhaps both? Either way, do you agree with these two propositions? Why? Why not?

2. Is not individual resort to violence in defense of human rights inherently contradictory? However much or little the right to revolution may be legally sanctioned, is it not true that the taking of life, if not also the large-scale destruction of property, never can be morally justified no matter what the purpose? Agree? Disagree? What would Paust say?

3. In *The Metaphysical Elements of Justice* (Indianapolis: Bobbs-Merrill Company, 1965, originally published in 1797), Immanuel Kant wrote:

> There can . . . be no legitimate resistance of the people to the legislative chief of the state; for juridical status, legitimacy, is possible only through subjection to the general legislative Will of the people. Accordingly, there is no right of sedition (*seditio*), much less a right of revolution (*rebellio*), and least of all a right to lay hands on or take the life of the chief of state when he is an individual person on the excuse that he has misused his authority. . . . The slightest attempt to do this is high treason, and a traitor of this kind, as someone attempting to destroy his fatherland, can receive no lesser punishment than death. (p. 86)

Do you agree? Disagree? What would Paust say?

4. In "The Legitimation of Violence" (*Collective Violence* ed. James F. Short, Jr., and Marvin E. Wolfgang [Chicago: Aldine-Atherton, 1972], 101), Sandra J. Ball-Rokeach poses the following pertinent questions:

> 1. How does violence become legitimated or how does it lose its legitimacy?
> 2. What are the manifest and latent functions of violence for individuals, groups, collectivities, or societies? For example, under what conditions is violence an effective way to bring attention to a cause, clarifying issues, or promoting inter-group communication? . . .
> 4. Is the threat of violence or violence itself an important facet of maintaining a democratic form of government? To what extent, for example, does the threat of violence provide organized minorities with bargaining power that they would not otherwise possess?

Applied to the promotion and protection of internationally guaranteed human rights, how would you answer these questions? How might Paust? Would your answers differ depending on the level of violence involved, for example, individual assault and battery, rioting, rebellion, insurrection, revolution? Would they differ depending on the violent actors involved, for example, militant civil disobedients, revolutionaries, terrorists, freedom fighters.

5. In *Why Men Rebel* ([Princeton, N.J.: Princeton University Press, 1970], 37) Ted Robert Gurr reasons that "[r]elative deprivation, defined as perceived discrepancy between value expectations and value capabilities" is among the prime explanations of collective violence, noting that

> [for] Aristotle the principal cause of revolution is the aspiration for economic or political equality on the part of the common people who lack it, and the aspiration of oligarchs for greater inequality than they have, i.e. a discrepancy in both instances between what people have of political and economic goods relative to what they think is justly theirs. (p. 46.)

After reviewing "analogous concepts" by contemporary theorists, Gurr goes on to consider "three other concepts frequently employed in the analysis of disruptive collective behavior that are not directly analogous to [relative deprivation] but that appear to be alternatives to it: dissonance, anomie, and conflict." Dissonance "is a concept widely used in individual psychology" that refers to "inconsistency between two cognitive elements or cluster of elements . . . that people . . . are motivated to reduce or eliminate." Anomie "is specifically a sociological concept" that refers to "a breakdown of social standards governing social behavior" which, in turn, can lead to "widespread deviant behavior and the establishment of alternative norms." And conflict may be defined as a condition in which "the source of [relative deprivation] is another group competing for the same values" or as a process of "interaction between groups in their respective attempts to alleviate [relative deprivation]."

What bearing does this theorizing have upon the revolutionary use of force in defense of human rights? Do social systems that produce relative deprivation, dissonance, anomie, or conflict forfeit legitimacy, in the Kantian sense, and, instead, legitimate such use of force? Why? Why not?

6. Herbert Marcuse has argued that violence is incorporated in oppressive institutions and that it is possible that logic and language will not suffice in reforming, transforming, or eliminating them. In *Counterrevolution and Revolt* (Boston: Beacon Press, 1972), he writes:

> The slogan "let's sit down and reason together" has rightly become a joke. Can you reason with the Pentagon on any other thing than the relative effectiveness of killing machines—and their price? The Secretary of State can reason with the Secretary of the Treasury, and the latter with another Secretary and his advisers, and they all can reason with Members of the Board of the great corporations. This is incestuous reasoning; they are all in agreement about the basic issue: the strengthening of the established power structure. Reasoning "from without" the power structure is a naive idea. They will listen only to the extent to which the voices can be translated into votes, which may perhaps bring into office another set of the same power structure with the same ultimate concern.
>
> The argument is overwhelming. Bertolt Brecht noted that we live at a time where it seems a crime to talk about a tree. Since then, things have become much worse. Today, it seems a crime merely to *talk* about change while one's society is transformed into an institution of violence, terminating in Asia the genocide which began with the liquidation of the American Indians. Is not the sheer power of this brutality immune against the spoken and written word which indicts it? And is not the word which is directed against the practitioners of this power the same they use to defend their power? (pp. 132–33)

Is there a level on which even incautious and reckless action against oppressive social structures seems justified?

7. In *Young India* (New Delhi newspaper, 17 July 1924), Mahatma K. Gandhi made the following assertions:

> They say "means are after all [just] means." I would say "means are after all everything." As the means, so the end. Violent means will give violent [results]. . . . There is no wall of separation between means and ends. . . . I have been endeavoring to keep the country [India] to means that are purely peaceful and legitimate.

Does Gandhi's view supply a workable axiom applicable to the pursuit of human rights? Why does he link "peaceful" means with "legitimate" means? Do you agree with Gandhi's objection to violence (*Young India*, 21 May 1925): "[B]ecause when [violence] appears to do good, the good is only temporary, the evil it does is permanent"?

SELECTED BIBLIOGRAPHY

Cancado Trindade, A. A. *The Application of the Rule of Exhaustion of Local Remedies in International Law.* Cambridge: Cambridge University Press, 1983. An examination of the right of individual petition in international human rights organizations, and the "local remedies rule" except "where ineffective or unreasonably prolonged."

Council on Foreign Relations, 1980's Project. *Enhancing Global Human Rights.* New York: McGraw-Hill, 1979. Focuses on indicators useful in assessing government behavior, on the role of NGOs in using them, and on strategies to modify the behavior of violator-governments.

Forsythe, David P. *Humanitarian Politics: The International Committee of the Red Cross.* Baltimore: Johns Hopkins University Press, 1977. An historical and analytical discussion of the origins, work, procedures, and accomplishments of the International Committee of the Red Cross.

Hannum, Hurst. *The Right to Leave and Return in International Law and Practice.* Norwell, Mass.: Kluwer International Legal Publishers for Martinus Nijhoff Publishers, 1987. Despite the fact that individuals frequently invoke it, for example, Soviet Jews and Chilean exiles, the right to leave and return has received little analytical attention. This author makes numerous suggestions on how NGOs can effectuate the realization of this basic human right.

Hurwitz, Leon. *The State as Defendant—Governmental Accountability and the Redress of Individual Grievances.*

London: Aldwych Press, 1981. A broadly comparative analysis of the various processes (judicial, administrative, political) by which citizens may complain of government action violative of personal liberties; includes an analysis of the methods of Amnesty International.

International Law Association, Australian Branch. *The International Status of Human Rights NGO's*. Sidney, Australia: Butterworths, 1978. Examines the status and participation rights of human rights non-governmental organizations in the United Nations and regional intergovernmental organizations.

Kramer, Daniel C. *Comparative Civil Rights and Liberties*. Lanham, Md.: University Press of America, 1982. A systematic description and assessment of individually initiated judicial action in defense of civil liberties (free speech, religious liberty, nondiscrimination, and criminal justice) in the United States, Britain, France, India, and the Soviet Union.

Larson, Egon. *The Flame in Barbed Wire: The Story of Amnesty International*. New York: Norton, 1979. A detailed and highly readable account of the origins of Amnesty International and the development of its policies on "prisoners of conscience" and avoidance of partisanship.

Levenstein, Aaron. *Escape to Freedom: The Story of the International Rescue Committee*. Westport, Conn.: Greenwood Press, 1983. Report on the fate of millions of political refugees since the Hitler era, and how private citizens banded together in the International Rescue Committee to alleviate the suffering of victims; cases include the homeless in Europe, Bangaladesh, the Carribbean, and Indochina.

Nanda, Ved P., James R. Scarritt, and George W. Shepherd, Jr. *Global Human Rights: Public Policies, Comparative Measures, and NGO Strategies*. Boulder, Colo.: Westview Press, 1981. Describes political science perspectives to efforts to develop human rights on a universal scale, including significant analysis of NGOs.

Power, Jonathan. *Against Oblivion: Amnesty International's Fight for Human Rights*. London: Fontana, 1981. An assessment of the work of Amnesty International, including its successes; also evaluates the role of private groups as actors in international relations.

Sakharov, A. D. *Progress, Co-existence and Intellectual Freedom*. Harmondsworth, U.K.: Penguin Books, 1976. A call for reform in the USSR and appeal for international detente and respect for human rights by the renowned Soviet dissident for whose freedom scores of NGOs have worked.

Schoultz, Lars. *Human Rights and U.S. Policy Toward Latin America*. Princeton, N.J.: Princeton University Press, 1981. Looks at U.S. foreign policy of the Carter administration, with special attention to the role of lobbying groups and human rights NGOs intent upon influencing policy toward Latin America.

Shestack, Jerome J. "Sisyphus Endures: The International Human Rights NGO." *New York Law School Review* 24 (1978): 89–123. A description of human rights action by private groups and an analysis of the multiple functions performed in international affairs by human rights NGOs.

Smith, Brian H. "Churches and Human Rights in Latin America: Recent Trends in the Subcontinent." *Journal of Inter-American Studies and World Affairs* 21 (1979): 89–128. Political science perspectives on the role of religious groups with international ties in influencing and responding to human rights problems in South America.

SELECTED FILMOGRAPHY

Banking on South Africa. Packard Manse Media Project, producer. 1982. 20 min., color. Demonstrates how bank loans by the United States and Canada to the government of South Africa support apartheid. Suggests ways to pressure banks to withdraw this support.

Breaking Ground for Freedom. P. Youzwa and S. Carscallen, producers. USA: Philippine Resource, 1984. 23 min., color; 16 mm, videotape. First documentary on the social revolution of peasant farmers in Luzon, Philippines; shows their efforts to organize to improve their livelihood through cooperative agriculture and their discussions of land reform and the need to change inequities of ownership.

Citizen: The Political Life of Allard Lowenstein. Mike Farrell, producer. USA: Cinema Guild, 1983. 72 min., color; 16 mm. Documentary that traces the career of the liberal New York congressman, assassinated in 1980, who was active in the civil rights movement and became an advocate of human rights and progressive social policy in his legal and political career.

Controlling Interest. California Newsreel, producer. USA: SoAfMedia/Michigan Media/UniCaExtMedia, 1977. 45 min., color; 16 mm. Documentary indictment of the role of multinational corporations and their efforts to oppress workers; focuses on disastrous social and economic conditions in the Third World where the corporations are prevalent.

Gathering Wealth Like Eggs. United Methodist Communications, producer. 1983. 15 min., color. Presents the hidden costs of transnational corporations and examines the need for corporate responsibility.

Sakharov. USA: Facets, 1984. 90 min., VHS videotape. Dramatization of the story of Russian physicist Andrei Sakharov and his wife, Elena Bonner, who were restricted and imprisoned in the Soviet Union for speaking out against violations of human rights and for social and political change. Made-for-television film, stars Jason Robards and Glenda Jackson.

Torture and the Urgent Action Network. USA: Facets, 1984. 17 min., color; videotape. Examines the phenomenon of torture and what individuals can do about it in Amnesty International-USA's Urgent Action Network; includes interviews with CBS News.

Appendix: Selected Documents

UNITED NATIONS CHARTER (1945) (Provisions bearing on human rights: Preamble, Articles 1, 2.7, 13, 55, 56, 62, 73–74, 75–85). Signed at San Francisco on June 26, 1945; entered into force on Oct. 24, 1945. 1976 Y.B.U.N. 1043

WE THE PEOPLES OF THE UNITED NATIONS DETERMINED

to save succeeding generations from the scourge of war, which twice in our lifetime has brought untold sorrow to mankind, and

to reaffirm faith in fundamental human rights, in the dignity and worth of the human person, in the equal rights of men and women and of nations large and small, and

to establish conditions under which justice and respect for the obligations arising from treaties and other sources of international law can be maintained, and

to promote social progress and better standards of life in larger freedom,

AND FOR THESE ENDS

to practice tolerance and live together in peace with one another as good neighbors, and

to unite our strength to maintain international peace and security, and

to ensure, by the acceptance of principles and the institution of methods, that armed force shall not be used, save in the common interest, and

to employ international machinery for the promotion of the economic and social advancement of all peoples,

HAVE RESOLVED TO COMBINE OUR EFFORTS TO ACCOMPLISH THESE AIMS.

Accordingly, our respective Governments, through representatives assembled in the city of San Francisco, who have exhibited their full powers found to be in good and due form, have agreed to the present Charter of the United Nations and do hereby establish an international organization to be known as the United Nations.

CHAPTER I. PURPOSES AND PRINCIPLES

Article 1

The Purposes of the United Nations are:

1. To maintain international peace and security, and to that end: to take effective collective measures for the prevention and removal of threats to the peace, and for the suppression of acts of aggression or other breaches of the peace, and to bring about by peaceful means, and in conformity with the principles of justice and international law, adjustment or settlement of international disputes or situations which might lead to a breach of the peace;

2. To develop friendly relations among nations based on respect for the principle of equal rights and self-determination of peoples, and to take other appropriate measures to strengthen universal peace;

3. To achieve international cooperation in solving international problems of an economic, social, cultural, or humanitarian character, and in promoting and encouraging respect for human rights and for fundamental freedoms for all without distinction as to race, sex, language, or religion; and

4. To be a center for harmonizing the actions of nations in the attainment of these common ends.

Article 2

7. Nothing contained in the present Charter shall authorize the United Nations to intervene in matters which are essentially within the domestic jurisdiction of any state or shall require the Members to submit such matters to settlement under the present Charter; but this principle shall not prejudice the application of enforcement measures under Chapter VII.

Article 13

1. The General Assembly shall initiate studies and make recommendations for the purpose of:

   a. promoting international cooperation in the political field and encouraging the progressive development of international law and its codification;

   b. promoting internation cooperation in the economic, social, cultural, educational, and health fields, and assisting in the realization of human rights and fundamental freedoms for all without distinction as to race, sex, language, or religion.

2. The further responsibilities, functions, and powers of the General Assembly with respect to matters mentioned in paragraph 1(b) above are set forth in Chapters IX and X.

CHAPTER IX. INTERNATIONAL ECONOMIC AND SOCIAL COOPERATION

Article 55

With a view to the creation of conditions of stability and well-being which are necessary for peaceful and friendly relations among nations based on respect for the principle of equal rights and self-determination of peoples, the United Nations shall promote:

   a. higher standards of living, full employment, and conditions of economic and social progress and development;

   b. solutions of international economic, social, health, and related problems; and international cultural and educational cooperation; and

   c. universal respect for, and observance of, human rights and fundamental freedoms for all without distinction as to race, sex, language or religion.

Article 56

All Members pledge themselves to take joint and separate action in cooperation with the Organization for the achievement of the purposes set forth in Article 55.

CHAPTER X. THE ECONOMIC AND SOCIAL COUNCIL

Functions and Powers

Article 62

1. The Economic and Social Council may make or initiate studies and reports with respect to international economic, social, cultural, educational, health, and related matters and may make recommendations with respect to any such matters to the General Assembly, to the Members of the United Nations, and to the specialized agencies concerned.

2. It may make recommendations for the purpose of promoting respect for, and observance of, human rights and fundamental freedoms for all.

3. It may prepare draft conventions for submission to the General Assembly, with respect to matters falling within its competence.

4. It may call, in accordance with the rules prescribed by the United Nations, international conferences on matters falling within its competence.

CHAPTER XI. DECLARATION REGARDING NON-SELF-GOVERNING TERRITORIES

Article 73

Members of the United Nations which have or assume responsibilities for the administration of territories whose peoples have not yet attained a full measure of self-government recognize the principle that the interests of the inhabitants of these territories are paramount, and accept as a sacred trust the obligation to promote to the utmost, within the system of international peace and security established by the present Charter, the well-being of the inhabitants of these territories, and, to this end:

a. to ensure, with due respect for the culture of the peoples concerned, their political, economic, social, and educational advancement, their just treatment, and their protection against abuses;

b. to develop self-government to take due account of the political aspirations of the peoples, and to assist them in the progressive development of their free political institutions, according to the particular circumstances of each territory and its peoples and their varying stages of advancement;

c. to further international peace and security;

d. to promote constructive measures of development, to encourage research, and to cooperate with one another and, when and where appropriate, with specialized international bodies with a view to the practical achievement of the social, economic, and scientific purposes set forth in this Article; and

e. to transmit regularly to the Secretary-General for information purposes, subject to such limitation as security and constitutional considerations may require, statistical and other information of a technical nature relating to economic, social, and educational conditions in the territories for which they are respectively responsible other than those territories to which Chapters XII and XIII apply.

Article 74

Members of the United Nations also agree that their policy in respect of the territories to which this Chapter applies, no less than in respect of their metropolitan areas, must be based on the general principle of good-neighborliness, due account being taken of the interests and well-being of the rest of the world, in social, economic, and commercial matters.

CHAPTER XII. INTERNATIONAL TRUSTEESHIP SYSTEM

Article 75

The United Nations shall establish under its authority an international trusteeship system for the administration and supervision of such territories as may be placed thereunder by subsequent individual agreements. These territories are hereinafter referred to as trust territories.

Article 76

The basic objectives of the trusteeship system, in accordance with the Purposes of the United Nations laid down in Article 1 of the present Charter, shall be:
    a. to further international peace and security;
    b. to promote the political, economic, social, and educational advancement of the inhabitants of the trust territories, and their progressive development towards self-government or independence as may be appropriate to the particular circumstances of each territory and its peoples and the freely expressed wishes of the peoples concerned, and as may be appropriate to the particular circumstances of each territory and its peoples and the freely expressed wishes of the peoples concerned, and as may be provided by the terms of each trusteeship agreement;
    c. to encourage respect for human rights and for fundamental freedoms for all without distinction as to race, sex, language, or religion, and to encourage recognition of the interdependence of the peoples of the world; and
    d. to ensure equal treatment in social, economic, and commercial matters for all Members of the United Nations and their nationals, and also equal treatment for the latter in the administration of justice, without prejudice to the attainment of the foregoing objectives and subject to the provisions of Article 80.

Article 77

1. The trusteeship system shall apply to such territories in the following categories as may be placed thereunder by means of trusteeship agreements:
    a. territories now held under mandate;
    b. territories which may be detached from enemy states as a result of the Second World War; and
    c. territories voluntarily placed under the system by states responsible for their administration.
    2. It will be a matter for subsequent agreement as to which territories in the foregoing categories will be brought under the trusteeship system and upon what terms.

Article 78

The trusteeship system shall not apply to territories which have become Members of the United Nations, relationship among which shall be based on respect for the principle of sovereign equality.

Article 79

The terms of trusteeship for each territory to be placed under the trusteeship system, including any alteration or amendment, shall be agreed upon by the states directly concerned, including the mandatory power in the case of territories held under mandate by a Member of the United Nations, and shall be approved as provided for in Articles 83 and 85.

Article 80

1. Except as may be agreed upon in individual trusteeship agreements, made under Articles 77, 79, and 81, placing each territory under the trusteeship system, and until such agreements have been concluded, nothing in this Chapter shall be construed in or of itself to alter in any manner the rights whatsoever of any states or any peoples or the terms of existing international instruments to which Members of the United Nations may respectively be parties.

2. Paragraph 1 of this Article shall not be interpreted as giving grounds for delay or postponement of the negotiation and conclusion of agreements for placing mandated and other territories under the trusteeship system as provided for in Article 77.

Article 81

The trusteeship agreement shall in each case include the terms under which the trust territory will be administered and designate the authority which will exercise the administration of the trust territory. Such authority, hereinafter called the administering authority, may be one or more states or the Organization itself.

Article 82

There may be designated, in any trusteeship agreement, a strategic area or areas which may include part or all of the trust territory to which the agreement applies, without prejudice to any special agreement or agreements made under Article 43.

Article 83

1. All functions of the United Nations relating to strategic areas, including the approval of the terms of the trusteeship agreements and of their alteration or amendment, shall be exercised by the Security Council.

2. The basic objectives set forth in Article 76 shall be applicable to the people of each strategic area.

3. The Security Council shall, subject to the provisions of the trusteeship agreements and without prejudice to security considerations, avail itself of the assistance of the Trusteeship Council to perform those functions of the United Nations under the trusteeship system relating to political, economic, social, and educational matters in the strategic areas.

Article 84

It shall be the duty of the administering authority to ensure that the trust territory shall play its part in the maintenance of international peace and security. To this end the administering authority may make use of volunteer forces, facilities, and assistance from the trust territory in carrying out the obligations towards the Security Council undertaken in this regard by the administering authority, as well as for local defense and the maintenance of law and order within the trust territory.

Article 85

1. The functions of the United Nations with regard to trusteeship agreements for all areas not designated as strategic, including the approval of the terms of the trusteeship agreements and of their alteration or amendment, shall be exercised by the General Assembly.

2. The Trusteeship Council, operating under the authority of the General Assembly, shall assist the General Assembly in carrying out these functions.

UNIVERSAL DECLARATION OF HUMAN RIGHTS
(1948) U.N.G.A. Res. 217A (III), 3(1)U.N. GAOR Res. 71, U.N. Doc. A/810 (1948).

PREAMBLE

Whereas recognition of the inherent dignity and of the equal and inalienable rights of all members of the human family is the foundation of freedom, justice and peace in the world,

Whereas disregard and contempt for human rights have resulted in barbarous acts which have outraged the conscience of mankind, and the advent of a world in which human beings shall enjoy freedom of speech and belief and freedom from fear and want has been proclaimed as the highest aspiration of the common people,

Whereas it is essential, if man is not to be compelled to have recourse, as a last resort, to rebellion against tyranny and oppression, that human rights should be protected by the rule of law,

Whereas it is essential to promote the development of friendly relations between nations,

Whereas the peoples of the United Nations have in the Charter reaffirmed their faith in fundamental human rights, in the dignity and worth of the human person and in the equal rights of men and women and have determined to promote social progress and better standards of life in larger freedom,

Whereas Member States have pledged themselves to achieve, in co-operation with the United Nations, the promotion of universal respect for and observance of human rights and fundamental freedoms,

Whereas a common understanding of these rights and freedoms is of the greatest importance for the full realization of this pledge,

Now, therefore,

THE GENERAL ASSEMBLY

Proclaims this Universal Declaration of Human Rights as a common standard of achievement for all peoples and all nations, to the end that every individual and every organ of society, keeping this Declaration constantly in mind, shall strive by teaching and education to promote respect for these rights and freedoms and by progressive measures, national and international, to secure their universal and effective recognition and observance, both among the peoples of Member States themselves and among the peoples of territories under their jurisdiction.

Article 1

All human beings are born free and equal in dignity and rights. They are endowed with reason and conscience and should act towards one another in a spirit of brotherhood.

Article 2

Everyone is entitled to all the rights and freedoms set forth in this Declaration, without distinction of any kind, such as race, colour, sex, language, religion, political or other opinion, national or social origin, property, birth or other status.

Furthermore, no distinction shall be made on the basis of the political, jurisdictional or international status of the country or territory to which a person belongs, whether it be independent, trust, non-self-governing or under any other limitation of sovereignty.

Article 3

Everyone has the right to life, liberty and security of person.

Article 4

No one shall be held in slavery or servitude; slavery and the slave trade shall be prohibited in all their forms.

Article 5

No one shall be subjected to torture or to cruel, inhuman or degrading treatment or punishment.

Article 6

Everyone has the right to recognition everywhere as a person before the law.

Article 7

All are equal before the law and are entitled without any discrimination to equal protection of the law. All are entitled to equal protection against any discrimination in violation of this Declaration and against any incitement to such discrimination.

Article 8

Everyone has the right to an effective remedy by the competent national tribunals for acts violating the fundamental rights granted him by the constitution or by law.

Article 9

No one shall be subjected to arbitrary arrest, detention or exile.

Article 10

Everyone is entitled in full equality to a fair and public hearing by an independent and impartial tribunal, in the determination of his rights and obligations and of any criminal charge against him.

Article 11

1. Everyone charged with a penal offence has the right to be presumed innocent until proved guilty according to law in a public trial at which he has had all the guarantees necessary for his defence.

2. No one shall be held guilty of any penal offence on account of any act or omission which did not constitute a penal offence, under national or international law, at the time when it was committed. Nor shall a heavier penalty be imposed than the one that was applicable at the time the penal offence was committed.

Article 12

No one shall be subjected to arbitrary interference with his privacy, family, home or correspondence, nor to attacks upon his honour and reputation. Everyone has the right to the protection of the law against such interference or attacks.

Article 13

1. Everyone has the right to freedom of movement and residence within the borders of each State.

2. Everyone has the right to leave any country, including his own, and to return to his country.

Article 14

1. Everyone has the right to seek and to enjoy in other countries asylum from persecution.

2. This right may not be invoked in the case of prosecutions genuinely arising from non-political crimes or from acts contrary to the purposes and principles of the United Nations.

Article 15

1. Everyone has the right to a nationality.

2. No one shall be arbitrarily deprived of his nationality nor denied the right to change his nationality.

Article 16

1. Men and women of full age, without any limitation due to race, nationality or religion, have the right to marry and to found a family. They are entitled to equal rights as to marriage, during marriage and at its dissolution.

2. Marriage shall be entered into only with the free and full consent of the intending spouses.

3. The family is the natural and fundamental group unit of society and is entitled to protection by society and the State.

Article 17

1. Everyone has the right to own property alone as well as in association with others.

2. No one shall be arbitrarily deprived of his property.

Article 18

Everyone has the right to freedom of thought, conscience and religion; this right includes freedom to change his religion or belief, and freedom, either alone or in community with others and in public or private, to manifest his religion or belief in teaching, practice, worship and observance.

Article 19

Everyone has the right to freedom of opinion and expression; this right includes freedom to hold opinions without interference and to seek, receive and impart information and ideas through any media and regardless of frontiers.

Article 20

1. Everyone has the right to freedom of peaceful assembly and association.

2. No one may be compelled to belong to an association.

Article 21

1. Everyone has the right to take part in the government of his country, directly or through freely chosen representatives.

2. Everyone has the right of equal access to public service in his country.

3. The will of the people shall be the basis of the authority of government; this will

shall be expressed in periodic and genuine elections which shall be by universal and equal suffrage and shall be held by secret vote or by equivalent free voting procedures.

Article 22

Everyone, as a member of society, has the right to social security and is entitled to realization, through national effort and international co-operation and in accordance with the organization and resources of each State, of the economic, social and cultural rights indispensable for his dignity and the free development of his personality.

Article 23

1. Everyone has the right to work, to free choice of employment, to just and favourable conditions of work and to protection against unemployment.

2. Everyone, without any discrimination, has the right to equal pay for equal work.

3. Everyone who works has the right to just and favourable remuneration ensuring for himself and his family an existence worthy of human dignity, and supplemented, if necessary, by other means of social protection.

4. Everyone has the right to form and to join trade unions for the protection of his interests.

Article 24

Everyone has the right to rest and leisure, including reasonable limitation of working hours and periodic holidays with pay.

Article 25

1. Everyone has the right to a standard of living adequate for the health and well-being of himself and of his family, including food, clothing, housing and medical care and necessary social services, and the right to security in the event of unemployment, sickness, disability, widowhood, old age or other lack of livelihood in circumstances beyond his control.

2. Motherhood and childhood are entitled to special care and assistance. All children, whether born in or out of wedlock, shall enjoy the same social protection.

Article 26

1. Everyone has the right to education. Education shall be free, at least in the elementary and fundamental stages. Elementary education shall be compulsory. Technical and professional education shall be made generally available and higher education shall be equally accessible to all on the basis of merit.

2. Education shall be directed to the full development of the human personality and to the strengthening of respect for human rights and fundamental freedoms. It shall promote understanding, tolerance and friendship among all nations, racial or religious groups, and shall further the activities of the United Nations for the maintenance of peace.

3. Parents have a prior right to choose the kind of education that shall be given to their children.

Article 27

1. Everyone has the right freely to participate in the cultural life of the community, to enjoy the arts and to share in scientific advancement and its benefits.

2. Everyone has the right to the protection of the moral and material interests resulting from any scientific, literary or artistic production of which he is the author.

Article 28

Everyone is entitled to a social and international order in which the rights and freedoms set forth in this Declaration can be fully realized.

Article 29

1. Everyone has duties to the community in which alone the free and full development of his personality is possible.

2. In the exercise of his rights and freedoms, everyone shall be subject only to such limitations as are determined by law solely for the purpose of securing due recognition and respect for the rights and freedoms of others and of meeting the just requirements of morality, public order and the general welfare in a democratic society.

3. These rights and freedoms may in no case be exercised contrary to the purposes and principles of the United Nations.

Article 30

Nothing in this Declaration may be interpreted as implying for any State, group or person any right to engage in any activity or to perform any act aimed at the destruction of any of the rights and freedoms set forth herein.

INTERNATIONAL COVENANT ON ECONOMIC, SOCIAL AND CULTURAL RIGHTS. Opened for signature on Dec. 19, 1966; entered into force on Jan. 3, 1976. U.N.G.A. Res. 2200 (XXI), 21 U.N. GAOR, Supp. (No. 16) 49, U.N. Doc. A/6316 (1967).

PART I

Article 1

1. All peoples have the right of self-determination. By virtue of that right they freely determine their political status and freely pursue their economic, social and cultural development.

2. All peoples may, for their own ends, freely dispose of their natural wealth and resources without prejudice to any obligations arising out of international economic co-operation, based upon the principle of mutual benefit, and international law. In no case may a people be deprived of its own means of subsistence.

3. The States Parties to the present Covenant, including those having responsibility for the administration of Non-Self-Governing and Trust Territories, shall promote the realization of the right of self-determination, and shall respect that right, in conformity with the provisions of the Charter of the United Nations.

Article 2

1. Each State Party to the present Covenant undertakes to take steps, individually and through international assistance and co-operation, especially economic and technical, to the maximum of its available resources, with a view to achieving progressively the full realization of the rights recognized in the present Covenant by all appropriate means, including particularly the adoption of legislative measures.

2. The States Parties to the present Covenant undertake to guarantee that the rights enunciated in the present Covenant will be exercised without discrimination of any kind as to race, colour, sex, language, religion, political or other opinion, national or social origin, property, birth or other status.

3. Developing countries, with due regard to human rights and their national economy, may determine to what extent they would guarantee the economic rights recognized in the present Covenant to non-nationals.

Article 3

The States Parties to the present Covenant undertake to ensure the equal right of men and women to the enjoyment of all economic, social and cultural rights set forth in the present Covenant.

Article 4

The States Parties to the present Covenant recognize that, in the enjoyment of those rights provided by the State in conformity with the present Covenant, the State may subject such rights only to such limitations as are determined by law only in so far as this may be compatible with the nature of these rights and solely for the purpose of promoting the general welfare in a democratic society.

Article 5

1. Nothing in the present covenant may be interpreted as implying for any State, group or person any right to engage in any activity or to perform any act aimed at the destruction

of any of the rights or freedoms recognized herein, or at their limitation to a greater extent than is provided for in the present Covenant.

2. No restriction upon or derogation from any of the fundamental human rights recognized or existing in any country in virtue of law, conventions, regulations or custom shall be admitted on the pretext that the present Covenant does not recognize such rights or that it recognizes them to a lesser extent.

PART III

Article 6

1. The States Parties to the present Covenant recognize the right to work, which includes the right of everyone to the opportunity to gain his living by work which he freely chooses or accepts, and will take appropriate steps to safeguard this right.

2. The steps to be taken by a State Party to the present Covenant to achieve the full realization of this right shall include technical and vocational guidance and training programmes, policies and techniques to achieve steady economic, social and cultural development and full and productive employment under conditions safeguarding fundamental political and economic freedoms to the individual.

Article 7

The States Parties to the present Covenant recognize the right of everyone to the enjoyment of just and favourable conditions of work which ensure, in particular:

(a) Remuneration which provides all workers, as a minimum, with:

(i) Fair wages and equal remuneration for work of equal value without distinction of any kind, in particular women being guaranteed conditions of work not inferior to those enjoyed by men, with equal pay for equal work;

(ii) A decent living for themselves and their families in accordance with the provisions of the present Covenant;

(b) Safe and healthy working conditions;

(c) Equal opportunity for everyone to be promoted in his employment to an appropriate higher level, subject to no considerations other than those of seniority and competence;

(d) Rest, leisure and reasonable limitation of working hours and periodic holidays with pay, as well as remuneration for public holidays.

Article 8

1. The States Parties to the present Covenant undertake to ensure:

(a) The right of everyone to form trade unions and join the trade union of his choice, subject only to the rules of the organization concerned, for the promotion and protection of his economic and social interests. No restrictions may be placed on the exercise of this right other than those prescribed by law and which are necessary in a democratic society in the interests of national security or public order or for the protection of the rights and freedoms of others;

(b) The right of trade unions to establish national federations or confederations and the right of the latter to form or join international trade-union organizations;

(c) The right of trade unions to functions freely subject to no limitations other than those prescribed by law and which are necessary in a democratic society in the interests of national security or public order or for the protection of the rights and freedoms of others;

(d) The right to strike, provided that it is exercised in conformity with the laws of the particular country.

2. This article shall not prevent the imposition of lawful restrictions on the exercise of these rights by members of the armed forces or of the police or of the administration of the State.

3. Nothing in this article shall authorize States Parties to the International Labour Organisation Convention of 1948 concerning Freedom of Association and Protection of the Right to Organize to take legislative measures which would prejudice, or apply the law in such a manner as would prejudice, the guarantees provided for in that Convention.

Article 9

The States Parties to the present Covenant recognize the right of every one to social security, including social insurance.

Article 10

The States Parties to the present Covenant recognize that:

1. The widest possible protection and assistance should be accorded to the family, which is the natural and fundamental group unit of society, particularly for its establishment and while it is responsible for the care and education of dependent children. Marriage must be entered into with the free consent of the intending spouses.

2. Special protection should be accorded to mothers during a reasonable period before and after childbirth. During such period working mothers should be accorded paid leave or leave with adequate social security benefits.

3. Special measures of protection and assistance should be taken on behalf of all children and young persons without any discrimination for reasons of parentage or other conditions. Children and young persons should be protected from economic and social exploitation. Their employment in work harmful to their morals or health or dangerous to life or likely to hamper their normal development should be punishable by law. States should also set age limits below which the paid employment of child labour should be prohibited and punishable by law.

Article 11

1. The States Parties to the present Covenant recognize the right of everyone to an adequate standard of living for himself and his family, including adequate food, clothing and housing, and to the continuous improvement of living conditions. The States Parties will take appropriate steps to ensure the realization of this right, recognizing to this effect the essential importance of international co-operation based on free consent.

2. The States Parties to the present Covenant, recognizing the fundamental right of everyone to be free from hunger, shall take, individually and through international co-operation, the measures, including specific programmes, which are needed:

(a) To improve methods of production, conservation and distribution of food by making full use of technical and scientific knowledge, by disseminating knowledge of the principles of nutrition and by developing or reforming agrarian systems in such a way as to achieve the most efficient development and utilization of natural resources;

(b) Taking into account the problems of both food-importing and food-exporting countries, to ensure an equitable distribution of world food supplies in relation to need.

Article 12

1. The States Parties to the present Covenant recognize the right of everyone to the enjoyment of the highest attainable standard of physical and mental health.

2. The steps to be taken by the States Parties to the present Covenant to achieve the full realization of this right shall include those necessary for:

(a) The provision for the reduction of the stillbirth-rate and of infant mortality and for the healthy development of the child;

(b) The improvement of all aspects of environmental and industrial hygiene;

(c) The prevention, treatment and control of epidemic, endemic, occupational and other diseases;

(d) The creation of conditions which would assure to all medical service and medical attention in the event of sickness.

Article 13

1. The States Parties to the present Covenant recognize the right of everyone to education. They agree that education shall be directed to the full development of the human personality and the sense of its dignity, and shall strengthen the respect for human rights and fundamental freedoms. They further agree that education shall enable all persons to participate effectively in a free society, promote understanding, tolerance and friendship among all nations and all racial, ethnic or religious groups, and further the activities of the United Nations for the maintenance of peace.

2. The States Parties to the present Covenant recognize that, with a view to achieving the full realization of this right:

(a) Primary education shall be compulsory and available free to all;

(b) Secondary education in its different forms, including technical and vocational secondary education, shall be made generally available and accessible to all by every appropriate means, and in particular by the progressive introduction of free education;

(c) Higher education shall be made equally accessible to all, on the basis of capacity, by every appropriate means, and in particular by the progressive introduction of free education;

(d) Fundamental education shall be encouraged or intensified as far as possible for those persons who have not received or completed the whole period of their primary education;

(e) The development of a system of schools at all levels shall be actively pursued, an adequate fellowship system shall be established, and the material conditions of teaching staff shall be continuously improved.

3. The States Parties to the present Covenant undertake to have respect for the liberty of parents and, when applicable, legal guardians to choose for their children schools, other than those established by the public authorities, which conform to such minimum educational standards as may be laid down or approved by the State and to ensure the religious and moral education of their children in conformity with their own convictions.

4. No part of this article shall be construed so as to interfere with the liberty of individuals and bodies to establish and direct educational institutions, subject always to the observance of the principles set forth in paragraph 1 of this article and to the requirement that the education given in such institutions shall conform to such minimum standards as may be laid down by the State.

Article 14

Each State Party to the present Covenant which, at the time of becoming a Party, has not been able to secure in its metropolitan territory or other territories under its jurisdiction compulsory primary education, free of charge, undertakes, within two years, to work out and adopt a detailed plan of action for the progressive implementation, within a reasonable number of years, to be fixed in the plan, of the principle of compulsory education free of charge for all.

Article 15

1. The States Parties to the present Covenant recognize the right of everyone:
   (a) To take part in cultural life;
   (b) To enjoy the benefits of scientific progress and its applications;
   (c) To benefit from the protection of the moral and material interests resulting from any scientific, literary or artistic production of which he is the author.
2. The steps to be taken by the States Parties to the present Covenant to achieve the full realization of this right shall include those necessary for the conservation, the development and the diffusion of science and culture.
3. The States Parties to the present Covenant undertake to respect the freedom indispensable for scientific research and creative activity.
4. The States Parties to the present Covenant recognize the benefits to be derived from the encouragement and development of international contacts and co-operation in the scientific and cultural fields.

PART IV

Article 16

1. The States Parties to the present Covenant undertake to submit in conformity with this part of the covenant reports on the measures which they have adopted and the progress made in achieving the observance of the rights recognized herein.
2. (a) All reports shall be submitted to the Secretary-General of the United Nations, who shall transmit copies to the Economic and Social Council for consideration in accordance with the provisions of the present Covenant.
   (b) The Secretary-General of the United Nations shall also transmit to the specialized agencies copies of the reports, or any relevant parts therefrom, from States Parties to the present Covenant which are also members of these specialized agencies in so far as these reports, or parts therefrom, relate to any matters which fall within the responsibilities of the said agencies in accordance with their constitutional instruments. . . .

* * *

Article 19

The Economic and Social Council may transmit to the Commission on Human Rights for study and general recommendation or, as appropriate, for information the reports concerning human rights submitted by States in accorance with articles 16 and 17, and those concerning human rights submitted by the specialized agencies in accordance with article 18.[1] . . .

1. Articles 17 and 18 are omitted here.

Article 21

The Economic and Social Council may submit from time to time to the General Assembly reports with recommendations of a general nature and a summary of the information received from the States Parties to the present Covenant and the specialized agencies on the measures taken and the progress made in achieving general observance of the rights recognized in the present Covenant.

Article 22

The Economic and Social Council may bring to the attention of other organs of the United Nations, their subsidiary organs and specialized agencies concerned with furnishing technical assistance any matters arising out of the reports referred to in this part of the present Covenant which may assist such bodies in deciding, each within its field of competence, on the advisability of international measures likely to contribute to the effective progressive implementation of the present Covenant.

Article 23

The State Parties to the present Covenant agree that international action for the achievement of the rights recognized in the present Covenant includes such methods as the conclusion of conventions, the adoption of recommendations, the furnishing of technical assistance and the holding of regional meetings and technical meetings for the purpose of consultation and study organized in conjunction with the Governments concerned.

Article 24

Nothing in the present covenant shall be interpreted as impairing the provisions of the Charter of the United Nations and of the constitutions of the specialized agencies which define the respective responsibilities of the various organs of the United Nations and of the specialized agencies in regard to the matters dealt with in the present Covenant.

Article 25

Nothing in the present Covenant shall be interpreted as impairing the inherent right of all peoples to enjoy and utilize fully and freely their natural wealth and resources. . . .

INTERNATIONAL COVENANT ON CIVIL AND POLITICAL RIGHTS.

Opened for signature on Dec. 19, 1966; entered into force on Mar. 23, 1976. U.N.G.A. Res. 2200 (XXI), 21 U.N. GAOR, Supp. (No. 16) 52, U.N. Doc. A/6316 (1967).

PART I

Article 1

1. All peoples have the right of self-determination. By virtue of that right they freely determine their political status and freely pursue their economic, social and cultural development.

2. All peoples may, for their own ends, freely dispose of their natural wealth and resources without prejudice to any obligations arising out of international economic co-operation, based upon the principle of mutual benefit, and international law. In no case may a people be deprived of its own means of subsistence.

3. The States Parties to the present Covenant, including those having responsibility for the administration of Non-Self-Governing and Trust Territories, shall promote the realization of the right of self-determination, and shall respect that right, in conformity with the provisions of the Charter of the United Nations.

Article 2

1. Each State Party to the present Covenant undertakes to respect and to ensure to all individuals within its territory and subject to its jurisdiction the rights recognized in the present Covenant, without distinction of any kind, such as race, colour, sex, language, religion, political or other opinion, national or social origin, property, birth or other status.

2. Where not already provided for by existing legislative or other measures, each State Party to the present Covenant undertakes to take the necessary steps, in accordance with its constitutional processes and with the provisions of the present Covenant, to adopt such legislative or other measures as may be necessary to give effect to the rights recognized in the present Covenant.

3. Each State Party to the present Covenant undertakes:

(a) To ensure that any person whose rights or freedoms as herein recognized are violated shall have an effective remedy, notwithstanding that the violation has been committed by persons acting in an official capacity;

(b) To ensure that any person claiming such a remedy shall have his right thereto determined by competent judicial, administrative or legislative authorities, or by any other competent authority provided for by the legal system of the State, and to develop the possibilities of judicial remedy;

(c) To ensure that the competent authorities shall enforce such remedies when granted.

Article 3

The States Parties to the present Covenant undertake to ensure the equal right of men and women to the enjoyment of all civil and political rights set forth in the present Covenant.

Article 4

1. In time of public emergency which threatens the life of the nation and the existence of which is officially proclaimed, the State Parties to the present Covenant may take measures

derogating from their obligations under the present Covenant to the extent strictly required by the exigencies of the situation, provided that such measures are not inconsistent with their other obligations under international law and do not involve discrimination solely on the ground of race, colour, sex, language, religion or social origin.

2. No derogation from articles 6, 7, 8 (paragraphs 1 and 2), 11, 15, 16 and 18 may be made under this provision.

3. Any State Party to the present Covenant availing itself of the right of derogation shall immediately inform the other States Parties to the present Covenant, through the intermediary of the Secretary-General of the United Nations, of the provisions from which it has derogated and of the reasons by which it was actuated. A further communication shall be made, through the same intermediary, on the date on which it terminates such derogation.

Article 5

1. Nothing in the present Covenant may be interpreted as implying for any State, group or person any right to engage in any activity or perform any act aimed at the destruction of any of the rights and freedoms recognized herein or at their limitation to a greater extent than is provided for in the present Covenant.

2. There shall be no restriction upon or derogation from any of the fundamental human rights recognized or existing in any State Party to the present Covenant pursuant to law, conventions, regulations or custom on the pretext that the present Covenant does not recognize such rights or that it recognizes them to a lesser extent.

PART III

Article 6

1. Every human being has the inherent right to life. This right shall be protected by law. No one shall be arbitrarily deprived of his life.

2. In countries which have not abolished the death penalty, sentence of death may be imposed only for the most serious crimes in accordance with the law in force at the time of the commission of the crime and not contrary to the provisions of the present Covenant and to the Convention on the Prevention and Punishment of the Crime of Genocide. This penalty can only be carried out pursuant to a final judgment rendered by a competent court.

3. When deprivation of life constitutes the crime of genocide, it is understood that nothing in this article shall authorize any State Party to the present Covenant to derogate in any way from any obligation assumed under the provisions of the Convention on the Prevention and Punishment of the Crime of Genocide.

4. Anyone sentenced to death shall have the right to seek pardon or commutation of the sentence. Amnesty, pardon or commutation of the sentence of death may be granted in all cases.

5. Sentence of death shall not be imposed for crimes committed by persons below eighteen years of age and shall not be carried out on pregnant women.

6. Nothing in this article shall be invoked to delay or to prevent the abolition of capital punishment by any State Party to the present Covenant.

Article 7

No one shall be subjected to torture or to cruel, inhuman or degrading treatment or punishment. In particular, no one shall be subjected without his free consent to medical or scientific experimentation.

Article 8

1. No one shall be held in slavery; slavery and slave-trade in all their forms shall be prohibited.

2. No one shall be held in servitude.

3. (a) No one shall be required to perform forced or compulsory labour;

(b) Paragraph 3(a) shall not be held to preclude, in countries where imprisonment with hard labour may be imposed as a punishment for a crime, the performance of hard labour in pursuance of a sentence to such punishment by a competent court;

(c) For the purpose of this paragraph the term "forced or compulsory labour" shall not include:

(i) Any work or service, not referred to in sub-paragraph (b), normally required of a person who is under detention in consequence of a lawful order of a court, or of a person during conditional release from such detention;

(ii) any service of a military character and, in countries where conscientious objection is recognized, any national service required by law of conscientious objectors;

(iii) Any service exacted in cases of emergency or calamity threatening the life or well-being of the community;

(iv) Any work or service which forms part of normal civil obligations.

Article 9

1. Everyone has the right to liberty and security of person. No one shall be subjected to arbitrary arrest or detention. No one shall be deprived of his liberty except on such grounds and in accordance with such procedure as are established by law.

2. Anyone who is arrested shall be informed, at the time of arrest, of the reasons for his arrest and shall be promptly informed of any charges against him.

3. Anyone arrested or detained on a criminal charge shall be brought promptly before a judge or other officer authorized by law to exercise judicial power and shall be entitled to trial within a reasonable time or to release. It shall not be the general rule that persons awaiting trial shall be detained in custody, but release may be subject to guarantees to appear for trial, at any other stage of the judicial proceedings, and, should occasion arise, for execution of the judgment.

4. Anyone who is deprived of his liberty by arrest or detention shall be entitled to take proceedings before a court, in order that that court may decide without delay on the lawfulness of his detention and order his release if the detention is not lawful.

5. Anyone who has been the victim of unlawful arrest or detention shall have an enforceable right to compensation.

Article 10

1. All persons deprived of their liberty shall be treated with humanity and with respect for the inherent dignity of the human person.

2. (a) Accused persons shall, save in exceptional circumstances, be segregated from convicted persons and shall be subject to separate treatment appropriate to their status as unconvicted persons;

(b) Accused juvenile persons shall be separated from adults and brought as speedily as possible for adjudication.

3. The penitentiary system shall comprise treatment of prisoners the essential aim of which shall be their reformation and social rehabilitation. Juvenile offenders shall be segregated from adults and be accorded treatment appropriate to their age and legal status.

Article 11

No one shall be imprisoned merely on the ground of inability to fulfill a contractual obligation.

Article 12

1. Everyone lawfully within the territory of a State shall, within that territory, have the right to liberty of movement and freedom to choose his residence.

2. Everyone shall be free to leave any country, including his own.

3. The above-mentioned rights shall not be subject to any restrictions except those which are provided by law, are necessary to protect national security, public order (*ordre public*), public health or morals or the rights and freedoms of others, and are consistent with the other rights recognized in the present Covenant.

4. No one shall be arbitrarily deprived of the right to enter his own country.

Article 13

An alien lawfully in the territory of a State Party to the present Covenant may be expelled therefrom only in pursuance of a decision reached in accordance with law and shall, except where compelling reasons of national security otherwise require, be allowed to submit the reasons against his expulsion and to have his case reviewed by, and be represented for the purpose before, the competent authority or a person or persons especially designated by the competent authority.

Article 14

1. All persons shall be equal before the courts and tribunals. In the determination of any criminal charge against him, or of his rights and obligations in a suit at law, everyone shall be entitled to a fair and public hearing by a competent, independent and impartial tribunal established by law. The Press and the public may be excluded from all or part of a trial for reasons of morals, public order (*ordre public*) or national security in a democratic society, or when the interest of the private lives of the parties so requires, or to the extent strictly necessary in the opinion of the court in special circumstances where publicity would prejudice the interests of justice; but any judgment rendered in a criminal case or in a suit at law shall be made public except where the interest of juvenile persons otherwise requires or the proceedings concern matrimonial disputes or the guardianship of children.

2. Everyone charged with a criminal offence shall have the right to be presumed innocent until proved guilty according to law.

3. In the determination of any criminal charge against him, everyone shall be entitled to the following minimum guarantees, in full equality:

(a) To be informed promptly and in detail in a language which he understands of the nature and cause of the charge against him;

(b) To have adequate time and facilities for the preparation of his defence and to communicate with counsel of his own choosing;

(c) To be tried without undue delay;

(d) To be tried in his presence, and to defend himself in person or through legal assistance of his own choosing; to be informed, if he does not have legal assistance, of this right; and to have legal assistance assigned to him, in any case where the interests of justice so require, and without payment by him in any such case if he does not have sufficient means to pay for it;

(e) To examine, or have examined, the witnesses against him and to obtain the attendance and examination of witnesses on his behalf under the same conditions as witnesses against him;

(f) To have the free assistance of an interpreter if he cannot understand or speak the language used in court;

(g) Not to be compelled to testify against himself or to confess guilt.

4. In the case of juvenile persons, the procedure shall be such as will take account of their age and the desirability of promoting their rehabilitation.

5. Everyone convicted of a crime shall have the right to his conviction and sentence being reviewed by a higher tribunal according to law.

6. When a person has by a final decision been convicted of a criminal offence and when subsequently his conviction has been reversed or he has been pardoned on the ground that a new or newly discovered fact shows conclusively that there has been a miscarriage of justice, the person who has suffered punishment as a result of such conviction shall be compensated according to law, unless it is proved that the non-disclosure of the unknown fact in time is wholly or partly attributable to him.

7. No one shall be liable to be tried or punished again for an offence for which he has already been finally convicted or acquitted in accordance with the law and penal procedure of each country.

Article 15

1. No one shall be held guilty of any criminal offence on account of any act of omission which did not constitute a criminal offence, under national or international law, at the time when it was committed. Nor shall a heavier penalty be imposed than the one that was applicable at the time when the criminal offence was committed. If, subsequent to the commission of the offence, provision is made by law for the imposition of a lighter penalty, the offender shall benefit thereby.

2. Nothing in this article shall prejudice the trial and punishment of any person for any act or omission which, at the time when it was committed, was criminal according to the general principles of law recognized by the community of nations.

Article 16

Everyone shall have the right to recognition everywhere as a person before the law.

Article 17

1. No one shall be subjected to arbitrary or unlawful interference with his privacy, family, home or correspondence, nor to unlawful attacks on his honour and reputation.

2. Everyone has the right to the protection of the law against such interference or attacks.

Article 18

1. Everyone shall have the right to freedom of thought, conscience and religion. This right shall include freedom to have or to adopt a religion or belief of his choice, and freedom, either individually or in community with others and in public or private, to manifest his religion or belief in worship, observance, practice and teaching.

2. No one shall be subject to coercion which would impair his freedom to have or to adopt a religion or belief of his choice.

3. Freedom to manifest one's religion or beliefs may be subject only to such limitations as are prescribed by law and are necessary to protect public safety, order, health, or morals or the fundamental rights and freedoms of others.

4. The States Parties to the present Covenant undertake to have respect for the liberty of parents and, when applicable, legal guardians to ensure the religious and moral education of their children in conformity with their own convictions.

Article 19

1. Everyone shall have the right to hold opinions without interference.

2. Everyone shall have the right to freedom of expression; this right shall include freedom to seek, receive and impart information and ideas of all kinds, regardless of frontiers, either orally, in writing or in print, in the form of art, or through any other media of his choice.

3. The exercise of the rights provided for in paragraph 2 of this article carries with it special duties and responsibilities. It may therefore be subject to certain restrictions, but these shall only be such as are provided by law and are necessary:

(a) For respect of the rights or reputations of others;

(b) For the protection of national security or of public order (*ordre public*), or of public health or morals.

Article 20

1. Any propaganda for war shall be prohibited by law.

2. Any advocacy of national, racial or religious hatred that constitutes incitement to discrimination, hostility or violence shall be prohibited by law.

Article 21

The right of peaceful assembly shall be recognized. No restrictions may be placed on the exercise of this right other than those imposed in conformity with the law and which are necessary in a democratic society in the interests of national security or public safety, public order (*ordre public*), the protection of public health or morals or the protection of the rights and freedoms of others.

Article 22

1. Everyone shall have the right to freedom of association with others, including the right to form and join trade unions for the protection of his interests.

2. No restrictions may be placed on the exercise of this right other than those which are prescribed by law and which are necessary in a democratic society in the interests of national security or public safety, public order (*ordre public*), the protection of public health or morals or the protection of the rights and freedoms of others. This article shall not prevent the imposition of lawful restrictions on members of the armed forces and of the police in their exercise of this right.

3. Nothing in this article shall authorize States Parties to the International Labour Organisation Convention of 1948 concerning Freedom of Association and Protection of the Right to Organize to take legislative measures which would prejudice, or to apply the law in such a manner as to prejudice, the guarantees provided for in that Convention.

Article 23

1. The family is the natural and fundamental group unit of society and is entitled to protection by society and the State.

2. The right of men and women of marriageable age to marry and to found a family shall be recognized.

3. No marriage shall be entered into without the free and full consent of the intending spouses.

4. States Parties to the present Covenant shall take appropriate steps to ensure equality of rights and responsibilities of spouses as to marriage, during marriage and at its dissolution. In the case of dissolution, provision shall be made for the necessary protection of any children.

Article 24

1. Every child shall have, without any discrimination as to race, colour, sex, language, religion, national or social origin, property or birth, the right to such measures of protection as are required by his status as a minor, on the part of his family, society and the State.

2. Every child shall be registered immediately after birth and shall have a name.

3. Every child has the right to acquire a nationality.

Article 25

Every citizen shall have the right and the opportunity, without any of the distinctions mentioned in article 2 and without unreasonable restrictions:

(a) To take part in the conduct of public affairs, directly or through freely chosen representatives;

(b) to vote and to be elected at genuine periodic elections which shall be by universal and equal suffrage and shall be held by secret ballot, guaranteeing the free expression of the will of the electors;

(c) To have access, on general terms of equality, to public service in his country.

Article 26

All persons are equal before the law and are entitled without any discrimination to the equal protection of the law. In this respect, the law shall prohibit any discrimination and guarantee to all persons equal and effective protection against discrimination on any ground such as race, colour, sex, language, religion, political or other opinion, national or social origin, property, birth or other status.

Article 27

In those States in which ethnic, religious or linguistic minorities exist, persons belonging to such minorities shall not be denied the right, in community with the other members of their group, to enjoy their own culture, to profess and practise their own religion, or to use their own language.

PART IV

Article 28

1. There shall be established a Human Rights Committee (hereafter referred to in the present Covenant as the Committee). It shall consist of eighteen members and shall carry out the functions hereinafter provided.

2. The Committee shall be composed of nationals of the States Parties to the present Covenant who shall be persons of high moral character and recognized competence in the field of human rights, consideration being given to the usefulness of the participation of some persons having legal experience.

3. The members of the Committee shall be elected and shall serve in their personal capacity. . . .

Article 40

1. The States Parties to the present Covenant undertake to submit reports on the measures they have adopted which give effect to the rights recognized herein and on the progress made in the enjoyment of those rights:

(a) Within one year of the entry into force of the present Covenant for the States Parties concerned:

(b) Thereafter whenever the Committee so requests.

2. All reports shall be submitted to the Secretary-General of the United Nations, who shall transmit them to the Committee for consideration. Reports shall indicate the factors and difficulties, if any, affecting the implementation of the present Covenant.

3. The Secretary-General of the United Nations may, after consultation with the Committee, transmit to the specialized agencies concerned copies of such parts of the reports as may fall within their field of competence.

4. The Committee shall study the reports submitted by the States Parties to the present Covenant. It shall transmit its reports, and such general comments as it may consider appropriate, to the States Parties. The Committee may also transmit to the Economic and Social Council these comments along with the copies of the reports it has received from States Parties to the present Covenant.

5. The States Parties to the present Covenant may submit to the Committee observations on any comments that may be made in accordance with paragraph 4 of this article.

Article 41

1. A State Party to the present Covenant may at any time declare under this article that it recognizes the competence of the Committee to receive and consider communications to the effect that a State Party claims that another State Party is not fulfilling is obligations under the present Covenant. Communications under this article may be received and considered only if submitted by a State Party which has made a declaration recognizing in regard to itself the competence of the Committee. No communication shall be received by the Committee if it concerns a State Party which has not made such a declaration. Communications received under this article shall be dealt with in accordance with the following procedure:

(a) If a State Party to the present covenant considers that another State Party is not giving effect to the provisions of the present Covenant, it may, by written communication, bring the matter to the attention of that State Party. Within three months after the receipt of the communication, the receiving State shall afford the State which sent the communication an explanation or any other statement in writing clarifying the matter, which should include, to the extent possible and pertinent, reference to domestic procedures and remedies taken, pending, or available in the matter.

(b) If the matter is not adjusted to the satisfaction of both States Parties concerned within six months after the receipt by the receiving State of the initial communication, either State shall have the right to refer the matter to the Committee, by notice given to the Committee and to the other State.

(c) The Committee shall deal with a matter referred to it only after it has ascertained that all available domestic remedies have been invoked and exhausted in the matter, in conformity with the generally recognized principles of international law. This shall not be the rule where the application of the remedies is unreasonably prolonged.

(d) The Committee shall hold closed meetings when examining communications under this article.

(e) Subject to the provisions of sub-paragraph (c), the Committee shall make available its good offices to the States Parties concerned with a view to a friendly solution of the matter on the basis of respect for human rights and fundamental freedoms as recognized in the present Covenant.

(f) In any matter referred to it, the Committee may call upon the States Parties concerned, referred to in sub-paragraph (b), to supply any relevant information.

(g) The States Parties concerned, referred to in sub-paragraph (b), shall have the right to be represented when the matter is being considered in the Committee and to make submissions orally and/or in writing.

(h) The Committee shall, within twelve months after the date of receipt of notice under sub-paragraph (b), submit a report:

(i) If a solution within the terms of sub-paragraph (e) is reached, the Committee shall confine its report to a brief statement of the facts and of the solution reached;

(ii) If a solution within the terms of sub-paragraph (e) is not reached, the Committee shall confine its report to a brief statement of the facts; the written submissions and record of the oral submissions made by the States Parties concerned shall be attached to the report.

In every matter, the report shall be communicated to the States Parties concerned.

2. The provisions of this article shall come into force when ten States Parties to the present Covenant have made declarations under paragraph 1 of this article. Such declarations shall be deposited by the States Parties with the Secretary-General of the United Nations, who shall transmit copies thereof to the other States Parties. A declaration may be withdrawn at any time by notification to the Secretary-General. Such a withdrawal shall not prejudice the consideration of any matter which is the subject of a communication already transmitted under this article; no further communication by any State Party shall be received after the notification of withdrawal of the declaration has been received by the Secretary-General, unless the State Party concerned had made a new declaration.

Article 42

1. (a) If a matter referred to the Committee in accordance with article 41 is not resolved in the satisfaction of the States Parties concerned, the Committee may, with the prior consent of the States Parties concerned, appoint an *ad hoc* Conciliation Commission (hereinafter referred to as the Commission). The good offices of the Commission shall be made available to the States Parties concerned with a view to an amicable solution of the matter on the basis of respect for the present Covenant;

(b) The Commission shall consist of five persons acceptable to the States Parties concerned. If the States Parties concerned fail to reach agreement within three months on all or part of the composition of the Commission, the members of the Commission concerning whom no agreement has been reached shall be elected by secret ballot by a two-thirds majority vote of the Committee from among its members.

2. The members of the Commission shall serve in their personal capacity. They shall not be nationals of the States Parties concerned, or of a State not party to the present covenant, or of a State Party which has not made a declaration under article 41.

3. The Commission shall elect its own Chairman and adopt its own rules of procedure.

4. The meetings of the Commission shall normally be held at the Headquarters of the United Nations or at the United Nations Office at Geneva. However, they may be held at such other convenient places as the Commission may determine in consultation with the Secretary-General of the United Nations and the States Parties concerned.

5. The secretariat provided in accordance with article 36 shall also service the commissions appointed under this article.

6. The information received and collated by the Committee shall be made available to the Commission and the Commission may call upon the States Parties concerned to supply any other relevant information.

7. When the Commission has fully considered the matter, but in any event not later than twelve months after having been seized of the matter, it shall submit to the Chairman of the Committee a report for communication to the States Parties concerned:

(a) If the Commission is unable to complete its consideration of the matter within twelve months, it shall confine its report to a brief statement of the status of its consideration of the matter;

(b) If an amicable solution to the matter on the basis of respect for human rights as recognized in the present Covenant is reached, the Commission shall confine its report to a brief statement of the facts and of the solution reached;

(c) If a solution within the terms of sub-paragraph (b) is not reached, the Commission's report shall embody its findings on all questions of face relevant to the issues between the States Parties concerned, and its views on the possibilities of an amicable solution of the matter. This report shall also contain the written submissions and a record of the oral submissions made by the States Parties concerned;

(d) If the Commission's report is submitted under sub-paragraph (c), the States Parties concerned shall, within three months of the receipt of the report, notify the Chairman of the Committee whether or not they accept the contents of the report of the Commission.

8. The provisions of this article are without prejudice to the responsibilities of the Committee under article 41.

9. The States Parties concerned shall share equally all the expenses of the members of the Commission in accordance with estimates to be provided by the Secretary-General of the United Nations.

10. The Secretary-General of the United Nations shall be empowered to pay the expenses of the members of the Commission, if necessary, before reimbursement by the States Parties concerned, in accordance with paragraph 9 of this article. . . .

Article 44

The provisions for the implementation of the present Covenant shall apply without prejudice to the procedures prescribed in the field of human rights by or under the constituent instruments and the conventions of the United Nations and of the specialized agencies and shall not prevent the States Parties to the present Covenant from having recourse to other procedures for settling a dispute in accordance with general or special international agreements in force between them.

Article 45

The Committee shall submit to the General Assembly of the United Nations, through the Economic and Social Council, an annual report on its activities.

PART V

Article 46

Nothing in the present Covenant shall be interpreted as impairing the provisions of the Charter of the United Nations and of the constitutions of the specialized agencies which define the respective responsibilities of the various organs of the United Nations and of the specialized agencies in regard to the matters dealt with in the present Covenant.

Article 47

Nothing in the present Covenant shall be interpreted as impairing the inherent right of all peoples to enjoy and utilize fully and freely their natural wealth and resources. . . .

OPTIONAL PROTOCOL TO THE INTERNATIONAL COVENANT ON CIVIL AND POLITICAL RIGHTS.

Opened for signature on Dec. 19, 1966; entered into force on Mar. 23, 1976. U.N.G.A. Res. 2200 (XXI). 21 U.N. GAOR, Supp. (No. 16) 59, U.N. Doc. A/6316 (1967).

THE STATES PARTIES TO THE PRESENT PROTOCOL

Considering that in order further to achieve the purpose of the Covenant on Civil and Political Rights (hereinafter referred to as the Covenant) and the implementation of its provisions it would be appropriate to enable the Human Rights Committee set up in part IV of the Covenant (hereinafter referred to as the Committee) to receive and consider, as provided in the present Protocol, communications from individuals claiming to be victims of violations of any of the rights set forth in the Covenant,

Have agreed as follows:

Article 1

A State Party to the Covenant that becomes a party to the present Protocol recognizes the competence of the Committee to receive and consider communications from individuals subject to its jurisdiction who claim to be victims of a violation by that State Party of any of the rights set forth in the Covenant. No communication shall be received by the Committee if it concerns a State Party to the Covenant which is not a party to the present Protocol.

Article 2

Subject to the provisions of article 1, individuals who claim that any of their rights enumerated in the Covenant have been violated and who have exhausted all available domestic remedies may submit a written communication to the Committee for consideration.

Article 3

The Committee shall consider inadmissible any communication under the present Protocol which is anonymous, or which if considers to be an abuse of the rights of submission of such communications or to be incompatible with the provisions of the Covenant.

Article 4

1. Subject to the provisions of article 3, the Committee shall bring any communications submitted to it under the present Protocol to the attention of the State Party to the present Protocol alleged to be violating any provisions of the Covenant.

2. Within six months, the receiving State shall submit to the Committee written explanations or statements clarifying the matter and the remedy, if any, that may have been taken by that State.

Article 5

1. The Committee shall consider communications received under the present Protocol in the light of all written information made available to it by the individual and by the State Party concerned.

2. The Committee shall not consider any communication from an individual unless it has ascertained that:

(a) The same matter is not being examined under another procedure of international investigation or settlement;

(b) The individual has exhausted all available domestic remedies. This shall not be the rule where the application of the remedies is unreasonably prolonged.

3. The Committee shall hold closed meetings when examining communications under the present Protocol.

4. The Committee shall forward its views to the State Party concerned and to the individual.

Article 6

The Committee shall include in its annual report under article 45 of the Covenant a summary of its activities under the present Protocol. . . .

CONTRIBUTORS

Philip Alston is professor and director of the Centre for Advanced Legal Studies in International and Public Law at the Australian National University.

Christian Bay is professor of political science at the University of Toronto.

Richard P. Claude is professor of government and politics at the University of Maryland, College Park, and founding editor and member of the advisory editorial board of *Human Rights Quarterly*.

Thomas M. Crowley is law clerk to Justice William D. Hutchinson of the Supreme Court of Pennsylvania and book review editor of the *American Journal of Jurisprudence*.

Richard N. Dean is an attorney with the New York law firm of Coudert Brothers and is based in Moscow.

Yoram Dinstein is professor of international law at Tel Aviv University, editor of the *Israel Human Rights Yearbook*, and a member of the advisory editorial board of *Human Rights Quarterly*.

Jack Donnelly is associate professor of political science at the University of North Carolina, Chapel Hill.

Richard A. Falk is the Albert G. Milbank Professor of International Law and Practice at Princeton University, Princeton, New Jersey, and is a member of the editorial boards of *Alternatives*, the *American Journal of International Law*, and *World Policy Journal*.

Tom J. Farer is professor of international law at the College of Law and School of International Service at American University, and is former chairman and member since 1980 of the Inter-American Commission on Human Rights.

David P. Forsythe is professor of political science at the University of Nebraska, Lincoln.

Animesh Ghosal is associate professor of economics at De Paul University, Chicago.

Mary C. Gosiger received her law degree from the University of Cincinnati College of Law, where she was an Arthur Russell Morgan Fellow of the Urban Morgan Institute for Human Rights.

Jack Greenberg is vice dean and professor of law at the Columbia University School of Law, and is a former director and counsel of the NAACP Legal Defense and Education Fund.

Kelly M. Hnatt is a third-year student at the University of Iowa College of Law.

Rajni Kothari is professor of political science at Delhi University, India, director of the Centre for the Study of Developing Societies, Delhi, and consulting editor of *Alternatives*.

Leo Kuper is professor emeritus of sociology at the University of California, Los Angeles.

David Lane is professor of sociology at the University of Birmingham, England.

Richard B. Lillich is the Howard W. Smith Professor of Law at the University of Virginia School of Law, Charlottesville, and a member of the board of editors of the *American Journal of International Law*.

Matthew Lippman is an associate professor in the Department of Criminal Justice at the University of Illinois, Chicago.

Evan Luard is a research fellow at Oxford University and has written extensively on international law and human rights.

Robin Ann Lukes is a graduate of the University of Iowa College of Law and currently is an instructor in legal writing at the Santa Clara University School of Law.

Jordan J. Paust is professor of law at the University of Houston Law Center.

A. H. Robertson is a former professeur associé at the University of Paris I, and is a member of the International Institute of Human Rights.

Katarina Tomasevski a fellow at the Danish Human Rights Centre, teaches at the University of Utrecht, Europa Institute.

Henn-Juri Uibopuu is professor of international law at the University of Salzburg, Austria.

Burns H. Weston is the Bessie Dutton Murray Professor of Law at the University of Iowa, Iowa City, and is a member of the board of editors of the *American Journal of International Law* and the editorial board of the *Bulletin of Peace Proposals*.

Index

Name Index